Shaking the Invisible Hand

Complexity, Endogenous Money and Exogenous Interest Rates

Basil John Moore

© Basil John Moore 2006

All rights reserved. No reproduction, copy or transmission of this publication may be made without written permission.

No paragraph of this publication may be reproduced, copied or transmitted save with written permission or in accordance with the provisions of the Copyright, Designs and Patents Act 1988, or under the terms of any licence permitting limited copying issued by the Copyright Licensing Agency, 90 Tottenham Court Road, London W1T 4LP.

Any person who does any unauthorized act in relation to this publication may be liable to criminal prosecution and civil claims for damages.

The author has asserted his right to be identified as the author of this work in accordance with the Copyright, Designs and Patents Act 1988.

First published in 2006 by
PALGRAVE MACMILLAN
Houndmills, Basingstoke, Hampshire RG21 6XS and
175 Fifth Avenue, New York, N.Y. 10010
Companies and representatives throughout the world.

PALGRAVE MACMILLAN is the global academic imprint of the Palgrave Macmillan division of St. Martin's Press, LLC and of Palgrave Macmillan Ltd. Macmillan® is a registered trademark in the United States, United Kingdom and other countries. Palgrave is a registered trademark in the European Union and other countries.

ISBN-13: 978–1–4039–9946–7 hardback
ISBN-10: 1–4039–9946–5 hardback

This book is printed on paper suitable for recycling and made from fully managed and sustained forest sources.

A catalogue record for this book is available from the British Library.

Library of Congress Cataloging-in-Publication Data

Moore, Basil J.
    Shaking the invisible hand : complexity, endogenous money and exogenous interest rates / by Basil John Moore.
       p. cm.
    Includes bibliographical references and index.
    ISBN 1–4039–9946–5 (cloth)
      1. Macroeconomics. I. Title.

HB172.5.M6523 2005
339—dc22   2005048133

10 9 8 7 6 5 4 3 2 1
15 14 13 12 11 10 09 08 07 06

Printed and bound in Great Britain by
Antony Rowe Ltd, Chippenham and Eastbourne

Contents

List of Tables	x
List of Figures	xi
Preamble: Complex Systems	xiv
Preface: Complex Adaptive Systems (CAS)	xvi

Part I   Complexity and Economics

1   Marshall's Tides   3
   1.1   Introduction: Marshall's tidal metaphor   3
   1.2   Haavalmo's probability revolution: "Let the data decide"   6
   1.3   Keynes' skepticism: unobservable variables   7
   1.4   Conclusions: the economy is a complex system   10

2   Complexity and Contingency   13
   2.1   An introduction to complex adaptive systems   14
   2.2   Some unique characteristics of complex adaptive systems: emergent properties, self-organized criticality, and sandpiles   17
   2.3   The relational structure of complex adaptive systems   20
   2.4   Science and complexity   22
   2.5   Challenges to modeling complex adaptive systems   25
   2.6   Are there limits to what we can know?   28
   2.7   The human brain   29
   2.8   Conclusions: an ode to pluralism   33
   Appendix: the Copenhagen interpretation   36
   Bibliography on complexity and chaos   39

3   Chaos Theory: Unpredictable Order in Chaos   43
   3.1   Chaos theory   43
   3.2   Application of chaos theory   49
   3.3   The innate instability of economic variables   56
   3.4   Determinism and predictability   59
   3.5   Five nontraditional truths   65
   3.6   Postmodernism and economics   68
   Appendix: prediction and domination   72

4	Econometrics, Data Mining, the Absence of a Stable Structure and the Pervasiveness of Contingency	75
	4.1 The absence of a stable structure and pervasiveness of contingency	75
	4.2 A brief survey of the econometric analysis of business cycles	77
	4.3 The methodology of modern econometrics	85
	4.4 The importance of stationarity	94
	4.5 Are economic time series time stationary or difference stationary?	96
	4.6 Conclusions: complex systems can be simulated but never solved	102
5	The Implications of Complexity for Economic Analysis	104
	5.1 Tensions in neoclassical economics	104
	5.2 "Misplaced concreteness" in neoclassical theory	108
	5.3 The non-probabilistic nature of fundamental uncertainty	112
	5.4 The case against equilibrium analysis	119
	5.5 Process analysis	122

Part II Some Thoughts on Economic Data and National Income Accounting

6	Sorites' Paradox: the "Looseness" of Economic Concepts	131
	6.1 The importance of quantification	131
	6.2 Sorites' dilemma: "loose" concepts	132
	6.3 Measurement in economics: "the excluded middle"	134
	6.4 The measurement and quantification of economic concepts	136
	6.5 The mismeasurement of National Income	138
	6.6 Eisner's total incomes system of accounts	144
	6.7 Unemployment, price levels, inflation rates, and growth rates	150
	6.8 Conclusions: where must we draw the line?	154
7	Saving is the Accounting Record of Investment	156
	7.1 Volitional and non-volitional saving	156
	7.2 Saving is identical to investment	159
	7.3 Widening the model: the government sector	162
	7.4 Words and terms: "saving" in economics is intransitive	164
	7.5 Volitional and non-volitional saving	167
	7.6 Conclusions: saving is the accounting record of investment	170
8	Capital Gains: Towards a Hicksian Definition of Income	174
	8.1 Most saving is non-volitional	175
	8.2 Hicksian income	177
	8.3 A Proposal for a "Capital Gains and Losses Addendum" to National Income Accouting	183

8.4	Estimates of Hicksian income	188
8.5	Conclusions: Hicksian income and saving behavior	192

Part III The Endogeneity of Money and Exogeneity of Interest Rates

9	The Endogeneity of Credit Money	197
9.1	Commodity, fiat, and credit money	198
9.2	The money-multiplier identity	202
9.3	The endogeneity of the high-powered base	205
9.4	Central Banks: the ultimate supplier of system liquidity	208
9.5	Conclusions: credit money and "convenience lending"	212

10	Commercial Bank Intermediation	215
10.1	Commercial banks as retailers of credit	216
10.2	Bank finance of working capital	222
10.3	A model of bank intermediation	224
10.4	The supply of credit money is endogenously demand-determined	230
10.5	Money market mutual funds	235
10.6	Conclusions: "horizontalism"	236

11	The Exogeneity of Interest Rates	238
11.1	Different theories of interest	238
11.2	Central Bank interest rate setting behavior	241
11.3	The US reserve supply process	243
11.4	The new consensus on monetary policy	247
11.5	Conclusions: bank rate is the exogenous policy instrument of the Central Bank	252
	Appendix: Keynes' changing views on interest rates	255

Part IV The Determination of Prices, Output, and Growth Rates

12	Markup Pricing and the Aggregate Supply Relationship	261
12.1	The impossibility of maximization	261
12.2	Markup pricing: the Post Keynesian theory of the firm	262
12.3	The limitations of empirical analysis	268
12.4	Survey evidence	270
12.5	The Post Keynesian theory of pricing	275
12.6	Conclusions: as a "stylized fact" the aggregate supply (AS) curve may be viewed as horizontal	278

13	The "Raffishness" of Mainstream Macroeconomics: a Post Keynesian Critique	281
13.1	The five "core" propositions of mainstream macroeconomics	281

13.2	A critique of the mainstream "core"	286
13.3	A fundamental critique of the mainstream theory of income determination	289
13.4	Post Keynesian AS–AD analysis	300
13.5	Conclusions: the central importance of changes in "animal spirits"	301

14 Interest Rates and Aggregate Demand — 303
- 14.1 The Post Keynesian case for aggregate demand management — 303
- 14.2 IS–LM analysis and the BR–AD diagram — 307
- 14.3 Process analysis: the BR–ΔAD diagram — 309
- 14.4 Process analysis: the ΔBR–ΔAD diagram — 313
- 14.5 The interest elasticity of aggregate demand — 316
- 14.6 The Japanese conondrum — 320
- 14.7 Conclusions: changes in Bank Rate are a good proxy for changes in "animal spirits" — 327

15 Monetary Policy: Non-Volitional and Volitional Saving — 331
- 15.1 The central role of monetary policy in AD growth — 331
- 15.2 Internal balance constraints on reducing Bank Rate to R_F — 340
- 15.3 External balance constraints on reducing Bank Rate to R_F — 345
- 15.4 Insufficient "saving" is never a constraint on investment — 348
- 15.5 The short run "exogeneity" and long run "endogeneity" of Bank Rate — 352

16 The Monetary Transmission Process — 359
- 16.1 Process analysis of how aggregate demand grows over time — 359
- 16.2 "Convenience lending": the non-volitional finance of deficit-spending — 363
- 16.3 "Convenience lending" and "convenience saving" — 366
- 16.4 The demise of the Keynesian "multiplier" — 370
- 16.5 The Quantity Theory of Money — 375
- 16.6 The simultaneous achievement of internal and external balance — 377
- Appendix: A critique of the Quantity Theory of Money — 378

V Open Economy Considerations

17 Using National Currencies in International Trade: the Case for Fixed Exchange Rates — 385
- 17.1 Open Economy Macroeconomics — 385
- 17.2 Consistent capital budget accounting for open economies — 389
- 17.3 The classical view of balance of payments adjustment — 396

	17.4 The Keynesian view of balance of payments adjustment	398
	17.5 Keynes' proposal for an international clearing union (ICU)	403
	17.6 Conclusions: the Bretton Woods system—success and failure	405
18	Using National Currencies in International Transactions: the Case for Flexible Exchange Rates	409
	18.1 The current international payments system: flexible exchange rates	410
	18.2 The case for flexible exchange rates	411
	18.3 The case against flexible exchange rates	413
	18.4 Endogenous speculation in flexible exchange rate regimes	420
	18.5 The deflationary bias in the current flexible exchange rates regime	424
	18.6 Empirical estimates of the deflationary bias	428
19	Using a Common Currency in International Transactions: the Post Keynesian Case for No Exchange Rates	433
	19.1 The Choice of a national payments medium: a critically important policy decision	434
	19.2 Efficiency gains from a common currency	439
	19.3 Stabilization gains from a common currency	441
	19.4 Post Keynesian open economy macroeconomics	442
	19.5 Currency unions	446
	19.6 Dollarization and Euroization	449
20	Financial Barriers to Demand-led Growth	454
	20.1 Why market economies are demand-constrained?	454
	20.2 Neoclassical supply-side models of economic growth	456
	20.3 Post Keynesian demand-led models of economic growth	460
	20.4 A demand-side explanation for the low growth rates of African economies	463
	20.5 Conclusions	472
Notes		474
Bibliography		522
Index		547

List of Tables

3.1	Five traditional and nontraditional truths	65
4.1	Sample autocorrelations of natural logs of annual data	99
4.2	Sample autocorrelations of first differences of the natural logs of annual data	99
4.3	Sample autocorrelations of the deviations from a time trend	100
4.4	Coefficient on lagged dependent variable nominal and real GDP, 1959:2–2003:1	101
6.1	Consumption and tangible and intangible domestic investment as percent of BEA GNP	146
6.2	Gross and Net Domestic Capital Formation as percent of BEA Gross and Net Private Domestic Investment and of own gross and net aggregates	146
6.3	Household and government capital services, household labor services and property, and labor incomes as percent of BEA GNP	147
6.4	Aggregates in relation to BEA GNP and rates of growth	148
8.1	Accounting net worth and market value of US Nonfinancial Corporate Business (1948–87)	189
8.2	Accounting net worth and market value of US Nonfinancial Corporate Business (1986–2001)	190
8.3	Balance sheet of households and nonprofit organizations (1986–2001) ($ Billions)	191
8.4	Change in household and nonprofit organizations, net worth, net investment and net holding gains (1986–2001) ($ Millions)	192
18.1	Bank Rate, growth rate, and the degree of external imbalance 1980–2000	432

List of Figures

3.1	The Koch curve	46
3.2	Exact and statistical self-similarity	46
3.3	Serpinski carpet and Menger Sponge	47
3.4	The Chaos game	48
3.5	Period doubling and chaos	50
3.6	The structure of chaos	51
3.7	Deterministic chaos	53
3.8	Deterministic chaos with displacement	53
3.9	How weather patterns diverge	54
3.10	The butterfly behind chaos	54
3.11	Lemming population as a stable system subject to exogenous shocks	57
3.12	Lemming population as a complex system with unstable dynamics	58
3.13	Hysteresis	62
4.1	Random does not imply pattern-less	76
4.2	Worm Trails	77
4.3	Slutsky's random series juxtaposed with business cycles	79
4.4	Changes in the Dow index look like random numbers, while the cumulation of a series of random numbers looks like the Dow	80
10.1	The balance sheet relation between bank loans, deposits and reserves	225
11.1	The US reserve supply process	245
13.1	The (C + I + G) relationship	289
13.2	The I–S ("Keynesian Cross") diagram	292
13.3	The IS–LM diagram	295
13.4	The mainstream AS–AD diagram	298
13.5	The Post Keynesian AD–AS diagram	301
14.1	The BR–AD diagram	308
14.2	The BR–AD diagram	311
14.3	The AD–AS diagram	311
14.4	The ΔAD–ΔBR relationship	314
14.5	The BR–ΔAD diagram	315
14.6	The ΔBR–ΔAD diagram	315
14.7	Interest rates, 1980–2000	321
14.8	The Nikkei index, 1980–2000	324
14.9	Monthly changes in the Nikkei index, 1980–2000	324
14.10	Commercial and residential land prices (1983 = 100)	325
14.11	Annual changes in land prices, 1984–2000	325
15.1	The BR–ΔAD relationship	340

15.2	AS and AD determination of Ṗ and ΔY	341
15.3	Phillips curves in developed and less developed economies	342
15.4	The BR–ΔAD relationship in developed and less developed economies	343
15.5	The ΔAD–ΔBOP relation in an open economy	347
16.1	The Keynesian multiplier	373
18.1	The ΔAD–ΔBOP relation in an open economy	425
18.2	BOP/imports vs Bank Rate	429
18.3	FOREXC/imports vs Bank Rate	429
18.4	BOP/imports vs GDP PC growth	430
18.5	FOREXC/imports vs GDP PC growth	430
18.6	Bank Rate vs GDP PC growth	431
18.7	Real Bank Rate vs GDP PC growth	431
20.1	GDP per capita growth rates 1980–2000	466
20.2	High and Low Income countries: real per capita growth rates, 1980–2000	467
20.3	Bank Rate, developed and developing economies	467
20.4	Average markups and spreads: High Income and Low Income countries	468
20.5	Four firm banking concentration ratios: High Income and Low Income countries	469
20.6	Indicators of "financial deepening"	471
20.7	Share of bank credit to the public and private sector	472

The fascination of scientific work does not lie in the craftsmanlike utilization of the tools of the science. It is admirable for the gymnast to put his splendidly disciplined body through intricate maneuvers, and it is no doubt equally admirable for the scientist to put his disciplined mind through a sequence of complex analytical or experimental maneuvers. The great fascination of scientific endeavor, however, is precisely the speculative pursuit of new ideas that widen the horizon of our understanding of the world. This endeavor is not at all like that of a graceful intellectual gymnast: on the contrary, the scientist is stumbling about in a jungle of ideas and facts that seem to defy system or logic ... Usually he fails to emerge with anything but scratches.

George Stigler, Nobel Memorial Lecture, 1982

It's an experience like no other experience I can describe, the best thing that can happen to a scientist, realizing that something that's happened in his or her mind exactly corresponds to something that happens in nature. It's startling every time it occurs. One is surprised that a construct of one's own mind can actually be realized in the honest-to-goodness world out there. A great shock, and a great, great joy.

Leo Kadanoff, quoted in Gleick, 1987: 189

Preamble: Complex Systems

This book was started in 1988, immediately after the publication of *Horizontalists and Verticalists*. I find this long period acutely embarrassing. Economists don't spend 17 years writing a book. The interval between thinking and writing about something and experiencing others' reactions to it has been frustratingly long. Although several chapters have been presented and published in conference proceedings the complete argument has never seen the light of day. I await its professional reception with keen anticipation.

The recognition that the world is a complex system came to me by way of a deep personal tragedy. While leading a family climbing holiday near St Moritz in 1970, a large boulder bounded down our gully directly into my not quite 10-year-old first-born daughter's head. This event profoundly altered my entire life path. My first marriage disintegrated. My enthusiasm for life disappeared. I was involuntarily hospitalized for depression. After being the teaching star of the department, my teaching evaluations plummeted. I was convinced that I would never write again. I continue to relive the memories of that event every day of my life and will take them with me to my grave.

I heard the boulder crashing down far above perhaps a minute before it reached us. As leader of our climbing party, I immediately shouted, *"Everyone get down!"* After I had found my own large boulder, of which there were many along both sides of our gully, I looked back to make sure that everyone was safe and secure. To my horror my daughter was now 20 feet below me in the middle of the gully. Due to the ambiguities of the English language, she had interpreted *"Get down!"* as *"Get down the mountain!"*

The boulder had surely lain undisturbed on that glacier for untold centuries! It was a glorious July morning. What was the probability that an unusually warm July sun should have loosened that boulder to bound down the mountain and occupy the same space as my daughter's small head, on that particular day, at that particular instant in time? We had been late leaving the hut and had briefly lost our path, which had delayed us a further few minutes. If we had not taken a second cup of coffee, had not lost the way, had hiked a little more quickly, or a little more slowly, Jessica would not have been in that fatal spot on that fatal instant. The probability of such an event was surely one in many, many millions. How could such a horror have happened to my young Jess, so beautiful, so full of promise, so pure, so magical, and so very, very, innocent?

I have now had 35 years to reflect on this event and have very slowly come to a deeper understanding that this is the way of our world. *"The best laid schemes o' mice an' men Gang aft a-gley."* The probability of any such single event is indefinitely small. But there are an indefinitely large number of such events that could possibly occur, so the probability of something horrible happening during one life-path is not so utterly insignificant. If and when such an unlikely event does happen, your life and the lives of many others can be changed forever.

We humans are unable to make sense out of such a world. We can never foresee what our future holds. (And a very good thing too. Imagine our own personal hell if we knew in advance when our own boulder was coming down!) Contingency. Things simply happen ... Just happen.

Science is forever a work in progress. Like a sculpture that is never finished, the body of scientific knowledge is continually remolded by many hands. I believe that once economists have recognized that the world is a complex system they will no longer be able to teach that economic agents rationally analyze the future until they reach an equilibrium defined as a position where all change ceases. They will no longer be able to believe in a world of omniscient rational agents making utility-maximizing judgments among all alternative outcomes.

But if rational decision-making is impossible how should we model economic behavior? This is the central question I address in this volume. My answer is we must reject linear equilibrium analysis completely and replace it with process analysis, and eventually computer simulation of nonlinear systems. As I have read more deeply into the literature of complexity I am continually amazed how well it fits my personal perception of reality. I warmly invite others to come down the same path. But please, get down behind a boulder.

I dedicate this book to my wife Sibs, with infinite gratitude for her sparkle, support and love. She is almost as glad as I am that this book is finally behind us. Let the games begin!

Moores End Farm, The Cape, South Africa, July, 2005

Preface: Complex Adaptive Systems (CAS)

> High up in the North, in the land called Svithjod, there stands a rock. It is 100 miles high and 100 miles wide. Once every thousand years a little bird comes to this rock to sharpen its beak. When the rock has been worn away, then a single day of eternity will have gone by.
>
> Hendrik Van Loon

> It is not to be forgotten that the explanations we offer are all our own artificial inventions in search of an understanding of real life. They are not hidden truths to be discovered.
>
> Trygve Haavelmo

1 Economies are complex systems

Over the past 50 years natural scientists in a multitude of disciplines have experienced increasing impatience with the reductionist thinking that has dominated science since Newton.[1] After dissecting everything into molecules, atoms, electrons, nuclei, and finally "quarks," physicists are finally turning that process inside out. Instead of looking for the simplest pieces possible they are now looking how these pieces fit together to form complex wholes. Microbiologists are beginning to grapple with life's essential mysteries: How do systems constituted of very simple particles and obeying very simple rules engage in such astonishing and unpredictable behavior? How do several quadrillion molecules organize themselves into entities that live, respond, and reproduce? In the brain sciences, neuroscientists are struggling to comprehend the essence of mind. How do the billions of densely interconnected nerve cells inside our brains give rise to feelings, thoughts, purposes, sensations, and consciousness itself?

Many investigators are now attempting to come to terms with the mathematical theory of chaos, the intricate beauty of fractals, and the weird inner order of liquids and solids. The old categories of science are beginning to dissolve and a new science is waiting to be born. Instead of a reductionist quest for the ultimate particles this new science is about systems, flux, change, the forming, and dissolving of patterns. Instead of ignoring everything that isn't uniform and predictable, the new science finds a place for individuality and the accidents of history. Instead of being about simplicity it is about *Complexity*.

Economics has lagged about one generation behind this loss of innocence in the natural sciences. But by the stagflation of the 1970s heterodox economists had become increasingly edgy about the mainstream paradigm and increasingly receptive to paradigm change. The neoclassical framework that had dominated graduate schools over the last generation appeared to have at last reached its high-water mark. Conventional economics had moved about as far away from the new vision of complexity as one could imagine. The mainstream view stressed the powerful discipline of market forces. Students were taught to focus on how prices equilibrated supply and demand to determine stable and unique equilibrium positions. Economic phenomena were distilled into timeless mathematical equations and rigorous ahistorical theorems were proved about them.

But, in the real world, time and history matter a great deal. Change, adaptation and evolution go on forever. Orthodox economics completely ignored the messy problems of the transitional present where systems are in chaotic flow before they reach a new "equilibrium" position. Theories were not considered "theories" until they were mathematicized and expressed rigorously and precisely.[2] The assumption of long-run equilibrium became in effect a nontransparent way of getting rid of all of the problems posed by time.[3]

Closed-form mathematical solutions where all change has ceased can occur only in linear systems, since nonlinear systems have no closed-form solution. Due to its general equilibrium orientation in order to achieve the possibility of a stationary solution mainstream economics was forced to make a number of extremely unrealistic assumptions: diminishing returns in production, everywhere-rising supply curves, homogeneous agents, diminishing marginal utility in consumption, all markets perfectly competitive, all firms with zero market power, negative feedback everywhere and the complete absence of externalities. Some critics have argued that education in economics has become *"little better than an indoctrination"* in economic theory.[4] But such restrictive assumptions had to be made to ensure that the vision of a hypothetical economic system tending towards a unique general equilibrium outcome, characterized by smooth trends, stability, and harmony, has a strong logical foundation and was not simply ridiculous. Even the modest introduction of increasing returns can be easily shown to lead directly to multiple possible outcomes.[5]

The vision of economies as complex systems is diametrically opposed to the mainstream paradigm. Description of complex systems can acknowledge and even embrace the existence of increasing returns in production, increasing utility in consumption, habit formation, scale economies, externalities, lock-in effects, unit roots, hysteresis, and extreme heterogeneity among both agents and techniques. Money becomes completely endogenous and short-term interest rates fully exogenous. The basic elements become patterns, possibilities and the continuous evolutionary change of technology, institutions, and market structures. Most relationships that occur over historical time are intrinsically nonlinear. In the real world the psychological foundations of "rational expectations" are bounded by ignorance. Perhaps most importantly in such a vision the future path of the system is unknowable in advance.

Mathematics is a kind of language that permits quantitative relationships to be expressed more clearly, systematically, and economically than with words. But economists have found it impossible to incorporate historical time into the mathematical language of general equilibrium analysis. In consequence mainstream economists are frequently accused by their critics of erring on the side of "rigor" at the expense of "relevance." But like "virtue," "rigor" has very strong positive connotations. Rigor is associated with more powerful mathematical formalization and analysis. In any mathematical analysis more "rigor" is always desirable. Even the harshest critics of mainstream economics are never heard to appeal for "less rigorous" analysis. "Less rigorous" has strong negative associations and implies analysis that is loose, sloppy, less precise, and less organized. Heterodox critics do not have a winning argument when they criticize mainstream theory for its "excessive" rigor.

The valid criticism of mainstream analysis is precisely the opposite. It is in fact far too simple. Its simplifying assumptions have been carefully chosen to yield clear and unique solutions. The mainstream paradigm completely fails to acknowledge the mysterious nonlinear complexity of economic behavior. By banishing complex phenomena it has been unable to provide enlightenment and increased understanding of the holistic richness and complexity of real world phenomena. As a result mainstream economics leads to conclusions that are faulty, and explanations that are both misleading and incorrect. In short mainstream economics provides an unsatisfactory and erroneous guide for the formulation of fruitful economic policy.[6]

Paradoxically it was the adoption of *positivism* that has led mainstream economists astray: *"The test of the truthfulness of a proposition lies in its ability to predict."* But the future behavior of complex systems is intrinsically evolutionary, unknowable, and unpredictable. Since accurate prediction is impossible, positivism is unable to discriminate among alternative hypotheses. Positivism has misled economists to build a theory that yields determinate equilibrium conclusions, and in the process to enormously oversell their predictive capabilities. It effectively denies economic agents the possibility to engage in free choice, along with the accompanying freedom to make mistakes.[7]

2 Pedagogy

This book argues that the subject matter of economics is intrinsically much more complex and therefore much more difficult to analyze and understand than the subject matter of physics. Unlike the group behavior of individual molecules, which can be accurately described in terms of objective probability distributions, the group behavior of individual human agents is intrinsically time-dependent and cannot be so described. Event probabilities as well as event outcomes are time-dependent, and the distributions as well as the outcomes continually change over time. Economic agents have free will and develop heterogeneous personal and mutually inconsistent expectations of future events. As one consequence economic processes creating more unemployment are frequently characterized by hysteresis. Unemployment leads to the deterioration of labor productivity. History is important in economics since outcomes depend on the history of the system.

Introductory students when first exposed to economics are at least at Wesleyan frequently a joy to teach. They come to economics with open and curious minds, and are quite capable of raising exquisitely discerning and uncomfortable questions for their instructor. One general line of such questions centers around economists' deeply ingrained habit of proceeding on the assumption that individual households and firms must be analyzed as if they are all "rational maximizers." For economists, agent behavior consists of choosing the appropriate action that "maximizes" some subjective function, "utility" for households, and "profits" for firms. Introductory students characteristically ask, *"Surely there are important additional non-strictly economic dimensions to agent behavior?" Are people really so simple?* Psychological, emotional and altruistic motives for households, and non-pecuniary motives such as risk, power, and prestige for firms obviously affect behavior. Yet all are excluded from the economists' models![8]

A second probing line of awkward questions concerns economists' ingrained habit of assuming that the analysis of complex economic phenomena can be distilled into simple mathematical equilibrium models that capture the "essential" features of the situation.

> *Surely there are many omitted factors which also influence behavior which we are unable to quantify? If this is so to what extent are "rigorous" economic models, which omit all non-quantifiable considerations, simply misleading? Can economic agents in the real world ever actually "maximize" utility or anything else?*[9]

Both types of questions will be explored in this book, and the manner in which they are fundamentally linked will be addressed.

Unfortunately, by the time most students have a couple of years of economics courses behind them such uncomfortable questions will have been either suppressed or forgotten. Those who remain unpersuaded and dissatisfied will have chosen another major. Those who stay in economics will have been socialized so they no longer focus on such embarrassingly sticky issues. Most university students take little more than one introductory economics course. The minority who continue are taught complicated techniques of economic theory and econometric analysis with no reference to the history of economic thought, and with little philosophical or methodological discussion of the validity of these powerful statistical techniques. Keen argues forcefully that modern economic students are in fact *"educated into ignorance."*[10]

Much has been said about these matters, but much remains unsaid. In order to be able to understand Henry James' "big, buzzing, blooming, confusion" around us it is obvious that economists must make assumptions that drastically simplify reality. Equally obviously, in order to simplify we must distort. But the manner in which we simplify is of crucial importance. As Joan Robinson often delighted in pronouncing:

> We must never make such heroic heuristic assumptions that any conclusion we can deduce becomes irrelevant once the assumptions that we have made are removed.[11]

3 Process analysis must replace equilibrium analysis

The single most fatal simplifying assumption that economists make is that economic actors can be viewed as having "perfect" information. This assumption must be made because in order to be able to "optimize" or "maximize" anything, agents must have full knowledge of all the alternatives, that is, "full" information. Once it is granted that such an optimum exists, we must only assume that economic actors are "rational" to enable them to find the unique position where utility is maximized. It is surely not fruitful to assume that agents act "irrationally"?

Chronological time cannot exist in comparative static equilibrium analysis. In consequence it is very easy to ignore the passage of time, and to focus on the mathematical attractions of the analysis. Most introductory economics textbooks consequently present a sanitized, antiseptic, conventional, closed, ahistoric, and apolitical rendition of economic behavior.

Economists enjoy intimidating other social scientists with the mathematical nature of their models and the "rigor" of their discipline. But most economists do not yet have the level of mathematical education necessary to confront the analysis of nonlinear systems. Economic theory as currently taught ignores the dynamic adjustment disequilibrium processes that occur over calendar time, and focuses solely on finding the solution of comparative static equilibrium outcomes. As one result, complexity and chaos theory have as yet made little impact on economics. This is in part because in order to fully understand chaos theory, you must have taken courses in second- and third-order nonlinear difference and differential equations, with which most economists are unfamiliar.[12]

This book represents one scholar's long (17 year) attempt to develop an alternative paradigm to comparative static equilibrium analysis. It concludes that the central constraint in economics is ignorance, not scarcity. One of its central themes is that economists must forgo the mathematical attractions of "rigorous" general equilibrium analysis. Once economists can be brought to recognize that economies are complex systems, it is an easy stretch to demonstrate that economic systems have no equilibrium solution and their outcomes can never be predicted.[13]

Part I, "Complexity and Economics" provides some introductory methodology. It attempts to define complexity, chaos theory, unit roots, and to elucidate what it means to state that economies are complex systems, and to explore the implications of complexity for economic analysis. It concludes that economists should explicitly acknowledge their inability to forecast the future behavior of the economy, and the narrow limits of their ability to comprehend complex phenomena. Even more than the meteorological universe the economic universe is complex beyond our wildest dreams. Economies are open systems whose longer run future behavior we will never be able to foresee, no matter how powerful and sophisticated our models. Like meteorologists economists must learn to build, simulate, and analyze nonlinear models. These will enable us to understand more completely *why* we cannot predict the future, and assist us to recognize the *order* inherent in the chaos.

Also like meteorologists economists must learn to confine themselves to making only short-run forecasts of ordinal changes in variables in complex systems over real (calendar) time. Economists are greatly aided in this enterprise by the fact that most economic variables do not change as rapidly over the very short chronological time units as do many meteorological variables. Unlike the weather, economies will be in broadly the same state tomorrow and even next week or next month as they are in today.

Most economic variables, with the important exception of asset prices traded on well-organized exchanges, are generated from data that are measured only at discrete monthly, quarterly, or even annual intervals. Within these short-run periods the ordinal change is generally small. When substantial it can frequently be accurately forecasted by ARIMA forecasts derived from the past behavior of the time series. Even though the economy is a complex system, like meteorologists economists can make forecasts about short-run ordinal changes in individual variables from their present value, without being required to forecast (or even fully understand) the longer run complex behavior the system undergoes.

I personally have found the recognition that economies are complex systems, together with the corollary that complex systems have no closed-form solution, to be enormously liberating in the amount of time that I must spend reading the literature. The deeper comprehension, that equilibrium analysis makes absolutely no sense for complex systems, gives one the superb freedom to completely ignore all articles or arguments, no matter how dressed up or how sophisticated the mathematics, that attempt to solve for an "equilibrium" value of either a variable or the system. The recognition that "equilibrium" is meaningless for complex phenomena permits all such work to be immediately discarded and seen for what it represents. The majority can be seen to be simply and literally intellectual "nonsense." Some are designed to impress and persuade by way of difficult elitist mathematical formulation. Some even exhibit a kind of intellectual exhibitionism, *"just look at all the difficult things I do here."*

In place of "equilibrium analysis" in logical time, like meteorologists economists must develop tools for "process analysis." They must attempt to explain and forecast only short-run *ordinal changes* in economic variables from their current position over real (calendar) time (one week, one month, one quarter, or one year), depending on the nature of the variable and the time period over which it is measured. Process analysis is sufficient to assist us to explain and understand although never precisely to predict most important short-run consequences of policy actions. Ordinal forecasts, greater or less, are fortunately a sufficient guide for most incremental policy formulation.

The remaining sections apply the technique of "process analysis" to a reconstruction of macroeconomic analysis for closed and open economies. Part II examines problems in the definition and measurement of economic concepts: consumption, investment, National Income, and in particular the relation between saving and investment. Part III summarizes the endogenous behavior of the money supply, and the exogenous (policy determined) behavior of interest rates. Part IV considers the monetary transmission process, the central inverse relation of interest rates to Aggregate Demand (AD), and the impossibility of optimum monetary policy. Part V emphasizes the huge advantages of using a common currency in international transactions, and the resulting severe financial constraints to AD growth and development in the worlds' poorest economies of multiple currencies. The case is made that institutional change toward a social contract is a necessary prerequisite if central banks are to successfully pursue enlightened monetary policy, and to lower interest rates to the levels necessary to generate full employment AD, without creating internal and external imbalance and inflation as an undesirable but inevitable by-product.

4 Endogenous money and exogenous interest rates

Mainstream economics currently operates with a fundamentally incorrect paradigm of the way modern economies function. The true direction of causality between money, wages, and prices is reversed.[14] The mainstream paradigm treats the central bank (CB) as controlling the monetary base and so determining the supply of money *exogenously* as its policy instrument. The quantity theory identity is adopted to summarize the implied causal relationships between changes in money and in prices and incomes. It is believed that if only wages were flexible, labor markets would clear and involuntary unemployment could be eliminated. If the money supply is exogenous, whenever the income velocity of money is reasonably stable it appears to be self-evident that an excessive rate of change of the money supply "governs" the rate of change of AD money income, the price level and the inflation rate.

The quantity theory paradigm did once have some relevance and validity in very early chronological periods of commodity and fiat money.[15] But it has absolutely no applicability for monetary analysis under current institutional conditions. In a world of sophisticated financial markets and complicated derivative instruments, quantity theory analysis is both wildly incorrect and directly misleading. It completely disguises the role of interest rates and the non-transparent but self-evident fact that the paramount policy goal of central banks should ideally be to maintain the lowest interest rate consistent with full employment and price level stability. It also totally hides the huge advantages enjoyed by countries that use a common currency in international trade.

In real world economies, wages have absolutely no tendency to "equilibrate" to establish "full" employment. To understand the true nature of the causal relation between changes in money wages and changes in income and output one must sharply distinguish the different institutional arrangements associated with commodity, fiat, credit, and international money. Today endogenous credit money is exclusively used in all economies.[16]

The policy disagreements between Post Keynesian and mainstream macroeconomists over monetary endogeneity hinge centrally around the direction of causality between key macroeconomic variables: money, income, prices, costs, and wages. Resolving the disagreement whether money is exogenous or endogenous requires isolating the direction of causal relationships between balance sheet and income variables: bank reserves, bank loans, bank deposits money income, and AD. It is now universally recognized that correlation does not imply causality. The direction of causality can only be conclusively demonstrated empirically by undertaking controlled experiments. Unfortunately, controlled experiments cannot generally be carried out in macroeconomics. Economists must use the real world as their laboratory, and, unfortunately, the real world is indefinitely complex.

The direction of causality inferred depends on the theory adopted. Theory is important, if only because different theories postulate different causal relationships. This book argues that Post Keynesian economists must develop "process analysis" as their nonequilibrium theoretical framework if they are to succeed in persuading the mainstream to adopt the endogenous money paradigm for the analysis of monetary change.[17] In the case of endogenous money the perception lag is compounded by an additional obstacle: bank reserves, bank loans, and bank deposits all move closely together empirically. Resolving the disagreement whether money is endogenous or exogenous requires isolating the true direction of causal relationships.

Unfortunately, it is impossible to establish the direction of causality among accounting identities with econometric analysis. Mainstream economists can continue indefinitely confidently to believe that the money-multiplier theory— *"Reserves cause deposits"*—is borne out by the empirical evidence. Reserve growth necessarily accompanies deposit growth. Experience has shown how extremely difficult it is to persuade mainstream economists to abandon exogenous money.[18]

This book attempts to incorporate monetary endogeneity and interest rate exogeneity centrally into macroeconomic financial analysis, and completely abandon equilibrium analysis. "Exogenous" generally means variables that are "policy-determined" by governments and their agencies. Economies are complex systems. The most that economic analysis can explain and forecast is limited to short-run ordinal changes in key macroeconomic variables, never "equilibrium" solutions for entire systems.

Central banks do not and cannot control the supply of credit money. But they do, can and must set the short term interest rate (Bank Rate) at which they provide liquidity to the system. Central banks are constrained in the Bank Rate they set by the fact that they are faced with both complementary and competing policy goals, full employment, rapid growth and price stability. As a result short-run CB rate-setting activity is always endogenously influenced and shaped over business cycles by the longer-run macroeconomic circumstances in which the economy finds itself.

5 The importance of identities and consistent capital budgeting

As Jim Tobin so often insisted, macroeconomic analysis must emphasize the central importance of identities in economic explanations and the critical importance of the correct formulation of the identities it chooses to emphasize. For questions concerning time, capital budgeting is an essential prerequisite for correct understanding of economic phenomena. Whenever assets have a long expected service lifetime, it is appropriate for units to borrow in the present to finance current asset acquisition so long as the value of the expected future services over the life of the asset exceeds the expected future interest cost of borrowing. Consistent capital budgeting must be performed for the government and the rest of the world sectors, as well as for the business and household sectors in the calculation of agent and sector deficits and surpluses. To be correctly informed as to whether a unit or a sector really has a deficit or a surplus, and about its relative size, the internal and external financing of expenditures for consumption goods and capital goods must be sharply distinguished.[19]

At present (2005) the US economy is widely believed to be running a huge external account deficit, the US government is widely believed to be currently running a huge budgetary deficit, and the US private sector is widely believed to be saving very little out of its income. But in the absence of consistent capital budgeting the calculation of these deficits and surpluses is thoroughly misleading. When assets are measured at current market prices, and capital gains on assets are included in the definition of National Income estimates, income and portfolio deficits can turn out to be surpluses. With consistent capital accounting, the US economy, the government, and the private sector may be shown currently to be both solvent and healthy.[20]

6 The art of persuading the academy[21]

John King has recently written an interesting *History of Post Keynesian Economics*. He concluded that although Post Keynesian theory has mounted a major challenge to orthodox economics it,

> has ultimately failed to supplant it. The object of this book is to explain why Post Keynesianism did not supplant orthodox macroeconomics.[22]

King maintained that the requirements for theoretical progress were,

> increased generality, scope, increased precision, increased rigor, elimination of error, elimination of inconsistency, increased simplicity and beauty, and the ability to predict novel facts.[23]

On the possibility of a future incorporation of Post Keynesianism into a broader heterodox coalition, Smithin has argued:

> Post Keynesianism cannot succeed if the expression is simply a generic term for any and all approaches to the subject which claim to oppose mainstream economics. ... Many of these "non-mainstream" approaches are flatly incompatible with one another in terms of both theoretical principles and of "world view," and are far from presenting a credible united front to potential converts.

Smithin concluded,

> "Embattled survival" is in my view, the only viable option ... [since] there is real analytical merit to the Post Keynesian tradition, ... [and] there are real issues of great importance that continue to divide the Post Keynesians from their mainstream opponents.[24]

Post Keynesian Economics has so far been unsuccessful in gaining acceptance by the mainstream. If a school of thought is measured by sociological considerations, as King has argued, its control of power, money, ranking, and prestige, Post Keynesian Economics has probably been in decline since the early 1960s.

In a review of King in the *JPKE* Davidson argued that a "small tent" definition of Post Keynesianism can meet King's requirements: Post Keynesians are all those who explicitly reject the three central classical axioms (the neutrality of money, gross substitution, and ergodicity).[25] Davidson argued Post Keynesians must become "institution-builders." In this context the present message is that central banks (CB's) when faced with fundamental uncertainty should:

1. Constrain speculative activities in all financial markets,
2. Smooth price movements and provide liquidity in equity as well as bond markets,
3. Set interest rates at the lowest levels that are consistent with price stability.

Davidson argues that the key to the Post Keynesian vision revolves around the recognition that the world is non-ergodic, so all distributions in economics are time-dependent. One cannot accurately predict future behavior on the basis of past observed distributions. Davidson believes it is possible to beat the classical mainstream on their own playing field if only Post Keynesians engage them in a debate. It is easy to demonstrate that the neoclassical axioms imply characteristics which, as Keynes put it,

> happen not to be those in which we actually live, with the result that its [mainstream theory]teaching is misleading and disastrous if we attempt to apply it to the facts of experience.[26]

But the problem is that so far at least little progress has been made in persuading the mainstream of the central significance of non-ergodicity for economic theory. Complex economies are non-ergodic. The present author is optimistic that the recognition that economies are "complex systems" (rather than "based on non-ergodic distributions") will provide a more persuasive foundation for the necessary paradigm shift, and finally enable Post Keynesians to mount a more convincing case to the profession.

Paradigm shifts occur only gradually, as the current senior generation retires. Once minds have been made up material mastered long ago in graduate school tends to become unquestioningly accepted. So long as dominating conclusive logical or empirical proof cannot be brought to the table there is little that can be done except to persuade the next generation.

It is however important to remain optimistic that in the long run "truth" will eventually prevail. As Keynes put it in the closing paragraph of the *General Theory*,

> If the ideas are correct ... it would be a mistake to dispute their potency over a period of time. ... The ideas of economists and political philosophers, both when they are right and when they are wrong, are more powerful than is commonly understood. Indeed the world is ruled by little else. Practical men, who believe themselves to be quite exempt from any intellectual influences, are usually the slaves of some defunct economist Madmen in authority, who hear voices in the air, are distilling their frenzy from some academic scribbler of a few years back[27]

In closing, I can do no better than quote another of my favorite economists, who has similarly experienced disappointment in her attempt to persuade the profession to change its ways:

> I have learned the hard way, over and over and over again, that most people are not always open to persuasion to what's right. It's a pity that this is true of your average professor carrying the New York Times as it is of your average Bubba carrying a six-pack, but there you are. It just goes to show that rhetoric is about something serious ... As Schopenhauer said: "It is quite natural that we should adopt a defensive and negative attitude towards every new opinion concerning something on which we have already an opinion of our own. For it forces its way as an enemy into the previously closed system of our own convictions, shatters the calm of mind we have attained through this system, demands renewed efforts of us and declares our former efforts to have been in vain."[28]

I would like to acknowledge in closing that my title is due to Adriaan van Zon and Joan Mugsken, "*Skill Biases in Employment Opportunities and Income Perspectives: Should We Try to Shake the Invisible Hand?*"[29]

I would also like to acknowledge the input of countless lively and loud Post Keynesian arguments with a great many Post Keynesian and mainstream economists.

In closing, I would like to express my gratitude to Wesleyan University, for permitting me to break all records in the number of leaves and sabbaticals taken in one academic lifetime. As my good friend and colleague Gerry Meier (who went on to Stanford) used to say, the faculty at elite small liberal arts colleges like Wesleyan, although unable to teach graduate students and keep up with all the specialized techniques of the research frontier, have the leisure to reflect at length, consider the big picture, and formulate apposite criticisms of the state of the discipline. This is precisely what I have here attempted.

Part I
Complexity and Economics

1
Marshall's Tides

> The next condition is that all the significant factors are measurable, and that we have adequate statistical knowledge of their measure … . If it is necessary that all the significant factors should be measurable, this is very important. For it withdraws from the operation of the method all those economic problems where political, social, and psychological factors, including such things as government policy, the progress of invention and the state of expectation may be significant. In particular, it is inapplicable to the problem of the business cycle.
>
> John Maynard Keynes, 1939

> It cannot be overemphasized that the social sciences like the life sciences are hypercomplex. Social phenomena are inherently far more difficult to understand than physical phenomena. As a result it is they which should really be called the "hard sciences."
>
> Edmund Wilson, 1998: 183

1.1 Introduction: Marshall's tidal metaphor

Alfred Marshall discussed the nature of "economic laws" in chapter 3 of his *Principles of Economics*. He asked: *"Why should the 'laws of economics' be less predicable and precise in their workings than the laws of physics?"* His answer was that economic forces work against a background of hugely complex forces. The most that can be expected of economic analysis is to capture *"tendencies"* induced by changes in economic variables. An increase in demand implies a *"tendency"* for prices to rise, *ceteris paribus*. This states that a rise in prices will occur, providing that none of the complicating factors imprisoned in the *ceteris paribus* clause work in the opposite direction with sufficient strength to cancel the effect of the increase in demand.[1]

To help the reader see what is involved in this idea in his third edition Marshall introduced the following simple analogy of the tides:

> The laws of gravity work in a highly regular way: so that the orbit of Jupiter can be predicted with great precision. In contrast the movement of the tides is much

harder to predict, because the tides are affected by two different influences. The primary influence is the gravitational pull of the sun and the moon. These can be modeled with great accuracy. But the tides are also influenced by meteorological factors, which are notoriously difficult to predict. They are also a secondary influence. By modeling the astronomical factors, we can arrive at a theory that affords us an adequate prediction, although always subject to some error.[2]

Unfortunately the tidal analogy is seriously misleading for economics. Since economies are complex adaptive systems there are no underlying stable regular relationships like the astrological factors in the tides. If Marshall's analogy were valid, we would have seen spectacular progress in economic modeling as has occurred in oceanography over the past hundred years.[3] We have not.

The theory of the tides was in a primitive and very unsatisfactory state when Marshall was writing his *Principles*. Only in the current century have researchers come to appreciate the importance of modeling the tides in each ocean as independent standing waves between continents. The solutions of the associated systems of equations with various simplified representations of the continental boundaries have led hydrologists to a whole new degree of precision. More recently the main advances have come with accurate modeling of the correction terms, to allow for the fact that the ocean is not of a uniform depth ("shallow water effects"). The problem of modeling the height and time of high tide has now been essentially resolved and research has shifted to more subtle problems, for example, modeling the way velocity of flow varies with depth.[4]

Marshall's bold claim that the workings of the market mechanism would pin down a unique outcome, as a function of a small number of observable variables subject to a small *"noise"* component in the manner suggested by the tides analogy, was not immediately accepted in the profession. Critics asked, "If we begin with only those few assumptions that we can readily justify, how can we know that this will provide a model within which a unique outcome is pinned down?"

The key exchange was between Marshall and Edgeworth. It was conducted in a microeconomic context, with reference to a single-product market in which a large number of rival firms competed. Marshall proceeded conventionally by first constructing a supply schedule, and then computing the intersection of supply and demand as a "unique" outcome.

Edgeworth proceeded more slowly. He first asked about the different strategies available to agents on either side of the market, and reached a much more pessimistic conclusion: prices will be indeterminate within a wide region. Within this region of indeterminacy no unique outcome can be pinned down by reference to the observable characteristics of supply and demand. Only when the number of agents in the market become very large does this region shrink to the unique competitive outcome defined by Marshall.[5]

In the interchange that followed, Marshall's prestige carried the day. The difficulties that Edgeworth emphasized were set aside as secondary complications. So long as we can safely assume that the world is approximated by a well-behaved model with a unique equilibrium outcome, the analogy of the tides holds good. The outcomes we observe are in fact the true "equilibrium" outcomes, but are accompanied by "random noise."

In the first half of the twentieth century economists began to make substantial strides in bringing together economic theory and empirical data. The idea was to formulate a deterministic theoretical model whose purpose was to represent the "true" underlying equilibrium mechanisms.[6] The passage from theoretical predictions to the data was bridged by attributing differences between predicted and actual values to "factors omitted from the model," and to "errors of measurement." This approach reflected the then prevalent view that economic data sets could not validly be described by reference to formal probabilistic models. Although statistical techniques such as least squares were frequently used to estimate the underlying relationship, these statistical procedures were not interpreted with reference to a probabilistic model. Concepts such as the "standard error" of estimated coefficients were not introduced.[7]

Although substantial efforts were devoted to such studies, their role remained highly controversial. How do we know that the relationships uncovered by such exercises transcend the particular data set under examination? If the forces that lay outside the model shift between one data set and the next, surely the estimated relationship would also shift? Robbins maintained,

> There is no reason to suppose that changes in the future will be due to the causes that have operated in the past ... there is no justification for claiming for [these] results the status of the so-called "statistical" laws of the natural sciences.[8]

Robbins' skepticism went hand-in-hand with his strongly expressed views on how far economists could validly proceed on the basis of *a priori* theoretical arguments. These assumptions were of an extremely weak kind which could safely be taken as compelling, for example, "consumers can arrange their preferences in an order," "there is more than one factor of production." Robbins believed that all generalizations of interest could be based on such fundamental assumptions, together with a few secondary assumptions chosen sensitive to the problem at hand.[9] So long as the theoretical claims were compelling, the task of the empirical worker was merely to estimate those parameters whose values were unspecified within the theory.

If we set aside his extreme skepticism as to the stability of the estimated parameters, Robbins' views find an important echo among many theorists today.[10] The pungency with which Robbins expressed his outlook reflected his battle with the leading empiricists of his day. The typical business cycle analyst then reversed the relative importance of theory and evidence: his job was simply to estimate the statistical regularities that existed in macroeconomic data in a manner that did not rest on any dubious *a priori* theoretical restrictions. Robbins regarded the failure of empirical analysis to even remotely predict the collapse of 1929 as a complete and total discreditation of the entire theoretical approach.

The views of Robbins and business cycle economists formed two extremes of the debate of the 1920s. Most economists took the middle ground position advocated by Marshall: the way forward was in the careful interplay of theory and evidence.

Theory alone was empty, while empirical investigations without theory are suspect. Marshall held that the interweaving of theory and evidence constituted "economics proper."[11] For those in the middle ground the question became simply "how best to proceed in confronting theory with evidence?"

1.2 Haavalmo's probability revolution: "Let the data decide"

By the 1940s two new strands of thought had emerged which together provided economists with a powerful new way of proceeding. The first was Samuelson's *Foundations of Economic Analysis*, published in 1947 although written a decade earlier. Samuelson showed how the vast bulk of theoretical analysis formulated by economists shared a common formal elementary structure. A series of "equilibrium relations" could be postulated and be assumed to hold between certain sets of variables. The solution of the system of simultaneous equations defined by these relations pinned down a unique equilibrium outcome. The impact of exogenous shocks to the system and the effects of exogenous policy variables could be modeled as a shift in one or more of the underlying parameters of the model. Comparison of the new equilibrium outcome with the old provided a prediction of the effects of the shock or policy variable in question. Samuelson's method of "comparative static analysis" appeared for the first time to provide the possibility of unification of the entire literature of economics within this new framework.[12]

Against this background Haavelmo published his now classic article, "*The Probability Approach in Econometrics*" as a 118-page supplement to the July 1944 issue of *Econometrica*. Haavelmo directly confronted the prevailing conventional wisdom which held that there was no basis for regarding economic data as being the outcome of some probabilistic scheme.[13] He argued that statistics has no valid interpretation except as they are related to some probabilistic scheme, and then proceeded to dispose of the popular misunderstanding that a probabilistic scheme was only applicable in situations where each observation was an independent draw from the same population.

Haavelmo's contribution was based on the recognition that the entire set of n observations could be interpreted as a single draw ("sample point") taken from an "*n-dimensional joint probability law*," the existence of which may be purely hypothetical. He fully recognized (and emphasized) that in practice agents' actions depended on:

> a great number of factors, many of which cannot be expressed in quantitative terms. What is then the point of trying to associate such behavior with only a limited set of measurable phenomena, which cannot be more than an incomplete picture ... ?[14]

Notwithstanding the complexity of the list of potential influences he argued that since some actions taken by agents have systematic and measurable consequences, it was: "only a natural step to attempt an approximate description of the behavioristic parameters."

For Haavelmo the apparatus of econometrics was essentially a diagnostic tool to be used in uncovering the workings of any systematic mechanisms at work, against a background of enormously complicating influences operating in a complex "noisy" world. Unfortunately this leaves open the question of whether there exists an underlying "true model" whose structure we can hope to uncover by incorporating Marshall's distinction between systematic influences and "noise". The heart of Haavelmo's concern was how to distinguish "deeper" regularities, whose appearance reflects some underlying "law," from "apparent" regularities that happen to crop up in particular data sets. (This would now be expressed as how to identify the underlying "structural equations" that lie behind the "reduced form relationships" observed in the data.)

Are there really two logically separable classes of mechanisms at work as reflected in Marshall's analogy of the tides, one yielding large systematic influences that can be captured in the equations of the model, and the other yielding only secondary random influences? To complete the description of the model we must assume a structure for the disturbance terms. The unruly list of potential influences can then be partitioned, and the noise part modeled as a set of random draws from some estimated distribution.

Suppose the analogy of the tides were accurate, and there in fact exists a "true" model linking an endogenous variable (y_t) to a vector of exogenous variables (x_{it}), plus a stochastic disturbance term (η_i), (where the subscripts x_{it} indicate data points). To obtain good estimates of the coefficients we need a data set where the values of x_{it} vary widely, leaving a clear trace of x's influence on y. But in practice we always work with only a limited set of data where many of the potentially relevant terms show little variability. In consequence the estimated equations are likely to indicate that only a limited subset of the x_i's are significantly different from zero. Attempts to replicate the model with new data sets are then likely to prove difficult. One of the "insignificant" x_i variables may have shifted to a new value, which again shows little variability within the new data set, but its effect is to induce a shift in other estimated coefficients. In principle what we must do is pool the data until we have a sufficiently large data set within which all the relevant variables exhibit a sufficiently wide range of variability, so as to lay bear the structure of the "true" model. But once we move beyond the setting in which the tides analogy is valid this task becomes impossibly difficult.

1.3 Keynes' skepticism: unobservable variables

Hayek and Keynes both very forcefully expressed grave doubts concerning the difficulty of Haavelmo's procedure of *"letting the data decide"* between candidate models. They emphasized that many important influences were inherently unobservable, impossible to measure, and sporadic in their operation. Hayek's objections were fatal and led him to a subjectivist conclusion and a dismissive opposition of the value of any econometric research.[15] Keynes' criticism of econometrics was much more measured. Nevertheless he strongly believed that in economics as a social science there would always be important variables that we are unable to measure and quantify. Keynes was concerned whether all relevant factors had been included in the equations, whether the factors were measurable and independent, whether the functional forms were appropriate, and whether the treatment of time lags and trends were satisfactory. He expressed these methodological doubts and objections in a review "Tinbergen's Statistical Testing of Business–Cycle Theories."

> If we were dealing with ... independent atomic factors ... acting with fluctuating relative strength on material constant and known through time we might be able to use the method of multiple correlation with some confidence for disentangling the laws of action.[16]
>
> Am I right in thinking that the method of multiple correlation analysis essentially depends on the economist having furnished, not merely the list of significant causes which is correct as far as it goes, but a complete list? For example, suppose three factors are taken into account. It is not enough that these should be in fact *verae causae*, there must be no other significant factor. If there is a further factor not taken into account of, then the method is not able to discover the relative quantitative importance of the first three. If so this means the economist is able to provide beforehand a correct and indubitably complete analysis of the significant factors. The method is one neither of discovery nor of criticism. It is a means of giving quantitative precision to what, in qualitative terms, we know already as the result of a complete theoretical analysis—provided always that it is a case where the other considerations to be given below are satisfied.[17]

Nowadays these objections of Hayek and Keynes are regarded as misplaced and unconstructive.[18] If the relationships are in fact nonlinear and if outcomes are heavily influenced by unobservable factors whose size we cannot measure, or whose impact we cannot pin down, how else should we proceed? Since we must judge between competing models of how the economy works, surely it is best simply to let the data decide?

If the economy were in fact like the tides metaphor, these robust dismissals of Keynes' objections would be justified. But if the economic universe were in fact as systematic as that, economists like oceanographers would long have converged onto a portfolio of well-founded theoretical models, as the hydrologists in the last century. Unfortunately economics is still far away from such a goal.

In the immediate postwar years of the 1960s based on the IS–LM paradigm economic performance and economists' confidence in the future progress of applied research had risen very high. But by the late 1970s this performance and confidence had completely disintegrated to be replaced by a new wiser and deeper skepticism.

The 1960s saw the first major challenge to mainstream Keynesian views on modeling macroeconomic activity. Friedman's early formulation of the Monetarist position appeared reducible to a set of claims which could be couched within the standard paradigm. Both Keynesians and Monetarists were content to use the identical IS–LM framework of equations to describe relationships between major macroeconomic variables. Differences between the two schools turned on the size of two key empirically estimateable parameters, the interest elasticity of the portfolio demand for money, and the interest elasticity of demand for investment goods, which determined the slope of the IS and LM curves respectively.

The stagflation of the 1970s produced a striking disappointment for the mainstream research program. Extended empirical research by proponents of both schools totally failed to resolve their differences. This failure was essentially due to the inherent noisiness of the data. Many factors obviously impinging on outcomes such as "animal spirits" were nonquantifiable, and so had to be left out of the model. Controlling for such influences involve more or less arbitrary decisions on which rival researchers were completely unable to agree. The stagflation of the 1970s was characterized by both high and rising inflation *and* high and rising unemployment. Growth rates fell but there appeared no clear long-run tradeoff between inflation and unemployment. It was falsely concluded that the Phillips Curves were vertical in the long run, and there was no long-run tradeoff between inflation and employment. This result had disastrous implications for Keynesian counter-cyclical aggregate demand (AD) management policy. The policy pendulum swung to Monetarist solutions, extremely restrictive monetary policy and extremely high interest rates, designed "to wring inflationary expectations out of the system."[19]

If the economy were merely a complicated and not a complex system and if all potential influences were measurable, there need in principle still be no problem. As data sets accumulate, with the use of proxy variables we might reasonably expect to converge bit-by-bit to ever closer approximations to the "true" model. Keynes and many others emphasized the extreme importance of ephemeral and nonmeasurable expectation factors for business cycles. Keynes' root explanation of business cycles was very simple: shifts in investor "animal spirits," which he seriously doubted could ever be accurately quantified. There may be some rare circumstances when the problem of model selection more or less disappears. But in general we never know what is the *"true"* model.[20] In macroeconomics the problems posed by factors that are unquestionably of major importance but are intrinsically nonmeasurable suggest that for most questions the problem of model selection is intractable.[21]

As Keynes insisted, in practice many of the x_is are impossible to measure quantitatively, even by way of "proxy" variables to control for their effects. When this is so the mere accumulation of more data does not help. We are stuck with the unpleasant fact that some of our systematic influences have slipped into the estimated "residuals," that is, into the "noise" component. One key question is then, "is it reasonable to expect the 'noise' terms to have nice statistical properties?"

When the equations don't have nice properties this is taken as an indication that there is at least one influence that we have failed to pick up. But to the extent that there are variables that we cannot measure, proxy, or control for, but which exert large and systematic influences on outcomes, their presence can easily induce continuous bias into the estimated model coefficients that we fit.[22]

Suppose we were in fact to impose the *"correct"* model, with all unobservable variables suppressed? Would there be any reason to suppose that our fitted residuals would have a "nice" structure, for example, the absence of serial correlation? Models that appear to fit for one time period suddenly break down for subsequent periods, leading to a search for hitherto unrecognized relevant factors. Put in this way the problem corresponds to the deep worries expressed by Haavelmo. Was it realistic to hope that model selection exercises could ever succeed in uncovering stable structural relationships?

1.4 Conclusions: the economy is a complex system

The essence of Marshall's tides analogy is captured by three properties:

1. A true model exists which captures a "complete set" of all factors that exert large and systematic influences.
2. All remaining influences can be treated as a "noise" component and modeled as a random drawn from some probability distribution.
3. The "true" model determines a unique equilibrium.

If the economy is a complex adaptive system none of these conditions hold. There is no sharp divide between measurable systematic (e.g. astronomical) influences and nonmeasurable (e.g. meteorological) factors treatable as "noise." With an indefinite number of exogenous variables, some having a larger influence and some smaller, in any finite data set we inevitably find that only a few of the variables are significant. Nonetheless whenever we re-estimate the model with a new data set there are always more variables sitting in the background that are subsumed in the noise component of the model we select. There exists no single "true" structural model of a complex economy.

The meteorological analogy is much more appropriate for economics than Marshall's tidal analogy. Meteorologists now recognize that meteorological phenomena must be modeled as nonlinear chaotic systems. Such systems exhibit many chaotic properties, such as "extreme sensitivity to initial conditions." Meteorologists have gained much deeper insight into weather behavior. They now understand *why* it is impossible to predict the weather more than a few days in advance. The meteorological universe has finally definitively been shown to be nonlinear.[23]

But the economic universe is unimaginably more complex than the meteorological universe. Unlike the homogeneous individual molecules of physics individual economic agents have consciousness, free will, and memory. Their individual behavior is extremely heterogeneous and their collective behavior can never be accurately forecast in advance, no matter how large the computer, how sophisticated the model, or how thorough the statistical analysis. Economies as complex adaptive systems (CAS) exhibit continual evolutionary technological transformation. History is a poor and untrustworthy guide to their future behavior. This is particularly the case for the analysis of business cycles, where changes in underlying moods and expectations with their associated unobservable and nonmeasurable dynamics are of critical importance.

Consider Galbraith's brilliant and vivid observation of the role of nonquantifiable expectations and mood swings in asset markets:

> The circumstances that induce the recurrent lapses into financial dementia have not changed in any truly operational way since the Tulipmania of 1636–1637. Individuals and institutions alike are captured by the wondrous satisfaction from accruing wealth. The associated illusion of insight is protected, in turn, by the oft-noted public impression that intelligence, one's own and that of others, marches in close step with the possession of money. Out of that belief, thus instilled, comes action – the bidding up of values, whether in land, securities, or, as recently, art. And so on to the moment of mass disillusion and the crash. The last, it will now be sufficiently evident, never comes gently. It is always accompanied by a desperate and largely unsuccessful effort to get out. ... There is nothing in economic life so willfully misunderstood as the great speculative episode ... When will come the next great speculative episode, and in what venue will it recur – real estate, securities markets, art, antique automobiles?
>
> To these [questions] there are no answers; no one knows. Anyone who presumes to answer does not know he doesn't know. But one thing is certain: there will be another of these episodes and yet more beyond. Fools, it has long been said are separated, soon or eventually, from their money. So, alas are those who, responding to a general mood of optimism, are captured by a sense of their own financial acumen. Thus it has been for centuries; thus in the long future it will also be.[24]

One unfortunate side effect of the dominance of the standard paradigm in the profession has been the tendency of mainstream economists to argue that the only "proper" kind of model is a complete model of the standard kind: The only correct way to test a theory is by examining restrictions on regression coefficients within the context of a model-selection exercise.[25]

But it is frequently more fruitful and enlightening to work in a looser framework and not attempt to specify a complete model of the standard kind. Different situations call for different approaches. *"Horses for courses"* as they say. In the future it may be found possible to build and simulate nonlinear models. But they will never successfully be able to predict the future.

This book makes the case that economies are complex adaptive systems and must be modeled as such. Once this is recognized the entire mainstream paradigm: general equilibrium, linear analysis, exogenous random shocks, closed-form equilibrium solutions, all fall like a house of cards and must be abandoned. The challenge for macroeconomics as a discipline is to develop a new dynamic nonequilibrium paradigm.

Note that recognizing that economies are CAS and throwing away equilibrium does not imply economists can say nothing about system behavior. Nor does it imply that anything is possible. A central goal of this book is to point the way toward a new nonequilibrium paradigm for macroeconomics, where "equilibrium analysis" is done by "process analysis". Economic processes evolve over time nonlinearly.

All economic variables must be dated and chronological time must be incorporated in an essential way. Sooner rather than later, economists will recognize "equilibrium" is useless and misleading. They will stop postulating and solving for "equilibrium" configurations. Economies are nonlinear, and "shocks" are endogenous and continual in their effects. Economic variables have unit roots in levels and not deterministic trends. Most economic distributions are fractal, have a memory and may be characterized as non-periodic. There are no constant "systematic" factors in economics like the planets, whose behavior may be captured and measured with statistical confidence. In economies nothing can be truly known in advance. Economies have no underlying "structure" and no unique "future" that can be discovered. Contingency is fundamental. In complex adaptive systems things happen … Just happen.

2
Complexity and Contingency

Some 165 million years ago dinosaurs were masters of Earth. Mammals, our direct ancestors, subsisted as best they could as small animals hiding in nooks and crannies to keep out of sight of voracious dinosaurs and assorted carnivorous monsters. But something happened some 165 million years ago ... that would change everything. ... A huge asteroid, weighing some 10,000 billion tons and about 10 km in size, crashed into the Yukatan peninsula. ... The impact had the explosive force of a billion megatons of TNT, or five billion times the power of the bomb that destroyed Hiroshima ... Earth shook heavily from the violence of this cosmic impact. The impact propelled more than a hundred thousand billion tons of vaporized rocks high into the atmosphere, leaving a giant crater 180 kilometers in diameter and more than 20 kilometers deep. The vaporized rocky material cooled off in the atmosphere and began falling back down to earth as hundreds of millions of small stones. A rain of gravel pelted the earth for the following hour. Atmospheric friction was such that the air became red hot. The nitrogen in the atmosphere began to combine with oxygen to form nitric acid, creating acid rain. Fires started to consume forests and spread rapidly over the entire planet ... The winds spread the dust particles all around the globe, and a huge black cloud covered the entire earth, blocking out the sun's light and preventing its heat from warming the planet. ... The consequences of this severe darkening of the skies and this deluge of acid rain were devastating to both plants and animals. A total of 30 to 80 percent of plant species were wiped out. The disappearance of plants and trees in turn triggered the demise of two-thirds of living species, including the dinosaurs which literally starved to death. ...

T. Thuan, 2001: 1, 43–4

Among the vast array of molecules that an organism can manufacture to serve its needs are simple carbon atoms of the methane series, composed entirely of carbon and hydrogen atoms. With one carbon atom, only a single kind of molecule is possible. With ten carbon atoms, the number is 75, with 20 it is 366, 319, and with 40 it is 62 trillion. Add oxygen atoms here and there on the hydrocarbon chains, to produce alcohol's, aldehydes, and ketones, and the number rises even more rapidly with molecular size. Now select various sub-sets, and imagine multiple ways they can be derived by enzyme-mediated manufacture. You have potential complexity beyond the powers of present day imagination. ...

The greatest challenge today, in all of science, is the accurate and complete description of complex systems. Scientists have broken down many kinds of systems. They think they know most of the elements and forces. The next task is to reassemble them, at least in mathematical models that capture the key properties of the entire ensembles. Success in this enterprise will be measured by the power researchers acquire to predict emergent phenomena when passing from general to more specific levels of organization. That in simplest terms is the great challenge of scientific holism.

Edmund Wilson, 1998: 85

2.1 An introduction to complex adaptive systems

We live in a world of truly astonishing complexity. Molecules interact with molecules to form cells, cells interact with cells to form organisms, organisms interact with organisms to form ecosystems, societies, and economies. Nevertheless it is extremely difficult to provide a working definition of complexity. There is neither something at a level below (micro-constituents) nor at a level above (a meta-description) that is capable of capturing the essence of complexity. One loose characterization is complexity is proportional to the degree of a phenomenon's improbability. Another is that complexity denotes more possibilities than can ever be actualized. These attributes hardly serve as definitions, but they do suggest that one should not be surprised that no simple definition of complexity is comprehensive. Instead of a definition, an outline of the most salient attributes of complex systems will be presented as an example of both the challenges and the prospects for economics offered by the new methods of the complexity sciences.

It is first useful to distinguish between "complicated," and "complex." If a system can be given a complete description in terms of its individual constituents and then analyzed by the method of reductionism, for example, televisions, computers, software programs, jumbo jets, or a snowflake, the system is merely complicated.[1]

A complex system is one in which the interactions between the constituents of the system, and the interaction between the system and its environment are such that the system as a whole cannot be fully understood solely by analyzing its micro components. The relationships among the components are not fixed but shift continually over time. The spontaneous self-organizing behavior of complex systems involves the nonlinear interaction of numerous uncontrollable forces. Complex systems evolve over the longer run in a manner far too complex ever to be successfully modeled. Even when successive events are formally linked chaotic behavior implies unpredictable outcomes. Analysis of the long-run behavior of complex systems is necessarily speculative and conjectural. Prediction of their future long-run behavior is impossible.

Complex systems are constituted by intricate sets of nonlinear relationships and feedback loops. They are inherently nonlinear and nearby trajectories can separate at exponential rates. Linear systems would explode, since for linear systems orbits that are locally unstable are globally unstable. But this is not true for nonlinear systems where local instability can coexist with bounded motion. Nearby trajectories separate exponentially, but are eventually folded back together and contained within a bounded region. This is the strange property of "hidden attractors."[2]

Complex systems are characterized by "sensitive dependence on initial conditions," possess "emergent properties," and interact with their environment. Many phenomena are emergent and exhibit properties that cannot be predicted or understood by examining the system's components. Since our world is bounded by uncertainty, empirical measurements have only a finite degree of precision. Initial conditions can never be precisely specified. Reality inevitably contains many unknown factors that we cannot hope to take into account. Any "laws" for complex systems no matter how complicated remain only approximations. Complex systems are open, and change unpredictably over time. Since our brains are all too finite, all comprehensible human models must be closed. This implies that only selected aspects of an open system can be modeled so our analysis of complex systems is necessarily incomplete.[3]

A complex system cannot be understood without considering its history. Two objectively identical systems when placed in identical conditions can respond in different ways if they have different histories. The history of a system is important, but not merely for understanding its current behavior. History co-determines the structure of a complex system. The evolutionary history of a system is not present in a way that can be "deconstructed." Although the history of the system is a determinant of its behavior, the history is continuously transformed through self-organizing processes. Only traces of history remain, distributed through the system. These traces do not correspond to facts, ideas, or symbols that can be "recalled from a filing cabinet." They constitute patterns of information, "smeared" over many units, stored in distributed fashion, and continually changing and altered by experience. Smith's metaphor of the "invisible hand" premises a disjunction between system-wide outcomes and the design capabilities of individuals. Market outcomes are the unintended consequences of individuals' actions rather than borne of national calculation and design.

Complexity theory may be formally defined as the search for algorithms that display common features across many levels of organizations. Commonalties assist in pruning all algorithms that can be conceived down to the ones that are present.[4] At their best models of complex systems can lead to understanding of the existence of a deeper new order and in the process account for emergent phenomena such as cells, ecosystems, and markets. Life itself is surely the most striking emergent property of complex systems. In constructing themselves from molecule, to cell, to organism, to ecosystem, living systems display deep laws of complexity and emergence, most of which lie beyond our grasp. Living organisms are self-assembling and adaptive, the most complex systems known. Most complexity theoreticians have thus focused their attention on biology, in particular the human brain.

The science of complexity is now like quantum theory stretching the cognitive capacity of humans to the breaking point. To understand how fertilized cells grow into complex organisms, or how the human brain generates language or creates consciousness, may be as far beyond our mental capacities as our ability to precisely track a water molecule as it falls over Niagara Falls. Science has in the past derived its power from the fact that its assertions can be checked against the real world, unlike the assertions of literature, religion, and art. Unfortunately this is no longer the case and the door is now for the first time open to "ironic" science.[5] Nonlinear systems have no closed-form solution, and human behavior cannot be fully defined by any mathematical model. There is no simple basic equation for life. Much of life is shaped less by deterministic laws than by contingent circumstances, or "serendipity." Science's faith in great unifying ideas is now dwindling. Society is gradually learning to accept a multiplicity of styles and views. The postmodern age is dawning: *Humanity is arriving at the end of certitude.*[6]

Reductionist approaches are inherently flawed for the analysis of complex systems. The behavior of a complex system cannot be deduced from even the most exhaustive formulation of its micro foundations, since complex phenomena are much more than the simple sum of their parts. A complex system cannot be "reduced" to a simpler one, unless it was not really complex to begin with. The "true nature" of complex systems cannot be revealed in terms of a smaller number of logical principles. Realistic models of complex systems must somehow "conserve" their complexity. In a sense they must be as complex as the system they model.[7]

The study of complex systems has uncovered a fundamental flaw in the highly successful and time-tested analytical method of reductionism. A complex system is constituted not by the sum of its components, but by the changing relationships among them. By "cutting up" a complex system reductionism destroys what it seeks to understand.

In classical reductionism the behavior of holistic entities is explained by reference to the nature of their constituents. The entities are viewed as collections of lower level objects and their interactions. Complex systems are also the collection of their elements. But their behavior can never be understood by a reductionist examination of their components. Analysis of complex systems must avoid the temptation of looking for a "master key." Due to the mechanisms by which complex systems structure themselves any single principle can provide only a partial inadequate insight. The analyst must be sensitive to self-organizing interactions and remain open to the play of patterns that perpetually transform both the system, and the environment in which it operates.

We appear to have arrived at a series of truisms: Complexity is complex. A complex system cannot be reduced to a simple one if it wasn't merely complicated to begin with. Complex problems can only be solved with complex resources. But these truisms do offer a powerful critique of reductionism. A complex adaptive system cannot be reduced to a collection of its basic constituents, not because the system is not constituted by them, but because the critical and changing relational information gets lost in the process. Strict quantification of the output is ordinarily infeasible for complex systems. Nonlinearity and incompressibility are central.

2.2 Some unique characteristics of complex adaptive systems: emergent properties, self-organized criticality, and sandpiles

Complexity results from the changing interactions between the components of a system and is manifested at the level of the system itself. Due to their complex patterns of interaction, complex characteristics "emerge" through interaction within the system.[8] Complex adaptive systems exhibit features such as "emergent properties" and "self-organized criticality." They are particularly associated with, although not confined to, living organisms.[9] Of particular interest for complexity is the human brain and all its products; consciousness, self reflection, languages, cultures, politics, arts, and economics.

Emergent properties are possessed by the complex whole, not by its parts. Take the case of a glass of water. There is nothing extremely complicated about a water molecule. Yet put a few zillion of these molecules together and you have a thing that shimmers, sloshes and gurgles. Collectively the molecules have acquired the property of "liquidity" or "viscosity" which none of them possess on their own. Unless you know precisely where and how to look for it, there is nothing in the fundamental equations of physics that even hints at such a property. Liquidity or viscosity is an example of an "emergent property." A critical current issue in molecular biology is which emergent properties can be explained in terms of their constituent parts, and which cannot.[10]

Water is as simple a molecule as one is likely to find. If it can withstand reductive analysis one need not worry about proteins and molecules of DNA. But as is well known water molecules undergo a "phase transition," when you cool them down or heat them up sufficiently. Quantum theory can provide a complete explanation of the structure of water in its gaseous phase but in neither of its condensed phases. None of the properties of water vapor are emergent. But all of the properties of liquid water and ice are irreducibly emergent.

An even less well-known and more astonishing emergent property of water is termed "critical opalescence":

> Critical opalescence is a strikingly beautiful effect that is seen when water is heated to a temperature of 374 degrees Celsius under high pressure. 374 degrees is the critical temperature of water, the temperature at which water turns continuously into steam without boiling. At the critical temperature and pressure, water and steam are indistinguishable. They are a single fluid unable to make up its mind whether to be a gas or a liquid. In that critical state the fluid is continually fluctuating between gas and liquid. The fluctuations are seen visually as a multicolored sparkling. The sparkling is called opalescence because it is also seen in opal jewels which have a similar multicolored radiance.[11]

Deciding which properties are emergent and which are not is far from easy. At each level of complexity new properties appear and for each stage new laws, new concepts, and new theories are necessary.

Self-organization is an "emergent property" of complex systems which enables them to adapt to cope with changes in their environment. Self-organization describes the emergence of macroscopic behavior through the activity of microscopic units responding to local information. A self-organizing system is suspended between active and passive modes. It reacts to the state of the environment and simultaneously transforms itself in response, affecting in turn its environment. The distinctions between active and passive, causal and caused then come under pressure. Self-organization is a self-transforming process: the system acts upon itself. A meta-level description may be constructed but can yield only "snapshots" of the system as it exists at given moments. The temporal complexities produced by the reflexive nature of self-organizing systems cannot be represented by any meta-description.[12]

The classical definition of stability holds that small causes produce small effects. But since relationships in complex systems are nonlinear this definition no longer holds. The notion of the "structure" of a dynamic system pertains to the mechanisms developed to receive, encode, transform and store information on one hand, and to react to such information by some form of output on the other. "Structure" evolves through a process of self-organization as a result of a complex interaction between the history of the system, the environment, and the present state of the system. Classical considerations term complex systems unstable. But for all living systems static "equilibrium" implies death.[13]

Poincaré suggested a probabilistic definition of instability. He defined unstable events as events that have no observable cause, "chance" events as opposed to "deterministic" ones. But complex systems reveal unpredictable behavior that is not the result of "chance." It is the result of (i.e. "caused by") the interaction of complex system factors. Although complexity contains structure, and so is not "randomness", it is nevertheless not describable in first-order logical terms:

> I find no alternative but to accept multiple, formally incompatible descriptions as a satisfactory explanation of many types of biological events ... a theory based on chance events, including those of quantum theory, ... serves only as an escape from classical determinism: it is not a theory of self-organization.[14]

The full comprehension of complex phenomena is likely to be forever beyond our mental grasp. Some scientists have suggested that for complex phenomena: *Insight seldom arises from complicated messy modeling but more often from gross simplifications.*[15]

Bak has developed the simple metaphor of the "sand pile" to illustrate how complex phenomena self-organize into "critical states." For sand piles minor disturbances like a few additional grains of sand can lead to avalanches of all sizes even catastrophes due solely to the dynamical interactions among individual elements of the system. A sand pile self-organizes into a "critical state." Avalanches can be understood, but never predicted from holistic descriptions of the properties of the entire pile. They cannot be modeled by reductionist descriptions of the properties of individual grains of sand.

> The metaphor of the sand pile helps us understand why it is impossible to predict the occurrence of complex phenomena such as earthquakes and business cycles. Like sand piles such events are contingent on minor local details of the historical configuration of the entire system. A reductionist approach cannot uncover the emergent properties possessed by a sand pile. The system remains posed at the critical state, as grains of sand interact and cause others to topple. We understand much about avalanches. They follow the Gutenberg-Richter power law, have fractal slopes emerge from the slides, and the slopes differ with different materials. But as Richter (the developer of the Richter scale) insisted: "Only fools, charlatans, and liars will predict earthquakes"[16]

The laws of physics are simple and can be expressed by mathematical equations. Sand piles are complex, and complexity is a "Chinese Box" phenomenon. In each box there is a new surprise. The underlying mystery of chaos is how does such incredible complexity emerge out of simple invariable relationships? What are the underlying properties of biological and social events that render them sensitive to minor accidental events? Solar flares, sand piles, earth temperatures, earthquakes, the water levels of the Nile, the English language, business cycles, stock prices, foreign exchange rates, speculative prices and an astonishing variety of other phenomena follow a deeper type of order termed "power law" distributions. These distributions may be chaotic, fractal, and characterized by scale-invariance. They may have no "characteristic" size. The frequency of events is inversely proportional to their magnitude.[17] Mandelbrot has found that stock prices follow a "Levy Distribution," characterized by "fat tail" power law distributions.[18]

A wide variety of phenomena follow different power law distributions. Economists traditionally have discarded large fluctuations as "outliers" and considered them "atypical." But economies are complex systems, where each agent has limited choices and "bounded rationality." Each attempts to do her best to increase her utility, based on her expectations of the future behavior of other agents. Each agent's decisions affect other agents, who adjust their expectations and behavior in turn to increase their expected welfare. Each agent's expectations of the future are influenced by the behavior of and the expectations of other agents. This yields a whole new deeper level of complexity and renders the prediction of future social and economic behavior impossible.

For nonliving complex phenomena, for example the relations between the planets and the geological history of the earth, self-organization takes place over eons and encompasses unimaginably lengthy transient periods. For all complex events the expression "we cannot understand the present without understanding its past" takes on deeper meanings. There are always many more small events than large events. But for complex phenomena, system changes are associated primarily with large, infrequent and catastrophic events.

Due to the inherent imprecision of language verbal descriptions tend to view events that occur with some degree of regularity as "periodic." But in all power-law phenomena strict periodicity is nonexistent. Complex events are clustered in time. After some time the longer you have waited at a given location for a certain phenomena, for example, a bus, the longer you can expect to wait. The longer a species has been in existence, the longer it can be expected to be around in the future.[19]

2.3 The relational structure of complex adaptive systems

Complexity is the result of a rich interaction of simple elements that respond to the limited information with which each of them is presented. Complexity emerges as a result of the pattern of interactions between the elements. All complex systems have the following relational structure.[20]

1. A complex adaptive system consists of very large number of individual elements. Conventional means of description (e.g. a closed system of equations) do not comprise a full understanding of the system.
2. To constitute a complex system individual elements must interact dynamically.
3. The interaction must be fairly rich, so that any element in the system influences and is influenced by many other ones.[21]
4. Interactions are local and nonlinear. Small causes have large effects, and vice versa. (Nonlinearity is a precondition for modeling complexity.)
5. Interactions have a short range, since information is received primarily from immediate neighbors. This does not preclude wide-ranging influences, since the influences may be mediated (enhanced or suppressed) along the way.
6. There are loops in the interactions, and the effects of any action may feed back on itself positively (enhancing) and negatively (inhibiting). Both kinds are necessary. (The technical term is "recurrency.")
7. A complex adaptive system is open and interacts with its environment. The border of a complex system is difficult to define since the position of the observer influences the scope of the system.
8. A complex adaptive system operates under conditions far from equilibrium. There must be a continual flow of energy to maintain the system and ensure its survival.
9. A complex adaptive system has a history. It evolves through time and its past is co-responsible for its present.
10. Each element in the system is ignorant of the behavior of the system as a whole, and responds solely to the local information available to it.

Economies are complex and self-organizing adaptive systems. Their structure continuously changes over time in response to a large number of factors: changes in technology, in the environment, in aggregate demand. Consider how the above ten characteristics of a complex adaptive system are manifest in economies:

1. There are a large number of individual agents. Each agent belongs to more than a single cluster of agents: for example, family, business, occupation, residential

area, political party, or recreational activity. Each occupies a different rank and status in the hierarchy of each cluster.
2. Economic agents do not know what other agents are thinking or doing. Their current decisions (investment expenditures in particular) are based on their expectations of the future behavior of other agents. Agents interact to earn and spend income, buying and selling, borrowing and lending, taking and giving goods and services. Means of payment are created and extinguished in the process. These relationships are all dynamic and continually changing.
3. Each agent interacts in many different markets with many other agents. Some are more active and important than others. Agents differ widely in the amount of purchasing power they control.
4. Economic systems are self-organizing and their structure adapts continuously in response to a large number of factors, for example, changes in technology, in the environment, in aggregate demand. Agents' interactions are nonlinear and small changes can have large effects.
5. Agents interact with other agents in their economic (not spatial) vicinity in highly specialized markets.
6. Agent behavior depends on their expectations of the future behavior, and so the future expectations of other agents. As the future becomes present, past expectations are confirmed or disappointed and expectations are continuously reformulated. Expected (*ex ante*) returns must be sufficiently positive if investment expenditures are to be undertaken. But realized (*ex post*) returns on investment may be positive or negative.
7. Agent expectations are contagious and self-fulfilling. Expectations of higher future activity lead to current increases in deficit spending which generate increases in the money supply, money income, nominal aggregate demand, and so higher *ex post* returns on investment projects. Expectations of future events may be formed extrapolatively or regressively, by different agents and by the same agent at different times.
8. Economies are open and are influenced by continual changes in tastes, output, income, production, technology, factor supply, political developments, and international relationships.
9. Economies never stand still. They are driven by continual changes in aggregate demand. Expectations of future events change continuously over time.[22]
10. Agents' expectations of the unknowable future state of the economy are based on each agent's expectations of others' expectations. Since they are based on fragile conventions they can be extremely unstable.

Economies are relational structure, and the above characteristics could easily be extended.[23] Changes in an indefinite number of variables, current and expected future levels of prices, quantities, legislation, institutions, interest rates, exchange rates, tax rates, public expenditures, property rights and laws can have significant effects. Some exogenous interventions by government and their short-run effects may be predictable in an ordinal sense.

2.4 Science and complexity[24]

The sciences have traditionally been grouped into two categories:

A. The natural or "hard" sciences, where quantifiable and repeatable events can be predicted from mathematical formulas, and explanatory hypotheses can be potentially falsified in controlled experiments.
B. The social or "soft" sciences, where due to the inherent variability and non-numerate nature of the subject matter controlled experiments are impossible, and only verbal narrative accounts of unique historical events are possible.

In physics, chemistry and molecular biology the chief method for gaining knowledge has been the laboratory. Parallel controlled experiments are carried out under rigorous controls holding specified variables and selected parameters constant. The traditional method of physics—controlled intervention and comparison with reproducible experiments followed by detailed predictions—is impossible in the social sciences, and in vast areas of the natural sciences. Laboratory experiments can play little or no role so scientists must gain knowledge by other means, primarily by observation and comparison of so-called natural experiments. Natural sciences like evolution, paleontology, cosmology and geology must be studied with the narrative tools of history. Outcomes concern unpredictable and singular contingent historical events where experimentation is impossible. Only storytelling is possible. Explanations can be offered *ex post* but never *ex ante*.[25]

Real numbers can be diced into infinitely fine gradations. But given the noisiness, fuzziness, flux, and openness of the world any apparent scientific precision is a sham. Computers may have the power to hasten the end of empirical science. With the help of powerful statistical methods and computers, astrophysicists have now learned how to overcome the n-body problem. Computers can now successfully simulate the short-run evolution of entire galaxies. But with the development of computers science may pass beyond our human cognitive limits.[26] Since we have only one universe to study, we are unable to do controlled experiments on it. We can never know what preceded the "big bang," or what exists beyond the borders of our universe.

In many areas of science, both "hard" and "soft," theoretical and applied, natural and behavioral, there is growing discontent with determinate analytical methods and descriptions. One early response was the rapid growth of statistical procedures. But most statistical models have not yet succeeded in breaking with deterministic models. As presently used statistics is the key tool in the process of uncovering the assumed underlying mechanisms of empirical phenomena that are being investigated. But the price paid, of averaging and so smoothing out most "noise" and with it most complex internal detail is conventionally completely glossed over.

Since Kepler's insistence that "to measure is to know" rigorous analysis in terms of deterministic laws rather than in terms of loosely ordered relationships has been characteristic of quantitative descriptions and calculations deemed necessary for science. But many real world phenomena in the life, behavioral and social sciences but also in physics and mathematics cannot be described or understood in terms of deterministic, rule-based, linear statistical processes. Quantum mechanical descriptions of sub-atomic processes are purely relational. On a more macroscopic level the significance of any atom is determined not by its basic nature, but by the relationships between itself and other atoms. It is the relations among atoms that determine the nature of matter.[27]

Thermodynamics as developed in the second half of the 19th century was the first successful attempt to deal with complexity in science.

> This was expressed in terms of the dissipation of energy, the forgetting of initial conditions, the evolution toward disorder. Classical dynamics, the science of eternal, reversible trajectories, was alien to the problems facing the 19th century, which were dominated by the concept of evolution.[28]

In classical mechanics time was reversible and so not part of the equation. In thermodynamics time plays a vital role. This is perhaps best expressed in the second law of thermodynamics: "over time the entropy of a system increases."

The concept of entropy is complex. It may be viewed as a measure of "disorder" in a system. As a system transforms energy, less and less remains in useable form, so "disorder" in the system increases. By replacing "energy" with "information" in the equations of thermodynamics, the amount of information in a message may be viewed as analogous to "entropy."[29] The more "disorderly" a message the higher is its information content. Consider a message consisting of a string of digits that is being transmitted one at a time. If the string consists of "fours" only, this will be quickly noticed at the receiving end. The next digit is fully predictable and will carry no new information. Although such a message is highly structured, its information content is very low. The less able is the receiver to predict the next digit in the sequence, the higher is the information content of the message. A message high in information content is low in predictable structure and therefore high in "entropy."

There is however an obvious problem. If information were defined as equal to entropy, the message with the highest information content would be completely random. Randomness must be then redefined in terms of "incompressibility," not "unpredictability." "A series of numbers is random if the smallest algorithm capable of specifying it to a computer has the same number of bits of information as the series itself."[30] In complex systems, randomness is not understood in terms of unpredictability, but in terms of the denseness with which the information is packed in the system. This provides an interesting definition of complexity: *The complexity of a series can be viewed as the size of the minimal program necessary to produce that series*.[31] To prove that a sequence is not random is easy. One has only to find a program that is shorter. But to prove that a sequence is random you have to prove that no shorter program exists. Such a proof is in general not possible. Randomness is falsifiable but not verifiable.[32]

There was no inevitability to the appearance of human life or any other form of complex life on earth. Life was single-celled for almost three billion years. It could surely have continued on for another billion without giving birth to multi-celled organisms? So long as we have only one form of life to study, questions such as whether Darwinism is a universal or merely a terrestrial law cannot be answered empirically. As a historical science, evolutionary biology can offer only retrospective explanations, never predictions. Where it lacks sufficient data concerning the evidence of antecedent sequences it can say nothing. We can never know the origins of language since this is a question of contingent prehistory.

Most scientists do not consider history, which deals primarily with particulars and contingency, as part of science. But history may be regarded as a different more complex type of science whose subject matter forces it to be an interpretative story-telling and ironic discipline. Rather than focus on the underlying complex structure and signals, history must focus on the particulars, the "noise." Historical sciences are concerned with chains of "proximate" and "ultimate" causes. This is a meaningless distinction in physics and chemistry, but is essential to our understanding of living systems in general, and human activities in particular. The most important question in understanding social phenomena is the "ultimate cause," which characteristically lies outside the domain of that science.[33]

In chemistry and physics the acid test of one's understanding of a system is whether one can predict its future behavior. Physicists have long tended to look down on fields that fail this test, for example evolutionary biology, which can provide *a posteriori* explanations but never *a priori* predictions. The characteristics of systems that frustrate prediction can be described in alternate ways. But the central answer is that they are all complex systems, characterized by interdependent variables operating in nonlinear relationships. Since each is the product of a different history, in a nontrivial sense each individual event is unique.

The difficulties in establishing cause-and-effect relations facing social and behavioral scientists are broadly similar to the difficulties facing astronomers, climatologists, ecologists, evolutionary biologists, geologists, and paleontologists.

> To varying degrees, each of these fields is plagued with the impossibility of performing replicated, controlled experimental interventions, the complexity arising from enormous numbers of variables, the resulting uniqueness of each system, the consequent impossibility of formulating universal laws, and the difficulty of predicting emergent properties and future behavior.[34]

Scholars in these fields must take advantage of natural experiments in the laboratory of history by comparing systems differing in the presence or absence of putative causal variables.[35] To the extent empirically observed variables can be quantified, for example economics, the relationships between them can be specified as algebraic equations, the observed relationships can be analyzed rigorously, and the interrelationships can be precisely estimated. But aside from the methodological criticisms and the econometric problems of inferring causation from correlation, bias, and missing variables, as will be addressed in Chapter 5 there remains the question of the extent that measured empirical quantities are adequate proxies for the theoretical concepts. We live in unique times. But all ages are unique. We assume that the exponential progress of science is a permanent feature of reality, but this need not be the case. Our understanding of complex phenomena depends on our ability to generate metaphysical pictures of what is going on.

Most of us do not deal well with existential problems about the fundamental questions of life. It is emotionally disturbing to view our existence as but one unlikely outcome among the zillions of other equally possible unlikely outcomes. We are unable to understand our world since we have nothing to compare it with.[36] Philosophy attempts to solve problems that lie beyond the scope of empirical inquiry. The great questions: "What is truth?" "What is consciousness?" "Does free will exist?" "How did life begin?" "How can we know anything?" are as unresolved now as they have ever been. One might argue that although these are real problems, they are beyond our cognitive abilities. We can compose them but we cannot solve them.[37]

2.5 Challenges to modeling complex adaptive systems

An empirical theory represents a statement about a phenomenon that can be confronted with reality, and possibly falsified. The theoretical description or "model" may be mathematical or verbal. If verbal the model can only be formulated with less precision. It cannot produce numerical measurements that can be estimated and confronted with the facts. Compared with mathematics verbal descriptions are more general but also much more cumbersome. They leave space for endless discussion as to what constitutes the better "fit" or description.[38]

Humans are born model-builders. At each moment in time our sensory systems scan our surroundings and our brain registers and compares the observations with images already formed and eventually reaches a preliminary conclusion. We understand what is going on in the world around us by telling stories (building "models") and comparing them with observations.[39] Whenever the variables of interest can be quantified, this permits "models" to be formulated rigorously in the form of algebraic equations.[40]

At this point problems arise. How should models of complex systems be tested and evaluated? So long as the systems they simulate are nondeterministic and inherently unpredictable even a "true" model cannot lead to accurate quantitative forecasts of future behavior. The requirement criteria for models must shift from being correct, in the sense of being able to predict accurately, to offering greater richness in the holistic understanding of complex processes.[41] Models are able to answer "how" questions, but never "why" questions.

Complex phenomena cannot be fully described with any simple model. The notion of "incompressibility" is fruitful. Complex adaptive systems cannot be reduced to a simpler model of their "basic" components because the changing relational behavior between the components gets lost in the process of reduction. To cope with the demands made upon them, complex adaptive systems must have two capabilities:[42]

1. They must be able to store information concerning the environment: representation.
2. They must be able to adapt their structure when necessary: self-organization.

A complete model of a complex adaptive system must have these capabilities. In order to be simulated and modeled the processes of representation and self-organization must be given some kind of formal description. The relationships between the elements of the system are continually changing under the influences of the external environment and so the history of the system. The system has to cope with unpredictable changes in the environment so its "structure" must be elastic.

The structure of complex adaptive systems is the result of the adaption of the system to the environment, not the result of any a *priori* design. Self-organization is only possible if the system can both remember and forget. Self-organizing systems involve higher order nonlinear processes and, at least until major disturbances occur, increase in complexity over time. Practitioners hope that the underlying structure may be sufficiently simple, in the sense of being governed by a sufficiently small number of degrees of freedom, that the model can yield increased understanding of system behavior.

The ability to accurately predict the future behavior of a system has long been the classic positivist criterion for successful theories. But complex adaptive systems adapt to changing open environments and cannot be successfully described by classical equilibrium theory. Predicting future behavior is impossible, so new criteria must be developed for model selection. A reductionist discourse is unable to elucidate emergent properties of complex systems. Complex macro behavior evolves from simpler micro interactions. Complex systems are the result of evolutionary processes. Systems that cannot adopt to new circumstances will not survive.

Complex phenomena can only be modeled with complex nonlinear systems, which implies computer simulation. The shift from prediction to understanding dictates that comparative evaluation of different models in terms of performance cannot be definitive. Once economists have a better understanding of the dynamics of complexity they will be able to start looking for similarities and differences between different complex systems, and will eventually develop a clearer understanding of the strengths and limitations of different models. Successful simulation of models of complexity cannot be expected until we are more familiar with the nature of complexity.

The past century of science has been overwhelmingly reductionist. Scientists have broken complex systems into simpler sub-parts, and broken these sub-parts in turn into ever simpler sub-parts. In the natural sciences the reductionist program has been spectacularly successful and will surely continue to be so. But it has left a deep difficulty. The "emergent properties" that characterize complex systems cannot be understood by intensive examination of their individual components.[43]

Physicists, whose subject matter is the simplest in science have succeeded farthest in this reconstitution. Quantum theorists are attempting to connect the collective behavior of electrons and other sub-atomic particles to the classical physics of atoms and molecules. But at higher levels of organization the difficulties of synthesis are indescribably more difficult. Entities such as living organisms exhibit indefinite variability. Each system changes during its development and evolution, leading to levels of complexity beyond the powers of present day imagination.

The astonishing increase in the capacities of computers may eventually permit our technology to simulate and even become more powerful than our ability to understand. Modeling techniques on powerful computers may allow us to simulate accurately the behavior of complex systems. But this does not imply that we will be able to fully understand them. If models are as complex as the systems they model, how can they result in any significant simplification of the system?[44]

Like biologists economists suffer from physics envy. They have attempted to build physics-like models leading from the microscopic to the macroscopic. But they have so far found it impossible to match their complicated models with the messy systems experienced in the real world. Armed with sophisticated mathematical concepts and high-speed computers, they can generate unlimited predictions and are able to create virtual worlds that evolve into more highly organized systems. Many scholars have become fervent advocates of complexity theory.[45] Many theorists believe not merely that deep laws exist but that their discovery is near.[46] They believe essential elements are already emerging from the exotic new mathematical theories of chaos, self-criticality, and adaptive landscapes. Such complexity theorists, *computer-oriented, abstraction absorbed, light on natural history, heavy on nonlinear transformations—think they smell success*.[47] Nevertheless there remains a problem:

> Wandering through the Cretan labyrinth of cyberspace they inevitably encounter emergence, the appearance of complex phenomena not predictable from the basic elements and processes alone, and not initially conceivable from the algorithms. And behold! Some of the productions actually look like emergent phenomena found in the real world. ... But how do they know that nature's algorithms are the same as their own, or even close? Many procedures after all may be false and yet produce approximately correct answers ... How do theoreticians know that their computer simulations are not just the paintings of flowers?[48]

In the case of the behavioral sciences it is not possible to quantify the degrees of freedom. The interactions are too varied, too complex, and too poorly understood to be modeled with mathematical precision. The real world is open and cannot be run on any computer. The hallmark of a truly complex system is that it cannot be completely captured by any simpler model. It is totally beyond our powers to simulate the behavior of complex economic systems, at least with our present technology. We have no choice but to fall back on simpler models. Our goal must be merely to develop models based on observed behavior that help us understand selected sub-aspects of complex systems.

Process analysis does not attempt to describe an entire complex system. It abstracts a small number of variables and formulates them into a dynamic model over historical time. Because of the nature of complexity even the best (most informative) models are never able to predict accurately and consistently the short-run behavior of the components. Social systems are ordinarily of such complexity that only ordinal (greater or lesser) behavior can be forecast. In many cases, for example speculative asset markets, we know why even the most short-term ordinal forecasts can never be accurate.

The goal of model building is not to discover invariant new "laws" to predict a system's future behavior. This is simply not possible. The goal is merely to increase our understanding of a system's holistic dynamics. Due to our limited intellectual capability, computer modeling of real time analysis must be confined to a finite number of variables. The models must be nonlinear and may but need not comprise computer simulations. All models must incorporate chronological time, all analysis must be dynamic, and all variables must be dated.[49]

2.6 Are there limits to what we can know?[50]

Science may eventually be able to provide a detailed map of all physical processes, but there are many things it will never be able to explain. The processes underlying human consciousness appear to be more paradoxical and difficult to grasp than anything in quantum mechanics. How can electrons act like particles in one experiment, waves in another and be in two places in the same time? What does it mean to say that mental states are correlated with electrical signals? Are mental functions accompanied by specific emotional states? How was the universe created? Could our universe be one of an infinite number of universes? Could quarks be composed of still smaller particles? How did life begin on earth? Will we ever find the answer to the deeper question that lurks behind all other questions—"Why is there something rather than nothing?"

An indefinite number of major scientific questions remain unanswered. But they tend to be questions that due to the limits of the human mind we will never be able to answer. In time science may approach literary criticism. Literary texts are "ironic" and have multiple meanings, none of which can be termed definitive. In the humanities arguments over meaning can never be fully resolved. The true meaning of a text is the text itself. One is left with an infinite regress of interpretations, none of which represents the final word.

Are there limits to science?[51] If science only addresses questions that can be answered, are there limits to what we can know? Is science infinite or is it as mortal as we are? Most questions concerning the meaning of life can only be answered ironically. It has been argued that the great era of scientific discoveries is now behind us. Further research may yield no fundamental revelations or revolutions but only incremental and diminishing returns. Researchers may be left to try to solve what Kuhn called "puzzles," problems whose solution buttresses prevailing paradigms. There is also the indisputable fact that science as an empirical and experimental discipline faces increasing cost constraints.

> We can only investigate nature by interacting with it. To do that we must push into regions never investigated before, regions of higher density, lower temperature, higher energy, smaller units. In all these cases we are pushing fundamental limits, and that requires ever more elaborate and expensive apparatuses. There is clearly a constraint imposed on scientific discoveries by the limits of human resources.[52]

The structure of our minds constrains both the questions we put to nature and the answers we may glean from them. Science's new answers simultaneously raise new questions, and humans have unlimited abilities to invent questions. No matter how far empirical science goes our imaginations can always go further. In raising questions that science can never answer e.g., "How do we know that our visible universe is not just one of an infinity of universes?" scientists can continue the quest for knowledge in the speculative mode, long after empirical science, the kind of science that answers answerable questions has ended.

Different paradigms may have no common standard for comparison and so are frequently incommensurable. The conversion of scientists to a new paradigm is both a subjective and a political process. It may involve sudden intuitive understanding, or simply waiting for the older "established" generation to pass on. Scientists are not mere knowledge-acquisition machines. They are guided by emotion and intuition and loyalty as well as reason and calculation, like all humans. The greatest scientists want above all to discover truths about nature.[53]

Some sciences like economics do not adhere to a single paradigm. They sustain several different paradigms in suspension and are unable to precipitate out the less successful. This is in part because they are unable to perform controlled experiments and rigorously test alternative hypotheses. It may also be because they address questions for which no single paradigm will suffice.

Unless complex systems can be quantified and measured, which for the reasons given earlier does not appear soon attainable, most hypotheses about the order of complexity are likely to remain empty of substantial content. A final theory of the universe if it could ever be formulated would not be meaningful in human terms.[54] On the brighter side one can argue that truth seeking rather than truth itself is what makes life meaningful. In science as in life it is the journey that matters, not the destination. "God is in the details."

2.7 The human brain

Some things humans will never be able to understand. The human brain does not have the language to deal effectively with complex phenomena. We see patterns where none exist; the numerical outcomes in roulette, the ink blots in Rorschach tests, the man in the moon. We are programmed to experience dynamical phenomena as periodic, when they are not: casinos, earthquakes, volcanos, business cycles, the level of the Nile. Whenever there are obvious deviations from periodicity, for example the absence of an event for a long time, we say the volcano has become "dormant," the fault is no longer "active," or business cycles are "a thing of the past." The human mind is unable to make sense out of the straight lines in log plots of power laws. We attempt to compensate for our lack of ability to perceive patterns properly by using words, but we use them poorly. Humans are inept at handling problems involving the interaction of large numbers of variables.[55] Some scientists have argued that the human brain was created for survival in a pre-industrial society, and is incapable of solving most complex questions.[56]

The root of the problem lies in the physical limitations of our brain. The cognitive abilities of all animals are shaped by their evolutionary history. A rat can be taught to navigate a maze that requires it to turn left at every second or even every third fork. But it can not be taught to turn at every fork corresponding to a prime number. Humans are subject to similar biological constraints and scientists are constrained by their cognitive limits.[57]

> Our brains were designed to understand hunting and gathering, mating and child rearing; a world of medium-sized objects moving in three dimensions at moderate speeds.[58]

Both the mind and its state of consciousness are "emergent properties," the collective activity of all the highly convoluted regions of the human brain.[59] Some scientific fields like the theory of the human brain may as quantum mechanics become too complex for even the most brilliant scientist to understand. We believe in Occam's razor, the simplest theories are the best theories. But this is because they are the only kind our puny brains can fully comprehend. The central task of science is to find those niches of reality that lend themselves to human understanding, given that most events are of a complex denseness unintelligible to human beings.

The human brain has evolved over thousands of generations to handle daily problems concerning simple numbers and proportions. Humans find it extremely difficult to grasp both the very big and the very small. Concepts such as "infinity," "infinitesimal," one "billion," "one hundred trillions," are impossible for anyone to comprehend. The human brain is also not well suited for complex problems requiring abstract reasoning.[60] The reason humans make consistent calculating errors lies in their genetic evolution. The human brain is a stone-age organ evolved over hundreds of millennia for hunter-gatherers. Only in the last few seconds of its existence has it been thrust into the alien and stressful environment of high-tech industrial society. Future research is likely to reveal that the brain sometimes operates as a powerful computer, and sometimes as an instant decision-maker ruled by powerful inborn heuristics.[61]

Our language capacity allows us to formulate questions endlessly and to resolve them in endless ways. But like rats, we are limited in our ability to resolve the questions we can ask. The innate structure of our minds imposes all too finite limits to our understanding of nature. Mountains and continents appear to be stable, but we now know this is not the case. Within a human lifetime nothing may happen in an earthquake fault zone. Dynamic phenomena are stationary over spans of millions of years. In comparison humans are literally "one-day flies."[62]

The human brain has long held a special place in studies of complexity. This is due both to its inherent structural complexity, and to the mind–body problem of consciousness: *"I think, therefore I am."* The human brain is the most complex structure in the known universe. It weighs only roughly three pounds, but contains more than one trillion cells. That number is of the same order as the number of stars in the milky way. But even this does not account for the brain's emergent abilities.

The human brain is commonly treated as a kind of computer or information processing system. From a strictly functional point of view the brain, that "three pound computer made of meat," consists of a huge network of richly connected neurons. Its fluffy mass is an intricately wired system of billions of neurons, each connected to other nerve cells by thousands of endings. Each neuron can be seen as a simple processor calculating the sum of all its inputs. Should the sum exceed a certain threshold, it generates an output which in turn becomes the input to the neurons connected to it.

Each connection is mediated by a "synapse" that causes the incoming signal either to excite or to inhibit the target neuron, and so determines the strength of the influence. Each neuron continually integrates up to 1000 synaptic inputs. The connection strength between two neurons increases in proportion to how often it is used. Communication between neurons is mediated by chemical transmitters released by specialized contacts called "synapses" which trigger a change in membrane permeability. Part of the mind's complexity is due to the diversity of its nerve cells. All cells contain the same set of genes, but individual cells express or activate only a small subset. The brain is not made up of interchangeable cells, and it is even possible that each individual neuron is in some sense unique.[63]

Many different kinds of transmitters have been identified in the brain, and this variety has enormous implications for brain function. Short-term synaptic changes associated with simple forms of learning are accompanied by molecular modification of proteins. Sensory systems are arranged in hierarchical manner and information is processed in parallel pathways. The human genome database reveals that the brain's structure is prescribed by over 3000 different genes. This is 50 percent more than in any other organ. Our mental system is capable of performing many specific highly complex tasks. Nevertheless at the level of the individual neuron no complex behavior is discernible.[64]

Critics of reductionist neuroscience argue that the brain is something organic, holistic, a living system, so it needs to be explained in terms of theories that deal explicitly in meaning and mindfulness. A self-making autopoietic system is one organized to respond to the world. Prod it and it will react homeostatically, striving to reach a new accommodation that preserves its integrity. A mechanical view of the brain says a chemical imbalance at nerve junctions causes the blues, so plug the gap with another chemical, like Prozac. But psychotherapy—treating the mind with conversation—can also restore neuro-chemical balances to normal. People under stress like nurses have the same neuro-chemical profile as the depressed, while feeling perfectly cheerful. There is no simple chain of cause and effect linking events on the cellular and the psychological level. The brain is too complex to control, but crude measures do sometimes work. A drug is frequently developed for one reason only to turn out to be a useful treatment for something entirely different. There is the famous case of chlorpromazine, originally meant as an allegy drug which became the first effective tranquillizer for schizophrenics.[65] Neuroscientists are mostly shooting in the dark with their crude knowledge of the brain. But if they scatter enough shots occasionally one may hit the mark. An Orwellian question is what happens when some of the expected steroids for the mind come along? Surely they will become impossible for students to resist? What about tiny scalp magnets that can induce electrical currents deep within the brain?

Plato compared humans to a chariot pulled by the two horses reason and emotion. Until now economics has been a one-horse show. But new technologies, such as functional magnetic resonance imaging, now allow second-by-second observation of brain activity, and allow researchers to identify regions of the brain used for different mental processes. The brain's response to short-term riches occurs largely in the limbic system that governs emotions. But the prospect of future rewards triggers the prefrontal cortex that is associated with reason and calculation. Choosing immediate gratification could be a sign that the limbic system is in charge. As is well known people apply different discount rates to short-term compared to future rewards. Most subjects prefer $100 now to $115 next month. But most also prefer $115 in thirteen months to $100 in twelve months.[66] When subjects play strategic games, and are attempting to anticipate the choices of other players, their brains show a high degree of coordination between the brain's "thinking" and the "feeling" regions.

Eventually we may know how many transmitters and receptors there are in the brain and where each one is concentrated. We will certainly learn much more about how some molecules are able to affect neuronal differentiation and degeneration. We already know that many neurotransmitters are common amino acids found throughout the body. The great challenge will be to determine how these molecules modulate the functional wiring diagram of the brain, and how this nerve set gives rise to mental phenomena. What does it mean to say that mental events are "correlated" with electrical signals? Identifying parts of the brain that control different economic actions is one thing. Determining how neural systems work together to create behavior, and how wide is the variation in brain patterns between different people is much harder.

Over the past half century the search for Artificial Intelligence (AI) provided a focal point for research on complexity. Rule-based systems initially constituted the classical approach. The behavior of a complex system was reduced to a set of rules which describe the behavior of the system at an abstract level. Symbols were used to represent important concepts, so the unnecessary detail of implementation can be ignored. Each symbol represents a specific concept, known as local representation. The set of rules was governed by a system of centralized control, the meta-rules of the system. This central system decides which of the production rules become active at every stage of the computation. If the central control should fail the entire system falls.

AI researchers differ on many points of detail including the scope and power of rule-based systems. There is a split between supporters of "strong" AI, who claim that formal systems can eventually provide an adequate model for all aspects of human intelligence, and supporters of "weak" AI, who regard formal systems as merely a powerful tool. Rule-based systems remain the central paradigm.[67] But to duplicate the mind in a machine, it will not be enough to perfect AI technology. Artificial emotion (AE), must also be synthesized.[68]

The astonishing growth of the capacities of digital and quantum-mechanical computers created expectations that it would be possible to construct computers capable of behaving intelligently, for example solving math problems or playing chess. But the important hallmarks of human intelligence: perception, imagination, intuition, movement, and use of language have proven complex beyond all expectation. No AI computing device yet built has capabilities even remotely close to those possessed by human beings. As a result although there have been a number of useful by-products, expectations for AI have recently been severely conflated.[69]

Connectionist systems termed "neural networks" have been constructed and enabled to "learn" simple tasks. This initially revived some expectations of the eventual possibility of AI. Nevertheless the brain's machinery remains forbiddingly alien. Only a minute fraction of its circuitry has to date been traced. The mind is an emergent property of the brains' electrical and metabolic activity, and emergent properties cannot be understood by considering the component parts one at a time. Subjective consciousness emerges from continuous exchanges between body and brain through nerve discharges and blood-borne flows of hormones, influenced by emotional controls that regulate mental set, attention, and selection of goals.

Due to the overwhelming complexity of information inputs through the human mind, it is unlikely we will ever be able to create an artificial human intelligence. Memory can be reducible to a series of molecular events.[70] But one of the trends that has enabled science to proceed so rapidly may actually lead sciences away from additional human understanding. When one switches to massive computer simulations one may end up with a model that can successfully model the particular phenomena one is interested in. But one then can no longer understand the model. A computer model that accurately modeled processes in the human brain will be as complex and inscrutable as the human brain itself.[71]

Edward Wilson has recently called for "consilience"; that is a concerted effort to unify the natural and social sciences.[72] The discipline to span the chasm will be evolutionary neuroscience, the study of the human brain. The brain viewed as an ordering machine imposes its structure on the things we perceive. But it did not evolve to cope with a microphysical environment. The brain processes all human experience through genetically self-structured pre-wired algorithms.[73] The process of Order→Chaos→Order has been identified as the fundamental algorithm of life, involving an intricate and complex interaction between proteins and nucleic acids common to all organisms as specified by their survival requirements and needs. The study of the biophysical-chemistry brain structure of the algorithm at the molecular and cellular levels is the province of *molecular neurobiology*.[74] Some have argued the protoreptilian structure was not replaced, but provided the substructure for subsequent brain development. The human brain may have evolved as a three-level interconnected structure inherited from the protoreptilian, mammelian, and neomammelian complex.[75]

2.8 Conclusions: an ode to pluralism

There is no question reductionism rules. In all disciplines scientists who use reductionist methods predominate in raw numbers, publish the most papers, are cited most frequently, and get the most grant money. Nevertheless if the world is a complex system, reductionism, as successful as it has been on a host of counts must be supplemented with holistic science. To understand nature in all of its vicissitudes, methods from the most reductionist to the least reductionist must be used. Like it or not, anti-reductionists are forced to advocate pluralism.[76]

Reductionists prefer to express their position in terms of laws, while anti-reductionists prefer to talk of processes, mechanisms, and systems. Reductionists emphasize causal explanations while anti-reductionists favor selectionist explanations, and emphasize structures and emergent properties. But even the most fundamental laws of physics require *ceteris paribus* assumptions and apply only to the most general characteristics of natural phenomena. We take laws governing planets as seriously as we do because they are special instances of more fundamental processes, the relation between masses. As general as these laws may be, we humans can solve them for only three and possibly four bodies at a time. Philosophers have argued that some sciences, like biology and the social sciences, have no "laws." The concept of self-organization carries inappropriate connotations, since numerous factors play a role in causal process. We have a tendency to select one factor as the cause, and demote all others to supplementary conditions. Social sciences are fundamentally historical in a sense missing in physical phenomena, since they necessarily incorporate in their subjects the historical elements of replication and selection.

It has incorrectly been argued macroeconomics must be built on "rigorous microeconomic foundations." But the social sciences and some natural sciences like biology differ fundamentally from physics in the role that selection and contingency play. Contingency is central in economies, since no invariant rules or patterns emerge in output to behavior. The output of the system **is** the history of the system and depends on previous outputs taken as inputs. Long-run accurate predictions are impossible. Economic decisions are typically discrete and not continuous.[77] Economies like sand piles tend to self-organize toward critical states, where earthquakes occur.[78] People living in a relatively poor society can lead healthier lives than people living in a richer society when the social difference between richest and poorest is sufficiently less. It matters by how much most people are in a society are poorer relative to the richest people.

Economic life may be viewed as analogous to a game of chess. There are about 10^{120} possible moves in chess. This is such a large number that it is impossible for any conceivable computer to examine all possible moves. As a result for human beings chess is effectively an open game. In interactive systems there exists no unique "best" move, since what is "best" depends on the behavior of one's opponents. Even so there are many poor moves, and chess masters can develop many heuristic relationships. Like chess, economies are "open" interactive systems. Given our limited analytical capabilities most interactive systems are effectively "open." Since we never have "complete" information, we are never able to "rationally" calculate optima or maxima positions.[79]

Economic agents must make do with heuristics or "rules of thumb." Since we always have incomplete information, human agents are unable to "maximize" anything. Complex systems exhibit phase transitions, where relationships never quite lock into place but yet never quite dissolve. The richness of these interstices allows complex systems to undergo spontaneous self-organization. Positive and negative feedback leaves room for creativity and change in response to new conditions. Groups of interacting agents, seeking mutual accommodation and self-consistency manage to transcend themselves, and in the process acquire emergent properties like languages and markets which they could never create or possess individually. For economies as for individuals the whole is incomparably greater than the sum of its parts. For economies as for individuals there is always room for improvement. *Ex post* complex adaptive systems make mistakes.

In trying to predict how markets will perform, agents must make guesses about how other agents will guess, and so on *ad infinitum*. Economic models should be peopled by agents who are uncertain about their future, know they are uncertain, and continually adjust their "internal models" in response to their perceived adjustments of the "internal models" of other agents. The economic realm is inherently complex, dynamic, co-adapting, psychological, and totally unpredictable.

These characteristics of complex adaptive systems have very important implications for how economists model economic behavior. The challenge for economists is to model imperfectly smart interacting agents, exploring their way into a bounded open space of possibilities and unable to calculate any "optimal" path.[80] If economics is to succeed in modeling and explaining intrinsically complex and path-dependent phenomena, it must become a high-complexity science. Economies must be modeled as open and adapting. Metaphors must be based on evolution rather than Newtonian physics. Economists will eventually understand the ways economic behavior is complex, and why economic outcomes are unpredictable. But they will be forever unable to foretell the future.

Economists are now finally beginning to focus on computer simulation. The Santa Fe institute held a famous conference with a group of physicists and economists in 1987. It was widely reported that the physicists were shocked by the degree to which economists relied on formal proofs.[81] They lectured the economists that they must not escape from the real world into excessive formalism, and the physicists won the argument. In the second conference economists applied much more *ad hoc* procedures, including computer simulation methods borrowed directly from statistical mechanics.[82] These will be the mathematical methods of the new complexity economics, less formalistic and more inductive than deductive.[83]

In intellectual disputes presenting the views of one's opponents sympathetically is not easy, since parody is too effective a strategy to reject. "Reductionism" was here used as an insult. But both sides acknowledge the rich interactive conception of all social systems. What at first seems hopeless disagreement, turns out on deeper examination to be primarily differences in emphasis. Mainstream reductionist comparative static economics is not all bad and has been responsible for increases in our understanding of the economy. But most complex phenomena do not lend themselves to formal deductive investigation. For that reason they have been largely ignored by mainstream economists.

The new consensus leads directly to pluralism. Depending on the questions being asked, both reductionist and holistic methods and approaches should be applied in a complementary manner to the analysis of complex systems. To quote a leading microbiologist,

> The reductionist method of dissecting biological systems into their constituent parts has been effective in explaining the chemical basis of numerous living processes. However many biologists now realize that this approach has reached its limit. Biological systems are extremely complex and have emergent properties that cannot be explained, or even predicted by studying their individual parts. The reductionist approach—although successful in the early days of molecular biology—underestimates this complexity, and therefore has an increasingly

detrimental influence on many areas of biomedical research, including drug development and vaccine development.[84]

Complex systems are defined as systems that possess emergent properties and which therefore, cannot be explained by the properties of their component parts. Since the constituents of a complex system interact in a nonlinear manner, the behavior of the system cannot be analysed by classical mathematical measures that do not incorporate cooperativity and nonadditive effects. This is another peculiarity of complex biological systems which exchange matter and energy with the environment and which are not in thermodynamic equilibrium.[85]

Appendix: the Copenhagen interpretation[86]

> The more the universe seems comprehensible, the more it seems pointless ... As we have discovered more and more fundamental physical principals, they seem to have less and less to do with us.
>
> Steven Weinberg, quoted in Horgan, 1996

Our inability to comprehend the behavior of complex systems, how "emergent properties" and "phase transitions" evolve and enable systems to exceed the sum of their components has a clear parallel in our inability to comprehend the mystery of quantum behavior. As is well known, electrons and photons can act as waves or particles depending on how they are observed. The theory of quantum mechanics is at the extreme limit of human comprehension. As Feynman said: If you think you understand quantum physics, this shows that you have not yet begun to understand it.[87]

In their attempts to understand the seemingly irrational behavior in the micro realm of quantum effects, in the late 1920s physicists led by Bohr and Heisenberg proposed a bold new conception of nature radically different from that of their precursors. This conception rejected presumption that nature can be understood in terms of elementary space–time realities. It maintained that a complete description of nature at the atomic level can be given only by probability functions. These referred not to fundamental microscopic space–time realities but only to the microscopic objects of sense experience. This radically new concept, termed the "Copenhagen Interpretation" was initially bitterly challenged but has now been accepted by most in the field.[88]

In his attempt to give a clear account of the essence of the Copenhagen Interpretation Stapp cited William James' pragmatic conception of what it means for an idea to be "true": *"an idea is true if it works"* The "truth" of an idea means its agreement with reality. James then raised the question "what is the 'reality' with which the idea agrees?" By definition all human ideas must lie in the realm of experience. But reality has parts lying outside this realm. James' question was, "How can an idea lying *inside* he realm of experience agree with something that lies *outside*?" James maintained that the relationship between an idea and "something else" can only be comprehended if that "something else" is also an idea. Ideas can only agree with other ideas. There is no way for a finite mind to comprehend an agreement between an idea and something that lies outside the realm of experience. If we want to know what it means for an idea to agree with a reality, we must accept that the reality lies in the realm of human experience.

Note that this is not in accord with our usual idea of truth. A great many of our ideas comprice what lies outside our realm of experience. The "truth" of such an idea depends on whether it "agrees" with something that lies outside the realm of experience. The notion of "agreement" suggests some sort of familiarity or congruence of things that agree. But things that are "similar" or "congruent" can only be things of the same kind.

Ideas and external realities are different kinds of things. Ideas are intimately associated with our brains. The structural forms that can inhere in our ideas depend on the structural forms of our brains. But external realities can be structured very differently from human ideas. There is no *a priori* reason to expect that the relationships that constitute and characterize the essence of external reality can be mapped in any simple direct fashion into the world of human ideas. When no such mapping exists, "agreement" between ideas and external realities becomes moot.

James argued that the only evidence we can have on the question whether human ideas can be brought into exact correspondence with the essences of external realities is the success of our ideas in bringing order to our physical experience. The success of our ideas in this sphere does not presume an exact correspondence of our ideas to external reality. The question whether the ideas "agree" with the external essences is of no practical importance. What is important is the success of the ideas in bringing order to our experience. If they do they are useful, even when they do not "agree" in an absolute sense with the external essences. Only agreement with aspects of our experience can be comprehended. That which is not an idea is as intrinsically incomprehensible as its relationships with other things.

This leads to the pragmatic Jamesian philosophy: ideas must be judged by their success in bringing order to the world of ideas and experience, rather than on the basis of some incomprehensible "agreement" with non-ideas outside of our experience. The significance of this viewpoint lies in its negation of the idea that the fundamental aim of science is to construct a "true" mental or mathematical image of the world. According to the Jamesian view the proper goal of science is to augment and order our experience. A scientific theory should be judged on how well it serves to extend the range of our experience and to reduce it to order. It need not provide a "true" mental image of the world itself.

James maintained that the structural form of the world cannot be placed in direct correspondence with the types of logical structures our mind can process. The objective world is not founded on conceptual abstractions, like "electrons" and "protons," but is founded on sense objects, the concrete sense realities of experience.

> This notion of a reality taken from ordinary experience, independent of either of us, lies at the base of the pragmatic definition of truth.[89]

James was accused of subjectivism—of denying the existence of an objective reality. James termed this charge "slanderous," and put forward in defense the following taxonomy:

1. Private concepts: which constitute subjective individual realities.
2. Sense objects: public sense realities, outside of and independent of the individual, that is, public and objective experiences.
3. Hypersensory realities: ultimate realities that exist independently of the human mind. Our knowledge of such things is forever uncertain.

The above excursion into James' philosophical pragmatism provides the background for Stapp's presentation of the "Copenhagen Interpretation." Stapp argued that Bohr linked his pragmatic view of science to the problem of communication:

> The task of science is both to extend the range of our experience, and reduce it to order ... In our description of nature the purpose is not to disclose the real essence of phenomena, but only to track down as far as possible the relations between the multifold aspects of our experience.[90]
>
> As the goal of science is to augment and order our experience, every analysis of the conditions of human knowledge must rest on considerations of the character and scope of our means of communication.[91]
>
> This is a clear logical demand, since the very word "experience" refers to a situation where we can tell others what we have done and what we have learned.[92]

Throughout Bohr's writing there is tacit acceptance of the idea that the external world exists. But there is no corresponding commitment to the idea that the external world is what we imagine it to be. The focus is simply on the descriptions of our physical experiments and the demand that they secure unambiguous communication and objectivity.

Bohr initially accepted the notion that nature contained a fundamental element of randomness or indeterminism:

> we have been forced ... to reckon with a free choice on the part of nature between various possibilities to which only probability interpretations can be applied.[93]

But he qualified his idea as follows:

> The fact that in one and the same well-defined experimental arrangement we generally obtain recordings of different individual processes makes indispensable the recourse to a statistical account of quantum phenomena. ... The circumstance that, in general, one and the same experimental arrangement may yield different recordings is sometimes picturesquely described as a "choice of nature" between such possibilities. Needless to say, such a phrase implies no illusion to a personification of nature, but simply points to the impossibility of ascertaining on accustomed lines directives for the course of a closed individual phenomenon. Here, logical approach cannot go beyond the destruction of the relative probabilities for the appearance of the individual phenomena under given conditions.[94]

In spite of doubts cast on our intuitive notions of space and time by the theory of relativity, the idea lingers that all physical objects that occupy space–time regions can in principle be divided into ever finer parts. But quantum theory is not a description of all the properties of nature located at infinitesimal regions of the space–time continuum. Strictly speaking it is not even a description of the external things which are hypersensory microscopic qualities. It is rather an operational description of what technicians see and do. The wave functions of quantum theory must be interpreted as only "symbolic devices" which scientists use to make predictions about what they will observe under specified conditions.

The fact that a "quantum" contains nothing that can be interpreted as a description of quantities located at points of an externally existing space–time continuum is evidence of its incompleteness. All we really know about the space–time continuum is that it is a useful concept for organizing sense experience. Man's effort to comprehend the world in terms of the idea of an external reality inhering in space–time continuum reached its culmination in classical field theory. Although satisfactory in the domain of macroscopic phenomena it failed totally to provide a satisfactory account of microscopic phenomena.[95]

James maintained the rejection of classical field theory in favor of quantum theory represented a rejection of the idea that external reality inheres in the space–time continuum. Space, like color and taste at root lies in the mind of the beholder. Can human ideas which in some sense are limited by the structural form of human survival ever fully comprehend science's ultimate essences? James' pragmatic view regards human concepts merely as tools for the comprehension of experience. Human ideas, being prisoners in the realm of human experience, can "know" nothing but other human ideas. James was pessimistic that man could ever grasp or know "absolute essences," what he termed "hypersensory realities."[96]

Hope can persist that man will perceive the world ever more clearly through his growing patchwork of complementary views about the general form of natural and social phenomena. But this world should not automatically be expected to be a resident of the three dimensional space of human intuition, nor to be describable in terms of qualities associated with points of a four dimensional space–time continuum. There may be no "one to one" connection between the outside world and our ideas about it. We can only make plausible inferences based on our experiences, but we can try to build a reasonable idea of the outside world beyond our sensory perceptions.[97]

Bibliography on complexity and chaos

Albin, Peter (1998) *Barriers and Bounds to Rationality, Essays on Economic Complexity and Dynamics in Interactive Systems*, Foley, Duncan (ed.), Princeton, Princeton University Press.
Anderson, Philip, Arrow, Ken, and Pines, David (1988) *The Economy as an Evolving Complex System*, Vol.5, Santa Fe Institute Studies in the Sciences of Complexity, Redwood City, CA. Addison-Wesley.
Arthur, Brian (1990) "Positive Feedbacks in the Economy," *Scientific American*, February, 92–99, in Arthur, Brian (1994) *Increasing Returns and Path Dependence in the Economy*, Ann Arbor, MI, University of Michigan Press.
Arthur, Brian, Durlauf, Steven, and Lane, David (eds) (1997) *The Economy as an Evolving Complex System II*, Redwood City, CA, Addison-Wesley.
Axelrod, Robert (1984) *The Evolution of Co-Operation*, New York, Basic Books.
Axtel, Robert (2005) "The Complexity of Exchange," *Economic Journal*, 115, F193–210.
Auyang, Sunny Y. (1998) *Foundations of Complex-Systems Theories: In Economics, Evolutionary Biology and Statistical Physics*, Cambridge, Cambridge University Press.
Backhaus, Juergen (ed.) (2005) *Entrepreneurship, Money and Coordination*, Cheltenham, Edward Elgar.
Bak, Per and Chen, Kan (1991) "Self-Organized Criticality," *Scientific American*, January, 26–33.
Bak, Per (1996) *How Nature Works: The Science of Self-Organized Criticality*, New York, Springer-Verlag (Copernicus).
Ball, Philip (1999) *The Self-Made Tapestry: Pattern Formation in Nature*, Oxford, Oxford University Press.
Barnsley, Michael (1988) *Fractals Everywhere*, London, Academic Press.
Bohr Niels, "Atomic Physics and Human Knowledge" (1934), in *Essays 1932–1957 on Atomic Physics and Human Knowledge(1963)*, and *Essays 1958–1962 on Atomic Physics and Human Knowledge* (1963) [reprinted 1987].
Boulding, Keneth (1978) *Ecodynamics: A New Theory of Societal Evolution*, Beverly Hills, Sage.
Brock, William and Nommes, C. (1997) "A Rational Route to Randomness", *Econometrica*, 65, 1059–95.
Cartwright, Nancy (1999) *The Dappled World: A Study of the Boundaries of Science*, Cambridge, Cambridge University Press.
Chaitlin, G.J. (1975) "Randomness and Mathematical Proof," *Scientific American*, 27 May, 47–52, 232, 5.
Chaitlin, G.J. (1990) *Information, Randomness, and Incompleteness: Papers on Algorithmic Information Theory* (2nd ed.), London: World Scientific Publishing, 14–19, 307–13.
Cilliers, Paul (1998) *Complexity and Postmodernism*, London, Routledge.
Colander, David (1996) *Beyond Microfoundations: Post Walrasian Macroeconomics*, Cambridge, Cambridge University Press.
Colander, David (ed.) (2000) *The Complexity Vision in Teaching Economics*, Cheltenham, UK, Edward Elgar.
Colander, David (2001) "Economics in 2050: How Did It Get This Way, and What Way Is It?," in *The Lost Art of Economics: Essays on Economics and the Economics Profession.* Cheltenham, UK, Edward Elgar, 169–81.
Coleman, P., and Pietronero, L. (1992) "The Fractal Structure of the Universe," *Physics Reports*, 213, 311–89.
"Commerce Complexity and Evolution" Conference Program and Papers, University of New South Wales, Vol. 1 & 2, February 12–13, 1996.
Corry, G.A. (1999) *The Reciprocal Modular Brain in Economics and Politics: Shaping the Rational and Moral Basis of Organization, Exchange and Choice*, New York, Plenum Press.
Corry, G.A. (2000) *Toward Consilience: The Bioneurological Basis of Behavior, Thought, Experience and Language*, New York, Kluwer.

Crutchfield, James, Farmer, Doyne, Packard, Norman, and Shaw, Robert (1986) "Chaos" *Scientific American*, 38, December, 46–57, 255, 6.
Davies, Paul (1987) *The Cosmic Blueprint*, London, Heinemann.
Davies, Paul (2002) "That Mysterious Flow," in A Matter of Time, *Scientific American*, September, 40–47, 54, 287, 3.
Dawkins, Richard (1986) *The Blind Watchmaker*, New York, W.W.Norton.
Day, Richard (1994) *Do Economies Diverge?*, Aldershot, UK, Edward Elgar.
Day, Richard (1997) "The Emergence of Chaos from Classical Economic Growth," in Omar, Hamoda, and J.C. Rowley, (eds) *Discrete and Continuous Systems, Cointegration and Chaos*, Cheltenham, UK, Edward Elgar.
Day, Richard (ed.) (1999) *Complex Economic Dynamics*, Cambridge, MA, and London, MIT Press.
Day, Richard (1999) "Economics, the State, and the State of Economics," in Sheila, Dow (ed.) *Essays in Honour of Brian Loasby, Vol 2, Contingency, Complexity and the Theory of the Firm*, Cheltenham, UK, Edward Elgar.
Dopfer, Kurt (ed.) (2005) *Economics, Evolution and the State: The Governance of Complexity*, Cheltenham, UK, Edward Elgar.
Dupré, J. (1993) *The Disorder of Things*, Cambridge, MA, Harvard University Press.
Durlauf, Stephen and Quah, Danny (1999) "The New Empirics of Economic Growth," in J. Taylor, and M. Woodford (1999) *Handbook of Macroeconomics*, Amsterdam, Elsevier.
Durlauf, Stephen (2005) "Complexity and Empirical Economics," *Economic Journal*, June, 115, F225–F43.
Feder, J. (1988) *Fractals*, New York, Plenium Press.
Finch, John (ed.) (2005) *Complexity and the Economy: Implications for Economic Policy*, Cheltenham, UK, Edward Elgar.
Franks, Nigel (1989) "Army Ants: A Collective Intelligence," *American Scientist*, 77, 139.
Frenken, Koen (2005) *Innovation, Evolution and Complexity Theory*, Cheltenham, UK, Edward Elgar.
Gell-Mann, Murray (1994) *The Quark and the Jaguar*, New York, W. H. Freeman.
Gleick, James (1987) *Chaos, Making a New Science*, New York, Viking Books.
Godel, Kurt (1931) [1967] "On Formally Undecidable Propositions of Principia Mathematica and Related Systems," in Jean Van Heijenoort (ed.) *I, From Frege to Godel: A Source Book Mathematical Logic, 1879–1931*, Cambridge, MA, Harvard University Press, 597.
Gould, Stephen (1987) *Times's Arrow, Time's Cycle*, Cambridge MA, Harvard University Press.
Gould, Stephen (1989) *Wonderful Life*, New York, W.W. Norton.
Gould, Stephen (1991) *Bully for Brontosaurus: Reflections in Natural History*, New York, W.W. Norton.
Green, B. (2003) "The Future of String Theory," *Scientific American*, November 289(5), 68–73.
Hacking, Ian (1990) *The Taming of Chance*, Cambridge, Cambridge University Press.
Hall, Nina (ed.) (1992) *Exploring Chaos: A Guide to the New Science of Disorder*, London, W.W. Norton.
Hayek, Fredrich A. (1967) "The Theory of Complex Phenomena," in *Studies in Philosophy, Politics and Economics*, Chicago, University of Chicago Press.
Hodgson, Geoffrey (1993) *Economics and Evolution: Bringing Life Back into Economics*, Oxford, Basil Blackwell.
Holland, John (1975) *Adaptation in Natural and Artificial Systems*, Ann Arbor, MI, University of Michigan Press.
Holland, John (1995) *Hidden Order: How Adaption Builds Complexity*, Reading, MA, Addison-Wesley.
Holland, John (1998) *Emergence*, Oxford, Oxford University Press.
Horgan, John (1996) *The End of Science*, New York, Addison-Wesley.
Hsieh, Ching-Yao, and Ye, Meng-Hua (1991) *Economics, Philosophy, and Physics*, New York, ME Sharpe.
Jen, Erica (1990) *Lectures in Complex Systems*, Santa Fe, NM, Addison-Wesley.

Kauffman, Stuart (1995) *At Home in the Universe*, Oxford, Oxford University Press.
Kauffman, Stuart (2000) *Investigations*, Oxford, Oxford University Press.
Kellert, Steven (1993) *In the Wake of Chaos*, Chicago, IL, University of Chicago Press.
Krugman, Paul (1996) *The Self-Organizing Economy*, Oxford, Blackwell.
Levin, Roger (1993) *Complexity*, New York, Macmillan.
Lorenz, Edward (1963) "Deterministic Non-Periodic Flow," *Journal of Atmospheric Science*, 20, 130–41.
Lorenz, Edward (1993) *The Existence of Chaos*, Seattle, WA, University of Washington Press.
Lovelock, James (2000) *Homage to Gaia*, Oxford, Oxford University Press.
Luhman, Niklas (1984) "Complexity and Meaning," in S. Aida (ed.) *The Science and Praxis of Complexity*, Tokyo, United Nations University.
MacLean, Peter (1990) *The Triune Brain in Evolution: Role in Paleocerebal Functions*, New York, Plenum Press.
Mandelbrot, Benoit (1977) *Fractals: Form, Chance and Dimension*, San Francisco, CA, W. H. Freeman.
Mandelbrot, Benoit (1982) *The Fractal Geometry of Nature*, San Francisco, CA, W. H. Freeman.
Mandelbrot, Benoit (1989) "Chaos, Bourbaki and Poincaré," *Mathematical Intelligencer*, Summer, 11, 10–12.
Markose, Sheri (2001) Book Review of *Computable Economics*, by K. Velupillai, *Economic Journal*, June, 111, 472, 468–70.
Markose, Sheri (2002) "The New Evolutionary Computational Paradigm of Complex Adaptive Systems: Challenges and Prospects for Economics and Finance," in Shu-Heng Chen (ed.) *Genetic Algorithms and Genetic Programming in Computational Finance*, Dordrecht: Kluwer Academic Publishers.
Markose, Sheri (2005) "Computability and Evolutionary Complexity: Markets as Complex Adaptive Systems (CAS)," *Economic Journal*, 115, 504, F159–F92.
Mirowski, Peter (1986) "Mathematical Formalism and Economic Explanation," in *The Reconstruction of Economic Theory*, Boston, Kluwer-Nijhoff.
Nicolis, Grégorie and Prigogine, Ilya (1977) *Self-Organization in Non-Equilibrium Systems*, New York, Wiley.
Nicolis, Grégorie and Prigogine, Ilya (1989) *Exploring Complexity: An Introduction*, New York, W. H. Freeman.
Pagels, Heinz (1988) *The Dreams of Reason*, New York, Simon & Schuster.
Peitgen, Heinz-Otto, and Richter, Peter (1986) *The Beauty of Fractals*, New York, Springer.
Penrose, Roger (1988) "On Physics and Mathematics of Thought," in Herkin R. (ed.) *The Universal Turing Machine: A Half Century Survey*, Oxford, Oxford University Press.
Penrose, Roger (1989) *The Emperor's New Mind: Concerning Computers, Minds and the Laws of Physics*, Oxford, Oxford University Press.
Pinker, Steven (1997) *How The Mind Works*, New York, Norton.
Prigogine, Ilya (1980) *From Being to Becoming*, San Francisco, CA, W. H. Freeman.
Prigogine, Ilya and Stengers, Isabelle (1984) *Order Out of Chaos*, London, Heinmann.
Prigogine, Ilya (1997) *The End of Certainty: Time, Chaos and the New Laws of Nature*, New York, Free Press.
Puu, T. (1997) *Nonlinear Economics Dynamics* (4th ed.), Berlin, Springer-Verlag.
Robson, Arthur (2002) "The Evolution of Rationality and the Red Queen," *Journal of Economic Theory*, 111, 1–22.
Rosser, J. Barkeley (1999) "On the Complexities of Complex Economic Dynamics," *Journal of Economic Perspectives*, 13(4), 169–92.
Rosser, J. Barkeley, (2000) *From Catastrophe To Chaos: A General Theory of Economic Discontinuities*, Vol I: *Mathematics, Microeconomics, Macroeconomics and Finance*, Boston, MA, Kluwer.
Rosser, J. Barkeley (2000) "Aspects of Dialectics and Non-Linear Dynamics," *Cambridge Journal of Economics*, 24, 311–24, with extensive Bibliography.
Rossler, M. (1976) "An Equation for Continuous Chaos," *Physics Letters*, Part A, 57, 397–98.

Ruelle, David (1989) *Chaotic Evolution and Strange Attractors*, Cambridge, Cambridge University Press.
Ruelle, David (1991) *Chance and Chaos*, Princeton, NJ, Princeton University Press.
Schachtel, E.G. (1959) *Metamorphosis*, New York, Basic Books.
Schroeder, M. (1991) *Fractals, Chaos, Power Laws*, New York, Freeman.
Scientific American (1992) "Mind and Brain." Special Report, September 2673, 48–58.
Shannon, C. (1948) "A Mathematical Theory of Communication," *Bell System Technical Journal*, 27, pp. 379–423, 623–56, July, October, 1948.
Smith, John Maynard (1982) *Evolution and the Theory of Games*, Cambridge, Cambridge University Press.
Stapp, Henry (1972) "The Copenhagen Interpretation," *American Journal of Physics*, 40(8), 1098–2116.
Stapp, Henry (1997) "Science of Consciousness and the Hard Problem," in Larry Vanderwert, (ed.) *The Journal of Mind and Behavior*, 171–91.
Stein, Daniel (1989) *Lectures in the Sciences of Complexity*, Proceedings of 1988 Complex Systems Summer School, Santa Fe, NM, Addison-Wesley.
Stewart, Ian (1988) "The Ultimate in Undecidability," *Nature*, 10, March, 115.
Stewart, Ian (1989) *Does God Play Dice? The Mathematics of Chaos*, New York, Penguin Books.
Stuart, Ian (1990) *Does God Play Dice?* London, Penguin.
Thuan, Trinh Xuan (2001) *Chaos and Harmony: Perspectives on Scientific Revolutions of the Twentieth Century*, New York, Oxford University Press.
Van Regenmortel, Mark (2004a) "Biological Complexity Emerges from the Ashes of Genetic Reductionism," *Journal of Molecular Recognition*, 17, 145–48.
Van Regenmortel, Mark (2004b) "Reductionism and Complexity in Molecular Biology," *EMBO Reports*, European Molecular Biology Organization, 5 (11).
Van Regenmortel, Mark and Hull, D. (2002) *Promises and Limits of Reductionism in the Biomedical Sciences*, London, Wiley and Sons Inc.
Vanderwert, L (ed.) (1997) "Understanding Tomorrow's Mind: Advances in Chaos Theory, Quantum Theory, and Consciousness in Psychology," Special Issue, *The Journal of Mind and Behavior*, Spring/Summer, 18 (2/3), 171–91.
Vetter, M., Stadler and Hayes, J (1997) "Phase Transitions in Learning," in L. Vanderwert, 1997, "Understanding Tomorrow's Mind: Advances in Chaos Theory, Quantum Theory, and Consciousness in Psychology," *The Journal of Mind and Behavior*, 18 (2/3), Spring/Summer, 335–50.
Von Foerster, H. (1985) "Entdecken oder Erfinden- Wie Lasst sich Verstehen Verstehen?" in H. Gumia, and A. Mohler (eds) *Einfuhrung in dem Konstruktwissmus*, Munich, 27–68.
Waldrop, M. (1992) *Complexity: The Emerging Science at the Edge of Order and Complexity*, New York, Touchstone.
Weinberg, Steven (1983) *The Discovery of Subatomic Particles*, New York, Scientific American Books.
Weinberg, Steven (1992) *Dreams of a Final Theory*, New York, Pantheon.
Wiener, Norbert (1961) *Cybernetics: or Control and Communication in the Animal and the Machine* (2nd ed.) Cambridge, MA, MIT Press.
Wilson, Edward (1994) *Naturalist*, Washington, DC, Island Press, Shearwater Books.
Wilson, Edward (1998) *Consilience: The Unity of Knowledge*, New York, Knopf.
Yorke, James A. and Li, T.Y. (1975) "Period Three Implies Chaos," *American Mathematical Monthly*, 82, 985–92.
Zimmerman, H.J. (1988) *Fuzzy Set Theory and Its Applications*, Boston, Kluwer-Nijhoff.
Zipf, George (1935) *The Psychobiology of Language*, Boston, MA, Houghton Mifflin.

3
Chaos Theory: Unpredictable Order in Chaos

> The new geometry mirrors a universe that is rough, not rounded, scabrous, not smooth. It is a geometry of the pitted, pocked, and broken up, the twisted, tangled, and intertwined. ... The pits and tangles are more than blemishes distorting the classic shapes of Euclidian geometry. They are often the essence of a thing.
>
> James Gleick, 1987

> Science keeps imposing limits on its own power as it advances: Einstein's theory of special relativity prohibits the transmission of matter or even information at speeds faster than that of light; quantum mechanics dictates that our knowledge of the microrealm will always be uncertain; chaos theory confirms that even without quantum indeterminacy many phenomena would be impossible to predict; Kurt Godel's incompleteness theorem denies the possibility of constructing a complete, consistent mathematical description of reality; and evolutionary biology keeps reminding us that we are animals, designed by natural selection for breeding, and not for discovering deep truths of nature.
>
> John Horgan, 1996

> We are the most complicated things in the known universe ... Physics is the study of simple things. Physics appears to be a complicated subject, because the ideas of physics are difficult for us to understand. ... We are ill-equipped to comprehend the very small and the very large; things whose duration is measured in pico-seconds or gigayears; particles that don't have position; forces of fields that we cannot see or touch, which we know of only because they affect things that we can see or touch ...
>
> Richard Dawkins, 1986

3.1 Chaos theory

Chaos theory was discovered by Henri Poincaré in 1899 in his attempt to find a solution to the gravitational attraction between a star and its planet (the n-body problem). He succeeded in proving that the problem had no analytical solution. Unlike conventional functions like sine waves, the planets follow complex a-periodic cycles which never exactly repeat themselves.[1] During the 1960s scientists with the first computers began to examine how natural systems like the weather change over time. To their astonishment they accidently found that many meteorological events were not haphazard. Lurking within them was a subtle form of order. They labeled this behavior "chaotic," and a new scientific field "Chaos Theory" grew up to explain nature's dynamics.[2]

Chaos theory has shaken science to its foundations.[3] Its central insight was entirely new and surprising. Very simple systems of nonlinear equations can exhibit elaborately complex and totally unpredictable behavior encompassing the endlessly detailed beauty of fractals. It has been argued that where classical science ends, chaos theory is only beginning.[4] Chaos theory is a young field of scientific inquiry whose boundaries have not yet been clearly defined.[5] It stretches across several established disciplines: physics, molecular and evolutionary biology, paleontology, meteorology, fluid mechanics, geology, chemistry and economics.

Chaos theory is formally defined as "the study of a-periodic behavior in nonlinear dynamic systems." The term "system" denotes a general description of the interacting relationship between variables. Time-varying behavior can only be modeled with dynamic systems. The models must be nonlinear and include a description of the instantaneous state of a system and a recipe for transforming the current state into a description of some future or past state.[6] Some scientists believe that nonlinearity and feedback contain all the necessary tools for encoding and unfolding structures as richly complex as the human brain.

Chaotic nonlinear systems have been characterized in many ways[7]:

A kind of order without periodicity;
Complicated, aperiodic, attracting orbits, of certain (usually low-dimensional) dynamical systems;
Apparently random recurrent behavior in simple deterministic (clockwork-like) systems;
Irregular, unpredictable behavior of deterministic nonlinear dynamical systems;
Dynamics freed from the shackles of order and predictability;
Simple processes that can produce magnificent edifices of complexity without randomness.

In the 1970s a new form of geometry emerged to describe these chaotic processes, termed "*fractals*" from the Latin (*fractus*) by their discoverer (Benoit Mandelbrot) to highlight their fragmented irregular nature. The degree of irregularity corresponds to the characteristics of the object in taking up space. Fractals constitute patterns that recur on finer and finer magnifications. They display self-similarity at every magnification, building up to shapes of unimaginable complexity. They are self-similar. Any small part of the structure looks identical to the whole.

Mandelbrot resurrected rather than invented the idea of dimension to isolate the crucial feature characterizing a fractal pattern: its fractal dimension D. Fractals quantify the scaling relation among patterns observed at different magnifications.

Euclidian space has three dimensions, a plane has two, a line has one, and a point has zero. For Euclidian shapes dimension (D) has a simple integer value: 1 for a smooth line, 2 for a completely filled two-dimensional area, 3 for a closed cube. But Euclidean measurements of length, depth, and thickness fail to capture the essence of irregular shapes. For fractal patterns the repeating fractal structure causes a fractal line to begin to occupy space as its D value rises. As the degree of complexity increases, the dimension of a fractal line approaches 2. The D value of a fractal line can vary between 1 and 2.[8]

In 1978 Mandelbrot published a bizarrely erudite and equation-studded book, *Fractals: Form, Chance and Dimension*. Within a few years this book and its expanded refined replacement, *The Fractal Geometry of Nature*, (which Mandelbrot called, *a manifesto and a case book*) sold more copies than any other book in higher mathematics.[9] Self-similarity may be exact, as in the case of mathematical equations, or statistical, as in the case of most natural fractals. Fractals have been found in a wide variety of phenomena: trees, mountains and clouds, even human lungs.

In a famous paper *"How Long is the Coast of Britain?"* Mandelbrot argued that the length depends on the scale of your ruler. As the scale becomes smaller the measured length of a fractal coastline increases without limit. A jagged coastline is an example of a fractal-like object. Viewed from afar, the coastline reveals peninsulas and bays. On closer examination smaller juts and coves are seen, which when surveyed even more closely reveal jagged borders. When the coastline is so jagged that with each magnification new details appear, the line describing the coast begins to "take up space" and becomes "fractal". Mandelbrot asserted:

> The notion that a numerical result should depend on the relation of object to observer is in the spirit of physics in this century and is even an exemplary illustration of it.[10]

This characteristic is shown in Figure 3.1 The Koch curve. It is constructed as follows: take a triangle with each side one unit long. Take the middle one-third of each side and attach a new triangle identical in shape but one-third the size. Repeat this transformation indefinitely. Every transformation multiplies the original length by four-thirds. The length of the circumference becomes: $3 \times 4/3 \times 4/3 \times 4/3 \times \ldots$ = infinity! Yet since the area remains less than the area of a circle drawn around the original triangle, an infinite line thus surrounds a finite area! The resulting object is more than a line yet less than a plane, greater than one-dimensional yet less than two-dimensional. Infinitely extended multiplication by four-thirds of the Koch curve gives a D of 1.2618.

Fractals are self-similar across scale and produce the identical detail at finer and finer scales. Many real world shapes have fractal qualities. The artificial tree in Figure 3.2a displays an exact repetition of patterns at different magnifications. For the real tree shown in Figure 3.2b the patterns do not repeat exactly, but their statistical qualities repeat.

Consider the Serpinski carpet in Figure 3.3. This is constructed by dividing a square into nine equal three-by three squares, and removing the central one.

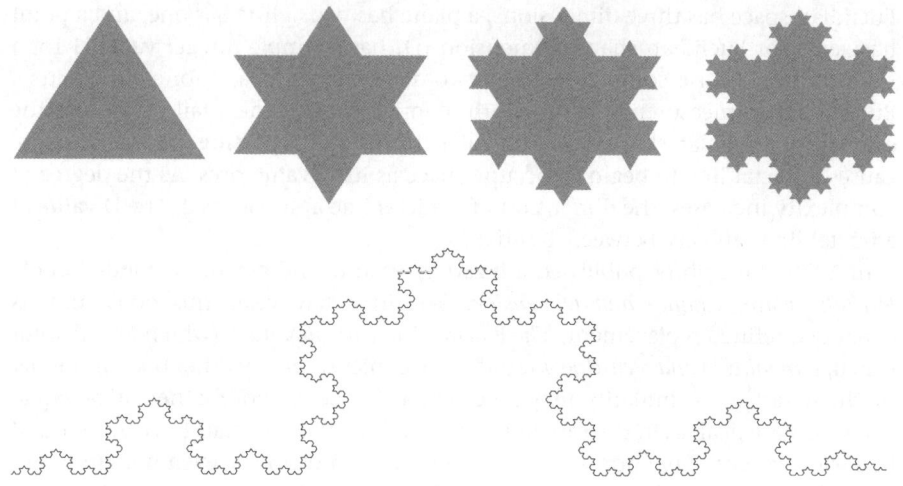

Figure 3.1 The Koch curve
Source: Gleick, 1987: 99.

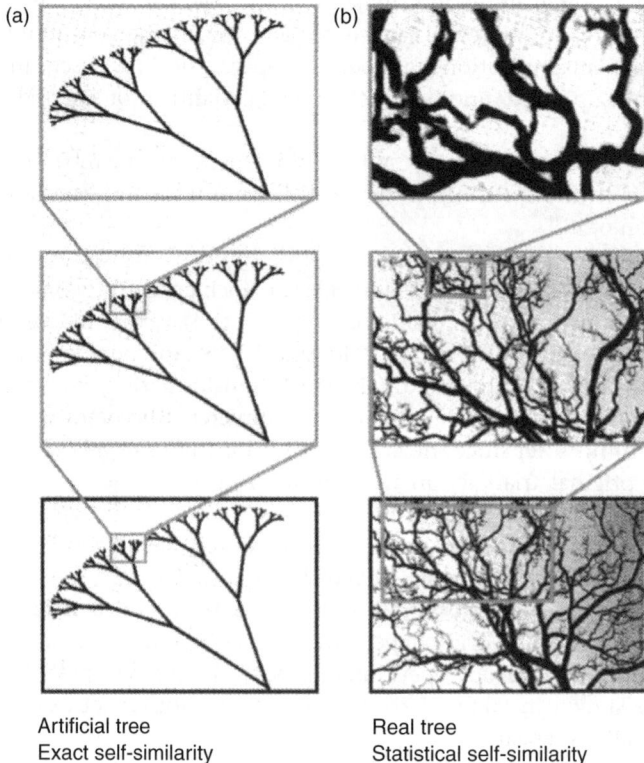

Artificial tree
Exact self-similarity

Real tree
Statistical self-similarity

Figure 3.2 Exact and statistical self-similarity
Source: Taylor, 2002: 118.

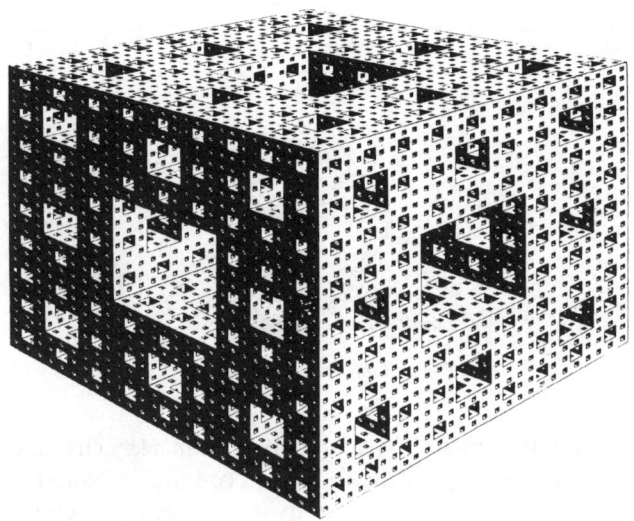

Figure 3.3 Serpinski carpet and Menger Sponge
Source: Gleick, 1987: 101.

Repeat this operation for each of the eight remaining squares putting a square hole in the center of each. Its three dimensional analogue is called the Menger Sponge, a solid-looking lattice with an infinite surface area and a zero volume.

It is possible to construct a Serpinski triangle in a similar fashion. Divide an equilateral triangle into four equal triangles remove the central one and repeat. This leads to the Chaos Game.[11] Start as shown in Figure 3.4 with three points that outline an equilateral triangle and label them (1,2), (3,4) and (5,6). Pick a point at random within or outside of the triangle shown in Figure 3.4(a). Now roll a fair die, and proceed halfway from the point to the angle of the rolled number (e.g. 6). Plot the new point as shown in Figure 3.4 (b). Using a computer, repeat these steps 10,000 times. Throw out the first 50 points as transients. One ends up in Figure 3.4 (c) with the Serpinski triangle. The shape is independent of the initial point. Random events are needed to play the game: the selection of the initial point and the roll of the die. The points are plotted in a random order, and the order is different each time the game is played. No matter where one starts one always ends up with the Serpinski triangle. The system reacts to random events in a deterministic manner. The Chaos Game shows how local randomness combined with system determinism creates a self-similar stable fractal structure.

48 *Shaking the Invisible Hand*

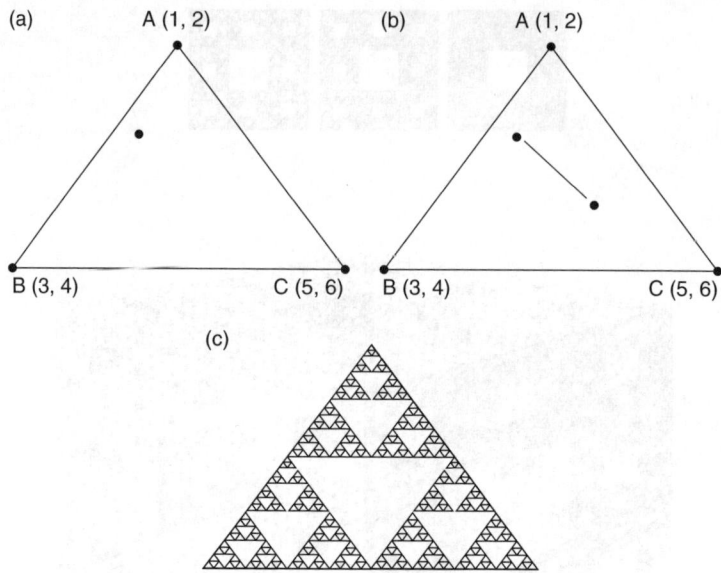

Figure 3.4 The Chaos Game

The unpredictability of chaotic systems derives from a key characteristic of non-linear systems: "sensitive dependence on initial conditions." Similar systems that start very close together end up very far apart.[12] Sensitive dependence on initial conditions explains why chaotic systems are unpredictable. The slightest degree of vagueness in specifying the initial state of the system grows to confront the researcher with enormous errors in calculation of its future states.

In principle a chaotic system is perfectly deterministic and predictable. Providing the initial situation can be precisely specified all future states follow from straightforward calculation. The problem is that for accurate empirical predictions the initial specification must be absolutely accurate. All variables must be measured to infinite decimal points, even to predict events an infinitesimal period into the future. Useful predictability would thus require an indefinitely large device for storing and manipulating data. Our inability to construct such a device is both a practical and a theoretical limitation. At what point does the number of decimal places required for accurate predictions become so great, that our inability to achieve such precision is no longer a matter of our limited resources, but becomes a physical impossibility, the way things are?[13]

Chaotic systems are not random, and random systems are not chaotic. Even if a pattern is impossible to discern, one cannot conclude that no pattern exists. Chaos theory discloses a particular region of logical possibility, closed to us not by physical law, nor by limited resources, but by the fact that we are finite beings. Even the most detailed inspection of the output generated by chaotic systems does not permit us to infer the equations and structure of the system that generated that output. Chaos theory compels scientists to reassess the methodological assumption that small errors always stay small, and to reconsider their motivation for making that assumption. The curious nature of chaotic unpredictability raises deep questions about scientific determinism. After chaos theory predictability must now be separated from determinism.[14]

It was traditionally assumed that randomness in a system was due to its extreme numerical complexity. But chaos theory reveals random system behavior need not involve a large number of degrees of freedom. The underlying structure of chaotic systems can be very simple, governed by only a small number of degrees of freedom. Systems with chaotic behavior share substantial commonality. Chaos theory highlights a new and authentically deep principle of nature: extremely complicated and outwardly random and indecipherable behavior can be determined by simple nonlinear order.

Chaos theory yields what is termed, "dynamic understanding," a holistic account of how order and unpredictability arise. It does not provide exact quantitative predictions, it eschews the use of rigorous deductive schemes, and does not develop general micro-reductive explanations. As a new area of inquiry, the study of chaos provides an occasion for reconsidering our methods for gaining knowledge about the world, our notions of what that knowledge should look like, and our conceptions of what kind of world we inhabit. Most importantly, chaos theory reveals that many phenomena can only accurately be modeled as nonlinear systems. The primary goal of scientific investigation becomes no longer prediction, but increased holistic understanding.

3.2 Application of chaos theory

The distinguishing mark of chaos theory is the presence of nonlinear terms in the equations which involve algebraic (power and multiplicative) functions of the variables. Until chaos theory most models were linear systems because they were very easy to manipulate and solve. System behavior was then both determinate and predictable. A-periodic behavior occurs whenever variables describing the state of the system do not undergo regular repetition of values. The system cannot be manipulated to yield a closed form "equilibrium" solution, since the nonlinearity of the equations rules out the possibility of closed form solutions. Mathematical modeling is the solution to understanding dynamical systems, since the impossibility of closed form analytical solutions necessitates computer simulation.[15]

In a Malthusian world of unrestrained compound growth, population rises forever upwards by a constant proportion (r) each year: $x_{t+1} = r\,(x_t)$. Since resources are limited, a term is needed to restrain growth when the population becomes large, for example due to death from starvation or predation. Mathematically inclined biologists developed a new discipline, ecology, using dynamical mathematical systems to analyze population growth and fluctuations. Ecologists used difference equations to capture the behavior of the population next year as a function of the population this year, $x_{t+1} = F(x_t)$. The behavior of the population may be derived through a process of functional iteration—a feedback loop with each year's output serving as the next year's input. By the 1950s ecologists had moved to the logistic difference equation: $x_{t+1} = r\,(x_t)(1-x_t)$. The term $(1-x_t)$ is included to keep growth within bounds. As x_t rises $(1-x_t)$ falls.[16]

With chaotic systems researchers are unable to make exact predictions of particular future states from present ones. They are only able to provide "qualitative" descriptions of system behavior. Most real world systems are nonlinear. Dynamical linear systems are unable to replicate the behavior of most actual systems, since what was previously considered "noise" is now recognized as constituting important information about system behavior.

The mathematician James Yorke and the biologist Robert May found to their astonishment that when they increased the growth rate *r* of the system it began to behave in an erratic manner and the quality as well as the quantity of the output changed. As the *r* parameter passed 3, population growth oscillated between two points in alternating years. As the parameter rose further, the number of points doubled, then again, and again. These bifurcations became faster until beyond a certain point periodicity gave way to chaos where the fluctuations never settled down.

Yorke analyzed this behavior in his famous 1975 paper "Period Three Implies Chaos." He proved that if a regular cycle appears in period three, the system will display regular cycles of every other length, but in addition will display completely chaotic cycles.[17] May used a bifurcation diagram to assemble his new results (Figures 3.5–3.6). When the growth parameter is below a certain value the population

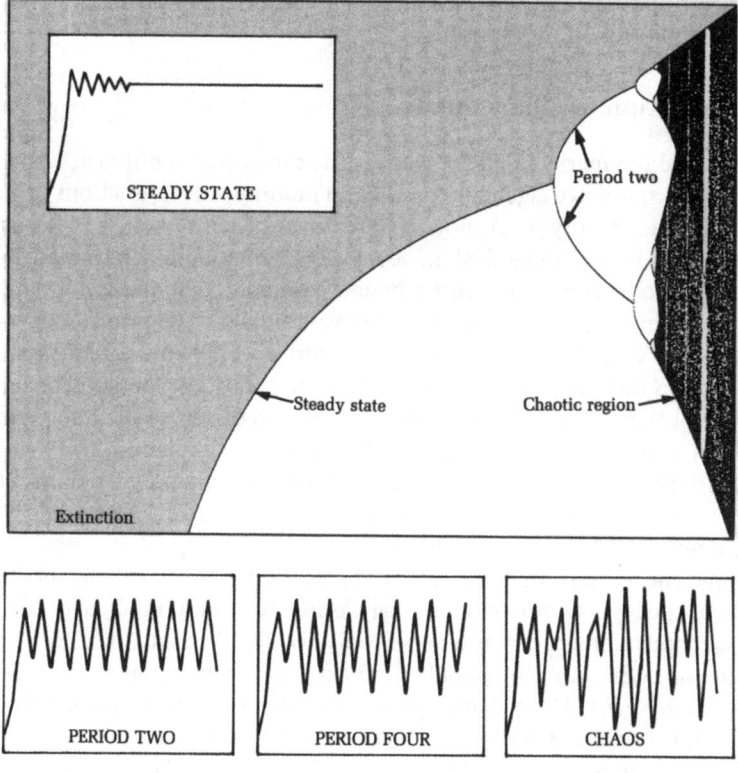

Figure 3.5 Period doubling and chaos
Source: Gleick, 1987: 71.

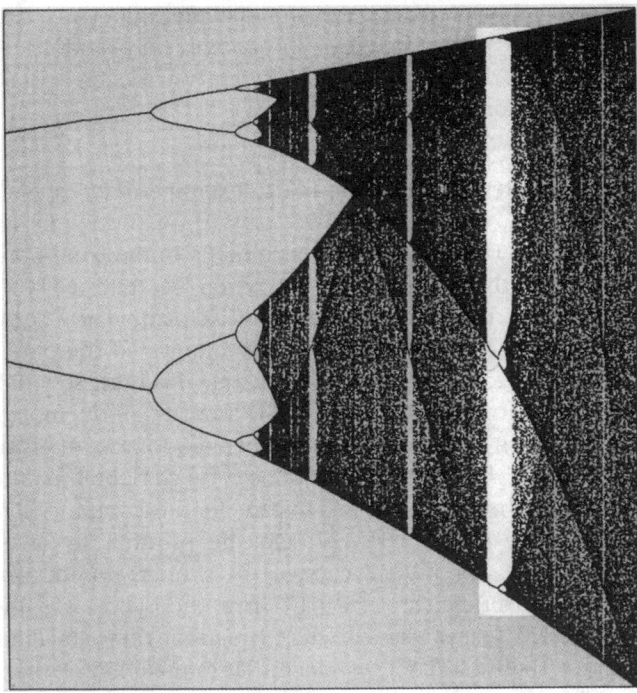

Figure 3.6 The structure of chaos
Source: Gleick, 1987: 74.

becomes extinct. When the parameter rises so does the equilibrium level of the population. When the parameter rises further the equilibrium splits in two. The bifurcations come faster and faster and the system turns chaotic. Even with the simplest equation the region of chaos has an orderly structure. At first bifurcations produce periods of 2, 4, 8, 16, ... then chaos ensues. As the system is driven harder, windows suddenly appear at odd periods. When portions of the chaos are magnified they resemble the whole diagram. The structure becomes infinitely deep.

Unstable a-periodic behavior may be found in very simple deterministic chaotic systems containing no explicit reference to chance mechanisms, and comprising only three differential equations. It was previously taken for granted that complex behavior, which shows no repeating patterns and responds abruptly to very small disturbances must reflect the reinforcing influences of countless different and complicated subsystems. The paradox of chaos is the existence of behavior so complex as to appear random, generated by extremely simple systems with very few degrees of freedom.

Human history is both complex and chaotic. It never exactly repeats itself and for long periods continues to manifest the effects of the smallest perturbations. Small changes have large effects. History books teem with examples of insignificant events that have led to momentous changes in the course of human affairs.[18]

A periodic chaotic behavior makes exact predictions impossible and produces deterministic outcomes that empirically appear completely random.

The groundwork for chaos theory was accidently discovered in 1963 by the meteorologist Edward Lorenz:

> One day in the winter of 1961, wanting to examine one sequence at greater length, Lorenz took a shortcut. Instead of starting the whole run over, he started midway through. To give the machine its initial conditions, he typed the numbers from the earlier printout. When he returned an hour later, he saw something unexpected, something that planted the seed for a new science. ... The new run should have exactly duplicated the old. ... Yet as he stared at his new printout, Lorenz saw his weather diverging so rapidly from the pattern of the last run that within just a few months, all resemblance had disappeared. ... he might as well have chosen two random weathers out of a hat. Suddenly he realized the truth. There had been no computer malfunction. The problem lay in the numbers he had typed. In the computer's memory six decimal places were stored: .506127. On the printout to save space just three appeared: .506. Lorenz had entered the shorter, rounded-off numbers, assuming that the difference—one part in a thousand—was inconsequential. ... Yet in Lorenz's particular system of equations these small errors proved catastrophic. ... .That first day he decided that long-range weather forecasting was doomed.[19]

Lorenz had been devising an extremely simple model of turbulent flow, as a prelude to developing a more complex model of atmospheric turbulence.[20] His model consisted of a thin sheet of water, held between two metal plates with one plate slightly hotter than the other. The temperature difference in the plates initiated a flow of water. Lorenz was using a simplified version of a well-known model of turbulent flow to explain the fluid's motion. His model had just three equations, three variables, and three constants to describe the fluid's motion in three directions. It would be hard to think of a simpler set of three equations.[21] Yet the behavior generated was indefinitely complex (Figure 3.7).[22] Figure 3.8 shows the time path of the east-west fluid displacement.

Figure 3.9 shows the resulting displacement from Lorenz's work. A very small change in any one variable leads rapidly to a very large change in the system's output. This illustrates the special feature of complex systems: "extreme sensitivity to initial conditions."

The pattern for any one variable appears erratic. But behind this apparent randomness lies a beautiful structure which only becomes visible when the three variables are plotted on one graph. Using a computer to plot the trajectory of his system, Lorenz created the first picture of a surprising new geometrical object: a "strange attractor."[23] A "strange attractor" is a self-similar fractal structure with a nonintegral dimension. Figure 3.10 shows the "butterfly" behind the superficial chaos.

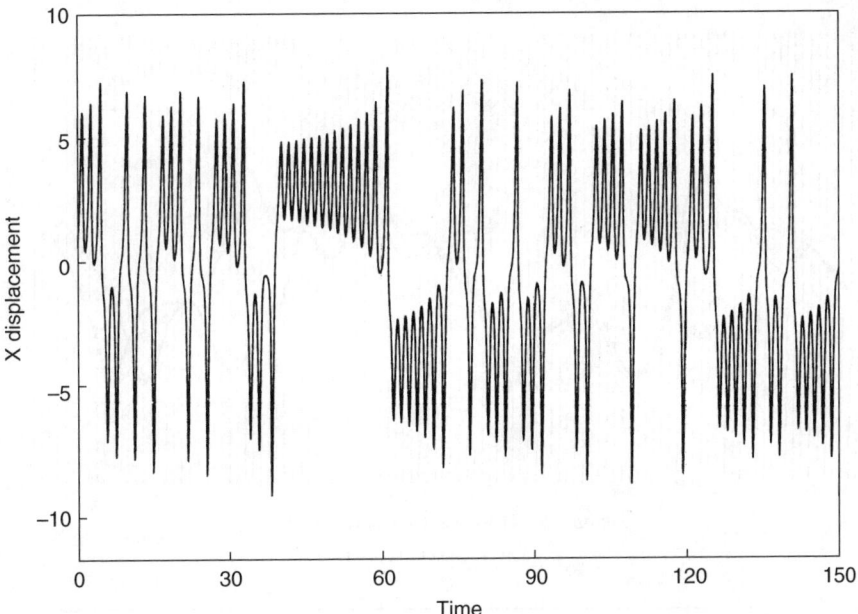

Figure 3.7 Deterministic chaos
Source: Keen, 2001: 181.

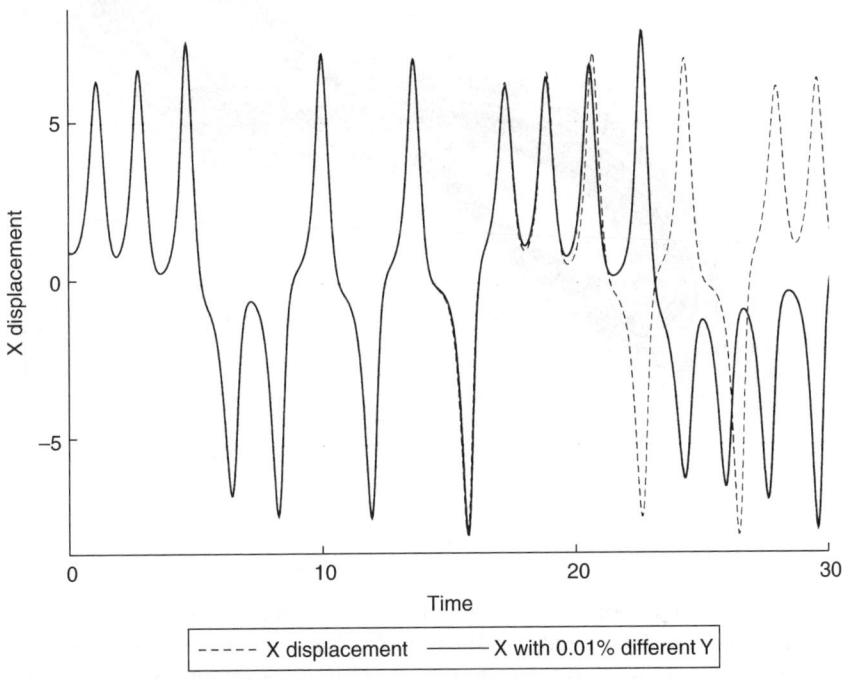

Figure 3.8 Deterministic chaos with displacement
Source: Keen, 2001: 181.

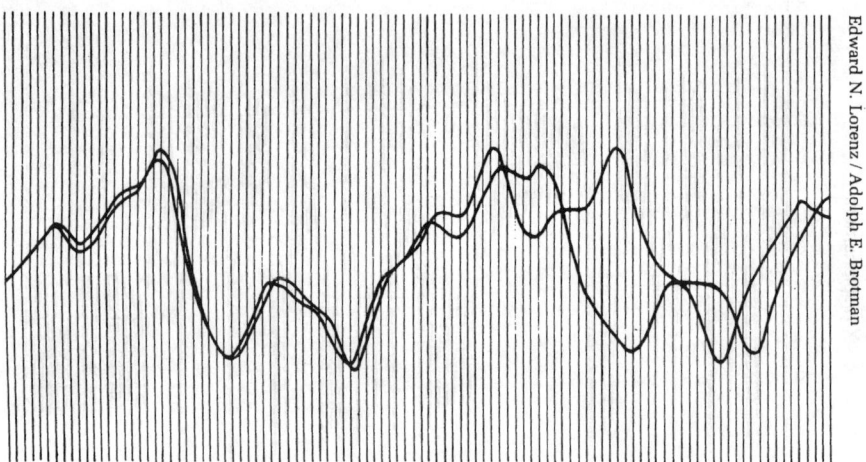

Figure 3.9 How weather patterns diverge
Source: Gleick, 1987: 17.

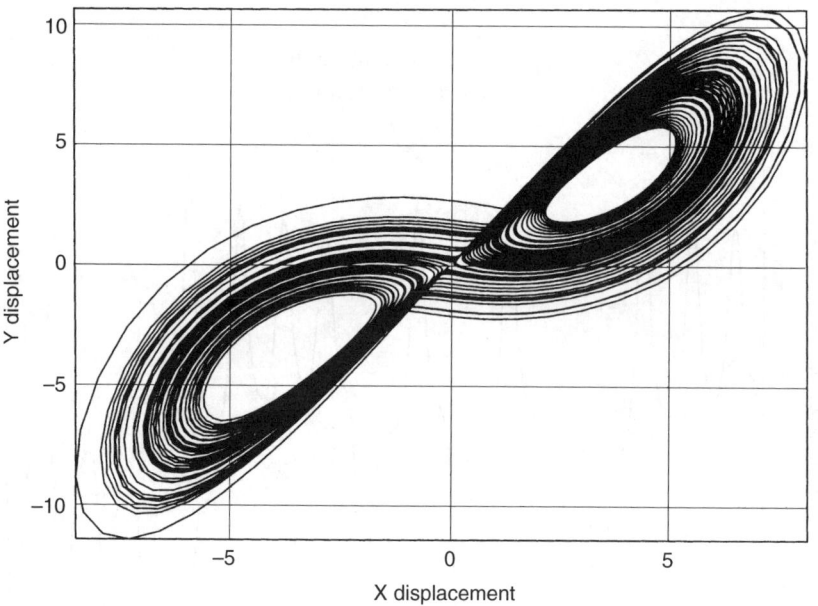

Figure 3.10 The butterfly behind chaos
Source: Keen, 2001: 182.

There are several important economics lessons from this discovery.[24] First, systems with unstable equilibria need not break down but can display complex cyclical behavior, much like real world economies. Second, if the equilibrium of the model is unstable neither the initial nor any final position can be an equilibrium position. Third, dynamic analysis does not plot movements from one unstable equilibrium position to another. Simple dynamic models display "far from equilibrium" behavior. Rather than equilibrium telling you where a system is tending, "equilibrium" positions tell you where the system can never go. Actual economies are always in disequilibrium as a result of their inherent complex structure, in the absence of any "exogenous" shocks. Even a system as simple as Lorenz's, with only three variables and three constants, displays incredibly complex dynamics due to the fact that the interactions between variables are nonlinear. Nonlinear relationships in differential equation models can lead to extremely complex bounded behavior.

Extrapolating from the model most economic variables are fractals. They are always in "disequilibrium" in the absence of external or "exogenous" shocks. For complex systems change is the only constant. All the abstruse mathematical conditions that economists have proven to exist for a system in equilibrium are irrelevant for complex economies. Comparative static analysis is not a simplified proxy for dynamic analysis. If system equilibrium is unstable a market economy can never reach an "optimal" position. The problem for complexity theorists is not how to eliminate the inherent instability in economic systems, but how to contain it within acceptable bounds by appropriate institutional change.

A central element of all chaotic systems is their total unpredictability. Chaotic phenomena guard the weather from falling into an ever-repeating rut, and give rise to the variations underlying evolutionary change. Systems characterized by sensitive dependence on initial conditions provide critically important sources of novelty and diversity. Small changes in conditions can result in dramatically different system outputs *vide* the well-known "*butterfly effect.*" A butterfly spreads its wings in Peking and two weeks later a hurricane arrives unannounced in Miami. Similariy if central banks provide sufficient system liquidity, a financial crisis may be averted.

Like quantum mechanics, chaos is another realm where our human understanding runs smack up against genetic limitations. It is as if nature decreed: "*Here you can go no further.*" No matter what we do, or how hard we try, we are forbidden from being able to predict the destiny of chaotic systems. Chaotic systems require impossibly exact accuracy for accurate predictions. While it is impossible to predict the outcomes of complex systems accurately, it is possible to describe the order they contain and the processes systems undergo.

Chaotic systems present a major challenge to the core methodological assumption that has long guided scientific practice. When confronted with an insoluble set of equations, we conventionally approximate with a simpler linear system whose behavior we are able to predict. In making this move we trust that slight discrepancies and higher order terms will not render our approximation worthless. If a small amount of vagueness in measurements leads only to a small amount of vagueness in predictions, small influences can be neglected. But sensitive dependence on initial conditions guarantees that all such approximations are worthless. As chaos sets in we encounter the inadequacy of our methodology, rather than the inadequacy of our laws. The complexity of a system may be defined by the complexity of the model necessary to simulate the behavior of the system. Chaos theory presents a limitation on the predictability of physical systems. Sensitive dependence requires physically impossible accuracy to perform any predictive task.

By presenting us with examples of tasks so difficult that the fact that we are finite beings makes us unable to accomplish them, chaos theory challenges the distinction between theoretical and practical impossibility.[25] Indefinitely small changes in starting conditions can result in dramatically different system outputs. Sensitive dependence undermines the methodological assumption behind the conventional strategy of approximation analysis and calls into question a number of central beliefs about the way of the world and how we should go about understanding it. If our world contains chaos even the smallest vagueness can blossom into open ambiguity. The challenge of chaos theory is to welcome this openness, and not see it as cause for regret. Some scholars regard chaos theory as containing within it the promise of the long desired reunification of the sciences.

People are genetically hardwired to discover regularities. They instinctively look for the periodicity wrapped in random noise. But by using the nonlinear equations of fluid motion the world's fastest CRAY supercomputers are incapable of tracking a turbulent flow of a cubic centimeter of liquid for more than a few microseconds. Physicists had good reasons to dislike a model that finds so little clarity in nature. Richard Feynman has expressed this paradox extremely forcefully:

> It always bothers me that, according to the laws as we understand them today, it takes a computing machine an infinite number of logical operations to figure out what goes on in no matter how tiny a region of space, and no matter how tiny a region of time. How can all that be going on in that tiny space? Why should it take an infinite amount of logic to figure out what one tiny piece of space/time is going to do?[26]

3.3 The innate instability of economic variables

Mainstream economics proceeds as if the instability and volatility of prices in well-organized financial markets is due to the advent of new information, which causes agents to change their expectations of future events. Fluctuations in equity values are believed to be due to the random arrival of new information that affects the market value of shares. By implication if there were no new information, there would be no change, and the market would remain quiescent at the current price. But there is a much more persuasive alternative explanation. The dynamics of financial markets is due to their internal nonlinear dynamical structure. Unfortunately, these two different explanations predict statistical outcomes that with present methods can be indistinguishable from one another.

The "efficient markets hypothesis" maintains that stock prices reflect all information publicly known about a particular stock.[27] Price fluctuations are explained as rational reactions by market participants to the random arrival of new information affecting the future prospects of companies. In an "efficient market" current share prices reflect all current information that concern the value of the companies. Changes in share prices thus must reflect new information coming in the market. In consequence efficient markets must follow a random walk, since new information by definition arrives randomly.[28]

Alternatively, share price fluctuations could be due to stock markets' own complex dynamics. The "inefficient market" hypothesis maintains that many investors are "noise traders," trading on how they believe other traders on average will expect the market to react to the news. "News" includes most importantly the most recent movements in the stock price. While there are three conceptually distinct sources of volatility, event-driven, error-driven, and price-driven, the efficient markets hypothesis models only the first. The second is the result of the market overreacting to news and then overadjusting once the initial mistake becomes obvious. The third is the phenomenon of the market reacting to its own volatility, building price movements on price movements the way neighborhood dogs keep yelping indefinitely after one of them has started. Haugen has argued that this endogenous instability accounts for most of all volatility: *a noisy stock market overreacts to past records of success and failure on the part of business firms, and prices with great imprecision.*[29]

Consider the following analogy from ecology. Lemming populations like stock markets are known to fluctuate wildly from year to year. There are at least two separate explanations for this. The environment in which they live may be so volatile, that it causes extreme fluctuations in the population from one year to the next. Or the environment could be stable, but the population dynamics of lemmings may be so volatile that it causes huge fluctuations in numbers from year to year.

Figure 3.11 shows a chaotic lemming population pattern generated by the first explanation. The equilibrium lemming population is normalized to 0.5 and has a

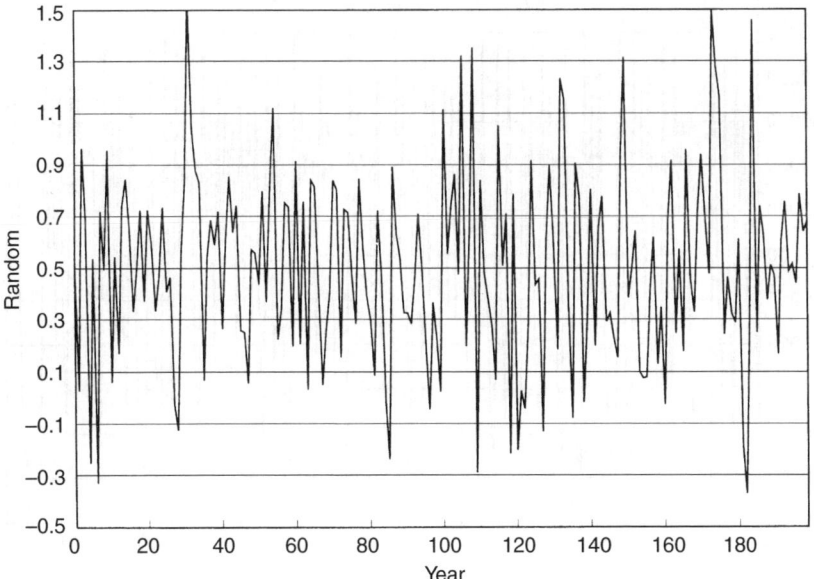

Figure 3.11 Lemming population as a stable system subject to exogenous shocks
Source: Keen, 2002: 245.

standard deviation caused by the environment of 0.35. Figure 3.12 shows a chaotic population pattern generated by the following complex system: each lemming has on average four offspring each season, and lemmings impose a burden on the environment proportional to the square of their number. This burden depletes the environment causing a rapid increase in the death rate when numbers are large. When numbers are small the environment recovers and can support a larger population.

If stock prices were in fact generated by a normal random process a fall or rise of more than 5 percent in one day would be exceedingly rare. If stock prices followed a normal distribution, the probability of such an event occurring even once in a century would be about 1 in 100. In fact there were over 60 such daily downward movements and more than 50 daily upward movements during the twentieth century. The fact that extreme five deviation movements occurred roughly 10,000 times more frequently than for a random process is very strong evidence that stock prices do not follow a random distribution.

Mandelbrot has argued that stock prices follow a fractal power law distribution. A fractal number is a nonlinear function of previous numbers in the series. Such fractal distributions are much more likely to generate extreme events than normal distributions. With fractal distributions a large movement is more likely to be followed by another large movement.[30] As may be seen it is difficult by inspection to determine whether shocks are exogenous (Figure 3.11) or endogenous (Figure 3.12).

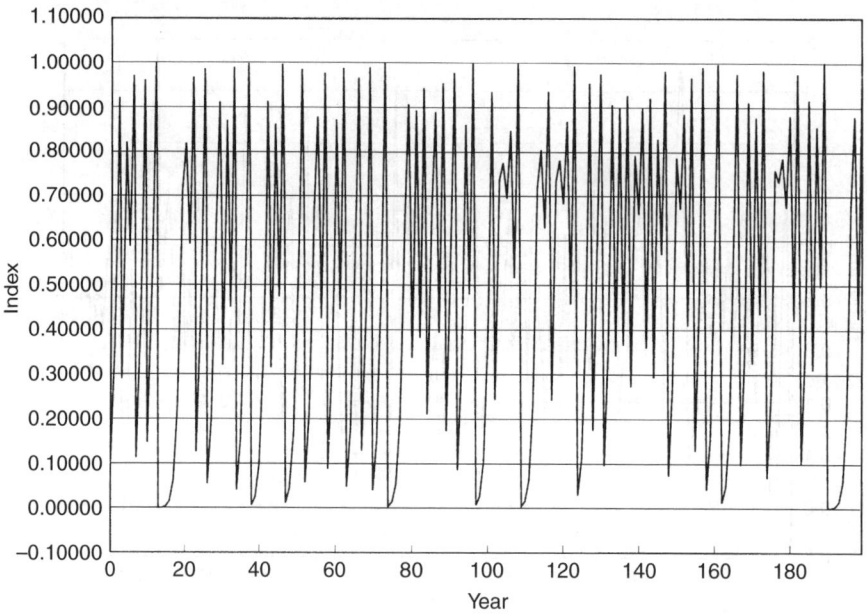

Figure 3.12 Lemming population as a complex system with unstable dynamics
Source: Keen, 2002: 245.

3.4 Determinism and predictability

It was long believed that a deterministic system and a predictable system were different names for the same thing. The interest in determinism has long been bound up with the ideal of predictability. Understanding something was viewed as synonymous with being able to predict its behavior. The goal of increased understanding was seen by practitioners as a quest for getting closer to total predictability. Positivism maintained that the success of alternative theories must be judged by their ability to successfully predict empirical events. A threat to the theoretical coherence of that goal was interpreted as a threat to the aim of science.

But improving something need not imply heading toward a "final" state. It is possible to make sense of science "progressing," without implying any hypothetical picture of the end of inquiry. One need that motivates determinism is the impulse to collapse past, present, and future into a co-present continuum: the desire to increase our ability to analyze problems rigorously and definitively by doing away with time.

Determinism binds the past and future irredeemably to the given present. All is given in one moment. It is as if the world were like a motion picture: the future coexists with the past and is fixed in exactly the same sense. Although the spectator does not know it, the future exists exactly as does the past. The future is known only to the producer of the film—the Creator. Determinism stems from a belief that a fundamental underlying order exists. This can yield "a feeling of intellectual repose stemming from the symmetries and certainties inherent in the mathematical analysis."[31]

Newton's world view presupposed an absolute separation of space and time. Space was viewed as purely Euclidian, an empty three-dimensional void, stretching infinitely in all directions. Time was viewed as an absolute phenomenon, existing somehow "outside" the universe so to speak. Einstein's introduction of a new universal constant, the speed of light, caused the collapse of Newton's conceptual separation of space and time. Einstein successfully proved that space, time and motion are all interrelated. Space–time is curved by the presence of matter. The shortest distance between two points is not independent of the distribution of matter in the space between them. Similarly chaos theory has presented us with a completely new phenomenon: purely deterministic models may be totally unpredictable.[32] Such systems cannot be studied by reductionism. One cannot understand the whole by adding up the parts, since the whole imposes rules on the parts and is greater than their simple sum. Complex phenomena may be more easily understood by first looking at the whole and then placing the parts within it.

The changing "Now" is our subjective window for experiencing the eternal "present" one instant at a time.[33] For those who see the openness of possible futures as fatally threatening to the orderliness and intelligibility of the universe, determinism is calmly comforting. Without it we must confront the possibility that events have no ultimate explanation, final reason, or larger meaning. They "just happen." On the other hand determinism is even more powerfully disturbing since it does major violence to our deeply held experiences of time, change, and free will. The fact that the historical evolution of the physical universe is fundamentally open leads some of us to a queasy inner feeling that encompasses both delight and panic: delight in the limitlessness of possibilities, panic that the world is completely open. This openness may appear to imply nihilism. We are adrift in a sea of indeterminate flux, hopelessly lost without even the theoretical possibility of sure predictability and ultimate explanation.

The critical point is that the recognition that the world is chaotic, open, and nondeterministic need not necessarily imply that perceived events are incapable of being explained. Research into chaos has provided us with the possibility of a fundamentally new level of understanding of nondeterministic processes. One of the difficulties in comparing analytical accounts of explanation with the understanding provided by chaos theory results from a conceptual mismatch. The items to be explained in the former are phenomena: facts, events, and "laws." The items to be explained in the latter are tendencies, patterns, and "order." Rather than answering "why" questions, chaos theory answers "how" questions: for example, how does unpredictable behavior appear? *The ultimate goal (of chaos theory) is to understand the characteristics of all kinds of time evolution encountered including those which seem totally disorganized.*[34]

By enabling us to construct simple models which although chaotic reveal order, chaos theory provides us with a new understanding of the appearance of unpredictable events. It helps us to think about observed aspects of the chaotic world around us in new, interesting and potentially insightful ways. It also allows us to set limits to the unpredictability we encounter and to understand how such unpredictability appears. The widespread occurrence of systems characterized by sensitive dependence on initial conditions has the implication that in our world very small causes can have very large effects. Chaos theory's goal is to explain how long-term patterns appear in system behavior, which in detail is completely unpredictable. How can chaos theory give us this understanding? The central answer must be by constructing and applying dynamic models. Since the world is a complex and open system it cannot be treated as if all descriptions are complete. Chaos theory shows how the interaction of components on one scale can lead to complex behavior on a larger scale that in general cannot be deduced from knowledge of the individual components.[35]

Chaos theory also argues against the universal applicability of reductionism: the belief that all properties of a system are reducible to the properties of its parts. Rather than proceeding by conventional scientific methods, which are microreductionistic, deductivistic, and ahistoric, the heart of chaos theory is dynamic model building. Models are simply idealized systems, defined by a set of equations and linked by various hypotheses to real world systems. The belief that reductionism is universally applicable in studying behavior relied on the construction of a deductive scheme which purported to yield rigorous proof of all theoretical propositions. Chaos theory now makes room for the astonishing insight that there may be no underlying deductive structure, no micro-foundation which generates models from a general set of propositions. Kaldor has termed the components of all dynamic, chaotic, and non-reductionist models in economics *"stylized facts."*[36]

> When approaching a theory, look first for the models and then for the hypotheses employing the models. Don't look for general principles, axioms, or the

like. ... It is not so much important to be rigorous as to be right. A way to be convinced (and to convince others!) of the rightness of a solution is a tried method of science—the experiment.[37]

In the social sciences controlled experiments are difficult or even impossible to perform. Computer simulations reveal the character of the dynamic behavior of a nonlinear system cannot be deduced from the equations that govern it. The recourse to analytical experiments whether conceptual or computer-simulated is not a matter of convenience, nor a tactic to finesse fearsome mathematical difficulties. It is based on the understanding that in all chaotic systems characterized by sensitive dependence on initial conditions, our empirical representation of initial conditions must be infinitely accurate to be able to forecast accurately. Since our computational resources are characterized by finitude, we must resign ourselves to the fact that we will never be able to forecast the future.

Scientists still lack a convincing picture of what constitutes time.[38] They are divided as to whether some incompletely understood process bestows a direction of time on the cosmos, or whether the human brain endows us with a sense of the passage of time.[39] The explication of how economic phenomena vary over time is the most critical challenge for economic analysis.[40] As Alfred Marshall famously maintained:

"The element of time ... is the center of the chief difficulty of almost every economic problem."[41]

Frank Knight formulated the paradox of time more insightfully as follows:

The existence of a problem of knowledge depends upon the future being different from the past, while the possibility of the solution of the problem depends on the future being like the past. ... Time is the center of "the chief difficulty of almost every economic problem."[42]

Mainstream economics has followed the general method of physics: the ahistoric and synchronic pursuit of understanding in terms of the properties of instantaneous states as represented by the characterization of a system in terms of its state at some point in time. As a result the methodology of mainstream macroeconomics has been exclusively equilibrium analysis: the characterization of economic systems in terms of a hypothetical position of "balance," where all markets simultaneously clear and all change ceases. The purpose of this methodology was to simplify analysis by doing away with the unsolvable problems presented by temporal change.

The assumption that a unique equilibrium position exists implies with it that "equilibrium" is independent of the particular transition path by which it is reached. In physics the general phenomenon of *"hysteresis"* has long been recognized. Over some range, there may be two or more possible states of the system, depending on its history. If this is the case knowing the exact equations of motion, including the exact value of the driving frequency, is insufficient to understand the behavior of the system.[43]

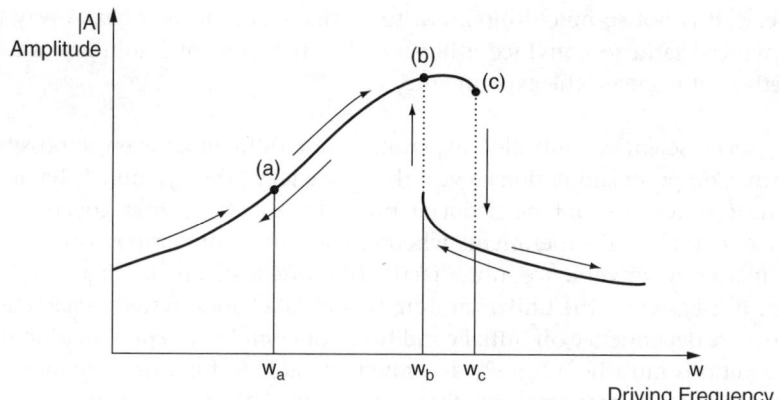

Figure 3.13 Hysteresis
Source: Kellert, 1993: 94.

As shown in Figure 3.13, if the system *"comes from below"* it has a relatively large amplitude of oscillation. But if it *"comes from above"* it has a relatively small amplitude. For systems where hysteresis exists the behavior of the system cannot be understood without knowing its history, at least in the limited sense of its past behavior.

Chaos theory has shown that to understand something is not the same as being able to predict it. Similarly, accurate prediction does not imply understanding the system. Ancient Babylonian predictions of lunar eclipses by means of sheer skill at observation and calculation offer a superb example:

> The Babylonians acquired great forecasting power, but they conspicuously lacked understanding. To discover that events of a certain kind are predictable, even to develop effective techniques for forecasting them, is evidently quite different from having an adequate theory about them, through which they can be understood.[44]

Everything has a history.

> Whether history is science or not, there can be no doubt that some sciences have essential historical aspects. Cosmology, geology, and evolutionary biology come immediately to mind.[45]

To the above group must be added the social and behavioral sciences, including expressly economics. It was long thought that being able to predict the behavior of a system was the same as understanding it. *"If you can properly predict the outcome, there is nothing to learn."* But it is now increasingly widely recognized that fully understanding how a system behaves need not imply we are able to predict its future behavior. For many phenomena prediction is impossible: weather, stock prices, foreign exchange, and all homogeneous assets traded in well-organized markets. Chaotic behavior makes detailed aspects of complex systems' future path completely unpredictable. Most social phenomena are aperiodic and hysteric. Periodic behavior is in fact quite boring, and in the life sciences is ordinarily fatal.

Chaos theory provides an enlightening account of how predictability goes out the window in the real world and puts a final nail in the coffin of the proposition that understanding implies predictability.[46] The assertion that chaos theory offers new qualitative predictive power does not refer to its ability to predict exact future values of the system, but only to explain holistic changes in the system's behavior. Chaos reveals only patterns and order, not strict regularities and invariant laws. The distinction is between specific quantitative predictions, which are impossible in all complex systems, and qualitative predictions, the recognition of the order that lies at the heart of dynamic systems theory.

> Dynamics is used more as a source of qualitative insight than for making quantitative predictions.[47]

Chaos theory permits us to construct dynamic models that can both yield qualitative predictions and account for their range of validity. It provides greater qualitative understanding by illustrating the geometrical mechanisms of stretching and folding, which account for the sensitive dependence on initial conditions responsible for unpredictable behavior. Rather than attempt to discover new fundamental laws, researchers have been led to the recognition that there may be:

> No universally valid law from which the overall behavior of the system can be deduced.[48]

Instead of a search for laws, chaos theory represents a search for *order*, which is a concept broader than law. Laws imply a deterministic universe and fuel the methodological goal of predictability. A rule-based conception of understanding seeks laws that dictate why things are constrained to turn out the way they do. Such an approach responds dismissively to chaotic behavior and assigns it entirely to outside causal influences (*"noise"*).

Chaos theory shows how patterns arise within unpredictable behavior. It provides an understanding of *"how it happens,"* not *"why it had to happen."* Chaos theory provides greater understanding of the ways in which unpredictable behavior and patterns appear. This counts as providing increased understanding by showing *"how"* chaos happens. The kind of understanding provided by chaos theory has been termed "dynamic,"[49] holistic, historical, and qualitative. It eschews deductive systems and causal laws.[50] It is holistic in that it studies properties of dynamic behavior inaccessible to microreductive analytical techniques. It is historical in that it studies how systems proceed in actual historical time, rather than in rest or *"equilibrium."*

Due to the complexity, openness and unpredictability of complex systems, to be intelligible chaos theory must massively simplify sense reality. In the physical sciences chaos theory takes the form of numerical simulations rather than deductive structures. Reduction in mathematical rigor does not imply sloppy data collection, nor vague appeals to intuition. The understanding we get from chaos theory may only be *"qualitative."* But this is not to be contrasted with *"mathematical."*

In the physical sciences the nonlinear dynamical systems approach gives no indication of reversing the process begun by Galileo, the mathematization of the world.

> Far from creating a space for the reappearance of qualitative properties in the sense of subjective, sensuous experiences, chaos theory strives to apply mathematical techniques to phenomenon like turbulence in clouds, that were once a repository for romantic notions of sublime Nature resisting the onslaught of human rationality.[51]

Models and not laws form the heart of modern science. Research into nonlinear complex systems will eventually lead to a new conception of nature embracing contingency and emergence. We now understand that different aspects of the world have very different types of understanding appropriate to them.[52] We must become cognizant of the fact that linear systems, though highly tractable analytically and capable of yielding precise closed-form solutions, are nonexistent in the real world outside of astronomy.

Since Newton, most models of science have been reductionist. But science works by metaphor and the metaphors used in science are now changing. Godel showed in the 1930s that even the simplest mathematical systems are inherently incomplete, in that they contain statements that cannot be proven true or false within the system.[53] In the 1970s physicists got analogous results from chaos theory. Simple nonlinear equations produced astonishing and completely unanticipated and unpredictable results. Scientists gradually came to realize that the subject matter of science is naturally and inherently messy and that this messiness is not created by the dirt on the glass of the microscope. The chaos revolution is the opposite of reductionism. Complex, unpredictable, emergent system behavior is now increasingly being understood as the product of simple nonlinear relationships.

To analyze the behavior of living phenomena, models must be nonlinear. Despite the basic theoretical assumption of continuity in nature, *natura non facit saltum*, the dynamics of self-organizing systems in fact do jump from one state of order to another. Concepts such as fluctuation, cycle, threshold, and saturation are intrinsically nonlinear and are only very roughly approximated by linear functions. The existence of nonlinear phenomena in the behavior of a system is a necessary condition for self-organizing processes. The importance of nonlinearity in the modeling of theoretical relationships cannot be overemphasized.

Linearity implies strict proportionality of responses to the stimuli. Yet this is never observed in living or social phenomena. In nonlinear systems the size of the input does not determine the size of the output. Minimal influences frequently can have maximal effects. In learning complex tasks, people commonly report an initial stage in which no advance is made despite high effort, followed by sudden improvement in which a new level of control is reached. Human learning is characterized by abrupt fluctuations and discontinuities in learning curves. These phases of arrested progress are termed "plateaus." A reorganization of simple skills appears to be necessary before their integration into more complex units is possible.[54]

So long as the system is linear the effects of separate factors are independent. The response of the system is proportional to the sum of the individual responses of the separate factors. In most economic models all relationships are linear in character.[55] Students of economics are taught early in their careers that so long as a series is continuous, even if the "true" relationship is nonlinear the systems' behavior can be approximated at any point by the tangent. This is correct for individual functional relationships. But such independence and proportionality are not true for unlinear systems. Nonlinear systems must be used to model the non-proportionality we clearly observe among the effects of separate system factors. Non-proportionality between inputs and outcomes is an important manifestation of nonlinearity where response is a complex function of the inputs. For chaotic systems the response function may be extremely sensitive. Minuscule changes in inputs can yield catastrophic changes in outputs. Nonlinear systems have "emergent properties" not explicit in the underlying elements. Confining modeling strategies to linear relationships is much too restrictive, since linear systems are unable to describe most of the counter-intuitive unpredictable behavior of real-world systems. The scale-free fractal nature of nonlinear low dimensional dynamics leads to unexpected changes in the system that mimic the complex dynamics observed in real time series. The property of chaos theory to be as crazy as the complex phenomena it models makes it an attractive descriptor.

3.5 Five nontraditional truths[56]

Nonlinear interactions in the complex dynamics of social phenomena call many of our traditional truths into question.[57] Much of our failure to understand events is due to the inapplicability of our unspoken assumptions rather than our inability to conceptualize truth about dynamic phenomena. In Table 3.1 five "traditional

Table 3.1 Five traditional and nontraditional truths

Traditional truths	Nontraditional truths
1. Scientific theories are essentially quantiative	1. Qualitative theories are as important for science as quantitative ones
2. Natural phenomena can be represented by analytic functions	2. Many natural phenomena are fractal and cannot be represented by analytic functions
3. Natural phenomena have fundamental scales	3. Many natural phenomena do not have fundamental scales, but are describable by scaling relations
4. The evolution of natural phenomena can be predicted from the equations of motion	4. The evolution and emergence of many phenomena are not predictable
5. Complicated processes can be reduced to the sum of their constituent parts	5. Complex processes are holistic and greater than the linear sum of their parts

truths" of science are contrasted with five "nontraditional truths." Most of the latter initially appear to erode the very foundations of the physical sciences.

1. The first traditional truth is that all scientific theories are quantitative. This often takes the form that if a theory is not quantitative it is not scientific. This perspective is both wrong and overly restrictive. All scientific disciplines accept the need for rigor and accurate quantitative measurement. But scientific theories may be qualitative as well as quantitative.[58] Many interesting phenomena in social science exhibit sharp discontinuities. Consider the crash in US stock prices in 1929, the fall of the Berlin wall, and the collapse of communism in Russia in 1990. Such discontinuities can only be modeled nonlinearly.

Complex systems frequently manifest periodic behavior that repeats itself after fixed intervals of time, generating a sequence of sub-harmonic bifurcations. Eventually the motion, after becoming more complex in each bifurcation suddenly becomes irregular. Consider the transition to chaos. A system may be regular for all values of a parameter below a critical value. Above this value the regular behavior is intermittently interrupted by a finite-duration burst during which the dynamics become qualitatively different. The bursts become more and more frequent as the parameter becomes larger, until chaos is reached and only the bursts remain.[59] Mathematics is merely one language among many that can be used to analyze complex events. *The first nontraditional truth is qualitative descriptions are as equally important as quantitative descriptions.*

2. The second fundamental truth asserts that all relationships can be represented by analytic functions. Since Lagrange (1759) celestial mechanics have been described by smooth, continuous, and unique functions. The evolutionary movement of physical systems are conventionally modeled by systems of dynamical equations and the solutions of such equations are thought to be continuous and differentiable, that is, analytic functions. From this comes one of the major assumptions of the physical sciences: understanding comes from careful description and prediction, not from the identification of teleological causation.

The purpose of modeling is to obtain a clear description capturing the essential features of the process being investigated. In physics some phenomena can be accurately described by exceedingly simple relationships.[60] But such relationships are not available outside the physical sciences. If phenomena do not have a fundamental scale, they cannot be linearized by a logarithmic transformation. Analytic functions are the solutions only to differential equations with well-behaved boundary and initial conditions. The time dependence of discontinuous phenomena and the structure of fractal geometric forms are determined by recursive algorithms not differential equations. Fractal processes do not possess a characteristic scale that can be represented by analytic functions. *The second nontraditional truth is many phenomena are fractal in character and not representable by analytic functions.*

3. The third traditional truth is all physical and social systems can be characterized along fundamental scales such as length and time. Such scales provide the meaning of the fundamental units in the physical sciences without which measurement cannot be made and quantification would be impossible. Recognition of the fractal complexity of the world requires us to reinterpret our existing data sets. If we consider closely an irregular time series, formed by first differencing economic time series, our first impression is typically the lack of organization in the first differences. But when we focus our attention on a small interval and magnify the series, two kinds of results typically occur. One is that the magnified region of the curve becomes smooth and no more irregularity is observed. When this happens the time series can be represented with an analytic function, since there exists the smallest scale below which there is no further variability. But a very common kind of result is that the more we magnify the curve, the more structure is uncovered. What is observed on one scale is repeated on adjacent scales, revealing more and more structure. There is no scale at which the variations in the data subside, and so there is no limiting smallest scale size.[61] The structure of many things is thus determined by the scale of the measuring instrument. *The third nontraditional truth is many natural phenomena are fractals with no fundamental scale, describable only by scaling relations.*

4. The fourth traditional truth is following Newton the time evolution of physical systems can be viewed as if determined by a system of dynamic equations. If one could completely specify the initial state of the system the solution to the dynamical equations uniquely determines the final state of the system. The final state can be predicted using the dynamical equations from a given initial state. The Newtonian model is valid for many short-run phenomena. But over longer time periods absolute predictability never holds for any variable. Mountains are constant and stable over medium time units, but over longer periods we now know how much they have changed. Chaos arises over longer time periods from the nonlinear structure of all physical systems.[62]

The time unit is central. Stock prices differ from other prices not due to their unpredictability but because their price change is continuous, so unpredictability holds over even the shortest time unit. As the time unit increases, more and more phenomena become intrinsically unpredictable. In economic systems the future price and supply of most commodities is largely unknowable over periods in excess of five to ten years.

A set of deterministic equations can generate erratic series that can satisfy all the conditions of randomness. Chaotic series have a fractal dimension, in the way an inverse power-law spectrum for a random time series has a fractal dimension. It is frequently not clear whether a fractal time series is generated by a low-dimensional deterministic nonlinear dynamical process or by a linear series plus an inverse power-law spectrum (colored noise). It is important to be able to distinguish between "chaos" and "noise" in any given time series. How we analyze the data and interpret the underlying process depend crucially on this judgment. A colored noise signal implies we must look for a static fractal structure that is moderating the noisy signal in such a way as to give rise to the fractal dimension. When the system is chaotic, the fractal dimension is related to the underlying nonlinear dynamical structure. As the time unit is increased for most systems the chaotic nature of the signal becomes more apparent and we have greater scope for constructing a holistic description of the underlying process.

Fractal structures are frequently described as the result of the geometrical operations of stretching and folding, exemplified by the baker's transformation creating folds within folds *ad infinitum*, resulting in a fractal structure in phase space.[63] The greater the magnification of any region of the attractor, the greater the degree of detail revealed. The solutions are extremely sensitive to the initial conditions. *The fourth nontraditional truth is deterministic equations of motion do not have predictable long-run final states.*

5. *The fifth traditional truth concerns the methodology of reductionism.* Science has historically followed a reductionist strategy: all the properties of a system are reducible to the properties of its parts. All systems and processes can be decomposed into their consistent elements. Each element should first be studied individually and then reassembled in order to understand the whole. The behavior of systems is determined by their structure which is assumed linear. Nonlinearities make no qualitative changes to the system's evolution. The effects of nonlinearities can be treated as perturbations and assumed weak effects. If a property is not contained in a system's fundamental elements it cannot emerge from their juxtaposition. Systems have no emergent properties.

Chaos theory provides a clear explanation of emergent properties which offer powerful counter-examples to all reductionist claims. Understanding complex processes cannot be achieved through detailed knowledge of its component elements, but only through the holistic simulation of the system. The failure of reductionism stems from the fact that for all complex systems the whole is a great deal more than the sum of its parts. Models that can successfully simulate real world phenomena are nonlinear, have no unique long-run solution, and can be simulated but not solved. Chaotic outcomes appear completely stochastic and unpredictable but the patterns they exhibit can be simulated on computers. Reductionism represents another god that has failed. *The fifth nontraditional truth is complex phenomena do not lend themselves to reductive analysis.*

3.6 Postmodernism and economics

Lyotard has defined postmodernism as *"incredulity towards meta-narratives."*[64] Instead of looking for a simple meta-discourse that can unify all forms of knowledge, we have to cope with a multiplicity of discourses determined locally, and not legitimated externally. The proliferation of discourses and meaning described in postmodern theory reflects the complexity of linguistic and social spaces. Different contexts and institutions produce different narratives not reducible to one another. The postmodern description of knowledge, as the outcome of a multiplicity of local narratives, is not an argument against scientific knowledge. It is an argument against the understanding of such knowledge as absolute. Lyotard has argued for a narrative understanding of knowledge, as a plurality of smaller stories that function well in the particular contexts where they apply. Rather than claiming the impossibility of knowledge, Postmodernism:

> refines our sensitivity to differences and reinforces our ability to tolerate the incommensurable. Its principle is not the expert's homology (sameness or correspondence) but the inventor's paralogy.[65]

Acknowledgment of system complexity implies the incorporation of continuous change, not as noisy epiphenomena but as the constitutive core of complex systems. Different groups tell different stories about their knowledge. Their logic does not constitute a logically structured and complete whole, but takes the form of different local narratives that are instrumental in allowing them to achieve their goals, and to make sense of what they are doing. These local narratives cannot be linked together to form any single grand narrative which "unifies" all knowledge. Postmodernism emphasizes that many stories even contradictary ones can be told about single events. The postmodern condition is characterized by the coexistence of a multiplicity of heterogeneous discourses.

Postmodernism is assessed differently by different parties. Many who have nostalgia for a unifying meta-narrative experience the postmodern condition as fragmented, full of anarchy, and meaningless. It leaves them with a feeling of vertigo. On the other hand many embrace postmodernism as challenging, exciting, and full of uncharted spaces. It fills them with a sense of adventure. Which of these two evaluations apply is determined by the extent one feels comfortable without fixed points of reference. The choice may be determined by psychological as much as theoretical considerations. A postmodern perspective need not imply relativism, but rather a greater inherent sensitivity to complexity. Instead of trying to analyze complex phenomena by reduction to their essential principles, postmodernism explicitly acknowledges more than a single exclusive story can be total about things that are complex.

A frequent argument against postmodernism is the claim that if narratives have only local legitimation, the resulting fragmentation of the social fabric relativizes knowledge. If there is no external "check" on any discourse, no local narrative can be criticized. Each discourse becomes independent of all the others leading to a situation where "anything goes."

Such an interpretation is explicitly rejected by Lyotard:

> The breaking up of the grand Narratives ... leads to what some authors analyze in terms of the dissolution of the social bond, and the disintegration of social aggregates into a mass of individual atoms thrown together into the absurdity of Brownian motion. Nothing of this kind is happening. ... A self does not amount to much, but no self is an island: each exists in a fabric of relations that is now more complex and mobile than before. Young or old, man or woman, rich or poor, a person is always located at "nodal points" of specific communication circuits, however thin these may be. Or better: one is always located at a post through which various kinds of messages pass. No one, not even the least

privileged amongst us, is ever entirely powerless over the messages that traverse and position him at the post of sender, addressee, or referent.[66]

The self is understood not in terms of atomistic units standing by themselves but in terms of a *"fabric of relations"* or a *"node"* in a network. The relationships are important not the node as such, so *"a self does not amount to much."* Lyotard's description of the postmodern condition is an accurate description of "networking" in contemporary society: the manner in which knowledge is produced and reproduced. These networks are too complex for any general overarching description. Society forms networks. Different discourses form "clusters" within these networks but cannot isolate themselves from the network. There are always connections with other discourses. Local narratives only make sense in terms of their contrasts and differences with surrounding narratives. Rather than being self-sufficient and isolated, discourses are in constant interaction battling with another for territory.

The argument that postmodernism results in isolation misses the target. Social fabric is not "designed." It evolves dynamically as a result of the way it responds to contingent information. The process is a complex one without any external design and involves many agents with nonlinear feedback relations between them. Agents cooperate to form "clusters" and compete for resources in the network.[67] Contingency is central. Counter-factual illustrations of the contingent nature of events provide a therapeutic query, the adequacy of nationalist histories celebrating a pre-ordained tryst with destiny.[68] The history of the system is vitally important for the way in which meaning is generated in any part. Social systems combat entropy and in the process generate meaningful structures, not noise. The methodological choice of "equilibrium" analysis constitutes the avoidance of complexity. It blinds us to the relational nature of complex systems and continual shifting nature of complex relationships.

> Consensus is a horizon that is never reached. Research that takes place under a paradigm tends to stabilize ... what is striking is that someone always comes along to disturb the order of "reason."[69]

> "To yearn for a state of equilibrium is to yearn for a sarcophagous."[70]

The role of science has traditionally been understood as "fixing" knowledge in a permanent grid. Experimental evidence was used to verify theories and sufficient verification assured a permanent place on the grid. But it gradually became clear that the conditions for objective verification were problematic. Experimental evidence could support a theory but could never prove it. Since it was only possible to disprove theories, the process of "verification" was gradually replaced by that of "falsification." If one could not add to the grid, one could at least disqualify unwanted members. The strategy of "throwing away" had the result of making the body of knowledge qualifying as "scientific" leaner and more impoverished. Everything complex was left aside and large parts of the totality of human knowledge were discarded as "unscientific": most of the arts, psychology, and the entire social and behavioral sciences. Pushed to its limits the theory of falsification implied that only abstract *a priori* truths were "scientific." This view has now at last finally been completely abandoned.

Complex systems access a constant flow of energy to change, evolve, and survive as living entities. The energy flow is necessary to fight entropy and maintain the complex structure of the system. Complex networks are finite. They can suffer from overload when confronted with too much novelty and in the process can be annihilated. Complex systems operate under conditions far from equilibrium. In complex systems equilibrium, symmetry, and stability imply death. There is no escape. We all learn to cope by being more discriminating and filtering out excesses. Society only survives as a process and is defined by what it does. In postmodern society this constant activity is pushed to ever-higher heights, with unsettling effects. All complex systems have a history. It is impossible even to think in the present without considering the past. We are continually creating society through our actions. No complete picture of its present state is ever possible.

Postmodernism's central message is that *consensus is impoverishing*. To proliferate knowledge we must proliferate discourses and not try to fix them onto a permanent grid. There is no immutable "method" that determines what forms part of the cannon and what does not. Postmodernism provides a framework for developing a "narrative" interpretation of scientific knowledge. Instead of being denotative, logical and cumulatively historic, scientific knowledge evolves through interaction and diversity. It is embedded in the context of the wider social network and depends on the authority of neither history nor the expert to legitimate it.

The idea of a normative scientific knowledge may be summarized as follows. The world we live in is complex, and this complexity is universal, diverse, and chaotic. Contingency is central to history. Descriptions of reality cannot be reduced to simpler and universally valid discourses. Different groups tell different stories about what they know and what they do. These narratives succeed if they are instrumental in allowing groups to make sense of what they are doing. The narratives are always local. Any attempt to link them to form unifying grand narratives will fail. All narrative paths share the characteristics of contingency, provisionality, and emergence. Our descriptions of the world must retain an inherent sensitivity for its complexity. Consensus is in fact never permanently achievable even as a local phenomenon limited in both time and space.

McCloskey has dramatically illustrated the importance narrative and rhetoric play in economic discourse.[71] Postmodernism suggests we must go further and recognize the narrative and inexact nature of knowledge itself. Economics can never represent the "totality of true economic knowledge." All basic axioms of economics are inexact and all economic assumptions are approximations.[72] Purely logical descriptions never exhaust the richness and contradictions of contingent complexity. Many stories, even contradictory ones, can be told about single events.

Economists must learn to accept the coexistence of a multiplicity of heterogeneous discourses. There is a kind of underlying "market test," "reality principle," or Darwinian "survival of the fittest" mechanism at work in science. Like all social networks, scientific knowledge self-organizes to ensure that in the long run only those narratives that make a difference will be perpetuated. The postmodern argument for a plurality of discourses represents the acknowledgment of complexity. Science has manned the battlements against the postmodern heresy that there is no objective truth only to discover postmodernism within the walls. Change is truly the only constant. Mainstream economists must learn to accept a plurality of approaches, and be more tolerant of heterodox views: *"Let a thousand flowers bloom!"*

Appendix: prediction and domination

Physics' deterministic view of natural phenomena is being overwhelmed by the increasing recognition of complex phenomena. These are found in the psychological and social sciences over the short run, and in the natural sciences over the very long run. The changes in perspective and metaphor developing in mainstream science over the past few decades are compatible with the view of the world that many heterodox life scientists, psychologists, historians, and institutionalists have long held. As old and new views coalesce nonlinear systems will assist us in understanding the chaotic features of social systems. Sensitive dependence on initial conditions serves not only to destroy but also to create. Even snowflakes are non-equilibrium phenomena, the product of the flow of energy from one state of nature to another.[73]

Instead of asking, *"Why has chaos theory only recently become the object of so much interest?"* it is more informative to ask, *"Why has it taken so long for scientists to focus attention on such phenomena?"* The existence of nonlinear systems characterized by sensitive dependence on initial conditions was first discovered by Poincaré at the close of the nineteenth century. The mathematics to study chaotic behavior was then available. Why did it take nearly a century for chaos theory to develop?

The nontreatment of chaos after the analytical tools were developed is widely attributed to the fact that nonlinear systems do not yield closed form solutions. Sensitive dependence on initial conditions is characteristic of all nonlinear systems. The possibility of system simulation on digital computers first made chaos accessible to scientific inquiry.

> [This fact] surprises us because it was invisible before the computer. With the computer it is easy to see and even hard to avoid. The computer is a viewing instrument for mathematical models that will, in the long run, be more significant than the microscope to a biologist or the telescope to an astronomer.[74]

While this is true it is not the sole answer. An important additional causal factor was societal interest in the control and exploitation of nature, which contributed to the institutionalized disregard of all physical systems not readily amenable to mathematical analysis:

> Cultural biases can profoundly affect the historical development of science, by influencing the scientific community's notions of what counts as an interesting or worthwhile scientific phenomenon.[75]

The resistance to analyzing complex and unpredictable behavior was attributable into part professional instruction. By training students to seek simple exact solutions, to disregard disordered behavior, and to focus their attention on linear models, scientific education screened off chaos as an object of study. The *zeitgeist* was created that only solvable systems were important. Students were steered away from nonlinear systems, which were regarded as uninteresting or exceptional.

> The engineer or scientist was taught to look for resonances and periodic vibrations in physical experiments, and to label all other motions as "noise."[76]

Linear equations were considered important simply because there were straightforward general methods for solving them. The emphasis on linear systems:

> may even have reached the point ... of scientists training themselves not to see nonlinearity in nature.[77]
> These particular things and the processes they underwent were important because they could be minutely and precisely known, rather than being known because they were important.[78]

Following physicists, economics instruction has traditionally focused on those systems that allow exact, stable, and periodic solutions. There has been a clear mutual interdependence between solvability and importance. Studies of the dynamical properties of models consist of finding an "equilibrium" solution and then conducting linear analysis to determine stability in respect of small disturbances. Explicit nonlinear dynamics were universally ignored as "noise."

But what made exact closed form solutions and stable general equilibrium behavior (the clockwork hegemony) so desirable as to justify the neglect of a wide range of analytical models and physical phenomena for an entire century? In part it was simply aesthetics. The fascinating beauty exerted by simple and exact solutions of linear systems led to their domination of the mathematical training of most scientists. As Von Neumann cautioned: "bad mathematical difficulties must be expected from nonlinear equations."

In physics exact closed form solutions which took the shape of routine mathematical expansions, that is, sine, cosine, log, were given the label "simple," and systems that admitted no such formula were labeled "intractable," "impossible to solve" and exiled for exhibiting behavior considered too irregular or complex.[79] Yet sine and cosine are not intrinsically "simple" concepts. Why did exact solvability which allows for precise quantitative predictions become the overriding sole aim of science? Mathematical and experimental tools were then available to study phenomenon not confined to this type of solution.

The metaphysical comforts of determinism contributed in a major way to the explanation of why random or "noisy" results were dismissed as unsuitable for scientific investigation. The desire for exact quantitative predictability accounts for the benefits ascribed to finding simple closed-form solutions. The notion that "science" should seek only straightforward causal mechanisms, expressed in micro-reductionist, ahistorical language reinforced the linear prejudice in its repression of "noisy" phenomena.

Ideology also played a role. The feminist philosophy of science has insisted that judgments about which phenomena are worth studying, and which kind of data are significant, depend critically on the social and linguistic practices of those making the judgments. Ideology operates in implicit ways, and indirectly shapes the choice of the scientific method used and the phenomena chosen as important. The superiority of one type of model over another is not determined solely by the availability of data. Model choice provides an arena where the contextual features of a culture influence science. Mathematical tractability is a crucial issue. In all sciences models that are tractable tend to prevail. But why do only certain results count as "solutions" while others do not? The criteria for a "successful" solution, a "good" theory, an "adequate" description depend critically on the practices accepted by the scientific community. Social and political commitments and ideology deeply affect these practices:

> Models are abstractions of particular abstracts of the assumed reality. Into the abstractive process go human assumptions and values as to the significant features of that reality.[80]

One long-held endeavor of science has been the prediction and control of natural phenomena. Not all forms of control are the same. The social interest in precise quantitative prediction and control contributed to the neglect of the study of chaotic behavior. The domination of nature was accomplished with the use of science and technology that relied on exact quantitative predictions. In order to bend phenomena to human needs, processes had to be reduced in complexity and simplified into predictable "laws." The domination of nature involves:

> making the world more predictable by reducing the chaotic complexity of real events and processes to regular procedures that can be controlled.[81]

Science has sought regular and predictable behavior to satisfy its socio-economic and cultural interest in dominating nature. These interests explain why exact closed-form solutions were considered the ideal type of solution to a scientific problem. Due to the prejudice in favor of linear systems chaotic behavior was screened off from study. Attention was primarily paid to those elements of the world that could be reduced to objects for human use. The notion that a solution to a problem must be a simple exact formula took hold so strongly because of the interest in social control:

> Modern science has as its main goal prediction, i.e. the power to manipulate objects in such a way that certain results will happen. This means that only those aspects of the object are deemed relevant which make it suitable for such manipulation or control.[82]

One of the most powerful metaphors in economics is the vision of the economy as an interdependent system. The economist is both investigator, seeking to discover its hidden interrelationships, and social engineer, seeking to ameliorate its faults. Such a mechanistic view of the economy provided the legitimating ideology for government "management" of the economy, and "social engineering." Feminist scholars have emphasized how much the ideology of nature and society as legitimate targets for government management and control have in common with gender ideology.

There are strong metaphorical parallels between the domination of nature, and the domination of women. Humans are purposive while natural processes are not, therefore nature may be subordinated. Men are stronger and more rational than women, therefore women may be subordinated. The vision of the economy as a mechanistic system functioned as a justification for persistent government domination over it. The wild disorderly features of the natural world such as the business cycle were perceived as needing to be tamed and subdued.

Machiavelli compared fortune to a violent, turbulent river. His added injunction offers at the very least much food for thought:

"Fortune is a woman and it is necessary, if you wish to master her, to conquer her by force."[83]

4
Econometrics, Data Mining, the Absence of a Stable Structure and the Pervasiveness of Contingency

> The statistician, when testing a relationship set up by economic theory, may draw unconditional and conditional conclusions. The unconditional conclusions, however, are only negative. ... If ... the correlation coefficient turns out to be too low (in comparison to the standard set before), the conclusion must be that the relation is incompatible with the facts. In other words the theory is incorrect, or at least incomplete. The positive conclusions that can be drawn do not appear when the theoretical relation is checked; it cannot be proved that a theory is correct. The correlation may be high: but other theories may also lead to a high correlation. ... If we want to draw positive conclusions, additional information is necessary.
>
> Jan Tinbergen, 1951

> The only truly exogenous factor is whatever exists at a moment of time, as a heritage of the past.
>
> Nicholas Kaldor, 1985

> On pessimistic days I doubt that economists have learned anything from the mountain of computer print-outs that fill their offices. On especially pessimistic days I doubt that they ever will.
>
> Edward Leamer, 1983

4.1 The absence of a stable structure and the pervasiveness of contingency

In seeking to understand, the human mind is predisposed to search for patterns. Pattern search and pattern comparison is the way humans make sense of the world. We cannot do otherwise. Our minds are programmed to find patterns even when there is no stable structure and no stable patterns to be found. "Random" means no stable underlying structural relationship. But it is not sufficiently appreciated that randomness does *not* imply the absence of patterns.

Consider the diagrams in Figures 4.1a and 4.1b. In one diagram the dots were entered completely randomly by a random number generator. In the other they

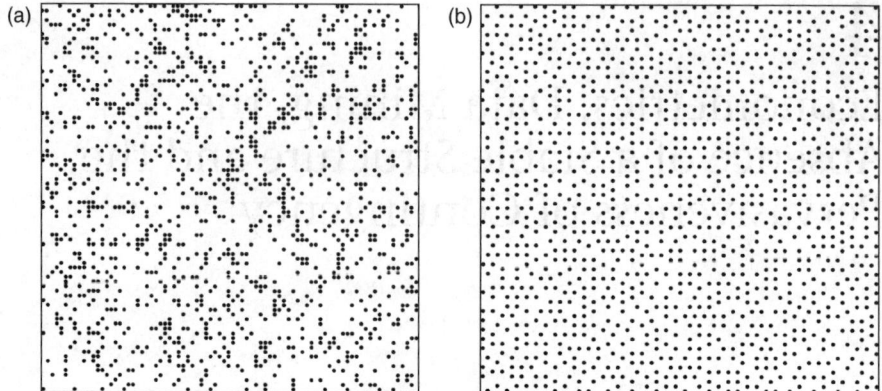

Figure 4.1 Random does not imply pattern-less

were constrained to satisfy a simple relationship. Examine both diagrams carefully. In which diagram do you perceive no hint of patterns? Which diagram appears to you to be most random? If you said 4.1b you would be in a large majority. But you would be also be … wrong!

Both diagrams were constructed by dividing the area into 83×83 equal squares and filling one-fifth of the squares with dots. In Figure 4.1a the computer was programmed to enter a dot in each square according to a random number generator. In Figure 4.1b the computer was also programmed to enter a dot according to a random number generator, subject to the following constraint.

If there was already a dot in any of the eight adjacent squares: above, below, at each side, or at any of the four corners, the square was left blank. In Figure 4.1b the dots were prevented from bunching and forming contiguous runs by construction. Patterns were thus prevented from appearing among the dots. In Figure 4.1a the random entry of dots was unconstrained: patterns, clustering, and all sorts of pseudo-relationships were allowed to freely blossom.

The point of this exercise is simply to demonstrate that "Randomness" does not imply the absence of patterns. We find vivid examples of random patterns in the skies every starry night, when the "Great Bear," the "Big Dipper," "Orion," the "Southern Cross," and the numerous other constellations about which humans have told astrological tales look down on us.

Examine the dots in Figure 4.2. They exhibit strange amoeba-like patterns or worm-trails. But Figure 4.2 was generated fortuitously in the process of constructing Figure 4.1. The dots were entered randomly in the squares subject to a looser constraint: if there was a dot in any one of the four adjacent squares above, below or to either side, the square was to be left blank (dots in the four diagonal corner adjacent squares were permitted). The completely unanticipated "Worm Trails" of Figure 4.2 were the result. Figure 4.2 is a striking example of how easily patterns can be produced by cumulating, smoothing, or otherwise averaging and massaging random series.

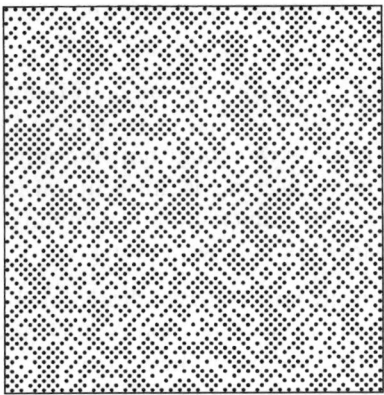

Figure 4.2 Worm Trails

With sufficient diligence it is always possible *ex post* to find patterns even when the series are completely random. But as is only too well known to all compulsive gamblers, these historic patterns are time dependent and fail to repeat themselves in subsequent periods no matter how clever or sophisticated the system used to discover them. When a series is truly random its future behavior cannot be predicted, no matter how apparent the patterns it may contain.

All relationships among social and economic variables are time dependent. The results from flipping a fair coin provide a familiar example. The probability of a head or a tail in flipping of a fair coin is precisely 0.5. But the sequence: H-T-H-T-H-T-H-T-H-T-H … is never observed. One instead observes runs of heads or tails, which although they may appear to be pattern-like are generated purely by chance, for example H-H-T-H-T-T-T-T-H-T-H-H-T-H … .

4.2 A brief survey of the econometric analysis of business cycles

At the beginning of this century economists William Jevons and Henry Moore, after many years of intensive and wide-ranging statistical endeavor, were able to independently persuade themselves that they had succeeded in finding strong empirical evidence that, in the case of Jevons, sunspots, and in the case of Moore, the position of the planet Venus, were clearly responsible for generating periodic 11-year and 8-year cycles in weather patterns which explained the dates of nineteenth-century financial crises.[1]

In a famous 1926 paper "Why Do we Sometimes Get Nonsense Correlations Between Time Series?" the English statistician George Yule rejected the conventional argument that a high correlation between two time series variables was due to "time" serving as proxy for "omitted variables" and so causing the two variables to move together.[2] Yule argued that the high correlations found in time series analysis were not "spurious correlations" due to correlated but omitted variables.

In fact there are no real correlations in the data. Any correlations found are simply "nonsense" correlations.

> Such correlations have no meaning at all; ... in nontechnical terms they are simply a fluke. If we could have had experience of the two variables over a much longer period of time we would not find any appreciable correlation between them. ... to argue like this is, in technical terms, to imply that the observed correlation is only a fluctuation of sampling, whatever the ordinary formula for the standard error may seem to imply.[3]

Yule argued that two critically important conditions are breached in the standard formula for the calculation of the correlation coefficient in time series. The first assumption is that each observation of the sample is equally likely to be drawn from any part of the aggregate population. The second assumption is that each observation in the sample is independent of the previous or subsequent observations. Yule argued that in time series successive observations are (rather obviously) drawn selectively from successive parts of the aggregate. In consequence time series observations are not truly "independent." If time series are in fact time-dependent and successive terms are historically related, the usual conceptions to which we are accustomed fail totally and entirely to apply.[4]

Yule demonstrated how easily time-series observations give rise to spuriously high correlations. He examined the correlation between two sine waves that differ by a one-quarter period. Over their whole length, these series have zero correlation. But over any short period of time they are correlated, and the observed correlation switches between +1 and −1. This produces a U-shaped frequency distribution of correlation coefficients, with the values furthest away from the true value (zero) being the most frequent.

> what looks like a good match to the eye would not seem at all a good match when subjected to strict analysis.[5]

In 1927 Eugen Slutsky designed a "crucial" experiment raising more deeply worrying reasons than "measurement errors" and the "omission of variables" why it has proven so difficult to isolate the cause of business cycles. By juxtaposing an index of English business cycles from 1855 to 1877 against another series generated by a simple 10-item moving average from a series of random numbers, Slutsky was able to demonstrate that business fluctuations can be extremely closely replicated by the simple cumulation of a series of random numbers.

> Is it possible that a definite structure of a connection between random variables could form them into a system of more or less regular waves? ... We wish to consider the rise of regularity from a series of chaotically-random elements because of certain connections imposed on them.

Slutsky believed he had found an inductive proof of our thesis that the summation of random causes may be the source of cyclic processes.[6] Figure 4.3 reveals the astonishing similarity between series of a moving average of random numbers, and a nineteenth-century series of British business cycles.

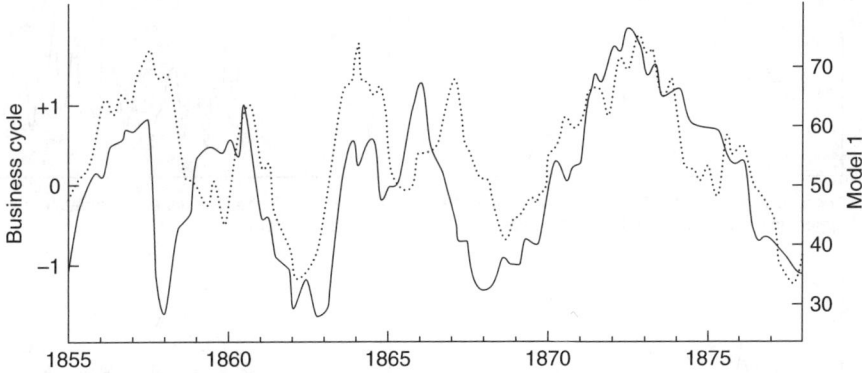

Figure 4.3 Slutsky's random series juxtaposed with business cycles
Source: Morgan, 1990: 81.

Other such "natural experiments" are the observed variations in stock prices. The theory of "efficient markets" maintains that all public information about the future value of securities is incorporated in a shares' current market price. If so, all changes in share prices must be attributed to "new" information coming on the market.[7] If such information is truly "new," it must occur randomly (if it did not occur in a random manner it would be known in advance, and so could not be "new" but would be anticipated and already reflected in share prices). The theory of "efficient markets" concludes that when markets are "efficient" it is impossible to predict future changes in share prices. Changes in share prices follow a random walk.

But this explanation can very easily be refuted in a manner analogous to Slutsky's experiment. Brealey cumulated a time series of random numbers whose variance was constructed to equal the average variance of stock prices. As shown in Figure 4.4 as Slutsky had demonstrated a series formed from the cumulation of random numbers (D) exhibits trends and cyclical movements that are indistinguishable from actual times series of stock indices (a).[8] Future changes in stock prices cannot be known in advance, changes in stock prices appear to be random.

Stocks differ from other goods and only in the extremely short time period over which price changes are observed. But over longer periods it is not possible to predict changes in the price of any good and service. Share prices differ from other goods because they are perfectly homogeneous, highly liquid, and traded in highly organized markets. Transaction costs are very low so their prices fluctuate over extremely short-run time periods, for example, minutes and hours. The essential short run unpredictability of stock prices holds for the prices of all goods and services over longer run periods. The period over which prices change is a function of the homogeneity, liquidity, and durability of the asset, and of the transaction costs which are a function of how markets are organized.

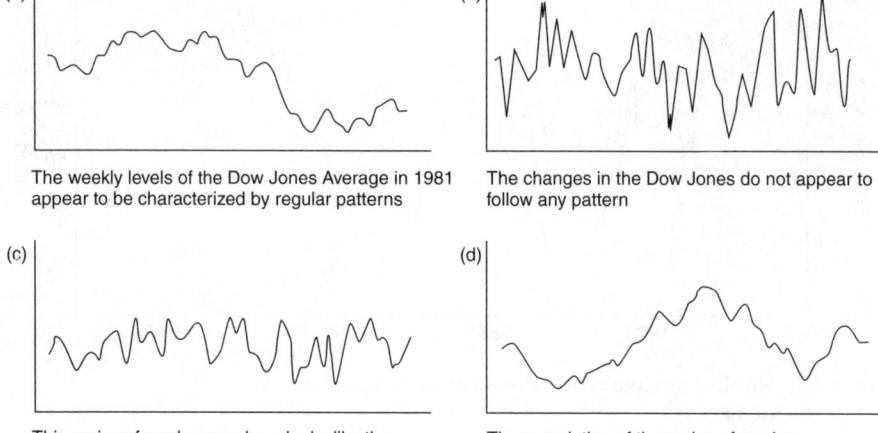

Figure 4.4 Changes in the Dow index look like random numbers, while the cumulation of a series of random numbers looks like the Dow

Source: Brealey, 1970, pp. 4–5.

The unpredictability of changes in stock prices has absolutely nothing to do with capital markets being "efficient", and establishing the "true" or "intrinsic" value of shares. It reflects the fact that economies are complex systems and the future change in the price or quantity of any variable cannot be forecast in the present. In all complex systems the future change in the price or quantity of any item cannot be known in the present. Stock prices differ from other prices not because the change in stock prices cannot be predicted in advance, but because stock prices change over much smaller units of time, every fraction of a second when the stock market is open. In "fix-price" markets where most produced goods are sold, firms "administer" the prices of their goods over their pricing period. The short-run change in prices is then to some extent predictable by the change in average variable costs. Providing the markup remains stable, the change in price in the current period is equal to the change in average variable costs in the previous period.[9]

Frisch's "rocking horse" model of 1933 encouraged economists to make random shocks an integral part of business cycle models. As Frisch graphically proclaimed, "When you hit a rocking horse with a club the movement of the horse will be very different to that of the club."[10] Random shocks, combined with the averaging effects of the institutional pricing structure, may be responsible for generating the observed cyclical oscillations in the economy.

In the 1920s and 1930s applied economists believed that real "laws" of economic behavior existed, and were waiting to be discovered in the data. The role of statistical measures was to measure the parameters of these underlying "laws." The law-like relationships that emerged were taken to be correct representations of the "true" underlying "laws" in the manner of Marshall's metaphor of the tides. Although economists had long used statistical methods, they had regarded probability theory as inapplicable to economic data. Empirical economists believed the measured relationships they discovered did not correspond to the theoretical "laws" of physics, and proposed a number of important reasons for this difference with which they grappled. They did not invoke formal inference procedures based on probability reasoning because they did not believe that economic data constituted the appropriate raw material to which probability reasoning could be applied.

Given the widespread belief that underlying law-like relationships existed, the two chief theoretical explanations given for the failure of measured relationships to correspond with the true underlying law-like relationships were "omitted factors" and "errors in measurement." Both frequently arose in applied work, since in economics it is widely recognized that the *ceteris paribus* clause of equilibrium analysis is never precisely satisfied. In applied work there are always "disturbing factors" that cannot be held constant and so cannot be completely accounted for. With all economic phenomena "errors in measurement" inevitably occur. Theoretical economists were not willing to acknowledge that the relationships econometricians discovered held the status of statistical "laws":

> They have no claims to be regarded as laws ... there is no reason to suppose that their having been so in the past is the result of the operation of homogeneous causes, nor that their changes in the future will be due to the causes which have operated in the past ... There is no justification for claiming for their results the status of the so-called "statistical" laws of the natural sciences.[11]

Economists rejected the use of probability theory because data from economic time series are obviously time-related. Each observation is closely related to previous and succeeding observations, so time series observations are clearly not independent of each other and controlled laboratory experiments are not possible. Many of the underlying relations are unquantifiable and change endogenously over the time period:

> Granting, as he [the statistician] must, that consecutive items of a statistical time series are in fact related, he admits that the mathematical theory of probability is inapplicable.[12]

Frisch was persuaded that due to the pervasiveness of multi-collinearity, multiple correlation techniques could not distinguish the "unique" relations between observed events. All variables were intrinsically subject to measurement error, so the theoretical significance of missing nonquantifiable variables could never be satisfactorily resolved. In consequence Frisch advocated nonparametric methods like principal components, cluster analysis and interviews:

> It is very seldom indeed that we have a clear case where the statistical data can actually determine numerically an autonomous structural equation ... We must

look for some other means of getting information about the numerical character of our structural equations. The only way possible seems to utilize, to a much larger extent than we do so far, the interview method. We must ask persons or groups what they would do under such circumstances.[13]

Frisch's dissatisfaction with econometrics paralleled Keynes' strong criticism of Tinbergen in the late 1930s. For Keynes the openness of social reality created two fundamental obstacles that prevented regression analysis being successfully applied to economic data. First, the potential for misspecification by leaving out unmeasurable but clearly significant variables, particularly changes in "animal spirits." Second, the arbitrariness of the imposed identifying restrictions, for example, Tinbergen's inclusion of differential lag lengths to increase goodness of fit. These objections led Keynes to a severely critical judgement of econometrics:

> The main *prima facie* objection to the application of the method of multiple correlation to complex economic problems lies in the lack of any adequate degree of uniformity in the environment.[14]
>
> It is a great fault of symbolic pseudo-mathematical methods of formalizing a system of economic analysis, ... that they expressly assume strict independence between the factors involved, and lose all their cogency and authority if this hypothesis is disallowed. Too large a proportion of recent "mathematical" economics are mere concoctions, as imprecise as the initial assumptions they rest on, which allow the author to lose sight of the complexities and interdependencies of the real world in a maze of pretentious and unhelpful symbols.[15]

Keynes' and Frisch's doubts were overwhelmed by Haavelmo's 1944 powerful "eureka" conversion to probabilistic reasoning. As previously described, Haavelmo's 1944 paper "The Probability Approach in Econometrics" initiated what has since been termed the "probabilistic revolution" in econometrics.

> Haavelmo's ... conversion to probabilistic reasoning ... radically changed econometric practice ... Probabilistic reasoning ... provided a formal alternative to ... informal and subjective inference procedures ... The choice of variables and models became a subject for economic theory and statistical tests. The probabilistic reasoning behind those tests was in contrast to Frisch's experimental and data-based approach to taking decisions on model content.[16]

Haavelmo explicitly recognized that although they made much use of statistical methods, most economists believed probability theory had little to offer to the analysis of economic questions. But he argued that since probability theory was the general body of theory behind statistical methods, it was not logically legitimate to use the latter without adopting the former:

> It has been considered legitimate to use some of the tools developed in statistical theory without accepting the very foundation upon which statistical theory

is built. For no tool developed in the theory of statistics has any meaning—except, perhaps, for descriptive purposes—without being referred to some stochastic scheme.[17]

Haavelmo maintained that the problems of non-independence of observations and nonhomogeneous time periods did not prevent probability theory from being applied to economic data, as had previously been widely believed. His key insight was the recognition that the relationship which existed between the population and the sample in probability theory provided the model for the correspondence between economic theory and passive economic data ("the sample selected by nature"). This simple reversal of the usual argument was the basis of his "probabilistic revolution":

> It is sufficient to assume that the whole set of, say n observations may be considered as one observation of n variables (or as a "sample point") following an n-dimensional joint probability law, the "existence" of which may be purely hypothetical. Then, one can test hypotheses regarding this joint probability law, and draw inference as to its possible form, by means of one sample point (in n dimensions).[18]

Since controlled laboratory experiments are impossible to conduct in economics, econometrics was a blunt tool for discriminating between different theories. Haavelmo maintained the essence of econometrics was to build, identify, estimate, and assess models which confirm the neoclassical precepts of optimizing behavior.

> The question is not whether probabilities exist or not, but whether—if we proceed as if they existed—we are able to make statements about real phenomena that are correct for "practical purposes."[19]

Neoclassical economic theory has been developed as a rigorous closed deductive system, subjected to the "exogenous shocks" of the real world. The theory is couched in terms of deductive event regularities. The truth claims of Haavelmo's approach reside in the ability of econometric models to account for predicted data regularities in a statistically significant way. But Haavelmo seems never to have entertained the notion that the economy, like the weather, was a complex system which could not be modeled with linear analysis, and any prediction of its future behavior was impossible.

The agenda of econometrics has been to conditionally attempt to confirm rather than to falsify maintained hypotheses. The "identification" of the appropriate economic relationships reflected the presupposition that *event regularities exist*, and can be discovered within a probabilistic parametric format. The magnitude of the key relationships between variables is identified by the empirically estimated coefficients. Peripheral "noise" influences can be captured through stochastic disturbance terms, and presented as if on average not affecting outcomes. Notwithstanding these explicit goals, econometrics has never been able to impose decisive demarcation and rejection among alternative theories.

The identification of causality remains paramount, but the direction of "causality" must be derived from economic theory, not empirical evidence. If relationships are to be identified outside sources of information must be used to impose restrictions. Since the *ceteris* never remain *paribus* in complex systems, it is impossible to prove empirically that theories are correct. Economic theories cannot be refuted by econometric results alone.

Following Haavelmo's lead and accepting the vision that economic phenomena are in principle predictable (linear), the Cowles Commission emerged in the postwar period with greatly increased confidence in the potential implications of structural estimation for theory choice. This new tradition formed the backbone of the standard textbook approach to econometrics.[20] But as Leamer has complained, Haavelmo's approach turned a "blind eye" to the identification issues raised by Keynes, Frisch, and others. *Haavelmo simply presupposed that a correct specification existed and could be found empirically.*[21] He insisted that because economists are unable to undertake scientific experiments they must make do with passive observations from "the laboratory of Nature's experiments."

Haavelmo clearly recognized that nature was influenced by many factors that are not accounted for by theory:

> If we cannot clear the data of such 'other influences', we have to try to introduce these influences in the theory, in order to bring about more agreement between theory and facts.[22]

But like Marshall Haavelmo never questioned that there existed fundamental underlying stable relationships in economic phenomena. The problem was solely how best to discover them. He freely acknowledged that the exact equations that characterized economic models could never be precisely satisfied in practice. The gap between exact theory and real life must be bridged by stochastic measurement errors. But he argued these could be specified as probability laws. Only by adopting probability theory could economists provide themselves with an adequate theoretical framework for conducting economic research and rigorous testing.[23] Properly formulated stochastic models must state the set of parameter values admissible. Since different probability models are always capable of explaining the same set of observed data, he admonished economists to remain skeptical concerning the truth value of their own hypotheses:

> Whatever be the "explanations" we prefer it is not to be forgotten that they are all our own artificial inventions in a search for an understanding of real life; they are not hidden truths to be "discovered."[24]

Tinbergen's econometric textbook presented the *"how to's"* of the Cowles Commission methodology, which directly adapted Haavelmo's insights. Tinbergen postulated five core assumptions that he believed necessary for econometrical work:[25]

1. Relations between variables are linear.

   "A very general mathematical theorem is of advantage in all these cases; ... that within a small range of variation nearly every function can be approximated by a linear one."

2. Relations between variables are invariant in time. This assures that estimated parameters will be constant for different values of t.
3. Parameters are structurally invariant with respect to other variables in the model.
4. It must be known *a priori* which variable is the *cause*, and which variable is the *effect* of the relationship. Similarly which variables are *endogenous* (determined within the model) and which are *exogenous* (determined outside the model) must also be known.
5. Models cannot be directly verified against "rival" models but only against "nature," by the use of the coefficient of determination (R^2), student-t ratios and F tests.

If economies are CAS the first four of these "core" assumptions are invalid. Tinbergen argued that two cases present themselves in the testing of economic theories. The predicted value of the variable is poorly correlated with the observed value of the variable to be explained. In this case the theory is erroneous or incomplete. The correlation between the predicted and observed values is high. In this case the theory is not contradicted by the facts.[26]

Tinbergen maintained three types of additional conditions must be present before any positive statement can be made from regressions having a high coefficient of determination.

1. There must be no significant determining factor omitted from the relationship. This reflects the contemporary belief that errors of omission were more important than errors of measurement.[27]
2. The estimated regression coefficients must have signs consistent with the economic theory being modeled.
3. Statements are conditional on the lag lengths of the variables being correct. Lag lengths need not be specified in advance but can be determined by trial and error in order to maximize the correlation between the variable to be explained and its predicted values.

These conditions attempt to assure that the relationship is properly specified. But so long as expectations are ungratifiable, the first condition can never be satisfied in econometric analysis.

4.3 The methodology of modern econometrics[28]

Modern econometrics represents the attempt to uncover Marshall's vision of the intrinsic real underlying structures that lie behind economic relationships. Most contemporary econometricians, at least in their written work retain the implicit belief that the economy is in principle law-like and so predictable. For example Christ long ago defined econometrics as,

> the production of quantitative economic statements that either explain the behavior of variables we have already seen, or forecast (i.e. predict) behavior that we have not yet seen, or both.[29]

Christ enumerated six properties desirable in economic models: relevance, simplicity, theoretical plausibility, explanatory ability, accuracy of coefficients, and forecasting ability.[30] A "good" model should exhibit all these properties. But if the economy is a complex adaptive system its behavior can never be fully understood or predicted. Unfortunately with so many excellent computing packages available, the modern research goal begins to combine the relevant economic theory and the building of models to produce the most persuasive econometric results. The existence of an indefinitely large number of plausible models, each of which can satisfy some or all these criteria, renders the problem of model selection strictly nontrivial. The methodology of econometrics relates to the established methods of defining and finding "good" models.

More recently Durbin defined econometric methodology as "how to's":

The knowledge or study of the methods or practices used in a scientific or other intellectual discipline; including:

(a) the part of training which deals explicitly with the "how to's" of a field, e.g. statistical methods and how to apply them; and
(b) the conscious awareness on the part of a practitioner of the often unconsciously implemented "how to's."[31]

But if economies are CAS there are no underlying law-like relationships that econometrics can discover. None of Tinbergen's five assumptions and none of Christ's six properties can be expected to hold. Given the profession's "*how to's*," it is not surprising that investigators have placed greatest weight on a combination of goodness of fit and consistency of the signs of the estimated variables with their theoretical expectation. Theory could be rejected if the data seemed inconsistent with it, as evidenced by low multiple correlation coefficients, student-t ratios, Durbin–Watson statistics far from 2, or parameters signs inconsistent with theoretical expectations.

The 1950s and 1960s witnessed a tidal expansion of theories and empirical studies and marked the high water mark for econometrics. A broad spirit of optimism and confidence in the future of econometrics prevailed. The underlying Cowles Commission assumptions and qualifications were rarely questioned. Econometrics was simply regarded as a set of techniques necessary to handle the relaxation of the assumptions of the General Linear Model required by the special problems faced by economists. No one questioned whether economic behavior was complex and intrinsically unpredictable.

Imagine the goal was to model the consumption function. An investigator must first prepare a set of potential regressors, for example, lagged consumption, current, lagged, and expected income (measured as a one-step-ahead prediction of income), income adjusted for changes in the value of assets, and current and lagged total wealth. Total income can be decomposed in two or more meaningful ways. All variables can be deflated by at least two different price indices, the retail price index and the cost-of-living index. The above give rise to 24 potential explanatory variables. This endorses the calculation of literally thousands of sensible-looking consumption functions, each defined for a particular choice of deflator and for a particular subperiod.

With modern high-speed computers they all can be estimated. Why not estimate them all, and choose the one with the best student-t and Durbin–Watson ratios combined with a high R^2? The ensuing running of countless regressions by different investigators, each attempting to chose the equation that had the best fit and was consistent with their *priors*, gradually became discredited, since it failed to provide believable results. The problems of model specification and selection were not addressed. A large gap developed between what theorists were developing "on the top floor," and what applied econometricians were doing to the data "in the basement."[32]

The results were soon seen to be heavily dependent on the particular researcher's own *priors*, and econometric work increasingly came to be viewed as unconvincing. Surprisingly the forecasting performance of the large scale macroeconometric models was poor, and quite inferior to naïve forecasts from single equation auto-regressive models.[33] Self-doubt became increasingly widespread, and eventually replaced the previous earlier position of self-confidence. Computing advances had removed the major obstacle to routine calculation and lead to the abuse of the Cowles Commission methodology. The intense skepticism towards standard econometric analysis is illustrated by the following remarks by one practitioner:[34]

> Even within the academic profession one is sensing a doubt as to whether the generation of more numbers for their own sake is fruitful. The ad hoc approach of many practicing econometricians to the problem of hypothesis testing and inference is illustrated by the popular image of much econometrics as a high R^2 in search of a theory. Garbage in—garbage out—is how many describe their own activity."[35]

"Data mining" has now become the central problem of econometricians. They have only an all too finite "history" of data as their laboratory, and are unable to conduct controlled experiments. Since data sets must be used to arrive at the final model specification, the widespread practice became:

(1) Take the widest possible set of variables which might eventually enter the model;
(2) Run numerous regressions, using as regressors various subsets of the entire set of "candidates";
(3) Select the "best" regression that combines the highest t-ratios with a high coefficient of determination.

Unfortunately neither R^2 nor student-t values are reliable as selection criteria since their values are under the control of the experimenter (Leamer, 1978; Lovell, 1983).

It has long been recognized that exclusive reliance on such statistics can lead to the selection of poor models (Theil, 1971). Johnston (1984) showed that although the R^2 associated with the "true" model will on average exceed that from an incorrectly specified model, "false" models can easily have R^2s greater than the "true" model. It became increasingly recognized that the mechanical choosing of models on the basis of their R^2 can result in the selection of a "false" model (Leamer, 1983). The R^2 criterion is not useful when making a selection from regressions with different dependent variables. Whenever a model is rewritten so that there is a change in the variation of the "dependent variable," there will be an associated alteration in the coefficient of determination. Values of R^2 belonging to different models with different explanatory variables cannot be directly compared since they have different distribution functions. Leamer concluded:

> diagnostic tests such as goodness-of-fit tests, without explicit alternative hypotheses, are useless, since if the sample size is large enough, any maintained hypothesis will be rejected. ... Such tests degenerate into elaborate rituals for measuring effective sample size.[36]

The credibility that can be ascribed to any reported econometric estimate is related to the process by which the equation was generated. If one were told that the functional form tested was derived on the basis of careful economic reasoning and that only one regression was fitted, one's confidence in the results would be much greater than if one were told the regression was the outcome of an extensive unstructured search, involving thousands of equations.[37]

The pure case of a well-reasoned economic argument leading to a single well-defined model estimated and tested just once from the available sample, conflicts directly with common sense. Econometricians will understandably desire to use their fixed data sample in a sequential way. Surely the sample evidence contained in estimated models should be useful in the improvement of our understanding of the processes that generated the data? In consequence "data mining" is inevitable. It has been argued by reflective scholars that the question is not whether data mining will be involved in modeling economic relationships, but how should the modeling be done? The goal should be to construct a structured and purposeful approach to econometric model building, and avoid the worst aspects of data mining.[38]

The confidence of the profession in textbook econometrics has recently become as illusory as it was in the 1920s.[39] As a result of the widespread incidence of data mining the standard approach advocated by the Cowles Commission has now broken down. Econometrics has for many lost its stature as the essential part of the scientific process of identifying demi-regularities on which theoretical inferences are based.[40] Theoretical disputes have seldom been successfully resolved by direct appeal to the data.[41] The above concerns have led to a general distrust of and dissatisfaction with econometrics. Many have concluded that applied econometrics: "has singularly failed to provide models that produced satisfactory out of sample predictions or resolved competing economic theories."[42]

Pagan argues that three distinct schools of econometrics have emerged to cope with the above problems:

1. Hendry's LSE approach,
2. Leamer's Bayesian approach, and
3. Sims' a-theoretical approach.[43]

Each approach shares the agenda of starting econometric analysis from some general representation of the data, and each offers criteria for model simplification.

1. Hendry's LSE approach. For Hendry as for Marshall, knowledge is the result of a complex interaction between deduction and induction. His approach involves the continual interaction between the theory and the subjective priors, and the data and the objective facts:

> The best is that theory delivers a model which happens to capture structure after appropriate estimation. ... structure potentially can be learned from empirical evidence without prior knowledge as to what exists to be discovered. ... economic theory is neither necessary nor sufficient for determining structure although it remains one of several useful tools for the econometrician. ... Economic theory is likely to prove a productive companion in empirical econometric research by suggesting directions for discovering structure, excluding unlikely contenders, helping to identify structure (in all three senses of uniqueness, correspondence and interpretation), and consolidating empirical findings ... although how one discovers useful knowledge remains an art rather than a science.[44]

A general model must first be formulated, reparameterized to obtain orthogonal explanatory variables, simplified to the smallest version compatible with the data and finally evaluated by extensive testing. The model must not exhibit serially correlated residuals and its parameters must be robust over subsamples. Weakly exogenous variables must be employed when possible, so their estimation has no influence on the estimation of the variables of interest. An attempt should be made to account for the results of rival models via "encompassing tests" so a notion of "critical theoretical evaluation" can be established. Precisely how the model is derived is less important. The basic criterion of appraisal is whether a model is useful or is not.

2. Leamer's Bayesian approach. Leamer in contrast adopts a Bayesian approach, and asserts the primacy of subjective factors in all reasoning. He argues that the official rhetoric of econometrics appeals to the "false idol of objectivity" which he believes has done great damage to economic science.

> Theoretical econometricians have interpreted scientific objectivity to mean that an economist must identify exactly the variables of the model, the functional

form and the distribution of the errors. Given these assumptions and given the data set, the econometric method produces an objective inference from a data set, unencumbered by the subjective opinions of the researcher.[45]

Econometrics must necessarily employ priors in establishing the sampling function and the prior probability density function. He argues econometricians must be explicit and "up front" about the role of *priors*. Not only are all econometric data nonexperimental:

> The misspecification matrix M is ... a pure prior concept. One must decide independent of the data how good the non-experiment is.[46]

Leamer's proscription is to formulate a general family of models, decide what inferences are important, express these in terms of parameters, and form prior distributions summarizing all information not in the data set. The sensitivity of inferences to a particular choice of distributions must be analyzed to explore their "*fragility.*" Subsets of variables may be focused upon but all possible linear combinations of what are considered to be prior "*doubtful*" variables must be explored. Extreme parameter values of a most favorable and least favorable character must be found for each of the variables of interest. When the restrictions required to obtain a narrower range of values are considered dubious, the results must not be treated as robust.[47]

The sensitivity analysis recommended by Leamer is implicit in the Hendry approach of testing "from general to specific models." Leamer's approaches differ in that Hendry recommends that inference concerning point estimates must proceed from the general model so long as the data indicate that the complete set of variables are significant. Leamer argues that such a procedure is extremely problematic since there are always conflicting grounds for inference, reflecting the differential weight placed both on judgment and on the critical evaluation of the data.

3. Sims' a-theoretical approach. Sims in effect rejects the possibility of ever processing successfully the unresolvable problems of variable exogeneity and identification. His approach confines itself to the analysis of reduced forms in a simultaneous "*vector autoregressive*" (VAR) context.[48] Vector auto-regressions involve the regression of each variable of interest on lagged values of itself and on all the other variables under scrutiny. The largest lag structure possible is started with and then simplified as in Hendry's approach. The objective of Sims' methodology is to provide structure-free conclusions revealed by the data itself. Sims' approach is an example of extreme inductivism and makes no attempt to discriminate between competing explanations and hypotheses. Sims' intention of emphasizing data description is basically designed to avoid the unresolvable problems of identification and theory choice.

Concern solely with reduced forms does not succeed in making Sims' approach theory-free. Sims' approach can be defended as providing partial support for a particular empirical *set* of economic relationships. He recommends the *"impulse response functions"* of orthogonal innovations be examined to trace out the time path of changes induced by changes in particular variables of interest. This involves rewriting the VAR in terms of a moving average representation of the errors associated with the other variables. The errors must be made orthogonal to enable the effects of individual shocks to be examined. Since most VAR work is undertaken with little explicit regard for theory, Sims appears to be diametrically opposed to Leamer. But Sims' approach shares Hendry and Leamer's concern to expose descriptively all sets of *"confluent"* relations. Darnell and Evons have concluded,

> There may be some empirical regularities (economic phenomena) deserving of further study ... [notwithstanding the fact that] ... VAR contributes nothing with regard to the scientific method of economics, nor, surprisingly, do its proponents pretend anything different.[49]

VAR has a potential role to play in all complex systems research that reject the hypothetical-deductive methodology of neoclassical economic theory. In identifying partial regularities, any narrative presupposes the existence of some order in the ubiquitous process under investigation without invoking the intrinsic condition of closure as a defense of econometric analysis. Although causal mechanisms exist, they continually evolve and get transformed. Inferences must be based on appeal to a wider set of insights than simply the statistics produced by econometric investigation. Pagan has argued:

> Our data are such that we cannot ignore the fact that the information therein may need to be extracted by a wide range of techniques borrowed from many different approaches.[50]

McCloskey has long insisted that confusing "statistical significance" with "economic significance" has now become a vice and tragedy of the highest order:

> most of empirical economics since the War has to be done over again. Literally most of the allegedly "scientific" findings of economics have to be redone with another method before anyone should believe them.[51]

McCloskey believes this confusion goes back to Klein's original 1943 mistake, to turn mechanically to statistics to answer the question, whether a coefficient is significant in the sense of being big or small.

> The role of Y in the regression is not statistically significant. The ratio of the regression coefficient to its standard deviation is only 1.812. This low value of the ratio means that we cannot reject the hypothesis that the true value of the regression coefficient is zero.[52]

But if economists could work with enormous sample sizes, the sampling variability of all estimates would approach zero. All coefficients would then be "significant." What would be the important economic variables? The scientific significance of effects summarized by the question, "how large is the effect?" is a quite different question from the problem, "how large is the sampling error?" The variation around the estimate of the average variation ($\delta/\sqrt{N}$) is not as important as the estimate of the magnitude of the variation itself (δ). Only the magnitude of the coefficient can tell you what is substantively significant for the problem at hand. The magnitude of the coefficient and not its statistical significance tells you what counts and what does not. The magnitude of the estimated coefficients is of more economic interest to economists than their precise "statistical significance." McCloskey emphasizes his fatal criticism is by no means new:

> Theoretical statisticians have always been aware that most economists tend to interpret "statistically significant" to mean "important for the problem at hand." They have warned repeatedly about this misinterpretation for decades.[53]

To form an opinion of the importance of this confusion McCloskey and Ziliak (1996) examined in detail all empirical papers published in the *AER* during the decade of the 1980s for their use of "statistically significant." They concluded that 96 percent of all papers misused "statistical significance." One result is that economists today no longer trust or believe in one another. As a result no important propositions in economics have ever been confirmed or rejected in a convincing way using the methods of econometrics. No minds have been changed. McCloskey concludes,

> Most allegedly empirical work in economics is unbelievable, or uninteresting, or both. It doesn't get down to the phenomena. It's satisfied to be publishable or clever by the sad standards of statistical significance. ... It's unbelievable, unless (because deans don't do their jobs) you have to believe temporarily to get tenure.[54]

Keynes similarly insisted that *weight*, the amount of relevant supporting evidence, is logically distinct from *statistical probability*, the degree to which particular empirical evidence supports a proposition. For Keynes, *weight* ultimately resided in logical theoretical justification. To avoid the problem of induction, a particular phenomenon must be examined in several different contexts. If phenomena appear to demonstrate a common element between various contexts, this commonality itself indicates its relevance and adds *weight* to a particular account. When different contexts reveal non-common elements the *weight* of an argument is decreased thus revealing our ignorance.

If *"qualitative"* evidence suggests that a particular form of stable process underlies events, this provides *prima facie* support for an econometric representation of that process. But the econometric method can only partially reveal the process. The interaction of theory and evidence must form the basis of econometrics given in the particular context. Econometric evidence can only add *"weight"* to particular knowledge claims in the manner stated by Keynes. Dow has taken this argument to the role of formal mathematics in formal modeling, and has argued:

> The allocation of resources to acquiring knowledge involves trade-offs. But there is no a priori reason why devotion of resources to formal mathematical models with limited application but certainty of conclusions, generates more knowledge than devoting resources to the wider realm of ordinary logic, and reducing the uncertainty attached to the wider realms of evidence which are accordingly admitted.[55]

Dow concludes:

> The case has to be made for each piece of analysis, because structural relationships may differ from one context to another. ... formal analysis in terms of partial systems needs to start with qualitative analysis in order to be justified, and combined with qualitative analysis in order to be applied. ... In general, Keynes's epistemology implies all theorizing be preceded by consideration of the applicability of particular arguments (assumptions, theories, techniques) to the circumstances under consideration.[56]

The inferences made possible by econometrics cannot be produced solely by statistical considerations. Econometrics can only produce tentative evidence of the *"demi regularities,"* requiring further research in a complex systems research program. Lawson has expressed this point of view flatly as follows:

> A stylized fact is a conceptualized phenomenon—typically a broad but not universal generalization about an event regularity—that is interpreted to hold in a way, or to a degree, such that the researcher regards as significant enough, given the context, that *prima facie* an explanation is called for.[57]

The confidence in textbook econometrics has now been shaken, and the importance of data mining has been widely recognized.[58] The fact that no major theoretical disputes have ever been successfully resolved by appeal to the data has led to an increasing dissatisfaction with econometrics.[59] One popular text has concluded:

> Applied econometrics: "has singularly failed to provide models that produced satisfactory out of sample predictions or resolved competing economic theories."[60]

These charges are primarily targeted at the breakdown of the traditional approach advocated by the Cowles Commission. Due to the increased incidence of data mining, econometrics has by now totally lost its shining stature as the center of the scientific process of identifying demi-regularities on which theoretical inferences can be based. The fall in computing costs has permitted economists increasingly to use simulation, trying out different theories and numbers to see which works best, as engineers routinely do in their calculations. VAR simulation of nonlinear systems will form the basis of the econometrics of the future, fully recognizing that economies are complex adaptive systems.

4.4 The importance of stationarity

The purpose of time series analysis is to study the time pattern of correlations among variables. The most critical question for the analysis of time series is whether the underlying stochastic process that generated the data is stationary (invariant with respect to time) or nonstationary (variant with respect to time). When the series is nonstationary, the characteristics of the stochastic process change over time and cannot be represented by a simple algebraic model. Only if the stochastic process is stationary it is valid to model the process as an equation with fixed coefficients estimated from past data. Nonstationary processes cannot be modeled with simple equations. All series must be transformed into stationary (or approximately stationary) processes before quantitative analysis begins.[61]

It is impossible to obtain a complete description of a stochastic process to precisely specify underlying probability distributions. The autocorrelation function that describes the correlation between neighboring data points in the series provides only a partial description of the process. It is useful to determine whether a particular value of the autocorrelation function is sufficiently close to zero, to test the assumption that the true value of all values of the autocorrelation function are zero. When this is the case we are dealing with a white noise process. When a time series is stationary, the autocorrelation function (ρ_k) falls off quickly as the number of lags k increases. If ρ_k does not fall off quickly, this is an indication of nonstationarity. Very few economic time series are stationary but most are homogeneous, and when differenced one or more times become stationary. In applied work it is never precisely clear how many times a nonstationary time series must be differenced to yield a stationary one. The researcher must make a judgment based on both experience and intuition.[62]

Since economies are complex systems most patterns in economic time series are nonstationary and path-dependent. If an economic time series is nonstationary, it does not revert to its previous long-run trend path following short-run disturbances. This is important because when variables have unit roots they do not have a finite variance, and a regression of one against the other leads to spurious results. When a series has a unit root the detrended series is not stationary.[63] The current level of a unit root series is simply the cumulation of past changes. The best estimate of its future value is its present value. How we characterize economic time series has deep implications for our understanding of the economy. If GDP has a unit root the effects of temporary demand shocks are permanent and do not dissipate over time.

The statistical issue is the appropriate representation of nonstationarity. A time series is the record of the values of a variable measured at different points in time.

These values may be recorded continuously or discretely and are influenced by temporal mechanisms. Most economic time series are not random walks, but most have unit roots. Their short-run levels at adjacent points in time are highly correlated. There is clear evidence of periodicity in the residuals from a linear trend in logs for most macro variables. But there is little evidence of periodicity in their first differences.[64] Empirical investigations of output deviations from trend overestimate the persistence and the variance of business cycles. Business "cycles" themselves may be endogenous aperiodic cycles in changing fractal distributions.

The two most salient features of aggregate output in developed economies are sustained long-run growth, and recurrent fluctuations around this growth path. As there are cyclical swings in output there are variations in the growth rate. This leads naturally to the question of the relative importance of changes in trend and cycles in explaining short-run movements in economic aggregates. Is there a link between the change in the long-run trend and the cyclical variation? Mainstream macroeconomics treats trends and cycles as if they were independent with different causes. Growth theories have been developed to shed light on the long-run forces determining secular trends, and business cycle theories have been developed to explain short-run fluctuations. Each attempts to shed light on how macroeconomic policy ameliorates swings between expansion and recession.

It has long been a standard practice to decompose real variables into their "secular" and "cyclical" components. In the case of real output the "secular component" falls in the domain of growth theory. Real supply-side factors, such as capital accumulation, population growth, and the rate of technological change, are viewed as the primary determinants of growth rates. The "cyclical component" comprises fluctuations around the trend line, and falls in the domain of business cycle theory. Changes in expectations and in monetary, fiscal, international, and other demand-side "shocks" are viewed as the primary determinants of cyclical fluctuations. Such cyclical forces are assumed to be transitory so all long-run permanent movement is attributed to the secular component.

Conventional or "classical" method of time series analysis has been to decompose a time series into its secular, cyclical, seasonal, and residual components. Intuitively this approach appeared both natural and logical. It is possible *ex post* to fit a trend line to any time series. Many series almost seem to cry out to have just such a line drawn through them to summarize broad underlying movements. The cyclical component is estimated from the residuals around trend. The seasonal component is calculated by estimating the magnitude of annual fluctuations. After all the above steps have been performed, all residual fluctuations are attributed to "stochastic" influences.

By construction the trend is the average movement of a series over a period. As a result, to the extent there is any short-run serial correlation, deviations around the trend by construction appear cyclical. The secular component appears to move only slowly in the short run, and the cyclical component appears to fluctuate around the secular trend line. This led to the very common practice of "de-trending" economic time series by regressing the series on time, to remove the trend component, and render the series "stationary."

For most economic variables their time series appears *ex post* to contain both secular and cyclical components. The first differences of such series are typically uncorrelated and resemble white noise. If this is the case the level of the series can be viewed as the cumulative sum of a series of random numbers. Since Slutsky, it has been widely recognized that a cumulation of a series of random numbers can be indistinguishable from real world time series.[65]

It has recently been demonstrated that the appearance of persistent secular movement need not imply the existence of a deterministic trend. The class of integrated stochastic processes exemplified by random walks exhibit similar secular and cyclical movements but do not follow any deterministic path. Such series appear to approximate a random walk with drift. The best estimate of tomorrow's value is today's value.

4.5 Are economic time series time stationary or difference stationary?

Economic time series characteristically exhibit variations that increase in mean and dispersion in proportion to their absolute levels. This motivates the transformation of series into natural logs. Long-term movements in most log series are well captured by straight lines, so it was long believed that the trend was linear in log-transformed data. Nevertheless two fundamentally different classes of nonstationary processes have recently been distinguished. The first class is a Trend Stationary (TS) process, where the trend is a deterministic function of time plus some stationary stochastic process with mean zero. Denoting the natural logs of the series by y_t and the deviations from trend by ε_t the linear TS class has the form:

$$y_t = a + bt + \varepsilon_t, \qquad (4.1)$$

where a and b are fixed parameters. As shown in equation 4.1 a TS process increases by a fixed proportion (b) every time period. The fundamental determinism of such a series is captured in the properties of long-term forecasts and the uncertainty around such forecasts. Any autocorrelation in ε_t can be exploited for short-term forecasting. But over long-term horizons all the information about future y_t is contained in its mean $(a+bt)$. Neither current nor past events alter these long-term expectations. The long-term forecast error is ε_t has a finite variance, bounding the uncertainty about such series over indefinitely distant future periods.

The second class is a Difference Stationary (DS) process, where the trend is a stochastic function of time, and the first or higher order differences are stationary. Most real world series with stochastic trends behave as if they have a unit root. They change on average in every period, and in each period the change deviates randomly from the average change. Regression analysis can produce spurious and misleading conclusions when performed on nonstationary fractal series that possess a stochastic trend.

A first order DS process written in natural logs takes the form:

$$(1-L)y_t = b + d_t + \varepsilon_t, \quad (L)d_t = (L)u_t; \quad \varepsilon_t - iid, \qquad (4.2)$$

where $(1-L)$ is the difference operator, and $(L)d$ and $(L)u$ are polynomials satisfying the stationarity and invertibility conditions. The simplest member of this class is a random walk, where all changes are serially uncorrelated, $d_t = \varepsilon_t - iid$ (identically independently distributed).

To see the fundamental difference between TS and DS classes it is more informative to express y_t in equation 4.2 as its value at some past reference point at time zero (y_0), plus all subsequent changes:

$$y_t = y_0 + bt + \Sigma d_t + \varepsilon_t \qquad (4.3)$$

Both equations 4.1 and 4.3 are linear functions of time plus the deviations from it. In equation 4.1 the intercept is a fixed parameter [a]. In equation 4.3 the intercept is the accumulation of specific past historical events; $[y_0 + \Sigma d_t]$. In equation 4.1 the deviations from trend are stationary. In equation 4.3 the deviations from trend are the changing cumulation of previous changes. Their variance increases without bound indefinitely as t grows.

A random walk is a special case of the DS process,

$$y_t = y_{t-1} + \varepsilon_t \quad \text{or} \quad y_t - y_{t-1} = \varepsilon_t \qquad (4.4)$$

where ε_t is a white noise process.

The error term (ε_t) is a stochastic iid process, with a zero mean and constant variance. Since $E(\varepsilon_t) = 0$, the one period ahead forecast is always value in the present period $\{E(y_{t+1}) = y_t\}$. Random walks are a special case of unit root processes. Most economic time series are not random walks but more complicated processes with auto-correlated error terms. Most economic time series are DS processes, have a unit root, and are autoregressive invertible moving average processes (ARIMA).

The DS class is fundamentally stochastic in nature while the TS class is fundamentally deterministic. The long-term forecast of a DS process is influenced by the particular past historical events. Since the variance of the forecast error increases without bound, the nonstationary nature of a DS process precludes the possibility of long-range prediction. When one assumes the TS class is appropriate, one is implicitly bounding uncertainty and restricting the relevance of the past to the future. Until Nelson and Plosser's 1982 article, most statistical procedures for fitting models assumed that time series would be stationary after detrending. But empirical tests are extremely sensitive to whether a series is stationary in levels or in first differences.[66] The crucial factor is that with DS processes, movements in short-run outcomes impact on long-term expectations. With TS processes short-run outcomes are disconnected and have no impact on long-term expectations.

In a path-defining article Nelson and Plosser (N & P) posed the question whether US macroeconomic time series were time stationary, as consistent with the deterministic time trend decomposition conventionally employed, or difference stationary.[67] To their astonishment they found they were unable to reject the hypothesis that all the macroeconomic series investigated were DS, i.e. nonstationary stochastic processes.

Nelson and Plosser developed extremely persuasive evidence that all the macroeconomic time series they investigated had a unit root. Such series, once disturbed have no tendency to return to their previous trend line. They concluded the secular movement observed in macroeconomic time series was stochastic not deterministic. As a result they pronounced that all models based on residuals from trend mis-specified.

To test whether a series is TS or DS, it initially appears one could simply run the combined regression of equations 4.1 and 4.2, and test the null hypotheses $\rho=1$, $b=0$.

$$y_t = a + \rho y_{t-1} + bt + \varepsilon_t \qquad (4.5)$$

Unfortunately such tests are seriously biased. The lagged dependent variable and the time trend are complexly interdependent. To demonstrate this bias, Nelson and Plosser conducted a set of Monte Carlo experiments where the generating process for the time series was a random walk (white noise). They found that customary testing procedures were strongly biased and rejected the null hypotheses in favor of stationarity far too often. The estimated distribution of ρ was centered on 0.9 when by construction it was 1.0. The estimated value of b centered on 0.1 when by construction it was 0.0. Standard testing procedures frequently reject the hypothesis of $\rho=1$ in favor of $\rho < 1$, and similarly reject the hypothesis of $b=0$ in favor of $b > 0$.[68]

To test for the applicability of the DS process, Nelson and Plosser calculated the autocorrelations of annual US macroeconomic time series transformed to natural logs (with the exception of the bond yield which is already a percentage), and compared them with a random walk process.

As shown in Table 4.1, the sample autocorrelations of a random walk start about 0.95, and decay slowly as the lag increases. The sample autocorrelations of most macro variables tested are similar to the autocorrelations of a random walk. The single exception was the unemployment rate (the difference between and the ratio of two macro variables, the labor force and total employment) which exhibited a lower first order autocorrelation and a more rapid decay, characteristic of stationary series.[69] The autocorrelations of first differences for all macro variables were quite low, and at longer lags displayed the insignificant autocorrelation characteristic of a random walk (see Table 4.2). A near-zero autocorrelation structure of first differences is inconsistent with a TS process.

The evidence against TS representation is reinforced by the autocorrelations of deviations from a fitted trend line. As previously discussed detrending unit root processes produces deviations that by construction show cyclical fluctuations. As shown in Table 4.3, for random walks the autocorrelations start at 0.8 and 0.9 and decline exponentially. The pattern across most of the macroeconomic time series

Table 4.1 Sample autocorrelations of natural logs of annual data[a]

Series	Period	T	r_1	r_2	r_3	r_4	r_5	r_6
Random Walk[b]		100	0.95	0.90	0.85	0.81	0.76	0.70
Real GNP	1909–70	62	0.95	0.90	0.84	0.79	0.74	0.69
Nominal GNP	1909–70	62	0.95	0.89	0.83	0.77	0.72	0.67
Real per capita GNP	1909–70	62	0.95	0.88	0.81	0.75	0.70	0.65
Industrial production	1860–70	111	0.97	0.94	0.90	0.87	0.84	0.81
Employment	1890–70	81	0.96	0.91	0.86	0.81	0.76	0.71
Unemployment rate	1890–70	81	0.75	0.47	0.32	0.17	0.04	0.01
GNP deflator	1889–70	82	0.96	0.93	0.89	0.84	0.80	0.76
Consumer price	1860–70	111	0.96	0.92	0.87	0.84	0.81	0.77
Wages	1900–70	71	0.96	0.91	0.86	0.82	0.77	0.73
Real wages	1900–70	71	0.96	0.92	0.88	0.84	0.80	0.75
Money stock	1889–70	82	0.96	0.92	0.89	0.85	0.81	0.77
Velocity	1869–70	102	0.96	0.92	0.88	0.85	0.81	0.79
Bond yield	1900–70	71	0.84	0.72	0.60	0.52	0.46	0.40
Common stock prices	1871–70	100	0.96	0.90	0.85	0.79	0.75	0.71

Notes:
[a] The natural logs of all the data are used except for the bond yield. T is the sample size and r_i is the *i*th order auto correlation coefficient. The large sample standard error under the null hypothesis of no autocorrelation is $T^{-1/2}$ or roughly 0.11 for series of the length considered here.
[b] Computed by the authors from the approximation due to Wichern (1973).

Source: Nelson and Plosser, 1982: 147, table 2.

Table 4.2 Sample autocorrelations of first differences of the natural logs of annual data[a]

Series	Period	T	R_1	r_2	r_3	r_4	r_5	r_6	S(r)
Random walk[b]		100	0.25	0	0	0	0	0	0
Real GNP	1909–70	62	0.34	0.04	0.18	0.23	0.19	0.01	0.13
Nominal GNP	1909–70	62	0.44	0.08	0.12	0.24	0.07	0.15	0.13
Real per capita GNP	1909–70	62	0.33	0.04	0.17	0.21	0.18	0.02	0.13
Industrial production	1860–70	111	0.03	0.11	0.00	0.11	0.28	0.05	0.09
Employment	1890–70	81	0.32	0.05	0.08	0.17	0.20	0.01	0.11
Unemployment rate	1890–70	81	0.09	0.29	0.03	0.03	0.19	0.01	0.11
GNP deflator	1889–70	82	0.43	0.20	0.07	0.06	0.03	0.02	0.11
Consumer prices	1860–70	111	0.58	0.16	0.02	0.0	0.05	0.03	0.09
Wages	1900–70	71	0.46	0.10	0.03	0.09	0.09	0.08	0.12
Real wages	1900–70	71	0.19	0.03	0.07	0.11	0.18	0.15	0.12
Money stock	1889–70	82	0.62	0.30	0.13	0.01	0.07	0.04	0.11
Velocity	1869–70	102	0.11	0.04	0.16	0.15	0.11	0.11	0.1
Bond yield	1900–70	71	0.18	0.31	0.15	0.04	0.06	0.05	0.12
Common stock prices	1871–70	100	0.22	0.13	0.08	0.18	0.23	0.02	0.1

Notes:
[a] The first difference of the natural logs of all the data are used except for the bond yield. T is the sample size and r_i is the estimated *i*th order correlation coefficient. The large sample standard error for r is given by $s(r)$ under the null hypothesis of no aggregation.
[b] Theoretical autocorrelation as the number of aggregated observations becomes large, result due to Working (1960).

Source: Nelson and Plosser, 1982: 148, table 3.

Table 4.3 Sample autocorrelations of the deviations from a time trend[a]

Series	Period	T	r_1	r_2	r_3	r_4	r_5	r_6
Random Walk[b]		61	0.85	0.71	0.58	0.47	0.36	0.27
Random Walk[b]		100	0.91	0.82	0.74	0.66	0.58	0.51
Real GNP	1909–70	62	0.87	0.66	0.46	0.26	0.19	0.07
Nominal GNP	1909–70	62	0.93	0.79	0.65	0.52	0.43	0.05
Real per capita GNP	1909–70	62	0.87	0.65	0.43	0.24	0.11	0.04
Industrial production	1860–70	111	0.84	0.67	0.53	0.40	0.30	0.28
Employment	1890–70	81	0.89	0.71	0.55	0.39	0.25	0.17
Unemployment rate	1890–70	81	0.75	0.46	0.30	0.15	0.03	0.01
GNP deflator	1889–70	82	0.92	0.81	0.67	0.54	0.42	0.30
Consumer price	1860–70	111	0.97	0.91	0.84	0.78	0.71	0.63
Wages	1900–70	71	0.93	0.81	0.67	0.54	0.42	0.31
Real wages	1900–70	71	0.87	0.69	0.52	0.38	0.26	0.19
Money stock	1889–70	82	0.95	0.83	0.69	0.53	0.37	0.21
Velocity	1869–70	102	0.91	0.81	0.72	0.65	0.59	0.56
Bond yield	1900–70	71	0.85	0.73	0.62	0.55	0.49	0.43
Common stock prices	1871–70	100	0.90	0.76	0.64	0.53	0.46	0.43

Notes:
[a] The data are residuals from linear least squares regression of the logs of the series (except the bond yields) on time.
[b] Approximate expected sample autocorrelations base on Nelson and Kang (1981).
Source: Nelson and Plosser, 1982: 150, table 4.

is strikingly similar to the DS process. All series, with the exception of the unemployment rate show close consistency with a DS process.[70]

The above tests strongly suggest that economic time series are not deterministic TS trends but are rather stochastic fractal trends characteristic of DS processes. Nelson and Plosser concluded their study as follows:

> The hypothesis that economic time series contain stochastic trends characteristic of the DS class of processes is not refutable from the empirical evidence ... If we are observing stationary deviations from linear trends in these series, ... the tendency to return to the trend line must be so weak as to avoid detection, even in samples as long as sixty years to over a century.[71]

A unit root in a time series implies that the coefficient on the lagged dependent variable is unity. Due to measurement errors and serial correlation empirical estimates of this coefficient are never precisely equal 1.00. The question then is, are the estimates of the coefficient on lagged dependent variables significantly different from unity?

Nelson and Plosser's striking findings provoked a cottage industry of studies to investigate whether economic variables were TS or DS. The consensus soon reached was that the hypothesis that US macroeconomic time series have unit roots cannot be rejected by the data.[72] These studies used the unit root tests of Dickey and Fuller. Real world time series processes are not random walks but are complex autocorrelated relationships. Their mean values change over time and the variance about the mean exhibits short-run autocorrelation. But for most economic time series the existence of a unit root cannot be statistically refuted. The challenge for the analyst is to construct a model to describe accurately the mean function and the correlation of economic variables over time.

Augmented Dickey–Fuller (ADF) tests essay the significance of the null hypothesis that the value of the coefficient is consistent with the series having a unit root. To avoid the previously described bias, the (ADF) test subtracts y_{t-1} from both sides of the combined equation 4.4, and takes the unit root as the null hypothesis *(DS H_0: $\rho=1$)* This is tested against the one-sided alternative *(TS H_1: $\rho < 1$)*. This augmented specification is used to test H_0 and H_1. The attempt is made to control for higher-order serial correlation by adding lagged difference terms of the dependent variable y to the right-hand side of the regression as long as they are significant.

$$y_t - y_{t-1} = \Delta y_t = a + (\rho - 1)y_{t-1} + bt + \delta_1 \Delta y_{t-1} + \delta_2 \Delta y_{t-2} + \cdots + \delta_{p-1} \Delta y_{t-p+1} + \varepsilon_t \qquad (4.6)$$

The Dickey–Fuller test is now very widely used but is unfortunately of limited power. The investigator must arbitrarily specify the number of lagged difference terms to add to the test regression needed to remove serial correlation in the residuals. She must also arbitrarily decide whether to include a constant, a constant and a linear trend, or neither, in the regression.[73] Finally the test only allows us to reject or fail to reject the null hypothesis that the dependent variable y has a unit root. The null hypothesis is rejected when the *t-stat* is less than the critical value of reported significance levels. But acceptance (failure to reject) of the null (DS) hypothesis does not provide formal disproof of the (TS) hypothesis.

Table 4.4 estimates of the magnitude of the ρ coefficient on the lagged dependent variable from the equation $y_t = a + \rho y_{t-1}$ using quarterly data for US nominal and real GDP for the period 1959:2–2003:1. As shown for both real and nominal GDP, the estimated coefficient on the lagged dependent variable is extremely close to unity to three decimal places.

The presence of "structural breaks" makes the testing for the order of integration of a series by ADF tests unreliable, and may lead to falsely accepting the null hypothesis of a unit root when the process is stationary.[74] Trend breaks give rise to spurious regressions, goodness of fit measures which are "too high," and generally make regression results difficult to evaluate. The distinction between a unit root and a trend break concerns the frequency of breaks in the trend. In unit roots

Table 4.4 Coefficient on lagged dependent variable nominal and real GDP, 1959:2–2003:1

Dependent variable	Lagged dependent variable	Constant	R^2	DW
1. RGDP	1.0055	12.1190	0.9999	1.39
	(650.36)	(1.397)		
2. NGDP	0.999	17.9467	0.9999	1.35
	(1350.69)	(48711)		

breaks occur frequently, while in a trend break they occur only once or twice in a sample period.[75] Note that as the time period is lengthened "structural breaks" occur more frequently. As a result in the longer run all time series increasingly resemble unit root processes.

All economic time series data are characterized by some type of *ex post* trend. First differencing leads to the loss of these long-run properties. When expressed in differences, the models characteristically have no long-run equilibrium solution. This has led the profession to concentrate analysis on whether DS economic series can be combined with other variables into a single series that is stationary. Series which exhibit such properties are termed *cointegrated*. Two time series are cointegrated only if they are integrated of the same order. Since their linear combination is stationary, cointegrated series will drift together over time. The short-run adjustment relationship prevents errors in the long-run relationship from becoming ever larger so all cointegrated series have an error correction representation.[76]

4.6 Conclusions: complex adaptive systems can be simulated but never solved

As at the Roulette table where they know perfectly well no systematic relationship exists, humans are programmed to look for and find patterns in dynamical outcomes. Runs and patterns are always present *ex post* in any time series. But the patterns found are always time-dependent and continually changing. Suppose that increases and decreases in a time series were generated by a random number mechanism where "heads" represent an increase and "tails" represent a decrease. Patterns that appear to fluctuate around "trends" can be produced by the simple aggregation of random sets of runs of heads and tails. One can never prove a series is random. All one can do is disprove the permanent existence of particular patterns.

Economies are complex adaptive systems and must be so modeled. Both the probability distributions and the outcomes of macroeconomic phenomena are path-dependent. Since complex systems have no closed form solution, their behavior can be modeled and simulated, but never "solved". There is no "correct" model of complex economic phenomena. In complex systems all relationships are nonlinear, variables can never be precisely quantified, and all variables are subject to measurement error. All attempts to forecast long-run outcomes must be abandoned. No theory can successfully forecast complex system behavior. Even ordinal forecasts are not always accurate. As a result theories cannot be evaluated by positivist criteria by comparing theories whose predictions are successful with theories whose predictions are not. No theory can accurately predict the future behavior of complex systems, so the methodology of positivism falls.

The observed secular movements in all complex macroeconomic series are endogenous. Detrending does not render series with unit roots stationary. All models based on residuals from linear time trends are mis-specified. No matter how "statistically significant" the relationship, all regression results calculated from time series with unit roots are spurious.[77] The mainstream decomposition of National Income into two separate components, "long run" forces explaining secular growth, and "short run" forces explaining cyclical fluctuations is imposed by the analyst and not inherent in the data. Mainstream classical decomposition is illegitimate for time series with unit roots. All relationships found are time-dependent, and peculiar to the particular historical period examined irrespective of their statistical significance. All economic phenomena are aperiodic, and all business cycles are statistical artitacts.

Econometric theory must be reconstructed to shed light on the complexity that generates economic data. Economists must become more tolerant of heterodox models, more critical of mainstream models and more cognizant that no single "true" model exists. The goal of econometrics must change from prediction to greater understanding. This is the best we humans can attain. Complex systems generate numbers that are extremely difficult and with present tools impossible to distinguish from random numbers. Variations in macro-economic phenomena reflect fractal distributions with endogenous a-periodic fluctuations, whose current values are nonlinearly related to past values.

The attempt to estimate simultaneous equation equilibrium models and stochastic errors should be abandoned and replaced by attempts to simulate complex processes. Any attempt to "close" complex systems by imposing final "equilibrium" outcomes is doomed. Cyclical fluctuations must be modeled as endogenous recursive processes, and econometricians must develop greater capability to model and simulate nonlinear systems. Their goal should be greater holistic understanding of the complex temporal trajectories exhibited in real world economies. Economists must always remember that the most important class of experiments is : "The stream of experiments that Nature is steadily turning out from her own enormous laboratory, ... which we merely watch as passive observers."[78]

5
The Implications of Complexity for Economic Analysis

> Monetary theory especially has to be developed in time, (with) future becoming present, and present becoming past, as time goes on ... One must assume that the people in one's model do not know what is going to happen, and know they do not know just what is going to happen. As in history.
>
> John Hicks, 1977

> In a world where all economic units are continually revising and rearranging their plans over time in their attempts to anticipate future events, equilibrium can never occur ... Time and equilibrium are incompatible.
>
> George Shackle, 1972

> The future waits not for its contents to be discovered, but for that content to be originated.
>
> George Shackle, 1980

> I should, I think, be prepared to argue that in a world ruled by uncertainty, with an uncertain future linked to an actual present, a final position of equilibrium such as one deals with in static economics does not properly exist.
>
> John Maynard Keynes, XXIX: 222

5.1 Tensions in neoclassical economics

Economists are confounded by the turbulence of economic events and are unable to answer most important questions posed to them. They are notoriously unable to forecast turning points in economic time series, to discern when a high price-earnings level of stock prices denotes a bubble; when economies will spin into catastrophic slumps; how to attain a higher rate of output growth; what forces shape changes in the distribution of income, or even if the average rate of increase in money wages next year will be higher or lower than the current rate. Economists are not only unable to predict future events. They have equal difficulty retrodicting past events. The causes of the Great Depression of the 1930s remain highly controversial.

The general high esteem that economists enjoy does not arise from a record of successful predictions. It stems primarily from the fact that business and government desperately want to know what the future will bring and have nowhere else to turn. Many who have wrestled at length with methodology have concluded that economics is not a science.[1]

Economists have attempted to resolve the aggregation problem from micro- to macro-phenomena by attempting to formulate increasingly "rigorous" microfoundations for macroeconomic models. This has involved introducing increasingly restrictive assumptions: for example, all economic distributions are ergodic, agent behavior is based upon rational utility-maximization, markets are perfectly competitive. But as two well-known economists have put it, the result has been "rigor without relevance."[2]

Economics is currently in methodological disarray. Its tests of "significance" are widely misused. Many of its theoretical models and existence proofs are irrelevant to real world problems.[3] Once it is recognized that economies are complex adaptive systems, it becomes evident that economic agents are unable to perform "rational utility-maximizing calculations." To maximize anything, agents must have complete information about all possible alternatives. But in complex systems agents are bounded by ignorance. Information is inherently incomplete and agents have neither sufficient information nor the process ability to optimize anything.[4] "Satisficing" behavior, making the most satisfactory choice out of those that are reasonably available, is the best we humans can do.

While it is the chief guide to economic behavior, self-interest does not dominate in all situations. Real world agents are buffeted by surges of competing emotions. The behavior of the *same* agent may at different times be careful or impetuous, considerate or insensitive, generous or selfish, loyal or spiteful, noble or sadistic, loving or cruel. For poorly understood reasons altruism and patriotism are sometimes powerful determinants.[5] People seldom act totally independently. Social influence varies widely by age and type of behavior. When faced with complete ignorance of possible future outcomes, economic agents follow easy rules of thumb in order to simplify the impossible task of judging among an indefinite number of alternative possibilities. The most common response to near complete ignorance is to imitate the behavior of others, as we do when evaluating a stock, or choosing a restaurant in a foreign country. Such heuristics frequently lead to systematic error. Economists are now attempting to consider systematically the psychological foundations of human behavior.[6]

A large number of distinguished economists have reflected critically on economists' application of methods to conditions for which they are unsuited: Marx, Veblen, Hayek, Keynes, Hicks, Schackle, Boulding, Kaldor, Vickrey, Tobin, Eisner, Solow, McCloskey, Davidson, Dow, and Lawson. Most have been exceedingly critical of unquestioned reliance on the neoclassical assumptions of perfect information and utility-maximization.

Marx put his criticism as follows:

> Individuals make their own history. But they do not do it just as they please ... but under circumstances directly encountered, given, and transmitted from the past.[7]

Hayek was driven to adopt an iconoclastic subjectivist orientation:

> Different rules apply to different individuals according to age, sex, status, or the particular state in which each individual finds itself at the moment.[8]

Economic methodology has been heavily influenced by Popper's writings on falsification, particularly his epistemological grounds for accepting or rejecting theories. Mainstream economists claim the methodological authority of Popper for what they do. But they are also disposed to follow current intellectual fashions and tend to be dismissive of heterodox views. They do not devote their full attention to Popper's central goal, the pursuit of objective truth:

> I guess it is the suppressed sense of our own fallibility that is responsible for our despicable tendency to form cliques and to go along with whatever seems fashionable, ... that makes so many of us howl with the wolves ... I hold that science ought to strive for objective truth, for truth that depends only on the facts ... truth that is above human authority, above arbitration, and certainly above scientific fashions.[9]

In the tradeoff between rigor and relevance, the case against modern economics is that it is either irrelevant, or wrong.[10] The unsatisfactory nature of the state of affairs in economics that has long been declaimed by heterodox economists is now increasingly acknowledged by mainstream economists. Twenty years ago a Nobel prize winner penned the following criticism of economics which is equally applicable today:

> Page after page of professional economic journal articles are filled with mathematical formulas, leading the reader from sets of more or less plausible but entirely arbitrary assumptions to precisely stated but irrelevant theoretical conclusions ... Year after year economic theorists continue to produce scores of mathematical models and explore in great detail their formal properties, and econometricians fit algebraic functions of all possible shapes to essentially the same sets of data, without being able to advance in any perceptible way a systematic understanding of the structure and operations of a real economic system.[11]

Equally significant are persistent and widespread theory/practice inconsistencies. Economists routinely apply methods and techniques that are logically inconsistent with the theoretical perspectives they claim to draw upon. McCloskey has sharply criticized this behavior:

> Economists do not follow the laws of enquiry their methodologies lay down. A good thing too. If they did they would stand silent on (most of) the matters about which they commonly speak ... [Economists] have two attitudes towards discourse, the official and the unofficial, or the explicit and the implicit.

The official rhetoric to which they subscribe in the abstract and in their methodological ruminations declares them to be scientists in the modern mode. But it is not a rhetoric that fits their actual practice. The opinion that economic theory has become largely irrelevant is held by an embarrassingly large share of the economics profession. The wide gap between economic theory and econometric practice might be expected to cause a professional tension. But in fact, ... we comfortably divide ourselves into a celibate priesthood of statistical theorists on the one hand, and a legion of inveterate sinner-data analysts on the other. The priests are empowered to draw up lists of sins and are revered for the special talents they display. Sinners are not expected to avoid sins, they need only confess their errors openly.[12]

A related tension is the excessively formalistic content of much of modern economic theory. Economists emphasize humans possess the capacity to exercise choice. Some even define the discipline as "choice theory." But they are extremely unreceptive to criticism that in all equilibrium models agent choice and free will are effectively denied. If choice means anything it is that individuals could have acted otherwise. The future is open. *Ex post* people make mistakes.

Yet this is precisely what formal equilibrium modeling cannot allow. Rational individuals are represented as if there were only one optimal course of action, so the outcome could not have been otherwise. If economists really believed that choice is a central feature of human life, they would be forced to jettison equilibrium theory where agent choice heterogeneity is not allowed.[13]

A final tension concerns economists' general contemptuous attitude toward methodology:

> Don't think about it, just get on with it. Those who can, do economics, those who cannot, do methodology.

Orthodox economists do not merely discourage methodology. Most are openly hostile to it in all its forms. A former President of the AEA well illustrates this smug contemptuous attitude:

> It has long seemed to me that students of the social sciences, especially sociologists, have spent too much time in discussing what they call methodology. I have usually felt that the man who essays to tell the rest as how to solve knotty problems would be more convincing if first he proved out his alleged method by solving a few himself. Apparently those would-be authorities who are forever telling others how to get results do not get any important results themselves.[14]

Many methodological disputes do amount to little more than empty distractions. Nevertheless serious methodological consideration is the precondition for sound theorizing. Contemporary mainstream economics is characterized by amazing heights of methodological inconsistency. The coincidence of a widespread acceptance of a scientific methodology combined with an inability to act consistently with it, warrants serious explanation.[15]

In summary, mainstream economics fares poorly on its own terms. It neither provides accurate forecasts of events, nor illuminates the real world in which we live. Of equal significance is the fact that although riddled with confusion and incoherence, the significance of these persistent theory/practice inconsistencies is with few exceptions only rarely acknowledged in the profession.[16]

5.2 Misplaced concreteness in neoclassical theory[17]

"Economic theory" is the most prestigious branch of modern economics.[18] In sharp contrast to complexity theory, mainstream neoclassical economic theory is deductivist, rigorous, and axiomatic, derived from a tight set of initial axioms and constant-event conjunctions. Each of the following axioms is centrally associated with mainstream neoclassical economic theory:

1. Individual behavior rather than groups or collectivities,
2. Economic exchange rather than production and distribution,
3. Optimizing behavior rather than satisficing or habit,
4. Perfect competition rather than oligopoly or monopolistic competition,
5. Constant or decreasing rather than increasing returns,
6. Well-behaved (differentiable, convex, or linear) functions (utility, cost, preference, production, profit) rather than nonlinear relationships,
7. Information sets that comprise perfect information (rational expectations) rather than admit uncertainty or ignorance,
8. The notion of "equilibrium" as the solution to the system.

Since the presumption of an axiom's centrality and universality is taken for granted, the defense of axioms is considered to be unnecessary:

> Axioms are not plucked out of the air. Far from distancing the theorist from what is somewhat mysteriously called the "real" world, they constitute claims about this world so widely agreed as to make further argument unnecessary.[19]

Many well-known mainstream theorists regard most of the above axioms as "inessential." Hahn has identified the following three "central" axioms as beyond question. All others are less secure and their acceptance only temporary: they can be discarded leaving the essential structure intact.[20]

1. The requirement that explanations are conducted in terms of individual behavior.
2. The acceptance of some rationality axiom.
3. The commitment to the study of equilibrium states.

The unquestioned reliance of economic theory on *deductivist* modes of explanation has led even some of its proponents to question its capacity for accounting for real world phenomena. In place of simple general premises and the "elegant" theorems they generate, Hahn has advised potential theorists to focus upon more complex and specific premises and embrace computer simulation.

> Not only will our successors have to be far less concerned with the general ... than we have been, they will have to bring to the particular problems they study particular histories and methods capable of dealing with the complexity of the particular, such as computer simulation. ... Not for them ... the pleasure of theorems and proofs. Instead the uncertain embrace of history and sociology and biology.[21]

Solow has argued that economic theory should be radically modified to accommodate the fact that individual decisions are conditioned by context-specific values and habits. He maintains that economists should pay more attention to matters of history, biology, and sociology:

> I am not prepared to abandon the exhaustive study of the implications of particular axiom systems, though I admit that I do not expect a lot from that sort of theory. What I am arguing against is the foolish belief that when it comes to studying the real world, there is only one useful system of axioms, and we already know what it is.[22]

The complexity of context-specific models has lead to increasing demands that economic theorists become experts in computer simulation. One cause of this dramatic change is the reluctant acknowledgment that the highly generalized models of "neoclassical economic theory" are in fact too general. Orthodox theory's focus on "General Equilibrium" has forced theorists to acknowledge the existence of insuperable problems in the concept of general equilibrium. For a general equilibrium outcome to occur all agents' plans must be mutually compatible. But if a specification of an economy allows one such equilibrium, it typically allows many. If each equilibrium is assumed unique, there is no mechanism in the standard orthodox specification to ensure how an economy gets there.[23]

Axioms of economic theory are postulated at an extremely general level. This encourages the assertion that a range of outcomes are possible. But the range of possibilities arises only because the models are not fully specified. Hahn has admitted that the claimed virtue of not predicting specific outcomes is simply a rhetorical device to mask what on orthodoxy's own terms is a state of ignorance:

> I want to argue that it is one of the virtues of theories derived from axioms more "fundamental" than those used in special theory that they really do not yield single-value restrictions on the world ... This is a virtue because the economist is thereby restricted from claiming more than he has reasons for claiming. The axioms have summed up what one regards as pretty secure empirical knowledge. The set of outcomes which is possible is simply the reflection of our lack of knowledge. A special theory can usefully narrow them down. But our confidence

in the special hypothesis is smaller than in the axioms. A claim of only one outcome should always include the proviso that, given our state of knowledge, there are always other possibilities.[24]

The deductivist nature of neoclassical economic theory based on strict event-regularities has been undermined by the recognition that the "axioms" of economic theory are postulated at a very general level, encouraging the assertion that many outcomes are possible. But the assumption of event regularity is in essence deterministic. In any open system there are always additional factors not included in the specified set of conditions which can influence outcomes. Hahn has stated this problem as follows:

> That people have preferences and try to satisfy them we treat as an axiom, while perfect competition, for instance, must count as an assumption ... That managers have preferences (to maximize some function of profits) is an axiom; that they take a particular form, for instance linear in expected profits, is an assumption ... If you want more out you have to put more in, you must supplement the axioms with assumptions, e.g. that production functions are Cobb Douglas.[25]

The insistence of equilibrium as a system level property derives from the logical dependence of deductive analysis on postulated strict event-regularities. Equilibrium is interpreted as a conceptual state where all actions and plans are mutually compatible and all the system's equations are mutually consistent.[26] But to ensure that a set of conditions is consistent with a particular outcome, it must be assumed that individual agents act in identical ways when analyzed under identical conditions.

Mainstream economic theory achieves this result non-transparently by three key assumptions:

1. By proceeding as if individuals were the sole unit of analysis.
2. By specifying the utility function (or production or profit function) as given, known and continuous, thereby ensuring the existence of a unique optimum.
3. By characterizing human nature in such a way that all individuals are rational utility-maximizers.

The central flaw in orthodox theory is not its general assumption that agents act in the rational pursuit of their own self-interest.[27] It is that rational behavior is defined in terms of *"actualities"* instead of *"potentialities."*[28] The flattening of potentialities into actualities combined with the refusal to recognize that market phenomena may be determined by causes other than those postulated by economic theory, follow directly from the logical dependence of deductivist theories on *strict event-regularities*. These regularities exhibit the law-like nature of constant-event-conjunctions: *"whenever x, then y."*

The persistence of mainstream economists' commitment to uncovering "laws" to predict and illuminate economic phenomena, in the face of their clear failure to be able either to predict or illuminate, follows from the overwhelming prestige of deductivism in the natural sciences. The legacy of positivism which portrays individual actors as homogeneous and passive, combined with the adoption of the positivist "successful prediction" criterion for the validity of hypotheses, serves to reinforce economists' commitment to strict event-regularities. The belief that economic theory *ought* to be more explanatory and must overcome its past explanatory failures underpins the recent movements toward computer simulation. Despite the repeated demonstration of the failure of officially sanctioned methods to predict or explain, the profession's uncritical adherence to positivism ensures that the deductivist methodology remains unquestioned. The identification of postulated event-regularities is regarded as *the essence of empirical science*, in spite of the fact that strict event-regularities never occur in complex systems.

Some theorists acknowledge that the theoretical postulates of neoclassical economics do not express the real mechanisms responsible for generating the outcomes recorded in economic data. Hahn has been highly critical of attempts to estimate formalistic models of economic theory using measured data of actual phenomena.[29] He views neoclassical theories as *"fictitious idealizations,"* and believes acknowledged fictions such as perfect foresight, perfect competition, or perfect mobility are justified on the presumption that the understanding of *"imagined economies"* facilitates insights into the workings of real economies. Hahn maintains that by using obviously fictitious assumptions, for example, infinitely lived agents, *"Everyone can see we are not dealing with any actual economy."*[30] Such assumptions provide an understanding of actual real world phenomena from a set of highly idealized aspects.

A second broad line of defense of *"acknowledged fictions"* is that they do not represent clear one-sided alternatives but are preliminary heuristic devices in the step-wise process of moving from simplified ideal concepts to concepts of greater reality and complexity. Neoclassical concepts like "perfect foresight," "perfect competition," "perfect mobility," and "omniscient agents" are obviously not features of the world we inhabit. But rather than *"fictitious idealizations,"* they can also with greater validity be regarded as *"misleading fictions."*

To be successful the method of successive approximation requires:

1. The factors considered in isolation are the sole "real" causal factors, and
2. Their effects contribute singly and interact linearly.

But complex systems are nonlinear, have "emergent properties," and are irreducible to their component parts. Complex systems do not combine components in a linear fashion. Components are combined nonlinearly and lead to qualitatively novel and emergent outcomes. The *"fictitious idealizations"* (*"misleading fictions"*) of economic theory are not justified by reference to any stepwise procedure. Any attempt to gain understanding of a complex system by reductionist examination of its components is doomed to failure, and can serve only to mislead.

Experimentation means intervening in the world, by controlling for all nonspecified causal factors, so the primary causal mechanisms can be identified and the theories about them tested. Due to the impossibility of manipulating most social structures controlled experimentation is not meaningful in the social sciences. Evidence of variable interdependence must be empirically discovered and not experimentally generated.

"Noise" is not the sole alternative to strict event-regularity. Over restricted regions of space-time, powerful mechanisms such as changes in interest rates, government spending, and taxes can dominate aggregate behavior and their effects shine through. The social system is open, but many broad mechanisms are continuously reproduced. These give rise to rough generalities and "partial" event regularities. *"Stylized Facts"* was Kaldor's term for phenomena that hold loosely empirically to the extent that a theoretical explanation is called for. Stylized facts are used by post-Keynesians to illuminate "partial" event-regularities.[31]

5.3 The non-probabilistic nature of fundamental uncertainty

Classical economists made a crucial simplifying assumption that shunted the train of economic theory onto a false spur: *"For simplification let us assume that economic agents act with perfect information."* It was explicitly recognized that such an assumption was completely unrealistic. (Economists know they cannot foretell the future.) But over the past century neoclassical economists have consciously attempted to follow physicists to "pierce the veil of everyday life" uncover the "underlying real structural forces" beneath. The assumption of "perfect certainty" was regarded as methodologically analogous to the similarly unrealistic assumption of "frictionless states" in physics. The messy second-order effects introduced by "uncertainty" for economic phenomena were assumed broadly equivalent to the messy second-order effects introduced by "friction" for physical phenomena.

Unfortunately the parallel is inexact. In making the assumption of perfect knowledge, neoclassical economists were forced (implicitly) to presume that external reality is deterministic. Economic behavior was assumed to be determined by immutable if unknown "laws," much like Newton's celestial planets. Mainstream economists have now completely abandoned the perfect certainty model. But they still implicitly presume the existence of a deterministic external reality describable by objective probability distributions. The external world is assumed deterministic. The passage of time and the particular traverse to equilibrium followed are considered irrelevant to the determination of final outcomes. The documentation of second-order details is regarded as historiography. The possibility of hysteresis (the dependence of the current value of a variable on its past history) is completely ignored for economic phenomena.[32]

Once the assumption of perfect certainty is abandoned, agent expectations of future events play the dominant role in determining agents' present behavior. The outcomes of present behavior only occur in future periods. To maximize utility agents must be able to make "rational" forecasts of future events, including the future outcomes of present decisions. To do this successfully they must be able to analyze sample data from the future. But since the future has not occurred, this is obviously an impossible condition. To get around this logical difficulty, classical economists were forced to make the very strong implicit assumption that events are "ergodic." (Ergodicity denotes the system where probability distributions remain constant over time.) The assumption of ergodicity is loosely analogous to assumption that the world is in a stationary state. All probability distributions remain stable and events regularly repeat themselves. It then appears possible to predict future events, by calculating their *ex post* probabilities.[33]

If the world is ergodic future outcomes become the shadow of past events. Economic agents would be able to make efficient forecasts of the future by analyzing the past. To be able to act "rationally" agents must calculate objective probability distributions for all events, and find the "certainty equivalent" value of future outcomes for all alternatives. If the world were ergodic, the future could be rationally forecast on a probabilistic basis by processing the information imbedded in past distributions. It is only for such a world that neoclassical economics is appropriate. All economies would then be completely supply constrained.

Mainstream economists have developed two distinct types of ergodic models:[34]

1. Ergodic certainty models: agents' knowledge of the underlying reality is complete. Agents know the certainty equivalent value of all variables. Examples are Classical Perfect Certainty models, some New Classical models.
2. Epistemological uncertainty models: agents' knowledge of external reality is incomplete. The world is ergodic, but highly complicated. Agents are unable to obtain reliable information about the future value of economic variables, due to inherent limitations in data-gathering, processing ability, and computing power. Examples are: Austrian theory, New Classical Sunspot and Bubble theories, New Keynesian Rational Expectations theories, Asymmetric Information and Coordination Failure models.

Epistemological uncertainty models have an individualist orientation. Agents are assumed to form subjective probabilities, which may but need not converge to the true objective probabilities. Agents whose subjective probabilities do not converge on the objective probabilities make persistent and systematic forecasting errors and will eventually go bankrupt. Markets are presumed to possess a kind of Darwinian natural selection process that weeds out inferior decision makers. Surviving agents will have learned to make efficient estimates. Their subjective expectations will conform to the real objective distributions.

The "long run," as it is defined by Neoclassical, Monetarist, New Classical, and Sraffian models is that future conceptual point where agents' expectations are fully satisfied, and so forecasting errors no longer occur. Friedman put this as follows:

> The long run equilibrium is one in which ... all expectations are realized ... and is determined by the ... quantity theory plus the Walrasian equations of general equilibrium. ... . It is a logical construct that defines the trend to which it [the actual world] is tending to return.[35]

Sraffian models conceptualize long run equilibrium as a "center of gravity" toward which the system is attracted but never actually reaches, due to the presence of continuous exogenous "shocks."

> Individual traders are bound to make significant forecasting errors ... while they are learning the dynamic laws significant forecasting errors of their environment ... during the period of transition of the economy towards a hypothetical equilibrium, if it ever reaches one, along which forecasting errors vanish eventually.[36]

> Most economists accept the natural rate hypothesis, which interpreted broadly states that classical economics is right in the long run ... economists today are more interested in long run equilibrium. The long run is not so far away that one can cavalierly claim, as Keynes did, that "in the long run we are all dead."[37]

"Rational Expectations" theorists do not assume that agents are omniscient and have complete knowledge of reality. Agents are simply presumed to be able to calculate subjective probabilities for future events. So long as the world is ergodic, these estimates will be statistically unbiased estimates of the objective probability distributions describing the future. So long as the future is like the past the collection of past data can be viewed as equivalent to drawing a sample from the future.

Space and time distributions calculated from past events are reliable estimates of the future *if and only if the stochastic processes are ergodic*. In this case, past data can be treated as a sample drawn from the future. But for non-ergodic processes space and time distributions do not converge. The distributions as well as the outcomes are time-dependent. Frank Knight described risk as events quantifiable in terms of objective probability distributions, but uncertainty cannot be expressed in probabilistic terms. It must be viewed as *"a probability distribution of probability distributions."* For all complex systems probability distributions are non-ergodic, time-dependent, and continuously changing over time.[38] Knight drew the following incisive distinction between risk and uncertainty:

> The practical difference between risk and uncertainty is that in the former the distribution of the outcome in a group of instances is known (either through calculation a priori or from the statistics of past experience), while in the case of uncertainty this is not true.[39]

The Arrow-Debreu formulation of Walrasian General Equilibrium is the conceptual progenitor of rational expectation analysis. For markets to be "complete," in addition to spot and forward markets for all commodities there must exist a set of futures markets for all commodities for every contingent future state of the world. The concept of Walrasian General Equilibrium is timeless. It refers to a position where all spot, forward, and futures markets are simultaneously in equilibrium. At this point all markets close, and all transactions cease. But in a world where all future prices in every future state of the world are known, all assets become perfectly liquid. Such a world has no function for money, so there would be no reason for money to exist. In such a world, if fiat money has no intrinsic use value it can have no positive value in exchange. If the real own rate of return on money were zero, no rational agent would hold money. The Arrow-Debreu Walrasian system thus depicts a perfect barter system in a world of perfect certainty, where all assets are perfectly liquid and there is no need for money.

The analytical appeal of *"Rational Expectations"*[40] is that it makes expectations endogenous, stemming from the natural process of learning involving the best use of all available information. Agents are assumed able to calculate the "true" objective distribution of all future outcomes, either from *a priori* calculations or past statistics. This can only be possible in an ergodic world where all probability distributions are given, time-independent and known with perfect certainty. The concept of "Rational Expectations" is logically confined to such imaginary worlds. By assuming the existence and uniqueness of General Equilibrium (GE), mainstream theorists (implicitly) endorse the belief that external reality is predetermined (life is like a movie). In an early paper Samuelson was quite explicit about this: "By imposing ergodicity, we theorists hope to remove economics from the 'realm of genuine history' and put it in 'the realm of science.' "[41]

Samuelson then believed the toughminded acceptance of ergodicity was the *sine qua non* if economics was to pursue the scientific method. He had not recognized that in an ergodic world with given objective probabilities, the future is predetermined.[42] Mainstream economists now renounce any belief in the existence of a predetermined reality. But so long as they use the concept of "General Equilibrium" as an analytical tool, they unknowingly display a tendency to retain it.[43] Whenever economists refer to "objective probabilities" they reveal they have not yet freed themselves from the axiom of ergodicity. The world is predetermined.

Mainstream economists have confused the importance that expectations be rigorously analyzed, for example, their elasticity estimated, heterogeneity among different agents examined, regressive or extrapolative formulation described, convergence over time determined; with the belief that expectations themselves must be determinate. Many incorrectly take the view that economic theory is useless under fundamental uncertainty. Lucas has infamously elected this position:

> In situations of risk, the hypothesis of rational behavior on the part of agents will have usable content, so that behavior may be explainable in terms of economic theory. In such situations, expectations are rational in Muth's sense. In cases of uncertainty, economic reasoning will be of no value.

But this is the argument of a drunkard looking under the lamppost for his keys, which he had dropped in the park, *"because this is the only place where I can see anything."* If one yearns to be "rigorous" and "scientific," one cannot admit the existence of complexity, since fundamental uncertainty cannot lead to deterministic outcomes. This does not imply *"economic reasoning is of no value,"* but rather that accurate prediction is impossible. Economists must bring complex tools to analyze complex systems. The recognition that economies are complex adaptive systems is something which economists eventually must come to terms with.

Keynes recognized that the absence of futures markets for most economic goods creates huge uncertainty and at times market failure:

> An act of individual saving means, so to speak, a decision not to have dinner today. But it does not necessitate a decision to have dinner or buy a pair of boots a week or a year hence, or to consume any specific thing at any specific date. Thus it depresses the business of preparing today's dinner, without stimulating the business of making ready for some future act of consumption. It is not a substitution of future consumption demand—it is a net diminution of such demand ... the expenditure of future consumption is so largely based on present experience that ... it may reduce present investment demand as well as present consumption demand.[44]

In the *General Theory* Keynes argued that the world was non-ergodic and complex although he did not use these terms. To emphasize their fragile and effervescent nature, he coined the term *"animal spirits"* for expectations that were formed under conditions of fundamental ignorance.

> The outstanding fact is the extreme precariousness of the basis of knowledge on which our estimates of prospective yield have to be made. Our knowledge of the factors which govern the yield of an investment some years hence is usually very slight, and sometimes negligible. If we speak frankly, we have to admit that our basis of knowledge for estimating a yield ten years hence ... amounts to little and sometimes to nothing, or even five years hence.[45]

Post-Keynesians believe economists must speak frankly: *"The economic emperor has no clothes!"* One year after the *General Theory* Keynes defended his earlier work by arguing that decisionmakers:

> Have no scientific basis on which to form any calculable probability whatever. We simply do not know.

Keynes believed in response to near complete ignorance decisionmakers fall back on three conventions:

1. We assume that *the present is a much more serviceable guide to the future* than a candid examination of past experience would show it to have been hitherto ...
2. We assume that the *existing state of opinion* as expressed in prices and the character of existing output *is based on a correct summing up* of future prospects ...
3. Knowing that our individual judgment is worthless, we endeavor to fall back on the judgment of the rest of the world which is better informed, that is *we endeavor to conform with the behavior of the majority or the average*.[46]

Nature continuously changes the number of black and white balls in the urn. Not only are the individual outcomes time-dependent but also the probability distributions from which they are drawn. The world is non-ergodic and economies are complex adaptive systems. Keynes put this as follows:

> A conventional valuation which is established as the outcome of the mass psychology of a large number of ignorant individuals is liable to change violently as the result of a sudden fluctuation of opinion due to factors which do not really make much difference to the prospective yield: since there will be no strong roots of conviction to hold it steady ... the market will be subject to waves of optimistic and pessimistic sentiment, which are unreasoning and yet in a sense legitimate where no solid basis exists for a reasonable calculation. ... It might have been supposed that competition between expert professionals, possessing judgment and knowledge beyond that of the average private investor, would correct the vagaries of the ignorant individual left to himself. It happens, however, that the energies and skill of the professional investor and speculator are mainly occupied otherwise. ... They are concerned, not with what an investment is really worth ... but what the market will value it at, under the influence of mass psychology, three months or a year hence. ... The social object of skilled investment should be to defeat the dark forces of time and ignorance which envelope our future. The actual, private object of most skilled investment to-day is "to beat the gun."... to outwit the crown, and to pass the bad, or depreciating, half-crown to the other fellow. ... For it is, so to speak, a game of Snap, of Old Maid, of Musical Chairs ... [47]

Fundamental uncertainty and the passage of time pose irresolvable problems. In the case of fundamental uncertainty agents are unable to form a "certainty equivalent" estimate for unknown phenomena, since not merely the outcomes but also the probability distributions are unknown and changing. For most goods agents are inevitably faced with the problem of forming expectations about the future expectations of other agents. No plausible set of assumptions can characterize a learning process that leads to a stationary equilibrium in a system with intrinsic and dynamic interdependency. Keynes caught the essence of this problem in his metaphor about the newspaper beauty contests:

> Professional investment may be likened to those newspaper competitions in which the competitors have to pick out the six prettiest faces from a hundred photographs, the prize being awarded to the competitor whose choice most nearly corresponds to the average preferences of the competitors as a whole; so that each competitor has to pick, not those faces which he himself finds prettiest, but those which he thinks likeliest to catch the fancy of the other competitors, all of whom are looking at the problem from the same point of view. It is not a case of choosing those which, to the best of one's judgment, are really the prettiest, nor even those which average opinion genuinely thinks the prettiest. We have reached the third degree where we devote our intelligences to anticipating

what average opinion expects the average opinion to be. And there are some, I believe, who practice the fourth, fifth, and higher degrees.[48]

Shackle introduced the concept of "crucial choice," where a decision once made radically changes the environment so the identical decision conditions can never be repeated.[49] Crucial choice decisions alter the subsequent probability distributions in unpredictable ways. Many important decisions possess this quality: choosing a career, selecting a spouse, having a baby, choosing to emigrate. Although the future created may be far from the future intended, the future is originated by agents and shaped by their crucial choice decisions. One unintended result is Schumpeter's process of *"creative destruction."* Austrian economists have emphasized that most important future consequences of present decisions are unanticipated by their innovators.[50]

Most mainstream economists believe that if only their theory and their data were "correct," they could successfully predict most economic events. The failure of models to predict successfully is met with a predictable set of responses: the desirability for better data collection, the necessity of increasingly sophisticated computer software, and the continuous revision of certain theories. Such responses primarily share the feature of allowing existing ways of doing economics to remain unchallenged. The recognition that economies are complex systems implies a radical transformation of economic methodology. Failure to predict does not indicate the failure of the theory but the complex nature of the system. Economists' disregard for the complexity of social reality has resulted in procedures being accepted as fundamental to economics that are inappropriate for analyzing economic behavior and opposed to fruitful analysis.

The major culprit is a mode of explanation based on the scientific conception of "law" as a "theoretical formulation." This is expressed in terms of a constant event conjunction, connecting outcomes with states of affairs and expressed as regularities of the form: "whenever event x, then event y." Under this conception explanation and prediction are the same. The former entails the deduction of an event after it has occurred, the latter prior to its occurrence. But law-like event regularities occur only in controlled deterministic systems. At the level of actual events complex systems never manifest law-like regularities.[51] Outside of astronomy, event regularities are never observed in nature. They occur only under the strictly controlled conditions of experiments, the product of human intervention.

Theoretical postulates of economics should be put in the following form: "Whenever event x then event y follows, *so long as conditions c hold.*" The social world is open. Agents could have acted differently than they did, in which case the choices and outcomes would have been different.[52] Most events are not predetermined. Choice presupposes that agents have some conception of what they are doing, and what they want to achieve. But intentionality is bound up with knowledgeability. Since strict event regularities are never encountered, agents inevitably must take actions for which the outcomes are uncertain.

Expectations may be regarded as "opinions," "estimates," or "conjectures" that are believed to be true *ex ante* but may turn out to be true or false *ex post.*

Uncertainty is always present concerning the falseness of these opinions, since the existing state of knowledge is insufficient to rule out more than a small range of possible outcomes. Cumulative errors occur, persist, and self-perpetuate. Contrary evidence conveys more information than corroborative observations. It is simply not possible for agents to discover their future by studying the past. They create their own future by their own current actions.

Many social structures have been developed to facilitate intentional action under conditions of fundamental uncertainty—languages, customs, rules of behavior, conventions, expectations—to encourage and constrain purposive human activities. Uncertainty about the future consequences of present action leads agents to imitate the behavior of others. The human predisposition to follow and to imitate others is deeply rooted.[53] People naturally converge on similar behavior known as "herding." This is an evolutionary adaptation that promoted survival in an uncertain world by allowing individuals access to the hard-won information of others.

> Men nearly always follow the tracks made by others and proceed in their affairs by imitation.[54]

> When people are free to do as they please, they usually imitate each other.[55]

When faced with a choice, how do agents determine which alternative is better? Each agent could decide independently and attempt a thorough analysis of all possible alternatives. But in view of the openness and complexity of the world such a strategy would be impossibly time-consuming, and for most questions impractical. Individuals rely primarily on the behavior of others, observational or social learning. In a complex world individuals acting in their self-interest take imitative and uninformed actions. Information cascades can be triggered by new information. Small differences in initial conditions make huge differences in final outcomes.[56]

Economic outcomes are inherently dynamic, and sensitive to historical and geographical initial conditions. The most students of behavior in complex systems can hope to do is attempt to identify the structures, mechanisms, and tendencies below the surface level of reality that result in change. Economists should look for order rather than laws. Due to their sensitivity to initial conditions it is never possible to predict the future path of complex systems. Social scientists must content themselves with building models that shed light on complex behavior. To theorize is to provide explanations whereby key aspects of phenomena are rendered intelligible. To theorize does not imply the ability to foresee the future.

5.4 The case against equilibrium analysis

Our perception of the world is shaped by the paradigm we use to interpret it. One goal of this book is to develop a powerful alternative to the neoclassical "general equilibrium" paradigm. To prepare the way consider the fatal flaws of equilibrium analysis. Most important is its unsatisfactory treatment of time. Pure decision theory ("catallectics": the science of choice) is formulated as a timeless optimization problem subject to constraints. The choice among anticipated outcomes of alternative actions is timeless logical calculus. A sharp distinction must be drawn between historical and logical time. The starting point of any nonequilibrium paradigm is the recognition that all economic phenomena occur in historical time.

The essential features of historical time may be simply stated:

(a) Time is intrinsically bound up with change. ("Instantaneous change" is an analytical fiction to avoid dealing with the problems created by the passage of historical time.)
(b) The future becomes for a fleeting temporal instant the present and then becomes the past.
(c) The past is given and cannot be changed.
(d) The future is open, but always bounded. Its particularities cannot be foreseen.
(e) Economic agents do not know what tomorrow will bring. Their rough working expectation is that prices tomorrow will be the same as today.

Equilibrium models are formulated in timeless systems of linear equations. When the equations are linear, providing the number of unknowns is equal to the number of equations, the system will have a unique solution, defined as the "equilibrium" position of the system. Much attention is paid by mainstream economists to proving the existence, uniqueness, and stability of equilibrium in economic models.

In mainstream economics, theorizing is built around the concepts of Partial (micro) and General (macro) Equilibrium:[57]

1. Partial Equilibrium. This denotes a model of a single agent or a single market with one or more dependent variables. Each equation in the model is partitioned into a dependent variable, a set of explanatory variables, and an error term. Only the relationship between the dependent variable and a small subset of possible explanatory variables are considered. The variables selected as "explanatory" are those believed to be causally the most important. All other explanatory variables and relationships are held constant under the *ceteris paribus* assumption.

The solution position for such a model is termed "Partial Equilibrium." This is defined as a position of balance, where the system is at rest, adjustment and change have ceased and all variables remain constant. Under the *ceteris paribus* assumption the analytical distinction is made between fast-moving variables, such as prices traded in well-organized financial markets, and slow-moving variables, such as institutions, the state of technology, and stocks of durable assets, whose value greatly exceeds annual production and depreciation so the proportionate change over short-run (quarterly or annual time) periods is small.

Slow-moving variables that change but little during the period under analysis may appropriately be held in the *ceteris paribus* box, and reflected by the constant term and the parameters in model equations. When an equilibrium model fails to describe empirical phenomena, it may be because the model is mis-specified, or because the terms being assumed constant in the *ceteris paribus* box have changed.

Since in the real world change is continual, a position of balance is never observed. This has the implication that an equilibrium model can never be empirically refuted. Failure to confirm can be due to the model being mis-specified, or to change in the terms assumed constant in the *ceteris paribus* box.[58]

2. General Equilibrium. (GE) It denotes a model of an entire economy. All markets and all variables in the economy are included and no variables are held constant. In GE models the system can not be partitioned between explanatory and dependent variables. All variables are assumed interdependent so it is not possible to identify causality. The solution to such a model is termed "General Equilibrium," defined as a conceptual position of balance where all markets clear and excess supply and demand have been eliminated. In GE change no longer occurs.

There are two closely related definitions of "equilibrium." The first is defined as a position of *balance*, where there is no tendency for any variable to change. The second is defined as a position where all markets *clear*. For a single market, "equilibrium" refers to the (timeless) point of intersection of the supply and demand curves in a perfectly competitive market. Since there is neither an excess nor a deficiency of demand, the price remains constant. General equilibrium is sometimes expressed in terms of the mutual consistency of expectations, since in GE expectations of all agents are simultaneously fulfilled. General equilibrium refers to a hypothetical situation where all markets in the economy clear, and all excess supply and excess demand are eliminated. If it is truly general, all markets and all behaviour must be included. There are no *ceteris* that remain *paribus*. But complex social systems are open and agent expectations of the unknown future continuously change over time. As a result the concept of a particular "general equilibrium" position toward which the economy is tending, and from which there is no further tendency to change, is unimaginable. It can never occur in historical time.

General equilibrium is a purely analytic and hypothetical statement and as such non-refutable by any empirical operation. Complex systems are open but we can only analyze closed systems. In complex systems the concept of equilibrium necessitates the inclusion of a *ceteris paribus* clause. All variables must be constant for "equilibrium" to occur. Partial equilibrium can be imagined for all closed systems. Variables not explicitly considered in the model must be held constant in the *ceteris paribus* clause if closure is to occur. But in complex systems change is continuous. Economists should distinguish slow-changing and fast-changing variables, and ensure only slow-changing variables are compounded in the *ceteris paribus* box.

In GE there are no *ceteris* that must remain *paribus*, so GE cannot be envisaged for complex systems. Historical time moves ineluctably forward and contingency plays a central role. Outcomes alter future paths in ways that can never be anticipated in advance. The future cannot be predicted from the past, since the future has not occurred and does not yet exist. Agents in one sense "create" their own future, so this future cannot be "discovered" in the present. It can never be known when regularities present in historical data will cease to hold. In complex systems change is the only constant. General Equilibrium, defined as a position of balance where all change has ceased, cannot occur in historical time. Time necessarily involves change in at least one variable, so GE is outside of time. It is in effect a non-transparent way of getting rid of the irresolvable problems raised by the passage of historical time.[59]

The recognition that economies are complex adaptive systems implies GE is logically inconceivable and cannot occur in complex systems. By taking recourse to the calculus of objective probabilities GE must "freeze" time and in the process assume away all the problems associated with historical time. If GE is defined as a position where nothing changes, a complex system must be dead. The existence of a unique equilibrium requires that uncertainty is reduced to calculable risk. Historical time is then transmogrified into logical time.

Such strong assumptions create inherent contradictions. In a world where agents are assumed able to form their expectations "rationally," fundamental uncertainty cannot exist. But in a world with no fundamental uncertainty there is no role for money. Money is not a good produced by labor and capital like other goods to provide utility to its owners. Money is a social convention like a language, that has evolved over aeons to facilitate exchange and production under uncertainty. If all agents possessed perfect certainty this implies that the value of all assets is known. But in such a world there is no need of money. If the present and future value of all goods are known, all goods are directly exchangeable for one another. Alternatively expressed, when all prices are known, all goods have a known value and so in a monetary economy are perfectly liquid so frictionless barter occurs. General equilibrium can thus apply only to a world of perfect information and perfect barter, where there are no transaction costs and agents have no need for money. In consequence GE systems logically have no role for money.

General Equilibrium, defined either as a position of balance or as a position where all markets clear, is inconceivable in complex systems. Equilibrium analysis attempts to simplify the problem of understanding the future by getting rid of historical time. But by focusing solely on "equilibrium" states, it ignores the events of the transition processes within which we are continually enmeshed. As a result, *"Equilibrium theory serves to conceal our ignorance and thereby accentuates our ignorance."*[60] For the analysis of social behavior in the complex world in which we live Walrasian GE analysis must be abandoned. Economic analysis should not entertain hypothetical GE positions, since in the real world such positions cannot even be imagined. Economists should rather analyze the dynamic historical processes within which we are continually enmeshed.

5.5 Process analysis

Complex systems have no closed-form solution. They never stand still, and can never approach a GE configuration. Successfully modeling the future behavior of an economy is forever beyond our grasp.[61] Fundamental uncertainty cannot be eliminated by the accumulation of additional knowledge. The unique feature of complex events are their non-repeatable quality. Change is continuous and intrinsic and is not attributable to "external shocks." The current values of variables reflect the current, previous, and expected future values of their own and other variables in continuously changing nonlinear fashion. Economists must give up "destination oriented" comparative static equilibrium analysis, with its fatal attempt to formulate deterministic future outcome, and must move to "history creating" process analysis, the examination of how systems change and evolve over calendar time.[62] The goal of process analysis is to explain the proportional change in first differences of selected variables. As is well known first differences are much more difficult to explain empirically than levels.

As shown in Chapter 4, economic time series have unit roots and the coefficient of the lagged dependent variable in autoregressive equations is not significantly different from unity. The best estimate of next period's value is the current period's value.[63] Process analysis focuses on explaining and when possible forecasting the sign (ordinal value) of the first difference of the dependent variable, over a short-run period. When the analyst is very lucky she may be able to successfully forecast cardinal changes in variables within a wide error band. This cannot be reduced to an objective statistical probability since distributions in economics are time-dependent.

Analysis can never hope to discover in the present the future "destination" of economic systems. No future "equilibrium" position exists. All variables are continuously changing at different rates over time. It can never be known when even the most stable historical relationship will cease to hold. No objective probability distributions exist on which expectations can be based. All distributions possess the uniqueness of the space–time position in which they occur. Economic agents cannot discover the future by studying the past. They must create their own future by their present and future behavior. Long-run analysis of complex systems is purely speculative. As the time period extends into the future, prediction errors rise exponentially.

Economic systems are complex beyond human comprehension. Any theory that takes complexity seriously must be a theory of processes through historical time. Economies must be modeled as complex systems and economists must focus on the temporal process in which change occurs. Variables must be explained in terms of short-run first differences (changes from their current level) with no attempt to close the process with any "equilibrium" outcome. It is impossible to forecast accurately the ordinal changes in economic variables over even the shortest of short runs. Agents' subjective probability distributions about future events are continually changing. This leads to "bubble" models where *prices change because they are expected to.*"[64]

To accurately model the future behavior of an economy is forever beyond our reach. Economists must content themselves with building dynamic models of complex subsystems using a select number of variables, not an entire economy. Short-run ordinal predictions (greater or less) may be successful, but accurate forecasts are impossible. No one can know today whether stock prices will rise or fall tomorrow, and changes in stock prices have important macroeconomic effects. All forecasts of cardinal quantities must include a wide range of indeterminacy which increases exponentially as the time horizon is increased.

Process analysis focuses on explaining and forecasting the ordinal value of the first difference of dependent variables over the shortest run. The current level of all variables is taken as given and may be regarded as predetermined. For most economic variables with sufficiently long time series the coefficient on the lagged dependent variable is not significantly different from unity. When variables have a unit root, the value of the coefficient on the lagged dependent variable is unity. The goal of process analysis is to explain and predict proportional changes (first differences) in all endogenous variables. As all empiricists know first differences of variables are much more difficult to predict successfully than levels. Complex systems' implications are highly destructive of the mainstream vision as to how economies function. When absorbed they will reshape the "trained intuition" of modern economists.

Economies are complex systems where strict event regularities do not occur. Economic outcomes reflect the consequences of volitional and non-volitional behavior of imperfectly informed agents who must each form expectations of other agents' behavior. Seen in this light it is not surprising that economic forecasters are unable to make accurate forecasts, and deductive theories are unable to illuminate economic behavior. Since economic events can never be precisely forecast, positivism, the ability to successfully forecast outcomes, is not an appropriate criterion for discriminating truth value among alternative economic hypotheses. Increased illumination and understanding of the dynamics of complex events is both possible and sufficient for successful stabilization policy.

Complex systems impose a different conception of "explanation" from the deductivist-constant-conjunction mainstream methodology. The goal of explanation for complex systems is not the scientific deduction of future events. It is rather the illumination of tendencies inherent in complex systems. Social science should be re-demarcated as *"dependency upon intentional human agency."*[65] Accepting that humans are continually faced by real choices, and frequently make "wrong" decisions is the first step in the recognition that the economic sphere is complex, sensitive to initial conditions, and pervaded by emergence and contingency. In economics there are no invariant "laws." Economists can at best hope to discover the "order" in the chaos.

The most telling point against mainstream methodology is that despite the enormous resources that have been allocated no stable event regularities have ever been discovered. Econometricians continually puzzle why carefully estimated relationships "break down," frequently as soon as new observations become available. Not surprisingly this has led to increased skepticism in the econometric profession concerning the validity of empirical results:

> I have a sense that most economists feel that conclusions from data sets are fragile. Somebody will add another variable, or they will control for some aspect of the time series phenomenon in some other way, which will yield a substantially different conclusion. One of the reasons we don't trust empirical work seriously is that there have been so many cases of fragile conclusions. Somebody claims to have found something and six months later a new equation is estimated, and the same finding seems to be reversed. It creates the feeling among economists that conclusions from data are very fragile.[66]

This unhappy situation is rendered intelligible as soon as economies are recognized as complex systems reflecting intentional human agency under fundamental uncertainty. The most order we can expect to find are semi-regularities, what Kaldor termed "stylized facts." Constant event-regularities (linear relationships) never occur. Is it possible to model rigorously complex systems in the absence of both strict experimental control and strict event-regularities to account for? Can we make a "science" out of imperfectly smart agents endowed with a range of discretionary free will, exploring their way into effectively infinite spaces of unknowable future outcomes where phenomena do not repeat with law-like regularity, and only partial event-regularities occur? Economic outcomes can never be accurately predicted. If you can never accurately predict, how can you have a science?

Scientists have only comparatively recently recognized that the goal of science is no longer accurate prediction, but increased comprehension and greater explanatory power.[67] Consider the science of meteorology. Like the meteorological universe the economic universe never settles down, and never precisely repeats itself. Within wide and variable bounds the weather is fluid and unpredictable. Meteorologists are unable to predict local weather events accurately more than a week in advance. But they are able to understand *ex post* most meteorological phenomena: the formation of weather fronts, jet streams, high and low pressure systems, and to explain how they dynamically interact to produce weather on a local and regional scale. What they are unable to do is to predict the future.

Unlike economists, meteorologists now understand why they cannot precisely predict future weather conditions. They have explicitly recognized that the weather must be modeled as a complex fluid system extremely sensitive to initial conditions, whose future behavior can never be precisely known in advance. Meteorologists now model the weather as a nonlinear system whose future behavior may be simulated but not "solved for."

Chaos theory has revealed many extremely complicated phenomena can be outcomes of extremely simple nonlinear systems.[68] Complex systems must be modeled with nonlinear equations, implying sensitive dependence on initial conditions, self-organization, critical states and all characteristics of complex systems that render accurate prediction impossible. Precise prediction is impossible for any complex system. But a "science" of meteorology exists independent of meteorologists' ability to predict future weather outcomes. Storms are like earthquakes. Meteorologists can never accurately forecast the occurrence of meteorological phenomena. But the goal of science is the greater understanding of complex phenomena which for many policy purposes is sufficient.

It is difficult and may prove impossible to rank complex systems in a cardinal manner. Nevertheless the social universe may be loosely termed more complex than the physical universe, since its agents are not homogeneous molecules but sentient and heterogeneous agents, endowed with intelligence, memory, self-consciousness, and most importantly within a circumscribed area free will, and with it the freedom to fail or to succeed. Each agent bases its behavior on its attempts to anticipate the behavior of others in a world where successful predictive ability is nonexistent. The group behavior of social systems is more time-dependent than most physical systems, and cannot be summarized in terms of stable *ex post* probability distributions.

Process analysis takes the existing position of variables as historically predetermined and attempts to explain their ordinal change over time. To analyze complex systems all variables and their interrelationships must be dated. Only ordinal changes (positive or negative, greater or less) can be explained due to the sensitivity of complex systems to initial conditions. Complex systems differ greatly in the chronological period over which changes occur. They may be loosely characterized as fast- or slow-changing systems. With fast-changing systems, jumps occur, and wide bounds must be imposed on predictions of cardinal changes for even the shortest of short runs.

The goal of the analysis of complex systems is to build dynamic models to explain changes (first differences) in selected variables over the short run. The detailed modeling of macro-system behavior is beyond our capabilities. Economists are unlikely to ever be able to precisely simulate the behavior of economies. Process analysis abstains from all attempts to impose future outcomes, destinations, or "centers of gravity."[69] Errors in forecasting increase exponentially as the time period is extended into the future. Formal modeling will remain unable to predict long-run economic behavior. All that can be attempted for long-run analysis is the exploration of alternative "scenarios." One must beware of all linear explanations of complex events.[70] In contrast to mainstream analysis, which attempts to model final "equilibrium" positions in logical time, process analysis models the short-run change in economic variables and makes no attempt to impose any "final" outcome.

Process analysis examines the manner by which economic variables change ordinally from their current value, taken as historically determined, to their value in the subsequent period. All variables are dated, and the concept of "equilibrium" is abandoned. For most variables only ordinal explanations and forecasts can be given. Distributions continually change over time and it is not possible to assign quantitative probabilities to summarize the uncertainty, The prices of many variables, for example equities and foreign exchange rates under flexible exchange rate regimes, change continuously whenever markets are open. For some financial variables markets are continually open in some part of the world. In this case it is impossible to precisely forecast even short-run ordinal changes. To the extent all variables and markets are interrelated for most variables short-run cardinal prediction is beyond our grasp.

Meteorologists now understand why they are unable to forecast the weather more than a few hours in advance. Complex systems exhibit sensitive dependence on initial conditions, called "the butterfly effect." Although real world economies are unimaginably complex, the first steps in computer simulation of simplified nonlinear models of real world markets and institutions exhibiting hysteresis and path-dependent dynamics of cumulative causation are now being explored. Once the profession fully recognizes that economies are complex systems, "history-creating" process analysis in real time will replace "equilibrium" analysis in logical time.[71]

Process analysis models the ordinal change of complex systems over calendar time without attempting to define any future "equilibrium" outcome. It attempts to explain why and how economic variables change from their current value to their value in the subsequent period. Different systems differ enormously in the speed in which they vary over time. For fast-changing variables such as equities, foreign exchange, and all homogeneous financial assets traded in well-organized markets, prices change and even "jump," whenever the market is open. For such variables even ordinal forecasts over very short periods are unlikely to be accurate. Prices of heterogeneous assets and commodities are slow-changing variables. In markets where prices change more slowly, accurate short-run ordinal and even cardinal forecasts are sometimes possible.[72]

Part II
Some Thoughts on Economic Data and National Income Accounting

Part II
Some Thoughts on Economic Data and National Income Accounting

6
Sorites' Paradox: the "Looseness" of Economic Concepts[1]

> We have to admit that there are lots of problems in the "utility" criterion of welfare that we economists love so well. Maybe utility comes from relative position, so universal progress is not possible. Maybe a lot of what we treat as final utility producing goods is instrumental, but we can't subtract them as intermediate or regrettably necessary. Fuel and utility bills? Soap? Warm clothes? On the other hand, the idea that there is no utility to work is probably wrong. As professors know, some work is fun. People do get satisfaction out of doing something well and being so perceived.
>
> James Tobin, in Eisner, 1989: 392

> We have sought to justify our economic concepts in terms of considerations that are appropriate to the natural sciences; not observing that what economics tries to do ... is essentially different.
>
> John Hicks, 1981

> Not everything that counts can be counted, and not everything that can be counted counts.
>
> Albert Einstein

6.1 The importance of quantification

How close an empirical grasp can economics get of the complex phenomena constituting the "economy"? Two separate questions may be distinguished:

1. How closely can economic theory capture underlying economic reality?
2. How closely can theoretical concepts be proxied by empirical measures?

The first question has been addressed in Part I, where the futility of attempting to analyze complex dynamic systems with comparative static equilibrium analysis has been emphasized, and the case made for process analysis. This chapter considers the second question. It will be argued that all economic concepts are intrinsically "loose." In the construction of empirical approximations to theoretical concepts economists never know precisely where to draw the line. Due to the continuously distributed nature of economic phenomena, all empirical approximation to the theoretical concepts is inherently arbitrary. Different types of phenomena are quantifiable to different degrees of accuracy and many are nonquantifiable.[2]

Quantification of empirical observations is the prerequisite for the scientific method. Only when sense observations lead to quantifiable data can the accuracy of empirical observations be verified, and the theoretical explanations offered be subjected to empirical refutation. There is nothing unique in the inherent nature of economic behavior that permits economics alone out of all the social sciences to be able to analyze its subject matter rigorously using the scientific method. Economics is unique only because market phenomena can be quantified in terms of prices and quantities. But the simplicity of the numbers that measure economic quantities is highly misleading, since the complexity of the underlying phenomena is disguised. Most central economic phenomena are essentially unquantifiable, for example, the utility agents receive from consumption and economic activities, and agents' expectations of the unknowable future, termed by Keynes "animal spirits" to emphasize they could not be proxied by objective probability distributions.

Quantification is possible for economic phenomena only because markets assign prices and quantities to marketable goods and services. It is the existence of markets, and not any special characteristic of economic phenomena, that explains why economics has been the sole social science discipline able to develop a rigorous theoretical core.[3] The ability to quantify their subject matter has enabled economists to build sophisticated theoretical models of economic behavior, raised economics to the status of "queen" of the social sciences, and made economists the envy of other social scientists.[4]

6.2 Sorites' dilemma: "loose" concepts

Markets generate the prices and quantities that permit heterogeneous goods and services to be quantified and compared. The resulting numbers appear to be "hard," objective and cardinal. But although economic data lend themselves to rigorous mathematical analysis and manipulation, the data generated by the price system are in fact extremely "loose."[5] Due to the complex continuously distributed nature of underlying economic phenomena, the nonarbitrary definition and measurement of any particular economic concept is impossible. For most economic quantities the most quantification can achieve is an ordinal ranking.

Measurement in economics is bedeviled by Sorites' paradox: "How must we classify continuously distributed phenomena?" This paradox has been posed colorfully by historians of science: *"How many hairs are there on the head of a bald Irishman?"*[6] Zero, one, two, three, twenty, fifty, one hundred? All are true, since over a wide range one additional hair does not negate the state of baldness. But were we to conclude that an additional hair makes no difference we are led immediately into absurdity.

The reason for the "looseness" of economic data is at root very simple. Economies are complex systems, and economic behavior and commodities are also complex.

At the micro level most economic phenomena are both ephemeral and continuously distributed over different dimensions. Since they are continually changing they cannot be "captured" by static analysis. Where the precise boundary is drawn for the empirical proxy to any theoretical concept must be arbitrarily imposed. It is impossible to draw a nonarbitrary line between "economic" and "noneconomic" activity, or to distinguish nonarbitrarily between different categories of economic activity, market and nonmarket, consumption and investment, work and leisure, income and output.

It has become a commonplace in which economists delight that all social phenomena have an "economic dimension." But the obverse of this observation is not so celebrated. All "economic" phenomena slide imperceptibly at the margin into other economic and noneconomic phenomena. In economics all numerical measurements are "loose" and never precisely correspond to the underlying theoretical concept they purport to measure. The boundary of any empirical proxy to any theoretical concept must always be arbitrarily imposed. Economists have no choice but to make arbitrary judgments when devising empirical proxy measures for any theoretical concept. They are inevitably faced with the question: "Where should I draw the line?" In economics there is frequently no single "right" answer to this question.[7]

Consider any important macroeconomic magnitude: "consumption," "income," "wealth," "investment," the price level, the wage level, inflation, unemployment. It is a meaningful empirical statement that an individual or a country is "rich" or "poor" in an ordinal and in a cardinal sense. It may be possible to refute such statements empirically. But it is not possible either to specify nonarbitrarily the precise empirical items that constitute "wealth" or "income," or the precise characteristics that divide agents into different economic categories. We will never be able to formulate a nonarbitrary definition of "rich" or "poor." We can estimate the mean and the variance of observed empirical distributions, and we can calculate the degree of measurement error, covariance and Gini coefficient. But we can never match any empirical proxy precisely to its theoretical concept.

Unlike the subject matter of other social sciences which are near-exclusively concerned with unquantifiable phenomena, in economics numerical distributions of quantifiable phenomena are everywhere. All market phenomena are operationally quantifiable and so it superficially appears obvious that the scientific method can be applied to economic phenomena exactly as done in the natural sciences. But since economies are complex systems there is an irreducible range of ambiguity around the operational estimate of any theoretical magnitude in economics.

The impossibility of defining a nonarbitrary logical boundary around empirical concepts is easily demonstrated. Economic concepts are continuously distributed, as are height, weight, color and many other quantities. Where one draws the line in any continuous distribution is arbitrary. When phenomena are continuously distributed, even when they can be measured precisely like height and weight, the classification of the distribution into any set of analytical classes is necessarily arbitrary.

Since they have no analogy to markets on which heterogeneous phenomena can be valued and compared, other social sciences must attempt to analyze unquantifiable complex phenomena. They may be able to observe that agents are "happy" or "unhappy," "contented" or "sad," "powerful" or "powerless." Such statements have clear descriptive meanings. But since they refer to nonquantifiable subjective phenomena, there is no empirical operation by which they can be objectively measured and quantified. The degrees of "happiness" or "unhappiness," or "power" or "powerlessness" is nonmeasurable on any scale.

The problem for the other social sciences is not merely that it is impossible to set precise refutable empirical boundaries to be able nonarbitrarily to distinguish different numerical categories. Their difficulties are hugely compounded because in all disciplines where quantification is impossible, one cannot design any operation by which the "truth" value of any statement can be either scientifically established, or empirically refuted. So long as the behavior under observation cannot be operationally measured, it is not possible to construct empirically refutable propositions about such behavior.[8] When concepts and terms are subjective they are merely matters of opinion, tastes, conventions and persuasion, like wine-tasting and art appreciation.

Like all continuously distributed phenomena, economic concepts cannot be nonarbitrarily empirically classified. But unlike the subject matter of all other social sciences, and like the subject matter of the natural sciences, numerical measurements can be made of empirical proxies for theoretical economic concepts. Particular explanations of observations can be subjected to empirical refutation via the scientific method. Only to the extent economic variables are exchanged on a market can the relationships between prices and quantities be analyzed via the scientific method, even though there is no intrinsic difference between marketed and nonmarketed commodities.

There remains a substantial range of ambiguity and arbitrariness around the particular empirical measurement of any theoretical concept. Economic phenomena are continuously distributed and are not isomorphic with their theoretical counterparts. Different economists may have different definitions and different empirical estimates of the same concept. Who is to say whose definition is more correct?

6.3 Measurement in economics: "the excluded middle"

As a result of the distributed nature of their subject matter most economic concepts do not obey Aristotle's law of the excluded middle: "A must be either P or non-P." In economics there is always some middle ground, where A can be both. Most economic concepts lie in this gray area where A may be either P or non-P. Economic data *appear* cardinal, "hard," and amenable to the mathematical manipulation of addition, subtraction, multiplication, division, and power laws. But economists must explicitly acknowledge Sorites' dilemma.[9] For all economic phenomena there is an unbridgeable gap between the theoretical concepts, which denote a clearly defined homogeneous (black or white) category, and their empirical counterparts, which reflect the dynamically changing, heterogeneous and multi-dimensional grayness of the real world. When making empirical proxies of theoretical concepts, economists can never know precisely where to draw the line.

When observation produces data that can be quantified, the relationships can be described with precision and analyzed using statistical tools. The precision yielded by mathematics is indispensable for the application of the scientific method, or for any rigorous analysis. Nevertheless many distinguished economists have emphasized how mathematics is widely mishandled in economics.[10]

Mathematics encourages the mistaken belief that only quantifiable aspects of phenomena are important. The rest are regarded as of lesser importance and ignored. Another implication of mathematics is that it encourages analysts' temptation to believe that human behavior can be "optimized." Due to the ever-present temptation to equate "logical validity" with "truth," mathematics encourages a false sense of certainty. It is easy to confuse the correct deduction of logical conclusions with the correct solution of real world phenomena. Mathematics is not a perfect substitute for language and its precision leads users to attribute and endow analogous precision to the phenomena they analyze. Once defined, the meaning of a mathematical symbol is permanently fixed. In contrast words can flirt with meaning, and be ambiguous where the relationships described are not well defined or understood. Language is indefinitely richer in descriptive vocabulary than mathematics and is much more comprehensive, sensitive, and flexible in conveying meaning. The drawback is that words are much less precise than mathematical representation and cannot be mathematically manipulated.

Mathematics is inapplicable for all nonquantifiable phenomena. Statements about feelings, tastes, qualities, expectations, intuitions, suspicions, future phenomena or any other nonquantifiable phenomena cannot be nonarbitrarily translated into quantitative statistical probabilities. Some may even be untranslatable into other languages. The replacement of words by symbols and numbers offers the tantalizing promise of superior deeper insight into real world interdependence. Mathematics allows us to describe complex systems concisely as a set of algebraic equations. But this does not imply that the numbers that can be found empirically accurately represent the symbols, nor that the equations formulated accurately describe the complex systems to which they refer.[11] It is not solely the problem of the huge number of equations that must be solved. The insuperable obstacle to mathematical quantification is that it is impossible to formulate nonarbritrarily objective probability distributions of unknown future events and agents' future reactions to them.[12] All complex systems are non-ergodic and their probability distributions as well as the inprobability outcomes are time-dependent:

> Underlying much of the practice of modern economics is the premise that the properties of the mathematical symbols used in models are isomorphic with the empirical relations they purport to represent; the belief that the two complex structures—the model and the reality to which it refers—can be mapped onto each other in such a way that to each significant part of one structure, there is

a corresponding part of the other, and each has the same functional role in their respective structures.[13]

The assumption that data and models are isomorphic is acceptable in physics solely because of the way physics is defined. Physics studies *only* phenomena that can be represented and analyzed mathematically, since physics defines itself as:

> The science devoted to discovering, developing and refining those aspects of reality that are amenable to mathematical analysis.[14]

In social sciences the relationships between the theoretical model and the empirical observations must be examined on a case-by-case basis. Isomorphism cannot be tacitly accepted. The greatest difficulty that economists face in the transition from theory to practice is the shift from the precise, well-defined and homogeneous concepts of logical and mathematical theory, to the heterogeneous, recalcitrant, nonlinear, distributed, fuzzy, and multidimensional complexity of empirical reality. The properties of complex systems make crystal clear that due to their "sensitive dependence on initial conditions," future behavior can never be accurately predicted from past observations. With the exception of astronomy, where the changes that continuously occur are extremely slow-moving, no scientific discipline can predict future events consistently and successfully outside of laboratory conditions.[15] System prediction is impossible, so the methodology of positivism collapses for the study of complex systems.[16]

6.4 The measurement and quantification of economic concepts

The conception of many economists that economics is (or should be) a science comparable to physics leads them to expect that economics should in principle be able to explain economic reality with the same precision that physics has demonstrated in explaining phenomena in the physical universe. In economics much more prestige is acquired in applying dazzling mathematical and statistical techniques to bad or indifferent data than in arriving at useful and valid results using low-tech descriptive or accounting reasoning. Due to the high prestige of mathematics in economics, there is an unconscious tendency to believe that mathematical rigor requires utmost precision in the numbers used. Quantification is the indispensable prerequisite for scientific analysis. But different aspects of reality are accurately describable within widely different margins of precision. Modern economists quite properly insist on the quantifiability of their variables. But they overlook the need to recognize and estimate the different degrees of precision attainable for different economic concepts.

There is unanimous agreement on the need to present the margin of error in econometric analysis. Sampling errors are regularly estimated and explicitly presented in empirical economic papers. But little or no attention is paid to formally assessing the different quality of different data sets. The different degrees of accuracy characterizing different time series are not explicitly acknowledged. Most economists regard the numerical measurement of different data series as if all were equally accurate or inaccurate.

Errors in parameters do not derive primarily from errors in measurement, even though these errors may sometimes be very important. They derive primarily from errors in how measured events are classified. Unlike accountants, who readily admit that their conventions are an imperfect and imprecise art, most economic theorists do not appreciate the degree of judgment that has entered into the classification of economic data. They tend to take all economic data at face value. Mainstream economists evade the deeper problems raised by complexity theory and fundamental uncertainty by proceeding as if the future could be represented as objective quantitative probability distributions, assuming that such distributions remain constant and imagining that future events are predictable from past observations with some given standard of error.

All market phenomena can be quantified into prices and quantities on a cardinal scale. But any such classification is arbitrary. The numbers generated appear "hard" and "objective" as numbers always do, and to lend themselves to rigorous mathematical manipulation. But for all economic concepts precision of measurement is impossible. For economic magnitudes the most that can be hoped for is a loose ordinal ranking. For many even an ordinal ranking is beyond our reach.[17]

"Economic" and "noneconomic" phenomena are distributed continuously over many different dimensions. Any precise boundary of an empirical approximation to a theoretical economic concept is necessarily arbitrarily imposed. As a result the numerical measurement constructed to describe any economic phenomena is necessarily "loose." The empirical proxies never correspond precisely to the economic concept they purport to measure. We are perpetually faced by the question: "Where must we draw the line?" Unfortunately the line is written in sand and our answers are arbitrary. The indefiniteness of individual commodities, and the inexactness of classes create "loose" concepts. Whenever data are continuously distributed we are unable nonarbitrarily to define the empirical boundary of economic concepts.

Unlike the subject matter of other social sciences, which are concerned with intrinsically nonquantifiable phenomena such as influence, power, character and values, markets generate empirically quantifiable prices and quantities. Market phenomena are numerical. It appears obvious that the scientific method can be applied to the study of economic phenomena as in the case of the natural sciences. The main difference is believed to be the absence of laboratories in economics to undertake controlled experiments. But the most important reason why it is not possible to conduct controlled experiments is because the most important variables' expectations cannot be quantified or held constant. Most economic phenomena are continuously distributed. There is always an irreducible range of ambiguity surrounding the operational proxy for all economic concepts.

In the physical sciences it seems reasonable to presume there exists some "true" objective value of the phenomena we are trying to measure. The average of the distribution generated by careful and repeated empirical measurement will approximate this "true" value. The data cluster around some central value with measurable objective error. Since absolutely precise empirical measurement of any quantity is not possible, scientific practice reports the results of all empirical measurements within standard margins of error.

In all theoretical systems the basic unit of analysis is the individual entity. This unit may be indivisible into parts, or may loose its individuality when divided and the parts separated. In economics, entities are households, consumers, firms, commodities, and markets. In theory the individual household or firm appears to be definite, homogeneous and given, sharply distinguishable from its background and from other individual units in space and time. But how is a family or firm defined? The precise empirical definition of an individual unit is always arbitrary. One may have no doubt whether a particular entity refers to an individual unit or a group. But doubt enters as soon as the heterogeneity of space and time dimensions are introduced.[18]

6.5 The mismeasurement of National Income

National Income Accounting provides an excellent illustration of the problems raised by Sorites' dilemma. Where should the dividing line be drawn between economic and noneconomic activity, or between consumption and investment? Theoretical concepts are impossible to precisely proxy empirically. Is the purchase of a house or a car consumption or investment? The correct answer is, it is both. But where must we draw the line? In economics we can never exactly know. Our attempt to classify complex distributed phenomena into homogeneous theoretical classes has been termed "stylized facts."[19] But in reality all "facts" in economics are "stylized."

It is impossible to define "income," "output," or any other economic concept with precision. In the National Income Accounts, Gross Domestic Product is defined as the value of all final goods and services purchased for consumption. Consumption is regarded as the penultimate ingredient of economic well-being, ignoring the value of all capital created for producing consumption and investment goods in the future. But market and nonmarket phenomena, like economic and noneconomic behavior merge imperceptibly into the other. It is operationally impossible to impose a nonarbitrary line between market and nonmarket or economic and noneconomic activity. Any dividing line drawn is arbitrary. The formulation of empirical proxies for economic concepts involves issues of judgment on which reasonable people have widely different opinions.

The construction of a National Accounting System must address the central issues categorized below:[20] As will be shown at the limit each must be arbitrarily defined.

1. The definition of final output and the production boundary.
2. The distinction between final and intermediate output.
3. The distinction between consumption and investment.
4. The appropriate valuation of production.

6.5.1 The definition of final output and the production boundary

What constitutes "economic output"? How must one draw the line between "economic" and "noneconomic" activity? The US Bureau of Economic Analysis (BEA) states. "The basic criterion used for distinguishing an activity as economic production is whether it is reflected in the sales and purchase transactions of the market economy."[21]

Simon Kuznets, the father of National Income Accounting, offered a more encompassing and deeper guide to the definition of final product:

> Final goals are provision of goods to ultimate consumers, the living members of society, and net additions to capital stock relevant to ultimate consumption current and future.[22]

Market transactions form the core of economic measurement and analysis. Markets generate prices that determine the relative value of different commodities, and enable intrinsically different and fundamentally incommensurate goods to be compared. But all accounting rules must in practice be qualified.

An important exception to the rule of including all final market transactions is the exclusion of all illegal transactions: drug trafficking, prostitution, gambling. In the United States these activities are currently valued at billions of dollars. There is no purely economic reason why illegal activities should be excluded from output. The reasons for their exclusion are political, ethical, and pragmatic. The pragmatic reason is perhaps most relevant. Since illegal transactions are never reported, governments have no official data on illegal transactions, An even larger proportion of legal transactions are either not reported or under-reported for the purpose of avoiding taxation, the "Informal" (Grey, Shadow, Unofficial, Subterranean) economy.

The informal economy is intrinsically hard to observe and measure, since it is untaxed and most activities are unrecorded. There are two basic approaches. One could ask people how much of their income and tax liabilities they refrain from reporting, or one could look at the results of spot tax audits. But people are unlikely to confess to breaking the law and tax inspectors do not check a random sample of the population. As a result the second method based on indirect detective work is preferred. One can compare data on cash transactions or on electricity or concrete consumption with official output figures, even though these are not proportionally related to income. If the use of cash or electricity or cement is growing faster than the measured economy, this indicates that the informal share of total activity is rising.

Using such techniques it has been estimated that in the year 2000 the informal sector on average was equivalent to 41 percent of the official GDP of developing countries.[23] In Zimbabwe the figure was 60 percent. In Brazil, Turkey, and South Africa about half of all nonfarm workers were in the informal sector.[24] The more complicated and more progressive taxes and regulations, the larger will be the informal sector as a share of GDP.[25] The informal sector is positively correlated with both the level of income inequality and the inflation rate, and is an index of the degree of alienation and social breakdown. It has recently been discovered that one cost for having a large grey economy is lower average productivity in the total economy. Gray firms tend to be micro-enterprises and want to stay that way lest they come to the attention of the tax authorities. Their small size limits their ability to participate in economies of scale and to make the most of new technology.[26]

Nonmarket output is an even larger proportion of GDP. This includes all economic activity performed in the home and all charity work done without compensation and leads to many well-known anomalies.[27] GDP is defined as final production for the market valued at market prices. National income is defined as the financial remuneration of the factors of production of that product. When we exclude production, we also exclude income earned.

The difficulty caused by the exclusion of non-market output is not solely that a large and variable proportion of total economic output is excluded thus reducing GDP. Inter-temporal and international comparisons are vitiated. The "true" availability of goods and services in less developed economies where much larger proportion is produced in the home is much closer to the level in developed economies than it appears in official accounts, which include only market activities. The rate of growth of total output is similarly exaggerated by ignoring nonmarket activities. With the expansion of market activities the accompanying reduction of nonmarket production is typically ignored.

6.5.2 The distinction between final and intermediate output

The issue of "double-counting" is central to National Income Accounting. It is resolved by restricting the measure of output to "final" product, defined as purchases of goods and services that are not resold and excluding all "intermediate" goods. For households and governments not in the business of reselling what they buy, all "personal consumption expenditures" and all "government purchases of goods and services" are considered "final." But for the business sector, final product is confined to purchases on capital account, defined as all reproducible assets lasting more than one year. Since measurement of the duration of services is arbitrary, investment services have conventionally been excluded from the National Accounts. Until recently the only business expenditures on current account that are included in GDP are changes in inventories, which are defined as investment.[28] All other goods and services purchased by business are considered nonfinal current expenditure.[29]

The lifetime of one year used to define capital assets is purely an arbitrary convention. If it were decreased or extended, recorded purchases on capital account would expand or contract. As the time unit defining capital goods is contracted towards zero, more intermediate goods are classified as final investment goods and measured GDP expands. Since estimated depreciation expands commensurately, estimates of net investment and net domestic product remain unaffected.

One implication of the "one year" definitional requirement for "capital goods" is that only investment "goods" are considered to the investment. Since it is impossible to estimate nonarbitrarily the expected lifetime of investment services, all investment services are excluded. When a business buys a computer this is considered an investment. When it purchases computer software this is considered a current expense. The exclusion of investment services is growing in importance as the share of services in GDP increases, biasing the rate of growth and the level of GDP downwards.[30] In the United States the increasingly serious underestimation of the contribution of computers was recently (November 1999) addressed by a comprehensive revision of the official National Income Accounts. This resulted in a substantial revision of productivity and growth figures.[31]

The identification of all government services expenditure as final product and all goods and services purchased by business as intermediate product, raises a host of anomalies and inconsistencies.[32] Most government activity is devoted to the provision of intermediate goods: direct services to business, and maintenance of the market system and infrastructure essential to private production.[33] Simon Kuznets strongly criticized the conventional classification of government provision for including:

> guns, planes, ships, roads, public buildings, judicial, legislative, and administrative services ... How much of all this is the cost of maintaining the social fabric, a precondition for net product rather than net product itself?[34] ...
>
> Only those parts of government activities of direct welfare to individuals as individuals (education, health services, and the like) can be considered as yielding net product.[35]

There is a very strong logical case for considering a substantial proportion of government output as "intermediate" and not "final" goods. The same argument can be applied to national defense expenditures. However necessary they may be judged national defense services are intermediate in character (apart from any satisfaction given to those who love military parades, or glory in arms displays). Logic is not the sole consideration behind the National Accounts. In most countries the elimination of defense spending from GDP would be politically unacceptable.[36] NIPA definitions make measures of final output subject to institutional arrangements limiting the validity of international and inter-temporal comparisons.[37]

The NIPA includes a number of "imputations" for goods and services not produced for market.[38] The largest relates to the value of rental services on owner-occupied homes (7 percent of GDP). Services furnished without payment by financial institutions are not insubstantial (2 percent of GDP). The comparable market transaction is easily available for both such imputations.[39]

Most nonmarket services are excluded in the National Accounts. But nonmarket household activity has some market counterpart. Estimates of the total value of nonmarket household output are enormous, as high as one-third of GDP.[40] The great bulk of government services are not produced for the market but distributed to the population without charge. In the National Accounts the value of government output is counted on the basis of the cost of market inputs of labor services. Since it ignores inputs for the services of capital and land its value is understated.

6.5.3 The distinction between consumption and investment

The broad importance attached by economic theory to investment contrasts sharply with the narrowness of the definition of investment in the NIPA. In the NIPA Gross Investment is denoted as, "Gross Private Domestic Investment," the sum of business expenditure on plant, equipment and inventories, the purchase of residences by households; plus "Net Foreign Investment."[41] The latter does not constitute physical investment in tangible assets as in the case of domestic investment. It is simply net claims on foreigners resulting from the excess of exports of goods and services over the value of imports, payments to foreigners in the form of government interest, and net transfers by persons and governments.

In the United States NIPA "investment" excludes all acquisition of tangible or physical capital by households with the exception of expenditures on houses.[42] The acquisition of intangible capital and all types of investment services by all sectors of the economy are excluded. Research and development expenditures by business are treated as intermediate products. Government expenditures for research are buried in, "Government purchases of goods and services." A strong case can easily be made that research and development expenditures represent a greater investment in future output than most expenditures formally considered in "Gross Investment."

Why should the vast amount spent on education, training and health, let alone on the raising of our children who create the human capital on which our future depends, not be treated as investment? Is it meaningful to say that "the U.S. is lagging far behind other nations in investment" when in the United States all expenditures on R&D, education, government capital, and household durables, which form a higher proportion than in most other countries are excluded from investment in the National Accounts? Does a country's capital investment decline when private capital formation shifts from business spending on plant and equipment to household spending on education and business spending on research?[43]

The theoretical interest in investment stems from its direct joint relation to both aggregate supply and to aggregate demand. Net investment when financed by borrowing represents the growth of aggregate demand and of capital which is an important variable in production and so aggregate supply. A more inclusive view of investment than the conventional definition of Gross Investment in the NIPA would clearly appear to be appropriate. But the question remains where should we draw the line, and when market transactions are not available, how should investment be valued?[44]

Natural resourses raise additional difficulties of their own. Economic activity that increases the value of land and natural resources could be viewed as investment. Investment might include all additions to the value of land and all changes in the value of natural resources as well as all real capital gains in physical assets.[45] Intangible investment may be characterized as all expenditure on services that make a contribution to future output. A more comprehensive measure of investment would more accurately indicate the proportion of output going to present and to future consumption. This would better explain productivity growth and better inform both the public and policymakers on the allocation between goods to this generation and the next.

A number of difficult conceptual and empirical problems arise in estimating investment in human capital.[46] Should we measure investment in education by the market costs of schooling, or by the discounted present value of future earnings? Should we include the (substantial) opportunity cost of the time of students, who if not in school would presumably be involved in market output? A considerable part of educational experience can be viewed as consumption. At least to some of the students, some of the time, school is fun. How do we determine what proportion of total education costs should be allocated to consumption and what proportion to investment?[47]

Similar difficult issues relate to health expenditures. What proportion should be viewed as maintenance and what proportion as investment? Another difficult question is what proportion of health expenditure contributes to productivity, and what proportion to a general improvement in the quality of life?[48]

6.5.4 The valuation of production

The market value of assets changes quite apart from investment expenditures and depreciation due to changes in asset prices. These changes stem from changes in expected future values of income, and changes in discount rates, risk, technology, exports, and exchange rates with other countries. The value of current assets changes inversely with changes in interest rates with no change in the expected future income stream from the capital goods. One kind of capital may change in value at the expense of another—for example, tangible as against intangible and human capital.[49] Changes in the terms of trade can hugely affect the aggregate value of a nation's capital and are frequently of much greater value than changes due to investment.

Asset valuations reflect the current market prices of tangible and financial assets and liabilities, including land and natural resources. Capital gains from asset revaluations represent additional purchasing power to asset owners, may be used to finance expenditure, and so constitute part of income, saving, and capital accumulation. In the treatment of reproducible tangible assets it is possible to rely on "replacement costs," based on the prices of the flows of current output. Appropriate price deflators must be applied to asset values to convert nominal to real capital gains.

The inclusion of net asset revaluations in measures of income and product entails a significant departure from conventional accounts. The latter focus solely on the direct output of current productive activity. Asset revaluations show sharp year-to-year variations, so it may be appropriate to separate capital gain income from other categories of income for certain kinds of analysis. For some purposes it may be appropriate to utilize measures that exclude revaluations. But where the focus is on saving and the accumulation of capital it proves seriously distorting to ignore them.[50]

144 *Shaking the Invisible Hand*

6.6 Eisner's total incomes system of accounts

Different economists have suggested different modifications to the conventional accounts. Some involve primarily the rearrangement of items in conventional NIPAs, but most modifications substantially affect the recorded levels of National Income and Output. Attempts have been made to account for "disamenities" of urban life, pollution, and the using up of natural resources. Terms of trade adjustments have been calculated for real GDP, to take account of changes in the relative price of imports and exports. The value of the increases in leisure time due to the shorter work week have also been included.[51]

Estimates of the value of leisure are acutely sensitive to the choice of the deflator for wages which carries with it implicit assumptions of the growth in the "productivity" of leisure. Calculation of investment in human capital is usually made on a cost basis as in conventional measures of investment of physical capital by business. But efforts have also been made to estimate the value of investment in human capital in terms of its presumed effect on the present value of expected income. These differ widely and it is by no means an obvious choice which concept is more appropriate.[52] Should housework be evaluated at what a household member could earn on the market, or what must be paid in the market for someone to do the housework?[53] It is difficult to see how quality differences in services performed can be held constant since the two are clearly different? The numbers in the National Income Accounts depend critically on judgmental questions about where to draw the line. As will be shown although each appear to be small judgmental issues on which reasonable people can differ, the total differences in the various account totals are nothing short of astonishing.

Robert Eisner undertook the Herculean attempt to implement many of the above extensions in his Total Incomes System of Accounts (TISA). Eisner calculated his revised estimates for total income and product for the United States in current dollars for all years from 1946 to 1981. He included income corresponding to all market and nonmarket economic activity, and compared them with the BEA totals. The differences in the different accounts were astonishing.[54]

Eisner's revised estimates of total product included such major items of nonmarket product as the services of government, household capital, unpaid household labor and the opportunity costs of students' time. He classified government services of national defense, roads, and police as intermediate goods. Some portion of commercial media services of television, radio, newspapers and magazines was counted as final product. Expenses related to work were subtracted from income and product, and the value of employee training and human capital formation were included. Output was valued as the value of all factor services from which it flows.

Eisner's TISA vastly increased total measured capital accumulation. His investment included in addition to BEA gross capital formation: the addition to inventories by government and government enterprises, the acquisition of durable goods and additions to inventories by households, and net investment in intangible capital reflecting expenditures on education, vocational training, research and development and improved health. In Eisner's revised TISA Gross Domestic Capital Formation amounted to 37 percent of GDP, more than double BEA's estimate of 16.1 percent. His Net Domestic Capital Formation was larger by a factor of 4 than BEA's estimate of Net private domestic investment.

The TISA reflects a substantial inclusion of nonmarket output of nonbusiness sectors, so the household share is greatly expanded. Households and nonprofit institutions accounted for only 3.3 percent of GNP in BEA while they accounted for 40 percent of GNP in the TISA accounts.[55] The biggest single items in TISA household income were imputations for unpaid household work ($981 billion) and opportunity costs of students' education ($284 billion). In the BEA accounts business accounted for 85 percent of GNP while in TISA the business share was less than 50 percent. The great bulk of TISA capital formation was intangible capital formation outside of the business sector. Consumption in the TISA grew one-third less rapidly than capital accumulation. This calls into question the repeated assertion that saving and investment rates in the United States are "too low" by both historical and international standards.

Some of the TISA imputations, for example estimated income on household and government capital and the value of nonmarket labor are necessarily speculative. In contrast market transactions which form the core of conventional accounts are exact where sufficient data is available. When no market transactions are available, as in capital consumption estimates in the conventional accounts and in the imputations for nonmarket income and product in the extended accounts, confidence in the estimated quantities is reduced. The tradeoff which can never be answered definitively is how much should be sacrificed in greater numerical accuracy in the interest of greater relevance? The question is again "Where should we draw the line?"

The gain from TISA is vastly increased comprehensiveness, essential to better understand and explain economic behavior. TISA makes clear that measurable investment activity is much greater than revealed in the conventional BEA accounts. The TISA estimates suggest extreme caution in theorizing about investment and consumption behavior from conventional BEA National Income concepts and data. BEA accounts exclude from investment most business and household expenditures for intangible capital formation, nonmarket income, and capital gains and losses on real and financial assets.

A few ambitious scholars have had the temerity and industry to develop alternative systems of extended national income and product accounts. Tables 6.1–6.4 summarize how these various alternative extended accounting systems compare to official BEA magnitudes.[56]

Nordhaus and Tobin imputed estimated income to government and household investment services, nonmarket work, and the value of leisure. They also eliminated a class of output classified as "regrettables and intermediate." As shown in Table 6.4, due primarily to their opportunity cost value of leisure their Measure of Economic Welfare (MEW) index was larger than BEA GNP by a factor of 2.7 and grew at about one-third lower annual real rate, 2.1 percent for the period 1947–65 compared with 3.7 percent for BEA.

Table 6.1 Consumption and tangible and intangible domestic investment as percent of BEA GNP

Account	Year	Consumption	Gross investment		
			Total	Tangible	Intangible
Nordhaus–Tobin, MEW	1965[a]	99.8[b]	38.9	—	—
Zolotas, EAW	1965	73.3[b]	—	—	—
Jorgenson–Fraumeni	1966	65.7[c]	290.1	27.8[d]	262.3[e]
Kendrick (1976)	1966	63.8[f]	66.1	39.8[g]	26.3[h]
Ruggles and Ruggles (1970, 1973)	1966	78.0	40.8	30.4	10.4
Eisner, TISA	1966	98.1	64.3	37.6	26.7
BEA	1966	61.5	16.6	16.6	0

Notes:
[a] 1958 prices.
[b] Excluding imputed values of leisure.
[c] Excluding value of time spent in non-market household production and leisure.
[d] Nonhuman investment.
[e] Human investment, tangible and intangible.
[f] 87.7 percent if value of non-market household labor, reported in Kendrick (1979) is included in consumption.
[g] Human and nonhuman; 32.2 percent excluding human tangible.
[h] 33.6 percent if human tangible is included.
Source: R. Eisner, *TOTAL INCOMES SYSTEMS OF ACCOUNTS*, 1989, table E.16, p. 122.

Table 6.2 Gross and Net Domestic Capital Formation as percent of BEA Gross and Net Private Domestic Investment and of own gross and net aggregates

Measure	Year	Percent of BEA		Percent of own aggregate	
		Gross	Net	Gross	Net
Nordhaus–Tobin, MEW	1929	194.6	−2.9	14.5	−1.0
Jorgenson–Fraumeni	1949	2,164.4	4,651.7	62.3	58.5
	1966	1,705.4	2,958.9	62.1	58.0
	1982	1,919.6	10,671.5	59.0	52.0
Kendrick (1976)	1929	339.1	306.7	43.1	21.5
	1949	371.9	279.7	41.4	17.2
	1966	385.5	361.6	50.5	31.6
Ruggles and Ruggles, IEA	1969	193.1	181.5	27.8	14.5
	1980	166.5	139.5	24.5	7.7
Eisner, TISA	1949	394.6	310.8	32.0	12.4
	1966	387.0	374.2	39.4	24.5
	1969	421.0	444.5	40.5	25.0
	1981	382.6	478.7	38.9	19.5
BEA	1929	100.0	100.0	15.7	6.9
	1949	100.0	100.0	13.7	5.7
	1966	100.0	100.0	16.6	9.4
	1969	100.0	100.0	15.8	8.0
	1981	100.0	100.0	16.1	5.5

Source: R. Eisner, *TOTAL INCOMES SYSTEM OF ACCOUNTS*, 1989, table E.17, p. 123.

Table 6.3 Household and government capital services, household labor services and property, and labor incomes as percent of BEA GNP

Account	Year	HHCS	GCS	HLS	Property income	Labor income
Nordhaus–Tobin, MEW	1965[a]	10.1	2.7	47.8	—	—
Zolotas, EWA	1965[b]	3.7	—	26.9	—	—
Jorgenson–Fraumeni	1966	—	—	—	33.9	429.3
Kendrick (1974)	1966	10.2	—	23.9	26.0	98.3
Ruggles and Ruggles	1966	12.6	3.0	—	24.3	63.0
Eisner, TISA	1966	11.9	7.0	35.4	25.6	102.2
BEA	1966	5.4[c]	0	0.5[d]	24.3	82.6

Notes:
HHCS = household capital services.
GCS = government capital services.
HLS = household labor services.
[a] 1958 dollars.
[b] 1972 dollars.
[c] Space rent of owner-occupied nonfarm dwellings.
[d] Compensation of employees in households.
Source: R. Eisner, *TOTAL INCOMES SYSTEMS OF ACCOUNTS*, 1989, table E.18, p. 124.

Real growth rates depend critically on the underlying price deflators. Since the real income is constructed by deflating nominal income, an upward bias in the price index results in a downward bias in real income which over time can cumulate to huge differences. Zolotas constructed an expanded measure of national income that he termed Economic Aspects of Welfare (EAW). His assumptions for constructing EAW were broadly similiar to Nordhaus and Tobin's MEW. As shown in Table 6.4 the ratio of EAW to BEA GNP was higher by up to 1.5 and the estimated growth rate was about one-third lower, 1.9 percent for the period 1965–77 compared with 2.8 percent for BEA.

Jorgenson, Kendrick, Richard and Nancy Ruggles and Eisner estimated a variety of alternative expanded income and product accounts. A major extension common to all (except the Ruggles') was the imputation of income and output for the non-market sector. Kendrick and Eisner imputed the opportunity costs of students' time at school. All included the services of household durables in consumption. All offered a broader measure of investment activity and included investment in intangible and human capital. Most calculated imputations for the estimated value of leisure. Nordhaus and Tobin, Zolotas, and Eisner subtracted large portions of government output categorized as "regrettables." Ruggles, Jorgenson, and Eisner highlighted the quantitative significance of including capital gain revaluations of existing assets and liabilities.

Table 6.1 summarizes how the extended alternative measures of consumption, investment and government expenditures differed from the level and composition in the BEA Accounts. The lowest estimate of the share of consumption in income was the BEA share of 61 percent of GNP. The Ruggles and Jorgenson share of consumption was 65–78 percent of BEA GNP, while for Nordhaus–Tobin and Eisner

Table 6.4 Aggregates in relation to BEA GNP and rates of growth

	Year	Ratio BEA/GNP	Years	Average annual percent growth ($)	
				Current	Constant
Nordhaus–Tobin, MEW-S[a]	1929	2.67	1929–47		2.57
	1965	2.01	1947–65		2.07
Zolotas, EAW[a]	1950	1.49	1950–65		2.37
	1965	1.22	1965–77		1.92
	1977	1.02			
Jorgenson–Fraumeni, Gross private domestic product	1948	4.50	1948–66	6.34	
	1966	4.68	1966–76	8.27	
	1981	4.74[b]	1966–81	9.62	
Kendrick (1979), GNP, adjusted	1929	1.54	1929–48	5.15	1.40[c]
	1948	1.59	1948–66	6.12	2.32[c]
	1966	1.59	1966–73	8.60	2.66[c]
	1973	1.64			
Ruggles and Ruggles, IEA, GNP	1969	1.12	1969–80[m]	9.65	2.76
	1980	1.15	1969–80[t]	9.78	3.14
Eisner, TISA, GNP minus net revaluations	1946	1.75	1946–66	6.26	2.79
	1966	1.63	1966–76	8.60	2.47
	1981	1.60	1966–81	9.34	2.52
BEA, GNP			1929–48	4.95	2.33
			1946–66	6.60	3.68
			1966–76	8.56	2.80
			1966–81	9.51	2.91

Notes:
[a] Constant dollars.
[b] Ratio of BEA *private* GNP in 1982 was 5.44.
[c] Gross National Income.
[m] Market transactions only.
[t] Total GNP.
Source: R. Eisner, TOTAL INCOMES SYSTEMS OF ACCOUNTS, 1989, table E.19, p. 125.

the consumption share was 100 percent of BEA GNP. It seems clear that the official BEA accounts underestimate total consumption spending. The expanded gross investment measures point to a considerably larger role for investment as a whole, and in particular a much greater role for intangible investment than the BEA. The various measures of investment exhibit even larger variations. By far the lowest gross investment share was the BEA estimate of 17 percent of BEA GDP. The investment share was about 40 percent of BEA GNP for Nordhaus–Tobin and Ruggles, about 65 percent for Eisner and Kendrick, and an astonishing 290 percent of BEA GNP for Jorgenson due to his inclusion of intangible investment including investment in human capital.

Table 6.2 reveals that the estimates of Gross and Net Domestic Capital Formation varied by proportions upto 10,000 percent of BEA values. As a percent of their own estimated GDP, which gives a better indication of proportions, investment varied from the BEA's estimate of 16 percent of GDP, to Ruggles 25 percent, Eisner's

40 percent, Kendrick's 50 percent, and Jorgensen's 62 percent. These extended estimates all agree that the share of investment in GDP is substantially higher than recorded in the BEA accounts. They also indicate a much smaller role for tangible business investment on which most attention is conventionally focused.

Table 6.3 reveals the extent labor's share of income is significantly expanded in the accounts of Jorgensen, Kendrick, and Eisner. Estimates of the value of nonmarket household labor services vary from 24 to 48 percent of BEA GNP. The expanded accounts collectively suggest a smaller role for business in economic activity and a much expanded role for households compared to BEA figures. They suggest a much larger role of intangible investment in education and health associated with the activity of households and governments. The magnitude of the estimated incomes aggregates in the different accounts exhibit enormous variation due to differences in both concepts and methodology.

Table 6.4 shows Nordhaus and Tobin's estimate of MEW is more than double BEA GNP, while Jorgenson's estimate is more than four times BEA GNP due to their inclusion of an opportunity-cost evaluation for leisure. The other estimates of GDP are all larger by 10–70 percent. The extended accounts similarly exhibit from one-half to two-thirds lower average rates of growth of revised real National Product over the postwar periods considered, 1929–47–65–77–81. Calculations of the real growth rates are particularly sensitive to the deflation procedures adopted.

The point of the above comparisons was simply to illustrate that because economic phenomena are continuously distributed, different classifications of the empirical counterparts to theoretical concepts calculated by different scholars show enormous variability. Careful scholars, making reasonable and eminently defendable decisions, produce estimates that can differ by astonishing orders of magnitude with respect to the level, composition and rate of growth of macroeconomic variables. As shown in Table 6.4 the different estimates of GDP differ not only by a few percentage points, but by 100s of percent. Some estimates of GDP were more than 4 times the official BEA amounts.

Another area where there are extremely wide differences in National Income estimates concern international comparisons of the GDP of different countries using different currencies. Traditionally countries' GDPs have been at official exchange rates, so as to express all countries GDP in terms of US dollars for purposes of comparison. But nontradables are typically 60–70 percent of GDP, and prices of nontradables in less developed economies are much lower than in more developed economies. As a result using official exchange rates hugely raises the inequality in international per capita GDP comparisons. There are truly enormous differences between real GDP calculated using purchasing power prices and official exchange rates. Real GDP of countries like China and India rise dramatically when calculated using purchasing power conversion. Whose and which estimate is more correct?[57]

No one would deny that the classification of economic magnitudes involves huge judgmental components, reflecting at root Sorites' dilemma "where must we draw the line"? Empirical research requires strong taxonomic and evaluative powers. Above all it requires a level of "sitz" power not teachable in graduate school and much less highly prized than "intellectual-muzzle-velocity" intelligence. Scholars such as Kuznets, Kendrick, Eisner, and Lebergott are highly esteemed in the profession. But although universally recognized as extremely valuable and even as constituting the life-blood of the profession, their work is viewed by most economists as deadly dull. Economists do not have laboratories and have little or no taxonomic training. The unrewarding task of empirical data collection and analysis (data grubbing) lies far from most economists' ideal. In most developing countries the figures produced by government statistical offices are highly questionable.

6.7 Unemployment, price levels, inflation rates, and growth rates

6.7.1 Unemployment

The state of being employed or unemployed is another area where Sorites' paradox applies. The state of being unemployed has two dimensions: a worker must be both without a paid job, and be actively seeking work. The second attribute, though much more difficult to define is equally important as the first. Most people who do not have a paid job, full time housewives, children, the old, the sick, the physically and mentally impaired, are officially considered not in the labor force.

The key phrase in the unemployment definition is "actively seeking work." How "active" must one define "actively"? Many workers without a job have given up looking for work. They may be discouraged by a long period of unsuccessfully work seeking and believe from past experience that there are no jobs to be found. But if they were offered a job they would take it, the so-called discouraged worker phenomenon. How many times per week must someone look to be included in the labor force? In many economies the inclusion of discouraged workers more than doubles the formal unemployment rate.[58] It is not possible to draw any precise line to measure the "true" amount of unemployment. In developing economies a large share of the labor force is in the "informal sector," made up of micro-enterprises, self-employment, family businesses, relatives, and paid employees. Their individual total sales revenues are so small that their incomes do not fall into any tax category and do not show up in the government's statistics.

6.7.2 The price level and the inflation rate

The price level is the weighted average of the prices of individual goods, where the weights are the relative quantities consumed. The goods chosen and their weights assigned vary with the particular price index. For the CPI the weights are the quantities of goods purchased in the market basket of the typical consumer. For the GDP deflator the weights are the quantities of all the goods and services produced in current output.

There many reasons why inflation rates are systematically overestimated by government census-takers.[59] There are literally millions of different types of goods and services available in modern economies. New products are being created all the time, existing ones are being improved, and others are leaving the market. In the United States the Bureau of Labor Statistics (BLS) collects monthly and bimonthly price quotations on 70,000 goods and services, at more than 20,000 retail outlets. But as the BLS has noted, it is extremely difficult to quantify "what's new in surgery this month."[60]

When a new product comes along that does not fit into an existing category, it is characteristically a decade or more before it is introduced into the CPI. The automobile was not introduced into the CPI until 1935, VCRs in 1987, and cellular phones in 1998. Demand is increasingly shifting to services where measurement of quality change is most difficult. Most goods and services are heterogeneous and their attributes can be measured over many dimensions. In the presence of rapid technological change in services, it is extremely difficult to separate the rates at which their quality and quantity is changing. This creates insuperable challenges for government statisticians. For durable goods quality changes must be measured in terms of the services provided, rather than in terms of physical changes in the good itself.

In the United States in 1998 the Boskin Commission divided up the CPI into 27 categories, and developed separate estimates of the quality change bias for each category. It estimated the total upward bias for the CPI inflation for the period 1995–96 was 1.2 percent, with a plausibility range between 0.80 and 1.80 percent.[61] In the case of services calculation of the rate of quality change was particularly difficult to estimate, and for many services the bias was impossible to measure. The fact that the share of services in GDP is increasing secularly, and now exceeds 60 percent in developed economies suggests that future estimates of GDP will become increasingly more imprecise. An increasing proportion of goods are sold through special sales promotions, discount houses and the internet at prices substantially below the list prices used by government enumerators. Enumerators collect prices during the week, and miss weekend sales prices. The Boskin Commission estimated that such factors alone give an upward bias to the inflation rate of 0.4 percent.

There is also the bias associated with the well-known index number problem. Laspeyres and Paasche indices have a reverse bias which the Fisher Ideal index attempts to ameliorate by taking the geometric mean of the two. The Boskin Commission estimated annual bias could be as high as 3.0 percent for medical and hospital services and 6.0 percent for appliances and electronic goods. It concluded,

> the major increase in longevity ... perhaps swamps everything else. ... our estimate of the current bias in the CPI is, ... probably seriously understated.[62]

There are many additional reasons why official estimates of the inflation rate will be biased upwards.[63] Individually the bias is typically small but it cumulates to a substantial proportion. Such bias contaminates all official estimates of the real growth of output, productivity, and wages.[64] Real income cannot be estimated directly, but must be calculated by first estimating nominal income, and then deflating the nominal values by a price index to put them in real terms. A bias of 1–2 percent in calculating the inflation rate sounds like a modest amount. No one would claim that GDP estimates are perfect. But when the inflation rate is being over-estimated by 1–2 percent a year, the error in real income growth can rapidly cumulate.[65] For example if the rate of growth of real income and real wages are underestimated by 2 percent per year, over a 20-year period this cumulates to an underestimation of more than one half the "true" growth rate of real income and real wages.

6.7.3 Global inequality of income: increasing or decreasing?

Is global inequality increasing or decreasing? This apparently straightforward question turns out to be much harder to answer than one might suppose. There are three broad areas of difficulty:

1. Measuring what people consume, especially the poorest people in the poorest developing countries.
2. Deciding what is the best way to value consumption to enable the most useful comparisons across countries and over time.
3. Determining what is the most appropriate basis of comparison? For example, is it more important whether inequality is widening among nations, or among all the individual people of the world regardless of the country they live in?

This third point deserves to be emphasized at the outset. Suppose that inequality were worsening across countries, that is, the gap between average incomes in the richest and poorest countries is widening. Also suppose that inequality was becoming more unequal within every individual country. Given that cross-country inequality is widening, and within country inequality is also increasing, it would surely seem to follow that global inequality measured across the world's individuals is also rising. Well, not necessarily. Even if the first two assumptions were true, global inequality measured across all the world's individuals could well be falling. How so?

Simply add a third assumption: a very few poor countries, which accounting for a large share of all the world's poor people, have been growing very rapidly, for example, China and India. Inequality could then be increasing within every country including China and India, and the gap between the very poorest countries (sub-Saharan Africa) and the richest countries (Europe and the United States) could also be increasing. Yet inequality measured across all the individuals in the world could be falling since average incomes in the two most populous poor countries were rising rapidly. Average incomes in China and India have in fact been growing at extremely rapid rates.

Suppose all the individual countries were ranked as scatter points on a diagram, with GDP per head in 1980 measured on the horizontal axis and growth in real per capita GDP from 1980–2000 on the vertical axis. If per capita incomes in poor countries were growing faster than per capita incomes in rich countries, the scatter points would follow a downward-sloping relationship. One could validly conclude that the poorer countries were catching up. But for the 20-year period 1980–2000 if such a scatter diagram is constructed the line of best fit slopes upwards. This implies that the richer countries have been growing more rapidly and the poorer countries have been falling behind. Can one conclude that cross-country inequality is increasing?[66]

Suppose that instead of dots, countries are represented as circles drawn in proportion to their population. India and China stand out by virtue of their vast populations, and since their growth record has been so much better than the poor country average. The population-weighted line-of-best-fit will slope downwards, implying both convergence and narrowing inequality. Once the rapid growth of China and India have been taken into account, together with the fact that these two countries account for such a huge share of the world's poor it is difficult to remain pessimistic about increasing global trends in inequality.

But the above discussion says nothing about poverty as such. Poverty is a relative concept and the data contain no information on how poverty is defined, how many people in any country are poor, or whether growth in a country is good for the poor people living there. The definition of a "poverty line" depends critically on the country one is considering. Ten thousand dollars a year may represent poverty in America, but riches beyond most families wildest dreams in China and India. One never knows where to draw the line.

Suppose one arbitrarily assumes that a household that earns less than $1 dollar a day (or $2 dollars a day) is poor, in any country. There is an important additional issue. Is it better to measure consumption using data drawn from National Income Accounts, or from data drawn from Household Surveys? Both levels of consumption and growth in consumption differ persistently according to which data source is used. The two sources differ systematically and by a wide margin. National Income Accounts give a much more optimistic view of growth rates and trends in poverty than do Household Survey data.[67]

When poverty is measured by the proportion of the population living on less than $1 a day, or $2 a day (inflation adjusted) using National Income Accounts data the proportion of the world's people living on less than $1 per day fell from 17 percent in 1970 to 7 percent in 1998, and the proportion living on less then $2 dollars a day fell from 41 percent to 19 percent.[68] Using an absolute headcount, the number of people on less than $1 a day fell by 200 million and on the count of less than $2 a day fell by 350 million in the same period. If these numbers are true the UN's 2000 Millennium Development Goal on poverty, to bring the number of people living on less than a dollar a day by 2015 to one half the number in 1990, has already been achieved!

But calculations based on World Bank estimates based on direct surveys of households show very little reduction in poverty. Chen and Ravallion of the World Bank put the proportion of the population living on less than $1 a day at 28 percent in 1987 (far higher than Sala-i-Martin's calculations), and in 1998 an only slightly lower 24 percent.[69] These huge differences in estimates are due to several factors. The World Bank attempts to measure "consumption poverty" as opposed to "income poverty." To the extent people manage to save, their consumption will be less than their income, so there will be more poor people on the Bank's definition. The Bank bases their estimates on specially designed Household

Surveys, rather than on National Income Account data. Using Survey data average growth in per capita consumption was less than 1 percent a year between 1987 and 1998, compared to more than 3 percent per year in the National Accounts. As Deaton very cautiously concluded,

> If the surveys are right there has been less growth in the world in the 1990's than we are used to thinking.[70]

The truth about global poverty presumably lies somewhere between the extremes suggested by the two methodologies. But combining them properly raises a host of extremely difficult technical issues.[71] One could perhaps conclude that the official World Bank data are too pessimistic on trends in poverty, and the truth is likely to be better than their figures indicate.[72]

6.8 Conclusions: where must we draw the line?

Quantification of the subject matter is a necessary precondition for any discipline to become a science. It is solely the existence of markets that permits prices and quantities of economic goods and services to be numerically measured. Such economic numbers appear to be hard, and to lend themselves to precise mathematical manipulation. Nevertheless due to the inherent complexity of economic phenomena the quantities recorded as proxies for most economic concepts are in fact extremely "loose." It is never possible to know precisely where to draw the line.

Estimates of the level of national income and output and their components and distribution by different scholars vary by hundreds of percentages. Estimates of their growth rate vary by even or greater proportional orders of magnitude. Our ability to measure the empirical proxy for theoretical economic concepts is subject to critical pragmatic and conceptual constraints. In a complex world no economic concept can be precisely quantified.

The message of this chapter is not that economic measurement should be de-emphasized. It is rather the reverse. The attempt to sharpen conceptualization and measurement must be pursued even more intensively. Only through empirical measurement can the different stories that economists tell be compared and tested against the real world.

But economists must stop deceiving themselves about the "scientific" status of their discipline. The behavior and phenomena that lie behind the reported numerical prices and quantities are indefinitely complex. Economists are not only unable to count or foretell the future. They are unable to count or fully understand the present or the past. There is still debate about the causes of the Great Depression. Our quantitative estimates of all economic phenomena are surrounded by a huge penumbra of ignorance and judgment. The notion that we are able to quantify economic variables within one decimal point is simply derisory.

Economists must explicitly acknowledge that economies are complex adaptive systems. They must abandon all attempts to formulate "equilibrium" growth models whose solutions purport to identify a "balanced" future path toward which economic agents or markets or systems are "tending." Economists must content themselves with refining process analysis, developing new nonlinear tools for analyzing complex nonlinear systems and simulating economic behavior to better understand the dynamics by which complex systems evolve. Economists' ability to forecast future events has been enormously oversold, both to the public and to the profession itself. Economics as a discipline should become much more modest in its pronouncements, because, in the immortal words of Sir Winston Churchill, "We have so very much to be modest about."

7
Saving is the Accounting Record of Investment

> In real life research is dependent on the human capacity for making predictions that are wrong, and on the even more human gift for bouncing back to try again. This is the way the work goes. The predictions, especially the really important ones that turn out, from time to time, to be correct, are pure guesses. Error is the mode. ... We all know this in our bones, whether engaged in science or in the ordinary business of life.
>
> Lewis Thomas, 1983: 82

> The accounting identities equating aggregate expenditures to production and of both to incomes at market prices are inescapable, no matter which variety of Keynesian or classical economics you espouse. I tell students that respect for identities is the first piece of wisdom that distinguishes economists from others who expiate on economics. The second? ... Identities say nothing about causation.
>
> James Tobin, 1997: 300

> The extent to which one sees one's destination before one discovers the route is the most obscure problem of all in the psychology of original work. ... It is the destination which one sees first, [though] a good many of the destinations so seen turn out to be mirages.
>
> John Maynard Keynes, Moggridge, 1992: 552

7.1 Volitional and non-volitional saving

Economists have long viewed saving and investment as independent behavioral relationships undertaken by households, firms, and governments. Business firms, the administrators of the economy's capital stock, are responsible for most investment spending. Households, the ultimate owners of the economy's private net worth, undertake most of the economy's saving. Governments tax and spend. They save by running a budget surplus and not spending all their income. But saving and investment are identical *ex post* as a national income identity. The unresolved question concerns the mechanism that brings these two allegedly independent volitional magnitudes into *ex post* equality?

The dilemma has conventionally been resolved by distinguishing *ex ante* (planned) saving and investment, which are not identical, from *ex post* saving and investment, which represent the definitional accounting identity. Classical and neoclassical economists have long regarded saving and investment *ex ante* as equilibrated in the market for loanable funds. Like commodities the supply and demand for funds were believed to be equilibrated by changes in their market price, which in the case of saving and investment is expressed as a rate of interest. Both saving and investment were regarded as the sum of the volitional decisions of individual savers and investors.

Keynes strongly disagreed with the neoclassical theory of interest. He argued that saving and investment were equilibrated by changes in the level of income and output, not by changes in interest rates. He argued an excess of planned investment over planned saving would cause aggregate demand (AD) to rise, and an excess of planned saving over planned investment would cause AD to fall. The level of income would continue to adjust until in equilibrium *planned* saving was equal to *planned* investment. The postwar "neoclassical synthesis" of IS-LM analysis combined both positions, and argued that in General Equilibrium (GE) both interest rates and income adjust to equilibrate saving and investment.

In the conventional mainstream view, saving establishes the physical limit of the resources available for investment. The Competitiveness Policy Council expresses this position clearly:

> Economic theory teaches us that the allocation of a nation's resources between consumption and investment is determined by saving. In practical terms, private individuals decide how much of their income to save rather than consume; private businesses decide how much of their earnings to retain rather than pay out as dividends; and governments decide how much to spend and tax, with government surpluses augmenting and government deficits diminishing the saving done in the private sector.[1]

Many mainstream economists would argue that so long as unemployed resources of labor and capital exist, the expansionary Keynesian investment-led multiplier-accelerator process will raise AD. But as the economy reaches its full employment potential it is believed that saving reestablishes the physical constraints on investment, so the logic of a saving-constrained expansion prevails in the long run. Mainstream economists hold low-saving ratios responsible for low rates of capital formation and low rates of growth for the economy. In response a host of policy measures have been proposed and enacted to increase public and private savings rates and encourage "domestic resource mobilization." Summers well-characterizes the mainstream view:

> It is widely recognized that low national saving is the most serious problem facing the U.S. economy. Low saving accounted for the trade deficit and the slow growth in standards of living that continued through the 1980s. Part of the reason for low national saving is the excessive federal deficit. But the low U.S.

saving rate is increasingly the result of insufficient personal saving by U.S. households.[2]

Post Keynesian critics of mainstream theory argue that saving, the difference between income and consumption, is determined by investment at all levels of income less than full employment. The difficult question then becomes how to determine when the economy reaches full employment. The argument tends to deteriorate into technical questions about how "saving" and "full employment" should be defined.[3] Tobin has argued:

> Experience recommends an eclectic view to which Keynes himself and even Pigou ... subscribed. Sometimes economies are in one regime, sometimes in the other. That leaves plenty of room for debate about their relative frequencies and for diagnosing which is the effective constraint at any particular time.[4]

The saving rate plays the central role in all equilibrium growth models by determining the economy's "natural" rate of growth. In a much-cited 1980 study Feldstein and Horioka found very high correlation between domestic saving and domestic investment for the industrialized OECD countries. They reasoned that if international capital markets were perfect, when domestic saving was added to a world saving pool and investment competed for funds in that same pool, there should be little or no correlation between a country's saving rate and investment rate. They interpreted their findings as evidence of the existence of severe imperfections in international capital markets.[5]

The core proposition that delineates the heterodox Post Keynesian view from mainstream views concerns the direction of the causal process by which saving and investment are equated.[6] Mainstream economists accept the classical position that economies are saving-constrained. Many would concede that over the short run movements in economic activity are dominated by movements in investment spending and AD. But over the longer run they believe the direction of causality is from saving to investment.[7] Saving is necessary to provide the resources for investment and so the constraining factor determining the rate of economic growth.[8] "The trend movement [in output] is predominantly driven by the supply side of the economy."[9]

Post Keynesians maintain in contrast that capitalist economies are always demand-constrained, and the direction of causation runs from investment to saving. The future is strictly unknowable and investment expenditures are shaped by investors' "animal spirits." The Keynesian argument is that by increasing AD investment creates the saving necessary to finance itself.[10] Output is viewed as demand-led and a unique long-run equilibrium "natural" growth path no longer exists.

Both the mainstream and its critics accept the National Income Accounting definition that saving is identical to investment *ex post*. Both agree on the desirability of increased saving for more rapid growth.[11] But they disagree strongly about policy. Mainstream economists put forward a set of supply-side policy recommendations, designed to stimulate additional saving and investment and lead to an expansion of aggregate supply (AS). Scarcity is viewed as the core economic constraint. Market economies are assumed to be supply-constrained and to operate near their production possibility frontiers.

In contrast Post Keynesians espouse a set of demand-side policy recommendations, designed to stimulate additional consumption and investment spending and expand AD. They maintain policy measures should be undertaken to raise the saving ratio only after full employment has been attained. Post Keynesians view insufficient demand as the central economic constraint. Market economies operate inside their production possibility frontier and are always demand-constrained.[12]

Both the mainstream and their critics agree saving and investment are independent behavioral relationships *ex ante*. This chapter demonstrates that since total saving is the accounting record of investment, investment is not determined by units' volitional savings. Saving is always identical to investment *ex post*, as an accounting identity. Since S and I are definitional identities the direction of causality between S and I cannot be determined by empirical analysis. An alternative explanation of the dynamic process of how saving, investment, and income are interrelated over real (historical) time must be developed.[13] This chapter addresses the causal relationship between saving and investment. It argues the true nature of the relationship between saving and investment has not as yet been grasped. Introspection and intuition to the contrary, aggregate saving is not as it appears to individual savers determined by the sum of volitional saving behavior. Saving is the accounting record of investment.

7.2 Saving is identical to investment

In a simple one-sector model it is trivial to demonstrate that aggregate saving is the accounting record of investment. But it will be demonstrated that so long as *capital budgeting is consistently carried out* this identity is maintained in all multi-sector models. The underlying ground for this position may be shown very simply as follows: All goods may be characterized as consumption goods, with an expected lifetime of less than one year, and investment goods, with an expected lifetime of more than one year. Consumption and investment exhaust the National Product. There are no other kinds of goods.

Once saving is recognized as the accounting record of investment it is no longer surprising that S and I are extremely highly correlated. If there were no accounting and measurement errors, as an accounting identity the two would be identical in all economies, no matter how simple or complicated the accounting. As the accounting record of investment a change in saving can never be the "cause" of a change in investment, no matter how high the correlation between S and I. The accounting identity that saving is identical to investment holds continually, however close or far away the economy is to its "full" employment ceiling.

The belief that aggregate saving is the sum of volitional saving decisions by individual economic units is simply a spectacular macroeconomic illustration of the "fallacy of composition." This fallacy has been reinforced by the unfortunate use of the colloquial verb "to save," with its very powerful transitive volitional connotations, for an economic term which is merely an intransitive accounting definition: "income not consumed." As economists know, it is a "fallacy of composition" that what is true for the part is necessarily also true for the whole. Total "saving" is the sum of total saving undertaken by individual "savers." But since saving is the accounting record of investment it cannot be the sum of volitional individual saving decisions. Aggregate saving is not the sum of individual savers volitional decisions to save. It follows that in all monetary economies most "saving" is "non-volitional."[15]

There are several ways of demonstrating that aggregate saving, defined as "income not consumed," is simply the accounting record of aggregate investment. First consider the familiar textbook demonstration why saving and investment are identical. In a simple one-sector model with no government or international trade, nominal income (Y) is defined as equal to the total value of final currently produced consumption (C) and investment (I) goods measured at current market prices.

$$Y \equiv C + I \tag{7.1}$$

This definition of consumption and investment is exhaustive. There is no additional third category of goods. All economic goods currently produced are either consumption or investment goods, even though as shown in the previous chapter it is never possible to know precisely where to draw the line.

Nominal saving (S) is defined as equal to all income not consumed:

$$S \equiv Y - C \tag{7.2}$$

Keynes (mistakenly) argued that a "fundamental psychological law" linked consumption spending with income earned, which can be expressed as a behavioral relationship termed the "consumption function." Equation 7.2 looks superficially like a saving function and is frequently so denoted in the textbooks.[16] But equation. 7.2 can be rearranged into a third identity, which simply states that all income is either consumed or saved:

$$Y \equiv C + S \tag{7.2a}$$

Equation 7.2a is another definitional identity. It no more implies the existence of a behavioral relationship between saving and income than equation 7.1 implies a behavioral relation between consumption and income. Equation 7.1 defines income measured as a flow of output, as the sum of consumption and investment goods. Equation 7.2a defines income measured as a flow of income, as the sum of consumption and saving. Equating 7.1 and 7.2a, saving is identical to investment.

$$S \equiv I \tag{7.3}$$

The above is the argument presented in all the textbooks. But its implications have not yet been fully grasped. It is universally recognized that $S \equiv I$ *ex post*. But in the internal paradigm of most economists and as explicitly categorized in many textbooks, *ex post* is interpreted as designating past events. *It is not explicitly recognized that* ex post *comprises the PRESENT as well as the past.*[17]

Equation 7.3 is simply an accounting identity. Saving is always identical to investment, irrespective of the time unit or the time period over which they are measured, or of how investment is defined. If investment is highly volatile over time, so is saving. It follows that for the economy as a whole there is no volitional behavioral "savings" relationship.[18]

The two saving identities, equation 7.2, saving is identical to income not consumed ($S \equiv Y - C$), and equation 7.3, saving is identical to investment ($S \equiv I$), logically imply that whenever the definition of income, consumption, or investment are changed so is "saving," without any volitional or even conscious behavior on the part of savers.[19] On purely pragmatic grounds due to the impossibility of precisely defining the relevant time period for services as described in the previous chapter, in the United States and in many other countries NIPA conventions arbitrarily exclude expenditures on services, training, and education as investment, since the time period of most services has to be arbitrarily imposed. In consequence NIPA methodology substantially underestimates the "true" amount of investment activity undertaken.[20]

Suppose in the attempt to better explain productivity growth investment expenditures were to be defined more inclusively, to include all expenditures on investment services and on human capital.[21] As shown in Chapter 6 recorded "investment" would increase substantially. Recorded "saving" also increases by an identical amount without any volitional decision on the part of savers. Saving is equal to investment as an accounting identity, so the quantity of saving changes whenever investment is redefined. Suppose that the price of investment goods were to fall relative to consumption goods, and real investment increases. Real saving would increase by the same amount, in the complete absence of any change in volitional saving behavior.[22]

Suppose saving were to be defined as what it is: net wealth accumulation, rather than what it is not: income not consumed. If income is not spent on consumption goods it must necessarily be spent on or held in the form of nonconsumption goods. When individuals "save" their net worth ownership increases. So long as all asset prices remain constant saving may be defined as the change in the unit's net worth. But when asset prices change, wealth owners receive capital gains and losses. Only if these capital gains are included in the definition of income can saving be defined as "income not consumed" and as "net wealth accumulation" measured in current prices.[23]

When saving is defined as the change in net worth, it can very easily be seen to be simply the accounting record of investment. From the National Balance Sheet the total wealth in an economy consists of all financial and tangible assets. Financial assets (IOUs) are the accounting record of the existing claims of creditor units against debtor units. Under double-entry bookkeeping, for every financial asset outstanding there is an identical financial liability. Apart from differences in valuation for the economy as a whole total financial assets (excluding equities) must equal total financial liabilities and so cancel out.[24] The Balance Sheet accounting identity holds in first differences as well for totals. The fact that saving is the accounting record of investment then becomes immediately obvious from the National Balance Sheet identity.

NATIONAL BALANCE SHEET

Δ Financial Assets XX	Δ Financial Liabilities XX
Δ Tangible Assets XX	Δ Net Worth XX
(Investment)	(Saving)

The total value of financial assets and the net change in financial assets are necessarily equal to the value of total financial liabilities and the net change in financial liabilities, since IOUs must necessarily sum to zero. The change in tangible assets is the definition of net investment and net worth is the definition of net saving. But how net worth is calculated depends on how assets are valued, whether at historical cost or at current market value. Saving changes both with changes in the volume of investment, and with changes in how investment is defined.[25] As the accounting record of total investment total saving is necessarily equal to net investment. As such total saving is not determined by the volitional behavior of savers but is largely non-volitional.[26]

Saving is the accounting record of investment. But if total measured saving were always identical to total measured investment this simple accounting identity would not have remained quasi-unrecognized by the profession for more than half a century. Even economists are not so obtuse. There are several powerfully extenuating reasons for the present unsatisfactory state of National Income Accounting, having to do primarily with the politicized nature of government statistics.

7.3 Widening the model: the government sector

One reason why saving and investment have not been recognized to be a simple accounting identity is because when the government sector and the rest-of-the-world sector are added to the model, the National Income Accounts have conventionally not been correctly extended. Current and capital transactions for the government and import sector have not been consistently distinguished as is done in the household and business sector. Due primarily to sloppy accounting procedures, it appears that the identity of saving and investment in multi-sector models no longer holds.

Total, private, public, and foreign saving are conventionally presented in macro-economic textbooks as follows:

$$Y \equiv C + I + G + X \text{ and} \qquad (7.4)$$
$$Y \equiv C + S + T + M \qquad (7.5)$$

Equating rhs it follows that:

$$I + G + X \equiv S + T + M \quad \text{or} \tag{7.6}$$
$$(I - S) + (G - T) + (X - M) \equiv 0 \quad \text{or} \tag{7.7}$$
$$(S - I) \equiv (G - T) + (X - M) \tag{7.8}$$

where G = Government spending, T = Government tax receipts, X = Exports, M = Imports.

From equation 7.8 private saving and investment differ by the size of the government deficit or surplus (G − T) plus the current account deficit or surplus (X − M). In multi-sector models it thus appears to be the case that private saving will be equal to private investment only if both the government sector runs a balanced budget (G = T) and the current account is also balanced (M = X). Since governments never exactly balance their budgets, and countries never exactly balance their current accounts private saving is never identical to private investment in the conventional NIAs. Whenever the government runs a budget deficit and the economy concurrently has a deficit on current account (the "twin deficit" problem as it was frequently termed in the United States), the inequality between the two can become substantial. It is then an easy reach for conservative politicians and mainstream economists to exclaim: *"government deficits are crowding out private saving."*

But capital budgeting must be applied consistently, not only to the government sector as the United Nations has long recommended, but also to the foreign sector which appears to have been completely overlooked. Current and capital components of income, consumption, investment, saving, government expenditures, and imports must be defined consistently. In the ROW accounts GNP must be replaced by GDP to designate the product of a particular geographic area. Once these changes have been made, saving becomes the accounting record of investment no matter how the model is extended, nor how many sectors are included.

7.3.1 Capital budgeting for the government sector[27]

Consider the government sector in isolation. Under the conventional National Income accounting, saving appears to differ from investment by the size of the government's deficit or surplus:

$$I - S \equiv (T - G) \tag{7.9}$$

But for consistent capital budgeting consumption and investment spending must be systematically distinguished in the government sector as is done in the private sector:

$$(I \equiv I_p + I_g), (S \equiv S_p + S_g), (C \equiv C_p + C_g), (G \equiv I_g + C_g), (S_g \equiv T - C_g)[28] \tag{7.10}$$

So long as capital budgeting is done consistently government saving becomes the accounting record of government investment, irrespective of how government spending is financed or the size of the government budget deficit. Distinguishing government consumption and capital expenditure and rewriting, equation 7.9 becomes:

$$I \equiv Ip + Ig \equiv S \equiv Sp + Sg \equiv Sp + (T - Cg) \tag{7.11}$$

Government saving is no longer the excess of total tax receipts over total expenditures. Government saving is the excess of total tax receipts over total government spending on consumption goods. Suppose at one extreme government tax receipts were equal to government consumption spending, so the government budget was balanced on current account $[(T - Cg) = 0]$. In this case all government investment is externally financed by borrowing. Government saving is then zero, and all saving is undertaken by the private sector. Total saving remains the accounting record of total investment:

$$I \equiv Ip + Ig \equiv Sp \equiv S \tag{7.12}$$

Conversely suppose at the other extreme government tax receipts equal total government spending, so the government budget is balanced on capital account $(T = Cg + Ig)$. All government investment is financed internally by government saving. Government borrowing is then zero, and private saving finances private investment. Total saving remains the accounting record of total investment.

$$S \equiv Sp + Sg \equiv Ip + Ig \equiv I \tag{7.13}$$

7.4 Words and terms: "saving" in economics is intransitive

A more insidious reason why the profession has failed to recognize that "saving" is simply the accounting record of investment is the unfortunate choice of the common verb *"to save,"* with its robust colloquial *transitive* meanings to designate an economic term that is an *intransitive accounting definition*. The result is perhaps the most damaging fallacy of composition ever to have confounded macroeconomics.

Since capital gains and losses are not included in the accounting definition of National Income, saving cannot be defined as what it is intended to be, the addition to the agents' net worth, unless all asset prices remain constant or unless wealth is valued at historical cost and not at current market prices. For this reason Keynes was forced to define saving somewhat clumsily what it was not, "income not consumed."[29] Keynes' definition of saving was not immediately unanimously accepted. Although now largely unread, a large economic literature appeared in the 1930s on the identity between saving and investment. This literature for the most part accepted the linguistic presumption that saving and investment were separate behavioral and volitional relationships and attempted to puzzle out and describe the manner how and why they were brought into equality.[30]

Economists have continued more or less unquestioningly to construe saving in the colloquial sense as an independent transitive behavioral relationship, and simply assumed saving was undertaken volitionally by different individual units. The colloquial meaning of the verb "*to save*" denotes a host of meanings, all except one pertaining to *transitive volitional individual behavior*. The confusion has been caused by the use of the verb "to save" with its strong transitive, volitional, behavioral overtones for an economic term that is intransitive and simply denotes an *accounting identity*.

Webster's Collegiate Dictionary lists 4 broad different meanings of the verb "to save" with 12 distinct sub-connotations:

1. TO SAVE
    (a) to deliver from sin.
    (b) to rescue or deliver from danger or harm.
    (c) to preserve or guard from injury.
2. TO AVOID
    (a) to make unnecessary.
    (b) to keep from being lost to an opponent.
    (c) to prevent an opponent from scoring or winning.
3. TO ACCUMULATE
    (a) to put aside a store or reserve.
    (b) to spend less ~, to economize, to abstain.
4. TO PRESERVE
    (a) to rescue or to deliver someone.
    (b) to put aside money.
    (c) to avoid unnecessary waste or expense.
    (d) to spend less money.

Note that each of the above meanings except 3(b) to spend less, to economize, to abstain refers to volitional action. With the sole exception of 3(b), each is deeply transitive. One always saves, avoids, accumulates, or preserves "something." When used in its colloquial sense it appears self-evident that saving "governs" investment. If investment demand is to be effective, it must somehow be financed. In order to be able to finance investment expenditures, economic units must *first* save and abstain from consumption. Since the term "save" is used in and implies two quite different meanings the problem is falsely posed. The confusion stems from the misleading association of the verb "to save," which in economics denotes an accounting identity which applies collectively to an economy with no implication of volition, with the common verb "to save," with the identical appellation but which applies to individual behavior, and is accompanied by a host of strong *volitional* and colloquial associations and overtones.

"Saving" defined as "income not consumed" appears superficially loosely equivalent to two of the four colloquial meanings of the verb "to save," "to accumulate," and "to preserve."[31] For individuals, saving appears to denote volitional and transitive actions. Its meaning superficially appears to be synonymous with to save or to spend less. Both can refer either to individuals or to the collective action of groups. But on reflection there is a subtle difference: "To accumulate" and "To preserve" are transitive. "To spend less" is intransitive.

Saving is regarded as "abstention from consumption." The dictionary defines "to abstain" as "to refrain deliberately, with an effort of self-denial from an action or practice." Economists have unfortunately retained this deliberative volitional meaning when thinking about saving. In its colloquial use "to save" applies to individuals' volitional actions. It is an extremely short logical step to associate the *volitional* meaning of "saving," "to accumulate"; with the *non-volitional* accounting identity, "to spend less than total income on consumption." But this association constitutes a serious error in logic that has had extremely deleterious consequences for the analysis of "saving" in macroeconomics.

The common sense conclusion appears to be:

(a) individuals volitionally decide on the amount they wish to save, and
(b) aggregate saving can be regarded as the sum of independent behavioral saving.

But this represents the fallacy of composition. What is true for the individual is not true for the group.[32] "Saving" is defined in macroeconomics as an accounting relationship, which may, but need not represent volitional behavior. Since "saving" is defined as the accounting *record* of investment it cannot logically be regarded as also the "*cause*" of investment.[33]

There is an important exception to the above statement, which has served to further add to the confusion. Changes in household saving when directed to the accumulation of previously produced and nonproducible financial or tangible assets, result in inverse changes in AD. Whenever such changes in AD have not been completely anticipated by firms, which in a complex world is typically the case, they "cause" (are responsible for) unintended changes in inventory accumulation and decumulation. The latter are recorded as changes in net investment and saving in the National Accounts. As a result it is correct to regard *unanticipated changes in business inventories (investment) as "caused" by unanticipated changes in household saving*.[34]

In overdraft systems unintended increases in business inventories are typically automatically financed by additional bank credit. They are also offset by firms as soon as they are perceived by volitional reductions in output as firms attempt to adjust inventories to their desired target ratio to sales. Only business *volitional* saving, representing the *planned* internal finance of planned investment projects constitutes the accounting record of volitional business changes in capital formation.[35]

So long as investment and saving are viewed as independent behavioral relationships, students and scholars alike are presented with an insuperable difficulty in comprehending how and why savings are always identical to investment. In modern economies "saving" and "investment" have now become increasingly specialized activities and are performed by very different economic groups. Unless planned saving and planned investment was exchanged as a market transaction so prices and/or incomes change instantaneously, how can the equality between saving and investment be continuously maintained?

The answer is that if saving and investment were indeed independent, behavioral relationships leading to such continuous equality would occur only in one case: when the planned saving and investment undertaken by each individual unit is also identical. But this happens to be the condition that is precisely satisfied in all barter economies where there are no financial assets, and all investment is internally financed. In economies without financial assets all economic units must necessarily run a balanced budget, and all investment must be internally financed. In this case total saving and investment are volitionally and simultaneously undertaken by individual units, and aggregate saving and investment in the economy are identical. The mainstream vision is then correct, but is applicable only to nonmonetary Crusoe economies.[36]

7.5 Volitional and non-volitional saving

Economists have loosely equated the *colloquial meaning* of saving, the volitional accumulation of wealth, with the *economic definition* of saving, the (not necessarily volitional) decision to abstain from consuming all one's income. On the surface they appear to be much the same thing. But closer examination reveals a crucial difference. Investment designates an increase in the quantity of capital in an economy. Saving is the accounting record of investment. All changes in investment result in identical changes in saving. But the accompanying saving undertaken may be either *volitional* or *non-volitional*. If investment is zero, so is saving.

In monetary economies all investment spending must be financed with money balances. The money balances used to finance investment spending may be acquired in two ways:

(1) internal finance (volitional saving) and
(2) external finance (non-volitional saving).[37]

When investment is internally financed the money to finance the investment must *first* have been saved before investment goods can be purchased. Such saving is volitional. Changes in volitional saving to finance real investment involve identical opposite changes in consumption and investment spending. Changes in volitional saving to accumulate internally financed currently produced investment goods result in equal opposite changes in consumption spending and leave the level of AD unaffected. Changes in volitional saving to accumulate previously produced and nonreproducible assets were termed "hoarding" and result in an inverse change in AD.[38] Such saving is volitional since agents volitionally decide how much to invest. But in modern corporations the volitional decision to finance investment by retained earnings is undertaken by business management, not by shareholders the ultimate owners of business firms. As a result saving associated with internal finance represents non-volitional saving from the point of view of the ultimate household owners of business corporations.

When investment spending is externally financed, the accompanying saving may be volitional or non-volitional, depending on whether external finance results in the creation of monetary or nonmonetary financial assets. The purchase of newly created nonmonetary financial liabilities such as currently issued stocks and bonds, which directly finance current investment spending, represents an increase in volitional saving. Non-volitional saving occurs whenever investment expenditures are externally financed by the issue of debt sold to the banking system and results in newly created bank deposits. Saving is then non-volitional, and need not be consciously regarded by the saving agents as saving since it need not involve any decision to abstain from consumption.[39] Whenever investment expenditure is financed by bank credit, newly created deposits are simultaneously accepted in exchange for goods. The money supply and AD both increase, without any accompanying volitional decision to increase "saving."[40] Deficit spending, deficit finance, and non-volitional saving cannot occur in nonmonetary economies. In nonmonetary economies all saving is volitional and transitive and all investment is internally financed. In non-monetary economies it may be concluded that saving "causes" investment. The mainstream view is correct. But only barter "Crusoe" economies fit the mainstream paradigm.[41]

Since saving is the accounting record of investment saving can never be in excess of investment, and investment can never be constrained by "too little" saving. Investment is constrained only by the inability to find sufficient finance for the amount of credit demanded, or by too high an interest charge for borrowing.

We are taught that saving is a supreme virtue, the sole path to increased wealth and greater economic security. It is true that in order to accumulate wealth, economic units must refrain from consuming all their income. Nevertheless in developed economies most saving is non-volitional. Only a small proportion of total saving is volitional.

Mainstream economists have been too inclined to accept the classical dichotomy between monetary and real behavior. They have been predisposed to believe that economic analysis must "pierce the veil of money" and focus on the underlying "real" phenomena that lie beneath. But there is no underlying "real" economy that exists independently of the nominal economy. There is only the nominal economy. Real variables are merely nominal variables which have been deflated by a price index by economists. Mainstream economists have failed to recognize the implications of the radical changes in business practices introduced by the development of credit money and overdraft systems for how money is created and for the causal relationship between saving and investment, and money and income.[42] In credit money economies, saving comprises both the volitional and non-volitional acquisition of money balances in exchange for externally financed investment goods. In credit money economies investment is no longer primarily internally financed, and saving is no longer primarily volitional. In most developed economies less than one half of total investment is internally financed and more than one half is externally financed.

Most investment spending with the sole exception of unintended inventory accumulation is volitional. Investment may be internally or externally financed. The internal financing of investment decisions reflects volitional decisions undertaken by the managers of private business firms and the personnel of public corporations. These are the administrators not the owners of the economy's real wealth and do not volitionaly undertake the accompanying saving. The accompanying saving is non-volitional, and is undertaken jointly by shareholders and citizens, the ultimate owners of the economy's wealth.

The saving that corresponds to internally financed investment by private corporations is non-volitional from the point of view of stockholders, the ultimate wealth owners. Volitional saving by ultimate wealth owners corresponds only to the internal finance of investment spending undertaken by non-incorporated small businesses. Such saving represents the volitional preferences of wealth-owners to save and invest some proportion of their income.

The purchase of previously existing financial assets by economic units constitutes saving from the viewpoint of individual economic units. But it represents portfolio-asset allocation and not income-saving allocation decisions from the point of view of the economy. From the viewpoint of the economy such "saving" does not finance or result in new investment spending. It determines the distribution of ownership of the existing net worth among private agents.

Ceteris paribus, volitional decisions to increase saving by surplus-spending units denote a volitional decision to reduce current spending on consumption. The attempt by surplus units to save in aggregate an amount in excess of total planned volitional deficit spending by deficit units leads to a decrease in the demand for currently produced goods and an increase in demand for previously existing assets. When surplus-spending units desire to acquire existing financial assets in excess of the quantity of new financial assets issued by deficit-spending units, the result is a reduction in expenditure on current output, AD, and income. This process was termed by Keynes the "paradox of thrift."[43]

In economics many expectations about the unknowable future are self-fulfilling. For most assets the future income stream is unknowable but nevertheless the present value must somehow be formulated. Expectations are formed largely by the extrapolation of recent behavior into the perceived future. A fall in current AD typically generates negative expectations about future AD, profits, and output, and in turn impacts negatively on current AD. As a result current decisions to volitionally raise surplus-spending and saving are likely to reduce current investment spending, by reducing current consumption spending. Conversely volitional decisions to raise current deficit-spending are *ceteris paribus* likely to raise the expected growth of AD. An increase in current spending leads to expectations of increases in future spending by other units, and so future growth of AD. Changes in current AD, by changing current expectations of future AD are typically self-fulfilling, and likely to result in future increases or decreases in consumption, investment, saving, and wealth accumulation.

Classical economists had a general equilibrium view of the economy. They believed an increase in volitional saving would reduce the level of interest rates by increasing the supply of "loanable funds," and the lower cost of capital would induce businesses to increase investment spending. Keynes was at pains to demonstrate how this classical argument was incorrect. He argued that the level of AD and income does not remain constant in the face of increases in planned saving but ordinarily falls *pari passu*. In *The General Theory* he argued that the level of interest rates was determined by the supply and demand for liquidity and not by the supply and demand for loanable funds. But he there assumed the money supply was determined by the monetary authorities.[44] Once it is recognized that the short term rate of interest rather than the money supply is the policy instrument of the monetary authorities, this opens the door to understanding how saving behavior can indirectly affect the level of planned and actual investment by inducing the central bank to change the interest rate it sets.[45]

7.6 Conclusions: saving is the accounting record of investment

Investment is the terrain, and saving is the accounting measure of that terrain. Investment spending depends on firms' current expectations of future quasi-rents and profits. These are compared with their current expectations of the present and future costs of labor and capital and the future cost and availability of finance. Aggregate saving is the accounting record of investment spending. Its quantity varies with investment and with how investment is defined. Investment is never limited by an "insufficiency" of saving since saving is simply the accounting record of investment. Apart from involuntary inventory changes the decision how much to invest is volitional. But in all monetary economies the decision how much to save is predominantly non-volitional.

The decision to increase volitional saving is recorded in the market for current output as a reduction in current consumption expenditure and so in AD. Increases in volitional saving do not, as the mainstream view has it, have the effect of raising the supply and lowering the cost of loanable funds. Increases in volitional saving are volitional decisions to reduce the level of current consumption spending and so reduce AD. To the extent current AD affects expected future AD, an increase in volitional saving is much more likely to reduce than increase current investment spending. Current investment falls whenever increases in volitional saving depress expected future levels of AD.

Total saving is the sum of volitional and non-volitional saving, and investment spending is internally and externally financed. The volitional saving associated with internal finance comprises strictly only the internal finance of volitional investment spending undertaken by unincorporated businesses. If income were to be redefined to include capital gains, internal finance of investment by business corporations would be accompanied by increases in non-volitional saving by shareholders.

When business units are incorporated and their shares are publicly traded, internal finance produces an increase in the market value of equities, resulting in capital gain income to shareholders. Shareholders do not spend most of their capital gain income, so most such saving is non-volitional. Volitional saving associated with external finance comprises primarily the volitional purchase of new issues of non-monetary financial assets by households. Non-volitional saving associated with external finance is associated with business borrowing from the banking system, and leads to the non-volitional accumulation of newly issued deposits by household and business savers.

As will be developed in Chapter 8 household saving associated with internally financed investment spending is much more transparent when a Hicksian definition of income is adopted. All capital gain income that is not consumed is then seen to result in equal increases in non-volitional saving. When increases in volitional saving by households are associated with equal reductions in consumption expenditures AD will initially fall, even though the money supply may initially rise to reflect bank finance of business' unintended inventory accumulation.

Non-volitional saving by households, businesses, and governments take the form of the passive accumulation of deposit balances ("convenience lending" of fiat money to the banking system) and the passive accumulation of corporate equities of greater market value. Non-volitional saving by bank depositors occurs whenever investment spending is deficit-financed by net new bank loans. Over time the passive expansion of deposits provokes a complex dynamic process of portfolio reallocation from shorter term to longer term financial assets.

Mainstream macroeconomics has traditionally regarded saving and investment as independent behavioral relationships undertaken by different groups.[46] The question then becomes, "what is the mechanism by which saving and investment are equilibrated?" The classical view was that the level of interest rates adjusted to a new "equilibrium" level where planned saving was again equal to planned investment. The Keynesian view was that the level of income adjusted to a new "equilibrium" level, where planned saving was again equal to planned investment. The neoclassical synthesis concluded that both interest rates and income adjusted until at the margin all variables attained a new "general equilibrium" configuration where all markets clear.

With identities the direction of causality gains increased importance. The recognition that saving is the accounting record of investment implies the direction of causality goes from investment to saving. Changes in investment "cause" changes in saving. With the exception of unplanned inventory accumulation all decisions to invest are volitional, and most saving behavior is primarily non-volitional. Investment can never be constrained by an "insufficiency" of saving, but only by an insufficient supply of credit or by too a high level of interest rates. Volitional and non-volitional saving are identical in that they are both the accounting record of investment. But there can never be a position of "general equilibrium" where planned saving by household is equal to planned investment by firms. In complex systems change is continuous.

Once thoroughly accepted, the recognition that saving is simply the accounting record of investment will have the effect of a neutron bomb on macroeconomic modeling. As soon as it is fully absorbed that there is no independent behavioral saving function, it will become clear that neither income, interest rates, prices, nor anything else has any tendency to approach a future "equilibrium" level, where the amount saving units plan to save is exactly equal to the amount spending units plan to invest. In complex adaptive systems most saving is non-volitional, and planned saving is never equal to planned investment. Saving is simply the accounting record of investment.

Volitional increases in planned saving do not provide additional resources to finance additional investment spending. They simply reduce the level of AD. Increases in volitional saving involving abstention from consumption result in a reduction in AD. If the reduction in AD due to increases in volitional saving leads to expectations of lower future AD growth, investment, AD and AS will fall. An increase in "planned saving" will then result in a reduction in "actual saving" (Keynes' "Paradox of Thrift"). If an increase in planned saving reduces planned consumption spending, and so the level of AD and current income, it will lead to a reduction in actual investment and saving.

Keynes' conclusion that income tends to some "equilibrium" level, where planned saving is equal to planned investment, was due to methodological error, the application of comparative static equilibrium analysis to a complex system. AD and AS are continually changing over time. Actual saving is identical to actual investment at every level of income and over every period of time, since saving is an accounting identity. Income does not adjust to eliminate differences between planned saving and planned investment. Income falls in response to increases in planned saving. This becomes obvious when an increase in volitional saving is described as an increase in abstinence from consumption. Planned saving is never identical to planned investment, and actual saving is always identical to actual investment. So long as output in the economy is below its potential full employment level, real income and AS change continually over time in response to continuous changes in AD. An increase in deficit-spending for consumption goods has the same one-for-one effect of increasing AD as does an increase in deficit-spending for investment goods. There is no Keynesian "multiplier."

One year after *The General Theory* was written, Keynes wrote:

> banks hold the key position in the transition from a lower to a higher scale of activity. ... The investment market can become congested through a shortage of cash. It can never become congested through a shortage of saving. This is the most fundamental of my conclusions within this field.[47]

Keynes was correct as to the "destination" of his vision. But he was mistaken in how it came about. An increase in planned saving need not result in a reduction in interest rates nor in an increase in investment spending. An increase in planned saving results initially in a reduction in consumption spending and in AD. It is more likely to result in a reduction in investment spending, unless it induces the central bank to lower interest rates and pursue a more expansionary monetary policy, to achieve its goal of full employment.

8
Capital Gains: Towards a Hicksian Definition of Income

What we want in economics are theories which will be useful, practically useful. That means that they must be selective. But all selection is dangerous. So there is plenty of room for criticism, and for the filling in of gaps, building some sort of bridge between one selective theory and another. There is plenty of room for academic work doing that sort of a job.

Sir John Hicks, 1967

To measure income it is a necessary prerequisite to know what it is you wish to observe. Facts are not so clear cut as in the natural sciences; they are often wrong. To get them "right" for the purpose at hand and the time period, economists need theory. Theory helps to focus one's attention, it helps one know where to look. It has a classificatory role. But this means the "facts" do not in the ordinary sense act as a check or test of the theory. Consistency of concepts is a necessary prior condition. The methodology is not that of econometrics but of an older craft: making sure that the facts are what the economists think they are. If it is income that you wish to measure, first work out what that income is. In the nature of things and because time passes there will never be a perfect set of "facts."

Dieter Helm, 1984: 14

If we accept the Haig – Hicks – Simon concept of income as that which can be consumed while keeping real wealth intact, saving is the difference between this measure of income and actual consumption. Both income and saving will then include real capital gains. To preserve the saving – investment identity investment would also have to include these capital gains. ... Inclusion of net revaluations in measures of income, product, and investment ... entails a significant conceptual departure from conventional accounts, which focus on the direct output of current productive activity. ... Different elements of revaluations have different implications for economic behavior. ... If for many purposes it may be best to utilize measures that exclude revaluations, it may prove for many purposes, particularly where the focus is on the accumulation of capital, seriously distorting to ignore them.

Robert Eisner, 1989: 17–18

Saving should be defined by reference to the underlying concept of wealth to which the saving is an increment. ... The most useful wealth concept is the market value of assets, not the cost-based measure of capital implied by the use of National income and product account (NIPA) saving.

David Bradford, 1991: 15–16

8.1 Most saving is non-volitional

As shown in Chapter 7 national saving is the accounting record of national investment. So long as capital budgeting is followed consistently saving is always identical to investment, irrespective of how complicated the model or how many sectors it contains.

We regard saving as volitional and are taught that an increase in saving is the path to increased wealth and economic security. It is true that in order to accumulate wealth economic units must refrain from consuming all their income. But in the conventional National Income Accounts income in the form of capital appreciation is excluded. In consequence it is not widely recognized that most saving in most monetary economies is non-volitional. Volitional saving constitutes only a very small proportion of total saving, confined to the portion of internal finance of investment that is directly undertaken by unincorporated businesses and households, and the portion of external finance of investment that takes the form of nonmonetary debt and equity issues sold to ultimate wealth-owners and purchased by nonmonetary financial institutions.

Business managers and government bureaucrats, the administrators not the ultimate owners of the economy's wealth, make most of the decisions concerning how and how much to invest and how it is to be financed. Most wealth-owners acquiesce passively to these decisions by not spending capital gain income. Investment spending is not determined by the volitional saving decisions of ultimate household wealth-owners. Most investment spending is financed completely non-volitionally by the passive accumulation of assets whose market values have risen. This financing takes two forms: first the holding of equities of higher market value reflecting corporate internal finance and increases in price–earnings ratios, and second the accumulation of newly created bank deposits created by new bank loans to finance increases in working capital.

Most "volitional saving" undertaken by ultimate household wealth owners does not constitute saving from the viewpoint of the economy. Most household "volitional saving" is devoted to the purchase of previously existing real and financial assets. As such it represents portfolio transactions that redistribute claims to the ownership of existing wealth. These transactions are properly recorded in the National Flow of Funds Accounts, not the National Income Accounts.

Saving is the accounting record of investment and both occur simultaneously. Use of a Hicksian definition of income combined with process analysis renders how private saving finances of private investment more transparent. All variables must be dated and expressed as first differences, and the institutional framework must be precisely acknowledged. Households are the "ultimate" owners of all private assets in capitalist economies. Private saving is undertaken by households, the ultimate owners of wealth. In capitalist economies most wealth is privately owned. Non-volitional household saving takes the form of the accumulation of newly created deposits, and of previously existing corporate equities whose market values have increased. Over longer time periods newly created deposits that provide working capital finance for the construction of investment goods are exchanged for higher earning and less liquid financial assets in wealth-owner portfolios.

From the viewpoint of individual households, "saving" comprises the volitional acquisition of previously existing tangible and financial assets. But from the viewpoint of the economy, these are portfolio transactions not income transactions that effectuate the redistribution of wealth ownership among wealth-owners. As such they are recorded in the National Flow of Funds Accounts, not in the National Income Accounts. The macroeconomic consequence of the devotion of current income to the accumulation of previously existing assets is to generate a surplus on current account and diminish AD for currently produced goods and services.

From the point of view of individual wealth-owners, all saving defined as income not consumed constitutes net wealth accumulation. But from the point of view of the economy, most such saving represents portfolio transactions not newly created wealth and net capital formation. How income is defined is critically important for understanding this process. Most household net wealth accumulation in most periods does not constitute net capital formation, but the appreciation of the market prices of previously existing assets. In the case of corporate equities increases in expected *future* earnings and dividends result in increases in *current* market values of expected future income streams, and constitutes capital gain income in the current period.

The inclusion of capital gain income in the definition of current income renders the saving process of households as the ultimate owners of societal wealth more transparent. In the case of public investment by government, if public assets do not have a market price, then net asset appreciation and net capital gain income are not recorded and no capital gain income is created. Capital gains and losses only accrue to economic agents when wealth values change, and are realized when assets are sold for money in portfolio transactions. When capital assets are publicly owned, they have no market price and it is not possible to measure the change in their value. When governments nationalize private property the market value of the total wealth economy is reduced.

According to official National Income and Product Account (NIPA) data the savings rate has declined precipitously in the United States during the past few decades. The consequences of such low saving rates are widely held to be extremely severe. This "collective profligacy" as reflected in "inadequate" saving rates has been blamed for a wide variety of macroeconomic ills.[1]

Macroeconomists are concerned with the link between saving and capital formation. "Inadequate" saving ratios are regarded as restraining capital formation and lowering the growth path of income, output, labour productivity and real wages. "Profligate" consumption spending is held responsible for the huge US current account trade deficits and the "forced sale" of large chunks of the US capital stock to foreign investors at "fire sale" prices. Many believe the recent low saving rates threaten the very foundation of US economic prosperity.[2]

But all such conclusions are mistaken. They are deduced from incorrect accounting conventions which assume savings is volitional, and ignore capital gain income. Changes in saving mirror changes in the current price of capital assets only if capital gains are included in income, and capital assets are valued at current market prices.

8.2 Hicksian income

In National Income Accounting (NIA) income is defined as the total value of factor payments made in the production of final output. Private saving is the residual left over from NIA income after deducting consumption and taxes. All capital gain income from asset revaluation is excluded from NIA data. The logical interdependency between consumption, income, and wealth is then no longer obvious or transparent. Defining any two of these concepts determines the value of the third. However which two of the three are most fundamental is not immediately obvious.[3]

There is widespread consensus among economists that consumption is the final goal and ultimate purpose of economic activity. From the viewpoint of welfare, few would disagree that "consumption" is the single most fundamental concept in National Income accounting. With regard to income and wealth, most economists would argue that income is more fundamental than wealth, since the change in wealth is equal to the excess of income over consumption. Suppose it is agreed that consumption and income are the two most fundamental macroeconomic variables. If income and consumption are taken as the most fundamental variables, then the question arises: "How should income most usefully be defined?"

There is widespread agreement that wealth is most informatively measured as the current market value of capital assets and not as the historical cost of producing them.[4] When consumption and income are taken as the two fundamental variables, and current wealth is defined as the accumulation of past saving, the change in wealth values over the period is identical to total saving over the period. But for such a definition of saving to equal the change in wealth values measured at current market prices, income must be defined to include capital gains and losses. If this is done, capital formation must be redefined to include capital gain income generated by changes in asset prices. If income is redefined to include capital gains the saving rates over the decade of the 1990s, rather than falling as is popularly believed, were substantially in excess of their long-run historical average.[5]

Is the decision to include capital gains in income reasonable? Hicks long ago made a powerful case for including capital gains in the definition of income:

> The purpose of income calculations in practical affairs is to give people an indication of the amount which they can consume without impoverishing themselves. Following this idea, it would seem that we ought to define a man's income as the maximum value which he can consume during a week, and still expect to be as well off at the end of the week as he was at the beginning.[6]

Hicks emphasized the extreme difficulties which accompany all attempts to define "income" *ex ante*. It is never possible to state with precision what a person's "true" income was over any particular time period, since the value of current income is dependent on the value of expected future income. As a result income is at root a subjective concept. There is no reason to believe that the future expectations of different individuals will be identical. But if they are not, the aggregation of incomes looses its objective meaning.[7] If income is defined as how much a person can consume during the current "week" and still expect to be as well off as at the beginning of the week, income is necessarily based on *ex ante* expectations. But nothing is said about the realization of these expectations. When these expectations are not realized income will be greater or less than expected. Agents will then receive "windfall" capital gains or losses.

Total Income in the NIPA accounts includes the total income generated by all factor services generated in current production, the sum of wages, interest, rents, and profits at current prices. Profits may be viewed as the residual of total revenue over total costs. Total factor income including profits thus constitutes the accounting record of current output. Such a definition of income has the enormous advantage of being measurable in two conceptually distinct ways:

1. As the value of all final goods and services produced in an economy during the period.
2. As the value of all factor incomes received and earned from current production during the period.

This permits the possibility of measuring current income as the sum of all final output, and as the sum of all current income earned in the production of final output. These two independent approaches have the huge advantage of enabling national income accountants to estimate the statistical error involved in each approach.

Nevertheles such a definition of income does not provide a measure of the amount that individuals could continue to consume in any period without eventually impoverishing themselves. As a result, although NIPA conventions may be more appropriate for investigating output, investment, capital formation, and growth issues, they are much less useful for understanding and explaining consumption and saving behavior. Hicks concluded,

It would seem that we ought to define a man's income as the maximum value which he can consume during a week, and still expect to be as well off at the end of the week as at the beginning. Thus when a person saves, he plans to be better off in the future; when he lives beyond his income, he plans to be worse off.[8]

As explained in Chapter 6 all economic concepts are by nature "Loose." Economists are forced to consider pragmatic considerations when defining the empirical proxy for any theoretical concept. In economics it is never possible to know exactly where to draw the line. The most appropriate proxy to any analytic concept comes down to a question of judgment. This was illustrated in the discussion of the measurement of National Income, where it was shown that small and reasonable differences in assumptions about how income should be defined lead to enormous differences in output measures.

The generally accepted definition of wealth is its current market price, representing the capitalized present value of its expected future income. Such a definition is most appropriate for property income, but much less sensible for labor income. Fluctuations in wages are difficult to anticipate in advance and so long as humans are not bought and sold, their present value cannot operationally be easily measured. Future labor income has no capitalized present value except in slave societies, and is unacceptable as collateral for credit.

Total income can be defined as the maximum nominal amount of money that can be spent during a period, maintaining the expected value of prospective future money receipts constant. But when interest rates change, the future expected interest stream and its capitalized present value move in opposite directions. This suggests related approximation: the maximum amount of money an individual can spend this week, and expect to be able to spend in each ensuing future week. When the rate of interest remains unchanged this comes to much the same as the first. But when the interest rate changes, the two cease to be identical. The second is a closer approximation to the central economic concept of income.

Suppose future prices are expected to change? A second approximation then suggests itself: the maximum *real* amount of money the individual can spend this week and expect to be able to spend the same amount in real terms in each ensuing week. Some correction of this sort into units of constant purchasing power is obviously desirable. But how must we to define "in real terms"? There is always the well-known index number problem, so the appropriate index to use is surrounded by a penumbra of uncertainty. In a world of rapid quality change it is clearly unacceptable to assume the future rate of change of all prices over all future time periods currently known. Any definition of real income thus necessarily is subject to a huge increase in the degree of indeterminateness.

Another complication arises when we consider durable goods. Strictly speaking saving is not the difference between income and consumption expenditure, but between income and consumption. When part of income is spent on durable goods, consumption expenditure includes consumption plus an investment in consumer durables. When part of consumption includes the consumption of durable goods purchased in the past, current consumption will exceed current consumer expenditure. Only in the steady state, when the acquisition of new consumption goods exactly matches the using up of old ones, will actual consumption be exactly equal to consumption expenditure. What must we do when these two things do not match? Even worse, in the absence of secondhand markets for heterogeneous durable consumer and producer goods, how do we know when they do match?[9]

We must revert to our central concept. If the individual is using up her existing stock of durable goods and not acquiring new ones, she will clearly be worse off at the end of the week if she can only plan the same stream of purchases as she could in the beginning. If she is to live within her income, she must plan to have a larger stream at the end of the week. How much larger can only be told from the central criterion itself. We are thus forced back on the central criterion: a person's income is what she can consume during the week, and expect to be as well off at the end of the week as she was at the beginning.

Hicks became extremely discouraged when considering the various approximations to individual income:

> We have come to see how very complex it is and how unattractive it looks when subject to detailed analysis. We may now allow a doubt to escape us whether it does, in the last resort, stand up to any analysis at all, or whether we have been chasing a will-o'-the-wisp.[10]

When we pass from the consideration of individual income to the consideration of social income, these doubts are fortified by others. We have established that income is a subjective concept, dependent on expectations about the future by the particular individual in question. Since in a complex world expectations are heterogeneous, there is no reason why the different expectations of different individuals should be consistent. If A's income is based on A's expectations, and B's income on B's expectations, when these expectations are inconsistent or self-contradictory, their aggregation has little meaning.

In the end Hicks became nihilistic about the entire enterprise.[11] He concluded that since the future was fundamentally unknowable, individuals were unable to distinguish between different streams of future consumption services. Since most of the events of any two different alternative consumption time paths are strictly unknowable, how much to save cannot be rationally calculated. At an even more fundamental level since utility is immeasurable it is not possible to directly compare different income and consumption situations:

> This conclusion seems unavoidable but it is very upsetting, perhaps even more upsetting than our doubts about the ultimate intelligibility of the concept of individual income itself.... It is hard to believe that the social income which economists discuss so much can be nothing else but a mere aggregate of possibly inconsistent expectations. But if not that, what is it?[12]

Hicks concluded the way to escape from this dilemma was to distinguish *ex ante* and *ex post* income. The previous definitions of income were all *ex ante*, the amount a person could consume during a week and still *expect* to be as well off as (s)he was at the beginning. Nothing was said about the *realization* of these expectations. Expectations of different wealth-owners about the unknowable future in a complex world are by nature heterogeneous. Asset market values represent the capital market's collective expectation of the discounted present value of future income streams accruing to owners of assets. When market expectations are not realized, the market value of the asset will be greater or less than expected. If we add or subtract these "windfall" gains or losses to our preceding definition of income, we get a new set of definitions of income *ex post*, which includes current capital gains and losses.

Hicks argued that so long as the *ex post* income of any one individual can be measured objectively, the *ex post* income of all individuals can be aggregated without difficulty. The rule that income *ex post* equals consumption *plus* the change in net worth has the advantage that it holds both for individual economic units and for the community as a whole. A definition of *ex post* income corresponds to each of the previous definitions of *ex ante* income. Income *ex post* may be defined as equal to the value of the individual's consumption *plus* the money value of the capital gains and losses accrued during the week. Income *ex post* is then equal to consumption plus the change in net worth. Providing we consider only property income and ignore the value of changes in human capital, which are neither operationally measurable nor marketable, income *ex post* ceases to be a subjective affair and becomes completely objective. The capital value of marketable assets at the beginning and end of any period is operationally an easily assessable figure.[13]

Provided we can measure *ex post* consumption, *ex post* income can be directly calculated. Since the *ex post* income of any individual is an objective magnitude the *ex post* income of all individuals in the economy can be aggregated without difficulty. The same rule that applies for individuals holds for the economy: Total *ex post* income equals total *ex post* consumption, plus net *ex post* capital accumulation. This becomes Hicks's simplest definition of income: "consumption plus the change in net worth."

But after carefully developing the above definition, Hicks was led to reject it as unsatisfactory for economic theorists. His grounds were that *ex post* concepts have no significance for conduct, on the general principle that: "bygones are forever bygones." Hicks unhappily concluded:

> Any one who seeks to make a statistical calculation of social income is confronted with a dilemma. The income he can calculate is not the true income he seeks; the income he seeks cannot be calculated. From this dilemma there is only one way out; it is of course the way that has to be taken in practice. He must take as his objective magnitude the social income *ex post*, and proceed to adjust it in some way that seems plausible or reasonable for those changes in capital values which look as if they have had the character of windfalls. This sort of estimation is normal statistical procedure, and on its own ground is

wholly justified. But it can only result in a statistical estimate. By its very nature it is not the measurement of an economic quantity.[14]

Hicks here came face to face with Sorites' paradox, the inability to non-arbitrarily define any continuously distributed analytical concept. But his nihilistic argument "bygones are forever bygones" does not hold for complex systems. It is true that individuals can do nothing to *affect* changes in asset values *ex post*. But this is not the issue. In a complex world past and current changes in observed variables are our only empirical basis for expectations of future changes. Bygones do have real effects for our current expectations of the future, and so for our future behavior.

There is a substantial literature on the effects of wealth and capital gains on consumption.[15] Capital gains and losses on marketable financial and tangible assets are one form of disposable income. Depending on the degree of ownership concentration of the asset in question and the asset's liquidity, marketability, and volatility, the marginal propensity to consume out of wealth and out of current capital gain income will be lower than out of current earned income. Consumption may also differ substantially among different types of assets. But the same can be said about consumption out of different types of income, for example, wages, rents, and dividends.

Conventional NI accounts measure output and income in terms of the current costs of resources used in production. Gross investment is the value of current income devoted to the production of goods to be used for future production. This is not the change in the market value of the capital stock. Asset values change independently of changes in investment expenditures due to depreciation, and due to changes in expected future incomes, prices, interest rates, technology, tastes, and uncertainty. The value of current wealth can change with no change in the mathematical expectation of future income when individual agents have heterogeneous expectations and horizons.

Some kinds of capital can increase in value at the expense of others, for example, human against tangible, or tangible against intangible. Changes in exchange rates and terms of trade can have substantial effects on the market value of a nation's income and capital stock. Over the years total changes in wealth values are substantially larger than net capital formation due to current investment. If the Hicksian definition of income is adopted, wealth is measured at current market values and saving is defined as net wealth accumulation. Income, investment, and saving then include holding gains and losses. To preserve the saving–investment identity investment must be redefined as net capital formation plus net asset revaluation, reflecting the net change in market prices of marketable assets. This is ordinarily practicable only for financial assets and housing. For most reproducible assets "replacement cost" based on current prices are all that is ordinarily available. Since human capital is neither marketable nor capitalized, capital gains on human capital cannot be known. Since human capital is not capitalized, capital gain income does not occur. The same holds for changes in the value of public assets, which have no current market value if they are not traded on any market.

The inclusion in income of capital gains from net asset revaluations entails a significant conceptual departure from conventional accounts which focus exclusively on the value of current productive activity. Changes in different asset prices may have different implications for consumption behavior depending on their liquidity and ownership concentration. Changes in exchange rates, terms of trade, and discount rates alter the wealth position of the nation and the distribution of national wealth among regions, generations, and agents.[16]

Saving decisions determine the distribution of net worth among individual economic units. The decision to volitionally increase saving by individual surplus-spending units can only be expressed as a reduction in spending for consumption goods. When the quantity of assets that surplus units demand to hold is in excess of the quantity of newly issued assets that deficit-spending units currently issue, surplus units acquire previously existing assets. This results in a reduction of AD, which may be offset by additional capital gain income. The extent of changes in demand for previously existing assets affect asset prices, and returns depends critically on the reaction function of the central bank (CB), in particular how they influence the Bank Rate it sets.

The future is fundamentally unknowable and changes in expectations about the future state of the economy have a self-fulfilling quality. A rise or fall in the rate of growth of expected future AD will lead to increases or decreases in current consumption and investment expenditures, current AD, and current GDP. Short-run expectations are typically formed extrapolatively, so increases in current AD typically generate positive expectations about future AD, leading to increases in current investment spending and future output. Exogenous decisions to reduce volitional saving and to increase planned deficit-spending raise current AD, and induce expectations of higher future AD. Exogenous decisions to increase volitional saving and planned surplus-spending conversely reduce the level of current AD, and lead to expectations of decreased future AD and so decreases in current consumption and investment spending.

8.3 A Proposal for a "Capital Gains and Losses Addendum" to National Income Accounting

Current NIPA, by defining National Income as identical to National Output, has the important advantage of providing government statisticians with two independent ways of estimating National Income from two independent data sources: as the value of all final goods and services produced and sold, and as the value of all income currently earned in the production of final output.

But it has the serious disadvantage that National saving is no longer equal to the net current change in National Wealth measured at current market prices. When current income is defined as the value of current output, and capital gains are excluded from the definition of National Income, then National Saving no longer equals National Net Wealth Accumulation measured at current prices. Keynes finessed this result by defining saving as what it was not: "income not consumed," rather than what it was: "the change in agents net wealth." Since nominal and real saving are no longer the accounting record of nominal and real capital formation, the saving-investment process becomes much less transparent.[17]

This non-transparency is created since saving defined as "income not consumed," is no longer equal to investment defined as "net capital formation." Most household "saving" in the NIPA, when defined as "income not consumed" represents the purchase of previously existing financial assets (stocks and bonds). Such "saving" constitutes portfolio allocation (Flow of Funds) transactions not National Income transactions.

Corporate business saving (retained earnings) concurrently generates increases in household capital gain income and so increases the value of household total assets and net worth. The resulting change in household income will be larger or smaller than the value of corporate retained earnings (savings), depending on the concurrent valuation ratio (the ratio of the market value to book value of corporate stock), and the concurrent price-earnings ratios at which stocks are capitalized and priced.

From the viewpoint of the economy most household "saving" so defined is devoted to the purchase of previously existing assets. It results in a redistribution of asset ownership, and is neither saving nor a record of net capital formation. Conventional household "saving" is a measure of portfolio (Flow of Funds) transactions, not National Income Account transactions.

Corporate business saving generates concurrent increases in household capital gain income. The increases in household wealth will be larger or smaller than the value of corporate retained earnings, depending on the current valuation ratio (the ratio of market value to book value and the price-earnings ratio). Household shareholders consume a much smaller proportion of their capital gain income than their wage and property income. The direct effect of an increase in volitional saving is an increased allocation of current income to the acquisition of previously existing assets, resulting in a reduction in the marginal propensity to consume, and a reduction in the level of AD.

A strong case can be made for a Capital Gains and Losses Addendum to the National Income and Flow of Funds Accounts to integrate capital gain income into NIPA. To more fully understand the events of the process by which saving finances invest in modern economies, it would be desirable to develop a set of Capital Gains and Losses Addendum to the NIA's. Such an Addendum would define GDI in the Hicksian sense to include net capital gain income on all marketable assets. Only then would saving equal the net accumulation of wealth at current market prices. By excluding capital gains, current NIPA income substantially underestimates saving in all periods (such as the 1990s) when capital gain income is substantial. Such a revised definition of the National Accounts is a prerequisite for a deeper understanding of saving and consumption behavior.

The following constitutes a list of suggestions for such an Addendum to National Income Accounting:

1. The goal is to define current income in the Hicksian sense and include capital gains and losses resulting from changes in the market prices of marketable assets. Saving defined as "income not consumed" then equals the change in net worth measured at current market values at both the micro-level and the macro-level for

individual economic units and for the economy. Under such a definition of income the change in net worth is identical to saving defined as abstention from current income. Saving may then be defined both as an "increase in net worth" and as "income not consumed."

2. When income is defined under present NIA conventions as earned income excluding all holding gains, and saving is defined as "income not consumed," most "saving" undertaken by individual households is not "saving" from the viewpoint of the economy. Most individual "saving" defined as "income not consumed" is devoted to the accumulation of previously created financial and tangible assets. It constitutes Flow of Funds (portfolio) transactions not National Income transactions.

3. When income is defined in the Hicksian sense to include capital gains and losses, and saving is defined as "income not consumed," saving is equal to the change in net worth measured at current market values. It then immediately becomes clear why there is no behavioral "savings function," either for individual units or for the economy. From the point of view of National Income, most household volitional "saving" does not represent "saving" in the National Income Accounting sense. Most "saving" by wealth-owners defined as "income not consumed" constitutes the purchase of previously existing and not newly created assets. The result of portfolio transactions is the redistribution of wealth ownership. As such they are portfolio transactions and properly recorded as "Asset Purchases and Sales" in the Flow of Funds Accounts, not as "Saving" in the National Income Accounts. Investment may be defined as the net change in capital assets measured at current market value. Saving and investment then include real capital formation plus the appreciation of asset prices.

4. Household "saving," defined as the accumulation of real or financial assets, constitutes current "saving" for the economy only to the extent it finances (a) current investment spending (the purchase of currently produced real capital goods), and (b) the purchase of newly issued financial assets that directly finance current investment spending by deficit spending units.

5. The production and sale of currently produced goods take calendar time. Bank lending provides firms' with increased working capital to finance increased purchases of factors of production and inventory accumulation during the production-sales period. Most household "saving" in the Hicksian sense is non-volitional and takes the form of: (a) the "convenience lending" of fiat money by bank depositors, and (b) the accumulation of corporate equities whose market values have risen due to internal investment and/or increases in the price/earnings ratio of corporate equities.[18]

6. Saving in the Hicksian sense that takes the form of an increase in "convenience lending" of fiat money to the banking system denotes the accumulation of newly created bank deposits by depositors. Individual depositors may hold newly created deposits only for nano-seconds. But depositors in the aggregate hold may realistically be viewed as collectively "demanding" newly created deposits for indefinitely long periods, for as long as the deposits remain in existence. Bank deposits are reduced when bank loans are repaid, and when banks sell

securitized loans and securities from their portfolios to non-bank agents outside the banking system.

7. Individual households and firms literally "do nothing" when making additional "convenience lending" to the banking system.[19] Depositors are always willing non-volitionally to accept (and so "demand") additional deposits. Whether the increases in "convenience lending" to the banking system denote convenience saving, convenience dissaving, or merely portfolio transactions is completely independent of depositor behavior. It depends on whether new bank loans finance increases in real investment spending, increases in consumption spending, the net acquisition of newly created financial assets issued to finance the acquisition of real or financial assets, or the net acquisition of previously existing real or financial assets. Newly created deposits are the accounting record of newly created bank credit. So long as bank deposits are generally accepted as a means of payment the aggregate quantity of deposits in existence is neither the result of nor directly caused by depositors' demand to accumulate deposits.

8. Credit money is not accepted (demanded) as a function of its price or its expected rate of return, as is the case with all nonmonetary goods. Expenditure of deposits by economic agents does not affect the quantity of deposits outstanding, unless used for the purchase of assets held by the banking system. It simply redistributes the ownership of the existing deposit stock among different agents.

9. Non-volitional saving comprises the passive accumulation by shareholders of equities with a higher market value due to the increased market price of shares. Such non-volitional saving results from shareholders literally "doing nothing," than non-realizing and nonconsuming the capital gain income generated by the appreciation of share prices due to retained earnings and higher P/E ratios.

10. After the production and construction of new net investment has been completed, the forms in which financial claims to wealth are held evolve dynamically. Bank loans and deposits are initially created by an act of short-term business borrowing from the banking system for working capital. Bank loans are used by household to finance "lumpy" consumption purchases involving the acquisition of houses, consumer durables, and lumpy consumption services such as travel, whose memories provide long-term utility. Business loans are repaid when the goods produced are sold by their producers and the receipts are used to repay bank loans. In this way convenience lending to the banking system is continually intiated and extinguished over time in the "monetary circuit."[20]

11. Bank deposits are created and retired through a dynamical process in the monetary "circuit," typically in exchange for riskier forms of wealth ownership with lower liquidity and higher pecuniary returns. Through a series of portfolio transactions longer-term debt and equity financial assets and liabilities replace shorter-term assets over time, as short-term debt instruments are repaid and exchanged for longer-term claims on property income.[21]

12. Equity ownership non-volitionally accumulates whenever business net capital formation and acquisition is internally financed and reflected in share price appreciation. Equity ownership accumulates volitionally when businesses issue new shares directly to nonbank units. In the US economy business retained earnings finance about one-half of total investment spending. The resulting net capital gain income, net wealth accumulation, and net saving by shareholders occurs non-volitionally as asset revaluation occurs.

13. Under a Hicksian definition of income, GDI may exceed or fall short of GDP. Capital gains and losses occur continuously and the value of current income and current output are no longer identical. NIA income equals total final consumption and investment spending measured at current market prices. Hicksian income equals total consumption plus net wealth accumulation measured at current market values and includes capital gain income from wealth revaluation. Like other income, capital gain income provides recipients with an increase in purchasing power which accrues exclusively to owners of marketable assets. Capital gain income is typically "realized" by borrowing against the asset rather than by asset sale. It may be associated with higher expenditures on consumption or investment goods, and increased purchases of previously existing assets. Capital gain income may also be spent on the purchase of previously existing financial goods and services. In this case AD for current output and income does not increase even though asset prices rise.

14. Financial assets represent legally enforceable claims on tangible, financial, and intangible assets. The current market value of claims varies continuously over time with changes in wealth-owner expectations of future "states of the world." The precise money value of total wealth, and so total income and the distribution of wealth ownership, is unknowable at any point in time and over any time period. Changing wealth values are dependent on continuously changing expectations of the unknowable future. Economists must explicitly acknowledge their inability to measure the value of income and wealth with precision.

15. Whenever economic agents realize capital gain income from asset revaluation and use the proceeds to purchase currently produced goods and services, the level of AD will increase. When individual households and firms devote current earned income to the purchase of previously created financial assets (including their own outstanding liabilities), previously produced tangible assets, and non reproducible assets, AD for currently produced goods and services will decline. Such transactions represent an "act of saving" for individual economic units. But for the economy they represent "portfolio" transactions, alternative "resting places" for generalized purchasing power held in different asset forms.

16. The net change in AD in every period is the outcome of opposing positive and negative stochastic flows and can never ever conceivably be known in advance. The allocation of current income to the purchase of previously existing assets results in a continuous reduction in AD. But such reductions are continuously offset by increases in AD due to the purchase of newly created goods financed by money receipts from the realization of capital gains from

asset-revaluation. AD is the result of dynamic stochastic processes and changes continuously over time.

17. The challenge for Flow of Funds Accountants is how best to record this complex dynamic process: how best to reconcile changes in the market value of financial and tangible assets stocks that occur continuously over time with the savings flows out of continuously changing disposable income that are recorded discretely over quarterly and annual time periods? Changes in asset market values generate concurrent changes in income, saving, and investment flows.[22]

18. The purchase of currently produced capital assets constitutes saving, investment, and net wealth accumulation both for the individual unit and for the economy. The purchase of previously created assets, whether real or financial, constitutes saving and net wealth accumulation for the individual units. But for the economy they represent merely wealth revaluation and redistribution. Most volitional household saving behavior is devoted to the purchase of previously existing financial assets. Although it is termed and regarded as "saving" by individual agents if it does not finance current real wealth accumulation, it does not represent "saving" for the economy. It constitutes rather a change in the distribution of ownership claims to existing wealth, and may be associated with a reduction or an increase in AD.

19. The accumulation of currently created money balances, and the accumulation of greater market value of equity, denote non-volitional saving by economic units and for the economy. Only when a Hicksian definition of income is adopted does "saving" represent the accounting record of net capital accumulation at both the individual and the aggregate level.

20. Accounting practices make no attempt to track continual changes in the market values of assets carried on the books of business firms.[23] Intangible assets financed by investment services are conventionally not capitalized and entered on the books, for example, expenditures on research and development, staff education and training, advertising and computer software, but are expensed as a current cost of production. Accounting data are designed to inform but not duplicate market valuations. Differences between accounting and market value definitions of wealth reflect differences in the measurement of corporate net wealth.

8.4 Estimates of Hicksian income

Table 8.1 shows the market value of tangible assets, equities, and the ratio of equities/net worth of US Nonfinancial Corporate Business based on 1988 National Balance Sheet data for the period 1948–1987.[24] Table 8.2 shows the same data for the period 1986–2001 based on 2002 National Balance Sheet data.

Net worth is defined as the difference between total assets and total liabilities after all adjustments. The accounting valuation of assets includes real estate at market value, reproducible assets at replacement cost (after adjusting valuation based on historical cost for changes in the acquisition costs of the same assets),

Table 8.1 Accounting net worth and market value of US Nonfinancial Corporate Business (1948–1987)

Year	Assets at market value or replacement cost ($ millions)	Market value of equities ($ millions)	Equities/net worth (percent)
1948	209,615	83,862	40.0
1949	219,672	92,205	42.0
1950	244,190	116,647	47.8
1951	269,211	138,250	51.4
1952	285,071	149,941	52.6
1953	300,142	144,776	48.2
1954	315,117	216,033	68.6
1955	342,531	269,173	78.6
1956	378,078	289,169	76.5
1957	403,297	242,470	60.1
1958	419,289	342,082	81.6
1959	439,972	361,299	82.1
1960	448,422	354,114	79.0
1961	461,733	428,294	92.8
1962	475,580	389,171	81.8
1963	489,970	456,076	93.1
1964	513,321	509,516	99.3
1965	543,746	553,720	101.8
1966	583,906	504,223	86.4
1967	621,655	651,678	104.8
1968	668,880	736,506	110.1
1969	729,963	646,230	55.5
1970	784,634	648,492	82.6
1971	856,111	758,897	88.6
1972	934,346	855,233	91.5
1973	1,048,013	678,436	47.3
1974	1,337,118	499,098	37.3
1975	1,491,060	684,337	45.9
1976	1,647,452	787,807	47.8
1977	1,717,268	748,002	41.2
1978	2,107,859	773,143	36.7
1979	2,419,386	933,373	38.6
1980	2,780,531	1,293,116	46.5
1981	3,109,641	1,214,845	39.1
1982	3,230,025	1,382,773	42.8
1983	3,327,399	1,638,730	49.2
1984	3,447,798	1,617,733	46.9
1985	3,503,026	2,022,648	57.7
1986	3,560,138	2,332,629	65.5
1987	3,657,167	2,331,322	63.7

Source: David F. Bradford, 1991. Board of Governors of the Federal Reserve System, 1988.

Table 8.2 Accounting net worth and market value of US Nonfinancial Corporate Business (1986–2001)

Year	Tangible assets at market value or replacement cost ($ billions)	Market value of equities outstanding (includes corporate farm equities) ($ billions)	Equities/ net worth (percent)
1986	4.339	1.978	45.6
1987	4.568	2.015	44.1
1988	4.882	2.217	45.4
1989	5.088	2.673	52.5
1990	5.087	2.530	49.7
1991	4.970	3.497	70.4
1992	4.678	3.828	81.8
1993	4.731	4.126	87.2
1994	5.125	4.142	80.8
1995	5.466	5.481	100.3
1996	5.902	6.367	107.9
1997	7.052	9.775	138.6
1998	7.510	11.607	154.5
1999	8.002	15.117	188.9
2000	8.594	12.741	148.3
2001	8.349	10.888	130.4

Source: Board of Governors of the Federal Reserve System, 2002.

and direct investment abroad based on historical cost. Liabilities include all debt, taxes payable, and foreign direct investment.[25] The accounting and current market measures of the value of firms have widely different numerical magnitudes, and exhibit surprisingly little tendency to fluctuate around any constant value.

The ratio of the market to the accounting value of the equity of US nonfinancial corporate business, termed by Kaldor the value "valuation ratio" and by Tobin the "Q ratio," has fluctuated markedly over the postwar period. From a value of 40 percent in 1948, the valuation ratio rose to a high of 110 percent at the stock market peak of 1968. During the stagflation of the 1970s the valuation ratio fell towards depression levels, reaching a low of 37 percent in 1974. Throughout the 1980s valuation ratios remained broadly stable, within a relatively narrow trading range of 40–55 percent. The valuation ratio then exploded during the stock market bubble of the 1990s. It reached a level of 100 percent in 1995 and at the peak of the bubble in 1999 market values rose to nearly double (190 percent) the accounting valuation. The valuation ratio fell back to 148 percent in the stock market crash of 2000, and 130 percent in 2001.

Some nonmarketable assets are impossible to quantify, most importantly human capital symbolizes the present value of an individual's future earning power. Since human capital cannot be sold or committed to lenders as collateral, market capitalization with its accompanying capital gains income does not occur. Capital gain income is generated only by the appreciation of marketable wealth.

But to explain household consumption behavior, estimates of human as well as nonhuman wealth are relevant.

It is sometimes argued that financial market prices are highly volatile and register merely "paper" gains and losses, not the accumulation of "real" value. But the determinants of all asset prices are market beliefs about the future income associated with the asset. All are inherently dependent on the depth and structure of this information. The value of assets such as equities has a transient and even ephemeral quality, and frequently leads to doubts about the efficiency of capital markets in resource allocation.[26] But our inability to predict future behavior cannot be avoided by focusing only on those variables which can be measured with relative precision. Whenever the expected future prices or quantities of goods change, so do the market value of physically unchanged stocks of assets. After "animal spirits," the most important factor determining wealth values is the rate of discount. This rate is dependent on the current Bank Rate set by the CB and the markets' expectations of future CB rate setting behavior.

Balance sheet data provide another demonstration of the inadequacy of conventional NIPA savings measures. Table 8.3 shows selected wealth and income data for U.S. households and nonprofit organizations: Balance sheets, total assets, tangible assets, real estate, consumer durables, financial assets, corporate equities, Mutual fund shares, total liabilities and net Worth, Disposable Personal Income (DPI), and household net worth as a percentage of DPI for the period 1986–2001. As may be seen household net worth averaged about five times the value of DPI over the past few decades, and rose to nearly seven times DPI during the stock market boom of the late 1990s.

Table 8.4 shows the change in household net worth, net investment, total holding gains, total holding gains on real estate, on equities (including mutual fund

Table 8.3 Balance sheet of households and nonprofit organizations (1986–2001) ($ Billions)

Year	Total assets	Tangible assets	Real estate	Consumer durable goods	Financial assets	Corporate equities	Mutual fund shares	Liabilities	Net worth	DPI
1986	18.315	7.146	5.719	1.390	11.169	1.418	333	2.591	15.724	3.198
1987	19.600	7.724	6.177	1.507	11.876	1.384	382	2.838	16.762	3.374
1988	21.401	8.398	6.713	1.641	13.003	1.640	401	3.123	18.278	3.653
1989	23.489	9.108	7.296	1.763	14.381	1.964	469	3.412	20.077	3.906
1990	24.200	9.324	7.405	1.866	14.876	1.795	368	3.701	20.498	4.179
1991	25.917	9.470	7.478	1.935	16.447	2.578	587	3.906	22.011	4.357
1992	27.089	9.733	7.666	2.005	17.356	2.923	728	4.104	22.985	4.627
1993	28.470	9.982	7.807	2.108	18.489	3.217	991	4.386	24.084	4.829
1994	29.472	10.319	8.021	2.226	19.153	3.069	1.047	4.737	24.736	5.053
1995	32.452	10.806	8.405	2.323	21.646	4.097	1.248	5.110	27.342	5.356
1996	35.367	11.425	8.925	2.415	23.943	4.651	1.583	5.462	29.906	5.608
1997	39.346	11.917	9.498	2.328	27.429	6.302	1.941	5.825	33.521	5.968
1998	42.287	12.785	10.269	2.427	30.503	7.174	2.406	6.320	36.968	6.356
1999	48.794	13.730	11.064	2.560	35.064	9.197	3.128	6.920	41.874	6.618
2000	48.810	15.130	12.282	2.732	33.680	7.317	3.125	7.507	41.303	7.180
2001	48.396	16.299	13.264	2.914	32.097	5.832	2.993	8.083	40.313	7.436

Source: Board of Governors of the Federal Reserve System, 2002.

Table 8.4 Change in household and nonprofit organizations, net worth, net investment and net holding gains (1986–2001) ($ Millions)

Year	Change in net worth	Net investment	Total holding gains	Holding gains real estate	Holding gains on equities (including mutual fund shares)	DPI	Total holding gains/ DPI (percent)	Subperiod averages gains/DPI (percent)
1986	1461.0	514.0	968,8	366.1	401.1	3198.5	30	
1987	1037.9	431.7	590.8	331.6	85.7	3374.5	17	28
1988	1516.7	513.2	1007.5	414.3	376.8	3652.7	28	
1989	1798.8	432.1	1389.3	465.8	444.5	3906.1	36	
1990	1421.3	592.3	−131.8	3.6	−171.0	4179.4	−3	
1991	1512.4	374.0	1093.3	−13.0	831.2	4356.9	25	
1992	973.9	526.3	476.0	81.8	328.0	4626.7	10	10
1993	1099.1	429.1	694.2	3.1	418.9	4829.3	14	
1994	651.6	503.2	140.7	64.6	−24.4	5052.7	3	
1995	2606.3	385.1	2308.4	238.3	1287.6	5355.7	43	
1996	2563.9	422.0	2138.6	362.5	979.2	5608.4	37	
1997	3780.3	353.1	3563.1	457.6	1886.4	5968.2	60	51
1998	3446.2	490.2	3091.0	535,1	1396.9	6355.6	48	
1999	4906.0	365.0	4574.1	564.6	2898.9	6618.0	69	
2000	−570,5	267.3	−700,8	958.1	−1636.6	7189.8	−10	−14
2001	−990.3	412.4	−1397.6	720.1	−1529.6	7436.0	−18	

Source: Board of Governors of the Federal Reserve System, 2002.

shares), DPI, and total holding gains as a percentage of DPI for the period 1986–2001. In most years, except 1990, 2000, and 2001 when capital gains were replaced by capital losses, the change in household net worth was two to six times the value of current net physical investment (new capital formation). During the bubble year of 1999 total holding gains exceeded net investment by twelve and one half times. For most years capital gains on stocks were greater than capital gains on real estate and in 1999 were more than four times as large. Capital gains averaged 28 percent of DPI for 1986–1989, and only 10 percent for 1990–1994. During the boom years 1995–1999 capital gains averaged more than 50 percent of DPI. In the bubble year of 1999 capital gains amounted to nearly 70 percent of DPI. Since the stock market bubble burst in 2000, capital gains became capital losses and on average amounted to −14 percent of DPI for the two years 2000–2001. The behavior of capital gain income plays a substantial role in the rise and fall in AD and consumption spending over the past 15 years.

8.5 Conclusions: Hicksian income and saving behavior

The calculation of Hicksian income including capital gains and losses on all marketable assets provides valuable new insights into the performance and volatility of the US economy over the past few decades. The high level of household net worth to income, and a high magnitude of household capital gain income in proportion to DPI indicate the importance of wealth values and capital gain income in explaining the strength of household consumption and investment expenditures during the boom of the 1990s, and its subsequent fall in the first decade of the twenty-first century.

The marginal and average propensity to consume out of wealth and capital gain income appear to be quite low. During the boom period 1995–2000 capital gains averaged more than 50 percent of DPI. The magnitude of the increase in consumption over this period compared to the total value of capital gains suggests that the MPC out of capital gain income was quite small, in the neighborhood of 1–3 percent. Such a low average propensity to consume suggests that the average and marginal propensity to save out of capital gain income is conversely very high, in the range of 97–99 percent. When income is defined to include realized and unrealized capital gains on marketable assets under a Hicksian definition of income, then the abstention from consuming capital gain income constitutes saving. Net wealth accumulation by wealth-holders out of capital gain income is much higher than their saving out of current earned income.

For AD to grow, economic units must spend more on currently produced goods and services in the current period than their total earned income and output in the previous period. Net deficit spending must be financed either out of previously existing money, or out of promises to pay money in the future. When the surplus-spending of one group exactly offsets the deficit-spending of other groups, the current level of AD remains unchanged. For the level of AD to increase above the level of income in the current period, deficit-spending units in aggregate must deficit-spend an amount in excess of the amount that surplus units are surplus-spending in the present period.

In every period the total deficit-spending of deficit-spending groups must, as an accounting identity, equal the total surplus-spending of surplus-spending units. The deficit-spending by debtor units must be identical to the surplus-spending of surplus units, since one unit's deficit is another unit's surplus. In a closed economy total deficit-spending is necessarily identical to total surplus-spending. Deficit-spending must somehow be financed, typically by borrowing against those assets whose market value has appreciated. But what has not been sufficiently emphasized is that most decisions to deficit-spend are volitional and involve an increase in spending on current output. Conversely most decisions to surplus-spend are non-volitional, and do not imply a decrease in concurrent spending. From the point of view of the economy the allocation of current income to the accumulation of currently produced capital assets represents an act of investment and saving. Saving is largely non-volitional on the part of shareholders, and occurs whenever increases in business investment spending are internally financed.

In most economies about one half of capital investment is financed externally by the issue of new financial assets, primarily the issue of debt (IOUs). In most periods new equity issue is largely offset by share repurchases. Increases in deficit-spending cause AD to rise, and increases in surplus-spending cause AD to fall. The allocation of current income to the accumulation of previously existing real or financial assets is an act of saving for individual economic units, but from the viewpoint of the economy represents a reduction in AD. The lower demand for consumption and investment goods lowers the level of AD, profits, income, and output.

Households as a group are net surplus-spenders, and on balance spend less than their total income on current output. Business firms are net deficit-spenders, and on balance spend more than their current income on current output. In a closed economy the aggregate amount that some units deficit-spend is identically equal to the amount that other units surplus-spend. When firms in aggregate deficit-spend an amount in excess of the surplus-spending by households, such net deficit spending is financed by additional bank credit and cause AD, the money supply, income, and output to increase. Conversely when the amount that households on balance desire to surplus-spend is in excess of the amount that business units desire to deficit-spend, net surplus-spending leads to net debt repayment, a reduction in AD and a fall in the money supply, output, and income. Planned deficit-spending by business debtor units is never equal to planned surplus-spending by household surplus units. AD changes continuously over time with no tendency to approach any equilibrium position of "rest" or "balance."[27]

Part III
The Endogeneity of Money and Exogeneity of Interest Rates

Part III

9
The Endogeneity of Credit Money

> Perhaps the greatest moment of triumph for the elementary economics teacher is his exposition of the multiple creation of bank credit and bank deposits. Before the admiring eyes of freshmen he puts to route the practical banker who is so sure he "lends only the money depositors entrust to him." The banker is shown to have a worm's eye view, and his error stands as an introductory object lesson in the fallacy of composition. From the Olympian vantage of the teacher and the textbook, it appears that the banker's dictum must be reversed; depositors entrust to bankers whatever amounts the bankers lend.
>
> James Tobin, 1963

> Monetary theory is less abstract than most economic theory, and cannot avoid relation to reality. ... It belongs to monetary history in a way that economic theory does not always belong to economic history.
>
> Sir John Hicks, 1967

> The central message of this book is that members of the economics profession currently operate with a basically incorrect paradigm of the way modern banking systems operate and of the causal connection between wages, prices, and monetary phenomena. The standard paradigm treats the central bank as determining the monetary base and hence the money supply. The growth of the money supply is held to be the main force determining the rate of growth of money income, wages, and prices. ... This book argues that the above order of causation should be reversed. Changes in wages and employment largely determine the demand for bank loans, which in turn determine the rate of growth of the money supply. Central banks have no alternative but to accept this course of events. Their only option is to vary the short-term rate of interest at which they supply liquidity to the banking system on demand.
>
> B.J. Moore, 1988

9.1 Commodity, fiat, and credit money

Money is the asset generally accepted as the means of payment and medium of exchange. Money also serves as a store of value and as the unit of account in which prices are expressed. The particular assets that are bestowed with general acceptability in exchange have evolved markedly over time, and are still evolving.[1] For conceptual clarity it is essential to distinguish the differences between commodity, fiat, and credit money.

Commodity money is a tangible asset. A wide variety of commodities have historically been used as money: cattle, salt, beads, shells, tobacco, rice, whale teeth, stone rings, and parrot feathers. Eventually commodity money evolved into coinage of the precious metals, gold and silver. These metals have properties highly attractive for the monetary asset: homogeneity, divisibility, durability, transportability, a high value to weight ratio, and reproducibility only under sharply increasing costs. As a result the supply in the very short run is given.[2]

Confidence in and general acceptability of gold and silver as exchange media evolved gradually over prehistoric time. Once confidence in their general acceptability was established, their drawback was the difficulty of verifying a coin's metal content. Due to frequent adulteration it proved impossible to keep "full bodied" coins in circulation.[3] The way around this problem was state intervention.[4] Fiat money maintains its value simply because it is declared by government "fiat" to be "legal tender" in settlement of debt and taxes. As the noninterest-bearing debt of the state, fiat money ceased being a commodity and became a financial convention.

Since it is nearly costless to produce, governments earn a substantial seigniorage from money issue, the difference between the face value of the coin and its cost of production. This led to a temptation for the issuers of money to issue money only partially backed by the money commodity. Governments had the unfortunate tendency to "over issue" fiat money to finance their expenditures during wars and financial crises. "Soft" money refers to coinage that is not fully backed, whereas "hard" money is fully backed by precious metals of equal value. Hard money has the advantage that the limited availability of precious metals prevents governments from increasing the money supply at their discretion. Advocates of "hard" money pointed to the hyperinflations of history as clear evidence of governments' fiscal irresponsibility.[5] With today's fiat money, a difficult-to-counterfeit but inexpensive-to-produce piece of paper is substituted for a valuable coin.

When commodities such as gold and silver served as money and when money was the debt of the government, it was easy to envisage an exogenous money supply independent of the forces influencing the demand for money. It then appeared reasonable to argue that if the money supply were exogenously increased or decreased, prices and incomes must rise or fall until the new supply of nominal money was willingly held. This was the institutional reality when the quantity theory was formulated by Locke and Hume in seventeenth-century England.

The quantity theory is simply an identity $MV \equiv PY$, where M is the money supply, V is velocity (PY/M), P is a general price index, and Y is real income.

The quantity theory asserts that like goods the value of money varies inversely with the quantity supplied. Locke's quantity identity appeared to provide a simple explanation for the broad doubling of prices observed in Europe over the century after gold was discovered in the New World. Implicit in quantity theory reasoning was the unquestioned assumption that the supply of money was exogenous.

Commercial banking originated in Renaissance Italy in the thirteenth and fourteenth centuries and gradually spread to northern Europe in the fifteenth and sixteenth centuries to finance the industrial revolution. The first Italian banks were goldsmiths who acted as brokers between lenders and borrowers of gold, the money commodity. Banking originated when these early goldsmiths first took the (strictly illegal) step of lending out someone else's gold that had been deposited with them for safekeeping. The crucial banking innovation was the making of bank depository receipts (IOUs) payable to "bearer" rather than to a named individual. This led to the surprising discovery that so long as confidence in the bank's solvency was maintained, a banking house of good repute could dispense completely with the issue of coin and issue its own instruments of indebtedness: "bank notes."[6]

Gradually bank notes and deposits became more widely used and checks transferring ownership of deposits became generally accepted in closing exchange transactions. Due to the growth of public confidence in the banks' "instant repurchase" clause—the promise to convert bank deposits into fiat money on demand—credit money gradually became accepted as the means of settlement to close transactions. To maintain its general acceptability in exchange, credit money depends on the public's certainty that deposits will be exchanged into legal tender on demand. Banking is based on a kind of confidence trick, and confidence is essential to the business of banking.

Over centuries the nature of money has dramatically evolved. Early in the nineteenth century most economists unambiguously regarded the money supply as the stock of gold. Bank deposits were regarded merely as "money substitutes" that enabled the gold base to support a larger volume of transactions. The quantity theory did not appear to require much change since the supply of gold was still viewed as determining nominal output. The main difference was that the variability of cyclical fluctuations was now greater, since the available gold stock would sometimes be more fully and at other times less fully used and so could support a more variable level of output. Fluctuations in output would then occur within a wider floor and ceiling around the underlying growth path of the gold stock.[7]

Bank deposits were initially considered to be simply a money substitute. So long as the banking system worked under given rules and maintained a fixed relation between the supply of bank notes and deposits, the nominal stock of bank money in circulation could continue to be regarded as exogenously determined by the underlying nominal stock of gold. It was not its "intrinsic" value, but its quantity relative to demand that gave gold its exchange value.[8]

The evolutionary development of banking built a pyramid of money-substitutes upon the base of metallic commodity money. These bank-created substitutes became closer and closer to money until finally the transfer of a banker's promise to pay was legally regarded as closing a transaction. At the end of the nineteenth century gold was still in use, but a huge superstructure of bank assets and liabilities had been built upon it. As long as countries abided by the gold standard their national currencies were convertible at fixed parities into other currencies based on their gold content. When precious metals and the fiat debt of governments constituted the money supply, it appeared self-evident that the money supply was independent of the forces influencing money demand.

The development of credit money introduced important complications for the view that the money supply could be regarded as exogenous and independent of demand forces. The question whether bank deposits should be viewed as a currency substitute which increased the velocity of base money, or whether they were a new component of the money supply in their own right, was the subject of considerable debate. At the end of the nineteenth century most economists including Marshall and Walras regarded the nominal value of money balances as determined by the underlying gold stock.

Over the twentieth century gold in private circulation gradually diminished, and became the asset of ultimate settlement for banks in international transactions. In the process currency plus bank deposits came to be regarded as the domestic money supply. If the quantity theory of money was to be retained, it was to the quantity of credit money that it must apply. Since the quantity of deposits bears a fixed relation to the supply of gold reserves this step was taken by most economists, and is still widely accepted today. But it is a fatal step, since it reverses the causal arrow between money and income and makes a profound difference as to how money prices and money incomes are determined.

The quantity of commodity money in existence denotes nothing about the outstanding volume of credit. Commodity money lies outside the lending and borrowing process. Commodity money is a material good not a financial claim. It carries no credit risk, pays no interest, has no capital uncertainty, and is perfectly liquid. It is an asset to its holder and a liability to no one. The supply of commodity money appeared to be exogenous. In the short run it is independent of changes in the demand for money and credit.

Fiat money is formally the liability of the government. The supply of fiat money is created by government deficit spending, financed by the issue of newly created money. Although it is a financial asset, the liability of the issuing government, the quantity of fiat money supplied does not directly depend on private units' demand for money. Commodity and fiat money have a supply existence independent of the demand for money. If money, were solely fiat money, it would be realistic to assume the existence of a physical stock of currency "out there" in the economy. So long as changes in this stock come about "outside" the private sector fiat money could be treated as exogenous. Changes in the supply of currency could then be regarded as "causing" changes in money income.[9]

Credit money refers to bank deposits, the liabilities of commercial banks. Unlike commodity and fiat money, the supply of credit money can no longer be assumed to be exogenously given. As retailers of credit, banks are price-setters and quantity-takers. Credit money is supplied by banks in response to changes in the demand for bank credit. Deposits increase whenever banks grant loans, so the money supply rises in response to increases in credit demand.

Proposals for a monetary constitution as to how central banks should regulate the supply of money have revolved around two concepts:

1. the *convertibility principle*, setting the price of some commodity, bundle of commodities, or debt; and
2. the *quantity principle*, setting the particular level or growth rate of the monetary quantity.

Fisher's and Keynes' decision in the 1920s to consider bank deposits as money rather than as money substitutes pushed the profession to reconsider the theoretical significance of the changed behavior of banking institutions. In the United States most economists continued to regard bank deposits as money substitutes until the Second World War.

But is the quantity of credit money supplied still controlled by the central bank? Changes currently occurring in the electronics payments mechanism are as revolutionary as the nineteenth-century introduction of bank checking accounts, and are creating just as much uncertainty about how money should be defined. Modern economies are in the initial stages of a comprehensive electronic funds transfer system (EFT) where computer networks instantaneously record and transfer funds globally. Electronic systems have no use for physical currency. The notion of money as an independent stock of financial assets generally accepted as a means of contractual settlement will soon become obsolete. Computerization of the payments mechanism will finally make crystal clear what is already the case. Central bank quantitative regulation of the money supply based on the *quantity principle* is impossible. Only the *convertibility principle* remains. The price set is not the value of money (1/P), but Bank Rate (BR) the rate at which the Central Bank (CB) lends money to the banking system.

Credit money is a financial asset to its owners (bank depositors) and a financial liability to its issuers (commercial banks). Unlike gold it is not created outside the banking system by the CB or the government. The supply of credit money is endogenously created by the extension of bank credit. Unlike commodity and fiat money credit money can yield interest. The term "money stock" becomes misleading, insofar as it implies the existence of a physical quantity of money "out there" in the economy. Credit money does not exist as given "stock." Its flow supply changes continuously over time, as the demand for bank credit and BR vary pro-cyclically over the business cycle.

Credit money is the liability of the issuing bank. It is backed by the banks' assets, which in turn are the IOUs of the bank's borrowers. A healthy economy requires a healthy banking system. Belief in the exchangeability of credit money into legal tender is a precondition for monetary exchange. Banks are **retailers** of credit not portfolio managers. The supply of credit money responds to changes in the demand for bank credit. Deposits ("Bank" or "Credit" money) are created and destroyed by the granting and repayment of bank loans. "Loans create deposits."[10]

Credit money can never be in "excess" supply, since additional loans are issued only in response to increases in demand for credit. If bank borrowers find themselves with an "excess" supply of deposits, they can repay their outstanding bank loans and their money balances are immediately reduced.[11] Credit money provides many of the services and takes on many of the characteristics of financial assets. It may carry credit risk, be capital uncertain, represent immediately available purchasing power and provide a host of transaction and financial services, including payment of interest. With the technological evolution of new forms of financial services, the dividing line between money and nonmonetary financial assets becomes increasingly blurred.

The process how credit money is supplied unfortunately is extremely non-transparent and regularly fools economists, politicians, journalists, textbook writers, and students.[12] In most countries the monetary authorities are formally delegated to control the money supply. Commercial banks are required to operate under strict rules imposed by the monetary authority. One of the foremost is the imposition of strict reserve requirements forcing banks to maintain a minimum ratio between their cash reserves and their deposit liabilities. These rules must be complied with and are completely firm. It appears self-evident that the story taught in the textbooks is correct. The supply of credit money is dependent on the supply of reserves, and the quantity of reserves is provided by the CB exogenously according to its policy goals. Central bank liabilities, outstanding notes and coin (legal tender) plus bank reserves (bank deposits held with the central bank) constitute the "high-powered base" that supports a multiple quantity of deposits.

Disputes concerning whether changes in the money supply play a *causal* role, or whether variations in money are the *effect* of economic activity, were central to the banking and currency school debate in the last century and have remained a persistent theme in the evolution of monetary theory ever since.[13] Current discussion of the quantity theory, after settling on some definition of how money is defined, considers how the factors determining the quantity of money supplied compare to the factors determining the quantity of money demanded by economic units. But the basis of the quantity theory is something so elementary that it is seldom explicitly considered: the belief that the supply and demand for money are independent as is the case of commodities.

Friedman's reinterpretation of the quantity identity, as a theory of the "demand" for money, led to the renaissance of monetarism during the 1970s. Its seemingly self-evident conclusion that changes in the supply of money determine changes in the level of prices and incomes depends for its validity on two assumptions: (1) the supply of money is exogenous, and (2) the economy eventually reaches a position of general equilibrium. Unfortunately neither of these assumptions are valid.

9.2 The money-multiplier identity

Mainstream macroeconomics maintains that the money supply is the policy instrument of the CB. Due to the "money multiplier" process the CB is believed to be able to increase or reduce the money supply at its discretion, by using open market operations to expand or contract the high-powered base. The money-multiplier theory is widely accepted in the mainstream literature, appears in all or most introductory macro-texts and is taught by most macro-economists not specialists in money and banking. Unfortunately it is incorrect.

Economists first recognized the existence of a "money-multiplier process" in the 1920s.[14] Given the empirical stability of the reserves/deposits ratio, since the CB is able to increase or reduce the base by open market operations, it was concluded that the money supply is an exogenous variable under the control of the CB. Central banks have not had a successful experience with monetary targeting. But most US economists still believe that if the Fed remained focused and tried sufficiently hard enough, it could ensure the money supply followed its target growth path.

The money multiplier holds that the CB initiates exogenous increases and decrease in the money supply by the open market purchase and sale of government securities. Open market transactions result in equal one-for-one changes in the high-powered base. Provided the base-money multiplier is stable the money supply changes by the same proportion as the base. *Ergo*, the CB controls the money supply.

The mainstream money-multiplier theory appears to be logical, persuasive, and amply supported by empirical evidence: Its essence may be briefly summarized as follows:

1. The money multiplier is an identity, the ratio of the supply of money (M) to the monetary base (B). As an identity, it is true by definition:
$$m \equiv M/B. \tag{9.1}$$
2. The money supply (M) is defined as the sum of currency (C) plus bank deposits (D):
$$M \equiv C + D \tag{9.2}$$
3. The high-powered base (B) is defined as the sum of currency (C) plus bank reserves (R), and constitutes the liabilities of the CB:
$$B \equiv C + R \tag{9.3}$$
4. As an accounting identity, CB total liabilities equal CB total assets. The high-powered base rises and falls with CB purchases or sales of government securities in the open market. By substitution of equations 9.2 and 9.3 into equation 9.1:
$$m \equiv (C + D)/(C + R) \equiv [(C/D) + 1] / [(C/D) + (R/D)] \tag{9.4}$$
5. Rewriting equation 9.1, the money supply is a stable "multiple" (m) of the high-powered base (B):
$$M \equiv mB \equiv [(C/D) + 1] / [(C/D) + (R/D)] \, B \tag{9.5}$$

From equation 9.5, the nominal supply of credit money (M) appears determined by three "proximate" factors:

1. the currency–deposit ratio (C/D), determined by the public,
2. the reserve ratio (R/D), determined by the banking system,
3. the high-powered base (B), determined by the CB.

Consistent with the General Equilibrium (GE) formulation of mainstream theory, money-multiplier theory concludes that money supply is jointly determined by the behavior of the public, the banking system, and the CB. So long as the above ratios vary within a narrow range, any effect of changes in the ratios on the multiplier can be offset by CB manipulation of the high-powered base. There is noticeable week-to-week variation in the money multiplier (m) over the short run. But for periods of one quarter or one year (m) is empirically highly stable. The effects of any changes in the multiplier (m) on the money supply (M) can be offset by appropriate changes in the Base (B) by the CB. The money supply appears to be firmly under the exogenous control of the CB.

The argument that the money supply is exogenous under the direct control of the monetary authorities, appears to be logically impregnable. But in fact it provides a striking example of how easily mathematical manipulation leads to the reversal of the "true" direction of causality and incorrect theoretical and policy conclusions.

The "proof" that the money supply is exogenous consists of two essential parts:

1. the identity ($M \equiv mB$), which is true by definition,
2. the empirical regularity ($m = k$), which is confirmable by empirical observation.

It is recognized that in addition to CB open market operations a large number of stochastic forces also affect the sources and uses of the base:

1. public holdings of currency,
2. the size of the "float" (checks in process),
3. the volume of discount window borrowing,
4. the quantity of excess reserves,
5. the size of government deposits,
6. net capital inflows.

The CB can offset these stochastic changes by "defensive" open market operations. Defensive actions account for the vast majority of all open market operations. It is recognized that the money multiplier (m), although normally stable, is not a constant, and at times varies significantly. Nevertheless so long as the CB is able to dominate net sources of the base by open market operations, it is able to realize its target growth rate for the money supply, admittedly not on a week-to-week basis but over longer periods such as one quarter or one year.[15]

When plotted in interest–money space, the mainstream money supply function appears vertical or at least steeply upward-sloping.[16] As a result the mainstream view has been termed the "Verticalist" position: the CB directly controls the money supply as its key policy instrument.[17] The authorities are presumed able to increase the base and the money supply by open market purchases (shifting the MS curve rightward), and to reduce the base and the money supply by open market sales (shifting the MS curve leftward).

Verticalist theory regards commercial banks as responding symmetrically to an excess supply or excess demand for reserves. By increasing or reducing their asset portfolios banks keep their cash-reserve ratio at the required level. Banks are viewed as portfolio managers (price-takers and quantity-setters) who manage their total assets to maintain cash reserves at the required ratio. Bank assets are (implicitly) regarded as marketable. Monetary change originates from policy-determined changes in the high-powered base. The direction of causality goes from changes in the base, to changes in deposits: "Reserves make deposits." When the money supply is observed to overshoot or fall short of the MS target this is attributed to CB stupidity and inefficiency, and/or political considerations.[18]

Unfortunately the money-multiplier demonstration of how central banks exogenously control the rate of growth of the money supply is logically and factually incorrect, and fatally misleading as a description of the money creation process. Money-multiplier analysis is largely responsible for the common misunderstanding that the direction of the causal relationship between monetary change and changes in prices and incomes is from money to income. It reinforces the widespread belief in the inflationary consequences of increases in the money supply within the economics profession.

Understanding the "true" direction of causality between reserves and deposits presupposes a realistic understanding of commercial bank behavior. Commercial banks are retailers of credit in highly oligopolistic markets. Like other retailers they are price-setters and quantity-takers. The quantity of credit they sell depends on the demand for credit they face. In all overdraft systems, changes in the quantity of bank credit granted are determined by changes in the demand for bank credit by credit-worthy borrowers. The rate of growth of the demand for bank credit (loans) determines the rate of growth of the supply of credit money (deposits).

In all overdraft systems the quantity of bank loans is determined by bank borrowers, not the banks or the CB. Banks assign a credit ceiling to individual borrowers, which sets maximum amount they are willing to lend. Bank borrowers decide the amount they wish to draw down. Central banks set BR, the marginal supply price of reserves to the banking system, not the money supply. The centrality of changes in the demand for bank loans, and the critical role of interest rates, are omitted and suppressed in the money-multiplier formulation.

The money multiplier (m) is simply an identity, the ratio of the money supply (M) to the high-powered base (B): $m \equiv M/B$. As such it is true by definition. When the identity is written: $Bm \equiv M$ and when the base is viewed as exogenous, it appears self-evident that exogenous changes in the base "cause" exogenous changes in the money supply: $\Delta Bm \rightarrow \Delta M$. But since the multiplier is an identity it remains true when inverted, and expressed as a quotient: $B \equiv (1/m) M$. In this case with equal logical force the identity can be read as implying the existence of "reverse causality." Changes in the money supply cause changes in the base, driven by changes in the demand for bank credit. Due to CB rate-setting behavior the high-powered base responds endogenously to changes in the demand for bank credit, bank demand for reserves, and the supply of money: $\Delta M (1/m) \rightarrow \Delta B$.[19]

9.3 The endogeneity of the high-powered base

CBs change BR according to their expectations of changes in the future state of the economy ("animal spirits"), in an attempt to achieve their stabilization goals of price stability, full employment ("internal balance"), and a stable external value of their currency ("external balance"). The supply of credit money is credit-driven and is horizontal as some markup on Bank Rate for all borrowers with unutilized lines of credit.

Changes in the supply of credit money do not depend on how banks respond to changes in interest rates, but on the interest elasticity of business and household demand for bank credit. The demand for short-term credit appears empirically very interest-inelastic. But this is explained because BR is changed positively with changes in the CB's estimate of changes in "animal spirits." When credit demand increases BR is raised, and when credit demand declines BR is lowered. When the demand curve shifts up, rates are changed. A rise in rates is associated with an increase in credit demand and a reduction in rates with a decline in credit demand. It is very difficult to disentangle the interest-elasticity of the demand for bank credit from bank lending data.

In developed economies the chief payment media are checks drawn against existing bank deposits or overdraft facilities, and bank credit cards drawn against overdraft facilities. Bank deposits represent bank IOUs for the loan of fiat money. Like fiat money bank deposits are generally acceptable as a payments medium due to the banks "instant repurchase" clause (the guarantee of transfer into cash on demand for all deposit liabilities.)[20] Bank deposits provide a much wider range of pecuniary and non-pecuniary services than fiat money: record-keeping of past transactions, security from theft, interest payments on deposits, overdraft facilities, financial advice, attractive buildings, and sometimes attractive tellers. As a result bank deposits thoroughly dominate fiat money for most exchange transactions.

The fatal error in the money-multiplier approach lies in the implicit assumption that because the high-powered base constitutes the liabilities of the CB, the CB has the ability to increase or reduce the size of the base at its discretion. The central ever-present responsibility of CBs is not to control the money supply, but to maintain the liquidity of the financial system. This fundamental liquidity-supplying system obligation completely dominates the goal of targeting any particular rate growth of the money supply. As ultimate supplier of system liquidity, CB's offset all sharp movements of security prices that would if not offset change the temporal flow price of liquidity.

The conventional view is that by open market purchases or sales of securities CB's exogenously increase or reduce the high-powered base. Although the base is no longer rigidly tied to an exogenous stock of gold it is regarded as under the direct control of the CB. But in the real world CBs are unable to increase or reduce the high-powered base at their discretion. Their job is continually to maintain system liquidity at the current level of security prices. Exogenous changes in the base would precipitate exogenous changes in asset prices and system liquidity. The CB must immediately offset all such changes by defensive CB open market operations in order to maintain asset liquidity and keep current asset prices near their previous levels.

The behavior of the monetary base and the money supply are completely endogenous in the real world. The supply of credit money is determined by the demand for bank credit by credit-worthy borrowers.[21] Under overdraft systems business and household borrowers have pre-arranged lines of credit with their bankers, up to some pre-arranged ceiling. Within these guidelines banks are price-setters and quantity-takers in their retail loan markets and are unable to increase or reduce their loan portfolios at their discretion. They are able to influence the quantity of loans demanded by varying the interest rate they charge, the collateral margin they demand, the credit ceilings they assign, the degree of borrower or loan risk they consider acceptable, the advertising they incur, and the attractiveness of their tellers. For borrowers with unutilized lines of credit who do not wish to borrow up to their permitted ceiling the quantity of credit granted is completely demand-determined.

The monetary authorities are unable to decrease or increase the high-powered base or the money supply exogenously at their discretion. If the demand for bank credit and the money supply is expanding more rapidly than desired the authorities cannot reduce non-borrowed reserves by selling securities in the open market. This would have the immediate effect of driving banks "into the bank" to borrow at the discount window to acquire additional borrowed reserves. Open market sales cause asset prices to fall and interest rates to rise. If the authorities wish to keep interest rates at their target level, they are forced to undertake offsetting security purchases.[22]

The interest cost of short-term loans is a very small proportion of the total cost of loan repayment. The demand for short-term bank credit is extremely interest-inelastic. Interest rates can rise precipitously without causing a significant short-run deceleration of loan demand and money growth. When the money supply is growing more slowly than desired the authorities could purchase securities on the open market to increase non-borrowed reserves. But the resulting excess reserves would soon drive market interest rates below their target toward zero bid. The authorities are forced to offset the security purchases and sell securities to keep interest rates at their targeted level. The CB's underlying responsibility is to set the short-term interest rate, and maintain the liquidity of the financial system. This involves smoothing all sharp fluctuations in security prices and accommodating all demand for increased bank reserves at the existing level of bank rate.

In most periods of loan expansion or deceleration the base "multiplier" remains reasonably stable. In consequence the relationship between changes in the base and changes in the money supply appears to be stable empirically. But the stability of the multiplier reflects the fact that changes in demand for base money are endogenously supplied on demand. The true direction of causality between reserves and deposits is the reverse of that envisaged by mainstream theory. Econometric techniques are unable to distinguish the direction of causality among accounting identities.

CB's target the level of interest rates as their chief policy instrument. Price-setting behavior may be illustrated diagrammatically as a horizontal credit supply function at a stable mark-up over BR. The particular BR set depends on the CB's goals for and its expectations of the future behavior of the economy, CB interest rate-setting procedure was long termed as its "policy reaction function" but recently has become known as its "Taylor Rule."[23]

9.4 Central Banks: the ultimate supplier of system liquidity

In the real world CBs do not exogenously increase or decrease the supply of credit money by expanding or contracting the high-powered base as the money-multiplier analysis asserts. CBs continually smooth security prices to ensure system liquidity at their targeted level of interest rates. As a result they are unable to target the supply of money. The CB sets BR and the supply of credit money varies endogenously with changes in demand for bank credit.[24]

The initial direct effect of an exogenous CB purchase or sale of government securities on the open market is to increase or reduce bank deposits and the non-borrowed reserves of the banking system. This part of the story told in the textbooks is correct. But unless they wish to raise or lower the level of short-term rates, CBs never undertake open market operations to exogenously increase or reduce total reserves or the high-powered base. Their overriding day-to-day responsibility is to maintain system liquidity at the target Bank Rate. Except when the target rate is changed open market operations are purely defensive. They are aimed at eliminating short-run fluctuations ("spikes") in security prices with the goal of ensuring the liquidity of the banking system and the economy at the Bank Rate selected to achieve the CB's macroeconomic targets.

Changes in net bank borrowing from the CB put immediate downward or upward pressure on interest rates. In their role of ultimate supplier of system liquidity, CBs continually smooth asset prices around their current values. They must continually pursue "defensive" open market purchases and sales of securities to maintain interest rates at their targeted level. All market shocks that would impact on asset prices must be deliberately offset and their effects on the level of security prices and interest rates eliminated.

CB open market purchases and sales of security raise or lower bank non-borrowed reserves, inducing banks to reduce or increase their borrowing from the CB. Central bank open market purchases of securities show up as immediate increases in bank excess reserves, and must immediately be reversed by open market sales if the overnight rate is to be kept at its current level. If CB security purchases were not offset by CB sales of securities or repose BR would fall toward zero bid. Since CBs must keep security prices and interest rates at their current level to ensure system liquidity they are unable to exogenously increase or reduce the reserve base. The supply of credit money is endogenously credit-driven at the Bank Rate (BR) set by the CB.

The CB's main policy instrument is the price of credit (BR) which it makes reserves available to the financial system. Over short time periods the interest cost is a very small proportion of the total costs of a loan, and the demand for short-term bank loans is very interest-inelastic. Huge swings in interest rates and accompanying huge fluctuations in asset values would be unavoidable if a CB attempted to hold the money supply or its rate of growth at some predetermined level over business cycle upswings and downswings. In a complex world where the future is unknowable, a CB's obligation is primarily to ensure the liquidity of the financial system. Liquidity requires that economic units can obtain money quickly, easily, and cheaply (particularly in times of crisis) by the sale of previously created liquid assets or newly created debt. To this end CBs keep BR at the targeted level that reflects their stabilization objectives for the economy.

The supply of credit money is determined by the demand for bank credit by credit-worthy borrowers.[25] Bank deposits are the accounting record of bank financial assets, and are equal to loans granted, securities purchased, and non-borrowed and borrowed reserves provided by the CB. The immediate effect of CB purchases or sales of securities on the open market is to increase or reduce total deposits and non-borrowed reserves of the banking system as the textbook story maintains. But this is not the end of the story and the belief that it is leads to a false understanding of CB behavior.

Unless they wish to change the level of BR, CBs never undertake open market operations to expand or contract bank total reserves, the high-powered base, or the money supply as the conventional view maintains. The central responsibility of CBs is to maintain the liquidity of the financial system. Unless the monetary authorities wish to change the level of interest rates, CB open market operations are purely defensive in nature. Their central object is continually to offset stochastic forces that change system liquidity.[26]

As the ultimate supplier of system liquidity CBs attempt to smooth out all short-run movements in financial asset prices. An exogenous increase in CB sales of securities *ceteris paribus* puts immediate downward pressure on security prices and upward pressure on interest rates. In response the CB must pursue offsetting open market purchases of securities to maintain interest rates at their targeted level. Conversely an exogenous CB purchase of securities puts immediate upward pressure on security prices and downward pressure on interest rates, to which the CB must respond by offsetting sales of securities. All exogenous forces whose impact is to affect system liquidity and increase or decrease the level of interest rates must continuously be offset by defensive operations to eliminate their effects on the liquidity of financial markets.

Open-market purchases and sales of securities by the CB increase or reduce bank non-borrowed reserves and induce banks to reduce or increase their borrowing from the CB. As an accounting transaction, CB open market purchases of securities show up as increases in bank excess reserves. This must immediately be reversed by open market sales to prevent the overnight rate from falling below target. If exogenous CB security purchases were not offset bank rate would fall to zero bid. Since they are targeting a particular level of interest rates, CBs are unable to increase or reduce the money supply at their discretion. Changes in the money supply endogenously reflect changes in bank assets since CBs must continually target BR.

The demand for bank credit determines the quantity of deposits supplied by the banking system. The CB's sole discretionary instrument is BR, the price at which it makes reserves available to the system. Since the demand for short-term bank credit is extremely interest-inelastic, huge swings in interest rates with accompanying huge fluctuations in asset values would be unavoidable if a CB attempted to keep the money supply or its rate of growth at some pre-determined value.

With the important exception of the United States in most countries commercial banks have automatic access to CB rediscount financing at BR to assure system liquidity. This has been termed the "classical" reserve system.[27] In practice CB open market operations maintain non-borrowed reserves slightly below the level of required reserves so as to keep the banking system "in the bank". This compels banks to use the CBs' accommodation facilities to borrow any residual reserves required and permits the authorities to maintain its target level of short-term rates.

The following is a particularly revealing quote by a prominent US central banker:

> The idea of a regular injection of reserves ... suffers from a naïve assumption that the banking system only expands loans after the system (or market factors) have put reserves into the banking system. In any given statement week, the reserves required to be maintained by the banking system are predetermined by the level of deposits existing two weeks earlier. ... Since banks have to meet their reserve requirements each week, ... and since they can do nothing within that week to affect required reserves, that total amount of reserves has to be made available to the banking system. The Federal Reserve does have discretion as to how the banks acquire this predetermined level of needed reserves. The reserves can be supplied from the contribution of open market operations and the movement of other reserve factors, or they can come from member bank borrowing at the discount window. ... Within a statement week, the reserves have to be there; and in one way or another, the Federal Reserve will have to accommodate the need for them. ... In the real world banks extend credit, creating deposits in the process. And look for the reserves later.[28]

The primary goal of CB operations is to smooth short-term fluctuations in interest and exchange rates to ensure financial markets are continuously characterized by liquidity and breadth. To keep non-borrowed reserves and so interest rates unchanged all exogenous factors must be offset by CB security purchases and sales.

In the 1970s and 1980s many CBs adopted a policy of announcing a "target" growth rate for particular monetary aggregates. But since CBs were unable to control the demand for bank loans they were unable to control the rate of change in the monetary aggregates. CBs frequently missed even their wide target bands for money supply growth.[29] Textbooks, contrary to monetary authorities, are unable to directly control either the quantity or the growth rate (nominal or real) of the high-powered base, total bank reserves, or the supply of credit money. The only variable CBs can directly control is the supply price at which they provide liquidity to the economy: BR, the overnight interest rate charged to the banking system for reserves.

In consequence of their inability to directly control the money supply—the variable for which they typically are given statutory responsibility—central bankers have been forced into a much noted propensity for "Delphic" pronouncements, characterized by carefully calculated vagueness, evasiveness, and obscurantism. This stems from their need to retain public credibility as the institution formally responsible for determining the rate of growth of the money supply, a variable whose movement they have only indirect power to influence. This is often compounded by the lack of formal authorization (and in some countries and some periods statutory prohibition) to set the variable they can, do, and must control, the level of short-term interest rates.

The supply of credit money varies directly in response to changes in the demand for credit. This reflects changes in agents' planned deficit spending and their future expectations about the economy. It is an illegitimate thought experiment to analyze the effects of a change in the supply of credit money, *ceteris paribus* holding all else constant. The supply of credit money, the demand for bank credit, the change in the wage bill, and the change in aggregate demand, are all intrinsically interrelated and vary *pari passu*. The essence of central banking is to provide an "elastic" money supply by "smoothing" (eliminating) sharp fluctuations in interest rates and exchange rates. As the residual supplier of system liquidity, CBs must provide the reserves demanded to meet all changes in the demand for bank credit and supply of bank deposits at the targeted interest rate.

The monetary authorities frequently find themselves in a serious dilemma. In order to fulfil their underlying commitment to orderly and liquid financial markets they are obliged to provide the banks with additional reserves at the target interest rate, even when the result is to accommodate more rapid monetary growth and so increased inflationary pressures in booms, or monetary contraction and deflationary impulses in slumps. Irrespective of the importance of their stabilization goals all a CB can do is adjust its interest rate target. As the residual supplier of system liquidity, in all closed economies the monetary authorities must set the marginal supply price of liquidity. They vary short-term interest rates procyclically over the business cycle in the attempt to steer the economy toward their desired set of macroeconomic outcomes, price stability, and full employment.

Commercial banks are retailers of credit. The business of banking is making loans. Lending denotes an exchange of IOUs and bank deposits are the banks' IOUs. Commercial banks purchase securities when they find themselves in a cash surplus position when their total deposits minus their required reserves exceed their total loans $[(D - R) > L]$. The CB's key role is to administer the marginal supply price at which it makes additional reserves available to the banking system. It has no choice as to the quantity of reserves it provides, but only the price and manner of their provision. If commercial banks are to meet their reserve requirements all deficiencies in required reserves must be supplied. Open market purchases or sales increase or reduce the volume of non-borrowed reserves and deposits in the banking system as an accounting relationship. Bank reserves are always supplied endogenously as demanded at the interest rate set exogenously by the CB.[30]

The above story conflicts directly with the monetarist policy proscription: CBs should supply the quantity of reserves necessary to achieve their money supply target and leave financial markets to adjust to this exogenous money supply. There are excellent reasons why no CB has ever adopted this monetarist proscription. The most important is because it cannot be done. The single most important constraint is that a CB's central obligation is the residual supplier of system liquidity.

CBs are unable to reduce the rate of money supply growth in a boom by reducing the supply of cash reserves to the system. All they can do is raise the marginal supply price of reserves and increase the general level of short-term interest rates. CBs are similarly unable to increase the rate of money supply growth in a slump. All they can do is lower the general level of short-term rates. By reducing rates and supplying excess reserves to the banking system, they may be able to expand the rate of money supply growth in a slump by inducing banks to purchase additional government securities. But they cannot force borrowers to borrow more or to spend additional amounts.

9.5 Conclusions: deposit creation money and "convenience lending"

The quantity of credit money is equal to the quantity of bank credit demanded by bank borrowers and granted by the banking system. Banks decide on the total amount they believe individual credit-worthy borrowers will be able to repay. Within their imposed overdraft credit ceiling, bank borrowers decide on the amount of credit they wish to borrow. The supply of credit money changes continuously over time with changes in the demand for bank credit. An increase in the demand for bank loans increases the supply of bank deposits. The repayment of bank loans reduces the supply of deposits.

The supply of bank credit may be viewed as "horizontal" in interest–money space at the banks' lending rate which is administered as a mark-up over the BR set by the CB.[31] So long as the mark-up is stable whenever the CB changes BR, the banks change their prime lending rate proportionally. Credit rationing is intrinsic to the lending process. Credit rationing is imposed by all lenders to prevent borrowers from borrowing themselves into bankruptcy and being unable to repay their loans. Private lenders will be unwilling to lend to borrowers whom they regard as un-creditworthy at any interest rate.

Bank deposits are the accounting record of bank loans. Loans are the single most important asset in bank balance sheets, and "loans create deposits." The quantity of bank deposits responds to changes in the demand for bank credit by borrowers who have been judged by their banks to be credit-worthy. Neither commercial banks, nor the CB, nor bank borrowers control the flow supply of credit money. The quantity of money changes continuously and endogenously over time with changes in the demand for bank credit. The *raison d'etre* of CBs is to maintain the good health and liquidity of the banking system. By raising and lowering BR the CB reduces or increases the quantity of bank lending and the money supply.

The demand for short-term bank credit is highly interest-inelastic. It varies with changes in business demand for working capital which in turn varies with the wage bill and expectations of future AD. The acceptability of bank deposits as a payments instrument depends on the public's confidence that deposits will be exchangeable for legal tender (fiat money) on demand in all future periods. Banks hold cash reserves in their portfolios to maintain the continuous convertibility of their deposits into cash. In most but not all economies CBs require commercial banks to maintain a minimum ratio of reserves to deposits.

Changes in required reserve ratios have no direct effect on the supply of credit money. By requiring banks to hold more noninterest-bearing assets in their portfolios, increases in reserve requirements act like a special tax on banking firms. Higher reserve requirements are widely disliked by the banking system since they reduce the share of earning assets held in bank portfolios, impair bank profits, and reduce the international competitiveness of the banking system. If required reserves were doubled, CBs would accommodate the banks' increased demand for reserves, and the quantity of reserves supplied would also double.[32]

Money is a social convention, not a commodity. Depositors do not have a demand to hold a particular quantity of deposits as a function of their price, income, wealth, relative prices of other assets, and interest rates as is the case with the demand for goods. Deposits are held as a buffer stock, to ensure agents maintain sufficient liquidity. Asset holders are always prepared to *accept* indefinite additional amounts of money in exchange for goods, irrespective of the level of interest rates. Increases in the supply of money are always accepted in exchange without a change in any price. General acceptability in exchange is the definition of money. An increase in deposits represents an endogenous increase in *"convenience lending"* by depositors of fiat money to the banking system.[33]

Individual depositors may hold an increase in deposits only for nano-seconds. But all the deposits that have ever been created must be held by someone. Depositors suffer no decrease in liquidity, and no abstention from consumption when they increase their lending of fiat money to the banking system in exchange for bank deposits. They typically do not even regard an increase in their deposits as an increase in their lending of fiat money to the banking system. *The demand to hold bank deposits by individual depositors is not a volitional decision.* It may be viewed as *"convenience lending,"* i.e. simply "doing nothing" when additional deposits are received in exchange other than depositing the checks in their bank accounts.

"Convenience lending" may alternatively be viewed as a "buffer stock" demand for money. The ratio of money-to-income and money-to-wealth held by depositors determines the income velocity of money. But the "demand" for money is not a volitional demand. Rather than having a volitional "demand" for money agents "accept" any money they receive. This is not the same as passively "demanding" goods as a function of their price. Asset holders have some desired ratio of money-to-income and money-to-wealth that they wish to hold, depending on the value of present and expected future interest rates. But money is always "accepted," in exchange, not "demanded."[34]

The money market is never in "equilibrium." The idea that the supply of money is determined by the demand for money represents a major fallacy of composition.

What is true for the individual is not true for the group. Individual agents are always willing to "accept" money balances in exchange, and the quantity of money accepted is always equal to the quantity of money supplied. But the supply of money is not determined by the "demand for deposits" by depositors but by the "demand for credit" by bank borrowers. The quantity of deposits supplied is determined on the asset-side and not on the liability-side of bank balance sheets. The supply of credit money outstanding is equal to the total quantity of deposits accepted by economic agents. But the supply of credit money is determined by the quantity of bank credit demanded by credit-worthy bank borrowers, not by depositors' "portfolio demand" for money balances.

The supply of credit money responds to changes in the demand for bank credit by borrowers who have been judged credit-worthy by their banker. In order for the money supply to be assumed as given, time must be stopped and the expectations of all agents "frozen." Only then would the quantity of bank credit demanded and the supply of credit money be constant. Unless all expectations are frozen a position of "general equilibrium" where all markets clear cannot occur in a money economy.

10
Commercial Bank Intermediation

It is assumed that the banks create just enough additional money for the industrial circulation ... to allow the absorption of the unemployed factors of production into employment at a steady rate ... This amounts to the banks' supplying the entrepreneurs with whatever they require over and above their profits to pay wages on the gradually increasing scale which is assumed.

John Maynard Keynes, 1930

Throughout the whole time money has been evolving. The change from metallic money to paper money is obvious, but there are other things going on, ... Even if we say that metallic money has given place to credit money we are still not getting to the bottom of what has happened. For credit money is just a part of a whole credit structure that extends outside money, ... There has been a change in the whole character of the monetary system, ... This evolution called as it proceeded for radical revision of monetary theory. As the actual system changed the theoretical simplification ought to have changed with it. We can now see that it did not change sufficiently.

Sir John Hicks, 1979

The individual desire to hold money reveals both doubt in existing conventions as well as increased confidence in one of them, namely money. ... This paradox can only be explained if it is allowed that agents attach meaning to beliefs external to the formal economic model of a monetary economy. Only when acting upon external beliefs rather than upon economic fundamentals are agents allowed to cut through the incompatibility between the trust in money and the mistrust in the persistence of existing institutions. ... In an economy where agents act upon their ignorance instead of their knowledge, trust represents an essential element in the coordination of the economic process.

Van Ees and Sterken, 2001

10.1 Commercial banks as retailers of credit

It is important to recognize at the outset that banks are "retailers" of credit in imperfectly competitive markets. They are not "portfolio managers." Like most retailers, banks are price-setters and quantity-takers in their retail markets. The quantity of credit that banks provide depends on the quantity of credit demanded by borrowers whom the banks have judged to be credit-worthy, and the lending rate set by the banks. In contrast to the mainstream view, it is not bank depositors but bank borrowers who initiate the changes in bank asset and liability portfolios.[1]

Like a language money is a social convention. Like a language the money supply cannot be controlled. But unlike a language the supply of money in existence at any time can be measured and quantified. The supply of credit money is endogenously determined by the quantity of credit that businesses and households demand from banks to finance their working capital requirements and to acquire longer term assets. Central banks (CBs) set Bank Rate as their chief instrument of monetary policy. As retailers commercial banks set their prime lending rate to credit-worthy ("prime") borrowers as a relatively stable mark-up over Bank Rate, and set their deposit rates as a relatively stable mark-down on Bank Rate.[2]

Bank loans are much like credit cards. Up to some pre-assigned credit limit borrowers and not lenders decide when and how much they wish to borrow. In developed financial systems most borrowers negotiate their credit commitments (overdraft facilities) with their bankers in advance of loan requests. Credit commitments entitle borrowers to draw down funds as demanded up to some pre-assigned ceiling, based on bankers' evaluation of borrowers' credit-worthiness.[3] When the economy is depressed and the demand for loans is flat, CBs purchase securities and provide banks with excess reserves. Banks also operate in highly organized securities markets, where they are price-takers and quantity-setters. Only in organized security markets do banks act like portfolio managers and decide on the different assets they wish to buy, sell, and hold.

Bank deposits are the accounting record of bank assets. The supply of credit money varies directly with the demand for bank credit. So long as money retains its acceptability as a means of payment the quantity of nominal money created is identical to the quantity of nominal credit supplied. Changes in borrower's current expectations of future aggregate demand (AD) induce changes in the quantity of credit demanded. No financial asset prices need change to induce a change in the quantity of credit demanded and deposits supplied. So long as money retains its generally "acceptability," there is never an excess supply of deposits.[4]

When borrowers require additional deposits to finance planned deficit spending they draw down their unutilized prearranged line of credit. The quantity of bank loans outstanding is determined by the quantity of bank credit demanded by borrowers whom banks have judged to be credit-worthy. Bank loans are predominately of short-term maturity, usually 30–90 days. Providing borrowers remain within their assigned credit ceilings, they are at liberty to repay and renew their loans at their initiative. The degree of risk that accompanies any individual borrower's promise to pay (IOU) is known only to the banker and the borrower. Bank loans are extremely heterogeneous, and so not traded on organized secondary markets. Banks set the lending rate charged and when the loan must be repaid. Credit-worthy borrowers determine the quantity of credit demanded so long as they remain within their overdraft ceilings. They decide if they wish to repay the loan when it comes due or defer payment and roll the debt over to the next period. To the extent short-term loans are rolled over bank loans become analagous to long-term floating-rate securities.

Bank assets consist primarily of the quantity of short-term loans in their portfolios. Bank loans represent the exchange of IOUs between the borrower and the bank. Borrowers exchange their IOUs for the bank's IOUs. The banks' IOUs in the form of demand deposits are generally accepted as payment in exchange for goods. Deposits are created in the act of borrowing from a bank, so "Loans make deposits." Due to their heterogeneous risks, bank loans are nonmarketable and no organized secondary markets exist on which they can be bought and sold.[5] The liquidity of a loan depends on its maturity and on the credit status of the borrower, which is known in detail only by the borrower and the bank. Banks also hold reserves of liquid assets and marketable securities. In addition to deposits they issue CD's, medium- and longer-term securities, and a host of derivative debt instruments.

When credit-worthy borrowers desire additional deposits, they can demand additional loans up to some assigned credit limit at the bank's lending rate. Banks administer their prime lending rates as a stable mark-up over "Bank Rate," the average overnight rate charged by the central bank for a loan of additional reserves. Bank Rate represents the marginal cost of short-term funds to the banking system.[6] Loans are like credit cards. Most borrowers possess unutilized credit and the supply of bank credit to most credit-worthy borrowers is seldom supply constrained. Potential borrowers who are judged uncredit-worthy will not be granted loans. All borrowers no matter how credit-worthy are subject to credit limits. No borrower can borrow indefinite amounts.

The absence of quantity restrictions on bank loans and deposits does not lead to the inflationary expansion of the money supply. Like goods the quantity of credit demanded is inversely related to the interest rate (price) charged. When the increase in AD is considered "excessive" or "insufficient" to meet their macroeconomic goals and money supply targets, CBs discretionarily raise or reduce Bank Rate. CBs decide whether the current level of Bank Rate is appropriate, depending on whether the current change in AD is considered "excessive" or "insufficient," based on the expected gap of the economy from their stabilization targets in the next period and their model of how the economy behaves. When plotted in interest–money space, the supply of credit money is horizontal at some mark-up over the Bank Rate set by the CB. This position is maintained until the current Bank Rate is changed and the money supply curve shifts up or down. The Post Keynesian theory of endogenous money and exogenous interest rates has been termed "Horizontalism."[7]

Commercial banks create credit money whenever they make additional loans to borrowers. Many CBs require commercial banks to hold some minimum ratio of cash reserves to deposits. This is not necessary for monetary control of interest rates. Reserves act as a tax on the banking system. In an increasing number of countries CBs have completely abolished legal reserve requirements; e.g. Canada, New Zealand, the United Kingdom. Banks would volitionally hold some positive ratio of cash reserves to deposits even without legal reserve requirements to maintain the instant convertibility of their deposits (credit money) into legal tender (fiat money) on demand, and ensure the general acceptability of their deposits in exchange.[8]

When a bank grants a loan to one of its customers it credits the borrower's account and its deposits rise *pari passu* with its loans. As borrowers spend the proceeds the recipients will either deposit the checks into their accounts at their own bank, or convert them into currency. Through each succeeding generation of transactions individual lending banks lose deposits created by their initial loans at clearing to other banks. But individual banks also gain deposits at clearing from the recipients of those borrowers at other banks who are also its depositors. So long as an individual bank keeps pace with the general rate of loan expansion of the banking system its net surplus or deficit position need not be affected by granting new loans. If it experiences more rapid loan demand or less rapid deposit growth than the system it will issue more or less CDs than it purchases, and become a deficit or surplus branch to rest of the system.

The degree to which individual banks retain the deposits created by increases in their loans depends on their size, number of branches, and their rate of loan expansion relative to the banking system. This relation between loans and deposits has been termed the "deposit-retention" function.[9] In the United States the leakage of deposits with loan expansion occurs much more quickly for bank purchases of wholesale marketable instruments than for loans to local businesses and households. Restrictions on branch banking in the United States make leakages to individual banks from loan expansion more rapid than in the banking systems of most other countries, where a few large branch banks dominate the market. If there were only one bank in the system the retention rate on deposits would be 100 percent. But even a national monopoly bank would face leakages of domestic and foreign currency.

Confidence is absolutely essential to the business of banking. The perceived risk of a bank's loan portfolio affects its supply of deposits. More conservative bank balance sheets and higher bank capital ratios attract more deposits. Deposit insurance partially eliminates this effect, as the surveillance exercised by depositors is replaced by the guarantees of the insurer.

In conventional mainstream theory, monetary change is assumed to be initiated by changes in the high-powered base originating from central bank open market purchases or sales of securities. This purportedly pushes the banking system into a "disequilibrium" position of portfolio imbalance. Changes in assets are viewed as made at the initiative of the banks in response to changes in their free reserve position. It is believed changes in the high-powered base determine changes in the volume of bank intermediation. Mainstream theory explains bank asset behavior in terms of portfolio theory. Bank portfolio management is interpreted as maximizing a utility function whose arguments include profitability, liquidity, and risk. Banks are assumed to decide on the optimum allocation of their assets between reserves, securities, and loans. As portfolio managers they are implicitly regarded as price-takers and quantity-setters in asset markets.[10]

But such an explanation confuses the direction of causality between bank reserves and bank deposits and ignores the critical difference between marketable and nonmarketable assets in bank portfolios. The historical *raison d'etre* of commercial banking was to make short-term business loans to finance the working and circulating capital credit needs of business firms. Only for marketable securities where developed secondary markets exist are banks price-takers and quantity-setters as the mainstream theory asserts. For the most important class of bank assets and liabilities, loans and deposits, banks are price-setters and quantity-takers.

Bank loans differ from private securities in two important respects:

1. Bank loans are nonmarketable financial instruments. An individual borrower's financial situation is known only to the borrower and her banker. From an outsiders' perspective the IOUs in bank portfolios are highly uncertain promises to pay, and extremely heterogeneous with regard to lenders' risk. In common with all heterogeneous assets trading is expensive and infrequent. No organized markets exist on which loans may be readily bought and sold. In spite of their short maturity bank loans are highly nonmarketable and so illiquid to bank borrowers. Their owners are unable to convert them into money easily, quickly, and cheaply.[11]

2. Bank loans are made at the initiative of borrowers, not the lending bank. Lenders have an important asymmetric information problem that can lead to serious moral risk. Bankers are outsiders, and know less about the clients' future prospects than the client herself. As a result price is an insufficient exclusion mechanism for the allocation of credit. Charging higher interest rates alters the composition of the applicant pool, toward borrowers who are willing to take on more risk. This is one reason why banks rely on credit rationing.

As price-setters and quantity-takers banks set their prime lending rate and attempt to meet all loan demand forthcoming from all credit-worthy borrowers who remain within their credit ceilings. Lending rates charged are administered at a stable mark-up over the expected wholesale cost of credit. The size of the mark-up varies with the degree of competition, and with the elasticity of loan demand in different markets. In most countries banking is highly concentrated. Bank credit markets are typically oligopolistic and price leadership is common. Due to the homogeneous nature of their products, all banks charge the same price so banks are "pure" oligopolists. The rate set depends on the lending and deposit rates set by the price-leading bank. In all banking systems price leadership in loan and deposit markets is widespread. There is a close relationship between the change in bank loans and the change in total deposits. The data suggest that a 1 percent increase in bank loans is broadly associated with a one-for-one increase in bank deposits.[12] The conclusion that the broad money supply is credit-driven is now strongly supported by a large empirical literature from many countries for many different periods.[13]

The supply of credit money is driven by the demand for bank credit. In overdraft systems banks assign borrowers a "credit line," "overdraft ceiling," or "credit limit." Banks set the credit line as their estimate of the maximum amount borrowers can safely service, based on their detailed estimate of the borrowers' three "Cs": Credit (Income), Collateral (Wealth), and Character (Credit History). Bank credit lines vary strongly pro-cyclically over the cycle, with cyclical variations in borrower and lender animal spirits. Banks are prepared to make credit available as demanded up to the borrower's credit limit.[14] Empirical studies suggest that in developed economies the credit-utilization rate fluctuates around 50 percent.[15]

Credit rationing is resorted to by lenders in all lending markets to prevent borrowers from borrowing themselves into bankruptcy and being unable to repay their loans. Credit rationing is intrinsic to the lending process. Lenders will always be unwilling to lend at any interest rate to borrowers whom they believe to be noncredit-worthy. Quantitative credit rationing, rather than credit allocation by price, is the chosen mechanism for allocating credit among different borrowers with highly diverse proposals, prospects, collateral, and borrowing records. As the interest rate charged increases, lenders' expected return will initially rise, reach a maximum, and decline. From the lenders' viewpoint a rise in interest rates has two negative effects:

1. An "adverse selection" effect, as less credit-worthy new borrowers are attracted.
2. An "adverse incentive" effect, as all borrowers are induced to select more risky projects.

Individual borrowers face an upward-sloping supply curve for funds, since:

1. As the level of borrowing by individual economic units increases, so does the probability of default. As borrowers debt/total assets ratio rises their net worth "cushion" shrinks, and lenders' risk exposure increases.
2. The rate that borrowers are willing to pay provides lenders with indirect information about the riskiness of their borrowing project.

In economies possessing well-developed overdraft systems quantitative lines of credit (overdraft limits) are assigned to prospective borrowers in negotiation with their bankers. Large borrowers typically have more than one banker, giving banks an incentive to satisfy all legitimate loan demands. Banks set the lending rate charged, and attempt to meet all legitimate loan demand forthcoming so long as borrowers remain within their predetermined overdraft limit. Bank lending is demand-determined, and changes in bank loans are made at the initiative of bank borrowers. From the point of view of an individual bank its loan portfolio is largely nondiscretionary. Banks are in the business of selling credit. Like all retailers they make their profits on the mark-up of the price charged over their average cost of funds. This is expressed as the "spread" between the rates earned and paid on the asset and liability side of their balance sheet. As sellers of contingent claims it is not surprising that banks have limited ability to control the volume of their lending.

Banks are willing to lend only to borrowers whom they believe are credit-worthy and able to repay their loans. Bank lending officers must make a discretionary judgment as to the maximum amount an individual borrower is able to repay. Most poor households and most small and new firms are severely credit-constrained. They form Keynes' "perpetual fringe of unsatisfied borrowers," since they are regarded by lenders as "noncredit-worthy." Such borrowers typically receive no bank credit because banks regard lending to them as too risky.

Banks must maintain the absolute confidence of their depositors that demand deposits will be convertible into cash on demand. Banks must balance profitability against liquidity. To maintain the instant convertibility of their deposits into legal tender, as is necessary for bank deposits to be generally accepted as the means of payment, banks hold defensive positions of cash reserves and liquid assets. The innovation of liability management (termed "liability-side liquidity") has substantially reduced bank demand for liquid assets. By issuing CDs banks are now able to purchase funds when they need them, rather than being forced to hold low-yielding liquid assets in their portfolios.

Bank assets and liabilities may be divided into retail and wholesale categories. In their retail markets banks are price-setters and quantity-takers. In their wholesale markets banks are price-takers and quantity-setters. Bank loans are traditionally very short term, 30–90 days. Bank liquidity comes from the short maturity of their loans rather than their individual liquidity. Over the past few decades, securitization has transformed bank ability to extend overdrafts and enabled them to finance loan demand at their discretion.

At the heart of the bank–customer relation is the confidential information banks learn about the income, balance sheet, business acumen, and future prospects of their individual clients in their role as creditor and financial advisor. From an individual bank's point of view retail loans and deposits are nondiscretionary variables, and most banks are quantity-takers in these markets. From the banks' point of view bank deposits are the accounting record of bank loans.

With the development and expansion of wholesale markets, commercial banks are increasingly becoming brokers, buying and selling negotiable assets and liabilities. An increased proportion of their revenues is derived from service fees rather than lending spreads. Lower lending spreads increase the demand for bank credit. The development of international financial markets has increased the degree of competition in wholesale banking operations. Due to scale economies larger banks typically earn higher rates of return on equity than smaller banks. In most economies banking tends to be highly concentrated. But statutes prohibiting intra- and inter-state branching are currently being abolished in many countries and merger booms are underway.

Credit rationing is intrinsic to all lending processes. Before they make a loan, lenders must decide the maximum quantity of credit they are willing to lend to each individual borrower. As the fiduciary agents of their depositors, banks will be unwilling to lend to anyone whom they suspect will be unable to repay their loan.[16] So long as borrowers remain within their assigned credit ceilings, the amount of loans taken out is the decision of the borrower not the bank. Bank credit commitments granted to prospective borrowers vary pro-cyclically with interest rates and business confidence over the cycle.

Generous bank credit lines for large borrowers provide important non-price means of attracting and competing for customers. In most developed financial systems the credit–utilization ratio (total loans granted/total credit commitments) fluctuates around 50 percent.[17] Credit-worthy borrowers thus have the potential roughly to double the supply of credit money at their initiative under existing credit commitments. Central banks, despite their ability to precisely supply bank reserves, are typically unable to directly quantitatively control the money supply. Their commitment to system liquidity and financial stability override their ability to control of the growth rate of the money supply. Increases in money wages lead to increases in the quantity of bank credit demanded and corresponding increases in bank deposits and the money supply. When costs and output stabilize, the level of bank borrowing and the money supply also stabilizes. The money supply is largely determined by business demand for working capital, and varies *pari passu* with the size of business inventories.[18]

10.2 Bank finance of working capital

The fundamental *raison d'etre* of banking was historically to supply short-term credit to meet business demand for working capital. It was no accident that commercial banking evolved in Renaissance Italy, before the advent of the "Industrial Revolution." Merchant traders had large demands for working capital to finance their inventories. The role of banks was to make short-term credit available to credit-worthy borrowers to satisfy the demand for working capital in trading. Merchant traders had a demand for working capital to finance the purchase of the inventories of the domestic goods they were planning to exchange for foreign goods in foreign markets. Such domestic currency could be repaid only after they had returned from foreign markets, and received domestic currency of greater value from the sale of foreign goods in domestic markets.

As factories and output expanded the industrial revolution created an insatiable demand for credit to finance increased working capital. The endogenous demand for working capital for manufacturing drove the development of modern banking.[19] The demand for bank credit by business has recently been overtaken in many developed economies by household demand for bank credit, to finance the purchase of lumpy consumer durables and houses, and to finance the household acquisition of financial portfolios as financial assets are accumulated to finance future deficit spending during retirement.

In market economies production costs must be incurred and paid *before* the receipt of sales proceeds. Business costs of production: the labor, raw materials, intermediate goods, and taxes constitute business demand for *working capital* for which finance must be obtained. Whenever factor prices or the quantity of factors demanded increase, businesses must obtain additional short-term finance to cover their increased working capital needs. Firms must pay all production and distribution expenses *before* they receive money from their sales proceeds. The owners of firms bear the residual risk that the goods produced in the future may not be demanded or sold at a profit.

Over any period t, profits (π_t) are defined as equal to sales revenues (S_t) plus changes in inventories (ΔI_t), minus production and sales costs (C_t) paid over the period. Inventory accumulation is a form of investment. The cost of producing inventories must be paid *before* sales receipts are received. Equation 10.1 is the accounting definition of current profits:

$$\pi_t = S_t + \Delta I_t - C_t \tag{10.1}$$

But this definition of profits does not constitute the net cash flow available from current operations. Current production costs have been incurred to produce goods that are not yet sold, as reflected in the build-up of business inventories. To calculate the cash flow, inventory accumulation (ΔI_t) must be deducted from profits. Accounting profits are available for distribution to owners in the form of cash income only after all working capital expenses have been financed by borrowing. Unless the company is able to finance its inventory accumulation with credit, unintended inventory accumulation reduces net cash inflow from production. When the cost of inventories rises rapidly during periods of high inflation and rapid sales growth, firms can find themselves in the position of making handsome profits on each sale, yet being continually faced with a cash drain, and continually requiring additional working capital finance.[20]

There are two dimensions to the working capital problem. The first is how do firms find suppliers of external finance when setting up new businesses. New firms have no established credit record to assure prospective lenders of their prospects for future repayment, so the need for equity finance is then most acute. When new firms are growing rapidly and lenders require all loans be fully collateralized, the demand for short-term external finance is crucial. This underlines the importance of well-defined property rights and banking practices for successful economic development.[21]

The second problem is in enabling established businesses to grow more rapidly. Whenever sales are growing, firms require additional credit to finance their growing stocks of inventories, irrespective of whether sales increases represent increases in real quantities or are the result of higher prices.[22] If inventory accumulation can be financed by bank borrowing the problem can be simply resolved. Over each time period new bank debt equals the increased value of inventories, and all accounting profits are turned into cash flow. Profits can then all be distributed in money to the owners while the firm can remain solvent. Its new debt is matched by the value of its quick assets (inventories). When interest rates rise, firms must pay increased interest charges to finance inventory accumulation. To maintain a steady flow of accounting profits, either the mark-up must be raised when interest rates are increased to cover increases in interest expense, or inventories must be valued inclusive of interest paid and mark-ups be calculated on total costs including interest. When inventories are completely financed by bank borrowing the value of inventories matches the value of bank debt.[23]

Firms attempt to maintain prices as a stable mark-up over their *historical* unit costs calculated by their accountants. When unit costs increase, so do prices. So long as they are based on a stable mark-up, prices of goods sold will rise *pari passu* with costs. Sales revenues rise with a lag depending on the length of the production-sales period. The excess of the increase in costs over the increase in sales proceeds represents the firms' additional demand for working capital, equal to the increase in the value of inventories. Whenever inventory accumulation is financed by bank credit, the result will be an equal increase in bank loans and the money supply.

Working capital finance is raised through a number of different sources: bank borrowing, nonbank borrowing, trade credit net profits, debt issue, equity issue, deposit reduction, and asset sale. Companies attempt to raise funds as cheaply as possible. The proportion of bank and nonbank financing selected depends on interest costs and the yield curve. In most economies bank loans are the most important source of business working capital finance.

For borrowers banks are price-setters and quantity-takers in their lending markets. Since household borrowing is positively related to wage income, increases in the wage bill typically have a greater than one-for-one effect on total bank lending. Banks lend both to firms and households. Firms borrow to finance working capital needs by taking out additional short-term bank loans. The largest component of working capital is the wage bill. Bank loans are repaid over the monetary circuit when firms realize their sales proceeds. Banks lend to households as well as firms, and in most developed countries the household share of bank loans is increasing.

Business demand for working capital includes wage and materials costs, taxes, and the accumulation of unfinished and finished inventories. Increases in net inventory accumulation generate demand for additional working capital finance and additional bank loans. Loan demand equations based on increases in working capital explain most of the variation in total business bank borrowing in developed countries where the equations have been estimated.[24]

10.3 A model of bank intermediation

Bank loans operate like credit cards. So long as individual borrowers remain within their pre-assigned loan ceilings, banks make credit available as demanded. Deposits are created when banks make loans. Borrowing is simply an exchange of IOUs: in exchange for the borrowers' IOU (a promise to repay the loan with interest at the due date), banks provide borrowers with their IOUs, bank deposits (a promise to repay the owner with legal tender on demand). This is sometimes referred to as the banks' "instant repurchase clause." So long as banks retain total

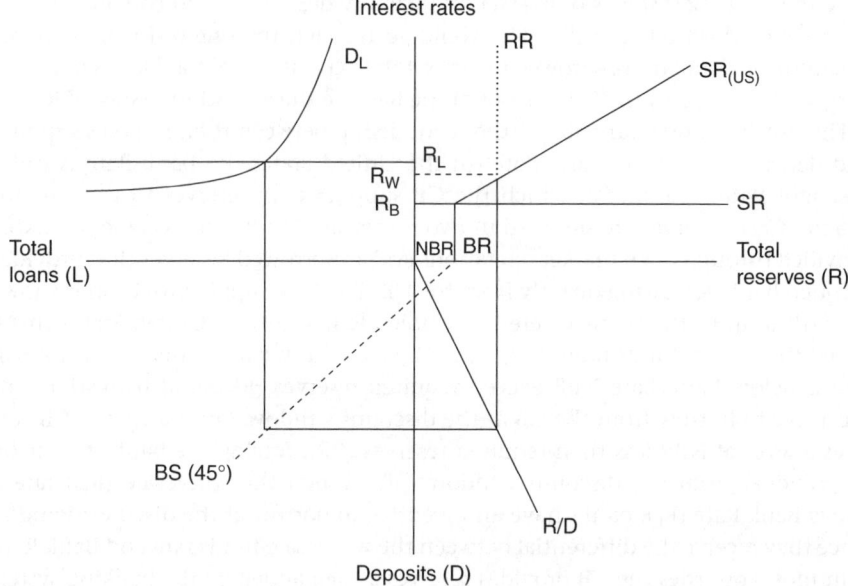

Figure 10.1 The balance sheet relation between bank loans, deposits and reserves
Source: Goodfriend, 1987.

public confidence that the "instant repurchase clause" will continually be upheld, deposits will be generally accepted as a means of final payment in exchange for real goods and services.

A diagrammatic presentation of the balance sheet relation between loans, deposits, and reserves is shown in Figure 10.1.[25] This diagram illustrates the balance sheet relationship between bank loans and bank deposits, and the endogeneity between credit money and the demand for bank credit. It also illustrates the non-transparent manner how the Federal Reserve previously described the federal funds rate as an endogenous market-determined rate, rather than an exogenous rate directly set by the Fed as its central policy instrument.

In the northwest quadrant of Figure 10.1, D_L represents the demand for bank loans by credit-worthy borrowers, inversely related to the loan rate charged (R_L). Since loans create deposits the southwest quadrant shows the balance sheet relationship between loans and deposits as a 45 degree line.

The banking system's balance sheet relation can be written as follows:

L + NBR = DD + TD = D or L = D − NBR

where L = Total loans, NBR = Non-borrowed reserves,

DD = Demand deposits, TD = Time deposits, D = Total deposits

The balance sheet relation (BS) has a slope of one, since every dollar increase in loans is matched by an equal dollar increase in deposits. If loans and deposits were the banking system's only asset and liability deposits would equal loans, and the balance sheet relationship (BS) would go through the origin. In the presence of bank capital and non-borrowed reserves, total deposits equal total loans plus non-borrowed reserves, so the X-intercept of the balance sheet relation (BS) is NBR.

The northeast quadrant shows the relationship between total reserves supplied and demanded and the Bank Rate (in the United States the Bank Rate is called Discount Rate), the rate at which the CB supplies cash reserves to the banking system. Cash reserves are supplied in two forms: as Non-Borrowed Reserves (NBR) provided through open market operations and as Borrowed Reserves (BR) provided through bank borrowing directly from the CB. The NBR supply provision is shown as vertical up to the point where the wholesale rate (in the United States this is called the federal funds rate) is equal to the CB's Bank Rate. When the wholesale rate is below Bank Rate NBR exceed required reserves (RR), and banks have no incentive to borrow from the CB at the discount window. Ordinarily the CB supplies a level of NBR less than required reserves (RR), forcing the banks to borrow the residual from the discount window (BR). When the wholesale (R_W) rate is above Bank Rate (R_B), banks have an incentive to borrow at the discount window since they receive the differential between the wholesale funds rate and Bank Rate.

In most countries the CB provides reserves as demanded by the banking system at Bank Rate. The supply of reserves is then horizontal at Bank rate (SR). But in the United States the Federal Reserve is unwilling to lend banks unlimited amounts at the Discount Rate, even when the bank has ample security. Instead the Discount Window imposes non-pecuniary costs of borrowing ("frown" costs) which rise with the volume and frequency of borrowing.[26] Banks borrow at the discount window up to the point where the non-pecuniary (frown) costs of borrowing offset the net interest saving over the wholesale (federal funds) rate. The supply of borrowed reserves in the United States becomes an upward-sloping relationship ($SR_{(US)}$).

Bank lending rates (R_L) are administered by banks at some mark-up over the wholesale rate expected over the lending period (R_W). Loan volume (L) and total deposits (D) are jointly determined by the public's demand for credit at the current lending rate (R_L). Since reserve requirements are lagged and calculated on bank deposits in the previous period, the quantity of required reserves (RR) is predetermined in each statement period. Total reserves demanded equal required reserves plus excess reserves and are interest-sensitive. By supplying only a portion of the total reserves demanded through open market operations in the form of non-borrowed reserves, the Fed forces the banking system to borrow the residual quantity in the form of borrowed reserves at the discount window. The federal funds rate was previously determined in this non-transparent manner because the Federal Reserve wanted the public to view interest rates as determined by market forces, and did not want to be seen as directly responsible for high levels of interest rates.[27]

The level of short-term interest rates is the monetary authorities' chief policy instrument. It is varied over the business cycle in the attempt to achieve the Bank's stabilization goals. The range over which short-term rates are varied pro-cyclically depends on the authorities' "policy reaction function" or "Taylor Rule." The expectations theory of the term structure concludes that long-term rates will equal the capital markets' expectations of average future short-term rates over the period, i.e the authorities future expected "policy reaction function" over different future periods.[28]

Banks are price-setters and quantity-takers in retail markets. As price-setters they set the rate they charge for loans (R_L), and the maximum amount they are willing to lend (overdraft limit) to different borrowers depending on their estimate of the borrower's credit-worthiness. As quantity-takers banks are prepared to meet the demand for credit by all credit-worthy borrowers. Similarly the banks set the rates they pay for deposits (R_D), and accept all funds supplied. From the viewpoint of an individual bank the volume of retail loans and deposits is completely demand-determined and so nondiscretionary. For the banking system the total quantity of deposits demanded is identical to the total quantity of deposits supplied. There can never be an excess supply of bank deposits.

The situation for individual banks is quite different. Due to the homogeneous nature of bank deposits the supply of deposit curves faced by an individual bank has a positive slope, unlike the situation for a single-bank system where all the deposits created are necessarily demanded. The demand for credit curves for individual banks is much more elastic than the banking system's demand for credit since borrowers shop around for the best lending rate. The rate charged will differ in different markets and for different classes of borrowers, depending on the degree of bank market power.

Individual banks have a local market of borrowers and lenders. They have no guarantee that the total quantity of loans they provide will be equal to the total quantity of deposits they receive. Unlike a single-bank system or the banking system as a whole, individual banks cannot assume all the deposits they create will be re-deposited. Some individual banks will find themselves with more deposits than loans, and so in a surplus position. Others will have more loans than deposits and find themselves in a deficit position. Some banks are characteristically in surplus positions and others characteristically in deficit positions. Surplus banks lend their excess funds to deficit banks by purchasing the CDs issued by deficit banks. If an individual bank finds that its demand for loans is in excess of its total supply of deposits, it will borrow additional funds by the issue of CDs to surplus banks, called "liability side liquidity." Deficit banks can also bid deposits away from other banks by raising the rates paid and services offered on deposits.

The total assets and liabilities of the banking system exceed the total volume of bank intermediation by the volume of inter-bank transactions between surplus and deficit banks. So long as bank concentration does not result in implicit pricing agreements among banks, competition for funds will induce profit-maximizing banks to raise the deposit rate paid and reduce the lending rate charged until the MC of additional deposits and the MR of additional loans equal the wholesale rate for marketable securities, the CD rate or Bank Rate.

Banks' willingness to take risk and the volume of credit commitments they are willing to extend to individual borrowers varies pro-cyclically over the business cycle. During recessions when animal spirits flag, CBs reduce short-term interest rates in the attempt to stimulate aggregate demand. Banks then lower their lending rates and their credit ceilings and raise their collateral requirements. Conversely during booms when animal spirits are strong CBs raise Bank Rate. Banks then raise their lending rates and their credit ceilings and lower their collateral requirements as perceptions of system risk recede.

Pro-cyclical variation in credit commitments accompanies pro-cyclical variation in interest rates, which depend on the CBs expectation of the position of the economy in the cycle and its policy reaction function. The variation in credit commitments increases the pro-cyclical variation in the volume of bank intermediation. Borrowers are faced with pro-cyclical variations in loan rates which dampens cyclical fluctuations in aggregate demand. But they are also faced by pro-cyclical variations in credit commitments, which operate to increase cyclical fluctuations in AD.

Banks can never be certain of borrowers' abilities to repay their loans. Depending on the conservativeness of their lending policies, banks are able to estimate their expected bad debt ratio over the cycle and mark-up the lending rate charged. Banks anticipate some level of bad debt losses *ex ante* no matter how conservative their lending policy. They can vary the mark-up of their lending rate over wholesale rates.[29] The volume of bank credit commitments varies pro-cyclically, increasing cyclical variations in the level of AD.[30]

Total bank assets and liabilities are linked through the bank balance sheet identity. Individual banks must match their demand for loans, with their supply of funds from deposits and from issue of CDs. For the banking system as a whole total assets equal total liabilities. But bank borrowers and bank depositors are different groups. For any individual bank there is nothing to ensure the total quantity of bank loans demanded will exactly equal the total quantity of bank deposits supplied. Initially when loans are granted bank deposits increase *pari passu* with bank loans. As borrowers spend the proceeds, individual banks are faced with leakage or accumulation of deposits at clearing from other banks. This generates interbank lending and borrowing through the federal funds and CD markets.

To be able to extend new loans based on previously granted credit commitments banks must be able to meet any net deficit of funds by borrowing in the wholesale markets. The wholesale market becomes the source and repository for marginal bank funds. Deficit banks, whose loan demand from borrowers exceeds funds supplied from depositors, are net sellers of CDs in the wholesale markets. Surplus banks, whose source of funds from deposits exceeds their loan demand, are net buyers. For the banking system as a whole, the net surplus of surplus banks equals the net deficit of deficit banks.

In times of cyclical expansion animal spirits are optimistic, deficit spending is high and new deposits are created and new loans expand at greater rates. Once created deposits are spent and redistributed among individual agents. Total deposits are reduced by the conversion of deposits into currency, the repayment of bank loans, and the sale of securities held by the banking system. Wholesale assets are equal to wholesale liabilities, so total loans, securities, reserves, and tangible assets are equal to total deposits and net worth.[31] The issue and purchase of wholesale securities affect the redistribution of funds within the banking system between deficit and surplus banks. Due to inter-bank borrowing and lending the total volume of assets and liabilities held by the banking system considerably overstates the total volume of bank intermediation.

The extent to which banks mark-up or mark-down the rates charged and paid to particular borrowers and lenders is governed by their degree of market power in individual markets, reflected in different elasticities of demand for funds. Oligopolistic banks set their administered retail lending rates equal to the rates set by other oligopolists. Profit-maximizing banks set the rate for funds in each retail market so their expected marginal revenue on loans is equal to their expected marginal cost of funds. In wholesale markets where they are price-takers, marginal and average cost and revenue schedules are identical, so the short-term wholesale rate becomes the banks marginal cost and marginal revenue curve. Profit-maximizing banks administer their retail lending and borrowing rates so that the expected marginal revenue from loans and marginal cost of deposits is equal to the wholesale rate set by the CB over the period. Short-term wholesale rates are highly volatile over the cycle, but administered lending and deposit rates are much less volatile. Administered rates are marked-up on the expected wholesale rate over the period of the loan.

Oligopolistic banking markets are characterized by price leadership. Bank lending and borrowing rates are normally sticky and characterized by explicit or implicit price leadership. Banks' perceived loan demand curve is "kinked" at the prevailing administered loan rate, and their perceived supply of deposits is "kinked" at the prevailing deposit rate. As a result there are discontinuities in marginal revenue and marginal cost curves around prevailing administered rates. So long as the variation in wholesale rates lies within this range banks do not adjust their administered loan and deposit rates. This explains the substantial stickiness of administered bank lending and borrowing rates, while Bank Rate set by the CB is varied more pro-cyclically over time.

So long as borrowers are within their credit limits an increase in the demand for bank credit results in an equal increase in lending to the banking system. Bank deposits are the accounting record of bank loans, so an increase in lending results in an equal increase in deposits. Providing bank deposits retain their moneyness, newly created deposits are always accepted in exchange for goods. The total quantity of deposits held by wealth-owners is identical to the total quantity of deposits supplied by the banks. Bank lending rates are administered over time and maintained at a stable mark-up over Bank Rate.

Business borrowing from banks depends on business demand for working capital. In bank lending equations the coefficients on the wage and materials bill are not significantly different from unity.[32] Theoretical analysis and empirical evidence confirm that the demand for short-term loans is interest inelastic. It is difficult to find significant negatively signed interest rate coefficients in estimates of loan demand, because CBs move interest rates pro-cyclically in pursuit of their stabilization goals. Interest rates and loan quantity rise and fall together over the business cycle. Single-equation estimates of the interest elasticity of loan demand are seriously biased since CBs adjust interest rates pro-cyclically over the business cycle.

Increases and or decreases in current rates normally lead to expectations of future rate movements in the same direction. This induces borrowers to accelerate borrowing during expansions and postpone borrowing during contractions. The demand for short-term credit is highly inelastic and the ability of the authorities to influence the change in business borrowing by varying the level of short-term interest is limited in the short run.

10.4 The supply of credit money is endogenously demand-determined

Commercial banks are price-setters and quantity-takers in their retail loan and deposit markets, so the volume of bank credit is demand-determined. Central banks administer the supply price of reserves to the banking system by varying the level of short-term interest rates pro-cyclically. The circumstances under which CB interest rate-administration takes place evolve sharply over time since agent behavior and monetary policy change continuously. Whether the supply of money is more accurately viewed as exogenously under central bank control or endogenously determined by market forces varies with the particular historical period considered.

In the United States during the great depression of the 1930s the demand for bank credit fell sharply and the money supply declined correspondingly. One-third of all banks failed, profit expectations were negative, and borrowers' "animal spirits" became severely depressed. By the late 1930s the Fed had reduced the nominal rates on Treasury Bills to 5 basis points, but in spite of the unprecedented low level of interest rates the authorities were unable to induce firms and households to borrow and deficit spend. The banks were faced with a falling demand for credit, and low lending rates failed to stimulate borrowing. There was a widespread perception that the economy had fallen into a "liquidity trap" which monetary policy was unable to ameliorate.[33]

By providing the banking system with huge excess reserves the authorities succeeded in inducing banks to purchase short-term and long-term government securities, in spite of their high prices and low returns. The money-base multiplier fell sharply and the money supply expanded by a reduced multiple of the reserve injection. In the 1930s cheap money policy failed to stimulate the economy. Nevertheless it could be argued that over this particular period the money-multiplier story had some validity. After 1929–33 the Fed succeeded in expanding the rate of growth of the money supply by its low interest rate policy, even though AD and GDP failed to respond.

By the late 1930s the Fed had reduced the Treasury Bill rate to 5 basis points, but rates on long-term government securities did not fall below a floor level of about 1.5 percent. This was due to market expectations that rates must rise in the future and capital losses on long-term bonds would be inevitable. No interest was paid on demand deposits, and bank lending rates never fell below 1.5 percent, the minimum spread required to cover the cost of bank intermediation. These positive floors in administered rates and constituted Keynes' much-discussed "liquidity trap." Rates could not be pushed below these levels no matter how much the CB increased excess reserves. Uncertainty whether the sharp price deflation experienced from 1929 to 1933 might return led to lender estimates of future capital losses if the level of rates rose in the future, keeping long-term nominal rates above 1.5 percent.

Private demand for bank credit continued weak throughout the Second World War. The banking system acquired ever increasing holdings of government securities issued to finance government deficit spending which supplanted private borrowing to finance private capital formation. After the war private loan demand quickly revived, money growth expanded rapidly, and inflation expectations were rekindled. Interest rates on government securities were initially kept at low levels. The Fed supported the high prices of government savings bonds issued during the war at low rates in response to wartime patriotism. Banks found themselves able to finance additional loans by selling government securities from their portfolios. Money supply growth was less rapid than loan growth, since loan acquisition was offset by the sale of government securities, and the income velocity of money rose.

After the Treasury–Federal Reserve Accord of 1951 the Fed was no longer obligated to peg the price of government securities at wartime levels. The level of short- and long-term interest rates drifted upwards. The "Availability Doctrine" held that due to the overhang of government securities in the banking system, interest rates did not have to be greatly increased to deter spending, since banks would then have to sell existing securities at a loss. Debt management was considered the active "third leg" of monetary policy. In 1953 the Treasury tilted the yield curve upward by issuing a series of long-term 30-year bonds. A protracted argument ensued about the term structure. Should the Federal Reserve intervene directly to reduce longer term rates by open market operations to purchase long-term securities, or should such intervention be left to debt management and the Fed confine itself to "Bills only" purchases?

The "locking in" effect of incurring capital loses on security sales failed to dissuade banks from dumping government securities to finance new loan demand, even though the banks had to report capital losses on their books. By 1960 the war-time overload of bank holdings of Treasury securities had been depleted. The federal funds rate determined the level of all short-term market rates. Differentials among short-term rates reflected differences in risk, marketability, and legislative tax treatment. With lagged reserve requirements, required reserves were based on the level of deposits in the previous period, so total reserves in each statement period were predetermined.

During the early 1960s the United States enjoyed a trade surplus but had a substantial negative current account balance of payments due to government foreign expenditures. The Treasury developed "Operation Twist," to retire long-term securities and issue short-term securities and flatten out the yield curve. Short-term rates were believed to be more relevant for international capital flows, while long-term rates were more relevant for the domestic economy since they directly affected the mortgage rate and the housing market as well as investment spending. It eventually became apparent that the effect of debt composition on the yield curve was much less than had been anticipated. Low long-term rates reflected market expectations of future short-term rates. This became known as the "expectations" theory of the term structure.

As short-term rates increased Regulation Q, which placed a zero ceiling on demand deposits and a low positive ceiling on time deposit rates became the "hammer" of Federal reserve policy. Commercial bank liabilities were the dominant saving instrument. When rates went up and impinged on these deposit rate ceilings, depositors fled to uncontrolled financial instruments. Commercial banks were unable to raise additional money and were forced to pull back on lending. The result was a mini-recession in the housing market. Due to the concentration of its impact on housing finance Regulation Q became a matter of intense political concern. In response to political pressure the Fed first relaxed and eventually removed all interest rate ceilings on saving deposits.

The effectiveness of Regulation Q was dampened by banks innovating additional techniques for raising money. To finance unutilized credit lines in 1960 banks initiated "liability management." By issuing newly created Negotiable Certificates of Deposits (NCDs), they could bid actively for surplus funds as credit demand dictated. Larger credit commitments were used as a competitive device and bank loans became increasingly granted at the initiative of borrowers not the banks. Central bankers found they had no choice but to make reserves available as demanded to satisfy higher level of deposits and required reserves. Their only control instrument was the supply price at which they made reserves available. By a process of bank arbitrage this determined the level of short-term interest rates and the supply of credit money became endogenously credit-driven.

Individual banks are never quantitatively constrained for reserves. They can always borrow additional funds at some price in the federal funds market, at the discount window, by the sale of securities, by issuing their own CDs, and by borrowing in offshore markets. Since 1968 the Fed used the federal funds rate as its chief operating instrument. The funds rate was predetermined for the subsequent reserve period. The Fed supplied the proportion of borrowed and non-borrowed reserves to maintain the funds rate at its chosen level. When it wished to tighten or ease monetary policy, it would increase or reduce non-borrowed reserves and raise or lower the federal funds rate.

During the stagflation of the 1970s, wages, prices, unemployment, and money supply growth all expanded at double-digit rates. The Fed came under huge criticism from Monetarists for being excessively accommodating to inflation, and permitting too-rapid growth of the money supply. It became generally agreed that the Fed's policy of interest rate targeting resulted in interest rates being raised too little and too late. By the late 1970s in the face of persistent double-digit inflation, it appeared that if the Fed were to succeed in controlling inflationary pressures, it must follow Milton Friedman's advice and directly reduce the rate of reserve growth.

In most countries bank reserves are provided as a tap issue at the central banks' rediscount rate. But in the United States the provision of additional reserves at the discount window has long been rationed. Interest is not paid on reserves, the discount rate is the lowest borrowing rate, and the Federal Reserve System administered commercial bank discount window borrowing "as a privilege and not a right." In addition to the pecuniary discount rate, discount window borrowing was subjected to non-pecuniary discretionary surveillance and general administrative hassle ("frown costs"). As an individual bank's borrowing at the discount window rose, its total costs of borrowing, the discount rate plus the non-pecuniary "frown" costs, rose sharply.[34] When faced with reserve deficits banks retain the option of borrowing excess reserves from other banks in the Federal Funds market, to avoid "frown costs" administered at the discount window.

On October 6, 1979 Federal Reserve Chairman Paul Volcker instituted a dramatic draconian new procedure of reserve supply. In response to Monetarist criticism the Fed switched gears, abandoned interest rate targeting, and commenced targeting non-borrowed reserves with the avowed goal of reducing the rate of growth of the money supply and "squeezing" inflation out of the system.[35] The Fed's announced that the rate of money supply growth would be reduced to the rate consistent with price level stability. It proceeded to supply a predetermined quantity of total non-borrowed reserves calculated as the amount that would enable the money supply to grow at the new "target" rate. Borrowed reserves and the funds rate were forced to adjust to the exogenous reduction in the growth of non-borrowed reserves. The Fed announced its intention to gradually lower the "target" growth rate of the monetary aggregates, to demonstrate to the markets that it was no longer willing to accommodate greater rates of inflation.

The difficulty the new regime immediately faced was that unacceptably high levels of interest rates were required to achieve the desired restraining influence. In spite of much higher rates borrowers continued to demand short-term bank credit, and banks continued to meet all valid loan requests. In response borrowed reserves soared and the federal funds rate and the discount rate rose to historically unprecedented levels, above 20 percent. As Volcker has recently admitted:

> I do not think that any of us embarking on this policy believed we were going to end up with bank lending rates at 21 percent in the United States.[36]

The result of this new policy was the opposite of a smooth landing. Deviations of the money supply from its target path produced sharp increases in borrowed reserves and large swings and fluctuations in interest rates. Short-term rates rose to historically unprecedented levels (23 percent), causing a wave of bankruptcies, the collapse of the stock and bond markets, the destruction of the savings and loan industry. The appreciation of the US exchange rate by 50 percent from 1979 to 1985 precipitated a debt crisis in many third world countries.

Then, in October 1982, money supply targeting was suddenly without fanfare abandoned. The Fed decided it had earned its reputation in the financial markets as an inflation fighter. After having been vastly exceeded, the monetary targets were suspended. The high level of interest rates had led to a sharp unanticipated fall in the income velocity of money. Rigid adherence to the monetary targets would have resulted in ever-higher interest rates and accompanying financial disaster. The financial innovation and deregulation associated with super-high interest rates had altered the income velocity of the different monetary aggregates, offering a convenient fig leaf for the policy reversal.

The Fed changed to a policy of targeting "the degree of reserve restraint" (in nonCentral bank-speak, targeting borrowed reserves). The Fed sharply de-emphasized and eventually abandoned targeting the rate of growth of the monetary aggregates. Using open-market operations to target "the degree of reserve restraint," and so indirectly the differential of the federal funds rate over the discount rate, represented in effect a return to the previous "dirty" interest rate targeting of the federal funds rate. By setting the discount rate, targeting the quantity of borrowed reserves, and administering the discount window, the Fed was able to control the level of the federal funds rate non-transparently.

Since the appointment of Alan Greenspan in the late 1980s the Fed has received much praise for its performance. Over the decade of the 1990s the economy enjoyed low and falling inflation rates, rapid economic growth, and a housing and stock market bubble. This provided capital gain income which combined with low and falling unemployment rates encouraged "animal spirits." There was much Monday morning quarterbacking of the Fed's unwillingness to raise rates more rapidly in the late 1990s, or to raise margin requirements to puncture the stock market bubble. But the economy greatly benefited from the prosperity and investment spending associated with the low interest rates of the 1990s boom, which unprecedently combined low and falling rates of unemployment, with low and falling rates of inflation. In response to the collapse in the stock market in 1999 the Fed reduced the federal funds rate in a short series of steps to the historically unprecedented postwar low level of 1 percent. The immediate response was a substantial fall in the value of the dollar. The economy showed signs of recovery in the election year of 2004 and the Fed raised rates moderately by a series of 25 basis points increases at each monetary policy meeting.

The policy of targeting the "degree of reserve restraint" was undertaken to disguise the linkage between the Fed's actions and the level of short-term interest rates. The goal was to shield the monetary authorities from political criticism of high rate levels and so provide them with greater autonomy to set future rates. But since 2000 this fig leaf has been abandoned. The Fed now explicitly sets the federal funds rate over the period until the next monetary policy meeting. It is universally recognized in the financial press that the Fed now sets the level of the federal funds rate at some target rate as its policy instrument until the next policy meeting, in spite of the liquidity preference and money-multiplier story told in the textbooks.[37]

The Fed has recently discovered two important new "transmission belts" of monetary policy, the behavior of asset prices (particularly housing and stock market prices) and the exchange rate, which were not previously considered of much importance for monetary policy. CBs have recently learned that the relationship between interest rates, money growth, inflation, stock prices and exchange rates are impossible to predict successfully in advance.[38] Sooner or later the market is dependent on Federal Reserve intervention. Market participants try to guess what the Fed will do and the banks try to minimize their use of base money. So long as no interest rate is paid on bank reserves, market participants will continue to economize on their use with great ingenuity. At the end of the day the CB is the only institution that can both satisfy the demand for currency and provide system liquidity. In the extreme case it can create liquidity without end, so long as there is no question about its credit status. This power gives the CB huge influence which the market respects. In consequence markets now respond quickly to the authorities' announced policy intentions.

10.5 Money market mutual funds

In many developed financial systems money market mutual funds (MMMF) constitute an increasing share of household checkable deposits. MMMF characteristically hold only short-term marketable securities, have few other expenses, and pay a higher interest rate on deposits than the commercial banks. From the point of view of depositors, mutual fund deposits that are transferable by check are a very close substitute for bank deposits. But the macroeconomic effects of nonbank MMMF intermediation on AD are very different from the effects of bank intermediation.

Increases in MMMF intermediation are initiated by bank *depositors*, who desire higher returns on their liquid assets than offered by the banking system. Bank depositors purchase money market funds deposits with previously existing bank deposits. These deposits are used by MMMF to purchase previously existing short-term money market primary securities in the open market. This does not reduce the supply of bank deposits so long as bank asset loans and securities are not reduced. The effect of MMMF intermediation is to transform highly liquid short-term primary securities (Treasury Bills and private corporate commercial paper) in wealth portfolios into even more highly liquid MMMF deposits which are similar to bank demand deposits as a payments medium. Increases in MMMF intermediation result in an increase in AD, to the extent greater liquidity and transaction services are attached to money-market deposits than to the Treasury Bills and commercial paper they replaced.

Commercial bank intermediation is initiated by bank *borrowers*, who desire to deficit-spend to finance working capital demand for currently produced goods and services and to acquire consumer durables and nonmonetary financial assets. The effect of bank intermediation is an increase in bank credit and bank deposits, which finances increases in deficit spending by bank borrowers, and results in increases in AD for productive factors and current output.

The result of MMMF intermediation is an increase in MMMF holdings of money market instruments and total MMMF deposits. But so long as the CB maintains short-term interest rates unchanged, the effect of greater MMMF intermediation on AD is minor: a slight differential increase in the liquidity of interest-bearing mutual fund deposits over the short-term money-market securities in MMMF portfolios. The increase in liquidity associated with an increase in MMMF deposits is comparable with the increase in liquidity associated with an increase in bank deposits. But the MMMF assets associated with MMMF intermediation are highly liquid, marketable and previously existing, while the assets associated with banks intermediation are illiquid, nonmarketable and newly created. The asset transmutation effect of commercial bank intermediation on AD is incomparably greater than the asset transmutation effect of MMMF intermediation.[39]

If the CB permitted the increased demand for money-market instruments to drive up short-term security prices and lower interest rates on securities, this would provide a substantial expansionary AD effect from MMMF intermediation. But the level of short-term interest rates is set by the CB as its chief instrument of monetary policy, and the CB does not permit increases in MMMF intermediation to lower the level of short-term rates, its main policy instrument. To the extent MMMF intermediation increases AD at a given level of interest rates, MMMF intermediation is likely to provoke the CB to pursue more restrictive monetary policy, and result in a higher level of short-term interest rates. The CB has the ability to offset any expansionary effects of increases in MMMF intermediation on AD by raising Bank Rate.

10.6 Conclusions: "horizontalism"

The "Verticalist" notion of an exogenous money supply encourages the view that inflation is a purely monetary phenomenon—"too much money chasing too few goods." An "excessive" rate of growth of the nominal money stock (above the underlying real growth rate of aggregate supply) is widely believed the chief "cause" of inflation. The underlying notion is that an "excess supply" of money "spills over," to create an "excess demand" for goods and services. Implicit in this view is the notion that the money supply is directly controlled by the CB and that inflation is due to an increase in AD. Such belief was natural when money was a commodity or created by government "fiat." It appeared reasonable to posit an exogenously determined stock of money which was held by economic agents. Prices and incomes would adjust until agents' total demand to hold real money balances was equal to the exogenous real stock of money in existence.[40]

But CBs are unable to increase or decrease the nominal supply of credit money exogenously by expanding or contracting the high-powered base, as the money-multiplier theory asserts. CBs target Bank Rate in an attempt to achieve their target rates of inflation and continuously smooth out fluctuations in the level of short-term rates to ensure system liquidity. CB's are unable to control the quantity of money in the economy. The supply of money changes continuously over time with changes in the demand for bank credit.

The effect of central bank purchases or sales of government securities on the open market is to increase or reduce total non-borrowed reserves of the banking system, and with them total bank deposits. This part of the story in the textbooks is correct. But unless CBs desire to raise or lower the level of short-term rates they never undertake open market operations to control the high-powered base. CB's overriding responsibility is to maintain system liquidity. This necessitates that CB open market operations be defensive in nature. CB open market operations are aimed at smoothing and eliminating short-run fluctuations in interest rates, to ensure the liquidity of the banking system and the economy.

Exogenous central bank open market purchases of securities show up as an immediate increase in bank excess reserves. These must be immediately reversed by open market sales to prevent the overnight rate from falling below its target range. If CB security purchases were not offset by equal concurrent sales of repos and securities, bank rate would fall toward zero bid.

Bank intermediation finances net increases in deficit-spending by firms and households. Banks create additional credit money by making additional bank loans. Increases in the volume of bank intermediation are driven by increases in the demand for credit by agents who desire bank deposits to finance additional deficit spending. Changes in the supply of deposits are determined by changes in the demand for credit. The money supply is fully endogenous in the theoretical, statistical, and control sense. Since changes in the money supply are throughly endogenous money cannot be an ultimate "cause" of changes in income, output, inflation, or anything else.

11
The Exogeneity of Interest Rates

> The banking system has no direct control over the quantity of money; for it is characteristic of modern systems that the central bank is ready to buy for money at a stipulated rate of discount any quantity of securities of certain approved types. Thus it is broadly true to say that the governor of the whole system is the rate of discount.
>
> John Maynard Keynes, 1930

> The rate of interest is the reward for parting with liquidity for a specified period. ... The rate of interest is not self-adjusting at a level best suited to the social advantage but constantly tends to rise too high. ... In a world, therefore, which no one reckoned to be safe, it was almost inevitable that the rate of interest, unless it was curbed by every instrument at the disposal of society, would rise too high to permit of an adequate inducement to invest.
>
> John Maynard Keynes, 1936: 167, 351

> We intend to retain control over our domestic rate of interest, so that we can keep it as low as suits our own purposes, without interference from the ebb and flow of international capital movements or flights of hot money.
>
> John Maynard Keynes, XXVII, House of Lords, 1944

> The General Theory's most momentous, radical and decisive service was to release the interest rate from its imprisonment in the mutual self-determinating equilibrium system of prices of goods in terms of goods, and to make it a response to uncertainty.
>
> George L.S. Schackle, 1983

11.1 Different theories of interest

The interest rate is the price of credit expressed as a percentage: the price paid for a loan of one unit of money in the present in return for a promise to repay one unit of money plus interest one year in the future. Classical economists analyzed the factors determining interest rates as *real* forces underlying the supply and demand for loanable funds.[1] They concluded that real interest rates were determined by the real forces behind the demand for investment and the supply of saving, conventionally summarized under the headings "productivity" and "thrift." Nominal interest rates comprised this *real* rate plus an "inflation premium," which reflected the expected future rate of inflation over the maturity of the particular security.[2]

The "Loanable Funds" theory of interest holds that the level of interest rates is determined at the intersection of an independent upward-sloping supply of loanable funds schedule and an independent downward-sloping demand for loanable funds schedule. Planned saving is positively related to the interest rate paid to savers, and planned investment is negatively related to the interest rate charged to borrowers. The real forces of "productivity" and "thrift" determine the supply and demand schedules and so the level of real interest rates. The "real" rate is what the interest rate would be in the absence of inflation.

Interest is regarded as the reward to be paid for foregoing and so abstaining from present consumption. The amount saved determines the resources available for investment. Both investment and saving are volitional. Volitional increases in saving shift the supply of loanable funds schedule rightward, reducing the level of interest rates. Volitional increases in investment also shift the investment schedule rightward, increasing interest rates. A lower (higher) interest cost of finance induces business firms to increase (reduce) planned investment spending.

Neoclassical economists believed that money was "neutral," and that agents had no money illusion. Nominal variables were determined by nominal variables and real variables were determined by real variables. Real interest rates were determined solely by real forces. The real rate is directly determined only in a barter economy where money does not exist. Once money is introduced it is necessary to distinguish two different rates of interest, the nominal and the real rate. The real rate *ex ante* or *ex post* is the nominal rate minus the *ex ante* or *ex post* inflation rate.

Wicksell was the first to recognize that the supply of credit money is credit-driven. Using comparative static analysis he argued that over the long run, market rates would adjust until in general equilibrium the real rate is equal to the "natural" rate, determined by real forces of productivity and thrift consistent with full employment and price stability.[3] Money rates below (above) the "natural" rate will provoke a cumulative rise (fall) in the money supply and after a lag a rise or fall in the price level. Wicksell and Walras viewed the quantity of capital, labor, technology, output, and income as mutually inter-determined in general equilibrium.

Unfortunately there are insuperable logical difficulties in defining a fixed value of real capital in Neo-Wicksellian theory having to do with how capital is measured. The value of the capital stock cannot be defined independently of the interest rate, but the interest rate cannot be determined until one has specified the quantity of capital. The problem arises because although capital is treated as an exogenous magnitude, its value cannot be defined independently of its price, the interest rate, which is determined only in general equilibrium. Wicksell's analysis treats capital as simultaneously exogenous and endogenous, so it is impossible to determine the interest rate. Wicksellian analysis is valid only for a nonmonetary (barter) one-commodity (corn) economy where it is possible to treat the "natural" rate of interest as the long-run center of gravitation for the system.[4]

Neo-Walrasian general equilibrium models treat the endowment of physical capital as a given quantity rather than a given value, so it is possible to derive own rates of return for each commodity. In this vision the uniformity of rates of return on capital are lost, but the Wicksellian indeterminacy of the quantity of capital is surmounted. In order to achieve determinate outcomes and avoid dealing with fundamental uncertainty, Neo-Walrasian general equilibrium (GE) analysis postulates that commodities are time-dated for each different future state of the world. A complete set of futures markets is assumed to exist for all such time-dated commodities in every future state of nature. Under such assumptions the future can be collapsed into the present. All decisions are made at the initial point in time and there is no business to transact at later dates.[5]

Unfortunately, money is an inessential addition to such models. In a world where contingent future contracts are possible in all markets, no one needs or wants money. Once the assumption of a perfect and complete array of contingent futures markets is dropped and our inability to predict the future is explicitly recognized, it is no longer possible to define any unique GE outcome. The economy then becomes a sequence economy where trading occurs at every date. Agents' current actions depend on the expectations of other agents about future events. If expectations are taken as exogenous, GE can be defined for every state of expectations. GE then becomes a continuously changing long-run gravitation point toward which the system is tending. The GE position changes with each change in expectations; so no unique GE position exists.

Real theories of interest implicitly assume that all essential forces that determine interest rates can be represented in a real exchange economy. Money is neutral, and it enters the analysis only in the role of a technical device to facilitate transactions by eliminating the necessity of an inverse coincidence of wants required for barter exchange to occur. So long as money functions normally it is assumed the economic process behaves as does a barter economy, so money is "neutral." Such a view lies behind Ricardo's assertion:

> Productions are essentially bought only by other productions. No man produces, but with a view to consume or sell, and he never sells but with an intention to purchase some other commodity. ... By producing, he necessarily becomes either the consumer of his own good or the purchaser and consumer of the goods of some other person.[6]

Such a statement holds only for barter economies. With credit money, current production may be purchased with newly created credit as well as with "other productions." Agents then need no longer save volitionally in order to provide the finance that other agents invest.

In the *General Theory*, Keynes developed a new "Liquidity Preference" monetary theory of interest, in which interest rates were determined by monetary and not by real forces. Interest rates were the rate that had to be paid to induce wealth-owners to hold bonds and forego the liquidity of holding money. Keynes argued the essential nature of capitalist production was not caught in the classical bloated vision of exchanging commodities and effort for money to obtain commodities (C–M–C). He adopted but did not develop Marx's vision that firms part with money to buy commodities and labor in order to end up with more money at the end of the production–sales process than they had at the beginning of the period (M–C–M).

> The firm is dealing throughout in terms of sums of money. It has no object in the world except to end up with more money than it started with. ... An entrepreneur is interested not in the amount of product but in the amount of money which will fall to his share.[7]

11.2 Central Bank interest rate setting behavior

In a closed economy the central bank (CB) is the monopoly supplier of legal tender and so able to set the marginal supply price of liquidity to the system. This rate (termed "Bank Rate" in most countries) is set as an exogenous policy instrument by the CB in its attempt to achieve its liquidity and stabilization goals.[8] The market rate on all other short-term financial assets is determined by Bank Rate (BR) through a process of bank arbitrage. The rates on different short-term securities differ slightly from BR, reflecting perceived differences in their risk, liquidity, maturity, transactions costs, and acceptability in satisfying "Required Reserves" status. As a result of bank arbitrage, all short-term market rates are kept at a stable differential with BR over time.

The rates charged for bank credit (bank lending rates) and the rates paid on bank deposits are administered by the banks and are not market-determined. Administered loan and deposit rates are set discretionarily by commercial banks at a relatively stable mark-up or mark-down on BR. As developed in Chapter 9, bank loan and deposit markets in all economies are highly oligopolistic, due to large economies of scale in banking. Changes in lending and deposit rates are typically initiated by the largest banks under price-leadership arrangements.

Nominal long-term market rates and the nominal yield curve are determined by a time arbitrage process based on capital market participants' expectations of future BRs and inflation rates. If future short-term rates were known with certainty, bank arbitrage would force the long-term rate to be identical to the known expected level of future short-term rates over the asset's maturity. Long-term rates reflect market expectations of the CB's future interest-setting behavior. In a complex world, if the CB wishes to reduce the current level of long-term rates, it must persuade wealth-owners that the levels of BR will be lower in the future. Nominal rates can never be set below Zero, the nominal return on currency, and no one will hold an asset with a negative return when currency yields a zero return. The real BR becomes negative when the inflation rate exceeds the nominal level of BR.

In closed economies the level of nominal short-term interest rates is set discretionarily by the monetary authorities as their chief instrument of monetary policy.

The authorities vary the rate pro-cyclically as they attempt to attain their future macroeconomic stabilization targets. This process can be demonstrated in terms of a flow supply and demand for loanable funds framework, and in a liquidity preference portfolio asset stock framework.

The central point is that in all closed economies the monetary authority sets the supply price of system liquidity. As the monopoly supplier of system liquidity, the CB must set the nominal level of BR. Monetary policy cannot be "neutral," since whatever nominal rate the CB sets has an effect. The authorities must set some rate, and they possess considerable discretion as to the rate they set. In complex economies there is no "natural" rate of interest, endogenously determined by market forces, and as there is no "natural" unemployment rate or "natural" growth rate. Real forces of "thrift" and "productivity" do indirectly influence the level of interest rates set by determining the effects that particular levels of or changes in BR have on aggregate demand (AD).

The BR rate that is set by the CB depends on its macroeconomic goals, its assumptions about how the economy behaves, and its expectations of the future course of target variables. Short-term rates are not adjusted by the monetary authorities one-for-one with changes in the inflation rate to keep the real rate constant. Depending on how the CB changes BR in response to changes in the inflation rate, the real rate will vary pro-cyclically or counter-cyclically over the cycle. In most periods, real rates have a higher variance than nominal rates. Nominal and real long-term rates depend on the markets' expectations of future inflation rates and on the authorities' expected future response or "reaction function" to the expected state of the economy. The nominal short-term rate set by the CB depends on its estimate of the future state of the economy, its stabilization objectives, and its model of the economy, including its estimates of the sensitivity of various economic behavior to changes in interest rates. Price stability recently has become the most important policy objective of most CBs. The CB is the sole government institution mandated with responsibility for the inflation rate.[9]

CBs use open market operations to maintain non-borrowed reserves slightly below required reserves so as to keep the banking system "in the bank." This compels the banking system to use the CBs' accommodation facilities and greatly facilitates CB's efforts to maintain short-term rates at a target level. Central bank price-setting behavior is directed at setting asset prices and interest rates, not asset quantities. In many mainstream textbooks such behavior is assumed to be rare or even pathological. Pegging interest rates at any level will be destabilizing over time as conditions change.[10] Nevertheless, rate setting or price "smoothing" behavior, sometimes termed "leaning against the wind," is undertaken by all CBs in all economies. Rate "smoothing" behavior must be distinguished from rate "pegging" behavior. Interest rate "smoothing" holds rates within a narrow band between CB rate setting periods. Rate "pegging" denoting a policy of holding rates constant over longer time periods, which is no longer practiced since it leads directly to disintermediation.[11]

CB interest rate smoothing is universally undertaken by all CBs to reduce uncertainty and promote liquidity in financial markets. Smoothing describes CBs' attempts to validate the general expectation in financial markets that the situation tomorrow will be the same as the situation today. "Liquidity" denotes that a liquid financial asset can be exchanged into money quickly, cheaply, and easily at every point in time. All Liquid financial assets are continuously exchangeable into money at a price close to the last price quoted. To ensure the liquidity of the financial system, all changes in short-term security prices must be smoothed. Gaps and "spikes" in time series of asset prices and rates are signs of temporary breakdowns in market liquidity.

Since Keynes's theory that effective demand determines the level of output has become generally accepted, CBs have been forced to accept responsibility for macroeconomic stabilization. All CBs move interest rates pro-actively in their pursuit of counter-cyclical monetary policy. In response to changes in current economic conditions, and to expectations of future economic conditions, CBs raise BR during business expansions and lower BR during business recessions. The underlying goal of the CBs is to move the economy toward their macro stabilization goals of price level and exchange rate stability and full employment. The goals of full employment and rapid economic growth are universally compromised in the attempt to achieve price level stability and external balance.

Whether CBs use price or quantity instruments is neither a policy option to be pursued or nor a tactical considerations dictat. Quantity controls on the supply of credit money are generally infeasible, since they cause security prices and interest rates to fluctuate sharply, impairing system liquidity. In contrast, quantity controls and quantity ceilings on the volume of bank credit are feasible, and were frequently resorted to in many economies in the postwar period. But in modern financial systems, quantity controls are now used only as a last resort, since it has been found that they generate unintended effects like financial disintermediation and other distortions, as private agents alter their behavior to avoid the controls.

CBs are unable to directly control the supply of credit money by varying the base and increasing or reducing the supply money, as the mainstream textbook account maintains. So long as CBs have a positive bank rate target, all exogenous purchases or sales of securities to inject or withdraw cash reserves are offset by defensive open market operations to keep BR on target. In all economies the provision of fiat money is the monopoly of the CB. So long as the market is "in the bank," bank arbitrage ensures that interest rates on short-term assets are maintained at a constant differential from BR. CB interest rate targeting is strongly supported by empirical evidence, and is now (2005) acknowledged and endorsed by all central bankers and financial journalists.[12] The CBs' "policy reaction function" in response to changes in the economy is now termed a "Taylor Rule," taken from Taylor's estimates of how the Federal Reserve adjusted interest rates when inflation and unemployment diverged from their targeted values.[13]

11.3 The US reserve supply process

In most countries, cash reserves are provided as a tap issue at the BR set by the CB. But in the United States the provision of cash reserves to the banks has long been rationed at the discount window and subjected to discretionary surveillance ("frown costs"). The discount rate is normally below the Federal Funds rate. It is considered a "subsidized" rate at which banks are not automatically entitled to borrow indefinite amounts. The Federal Reserve treats bank discount window borrowing as "a privilege and not a right." Substantial borrowing at the discount window is reserved for banks who find themselves for whatever reasons with a temporary urgent need for liquid funds.[14]

When an individual bank's borrowing at the discount window is considered "too frequent," or the amount demanded is considered "too large," the rate the Fed imposes for lending at the discount window {the pecuniary costs (discount rate) plus the non-pecuniary "frown" costs} is sharply increased.[15] Banks have the option of borrowing the excess reserves of other banks in the Federal Funds market with no "frown costs." In consequence individual banks are never quantitatively constrained for reserves. So long as they are solvent they are able to obtain additional funds at some price: at the discount window, in the federal funds market, by the sale of existing securities, by issuing their own CDs or longer term debt securities, and by borrowing in offshore markets.

As shown in Figure 11.1, in the period from the 1970s to the 1990s the Fed set the federal funds rate non-transparently:

1. It exogenously set the discount rate (R_D), the rate at which it lends additional reserves to member banks through the discount window as its policy instrument.
2. By varying the supply of non-borrowed reserves (NBR) relative to required reserves (RR) by open market operations, it was able to determine the degree that the banking system was "in the bank" and so the banks' demand for borrowed reserves (BR) ("degree of reserve pressure").
3. By its surveillance and regulation of the discount window ("frown costs" attached to additional discount window borrowing) it set the *slope* of the reserve supply function (SR).
4. By setting the discount rate (R_D) and targeting the "degree of reserve restraint" (BR) the Fed was able to determine both the level and the slope of the reserve supply function (SR). The federal funds rate (R_{ff}) was kept within a narrow band determined by the intersection of the demand for borrowed reserves (BR) and the reserve supply function (SR).
5. The federal funds rate was kept at its target level by continuous open market sales and purchases of Repurchase Agreements (Repos) to provide the required degree of reserve restraint to permit the Fed to hit its interest rate target.

In the 1990s the Fed gradually abandoned the above policy, which had concealed its responsibility for setting short-term rates. It now (2005) explicitly targets and announces the level of the federal funds rate over the period until the next open market committee meeting. The Fed purchases Repos whenever the funds rate threatens to rise above target and sells Repos when the funds rate threatens to fall below target. In their role as residual supplier of system liquidity, the monetary authorities must supply reserves to the banking system as demanded.

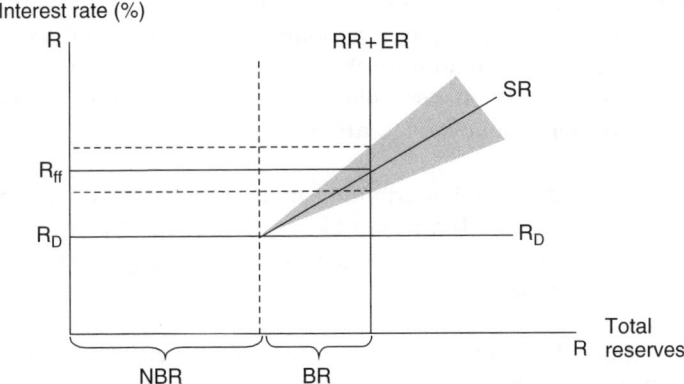

Figure 11.1 The US reserve supply process

CBs are unable to directly reduce money supply growth by reducing the supply of cash reserves provided to the system due to their overriding commitment to system liquidity. To reduce the rate of money growth they can only raise the marginal supply price of liquidity to the banking system by increasing the federal funds rate, and attempt to deter lending and borrowing by raising the cost of reserve funds. They are similarly unable to directly control the money supply. To raise the rate of money growth they can only reduce the banks' marginal supply price of liquidity by reducing BR, and inducing economic units to borrow more by reducing the price of bank credit. CBs cannot force borrowers to borrow or to spend additional amounts. CBs only indirectly influence money supply growth by varying interest rates pro-cyclically over the cycle.[16]

The quality of credit money is credit-driven, and is not exogenously set by the monetary authorities. The authorities directly set prices but not quantities: Bank Rate, the Federal Funds rate, and the exchange rate. The money supply responds endogenously to changes in the demand for bank credit. In all overdraft systems, banks assign individual borrowers a line of credit, based on their estimate of the borrower's credit-worthiness and ability to repay. So long as borrowers are within their assigned credit limits, banks are price-setters and quantity-takers in their retail loan markets. In developed economies the credit-utilization rate for bank borrowers fluctuates around 50 percent.[17] The supply of money is endogenously demand-determined and credit-driven.

The textbook story argues that by flooding the capital markets with base money, CBs cause interest rates to fall. Conversely by contracting the monetary base they cause interest rates to rise. But this story is directly contradicted empirically. The short-run relationship between changes in money and changes in interest rates is positive, as predicted by endogenous money and exogenous interest rates theory and not negative as predicted by textbook liquidity preference theory. The monetary authorities vary the level of short-term market rates pro-cyclically at their discretion over time, in their attempts to hit their stabilization goals.

In the United States, Federal Reserve rate setting policy has recently become much more transparent. The Fed now announces at its discretion the level of the federal funds rate that will hold until the next Open Market policy meeting and rates adjust immediately. Monetary policy has attained an almost mystical status. As previous Governor Paul Volker recently exclaimed,

> You have to wonder whether anything more is necessary these days than a pronouncement that the Fed would like to change the federal funds rate by x percent. The Fed does not actually have to do anything. The rate will immediately change by x percent.[18]

The expectations theory of the term structure links the current long-term rate to the expected future short-term rates over the life of the instrument in an intuitively appealing manner. The nominal LT rate is an appropriately weighted average of expected future ST rates plus the addition of a positive or negative risk and maturity premium. If future rates were known with certainty, the expectations theory conclusions that nominal LT rates are the weighted average of expected future ST rates would follow directly as a simple arbitrage condition. Under uncertainty, a positive or negative maturity premium must be added since ST and LT securities are not perfect substitutes. Market expectations of the future cannot be measured directly. The yield curve varies over time with changes in expected future rates.

When the CBs announce a change in BR, this directly influences market expectations of future inflation and of future long-term real rates. Since the expected future rates of inflation and Bank Rate are heterogeneous, and cannot be directly measured, it is not possible to directly test the expectations theory empirically. Agents' expectations of future events are highly heterogeneous. At any moment of time there is a distribution rather than a single-valued estimate of *ex ante* long-term real rates. The average expected future level of real rates or the inflation rate cannot be measured directly.

The CBs' ability to influence long-term real rates depends on their ability to persuade capital market participants that they will carry out their announced future policies. This governs their ability to shape market expectations of future BR and inflation rates. In the case of expansionary monetary policy the CB's ability to target a low level of real LT rates is greatly eased by expected inflation, since expected inflation lowers the *ex ante* real rate on a one-for-one basis. Conversely, when the economy is experiencing deflation, since CBs cannot reduce nominal ST rates below zero, the return on currency, they are unable to reduce the real BR below the expected deflation rate. Whenever deflation is anticipated, CBs are unable to attain lower LT real interest rate targets. Expected deflation raises *ex ante* real rates. When the rate of expected deflation is high, the *ex ante* real LT rates will also be high; so the effectiveness of expansionary monetary policy will be severely impaired. For this reason deflation is widely disliked by all central bankers.

The CB sets the *nominal short-term rate* it charges banks for supplying additional reserves. But for most investment spending decisions the *long-term real rate* is more relevant for most borrowers than the short-term nominal rate. Expected future nominal long-term rates determine the current market values of debt and equity instruments, and so portfolio allocation decisions. Expected real long-term rates govern most real investment decisions. To the extent the *ex ante* inflation rate is predetermined over the short run, by setting the *nominal* short-term rate the CB effectively sets the *real* short-term rate. The fact that the CB directly controls the *nominal* short-term rate, but investment spending is primarily a function of the *real* long-term rate, is an important factor contributing to the looseness of the relationship between changes in short-term rates and changes in investment spending and AD.

The most important function of the CB is to ensure the liquidity of the financial system. CBs continuously intervene to smooth out fluctuations in the prices of financial assets. The second most important function of CBs is to set the level of short-term interest rates at the appropriate level to achieve its stabilization goals: price stability, full employment, and current account balance.

11.4 The new consensus on monetary policy

A number of CB conferences have recently agreed a new consensus has emerged on monetary policy.[19] Over the past decade, "Inflation Targeting" has generated considerable support among central bankers, and has been adopted by many industrialized countries, the ECB and even some developing economies. In the early postwar period there was a considerable debate about the strategies for conducting monetary policy, in the "rules" versus "discretion" debate. Rules are automatic, and advocates of rules stress the "discipline" and "credibility" that they create. But it is now recognized that there is no such thing as an absolute rule for monetary policy. When a crisis time comes, any "rule" must be discretionarily altered. All monetary regimes are discretionary, but the discretion is a matter of degree. Advocates of "inflation targeting" argue it provides a framework of "constrained discretion."[20] By imposing both a conceptual structure and an inherent discipline, it combines the advantages traditionally ascribed to rules, without eliminating discretion.

Mainstream macroeconomists believe in the long run the inflation rate is the sole variable monetary policy can affect. According to this view, the stagflation experience of the 1970s demonstrated there is no long-run tradeoff between inflation and unemployment.[21] Activist monetary policies had assumed it was possible to maintain a *permanently* lower average rate of unemployment by engineering higher AD and accepting a higher rate of inflation. The severe 1981 recession was the result of highly restrictive monetary policy in response to the stagflation of the 1970s. Stagflation was supplemented by intellectual developments, in particular Milton Friedman's insistence that monetary policy works only with "long and variable lags" and Friedman and Phelps's argument that in the long run there is no tradeoff between inflation and unemployment.[22] Most advocates of inflation targeting would not deny monetary policy has powerful effects on employment and output. But they argue that the benefits of higher output and employment are largely transitory, while the inflationary costs are permanent. CBs are prone to opportunistic behavior, which leads in the long run to higher inflation with no higher output and employment.[23] Periods of rapid inflation are clearly detrimental to output and efficiency. Whether moderate inflation is harmful is more controversial. Economists have found that only "Inflation crises," when inflation reaches very high levels, have significant negative effects on growth. Many studies have found that higher inflation is associated with lower rates of productivity and growth.[24]

In recent years many central bankers have treated even relatively low rates of inflation as a problem, in part due to the public's confusion over what causes inflation and how to adjust for it. Given compound interest, over a 30–40 year period even slight differences in annual inflation rates have a large effect on the purchasing power of a currency, making it difficult to assess future price levels and distorting the production and investment decisions of firms.

The Bank of England has now explicitly adopted an endogenous view of the money supply. It regards the stock of money as entirely credit-driven, and the money supply as totally endogenous. Money no longer enters causally anywhere in the UK model of the economy, and the Bank of England no longer mentions the money supply in policy statements. It has explicitly recognized that it does not control the money supply but sets Bank Rate, and leaves the system to adjust.[25] It recently stated:

> Sustained increases in prices cannot occur without an accompanying increase in the money stock. But that does not mean that money causes inflation. When the short-term nominal interest rate is viewed as the policy instrument, both money and inflation are jointly caused by other variables.[26]

Both academics and practitioners now agree that the short-term interest rate is the CB's chief instrument of monetary policy. The policy rules and the "inflation targeting" literature have adopted the "Taylor Rule" approach to the formulation of monetary policy. It is now widely agreed that monetary policy operates through changes in Bank Rate, rather than changes in the money supply, through a complex process that alters the whole structure of interest rates to which agents respond by adjusting their portfolios.

Changes in interest rates affect AD through several different channels: investment, consumption, credit markets, asset prices, exchange rate, wealth values, general expectations, investor confidence, which are all influenced by inflationary pressures. Inflation targeting has now been widely accepted by CBs. The effect of monetary policy on inflation runs through the effects of changes in interest rates on consumption and investment spending, aggregate demand, exchange rates, and the indirect impact of changes in AD on the pace of inflation. In developing economies such as South Africa, where inflations primarily cost and import inflation, unemployment rates are extremely high, CB "inflation targeting" is less successful. It serves primarily to raise the level of interest rates and the exchange rate, and depress the level and rate of growth of AD.

The level of market short-term rates determines the marginal supply price of liquidity set by the monetary authorities (BR). The ability of CBs to influence AD depends on the interaction of BR with various short- and long-term market rates and on their interaction with the financial and real behavior of the economy. In the United States, the banks' mark-up of prime rate over the federal funds rate lies within a narrow range of 1–3 percent. Most administered rates vary less through the cycle than the federal funds rate. As a result, interest rate mark-ups exhibit counter-cyclical variation, rising during recessions when Bank Rate is sharply reduced, and falling in expansions when Bank Rate is increased. The primacy of the federal funds rate in determining the level of short- and long-term market rates has recently been thoroughly explored with Granger–Sims causality tests. One-way causality had been found to exist from the federal funds rate to other short-term market rates.[27]

The effectiveness of changes in interest rate on the economy is primarily estimated through the simulation of macroeconomic models. In a recent US study using instrumental variables, over the 1990s a reduction in the federal funds rate of 1 percent for one year was associated with an increase in output of 0.8 percent after 4–8 quarters.[28] In another study by the Bank of England, a 1 percent rise in Bank Rate for one year was found to lower GDP by 0.2–0.3 percent after about two years and reduce inflation by around 0.2–0.4 percent over a two-year time period, depending on the subsequent responses of interest rates in response to the evolving inflation rate.[29]

By raising capital costs, higher interest rates have a tendency to raise business mark-ups, the price level, and the inflation rate. There is a direct effect on the cost of credit and home mortgages as reflected in the official inflation rate. It has been estimated that elasticity of demand for business investment with respect to the real cost of capital is unity, but it takes six years for 50 percent of the effect to be experienced and ten years for 70 percent to occur.[30] If capacity shortage is a significant source of inflationary pressure, raising interest rates adversely influences productive capacity and adds to future inflationary pressure over the longer term.

The relationship between the CBs' affect on short-term and long-term rates is strikingly different.[31] Granger–Sims tests exhibit strong one-way causality from long-term rates to short-term rates, including the federal funds rate. There is both persuasive theoretical and empirical evidence that short-term interest rates are exogenously determined by the federal funds rate. Granger–Sims tests must be interpreted as "informativeness" tests rather than "causality" tests. (No one would argue that changes in share prices "cause" changes in corporate profits. Long-term interest rates "Granger-cause" short-term interest rates in the same way that share prices "Granger-cause" corporate profits.) Such "causality" tests rather reveal that future values of short-term rates are "informative" in predicting present values of long-term rates, in the way future corporate profits are "informative" in predicting present share values, as is consistent with the "expectations" theory of the yield curve. Current long-term rates are based on market participants' estimates of the future values of short-term rates over the maturity of the financial instrument.

By manipulating the magnitude of the banking system's reserve deficiency and its demand for borrowed reserves, central banks are able to move Bank Rate to any level they desire. By changing the supply relative to the demand for non-borrowed reserves, the Fed can indirectly and non-transparently determine the level of the federal funds rate. Note that CB open market operations do not increase or reduce the size of the high-powered base, but merely change the composition of the base between borrowed and non-borrowed reserves. "Increasing the degree of reserve restraint" is simply "CB-speak" for increasing the proportion of total reserves that banks must borrow from the CB.[32]

A rise in investment spending and the size of the government fiscal deficit is incorrectly believed to put upward pressure on interest rates, by increasing the demand for funds. Similarly, a fall in the saving rate or an outflow of foreign capital is believed to have a similar effect of reducing rates by reducing the supply of funds. This story, which for political convenience used to be told by central banks, was perhaps applicable before the advent of central banks but is no longer accurate. The level of short-term interest rates is not a market-determined price but is directly set by the CB. Higher interest rates are always unpopular and even nonelected officials must tend their political fences. Central bankers are widely known for their Delphic utterances.[33]

In closed economies the CB must set BR, the supply-price of liquidity to the banking system and the economy, since it is the monopoly supplier of legal tender and system liquidity. In its role of lender of last resort, the CB must provide the quantity of reserves demanded by the banking system to meet its cash reserve requirements. In the process the CB must select the price at which it makes reserves available. In open economies, depending on the exchange rate regime in force and on the degree of capital mobility, domestic CBs share their rate-setting responsibilities with foreign CBs. At the limit when the exchange rate is fixed, the CB loses all ability to set the domestic BR.

Drawing a horizontal money supply at the interest rate set by the CB is intended to represent graphically that the CB is a price-setter due to its overriding obligation to provide system liquidity. It is not to be interpreted as implying an infinite money supply. In closed economies the price of liquidity (BR) is set by the CB, and the quantity of credit money supplied is determined by the demand for bank credit.

The growth of the money supply is the consequence and not the cause of inflation. In most economies the money supply grows broadly in line with inflation. But the sources of cost inflation lie in labor and factor markets, whenever money wages rise more rapidly than average labor productivity growth. Inflation is not created because the nominal growth of the money supply exceeds the real growth rate of the economy, despite the high correlation between the two variables.

Money supply endogeneity in no sense implies that monetary policy is unimportant, or that CBs have no influence on the money supply. It simply asserts that the CB sets the short-term interest rate and does not directly increase or decrease the money supply by the open market purchases or sales of securities. By altering the level of short-term interest rates, the CB can shape market expectations of the future behavior of inflation, exchange rates, and the change in AD. In this manner it influences the quantity of credit demanded and the quantity of money created and supplied.

The CB has the overriding obligation to ensure the financial system remains liquid. A liquid system accommodates changes in demand for credit and so monetary expansion at existing interest rates. All a CB can do in response to more rapid monetary growth than it desires is to raise the rate it charges banks for additional liquidity (BR). It has no choice but to provide reserves as demanded in its role as residual supplier of system liquidity. Commercial banks do not generally change their lending rate independently of changes in BR in response to changes in the demand for credit. Competition forces them to maintain the differential of their lending rates at a highly stable mark-up over BR.

Exogenous open market purchases of securities provide the banking system with additional reserves. Since the CB continuously targets the short-term interest rate, the effects of exogenous open-market purchases are immediately reversed before the reduction in banks' reserve deficiency exerts a lowering effect on interest rates. Once a particular level of interest rate has been targeted, the supply of reserves becomes totally endogenous. In economies with developed financial markets, open-market transactions are conducted primarily with "repos." The effects on borrowed reserves and on the base are then automatically reversed and need not later be offset by sales. Interest rates may rise when the level of investment or government spending increases, but they need not. They may also fall, as occurred in the United States over the decade of the 1980s. The behavior of interest rates depends solely on the central bank's "policy reaction function," or "Taylor Rule," and how it is interpreted in capital markets.

In a world where there are no financial assets, deficit spending is impossible, and economic units are confined to the strait-jacket of a balanced budget. In such a world, saving takes precedence over investment, and thrift and time preference are the determining factors shaping the level of interest rates.[34] But in a credit money world, whenever deficit spending is financed by bank borrowing the recipients of checks who accumulate the newly created deposits automatically become non-volitional "convenience lenders" to the banking system. The newly created deposits provide the "non-volitional saving" identical to the deficit-financed investment expenditures.

If a CB wishes to raise the level of AD, to increase investment spending and move the economy closer toward its full employment potential, it must reduce the target level of BR. In open economies the level of interest rates set by the CB and its differential over the rates set by other CBs is of critical importance for short-term capital inflows, the level of the exchange rate, the size of AD, the output gap, and so the expansion of AD and the economy.

Changes in the money supply are governed by changes in the demand for bank credit, i.e. by the asset and not the liability side of commercial bank portfolios. The money supply increases and decreases with loan creation and contraction when banks buy and sell financial assets. Increases in deposits represent a non-volitional increase in depositers "convenience lending" to the banking system.

Many economists appear not to have recognized that the level of short-term interest rates is no longer determined by supply and demand phenomena. In all closed economies, and in all open economies with flexible exchange rates, the level of BR is the CBs' central exogenous policy instrument. The long rate depends on market expectations of the future behavior of BR and the goals of the monetary authorities. CBs cannot control the money supply. But they must and do control the supply price of liquidity. CBs set the BR at which they provide liquidity to the banking system.

11.5 Conclusions: bank rate is the exogenous policy instrument of the Central Bank

The overnight wholesale rate of interest at which the CBs lend reserves to the commercial banks is the key instrument of monetary policy. This short-term lending rate (termed in most countries Bank Rate, or the repo rate; in the United States the federal funds rate) is administered by CBs in their role of residual monopoly supplier of system liquidity. Nominal long-term interest rates depend on market expectations of future short-term rates, i.e., of expected future CB interest rate policy. Nominal market interest rates "rule the roost" since they set the floor rate of return, which expected nominal marginal efficiencies on capital must exceed if projects are to be taken up. Given the level of Bank Rate administered by the CB, prevailing inflationary expectations determine the subjective *ex ante* real rate that is incorporated in economic decision-making.

Central banks directly set BR, the short-term supply price of system liquidity. Long-term rates and the yield curve are determined by market arbitrage. Long-term rates adjust to equal market participants' average expected level of future short-term rates over the maturity of the asset, plus a positive or negative risk and term premium to reflect the relative time- and maturity-preferences of different asset-holders and asset-issuers. The CB exogenously sets BR, the rate at which additional bank reserves are supplied, and the volume of reserves supplied is endogenously demand-determined. The causal chain is as follows:[35]

1. The CB sets BR exogenously as its central monetary policy instrument. The rate set depends on its estimation of the future position of the economy, its policy goals, and its reaction function (Taylor Rule).
2. Banks quickly adjust their administered lending and deposit rates in response to changes in BR. Short-term market wholesale rates adjust to maintain the required risk and maturity differentials.
3. The private sector determines the volume of bank borrowing at the BR rate set by the CB. This determines the money supply and its various components, demand, time, and wholesale deposits, and the volume of reserves demanded to support this level of liabilities.
4. The CB adjusts non-borrowed reserves by open market operations to provide the quantity of non-borrowed reserves demanded by the banks at the BR it sets.

5. Depending on CB open market operations and the total volume of reserves supplied, the banks calculate how much they must borrow from the CB to meet their reserve requirements and their demand for excess reserves.
6. The quantity of the monetary base (B) and the money supply (M) are endogenously determined in a complex process of bank portfolio adjustment. They are ultimately driven by animal spirits and so the market reaction to the level of BR rates set by the CB.

Most introductory economic textbooks present a diametrically opposite chain of events:

1. The CB sets the volume of the monetary base (B) through open market operations as its exogenous variable.
2. The banking system determines the money supply via the money-base multiplier, which is dependent on portfolio choices between currency and deposits and desired reserve ratios.
3. No mention is made of the demand for credit. The implicit assumption is that banks adjust the quantity of deposits by buying and selling marketable and nonmarketable assets, until actual reserves are brought into equality with required reserves.
4. The supply of money is determined by steps 2 and 3. The nominal level of short-term interest rates is endogenously determined by market forces so as to bring money demand and money supply into equality.

Apart from Post Keynesians, few economists have recognized the serious error that persists in mainstream monetary theory. All practicing central bankers now recognize that the short-term interest rate is their key policy instrument. Under Volcker the US Fed adopted the language of monetary base control for political reasons during the years of non-borrowed reserve targeting, from 1979 to 1982, to be able to achieve levels of interest rates above the political tolerance levels of Congress. The Fed continued to use interest rates as its fundamental policy instrument, even though its activities were dressed up behind the mask of monetary base control. There was a degree of play-acting and even deception, which became worse during the period of targeting the level of borrowed reserves.[36] The unformulated rationale was that Congress and the president would not have abided the level of interest rates necessary to restrain inflation. Goodhart has incisively observed,

> A persistent theme of political economy in the post-war world is that politicians have been reluctant to accept levels of interest rates sufficient to maintain price stability. The present fashion for central bank independence helps to resolve this problem by having the politicians set the target for price stability, and have the monetary policy authority use its technical judgement and abilities to set the interest rate independently ... [this] did lead some politicians to become confused about the nexus between money, interest rates and economic developments. ... In 1973 Prime Minister Heath ... ordered the Bank to find a

way to restrict monetary growth without bringing about any further increase in interest rates; hence the advent of the "corset." ...

Mrs Thatcher was more of a true believer in the importance of monetary control. It is to her credit that she always refused to countenance direct (credit) controls. Nevertheless the difficulty of sorting out the money supply/interest rate nexus was clearly apparent in the numerous fraught meetings with Bank officials in the early 1980s. The initial part of the meeting would usually consist of a tirade about the shortcomings of the Bank in allowing £M3 to rise so fast; were Bank officials knaves or fools? Then, in the second half of the meeting, discussion would turn to what to do to restrain such growth. In the short run, with fiscal policy given, and credit controls outlawed, the main option was to raise short-term interest rates. At this point the whole tenor of the discussion would dramatically reverse. Whereas in the earlier discussion Mrs Thatcher would have been strong on the need for more radical action on monetary growth, and the Bank on the defensive, when the discussion shifted to the implications for interest rates the roles suddenly reversed.[37]

There has long been a sharp division between bank practitioners, who see themselves as setting rates and responding passively to the cash-flow requirements of borrowers and depositors, and academic economists, who allot banks a much more active role in initiating changes in monetary quantities. Most economists have assumed that CBs set the high-powered monetary base and so the money supply exogenously, but short-term interest rates were endogenously determined in money markets. Post Keynesians have insisted that CBs directly set short-term interest rates according to their reaction function (Taylor Rule), and the monetary base (B) and the money supply (M) become endogenous variables.[38] This has long been understood by CB practitioners, who have viewed the monetary base not as a multiplier but as a divisor, and working backwards determining not M but B. The ECB has chosen a monetary aggregate target as the "pillar" of its policy. But it has explicitly recognized that the week-to-week operational instrument is the level of short-term interest rates.[39]

Prices are cost-determined in all markets in which firms possess market power. In order for increases in bank borrowing, money supply growth, AD, and employment expansion not to result in higher inflation, either an explicit or implicit social contract or incomes policy must be in place. Otherwise, increases in the demand for labor and reductions in the unemployment rate lead to money wages increases in excess of the average rate of growth of labor productivity. In order for the price level to remain stable, so long as the average mark-up is given, unit labor costs must remain constant. For long-run price stability, money wage growth must be moderate and must not exceed the rate of average labor productivity growth. In the absence of a social contract this is achieved in many countries by the threat of international competition and cheaper imports in fixed exchange rate regimes.

Most CBs are explicitly directed by their governments to target the inflation rate. In the absence of a social contract or stiff international competition, this requires that CBs must keep the level of Bank Rates at a sufficiently high level, to keep AD growth sufficiently low, and the unemployment rate sufficiently high, to prohibit labor from being able to increase money wages more rapidly than productivity in response to improvements vis-à-vis business in its bargaining position. The result of CB "inflation targeting" has been a reduction in inflation rates. But it has come about through old-fashioned Phillips Curve effects, the deterioration of unions' role in wage bargaining due to higher unemployment, and the threat of international competition. The result has been a significant reduction in labor's share of national income.

Appendix: Keynes's changing views on interest rates

In the *General Theory* Keynes argued that the level of income was determined by "effective demand." Since he had argued that output adjusted to equilibrate planned saving with planned investment, he was forced to develop a new theory of interest rates. In the *General Theory*, he developed his new "Liquidity Preference" theory of interest. He argued that interest rates were determined by monetary forces in financial markets and the supply and demand for the stock of "liquidity," and were not determined in goods markets by the flow supply of saving and demand for investment.[40] He argued that CBs indirectly controlled the level of short-term interest rates by varying the proportion of money and bonds in wealth portfolios.

In order to simplify his argument that income was determined by "effective demand," in the *General Theory* Keynes assumed that the supply of money could be regarded as set by the monetary authorities. Since he had argued that the level of output was demand-determined, in order to escape from the logic of the Quantity Theory he was forced to argue that the income velocity of money varied widely and pro-cyclically over the business cycle. For most countries during the Great Depression this assumption was empirically fairly accurate. But after his death it left this macroeconomic theory open to serious attack. In the 1950s and 1960s Milton Friedman was able to demonstrate successfully that for all periods except the Great Depression of the 1930s the income velocity of money was much more stable than the Keynesian multiplier.[41]

In the *General Theory*, Keynes attempted to demonstrate logically why the neoclassical loanable funds theory of interest was incorrect. He argued that saving and investment were not independent behavioral relations, but accounting identities that did not have to be equilibrated by changes in the rate of interest.[42] Keynes there developed a monetary theory of interest rates. He argued that the short-term interest rate was the rate that had to be paid to investors to bribe them to forgo holding money in their portfolios. He termed his new theory the "Liquidity Preference Theory of Interest." By changing the money supply the CB was able to vary the interest rate inversely.

This led to the long and still unresolved controversy between adherents of "loanable funds" and "liquidity preference" theories of interest. In his later post–*General Theory* writings Keynes abandoned his "liquidity preference" theory of interest, and insisted that the interest rate was an exogenous policy variable. The monetary authorities could set "any interest rate they desire."[43] It is now increasingly being recognized that the short-term rate is an exogenous instrument of CB monetary policy. But the high-powered base-money multiplier theory, about how the CB exogenously determines the money supply, still appears in most introductory and intermediate mainstream texts on money and macro economics.

In the *General Theory*, Keynes argued that an exogenous rise in investment spending would cause the level of income to rise by a multiple amount. Income would increase until planned saving had risen sufficiently to equal to the new higher level of planned investment. This was the famous investment "*multiplier*" analysis he had adopted from Richard Kahn. In 1937, Ohlin developed a profound criticism of Keynes's analysis by incisively demanding:

> How is the original increase in investment financed, before the level of income has increased?

Keynes replied to Ohlin's criticism in his 1937 article "Alternative Theories of the Rate of Interest." He there introduced his *"finance motive"* and argued:

> If investments are proceeding at a steady rate, the finance (or the commitments to finance) required can be supplied from a revolving fund of a more or less constant amount. ... If decisions to invest are increasing, the extra finance involved will constitute an additional demand for money.[44]

Keynes believed that so long as the level of income remained unchanged, the finance released from *"ex post* output" was sufficient to finance *"ex ante* output." But he maintained that when investment spending was increasing, the "finance" motive constituted an additional motive for holding money, which could be lumped together with the transactions motive.[45] In a later article in the same year, "The Ex Ante Theory of the Rate of Interest," Keynes felt sufficiently confident to declare:

> Just as an increase in actual activity must (as I have always explained) raise the rate of interest, unless either the banks or the rest of the public become more willing to release cash, so (as I now add) an increase in planned activity must have a similar, superimposed influence"[46]

With characteristic flourish Keynes proclaimed that his newly discovered "finance motive" was "the coping stone" of his liquidity preference theory of interest. He was pleased to be able to show how increases in *planned* future activity could lead to *actual* increases in the *current* rate of interest. He added:

> The banks hold the key position in the transition from a lower to a higher level of activity. If they refuse to relax (i.e. to provide additional finance), the growing congestion of the short term market or the new issue market, ... will inhibit the improvement, no matter how thrifty the public purpose to be out of their future income. ... The investment market can become congested through shortage of cash. It can never become congested through shortage of saving. This is the most fundamental of my conclusions within this field.

In the 1930s, Keynes's central goal was to defend and reformulate his new theory of effective demand. He had persuaded himself that this required that the "loanable funds" theory of interest be repudiated and replaced by his new "liquidity preference" theory. The main point of his argument in the *General Theory* was to demonstrate that interest rates would not automatically adjust to equilibrate the supply and demand for loanable funds or saving and investment to assure full employment, as the classical theorists had maintained. His argument was that interest rates adjusted to equilibrate the supply and demand for liquidity. In his vision the interest rate was 'monetary' and not a 'real' phenomenon.

In the *General Theory*, Keynes's central message had been that interest rates would not automatically adjust to equilibrate saving and investment at full employment. CBs could control the level of interest rates by varying the supply of reserves. He then believed that the authorities controlled the level of interest rates indirectly, by their ability to pursue open market operations and control the money supply. His liquidity preference theory led him to the recognition that the cheap money policy had the potential to lead to the gradual "euthanasia" of the rentier, and to an enormous sea change of much else besides:

> If nations can learn to provide themselves with full employment by their domestic policy, there need be no important economic forces calculated to set the interest of one country against that of its neighbors. ... International trade would cease to be what it

now is, namely, a desperate expedient to maintain employment at home by forcing sales on foreign markets and restricting purchases, which, if successful, will merely shift the problem of unemployment to the neighbor which is worsted in the struggle, but a willing and unimpeded exchange of goods and services in conditions of mutual advantage[47]

By 1937, Keynes believed the finance motive was not merely an additional motive for demanding money, but offered a potential for the reformulation of the liquidity preference theory of interest. With hindsight wisdom this may be seen to constitute another stage in his *"long struggle of escape"* from orthodoxy. By 1938, Keynes had reached the following intermediate stage. He had abandoned the *General Theory*'s assumption that the money supply could be regarded as exogenous, and had returned to his original 1930 *Treatise* position that the supply of credit money was credit-driven. In the *General Theory*, Keynes had accepted the classical argument that the rate of interest in equilibrium was equal to the marginal of capital. But he insisted the direction of causality was reversed:

> The output of new investment will be pushed to the point at which the marginal efficiency of capital becomes equal to the rate of interest. What the schedule of the marginal efficiency of capital tells us is, is not what the rate of interest is, but the point to which the output of new investment will be pushed, given the rate of interest.[48]

In the *General Theory*, Keynes's avowed goal was to develop a theory

> of a monetary economy where monetary disturbances don't wash out over the long period. The introduction of money leads to a different long period conclusion.[49]

Unfortunately, Keynes was unsuccessful in the *General Theory* in fully developing the essential differences between a commodity money and a credit money economy. This stemmed from his fateful decision to let "technical monetary detail fall into the background" and assume "the quantity of money is determined by the action of the central bank."[50]
Had he adopted his earlier position in the *Treatise* that

> the central bank lacks direct control over the quantity of money—the governor of the whole system is the rate of discount.[51]

a much simpler explanation of the level of interest rates would have been available. In the *Treatise*, Keynes had recognized and developed the endogenous nature of credit money. He modeled how bank loans and the money supply expanded when additional workers were hired in the expansion phase of the cycle. In response to the increase in employment and in business demand for additional working capital, he argued:

> It is assumed that the banks create just enough additional money for the industrial circulation, after allowing for any fluctuations in the amount of the financial circulation, to allow the absorption of the unemployed factors of production into employment at a steady rate ... this amounts to the banks' supplying the entrepreneurs with whatever they require, over and above their profits, to pay wages on the gradually increasing scale which is assumed.[52]

Under an overdraft system, increased demand for bank credit implies that the "liquidity preferences of the banks" do *not* remain unchanged, as Keynes had argued in the *General Theory*. By the time of his 1937 articles, Keynes was halfway there. He had explicitly recognized that an overdraft system was

> the ideal system for mitigating the effects on the banking system of an increased demand for *ex ante* finance.[53]

He had also formally recognized that

> to the extent that the overdraft system is employed, and unused overdrafts are ignored by the banking system, there is no superimposed pressure resulting from planned activity over and above the pressure resulting from actual activity. In this event, the transition from a lower to a higher scale of activity may be accomplished with less pressure on the demand for liquidity and the rate of interest.[54]

It was from there but a short step to the recognition that the rate of interest was the key policy instrument of CBs. Simply change "less pressure" to "no pressure" in the above passage, and he was there. Thanks to his position in the Treasury during the Second World War, Keynes finally recognized that CBs could set the interest rate at whatever level they wished. By the end of the war he had completely abandoned his liquidity preference argument of the *General Theory*, and had recognized that the rate of interest was the main exogenous policy instrument of the monetary authorities:

> The whole management of the domestic economy depends on being free to have the appropriate rate of interest, without reference to rates prevailing elsewhere in the world.[55]

Had Keynes had the opportunity to write a second edition of the *General Theory*, it would have been a very different and much improved book. He would have explicitly recognized the endogeneity of the supply of credit money, and discarded the "liquidity preference" theory of interest for the recognition that short-term interest rates are the main exogenous instrument of the monetary authorities. One year before his death, Keynes conclusively stated his final position: interest rates were the chief exogenous policy instrument of the CB.

> The monetary authorities can have any rate of interest they like. ... Historically the authorities have always determined the rate at their own sweet will, and have been influenced almost entirely by balance of trade reasons and their own counter-liquidity preference.[56]

Part IV
The Determination of Prices, Output, and Growth Rates

Part IV

12
Markup Pricing and the Aggregate Supply Relationship

> If ten men are to be set to dig a hole instead of nine, they will be furnished with ten cheaper spades instead of nine more expensive ones: or perhaps if there is no room for him to dig comfortably, the tenth man will be furnished with a bucket and sent to fetch beer for the other nine.
>
> Sir Dennis Robertson, 1931: 226

> The outstanding fact is the extreme precariousness of the basis of knowledge on which our estimates of prospective yields have to be made. Our knowledge of the factors which will govern the yield of an investment some years hence is usually very slight and often negligible. ... In fact those who seriously attempt to make any such estimate are often so much in the minority that their behavior does not govern the market. ... If human nature felt no temptation to take a chance, no satisfaction (profit apart) in constructing a factory, a railway, a mine or a farm, there might not be much investment merely as the result of cold calculation.
>
> John Maynard Keynes, 1936: 149–50

> The firm is dealing throughout in terms of sums of money. It has no object in the world except to end up with more money than it started with. That is the essential characteristic of an entrepreneur economy.
>
> John Maynard Keynes, XXIX, 89

12.1 The impossibility of maximization

Neoclassical theory is based on the assumption that all individual economic agents are rational utility-maximizers. Agents are not assumed to have perfect information. But they are assumed to be able to form objective probability distributions of *all unknown future states of the world*. If they can do this they must simply select the alternative with the highest expected outcome to maximize utility.[1] The binding constraint on economic agents stems from the ultimate fact that resources are scarce relative to wants. "Scarcity" is the central problem of economics.

But in order to "maximize" anything agents must know, or be able to discover, all possible alternatives of every possible decision to select the optimum outcome.

Economists term such situations "full information." But "full information" is in effect a non-transparent surrogate for the classical economists' assumption of "perfect certainty." When the objective probabilities of all possible alternatives are known, optimal behavior may be defined as simply selecting the outcomes where the expected marginal costs equal or exceed the expected marginal benefits of any action. "Rational choice" appears easy and even obvious. Surely no one can argue for irrationality against rationality?

But in a complex world, not only is the future unknowable, but also the alternative outcomes of any action can never be known in terms of objective probabilities. In the presence of fundamental uncertainty, utility maximization is impossible. Knowledge is limited and agent rationality is "bounded." The binding constraint is not scarcity but ignorance. Agents can only "satisfize," that is select those alternatives whose expected consequences appear satisfactory. Rather than "maximize," they follow heuristic "rules of thumb."

When faced with the unknown future consequences of present actions, agents decide what to do by largely relying on social conventions. The most important of these is to simply *"follow the crowd."* Agents' expectations of the future are profoundly influenced by the expectations of other agents. For highly organized markets, with low transactions costs and high leverage, the successful prediction of even very small price changes can be very profitable. Optimal holding periods become very short so agents have no choice but to try to *"beat the gun."* Keynes' newspaper beauty competition is a precisely accurate metaphor for stock markets. Agents must choose not the stock they think will be most profitable, but the stock they think most others think will be most profitable. Since they know that all other agents will be doing the same thing, they must dig even deeper and attempt to choose the stock that other investors think will be most profitable. This process may be continued into impenetrable higher levels of complexity.[2] Markets are not driven by external "shocks," but by how agents perceive these "shocks." Agents are thus forced to make subjective estimates of other agents' subjective estimates.[3]

Post Keynesians maintain that utility maximization is pure fantasy. Complex systems behavior cannot be successfully modeled with comparative static utility-maximizing equilibrium analysis. Economics must take an "open-system" rather than a "closed-system" view of the world and pursue *realistic* but not rational-deductive analysis of decision-making. Post Keynesian methodology shares a common groundwork with the psychological methodology of behavioral and institutional economics.[4]

12.2 Markup pricing: The post Keynesian theory of the firm

Future economic behavior is inherently unpredictable and the comparative static utility-maximizing analysis of neoclassical economics is thoroughly misleading. Post Keynesian theorists adopt a realistic open-system methodology and refrain from attempting to deduce "optimum" outcomes.[5] The Post Keynesian theory of the firm draws heavily on institutional studies and emphasizes the importance of changing cost conditions rather than demand elasticities to explain firm pricing behavior.

The early studies of Hall and Hitch of the Oxford Economists Research Group drew heavily on case-study evidence of business behavior.[6] They concluded that firms did not "maximize" profits by the equalization of marginal revenue and costs because future-demand and marginal-revenue curves were unknown. Instead prices were administered on a "full cost" theory of pricing:

> prime (or direct) cost per unit is taken as the base, a percentage addition is added to cover overhead, ... and a further conventional addition ... is made for profit.[7]

Hall and Hitch examined the dynamics of firm interaction by interview studies. They were led to the discovery that in oligopolistic markets firms view their demand curves as "kinked" at the existing price, implying a discontinuity in perceived marginal revenues. Firms do not have sufficient information to calculate the profit-maximizing price where MR = MC, since future demand and so MR curves are unknown. They instead follow average cost pricing and simply add a markup to average variable costs to cover estimated overheads, letting profits be the residual. They insisted it was not possible to formulate precisely all the factors that determine the mark-up since they are historically highly specific, time-dependent, and vary markedly over time. Mark-ups are fundamentally constrained by competitive pressures, since

> the same prices for similar products rule within the group of competing producers.[8]

Prices are administered for some future time period whose length depends both on the product and the technology used in the industry. Prices vary primarily with changes in costs, so long as

> none of the competitors form an idea of a profitable price which is markedly different from existing prices.[9]

Prices are set for discrete periods of time as a mark-up on "direct costs" (average variable costs), by adding an allowance for expected overheads and target profits. The prices set are constrained by potential and actual competition. The key point is that prices vary primarily with changes in costs, not changes in demand.

Andrews, another early member of the Oxford Economists Research Group, relied chiefly on case-study evidence as the basis for his theorizing. Andrews introduced the concept "normal-cost" pricing. He distinguished between direct (variable) costs and overhead costs and argued that the prices of factors of production could be taken as constant in the current planning period, since they reflected contractual agreements signed prior to production:

> The normal situation is that the businessman will plan to have reserve capacity, his average cost curve falling for any outputs that he is likely to meet in practice,

and his average direct costs, which ... [are] ... of crucial importance in the theory of pricing, normally being practically constant for very wide ranges of output. The present theory differs from accepted doctrine precisely in that it considers the constant level of average direct costs and the reserve capacity on which it is based, to be normal phenomena, irrespective of the degree of competition which the firm has to meet.[10]

Most oligopolistic companies plan to maintain a target level of excess capacity. This is a strategic phenomenon designed both to meet uncertain demand contingencies and act as a powerful barrier to entry.

> As a general rule, the businessman will not wish to produce at all near the theoretical capacity of his plant. ... Many things ... may cause a proportion of the plant to be idle at any one time, and a reserve, over and above the equipment which is strictly necessary for the planned output, will have to be kept to allow for these contingencies. ... It is the short run cost curve that the businessman sees as immediately relevant and which he acts on. In analysis, therefore, with reference to practical pricing policy it should be our starting point.[11]

Changes in costs associated with significant changes in output do not affect pricing policy, for example overtime rates. Fall in costs due to scale economies lead to expectations of greater profits and are the key reason, besides providing additional deterrence to potential competition for planned new investment. A businessman normally bases prices on "direct" (average variable) costs of production:

> He will be able to make fairly accurate estimates of his average direct costs, and, in order to get the quoted price, these will be grossed up by a definite amount which ... will equal the average contribution that the businessman will require each unit of product to make towards covering the overhead costs of the business and making a profit. ... This principle of pricing will be called the Normal Cost Principle, since the businessman in fixing his price in this way appears to act on the idea that such a price will normally enable him to cover his costs.[12]

Company pricing policy is a simple markup on average variable costs. The markup is stable and normally adhered to. It includes an allowance for overhead costs and a target level of profits. Actual profits depend on the level of sales achieved in the period. If output is known to fluctuate widely, this is allowed for in price determination. Businessmen do not revise their costing margins to allow for changing overheads as sales fluctuate. Realized profits absorb all "normal" fluctuations in demand. The general rule is that the "right price" is first set and all demand forthcoming is then supplied.

Andrews argued that competition is a critical factor in determining the "normal" level of profits:

> The general situation, then is that so long as its price is right, an established business will have a more or less clearly defined market, and will be protected

from the efforts of would-be competing businesses to cut into that market. ... But the necessity that the business should quote the right price will be paramount. The right price in the long run cannot be higher than its competitors would quote.[13]

Kalecki usually distinguished two different types of pricing behavior in modern economies, the "flex-price" sector and the "fix-price" sector. Prices of agricultural products and raw materials were demand-determined and were "flex price" as neo-classical theory maintained. In contrast prices of finished manufactured goods were cost-determined, and so "fix price." In the core oligopolistic manufacturing sector, prices are set at a fixed markup over direct or variable costs over future short-run periods. Profits are not "maximized" over the long run. The long run is merely a sequence of short runs.

> the long run trend is but a slowly changing component of a chain of short run situations.[14]

Over the course of time as long-run expectations are disappointed, firms will gradually adjust their prices.[15] At the level of the firm, prices are set as a markup on average direct costs, with explicit reference to the prices and markups set by other firms in the industry. Prices vary directly with the level of average direct costs and are constrained by the price set by the competing group of firms in the industry.

For any specific firm markups are constrained by the degree of monopoly in the industry and by the threat of new entrants. Depending on the context, two firms may compete more fiercely than ten firms in another industry.

> In view of the uncertainties faced in the process of price fixing it will not be assumed that the firm attempts to maximize its profits in any precise sort of manner.[16]

Kalecki's price equation may be written as follows:

$P = (1+\mu)(wn/y) = (1+\mu)(w/(y/n)) = (1+\mu)(w/a)$ where

P = the price of output in the firm/industry
μ = the percentage markup over unit labor costs
w = the average money wage
n = employment
y = real output
wn/y = unit labor costs
y/n = average labor productivity (a).

This pricing equation is at the aggregate level and ignores all differences between industry averages and individual firm prices, how prices are affected by product differentiation, and so on. In addition, by treating all firms as vertically integrated, the flex-price raw material sector and inter-firm transactions sector disappear from view. This equation reflects the fundamental indeterminacy in Kalecki's work concerning the markup pricing process. In his own words, his price equation and "degree of monopoly" summarize *tendencies* and *possibilities*. They do not purport to provide a determinate deductive analytical account of the pricing process.

Once product differentiation is allowed for, what constitutes the "competing group of firms" becomes an intractable problem. Kaldor concluded that given the subjective elements involved in determining and defining the substitutability of products, any precise grouping of firms into an "*industry*" was arbitrary. There is no *necessity* for prices to change when overheads change. If overheads rise in relation to prime costs in a depression this may then result in a squeeze of profits . A tacit agreement among firms may develop to raise prices to protect profits. But as Kaldor recognized in the following *caviat*,

> This is the basic tendency; however in some instances the opposite process of cut-throat competition may develop in a depression.[17]

Means argued that in large modern corporations prices were "*administered*" and not determined under auction conditions as implied in neoclassical theory. He also relied primarily on case-study evidence for his pricing theory. Administered prices were set before transactions occur, and held constant over the sequential transactions period. Price adjustment was discontinuous, and much less frequent than in markets where prices are market-determined. Means insisted:

> Basically, the administered price thesis holds that a large body of industrial prices do not behave in the fashion that classical theory would lead one to expect.[18]

The key point of Means's "*administered price*" thesis was that the structure of modern production, being so divorced from the tenets of neoclassical price theory, ensured the inflexibility of prices to increases and decreases in the overall level of AD, though not absolute price rigidity. In a recession prices could fall slightly, show no substantial change, or even rise. Pricing is conducted in terms analogous to full or normal cost pricing. The price was set for some time period over a future series of transactions. Changes in demand primarily determine changes in the sales volume, not changes in the price charged.[19]

Eichner maintained that in modern economies the "megacorp" (the dominant price leaders in each industry) were characterized by the separation of ownership and control. Dividends were regarded as a quasi-contractual cost required for shareholder appeasement. In the oligopolistic sector, prices were marked up to provide the required finance for business investment expenditure out of retained earnings. Eichner termed this the "*corporate levy*."[20] With regard to flexibility in price setting, he concluded,

> Oligopoly being in a certain sense a description of behavior that has been learned over time, firms in oligopolistic industries can be expected to

have had sufficient experience with the untoward effects of price shaving to eschew it as a competitive weapon in all except periods of unusually depressed demand.[21]

The above models all conclude that prices at the firm level are much less sensitive to changes in demand than to changes in costs. Changes in unit wage costs play the dominant role in price changing behavior via the markup procedure. These models echo the empirical literature in industrial organization. While these models differ at the concrete level they share common qualitative predictions reflecting the "demi-regularities" of pricing behavior under uncertainty.[22]

Consistent with Kalecki's position that increases and decreases in overheads may or may not affect prices, these are not tight deductive systems. They share an indeterminacy consistent with an open system view of the economy. When average direct costs are constant, markup pricing assumes that marginal costs are constant. The markup process is then logically equivalent to maximizing profits by equating marginal revenue and marginal costs. Nevertheless this equivalence misses the central point of the analysis. In the presence of incomplete information about the future, in particular within a wide range near total ignorance of the future marginal revenue curves, firms cannot "maximize" profits. They can only "administer" prices and maintain them over finite pricing periods.

The above accounts reflect the ontological views of Post Keynesian theorizing in a complex world. Sylos-Labini has argued that Kalecki's formulation was the "full-cost principle, in its simplest form."[23] Steindl described Kalecki's theory as *"a framework rather than a general model."*[24] Lavoie concluded that once it is recognized that businessmen must deduce some estimate of output to calculate average overhead costs,

> the simple mark-up of the Kaleckian type, full cost pricing a la Hall and Hitch, or target return pricing (a la Eichner) ... are just different forms of a general pricing procedure.[25]

Economists working in the realist tradition insist that abstraction must attempt to capture the essential *"real"* aspects of complex systems rather than fictional *"ideal types."* Case-study investigations add weight of evidence to the Kaleckian vision of markup pricing and give it enhanced credibility as a microeconomic account of pricing reflecting actual firm behavior. A variety of studies differing somewhat in concrete character is consistent with the realist "open system" methodological approach to theorizing about complex systems.[26]

The work of Hall and Hitch, Andrews, Means, Kalecki, and Eichner is all of a case-study nature. They attempted to investigate why prices do not behave in the way predicted by the neoclassical market-clearing mainstream vision. It is not surprising that work born out of this realist point of view is consistent with the ontological vision of complexity. Post Keynesian theory is centrally about uncovering, identifying, and elaborating the presence of nondeterministic order, demi-regularities, and "stylized facts" inherent in complex systems.[27]

12.3 The limitations of empirical analysis

Econometric evidence attempts to quantify the manner that prices are related to unit costs and the extent that demand exerts a direct effect on markups and prices to provide quantitative estimates of the system's "demi-regularities." These issues are conventionally addressed in terms of the following simple general model:

$$P_t = p\,(C_t, D_t)$$

where P = price, C = proxies for unit costs, and D = proxies for demand pressure.

A wide variety of different specific formulations of the Post Keynesian model have been formulated. Costs have been restricted to labor costs with and without raw-material costs. Current and lagged costs and demand factors have been included in regressions. Demand pressure has been included as GDP and as an excess demand proxy. Firm behavior has been modeled in terms of competitive and oligopolistic/monopolistic views of price determination.

McCallum estimated a conventional competitive pricing model. By imposing lags between product and labor demand, he concluded that "*the pure excess demand hypothesis*" accorded very well with the empirical evidence.[28] McFetridge, using a mixture of cost-based and excess-demand components, concluded that markups adjusted to changes in demand conditions, and prices adjusted to take account of changes in unit costs.[29] Eckstein and Fromm (E & F) attempted to resolve the issue whether prices are better explained by a demand and supply competitive price mechanism or by full-cost pricing procedures.[30] They included estimates for unfilled orders, inventory disequilibrium, standard unit labor costs divided by "normal" output per head, and industry operating rates. Due to the presence of common time trends, they recognized their price-level equations were susceptible to severe multi-collinearity problems The price-change equations included large errors of measurement since the magnitude of quarterly changes in prices was extremely small. E & F found the *combination* of a competitive pricing mechanism (an excess-demand formulation) together with an oligopolistic mechanism (where prices are set with reference to normal costs) was "superior to equations using either approach in isolation." As a result they concluded that price levels were jointly well explained by both cost and demand elements.

One of the more complete investigations of the normal cost hypothesis was provided by Godley, Nordhaus, and Coutts et al.[31] Using quarterly data they intensively examined seven broad industry groups. They sought to predict changes in actual prices from changes in "*normal costs prices*," where their normalization equations expressed prices as a constant markup on normal unit costs. They concluded that demand pressure had a small but statistically insignificant effect on prices. Smith used their same data, but respecified their normalization procedures. He concluded that after their equations had been respecified the demand proxies had the expected signs and were all significant.[32]

Sylos-Labini examined the effects on changes in aggregate prices of changes in demand and costs for five different countries for the period 1954–73 using annual data.[33] He found that price changes were only weakly influenced by changes in demand, proxied by the degree of capacity utilization.

Sawyer pointed out the significance of industry heterogeneity in pricing behavior and used actual unit costs in a two-stage procedure to avoid simultaneous equation bias.[34] He found that adding demand to normal cost did not increase the performance of his equations. Sawyer interpreted his results as offering strong support for the normal cost hypothesis. Geroski and Fedderke reached similar conclusions and emphasized the significant heterogeneity in different industries' pricing behavior.[35]

The most obvious conclusion of the above summary of empirical studies is perhaps simply that no clear consensus has been reached. Unit costs are ubiquitously the most significant determinant of pricing behavior. There is strong evidence that demand also plays a role, but the results are typically selectively reported. Dorwald's survey of the studies interpreted the evidence as being broadly neoclassical, since he found that demand as well as costs affected prices.[36] But Reynolds' survey of the same year concluded, "*short-run fluctuations in demand are primarily met by changes in output.*"[37] In fact both statements are true. The econometric literature provides ample support for a Post Keynesian account of pricing, emphasizing the role of costs over demand. But it just as clearly does not completely rule out demand effects on prices as a Post Keynesian demi-regularity.

Keynesian pricing theory insists that pricing procedures are not the result of a profit-maximization process. They involve simply adding a markup to a measure of average variable costs. Based on the econometric evidence a model that links prices to average variable costs offers most insight into real world processes of pricing. But extreme caution must be exercised. Selection of one set of results with "*acceptable*" statistical characteristics can indicate a radically different view of pricing determinants from an other set of "*acceptable*" results. The empirical divide in interpreting the results is reinforced by the data mining that is endemic to the "*average economic regression*" approach.[38] Radically different accounts of pricing are frequently reported by different studies, using the same data set. One general econometric problem arises from the treatment of time. Backward-looking "*normal cost pricing*" is empirically very difficult to distinguish from forward-looking "*rational expectations pricing.*" There is little to chose econometrically between Kalecki's nonoptimizing formulation of pricing decisions and neoclassical optimizing interpretations of an identical set of data.

It is impossible to establish unambiguously the "*correct*" view of pricing solely by econometric means. Econometrics is a "closed system" form of reasoning and as such cannot provide decisive demarcation between different theories of pricing. In contrasting the positivist ideals of neoclassicals with the more open methodology of complex systems no single hypothesis can be demonstrably shown to be *the* correct hypothesis. Certain insights simply appear more persuasive and compelling than others, and to offer fundamental empirical foundations to the demi-regularities found in economic phenomena.[39]

In his study of whether prices are cost- or demand-determined in UK manufacturing Downward made a careful attempt to reconcile the time series practices of Leamer, Hendry, and Sims.[40] He first defined all monthly data in logs and regressed each variable on lagged values of itself and on the other variables, manufacturing prices, costs and output respectively. Only lag one was significant for all variables. Both costs and demand were clearly significant, but cost effects were three times as large as demand effects. The short-run effects of cost changes were small: a 1.0 percent increase in costs led to only a 0.1 percent increase in the index of prices in the following month. These small short-run effects are magnified over time by the dominant influence of the lagged dependent variable. Downward's results reveal the extent manufacturing prices in the aggregate display inertia. The previous months' prices are carried forward to the current month, with small price adjustments made in response to lagged monthly changes in both cost and demand variables.

12.4 Survey evidence

Econometrics does not permit the direct testing of one theory against another. Most of the prominent theories of price stickiness rely on variables that are either unobservable in principle or are unobserved in practice. There exists a large literature of survey evidence on pricing behavior. Hall and Hitch developed the original theory of the kinked demand curve and concluded that most firms set prices by adding a markup to full costs from case-study methods. Based on survey evidence. Early concluded that price-cost markups were not fixed but depended on the elasticity of demand and *"expected competitive pressures."*[41] Kaplan and Lanzillotee's questionnaire study found that about one-half of their respondents set prices to achieve a target rate of return.[42] Gordon conducted a survey that found pricing-to-market (meeting the competition) and markups based on *"full costs"* (although the definition of fixed costs varied widely across firms).[43] Samiee found from survey evidence that satisficing goals such as *"satisfactory return on investment,"* *"target return on investment,"* and *"maintain market share"* ranked higher than *"profit maximization"* as explicit objectives of business pricing.[44]

In view of the failure of econometric evidence to provide answers to why prices are so sticky in nominal terms and the decidedly mixed evidence from previous surveys, Blinder (1998) undertook a study to directly interview business management why prices were so rigid in the US economy.[45] He developed a questionnaire designed to test 12 different explanations of price rigidity, simply taking for granted that, apart from agriculture, all firms in the sample were price-setters. A stratified random sample of 200 firms was selected, and structured interviews of the heads of small companies and the appropriate officers of large companies were conducted by Blinder and his students.

Blinder's basic results were quite startling. He found that less than one half of all firms changed prices more than once a year, and less than 10 percent of his firms repriced more than once a week. There is an auction market sector, but it is quite small.[46] The reasons the firms gave why they did not change prices more frequently varied: *"antagonize customers"* and *"competitive pressures"* topped the list, but *"costs of changing prices," "infrequent changes in costs," "coordination failures,"* and *"explicit and implicit contracts"* were each well supported. Management-estimated lag of three months elapses before prices were changed in response to cost or demand changes. No evidence was found that prices adjust more rapidly upward than downward or that firms respond more rapidly to cost than demand shocks.

The variances across firms in adjustment lags were larger than the mean lag, indicating large variations in the speed of price adjustment. Firms in services adjust prices most slowly, and firms in trade adjust most rapidly, with manufacturers and services in between. The median number of price changes per year in trade is three, but only one in manufacturing and services. Most firms reported periodic reviews of price adjustment, and annual reviews were by far most common. Once-and-for-all and not step-wise adjustments were the norm. About 25 percent of prices are set by nominal contracts. Most firms rarely offered discounts and two-thirds of respondents reported that most sales were made under implicit contracts. The mean percentage of sales going to regular customers was 85 percent and the median was over 90 percent. Sales to non-repeat customers thus appear almost small enough to be ignored.[47]

The vast majority of firms (80 percent) reported they did not take inflation forecasts into account in their price setting behavior. This implies strong *"money illusion."* A large majority of firms viewed their demand as very inelastic (84 percent reported their estimated elasticity of demand was less than unity!), offering strong grounds for management's general reluctance to cut prices. The mean response was that 44 percent of total costs were fixed, and 56 percent were variable. Fixed costs are much more important in management's perception than in economic theory.[48] On average about 50 percent of output is produced to order and 50 percent to stock, but there are substantial differences in this proportion among industries. Most wholesale and retail firms produce to stock, while durable goods are most commonly produced to order.[49]

Mainstream economists traditionally envision demand curves as shifting along upward-sloping supply curves. But less than 10 percent of firms reported they produced under rising costs, more than one half reported they produced under constant costs, and 40 percent reported declining average cost relationships. This takes much of the mystery out of price stickiness.

In summary:

1. The modal commodity is repriced once a year.
2. More than three quarters goods are repriced less frequently than quarterly.
3. Prices are most sticky in the service sector and industry, and least sticky in trade.
4. More than two-thirds of all firms reported implicit contracts (85 percent).
5. The majority of sales in industry are made to regular customers.
6. A huge majority (more than 90 percent) of firms report producing under constant or declining costs. (less than 10 percent report producing under increasing costs)
7. Fixed costs were nearly half (45 percent) the total costs.

These answers paint a very different picture of the cost structure of the typical firm than the one found in mainstream textbooks. Blinder attempted to summarize the 12 different theories of the cause of price stickiness on a four point scale: (1) *"totally unimportant,"* (2) *"minor importance,"* (3) *"moderately important,"* and (4) *"very important."* Five theories were found to have substantial support, defined as an average rating above two. The other seven had an average rating under two and were reported either as of minor importance or as totally unimportant.

The five winners listed in order of importance were:[50]

1. The kinked demand curve, firms wait for other firms to go first (*"Coordination failure"*): 2.8
2. Price rises are delayed until costs rise (*"Cost-based pricing"*): 2.7
3. Firms vary non-price elements, delivery lags and service (*"Non-price competition"*): 2.6
4. Firms tacitly agree to stabilize prices (*"Implicit contracts"*): 2.4
5. Prices are nominally fixed by contract with clients (*"Explicit contracts"*): 2.1

The above five theories provide a good explanation of price stickiness for the majority of firms in most industries. *"Costly price adjustment"* and *"Pro-cyclical demand elasticity"* theories were ranked quite low. Even though more than half the firms stated they produced under conditions of broadly constant costs, *"Constant costs"* were not ranked highly as a major factor behind price stickiness. *"Pricing points"* and *"Inventory adjustment"* theories similarly received very poor ranking. *"Hierarchical delays"* and *"Judging quality by price,"* in spite of much theoretical debate about the latter, received extremely low support, ranking lower than a mean score of 1.5. (This is equivalent to more than one-half firms rejecting the theory outright and the remainder regarding it as of only *"minor importance."*)

Differences across sectors were small. The top four theories were the four most important theories in all sectors. Industry dummy variables were significant for all the less important theories. Some theories were significantly positively correlated, for example, cost-based pricing and constant MC. Surprisingly the theories did a better job of explaining upward than downward price stickiness.

Kinked demand curves, cost-based pricing, use of non-price variables to clear markets, implicit and explicit contracts were the five most important explanations for sluggish price adjustment. Decision-makers resoundingly rejected the theory that price cuts were deterred because customers judge quality by price, and that bureaucratic delays slow down price changes. There was little evidence in support of the proposition that prices are stickier downward than upward. Two-thirds reported they entered into implicit contracts and these agreements were important sources of sticky prices, supporting Okun's theory of the *"invisible handshake."* Less than 20 percent reported that customers judged quality solely by price. Firms delay price adjustments longer when cost shocks are small, transitory, and firm specific. Even when they see cost increases underway they delay price increases, and they raise prices in less than half the cases. This is largely out of fear of *"antagonizing customers"* and loss of market share, when prices are raised ahead of their competitors.[51]

The neoclassical view that firms produce with an upward-sloping MC curve was rejected by 90 percent of firms! More than one half reported that variable costs of producing additional units were constant, while 40 percent reported declining marginal costs. Surprisingly, most firms rated constant marginal costs as of minor importance as an explanation for price stickiness. The theory that marginal costs were constant found strong support primarily for firms in the wholesale and retail sector who try to hold inventories at some desired sales-ratio, and have binding if implicit contracts with their customers. Retail firms were constant costs biggest supporters with more than one quarter saying that constant MC's were a very important cause of price stickiness.[52]

Coordination failure clearly leads to price rigidity. Each firm adjusts its price if it expects other firms to do so but holds its prices fixed if it does not expect other firms to change their prices. More than 60 percent of the firms surveyed and more than 70 percent of all firms in trade rated coordination failure moderately or very important as an explanation of sluggish price-adjustment. The theory of kinked demand curves holds up extremely well, and it was the single most important explanation of price stickiness. Blinder's results strongly endorse the *"kinked"* demand curve conclusion that sticky prices are the rule and not the exception.

Price adjustment lags an average three months behind changes in costs, and an even longer period behind changes in demand. Prices react more quickly to cost shocks that are permanent, industry-wide, and large rather than small. Prices are stickier than average when firms enter into implicit contracts with their customers, have relatively large fixed costs, and experience significant coordination failures in changing prices. Prices are less sticky among firms in trade and for firms whose business is more cyclically sensitive. Almost half of all prices are changed less frequently than once a year. Annual price reviews are by far the highest median period.

Another big surprise was that less than one quarter of firms consider economy-wide inflation in setting their nominal prices. Most prices are held constant for some time, eight-and-a-half months in the median case. This implies the existence of significant money illusion. The view that price setting is not anticipatory is reinforced by the finding that even though many firms report being able to *"clearly forecast price increases for labor and other things they buy,"* less than half of these firms *"raise their own prices in anticipation."*[53]

A strong majority report having *"a customary time interval between price reviews."* A similar large majority report that they typically make price changes all-at-once, rather than in a series of small steps. The survey responses suggest that firms do not deal with fixed costs of price adjustment by adopting state-dependent (S.s) strategies in the manner optimizing theory suggests. They set up instead a schedule of periodic price reviews, which they simply ignore when they are found inappropriate.[54]

The following 13 empirical facts inform business pricing strategies in general and price stickiness in particular:[55]

1. About 85 percent of all the goods sold in the US nonfarm business sector are sold to *"regular customers,"* primarily other firms. Most sales (70 percent) are business-to-business rather than business-to-consumers.

2. About one quarter of output is sold under contracts fixing nominal prices for nontrivial periods of time. About 60 percent of output is covered by Okun-style implicit contracts which slow down price adjustments. Contractual rigidities are extremely widespread.

3. Firms typically report high fixed costs relative to variable costs. Very few report the upward-sloping marginal cost curves ubiquitous in mainstream economic theory. Constant or downward-sloping cost curves are much more common, calling into question the common presumption that prices move strongly pro-cyclically.

4. The top five theories were a kinked demand curve (coordination failure) and four theories with a distinctly Keynesian flavor: cost-based pricing with lags, non-price competition, implicit and explicit contract theory. Differences in the ranking of the theories by industry and by firm size were typically not large, offering a ray of hope for a general theory of price stickiness, but heterogeneity of firm response was widespread. The top theory scored only 2.77, somewhat short of *"moderately important"*—so theorists still have a long way to go.[56]

5. The cornerstone of Keynesian macroeconomic theory is the existence of nominal wage and price rigidity. This combines money illusion, the nominal part, with wage-price stability, the price rigidity part. Blinder's survey very strongly reinforces the Post-Keynesian, administered-prices view of the world.

6. The survey evidence for price stickiness is overwhelming and for money illusion only slightly less so. The absence of anticipatory price increases and the failure to pay attention to economy-wide inflation forecasts point strongly in this direction. A simple macro model with a one quarter lag in price-setting is the baseline case.

7. No single simple theory of price rigidity clearly emerges, although several hybrid models have wide support. Price increases are prohibited by written contracts in a significant minority of cases. Many firms that are not explicitly constrained are deterred from raising prices by the concern that competitors may not follow suit.

8. Cost increases are industry-wide rather than firm-specific and serve as convenient signals that other firms are also under pressure to raise prices. Many firms have implicit contracts with their customers, which prohibit them from raising prices when demand rises and allow them to raise prices only when costs increase.

9. Firms typically delay price increases some time after costs have risen. Firms do not practice anticipatory pricing even when they clearly see cost increases coming. This may be because production takes time and prices are based by accountants as a markup on *historical* costs.

10. Firms typically hold their prices stable until the next scheduled pricing review. Once they decide to raise prices, they do so all at once rather than in a sequence of small steps. Price increases are lagged and firms employ various forms of non-price competition to close gaps between supply and demand: variations in selling effort and service, shorter or longer delivery lags, changes in the quality of service and in advertising expenses.

11. Blinder's survey revealed an extremely strong reluctance to not *"antagonize"* customers. This was used to justify firms' decision against more frequent price adjustments and explain why they base prices on historic costs and not anticipated future costs. Firms feel entitled to raise prices when other firms raise them as well. The most frequent explanation why firms prefer to change some non-price attribute of their goods rather than change prices was that *"it does not antagonize customers so much."* More than 120 of the 200 firms offered this answer at least once without prompting from the interviewers.[57]

12. Most customers are other businesses not consumers and have nonnegligible costs of price adjustment. Price adjustments by sellers frequently impose highly unwelcome costs on buyers. There is also the "fairness" or "equity" issue. Buyers deem it "unfair" when prices are raised too frequently, too rapidly, or in response to anticipated demand increase. Such a notion of opportunistic unfairness implies money illusion during inflation and is one reason why price stability was given high marks. If customers are "antagonized" by price variability, it is in firms' self-interest to take this into account in their pricing even if it implies a reduction in real earnings. This provides another reason why inflation is widely resented.

13. Under moderate inflation there is little price indexing, but explicit and implicit contracts apply to nominal prices and wages. Firms declare they rarely refer to economy-wide inflation forecasts. Most hold their nominal prices constant over their pricing periods, implying the existence of strong money illusion.

In a not-quite-rational world, a *"rational"* firm that raises its nominal price to keep its real price constant is likely to antagonize its customers. As a result it will suffer a reduction in its goodwill and its sales, even when its nominal price is only raised enough to maintain the real price constant. Firms frequently told Blinder's interviewers they were loath to raise prices because by so doing they would *"antagonize"* their customers.

In a not-quite-rational world quasi-rational behavior thus becomes *"rational."* This suggests why firms leave prices constant in the face of cost and demand shocks and prefer to compete by non-price means. Even though non-price behavior entails real resource costs, which price competition appears to avoid, the loss of goodwill from frequent price changes is sufficiently large so that leaving prices constant is perfectly rational.

12.5 The Post Keynesian theory of pricing

Classical economists took the theory of diminishing marginal physical productivity directly from agriculture where variable factors are used with one or more fixed factors. In agriculture most markets can be assumed perfectly competitive, and most agents can be assumed price-takers. Unfortunately the agricultural analogy fails to generalize to manufacturing. In agriculture the flow of services from the land are not distinguished from the stock of land since the services from land are continuously provided and not turned off for the night.[58] Diminishing returns support the existence of a negative slope for the productivity of the variable factor assuming the competitive markets of traditional theory. Supply curves are positively sloped and rise due to diminishing returns. A rising marginal cost (MC) curve and a falling marginal physical product (MPP) curve are necessary to derive perfectly competitive general equilibrium. Such an outcome banishes fundamental uncertainty, monopoly, public goods, and all external considerations.

A range of first increasing returns and then diminishing returns produces the U-shaped average variable cost (AVC) curve of traditional mainstream micro theory. The MC curve intersects the AVC curve at its minimum point. But this prediction is refuted by centuries of observation, which invariably show the AVC/MC curve as horizontal over relevant ranges of output. The traditional derivation of diminishing returns requires that the fixed factor be held constant, hence Robertson's ten cheaper spades.[59] But although the capital stock of land is fixed, the capital services on land are divisible. When both capital services and labor services are variable, they are used in fixed proportions, so the law of diminishing returns and variable proportions is no longer realistic. Clark's development of marginal productivity theory provided the mathematical solution to the adding-up problem of distribution theory. But the cost was neglect of the essential differences between stocks of capital and flows of capital services.[60]

The U-shaped cost curve should be replaced in price theory by a horizontal AVC curve that becomes vertical when full capacity is reached. In a world where future demand is highly uncertain this provides a compelling argument why firms attempt to maintain excess capacity. With constant or declining AVC a determinate solution requires a downward-sloping demand curve in short run equilibrium. Only a declining MR can intersect horizontal MC and AVC curves. But this brings the problem of monopolistic competition into the midst of competitive general equilibrium and spoils the logical coherence of the crown jewel GE analysis. Profit maximization is impossible in complex economies where future demand is uncertain. Firms have far from perfect information and are particularly uncertain about what their marginal revenue curve will be in the next period. As a result they are unable to calculate or equate their MR and MC curves.

Firms are compelled to grow if they want to maintain their share of the market. Profits and retained earnings are necessary to provide finance for capital accumulation. In order to be able to raise external finance, firms must demonstrate their capacity to generate current profits for creditors. Shareholders are non-residual factor claimants against the firm and dividends are quasi-contractual obligations. Firms have a de jure obligation to make interest payments but a de facto obligation to pay dividends. Robinson has argued,

> An obligation to pay interest is a contractual agreement, while the amount of dividends and personal profits paid out is at the discretion of the entrepreneur.

> But neither the obligation nor the discretion is absolute in practice. ... dividends fluctuate less than earnings because entrepreneurs are reluctant to reduce dividends, ... and reluctant to increase them. ... Thus ... to an important extent dividends behave like interest.[61]

Kalecki's principle of increasing risk was based on the observation that the higher the leverage ratio, the higher the proportion of investment expenditures that will be financed by outside funds, the larger will be the fluctuation of net earnings (net of interest payments) and the more difficult will it be for the firm to borrow in the future:

> The expansion of the firm depends on its accumulation out of current profits. This will enable the firm to undertake new investments without encountering the obstacles of the limited capital markets or "increasing risk." Not only can savings out of current profits be invested directly in the business, but this increase in the firms' capital will make it possible to contract new loans.[62]

Internal and external finance should be viewed as complements rather than as substitutes. If a firm desires to grow at a more rapid rate it must increase its profit rate, since it must consider as given the rates at which it pays for debt and equity capital and its admissible leverage ratio. This is termed the firm's *"finance constraint."*[63] Insofar as there is separation of ownership and control, corporate managers have considerable discretion over the size and direction of business expenditures. Firms trade off research and advertising expenditures, which raise expected future growth rates but lower current profit rates, with prices and profit margins sufficient to generate finance for dividend payments. They must leave sufficient retained earnings to provide internal finance and sustain the ability to raise outside finance.

Shareholders have a critical agency problem. How can they best ensure management will take decisions in the best interests of the shareholders? To maximize expected share price, managers are constrained by the tradeoff implicit in stock market valuations between expected profit rates and expected growth rates. A firm may be regarded as choosing between alternative profit rates and growth rates along an "expansion frontier" that after some point becomes downward sloping. This imposes powerful external discipline on corporate management. As a firm moves away from the capital markets' "revealed preference" between the combination of earnings and growth rates that maximize the share price, share prices fall, and the threat of a hostile takeover increases. This process constitutes the well-known "market for corporate control."

Blinder found that AVC curves are horizontal up to the level of full capacity operation. Firms invest to establish full capacity output at a level sufficient for favorable expectations of current demand plus a margin of excess capacity. The amount of planned excess capacity depends on management's expectations of the growth and variance of fluctuations in expected future demand and their desire to discourage future entry into the industry. Firms set their price as a markup over AVC to cover all fixed costs to attain their desired profit rate/growth rate tradeoff.

Survey results reveal that in the United States AVC are roughly one half (45 percent) of unit costs at current output levels. This implies that for the economy as a whole the markup on AVC averages about 100 percent. Firms are very uncertain of the position and the slope of their future demand curves, which may be represented as a band between a most favorable and a least favorable demand scenario. Firms must choose the markup over AVC at which they set their prices that must cover fixed costs plus target profits. Since prices must be consistent with the prices charged by competitors. Markups vary widely within a single industry reflecting differences in AVC.

Firms attempt to achieve a target level of profits when they set their markup. The AVC plus the markup determines the administered price. Taking into consideration prices set by its competitors, firms set the markup and price they estimate will achieve their profit target at their expected sales quantity. When sales exceed their estimates, profits will surpass the target level. When sales are below estimates, profit targets will not be attained. Profits consequently fluctuate procyclically over the cycle. If demand falls so low that sales are below the firm's break-even point, the firm must decide if it has the financial resources to continue to operate for some period or whether it should shut down.

12.6   Conclusions: As a "stylized fact" the aggregate supply (AS) curve may be viewed as horizontal

Profits are the overriding objectives of firms—they can neither survive nor grow without them. But prices are not set to achieve the single goal of profit maximization. This is not due simply to the fact that firms cannot foresee all the future consequences of their actions. The notion of profit maximization assumes that cost and demand conditions can be taken as given. But neither costs nor demand are given in firms price-setting behavior. Prices are "strategically determined" rather than "cost-determined." Some Post Keynesians have argued,

> It is the strategic determination of prices and the conception of the firm that underlies it that gives the Post Keynesian theory its realism and significance.[64]

The firm is the center of the Post Keynesian theory of prices. Prices on average are marked up over average variable costs of production. Nevertheless the transmission of costs into prices is not a mechanical relationship, and prices are not determined by costs alone. Prices depend on changes in the markup as well as changes in average variable costs. The markup is fixed neither by the particular product nor by the conventions of the industry. Markups vary substantially among industries and among different firms in the same industry. Firms' price-setting decisions consider the effect current price changes have on future sales. Prices affect the demand for the product rather than simply reflect it. The price set attracts customers and promotes sales. Prices operate to shift demand curves as well as to move firms along them.

Prices are generally set as a stable markup over AVC to achieve some target rate of profits. So long as the markup remains constant, prices will rise at a rate equal to the average rate of increase in AVC in the previous pricing period. For most firms the markup is relatively stable over time, but it can vary considerably among different firms. Since labor is the largest single cost, the change in AVC is closely proxied by the change in unit labor costs (ULC). So long as markups remain stable the rate of inflation may be decomposed into the excess of the rate of increase in average money wages, over the growth rate of average labor productivity. In open economies a term must be included to reflect the rate of inflation of imported goods. This is conventionally expressed as the change in import prices that may further be decomposed into the rate of imported goods inflation, the rate of depreciation of the exchange rate, and the share of imports in GDP.

To summarize, the inflation rate is based on the historical growth of ULC. It is predetermined for individual firms over their short-run pricing period by the growth of ULC in the previous pricing period. Prices are set by individual firms as a markup over ULC and are held constant over the current pricing period. In the United States roughly one half of all firms change prices or less frequently once a year pricing decisions are uncoordinated among firms. The rate of inflation for the economy over the period is the weighted average of the change in prices by all firms in the economy.[65]

In fix-price markets, supply adjusts to changes in AD primarily by changes in output, not by changes in prices. This is reflected by wide changes in capital-utilization ratios that in the United States fluctuate between 70 and 85 percent over the business cycle. Firms hold inventories and build in an average level of excess capacity of 15–25 percent, to be able to meet unexpectedly high levels of future demand. Most firms operate well below their capacity ceilings.

In fix-price markets there is no price level or inflation rate that "equilibrates" supply and demand or "clears" the market. Neither prices nor output have a tendency to adjust to any "equilibrium" level. Fix-price markets never "clear," and sales, inventories, and excess capacity vary continuously over time. So long as firms have excess capacity, and remain price-setters and quantity-takers output is demand-driven. The quantity supplied varies continuously with changes in AD. The inflation rate is predetermined by the average change in unit costs in the previous pricing period.

The very notion of a "market clearing" price must be reformulated. When prices are administered on a markup basis, the AS curve may be viewed as horizontal. Firms hold inventories and build in excess capacity to meet unexpected variations in demand. A horizontal AS curve implies that the rate of change in prices is predetermined by changes in average costs in the previous pricing period. Prices respond weakly to changes in current demand. As a broad simplification, changes in prices are caused by changes in costs and changes in output are caused by changes in demand. The level of output is determined by the level of aggregate demand, and AS is equal to AD at every level of output.[66]

Wage rates are determined by domestic labor market conditions while primary commodity prices reflect conditions in world markets. Kalecki (1971) treated primary commodity prices as determined by supply and demand forces in contrast to finished goods prices, which were determined by administered markup pricing. Primary commodities are used as raw materials in the manufacturing process of finished goods. Industrial production rises with aggregate demand, while primary production may be supply-constrained in expansionary boom periods.

The Post Keynesian explanation of inflation emphasizes the conflict between workers and employers over dividing a nation's money income. This may be extended internationally to conflict between primary producers in developing countries and manufacturers who are predominately located in the developed countries.[67] Over the twentieth century the rate of change of the US producer price index (a measure of finished goods inflation) increased by about the same amount as the combined rate of unit labor cost increase and the rate of primary commodity price decrease. There was complete pass-through of inflation in input prices to inflation in finished goods, exhibiting the fundamental proposition of markup pricing. AD growth has a slight negative impact on markups in manufacturing, and hence a slight negative impact on finished goods inflation.

Although higher unemployment reduces and delays money wage growth, and thereby leads to lower inflation the impact is both delayed and temporary. A sustained reduction in inflation requires a secularly rising rate of unemployment. A reduction in world economic growth would lead to a sustained reduction in inflation, by reducing the rate of increase in commodity prices. But this would further reduce the share of world income received by producers of primary commodities who reside primarily in developing economies.

13
The "Raffishness" of Mainstream Macroeconomics: a Post Keynesian Critique

> Its not so much what folks don't know. as what they know, that ain't so.
>
> Will Rogers

> These days macroeconomics has become more popular than it used to be. I can remember when many economists liked to say: "I just don't understand macroeconomics." There was a definite implication that something must be wrong with macroeconomics, not with the observer. Of course macroeconomics cannot be "exact." It has to work by rough analogy and empirical compromise. Maybe a certain raffishness is inevitable. Most economists work on micro-economic problems with increasing use of new microeconomic data. But now it is widely understood that macroeconomics is at the heart of economics; it will not do to be snooty about it. This centrality will continue, for the best possible reason: the need to understand current events, especially unfavorable ones, and to formulate policies—even benign neglect is a policy—to deal with them.
>
> Robert Solow, 2000: 151

> Nothing is quite as difficult as not deceiving oneself.
>
> Ludwig Wittgenstein

13.1 The five "core" propositions of mainstream macroeconomics

In the 1997 AEA meetings a session was organized on the topic, "Is There a Core of Practical Macroeconomics That We Should All Believe?" The five panelists (O. Blanchard, A. Blinder, M. Eichenbaum, R. Solow, and J. Taylor) each answered with a resounding "YES." Each panelist summarized his vision of the "core" and a significant consensus was exhibited.

These statements of the current state of macroeconomics by five leading proponents illustrate the extent mainstream economics has ignored Keynes' central message that the world is fundamentally uncertain and reverted to what Joan Robinson called "the bastard neoclassical synthesis." They also reveal the extent mainstream economics has lagged behind recent methodological developments in complex adoptive systems (CAS) in the natural sciences.

This chapter summarizes the core mainstream propositions and describes why they are empty, misleading and wrong. It then outlines an alternative set of Post Keynesian core propositions which will be developed at greater length in subsequent chapters. Post Keynesians maintain the mainstream General Equilibrium (GE) paradigm is fatally flawed for the analysis of economic behavior in a complex world and most of the subsidiary framework is tautological. Comparative static equilibrium analysis has shunted economics onto the wrong track, inhibited its development, and marginalized its ability to contribute to macroeconomic policy. In macroeconomics the use of equilibrium analysis has been responsible for the reversal of the true direction of causality between money and income. Changes in the money supply do not "cause" changes in money income. "Process analysis" offers a superior paradigm for the analysis of complex macroeconomic phenomena and a more useful methodology for the formulation of macroeconomic policy. A paradigm shift in macroeconomics is long overdue.

The AEA panelists all agreed contemporary mainstream macroeconomics incorporates the following five "core" propositions:

1. In the short-run movements in economic activity are dominated by movements in aggregate demand (AD):

    Fluctuations around the trend growth of potential output are predominately driven by aggregate demand impulses[1]

2. In the long run the economy returns to its steady-state trend growth path:

    The trend movement is predominately driven by the supply side of the economy.[2]

3. Price rigidities are the main explanation why fluctuations in aggregate demand generate short run fluctuations in real output:

    Wages and prices are not flexible enough to clear their markets more or less continuously.[3]

    Nominal rigidities are why macroeconomics looks so different from microeconomics.[4]

4. There is a short-run tradeoff between unemployment and inflation. All panelists were agreed on the existence of a short-run tradeoff with the exception of Solow who did not address policy issues. But all agreed that this tradeoff disappears in the longer run, when the PC becomes vertical and the economy returns to its steady state path:

    There is no long term tradeoff between the rate of inflation and the rate of unemployment.[5]

5. IS–LM is the most appropriate model for analyzing and understanding the effects of AD changes on the economy:

    Right or wrong, the IS–LM model and its intellectual cousins, the Mundell-Fleming model and the various incarnations of AS–AD models, have proved incredibly useful at analyzing fluctuations and the effects of policy.[6]

[*Most contemporary models*] are modified or extended versions of something like IS-LM.⁷

There was disagreement about details of the IS–LM model. Blinder, reflecting his stint as Vice Chairman of the Fed, was critical of the mainstream IS–LM theory of exogenous money and endogenous interest rates. He was the sole mainstream economist to support the Post Keynesian theory of endogenous money and exogenous interest rates. Unfortunately his support was not grounded on the Post Keynesian theory of endogenous money, but on *"rapid financial innovation,"* resulting in *"ferocious instabilities in both money demand and money supply."*

Textbook descriptions normally pair a downward-sloping IS curve with an upward-sloping LM curve, relating real output to the nominal interest rate. Unfortunately there is by now strong professional consensus that the once reliable LM curve fell prey years ago to "ferocious instabilities in both money demand and money supply," themselves the product of rapid and ongoing financial innovation. The LM curve no longer plays any role in serious policy analysis, having been supplanted by the assumption that the central bank controls the short-term nominal interest rate. It is high time we changed our teaching in this way too.⁸

There was underlying agreement about the general validity of the IS–LM framework. Each panelist with the exception of Blinder viewed the money supply as exogenously controlled by the central bank (CB). Each, again with the exception of Blinder viewed the level of interest rates as the endogenous outcome of portfolio balance (stock) and/or loanable funds (flow) market-clearing processes.

As the sole advocate of the real business cycle school, Eichenbaum held that US monetary policy,

was characterized surprisingly well by what is sometimes referred to as a Taylor rule. The key features of that rule are that it calls for the Fed to raise the federal funds rate when inflation exceeds some target level or when real GDP growth exceeds its target level⁹

This sounds superficially very much like endogenous money and exogenous interest rates. But it is not. Mainstream economics has not yet freed itself from the view that the money supply is exogenous. As Taylor himself noted when arguing that monetary policy should be evaluated as a rule rather than one-time isolated changes,

To be sure there is some debate about the form of the policy rules: Should the interest rate or the money supply be the instruments in the rule?¹⁰

No panelist recognized that the short-term interest rate is *necessarily* exogenous. As was shown in Part III, CBs are the monopoly supplier of system liquidity and do not have a choice between price or quantity instruments. As the residual lender of last resort the CB must set the interest rate at which it makes liquidity available to the system. The general level of short-term interest rates is not "market-determined." The level of short-term rates is the exogenous instrument of monetary policy. The key short-term rate, termed in most countries "Bank Rate" or "repos rate" (in the United States the "federal funds" rate) is set by the CB as the key instrument of monetary policy.[11] Long-term rates depend on capital market participants' current expectations of future levels of the short-term rate and so of the CB's future rate policy.

No panelist explicitly recognized that the supply of credit money is *endogenous*. Monetary endogeneity implies that real and monetary variables and so the IS and LM curves are inherently interdependent. During expansions, increases in the demand for bank credit increase the nominal supply of credit money which finances increase in nominal deficit-spending and capital formation. Increases in the money supply cause both the LM and the IS curves to shift rightward. During contractions the demand for bank credit falls, and the above process proceeds in reverse: the money supply, bank credit, investment and AD fall and the LM and IS curves shift leftwards. Money, prices, wages, money income and the IS and LM curves all vary together, driven by (nonmeasurable) changes in animal spirits (current expectations of future AD and future CB policy) and concurrent changes in unit costs.

As shown in Chapter 12 *unit prime costs (average variable costs) for the economy are determined by the excess of the average rate of increases in money wage over the average rate of growth of labor productivity*. In open economies the average change in imported commodity prices, the interest rate differential between domestic and foreign rates, and other open economy factors affect exchange rates and also play a role. Post Keynesians can easily demonstrate that AD and aggregate supply (AS) are intrinsically interrelated. As a stylized fact *changes in prices are caused by changes in average variable costs (supply-side considerations)*, while *changes in quantities supplied are caused by changes in expected future sales (demand-side considerations)*.

All panelists emphasized the central importance of expectations in determining the response of the real economy to policy measures. A sharp division was exhibited whether expectations should be modeled rigorously, "*as grounded on individual inter-temporal utility maximization*,"[12] were "*formed adaptively*,"[13] or were instead best handled "*ad hoc in a common sense way.*"[14] Deep disagreement was expressed about the concept of "Rational Expectations." It was agreed that the Rational Expectations argument remained unsettled:

> The danger with the Rational Expectations hypothesis is that it is too often directly wrong.[15]
>
> Where expectations can be measured directly, they do not appear to be "rational" as economists use that term (see M. Lovell, 1986).[16]

None of the panelists appeared to recognize that the mainstream procedure of conceptually isolating short-run and long-run phenomena constitutes serious methodological error. The first proposition states that demand forces have powerful effects *over the short run*. The second proposition states that *in the long-run* the PC becomes vertical and the economy returns to its underlying secular growth path. But it is not possible for AD impulses to have strong effects on output over the "short run" and be neutral and so have no effect over the "long run," since the long run is simply a consecutive cumulative series of short runs.

Solow raised the yawning theoretical lacuna between these two propositions:

> the lack of real coupling between the short-run picture and the long-run picture. Since the long run and the short run merge into one another, one feels they cannot be completely independent " ... [can]" a major episode in the growth of potential output ... be driven from the demand side? Can demand create its own supply? ...

Unfortunately Solow answered his own question in the negative:

> The demand-driven growth story sounds quite implausible to me under current conditions, but it is an example of the kind of question that needs to be asked.[17]

Once the existence of unit roots in economic time series has been fully absorbed, it becomes obvious how short-run demand-side "shocks" can have permanent long-run effects, and gradually becomes crystal clear how long-run output growth is demand-driven. In all time series containing unit roots any trends found are time-dependent and vary stochastically over time. Deterministic long-run trends are imposed by the analyst, since unit roots time series do not contain determinate long-run "trend" behavior.[18] The conclusion that the economy returns to its "natural" equilibrium path in the long run governed purely by supply-side factors implies that economies follow a deterministic trend path.[19] This conclusion is disproved by the recent discovery that the existence of unit roots in all macroeconomic time series cannot be empirically refuted.[20]

All panelists, with the exception of Solow, agreed that monetary policy was more important than fiscal policy in the management of AD:

> the inability to find a successful way of formulating discretionary fiscal policy as an implementable rule ... has led even most Keynesians to be sceptical of attempts to use fiscal policy to stabilize business cycles

There were wide differences in panelists' views regarding fiscal policy. All, with the exception of Solow, shared the belief that a positive fiscal mutiplier was suspect. New evidence appears to suggest that in the short run deficit reduction can promote growth.

> The notion that what used to be called "contractionary" fiscal policies may in fact be expansionary is fast becoming part of the conventional policy wisdom, mostly on the basis of a single observation: the success of the Clinton budget plan in 1993.[21]

Expectational effects of fiscal policy may reverse standard Keynesian effects, even in the short run.[22]

Eichenbaum was the sole theorist with the mental fortitude to carry the belief in a vertical PC to its logical conclusion—in the long run both monetary and fiscal policy are neutral in their effects. Eichenbaum maintained that observed short-run fluctuations in AD cannot be attributed to monetary "shocks." This led him to the conclusion that Friedman's monetary "rule" was suspect and sub-optimal. The implication of accepting the view that long-run growth is independent of short-run demand factors (money and interest rates) and depends solely and uniquely on supply-side factors (labor force and labor productivity) is that unless they have supply-side effects, monetary and fiscal policy are neutral in the long run. Real Business Cycle models no longer embody the recommendation that fiscal policy should be used for stabilization purposes, Eichenbaum was the sole panelist to carry the argument to its logical conclusion: "Monetary policy is neutral in the long run."[23]

The rediscovery of endogenous growth theory has provided a popular option for mainstream theorists to disown the logical implication that the assumption that the long-run PC curve is vertical implies long-run policy neutrality. Several panelists emphasized that many major long-run supply-side phenomena, for example the decline in potential GDP growth since 1973, remain an unsolved mystery.[24] No panelist recognized that in a complex world, expectations cannot be summarized in terms of objective quantitative probability distributions. Due to agent ignorance under fundamental uncertainty expectations can never be formed *"rationally."* Since agent behavior is bounded by ignorance, agents cannot undertake "utility maximization." No one recognized that if the economic universe is nonlinear and characterized by sensitive dependence on initial conditions, no general equilibrium outcome can be envisaged. No one emphasized that as complex adaptive systems (CAS) economies cannot be modeled reductively, but can only be modeled as nonlinear systems which may be simulated but never solved.

13.2 A critique of the mainstream "core"

The first mainstream proposition: *"In the short run movements in economic activity are dominated by movements in AD,"* is the sole component of the mainstream "core" with which Post Keynesians are in unqualified agreement. All other "core" propositions are false. The second mainstream proposition is clearly incorrect. As a complex adaptive system GDP does not follow steady-state long-run growth paths. GDP like all other macroeconomic variables has a unit root, so it is incorrect to assume that GDP fluctuates around a deterministic trend. For all series that have unit roots short-run shocks have *permanent* effects on future values of the variable. Any trends found are "stochastic" and time-dependent, the result of the particular historical events that occurred over the period. The future growth rate of complex systems is nondeterministic and can never be known in advance.

The third and fourth propositions, concerning the importance of price rigidities for output fluctuations, and the existence of a vertical long run Phillips Curve, are also false. In all modern economies prices in the fix-price sector prices are set as a stable markup on unit variable costs. Once it is recognized that the supply of credit money is endogenous it becomes immediately apparent that inflation cannot be explained by quantity theory logic. Monetary causality *presupposes* an exogenous money supply. Post Keynesians regard inflation as primarily cost inflation. The "core" inflation rate is equal to the excess of the average rate of money wage increase over the average rate of labor productivity growth. Post Keynesians strongly repudiate all quantity theory (Monetarist) explanations of inflation incorporating a vertical long run Phillips Curve.

The behavior of money wages is the outcome of a process of conflict and negotiation between labor and capital over the distribution of income. Workers with market power attempt to raise their money wage rates to offset past increases in finished goods prices, and to keep their real incomes rising at the average growth rate of labor productivity. Firms with market power attempt to raise their markups to achieve higher returns on capital. The Post Keynesian aphorism is: "Inflation is always and everywhere a symptom of the struggle over the distribution of income."[25]

The mainstream neoclassical synthesis (NCS) includes a number of serious methodological errors:

1. The third proposition that price rigidities explain fluctuations in real output illustrates the professions' regression to the core neoclassical paradigm that Keynes was at such pains to refute in the 1930s, but has since been readopted as Joan Robinson's "bastard Keynesianism." "If only wages and prices were sufficiently flexible, all markets would clear, and we would be back in the neoclassical vision of homeostatic full employment equilibrium."

This is directly opposed to Keynes' carefully articulated argument in Ch. 19 of the *General Theory*, "Changes in Money Wages," where he detailed at length why the root cause of unemployment was not price inflexibility but AD deficiency. For Post Keynesians price inflexibilities and market imperfections are not the central explanation for unemployment. As Keynes argued the chief result of greater money wage flexibility would be a more rapid cumulative deflationary spiral. Keynes concluded:

> the maintenance of a stable level of money wages ... on a balance of considerations [is] the most advisable policy for a closed system.[26]

2. The second methodological error stems from the fact that neoclassical equilibrium theory has no satisfactory way of dealing with *time*. As Hicks emphasized in his later papers the neoclassical GE vision of timeless market exchange, in a single market where individual maximizing agents are assumed to exchange goods, labor, money and bonds with one another, is

> a thoroughly unsatisfactory characterization of the sequence of events that carry production economies through a complex traverse from the partially known present towards the unknowable future.[27]

3. The mainstream model formulates a hypothetical production function, but deduces no conclusions from the fact that *production occurs over chronological time*. The chief significance of the passage of chronological time in a production economy is that *firms must pay their labor and materials bills in the present*, before *they have received their future sales receipts from the goods and services the factors produce*.[28] This generates business demand for working capital finance from the banking system.

4. To assure that all future working capital requirements are financed, firms negotiate long-term credit commitments (overdraft agreements) with their bankers to assure access to future loans. Increases in planned output generate increased demand for working capital finance to pay for increased factors of production during the production-sales period. Bank lending leads directly to increases in the money supply. Money supply expansion is fully endogenous in response to increases in demand for bank credit, which in turn is due to business expectations of higher future sales. The resulting money growth finances the expansion of the AD and AS curves. Changes in the money supply typically precede changes in money income, with no Monetarist Granger-causality implication that monetary change *"causes"* income change.

5. The upward-sloping LM curve of the IS–LM model logically requires that the money supply be exogenously controlled by the CB. The construction of the LM curve assumes the CB sets the money supply as its policy instrument. The CB is assumed to control the money supply by open market operations which increase or reduce the high powered base. The transactions' demand for the given money supply rises with income, causing interest rates to rise and the LM curve to slope upwards. In the IS–LM model there is no role for business demand for bank credit to finance working capital and endogenously increase the money supply.[29] A deeper criticism of IS–LM analysis is that the IS and LM curves are intrinsically *interdependent*.

6. Mainstream theory takes as axiomatic that prices send the key signals to agents. However in modern economies the prices of most goods and services constituting GDP are not determined in perfectly competitive auction markets by impersonal supply and demand forces. Most GDP transactions concern intermediate goods, most firms sell primarily to other firms, and most firms possess market power. Most GDP prices are discretionarily administered and subject to a flock of contractual commitments and implicit constraints. Mainstream theory overlooks that the price system has requirements more fundamental than resource allocation: the need to motivate workers and to not antagonize customers create a host of wage and price pseudo-irrationalities and rigidities: implicit long-term contracts, sticky wages and prices, information asymmetries and moral hazards. *In a non fully-rational world, non fully-rational behavior is rational.*

7. Mainstream theory recognizes that expectations are the key variable driving agent behavior. But the critical expectations for investment spending concern future sales quantities not future prices. Mainstream theory regards "supply shocks" as the chief disturbance. But the proximate driving force of changes in AD is changing agents' expectations of other agents' behavior. AD depends on agents' expectations how future "shocks" will be perceived by other economic agents.

Economic outcomes are complex beyond our wildest comprehension. *Agents base their behavior on their current expectations of how other agents will form their future expectations.*

13.3 A fundamental critique of the mainstream theory of income determination

The mainstream theory of the determination of GDP in mainstream textbooks is traditionally summarized in four diagrams: the (C+I+G) diagram, the "Keynesian Cross" (S–I) diagram, the IS–LM diagram, and the AD–AS diagram. Each of these presentations is fatally flawed:

13.3.1 The (C+I+G) diagram

In the (C+I+G) diagram shown in Figure 13.1, AD is measured on the vertical axis and AS is measured on the horizontal axis. AD is represented by the (C + I + G) line. [C = consumption spending, I = investment spending, and G = government spending on public goods] At all points on the 45° line the vertical magnitude (AD) is equal to the horizontal magnitude (AS). Prices and wages are assumed to be stable in the short run.

In Figure 13.1 investment and government spending for simplicity are assumed exogenous and independent of current income. In the simplest model the slope of the (C + I + G) relationship (the marginal propensity to spend—MPS) is equal to the marginal propensity to consume (MPC). For stability it must be assumed that the MPC is less than unity. This assures that the slope of the AD curve is less than 45° and intersects the AS curve at a finite level of income. The (C + I + G) curve shows how AD for currently produced goods varies with changes in current income depending on the economy's MPC. All market economies are recognized as demand-driven in the short run.

In the mainstream theory of income determination the "equilibrium" level of income (Y_{Eo}) is defined as the point E_o where the ($C+I_o+G_o$) line intersects the 45°

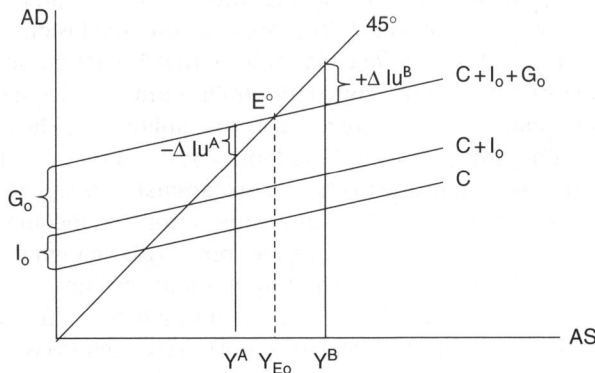

Figure 13.1 The (C + I + G) relationship

line. AS is equal to AD in equilibrium since all markets are assumed to be competitive, and inventories continually adjust to changes in demand. The "equilibrium" level of income is defined as that level where there no tendency for income to change.

The conclusion that this is an "equilibrium" level of income is demonstrated to undergraduates by showing that at all other levels of output, AD is not equal to AS so the level of income will change.[30] Suppose the current level of income were Y^A, less than the equilibrium value Y_{Eo}. At the lower level of income Y^A the (C+I+G) line exceeds the 45° line, which is a proxy for AS. The level of output is then below the level of aggregate demand for goods and services. Firms find that current demand exceeds current production and experience *unintended inventory decumulation* ($- \Delta Iu^A$). They respond to the unanticipated fall in inventories by hiring additional workers and purchasing additional intermediate goods and factors of production to replenish their inventories. Income and employment continue to increase until the new "equilibrium" position is reached (Y_{Eo}) when AD is equal to AS, and there is no further tendency for income to rise.

Conversely suppose the current level of income were Y^B above the equilibrium value Y_{Eo}. At that higher level of income Y^B the 45° line which is a proxy for AS exceeds the (C+I+G) line (AD). Firms find that current demand is less than current supply, and experience *unintended inventory accumulation* ($+\Delta Iu^B$). They respond to the unanticipated rise in inventories by laying off workers and purchasing less intermediate goods and factors of production to reduce the level of their inventories. Income and output will fall until a new "equilibrium" level of income is reached (Y_{Eo}), when AD is equal to AS and there is no further tendency for income to fall.

Mainstream macro models present three alternative ways of demonstrating an "equilibrium" level of GDP. As the position where:

(1) AD equals AS
(2) Planned investment equals planned saving
(3) Planned surpluses equal planned deficits.

The accounting identity between saving and investment and surpluses and deficits was discussed in Chapter 7. The mainstream conclusion that unanticipated changes in inventories drive changes in output is correct. But mainstream analysis confines itself to comparative static equilibrium, and devotes much effort to exploring the conditions necessary for such an equilibrium to be unique, stable, and feasible (non-negative). In complex adaptive systems the AD curve (C+I+G) shifts continuously over time due to changes in "animal spirits," agents' heterogeneous expectations of unknowable future expectations of income and prices.[31] Expectations about the unknowable future are continually changing, so economies can never approach any future stationary "equilibrium" position.

Production takes chronological time and the future demand for goods and services can never be known in advance. Firms must make their decisions in the present about how much to produce in the future, and must set the supply price in the present that will hold over their future pricing period. Firms are never sure what the future demand for their products will be and what amount they will be able to sell. As developed in Chapter 12 in the entire fix-price sector firms are price-setters and quantity-takers. For individual firms the short run AS relationship may be represented as a horizontal line over the current average pricing period. Prices are administered as a markup over average variable costs. Businessmen know they do not know what their future demand curve will be. For all storable goods they will hold sufficient inventories to increase the likelihood they will be able to meet all anticipated future increases in demand, taking into account the expected future storage costs involved. They also build in sufficient excess capacity to be prepared for long-run future demand increases that are not presently known, but anticipated.

Labor is by far the most important factor in terms of total cost. For most firms average variable costs are closely approximated by unit labor costs. The markup over unit costs is ordinarily stable in the short run. The rate of change in average money wages in excess of the rate of change in average labor productivity determines the "core" rate of inflation. As a stylized fact, the short-run AS curve may be represented as a horizontal line in inflation-output space.[32]

Changes in prices are determined by changes in average variable costs, and changes in nominal output are determined by changes in AD. AD changes continuously from one period to the next with agents' changing expectations of the unknown future. Deficit spending is accompanied by parallel changes in the velocity of money. If velocity is constant deficit spending must be accompanied by an identical change in bank borrowing to finance the deficit-spending undertaken, and result in an identical change in the money supply. The factors determining the volume of deficit spending over the current period are agents' expectations of AD in future periods, agents' current money balances, and the interest rate they expect to be charged to finance their deficit spending.

Post Keynesians agree with the mainstream that unintended inventory accumulation and decumulation provide the signals for firms to adjust their production in the current period to anticipated changes in future demand. But they insist this adjustment process never comes to an end. Changes in demand occur continuously, as AD shifts over every future period reflecting continual changes in animal spirits. The system never settles down and an "equilibrium" position is never attained nor even approached. Complex systems have no tendency to approach any future position of "balance" where all change ceases. The C+I+G diagram may be retained as an introductory teaching device, so long as the point of intersection with the 45° line denotes the "current" (continuously changing) level of income and not a future "equilibrium" level of income.

13.3.2 The "Keynesian Cross": the I–S diagram

The second workhorse macro diagram of mainstream analysis is the "Keynesian Cross" I-S diagram. As shown in Figure 13.2 planned saving and investment are measured on the vertical axis and current GDP is measured on the horizontal axis. Planned investment and planned saving are regarded as independent behavioral relationships, undertaken by two different groups, firms and households. Both

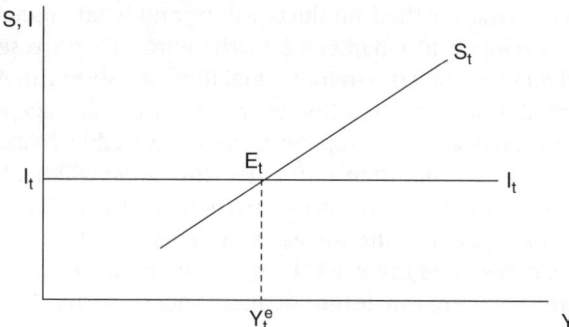

Figure 13.2 The I–S ("Keynesian Cross") diagram

households and business managers are assumed to act to maximize expected utility. Investment spending is undertaken by firms, although in the National Income Accounts (NIAs), household purchases of homes [though not consumer durables] are included as "investment" spending.

The quantity of planned investment undertaken depends on "animal spirits," which summarize business's heterogeneous expectations of future profits and their future costs of capital. To simplify the argument, investment spending is assumed to be solely determined by changes in "animal spirits," which are assumed independent of changes in current income. Investment is then "exogenous" and may be drawn as horizontal. [If investment were assumed positively related to income, the investment function would have a positive slope equal to the marginal propensity to invest.] The level of income is assumed to adjust until the quantity of planned saving undertaken by household wealth-owners is equal to the quantity of planned investment undertaken by business managers (E_t).

Saving defined as the difference between income and consumption is undertaken by both households and so firms. Households are recognized to be the ultimate owners of businesses and so of the economy's capital stock. In most developed economies firms finance broadly half their total investment expenditures internally out of retained earnings. Saving for the economy is regarded as a function of current and expected future income, summarized by the economy's "marginal propensity to save," the slope of the saving function (S_t). The analysis concludes that in response to a change in investment spending income will increase by a *multiple* of the change in investment. The multiplier is the inverse of the slope of the savings relationship ($1/s_t$). In order for the model to have a finite determinate equilibrium it is assumed that household marginal propensity to save out of disposable income (MPS) exceeds business marginal propensity to invest (MPI) out of current profits.

The level of income is assumed to adjust to its "equilibrium" level (Y_t^e) where planned saving by households is exactly equal to planned investment by firms. Both saving and investment are regarded as independent volitional behavioral relationships, and income adjusts to equilibrate the two. Investment spending is assumed to be more volatile than household saving, since it is governed by continually shifting investor "animal spirits" surrounding the unknown future profitability of current investment. Cyclical shifts in the investment schedule are represented by rises or falls in I_t, and produce cyclical fluctuations in GDP. Planned investment varies pro-cyclically over the cycle. Shifts in exogenous investment spending are the motor that drives cyclical fluctuations in GDP.

Once it is recognized that saving is the accounting record of investment, the error in the above account becomes self-evident. Since saving is the accounting record of investment there is no independent volitional saving function for the economy. Actual saving is identical to actual investment as an accounting identity, at every level of income, rate of interest and moment of time. An independent saving "function" does not exist. Saving is an identity, the accounting record of investment spending, and is therefore coterminous with the investment function.

One implication of the above is that saving is volitional only for a small proportion of the economy. In developed economies about one half total investment spending is financed internally out of retained earnings. The accompanying non-volitional saving takes the form of stockholders literally "doing nothing," and passively "abstaining" from taking a decision to sell those assets whose market values have increased and consume their capital gain income. Agents then have assets in their portfolios with a higher market value at the end of the period than at the beginning. Agents who find themselves with a higher net worth due to capital gain are from the viewpoint of the economy "non-volitional savers" over the period.

Similarly about one half of business investment spending is financed externally by the issue of marketable and nonmarketable debt and equity instruments. These are primarily sold to financial institutions who finance their purchases of primary securities with money generated by the issue of their own "secondary" securities. Some "primary" nonmonetary financial assets, such as stocks and bonds, are volitionally purchased by households. But the largest single component of external finance takes the form of firms borrowing from banks to finance their working capital needs. This involves the issue by business units of nonmarketable loans (IOUs) to the banking system, and is accompanied by an identical increase in bank deposits and the money supply. A non-volitional increase in "convenience saving" is undertaken by all depositors whose deposit balances increased over the period. The only "volitional" saving undertaken is by households who volitionally abstain from consumption to purchase newly issued primary and secondary non-monetary financial assets, issued by nonfinancial firms and nonbank financial intermediaries to externally finance current investment.

Saving is the accounting record of investment spending. Changes in investment automatically create its own saving with no required "equilibrating" adjustment in the level of income, interest rates, or anything else. In modern economies most saving is non-volitional, the excess of total investment over total volitional saving. As an accounting identity, total saving is identical to total investment. There is no independent volitional total saving function and no unique "equilibrium" level of income, where "planned" saving of households is equal to "planned" investment of firms.[33] "Planned" saving is never equal to "planned" investment. Consumption and investment change continuously over time. When firms are price-setters and quantity-takers the AS relation may be represented as a horizontal line in inflation-output space at the current "core" inflation rate. In closed economies the "core" inflation rate is equal to the change in average variable costs, the excess of the average rate of money wage growth over average rate of labor productivity growth. So long as firms are price-setters and quantity-takers the change in output is identical to the change in AD (total consumption, investment, and government spending), apart from any temporary unintended changes in business inventories .

As will be developed in Chapter 14 the AD curve may be represented as a vertical fractal band in inflation-output space. The Keynesian Cross diagram of mainstream theory is both false and misleading. It assumes that investment and saving are volitionally and independently determined by different groups, businesses and households, or savers and investors. The level of income is assumed to adjust until in equilibrium the planned saving of the surplus groups is exactly equal to the planned investment of the deficit groups.

The "Keynesian Cross" should be abandoned as a teaching tool. The level of income in the economy does not adjust until planned investment by one group is equal to planned saving of another group, or planned deficit-spending by business units is equal to the planned surplus-saving of household units. Saving is identical to investment and total surpluses are identical to total deficits, by definition, at every level of income and interest rates. They are simply accounting identities. Income grows when AD increases and falls when AD decreases. The level of income is continuously demand-determined. In the fix-price sector the AS relation becomes horizontal when firms are price-setters and quantity-takers.

13.3.3 The IS–LM diagram

All AEA panelists agreed the theory of income determination taught at the intermediate level in most mainstream macroeconomic courses was some variant of the workhorse IS-LM diagram. In the textbook presentation of IS-LM, income is measured on the horizontal axis and interest rates are measured on the vertical axis (Figure 13.3). But there are fatal logical defects in the derivation of both the IS and the LM relationships.[34]

The Investment–Saving relationship (the IS curve) is defined as the different combinations of interest rates and income that are consistent with "equilibrium" in the goods markets, where "planned" saving equals "planned" investment. The IS curve is traditionally drawn as downward-sloping, since lower interest rates stimulate investment and raise AD. It is recognized that in periods of economic expansions when "animal spirits" are buoyant, investment demand may respond more strongly to increases in income than to the supply of saving, the marginal propensity to spend will exceed unity and the IS curve may slope upward.

Expectations of future economic behavior, and with them planned saving and investment change, continuously over time. In monetary economies, total saving

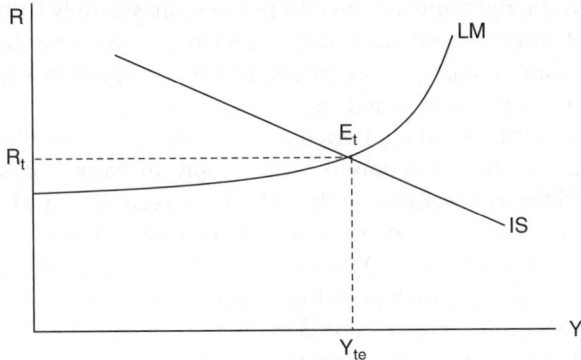

Figure 13.3 The IS–LM diagram

is not a volitional relationship. Actual saving is identical to actual investment at every level of income, interest rates and time period since S = I is an accounting identity. Savers and investors are different groups. Planned saving by some groups is never identical to planned investment by other groups. The IS curve, defined as those combinations of interest rates and income where "planned" saving is equal to "planned" investment, delineates an ordering of nonexistent GE combinations.

The problem is not simply that the IS curve is very difficult for students to grasp pedagogically. The IS curve is difficult to teach because it is a complete nonsense. An IS curve, defined as the set of combinations of S and I that result in "equilibrium" in the goods markets, can neither exist nor be logically imagined. It is neither a logical concept nor an empirical relationship but a fantasy and should be banished from the textbooks. Since investment spending responds inversely to the level of interest rates, the IS curve may be fruitfully resusicated as a downward-sloping AD relationship in interest rate-output space.

The Liquidity–Money relationship (the LM curve) denotes the different combinations of interest rates and income consistent with "equilibrium" in the money markets, where the demand for money is equal to the supply of money. The money supply is assumed exogenously set by the CB. The LM curve is conventionally drawn as horizontal at low levels of income, where interest rates have reached a positive floor level that cannot be reduced by raising the ratio of money to income (Keynes' liquidity trap). At levels of interest rates above the floor level the LM curve is upward-sloping. The slope of the LM curve is positive since the "transactions" demand for money increases with income, and the money supply is assumed given as an exogenous policy instrument.

The level of interest rates must rise to keep the sum of the "transactions" plus "asset" ("portfolio") demand for money equal to the assumed fixed stock of money. The implication of an upward-sloping LM curve is that for any given money supply set by the CB, interest rates rise endogenously during expansions, and fall endogenously during contractions. An increase in the money supply shifts the LM curve to the right and a reduction in the money supply shifts LM curve to the left. IS–LM analysis embodies the monetarist conclusion that exogenous changes in the money supply cause prices, incomes and AD to adjust over time, with a long and variable distributed lag.

The LM curve is thus as fatally flawed as the IS curve, but for different reasons. In developed credit money economies the supply of bank deposits is endogenously credit-driven as developed in Part III. Mainstream theory assumes that the money supply is exogenous so the direction of causality goes from monetary change to income change ($\Delta M \rightarrow \Delta Y$). As stated this is a reversal of the true direction of the causal arrow, which goes from changes in income to changes in the money supply ($\Delta Y \rightarrow \Delta M$), termed "reverse causation" when money is endogenous.

The IS–LM diagram represents comparative static equilibrium analysis which as developed in Part I is unenlightening for complex adaptive systems. In mainstream theory the intersection of IS and LM curves determines the level of income and interest rates in "GE" (E_t). At this point all real and financial relationships are assumed in equilibrium, planned saving is equal to planned investment, and the quantity of money supplied is equal to the quantity of money demanded. The level of nominal interest rates is assumed endogenously determined to satisfy both the supply and demand for loanable funds, and the supply and demand for income and output. The money supply is assumed to be set exogenously by the CB as its key monetary policy instrument through control of the high-powered base. The intersection of the IS and LM curves (E_t) determines the level of income (Y_{te}) and interest rates (R_t) consistent with equilibrium in the goods and the financial markets.

IS–LM analysis solves for the level of income and interest rates in "GE." But complex systems can never attain a GE position. GE can only exist in "logical time" where nothing changes and no agent expects the future to be different from the present. It is logically illegitimate to hypothesize different "GE" outcomes, at different levels of interest and output, as implied in the construction of the IS–LM diagram. The IS and LM curves represent illogical hypothetical relationships, which cannot hold for complex systems and have no relevance for real world economies.

IS–LM analysis does not provide an accurate explanation of how changes in interest rates and the money supply are related to changes in income, output, and prices. Its central message is the exact opposite of the truth. The supply of credit money is not set exogenously by the CB, but is determined endogenously by the demand for bank loans by borrowers judged to be credit-worthy. The short-term rate of interest is not market-determined by wealth-owner decisions to invest and to deficit spend, but exogenously set by the CB as its chief instrument of monetary policy, and held constant at this level over short-run periods between monetary policy meetings.

Complex economies must be modeled as nonlinear systems where no closed form "equilibrium" solution exists. Their future behavior can be simulated but never accurately foretold or "solved for." The IS–LM diagram is even more logically flawed as a teaching tool than the "Keynesian Cross" diagram. Once it is recognized that saving is the accounting record of investment, it becomes self-evident that saving is identical to investment at every level of investment, income, and interest rates. There is neither a downward-nor an upward-sloping IS curve. There is in fact no IS curve, since it is on inconsistent construction. In modern economies the supply of credit money is endogenously credit-driven by the demand for credit, so the CB cannot exogenously control the supply of credit money. There is no upward-sloping LM curve. The interest rate is exogenously determined by the CB, and not market-determined as implied by IS–LM analysis. The LM curve is a horizontal line at the bank lending rate (R_L), which is a markup on Bank Rate set by the CB.

The IS–LM direction of causality, from changes in the money supply to changes in income, reverses the "true" direction of the causal arrow between money and income. The supply of credit money is endogenously determined by the quantity of bank credit demanded by credit-worthy borrowers. Changes in the money supply temporally precede changes in income and output, but are not the "cause" of changes in income, output, prices, inflation, or any other macroeconomic variable. As an endogenous market-determined variable the money supply changes with changes in the amount of credit demanded, depending on the interest elasticity of the demand for credit the change in animal spirits, and the change in Bank Rate set by the CB.

The IS–LM diagram should be banished from the textbooks as a confused GE fantasy. The supply of credit money is endogenously determined by the demand for bank credit by credit-worthy borrowers, not directly controlled by the CB by varying the high-powered base. The level of short-term interest rates is not endogenously determined over the business cycle. CBs set Bank Rate exogenously as their chief policy instrument, and vary it pro-cyclically over the business cycle. Bank lending rates are administered as a stable markup over Bank Rate. By setting the supply price of credit to the economy the CB affects the quantity of credit demanded, and the quantity of credit money created.[35]

Once interest rates are recognized as the CBs chief exogenous policy instrument the LM relationship becomes a horizontal line at the bank lending rate (R_L) which is a stable markup on Bank Rate (BR) set by the CB. The recognition that the credit money supply is endogenously credit-driven, and the level of short-term interest rates is exogenously set by the CB, permits the effects of changes in interest rates on the money supply, AD, and income, to be analyzed using process analysis. The IS curve becomes a downward-sloping AD relationship in interest rate-output space. This provides a clear and simple explanation why market economies are typically demand-constrained.[36] CB's set BR too high for a full employment level of AD.

13.3.4 The AD–AS diagram

Mainstream textbooks also present the Keynesian theory of income determination in the form of AD and AS relationships. As shown in Figure 13.4 the AD curve is conventionally portrayed as downward-sloping in price-output space. A lower

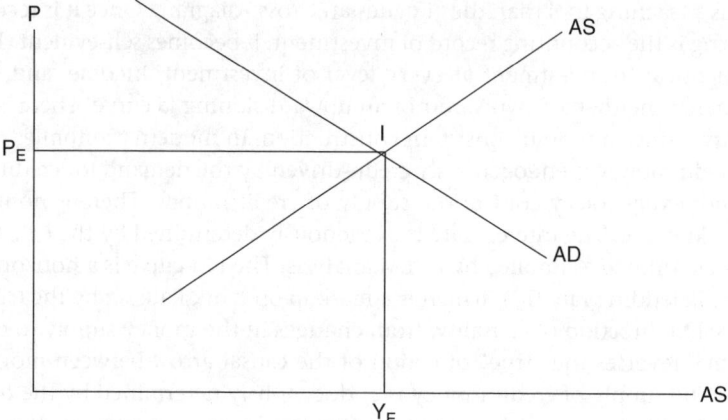

Figure 13.4 The mainstream AS–AD diagram

price level is assumed to be associated with a higher AD, due to the "real balance" or "Pigou" effect. The AS curve is portrayed as upward-sloping in price-output space, on the assumption that additional output will be supplied only at higher prices due to the presence of diminishing returns.

As shown in Figure 13.4, the AD curve is conventionally portrayed as a downward-sloping sum of the aggregate demand for individual goods. But the demand for individual goods slopes downward due to the *substitution and income effects*, which are generated by changes in relative prices. Neither is applicable to the AD relationship, since P represents the Consumer Price Index (CPI) or the GDP deflator, a quantity-weighted index of individual prices unaffected by changes in relative prices. Mainstream theory assumes the nominal money supply is exogenously controlled by the CB as its monetary policy instrument, and interest rates are endogenously determined by loanable funds and liquidity preference considerations.

The Real Balance (Pigou or Wealth Effect) is assumed to increase AD when P falls since the real value of money balances rises when prices fall (M/P) assuming that the nominal money supply (M) is given. The increase in the real value of the (given) nominal stock of money balances is assumed to raise real wealth values, and reduce the level of interest rates, leading to an expansion of AD. So long as prices and wages are perfectly flexible, it is assumed prices will continue to fall until full employment is reached, and the price level stabilizes at a new lower level. The uncomfortable fact that all empirical estimates of the magnitude of the Real Balance effect are small in the extreme is ignored in theoretical expositions of the Real Balance effect.[37]

Once the money supply is recognized as endogenously credit-driven, the Real Balance effect vanishes. The money supply is driven by business demand for bank loans to finance their working capital needs, and by household demand to finance the accumulation of houses and of consumer durables. In consequence the level of wages and prices, and the demand for credit and the money supply, co-vary together. As a "stylized fact" AD may be viewed as *vertical* in price-output space. AD is determined by animal spirits and BR, and is not related to the price level.

Mainstream analysis portrays the AS curve as an upward-sloping relationship in price-output space. All markets are assumed to be perfectly competitive and production is assumed subject to diminishing returns. Marginal costs rise with unit costs as AS increases with increases in AD. The rate of change of prices and output are assumed to respond to the shape and position of the AS and AD relationships which determine the new point of intersection.

As shown mainstream AD and AS curves resemble the supply and demand curves for a single commodity produced under perfect competition. It is thus not surprising that mainstream analysis concludes that if only prices were sufficiently flexible, market economies would tend to full employment. Due to its commitment to comparative static equilibrium analysis, mainstream analysis focus on the technical conditions necessary for the economy to adjust to full employment equilibrium. Individual prices are assumed to vary in response to changes in unit costs, as driven by changes in supply and demand in individual markets. Relative prices vary with differential rates of technological change in different industries. Over longer run periods the AS and AD curves are regarded as interdependent. Supply "shocks" can be distinguished from demand "shocks" by holding the AS or the AD curve constant, and shifting the other curve to examine the "comparative static" properties of shifts in AS or in AD on prices and output.

Classical economists believed that if only prices and wages were sufficiently flexible a negative shock, that is a leftward shift in the AD curve, would initially cause demand and output to fall, and unemployment to rise. But so long as wages and prices are flexible, unemployment and an excess supply of labor would cause wages, other factor prices and goods prices to fall. This would continue until factor and goods markets finally equilibrate at full employment.

So long as wages are flexible, it is believed an excess supply of labor (unemployment) would cause money wages to fall. Unit costs and prices will decline, raising the real value of money balances, and increasing the economy's real wealth. This process will continue until the price level has reached a sufficiently low level, and the real supply of money (M/P) is sufficiently high, that AD intersects AS at the full employment level of output and real wages stabilize at the level of the real marginal product of labor. The economy is viewed as a homeostatic system which once disturbed has a tendency to return automatically to full employment equilibrium, without any required government AD or AS intervention.

Post Keynesians argue that the mainstream vision of an economy as a single market, with a downward-sloping AD curve and an upward-sloping AS curve, is both incorrect and fatally misleading as a characterization of market economies. Product and factor markets are interrelated but separate market prices are based on unit costs and investment is intrinsically forward looking. If wages were perfectly flexible firms would not know the levels of future prices, and the degree of uncertainty about nominal future returns on current investment projects would be enormously increased. The assumption that if only wages and prices were more flexible, the system would adjust until the AS and the AD curve intersected at full employment in GE, is pure classical fantasy. GE is an unhelpful fiction, not a simplifying assumption.[38] Both the upward-sloping AD curve, and the downward-sloping AS curve, should be banned from the text books.

13.4 Post Keynesian AS–AD analysis

Kalecki was the first to argue it was incorrect to portray the economy's short-run AS curve as upward-sloping. This would only be true if all industries were perfectly competitive, all firms operated under increasing costs and all markets were flex-price. In the dominant fix-price manufacturing and service sectors, most firms possess market power, most markets are imperfectly competitive and most prices are administered at a markup over *historic average variable costs*. Firms set their markup in an attempt to achieve a target rate of profits. Markups differ widely over firms and industries but in the short run the average markup for the economy is stable. Wages are by far the largest component of costs and as a first approximation average variable costs are well-approximated by ULCs.[39]

The pricing period over which firms hold prices constant is the average production-sales period.[40] As the monopoly supplier of system liquidity, the CB sets Bank Rate exogenously as its chief policy instrument. The quantity of bank loans granted and the supply of credit money created are endogenously credit-driven. The quantity of deposits created depends on the influence of animal spirits on credit demand, the interest-elasticity of the demand for bank credit, and the level of Bank Rate set by the CB.

This construction permits the independence and interdependence between AD and AS to be represented diagrammatically. As a stylized fact as shown in Figure 13.5 the AS curve may be viewed as *horizontal* in price-output space. In the flex-price sector, which is confined to agriculture and natural resources, prices are flexible, markets are competitive, and firms lack the ability to administer prices. But in most developed economies the flex-price sector accounts for less than 5 percent of GDP. In the fix-price sector, which accounts for more than 95 percent of GDP in developed economies, prices are administered at a stable markup over historic (accountants') unit costs. In product markets most firms are price-setters and quantity-takers. In factor markets both firms and unions attempt to be price-setters, and money wage rates are negotiated between workers, unions, and employers. The rate of inflation is largely predetermined in the current pricing period, and the "core" inflation rate equals the excess of the average rate of money wage growth over the average rate of labor productivity growth in the previous pricing period.

With endogenous credit money, the money supply, money wages and prices vary together. Since the real value of money balances is largely independent of the price level, there are no "income," "substitution," "wealth," or "real balance" effects. Real world economies are not homeostatic and have no tendency to approach a full employment "equilibrium" level of output. Once the short-term interest rate is recognized as under CB control, and the money supply is recognized as endogenously credit-driven, AD does not vary inversely with the price level. As a stylized fact the AD curve may be represented as *vertical* in inflation-output space, as shown in Figure 13.5.

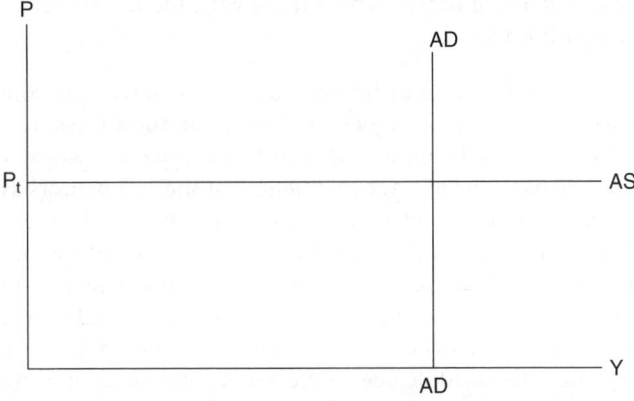

Figure 13.5 The Post Keynesian AD–AS diagram

The AD curve shifts to the right and left with changes in the demand for bank-financed deficit-spending, and accompanying changes in the supply of credit money. The behavior of AD is time-dependent and varies cyclically over the cycle with changes in "animal spirits." Firms respond to changes in AD by expanding or contracting output. So long as unit costs remain constant and there is excess capacity the level of AD has little direct effect on the inflation rate.[41] The AS function may be portrayed as *horizontal* in inflation-output space and the AD function as *vertical*. So long as the average markup remains stable, the "core" inflation rate is equal to the excess of the average rate of growth of money wages over the average rate of growth of labor productivity in the previous period.

13.5 Conclusions: the central importance of changes in "animal spirits"

The mainstream "core" paradigm is fatally flawed. Process analysis, which incorporates endogenous money and exogenous interest rates in calendar time, will be shown in the next chapter to offer a more insightful framework for macroeconomic analysis and replace comparative static GE analysis for policy evaluation. Mainstream C+I+G, S–I, IS–LM, and AS–AD analysis all have been critically evaluated and, each was shown to be fatally flawed. Economies are complex adaptive systems whose behavior is far beyond our ability to fully understand or anticipate. They have no tendency to approach any pre-determined "equilibrium" position. Changes in economic variables are not as is commonly believed due to "exogenous shocks." Complex nonlinear systems endogenously produce cyclical fluctuations, which cannot be distinguished econometrically from "random" shocks.

Expectations drive the economy. Agent expectations are fundamentally concerned with the present and future expectations of other agents about future events, all of which change continuously over time. At the most basic level *individual agents are faced with the insoluble problem of attempting to anticipate the changing expectations of other agents*. Keynes termed this complex process "animal spirits." Each economic agent is faced with the insoluble task of Keynes' newspaper competition:

> ... professional investment may be likened to those newspaper competitions in which the competitors have to pick out the six prettiest faces from a hundred photographs, the prize being awarded to the competitor whose choice most nearly corresponds to the average preferences of the competitors as a whole; so that each competitor has to pick, not those faces which he himself finds prettiest, but those which he thinks likely to catch the fancy of the other competitors, all of whom are looking at the problem from the same point of view. It is not a case of choosing those which, to the best of one's judgment, are really the prettiest, nor even those which average opinion genuinely thinks the prettiest. We have reached the third degree where we devote our intelligences to anticipating what average opinion expects the average opinion to be. And there are some, I believe, who practice the fourth, fifth and some higher degrees.
>
> Even apart from the instability due to speculation, there is the instability due to the characteristic of human nature that a large proportion of our positive activities depend on spontaneous optimism rather than on a mathematical expectation, ... Most ... of our decisions to do something positive, ... can only be taken as a result of *animal spirits*—of a spontaneous urge to action rather than inaction—and not to the outcome of a weighted average of quantitative benefits multiplied by quantitative probabilities. Enterprise only pretends to itself to be mainly actuated by the statements in its own prospectus, however candid and sincere. Only a little more than an expedition to the South Pole is based on an exact calculation of benefits to come.
>
> We should not conclude from this that everything depends on waves of irrational psychology. ... We are merely reminding ourselves that human decisions affecting the future, whether personal or political or economic, cannot depend on strict mathematical expectation, since the basis for making such calculations does not exist; and that it is our innate urge to activity which makes the wheels go round.[42]

The mainstream IS–LM model has been shown to be fatally flawed.[43] At the deepest level this is due to the fact that complex economies have no tendency to approach any future "equilibrium" position. Economic behavior must be analyzed by recognizing that agents have imperfect information, are faced with fundamental uncertainty, and act over calendar time. Unlike economists, economic agents know that they cannot predict the future. Most "saving" is not volitional as it appears at the micro level to individual agents. From the view point of the economy, total "saving," that is abstaining from consumption, is merely the accounting record of total investment. The recognition that economies are complex adaptive systems (CAS), and saving is simply the accounting record of investment, will act as a neutron bomb in demolishing the general equilibrium foundations of mainstream C+I+G, S–I, IS–LM, and AS–AD analysis.

14
Interest Rates and Aggregate Demand

> A large portion of our positive activities depend on spontaneous optimism rather than on mathematical expectation, whether moral or hedonistic or economic. Most ... of our decisions to do something positive ... can only be taken as a result of animal spirits: of a spontaneous urge to action rather than inaction, and not of the outcome of the weighted average of quantitative benefits multiplied by quantitative probabilities. Enterprise only pretends to itself to be mainly actuated by the statements of its own prospectus, however candid and sincere.
>
> John Maynard Keynes, 1936: 161–2

> In a world that is always in equilibrium there is no difference between the future and the past, and there is no need of Keynes.
>
> Joan Robinson, 1974: 28

> The macroeconomics which has followed the *General Theory* in time has not followed it in spirit.
>
> Victoria Chick, 1983: v

14.1 The Post Keynesian case for aggregate demand management

Keynes argued that even perfectly competitive flexible prices and wages do not transform market economies into homeostatic systems that maintain dynamically stable equilibrium states without direct government intervention. Real world economies have no natural tendency to approach full employment equilibrium. Flexible wages and prices alone do not eliminate the destabilization produced by exogenuous shifts in animal spirits, as is the case with a single market. The demand for factors is dependent on profit expectations and reflects the dynamic relationship between wage rates and the prices of goods. Coordination between prices and wages is essential for the successful performance of all market economies since their ratio determines the real wage (W/p) and profits.

The direct result of greater flexibility of wages and prices is more rapid rates of inflation and deflation, greater fluctuations in real wages, and greater countercyclical variation in real interest rates. This results in greater variability in and greater uncertainty about the future behavior of prices, incomes, real wages, and the change in aggregate demand (AD). This increased uncertainty would greatly increase business risk and lower investment demand. Countercyclical variation of real interest rates raises the variability of cyclical fluctuations in income and output. Keynes argued the unintended result of more stable money wage rates would be more stable price levels, and a corresponding reduction in uncertainty about future profits.[1]

To demonstrate that AD deficiency and not wage inflexibility was the central problem of macroeconomics, in the *General Theory* Keynes adopted most of the standard neoclassical assumptions: perfect certainty, perfect mobility, perfectly competitive markets, diminishing returns and increasing marginal costs, and derived the familiar upward-sloping aggregate supply (AS) relationship for the economy. By denominating all variables in wage units, he was able to show that even perfectly flexible wages would not assure full employment, when the underlying cause of unemployment is AD deficiency.[2] In his 1939 rebuttal of Tarshis's and Dunlop's claim that imperfectly competitive supply-side market conditions were necessary for involuntary unemployment, Keynes expanded his *General Theory* argument to demonstrate that effective demand can occur at any level of employment.[3]

In the real world money wages are far from perfectly flexible. In most countries money wages are extremely sticky downward, due to "implicit contracts" that evolve in all long-term relationships. Price-setting firms are never sure of the future demand, for their product. Nevertheless they must somehow estimate their future sales proceeds, before they can mark up their prices. In the face of an unknown future, firms are unable to calculate their future marginal revenue schedules, and cannot "maximize" profits. As developed in Chapter 12, firms mark-up prices above unit costs in an attempt to achieve a "target" rate of return on equity, assuming a conservative level of future aggregate demand. Non-service firms also hold inventories to meet unanticipated increases in future demand.

In fix-price economies changes in inventories play a critical signaling role. For all storable goods, the first signal to a firm of an increase or decrease in ΔAD is a fall or rise in inventories. As soon as a fall in inventories is noticed, firms immediately replenish their stocks by ordering more goods from their suppliers and by increasing output. In oligopolistic markets firms hold inventories and build-in excess capacity to ensure their future supply will be adequate for most unexpected increases in demand, and also to deter new firms from entering the industry.

Keynes insisted that in all market economies the level of output was effectively constrained not by scarcity, but by the lack of effective demand. But he was unable to demonstrate analytically the underlying reason why AD was typically insufficient. His attempt to explicate the demand-led process of income change using comparative static equilibrium analysis was ultimately unsuccessful. First assumed an initial "equilibrium" position where AD was equal to AS, planned saving was equal to planned investment and there was no tendency for income to change. In response to an exogenous increase in ΔAD, he argued that an unanticipated fall in inventories would stimulate an increase in output, which would then induce more consumption spending, and lead to a "multiple" increase in income. The economy would eventually find itself in a new equilibrium position, where ΔAS was equal to the now higher ΔAD and planned saving was equal to the now higher level of planned investment. In response to an exogenous fall in AD, the multiplier process would operate in reverse. AD and AS would both decline by a multiple of the reduction in exogenous spending.

But as previously argued, comparative static equilibrium analysis is not applicable to complex adaptive systems. In CAS change is continuous and "equilibrium" positions are never observed. Keynes introduced the term "animal spirits," to characterize the ever-changing non-quantifiable processes determining agents' expectations about other agents' expectations about unknowable future events.[4] He distinguished short-term expectations, which were inductively based on recent experience and so continually in flux, from long-term expectations, which were made deductively and changed much less frequently. Expectations of the unknown future are weakly held and strongly influenced by the perceived views of others. Due to the phenomenon of crowd psychology they are likely to change by larger amounts.[5]

In the fix-price sector firms are price-setters and quantity-takers. Prices are set by firms at stable markup over historic unit costs in the attempt to earn a target rate of return on capital. For all firms that are quantity-takers, current output is always demand-constrained. The level of output is determined by what Keynes termed "Effective Demand" and is now termed "Aggregate Demand" for currently produced final goods and services (C + I + G + X − M). So long as firms are quantity-takers, AS changes one-for-one with changes in AD. So long as average money wages do not increase more rapidly than the growth rate of average labor productivity, unit labor costs and prices remain constant in closed economies. So long as unit costs and markups remain constant, changes in AD leave prices and the "core" inflation rate unchanged. The "core" inflation rate is equal to the excess of the average rate of increase in money wages over the rate of growth of average labor productivity.

Over longer periods relative costs and relative prices also change, reflecting differences in wage and productivity growth rates in different sectors. But so long as the average rate that money wages increase does not exceed the average rate of labor productivity growth, the rise of prices in sectors where productivity growth is below average will be broadly offset by the fall of prices in sectors where productivity growth is above average, and the price level will remain broadly stable.[6] The rate of change in nominal GDP is jointly determined by the rate of change in real output ($\dot{y}$) and the rate of inflation ($\dot{p}$). The change in wage rates, average productivity, and ULCs (and in open economies the change in import prices) jointly determine changes in the inflation rate. The change in real aggregate demand (ΔAD/p) determines the change in real output ($\dot{y}$) and employment ($\dot{N}$).

In the absence of cost inflation, the optimum role of the monetary authorities is simple and unambiguous. In economies where prices rise only after output has reached the economy's full employment capacity, the authorities are able to manage AD to simultaneously assure full employment and price stability. The reason full employment output is so rarely observed in the real world is because as unemployment falls, worker bargaining power increases, and money wage increases exceed the rate of labor productivity growth. Such cost inflation typically occurs **before** the economy's potential full employment output level is reached. In response to current and expected future wage increases, central banks (CBs) are forward looking, and raise BR preemptively in an attempt to reduce anticipated inflation. In response AD declines, inflation and unemployment rates increase, and the growth rate of the economy falls, producing the unpleasant phenomenon known as "stagflation."

Excess demand inflation occurs only very rarely in peacetime, when AS is disrupted by shortages of food, oil, fuel, or other flex-price goods. When a rise in flex prices is expected and becomes incorporated into the demand for credit and the supply price of labor, and money wages rise to keep real wages constant, excess demand inflation soon leads to cost inflation. This is why CBs, if they are to be successful in reducing inflation, must be credible and able to influence agents' expectations of future inflation. With cost inflation prices do not rise in response to increases in AD, but in response to actual and expected future increases in unit labor costs, whenever money wage increases exceed average labor productivity growth.

Market economies characteristically operate well below their production-possibility frontiers. Scarcity is not the central problem in developed economies. The central problem is ignorance, which stems at root from the complexity of resource coordination. Businesses can never accurately estimate their future demand, and so never know the "appropriate" level of investment spending that maximizes their future profits. Businesses must be conservative in their estimate of future sales, since unsold goods have a cost and reduce business profits. In consequence most developed economies are characterized by less than full capacity utilization and both open and disguised involuntary unemployment.

Keynes insisted that market economies do not tend to self-equilibrate at a full employment level of output. He proceeded to invert Say's Law and argued "demand creates its own supply." In Keynes view the Achilles' heel of capitalism was that AD was characteristically insufficient to purchase the economy's potential full employment output. He also attributed AD deficiency to insufficiently expansionary government AD management.

The chief goal of CB monetary policy is price stability. CBs are constrained in their ability to reduce BR and expand AD, because to achieve stable prices they must undertake pre-emptive policies to prevent money wages from increasing at a rate in excess of average labor productivity growth. If CBs operate under an "inflation targeting" regime, they must assure the economy is in "internal" and "external" balance before they can undertake expansionary policy and lower BR.[7] In most countries there are very strong political, ideological and sociological forces that support conservative AD management policy. Inflation is centrally about conflict over the distribution of income. Excess supply of labor serves to keep workers disciplined, off the streets, and "in their place." Such conditions are generally regarded with approval by business elites who through ownership of the media are able to create a "zietgheist" that leads voters to support polices that are not favorable to the self-interest of labor but to the self-interest of capital.[8]

14.2 IS–LM analysis and the BR–AD diagram

Post Keynesian economists have embraced endogenous money and exogenous interest rates for about 30 years. Nevertheless the IS–LM diagram with its explicit assumption of monetary exogeneity and interest rate endogeneity, remains widely accepted by most mainstream economists and continues to appear in most money and banking and macroeconomic textbooks. Most central bankers, financial market participants and financial journalists now (2005) fully recognize that the supply of credit money is endogenously credit-driven, and is not controlled by the CB through the monetary base-multiplier relationship of the textbooks.

Post Keynesians have long insisted that interest rates do not adjust to equilibrate saving and investment, or the supply and demand for "loanable funds," as the textbooks maintain. BR is now widely recognized as the key instrument of monetary policy, exogenously set by the CB to achieve its stabilization targets and held constant between monetary policy meetings. CBs spend much effort in attempting to forecast the future direction of the economy, which at root is driven by changes in unquantifiable "animal spirits." CBs are explicitly forward-looking. They adjust BR based on their expectations of the future state of the economy. By a bank arbitrage process, BR determines the level of all other short-term market rates. Long-term rates are arbitraged over time, and reflect the capital markets' expectations of the levels of BR that the CB will set in the future, plus a positive maturity premium reflecting differences in maturity, risk, and time preference among debtors and creditors.

The academic profession currently seriously lags practitioners in the teaching of endogenous money. In IS–LM analysis the upward-sloping LM curve, defined as all positions where the demand for money is equal to the supply of money is based on the assumption that CBs set the money supply as their exogenous policy instrument through the high-powered base-money-multiplier relationship. Once the money supply is recognized as endogenously credit-driven and BR is recognized as the CBs exogenous instrument of monetary policy, the LM curve becomes a horizontal line at the BR set by the CB.[9]

The IS curve, defined as all positions where planned saving is equal to planned investment, is also false but for different reasons. Saving is the accounting record of investment, so actual saving is identical to actual investment at every level of income, interest rate and time period. Planned saving is never equal to planned investment and the IS curve is a nonsense relationship. The implied message of IS–LM analysis, *"changes in the money supply cause changes the level of interest rates and income,"* represent a reversal of the "true" direction of causality between money and income. It provides a classic example of the "reverse causation" error resulting from the confusion of identities with behavioral relationships.

In short, IS–LM analysis is confusing and false as well as nontransparent. As a guide to understanding the interaction between money, interest rates, prices and incomes, IS–LM analysis is a misleading fiction and should be banished from the textbooks. S = I is an accounting identity true at every level of income. The downward-sloping IS curve is instead a portrayal of the AD relationship in interest rate-output space. The underlying truth buried in the downward-sloping IS curve is that AD is inversely related to the level of interest rates. The downward sloping IS curve is an important mainstream acknowledgement that AD is inversely related to BR.

A downward-sloping AD relationship is contrary to the positive empirical relationship observed between changes in BR and changes in investment and consumption spending. But the econometrics of the AD relationship in interest rate-output space must be re-examined. Once BR is recognized as the CB's exogenous policy instrument, whose level is discretionarily and pro-cyclically set over the cycle, it can be clearly shown AD is a downward-sloping function in interest rate- output space.

In Figure 14.1 the BR set by the CB is measured on the vertical axis, and AD is measured on the horizontal axis. The slope of the AD curve represents the interest-elasticity of AD. The position of the AD curve shifts right and left over the business cycle with changes in "animal spirits." In period t, BR set by the CB (BR^t) is associated with a particular level of aggregate demand (AD^t). As BR is reduced towards zero, AD expands as BR asymptotically approaches the horizontal axis. When firms are price-setters and quantity-takers, output, is demand-driven and changes in AD produce an identical changes in GDP.

Figure 14.1 illustrates why output in market economies is typically demand-constrained: *Central banks typically set BR at too high a level (BR^t) to achieve a full employment level of AD. CBs fail to set BR at a sufficiently low level (BR^F) to increase AD to the full capacity-full employment level of output (Y^f) of the economy.* This simple insight is of utmost importance for understanding monetary policy.

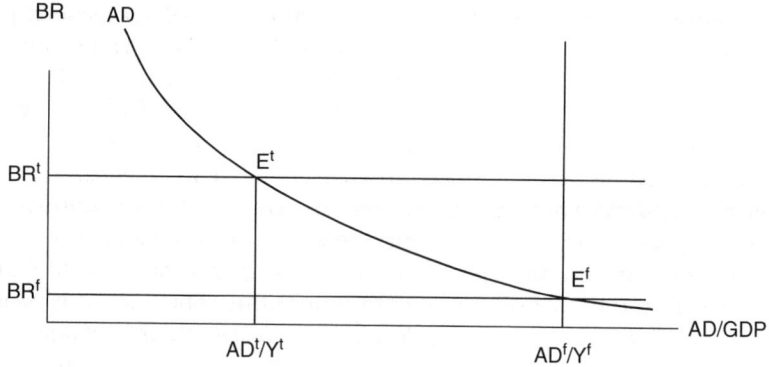

Figure 14.1 The BR–AD diagram

Chapter 15 examines the various economic-historical-ideological-sociological-institutional reasons why CBs have an aversion to cheap money and why they typically set interest rates at too high a level to generate full employment AD. It will be argued that so long as economies are demand-constrained, *the primary goal of the monetary authorities should be to reduce BR to the lowest level consistent with stable prices and zero excess demand inflation* (BR^F). *Lower rates and cheaper money are generally in the public interest.*[10]

Figure 14.1 is comparative-static equilibrium analysis, and purports to solve for the "equilibrium" level of aggregate income that occurs at different rates of interest (e.g. E^t and E^f). But the use of comparative static equilibrium methodology has been explicitly rejected as false and misleading for the analysis of complex systems. Figure 14.1 must therefore now be reformulated in terms of process analysis to determine the *future change in aggregate demand* (ΔAD) associated with the *current level and the current change in the interest rate* set by the CB.

14.3 Process analysis: the BR–ΔAD diagram

If economies are in fact typically demand-constrained, why do so many CBs have a bias in favor of tight money? CBs are typically mandated by governments to attempt to achieve price stability, full employment, and rapid growth as their stabilization targets. Since economies are complex adaptive systems, to understand more comprehensively the role of interest rates and finance in economic growth it is necessary to replace comparative static equilibrium analysis with process analysis. The goal of process analysis is to elucidate how complex systems behave over calendar time, and if possible predict future ordinal changes in the variables considered. Process analysis examines the process how deficit spending is financed, and how AD and AS change over the short run.

In process analysis all variables must be dated. No attempt is made to discover future "equilibrium states." Process analysis takes the current value of all variables as given (predetermined), and attempts to explain the ordinal change in variables over the shortest period for which data are available. Economies consist of slow-changing and fast-changing variables, so different goods differ widely in the time period over which change occurs and is measured. For variables in the National Income Accounts (NIAs) the chronological time unit is one quarter or one year, depending on the country and data availability. For prices of most individual goods the time period over which change occurs can be measured over a much shorter period, monthly, weekly or even daily. For homogeneous financial assets traded on well-organized markets with very low transaction costs, the time unit over which change occurs and is measured may be extremely short: one hour, one minute or even instantaneously in continuous time.

If process analysis is to have substantial explanatory power, ordinal change in variables must be measured over the shortest time period over which data are available. In well-organized financial markets for equities, foreign exchange and a host of financial derivatives, trading and price changes occur continuously whenever the market is open. When transactions cost are a very small proportion of the value of the transaction, the successful prediction of even extremely small ordinal percentage changes in price can exceed transactions costs and yield a profit. Agents in such markets continuously speculate and trade about future short-run price movements, and prices move continuously whenever the market is open. Changes in current prices reflect changes in wealth-holder expectations of future prices. The successful prediction of the future ordinal change is possible by the experienced agents who are able to recognize consistent order and patterns in past transactions. For all assets where trading is continuous, any price pattern that is discerned is immediately exploited by speculators, and reflected in changes in the current market price.

In such markets current prices equal markets participants' collective expectation of the price in the subsequent period, outside a small range determined by transactions costs. When the current price is equal to the markets' expected price in the next period, the expected change in price will be zero after allowing for transactions costs. For fast-changing variables it is possible for experienced speculators to forecast ordinal changes in the next transaction with some confidence based on observed behavior. But it is not possible to forecast accurately ordinal changes over very short chronological periods such as one hour, since these prices represent the net cumulative change of thousands of interdependent individual transactions. When future changes in price cannot be known in advance, the market is termed "efficient." But such markets differ from "inefficient markets" primarily because price changes can be measured much more frequently in calendar time. Many transactions occur over very short calendar periods such as one week, one day, one hour, or even one minute. The complexity of summing a series of interdependent dynamic changes is enormously amplified, and the cumulative change is unpredictable. But if transaction costs are sufficiently low, leverage can yield profits from very slight predictive advantages.

Comparative static equilibrium analysis is not merely useless for complex systems, it is actively misleading.[11] Macro-economic variables have no tendency to approach any future "equilibrium" level or growth rate. Changes in autonomous spending have no determinate "multiplier" effect on future income. When firms are price-setters and quantity-takers, the short-run rate of change in prices is largely predetermined by changes in past costs. For the economy as a whole the change in AD determines the change in AS apart from unintended changes in inventories.

Economies never approach any "equilibrium" position, where "planned" saving is equal to "planned" investment. Change is continual, unanticipated, and exogenously and endogenously generated. Actual saving is identical to actual investment since saving is the accounting record of investment. But planned saving is never exactly equal to planned investment, except by accident. Providing inventories remain unchanged at their target levels, and there is no quantity rationing, the change in AS (ΔAS) is equal to the change in AD (ΔAD) over every period.

The BR–ΔAD diagram of Figure 14.2 is the BR–AD diagram of Figure 14.1 revised for process analysis. The level of BR is measured on the vertical axis. The current level of AD (GDP) is taken as predetermined on the horizontal axis so the origin denotes a position of zero change in AD. Positive or negative changes in AD from its current value ($+/- \Delta AD^{t+1}$) are measured to the right or the left of the origin. The time unit is the shortest period for which change in GDP is recorded, one-quarter for developed countries, but one year for many developing economies.

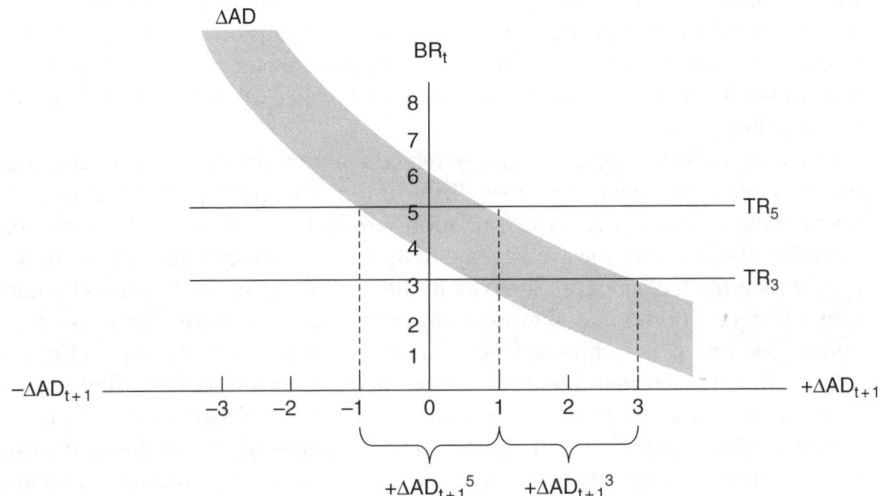

Figure 14.2 The BR–AD diagram

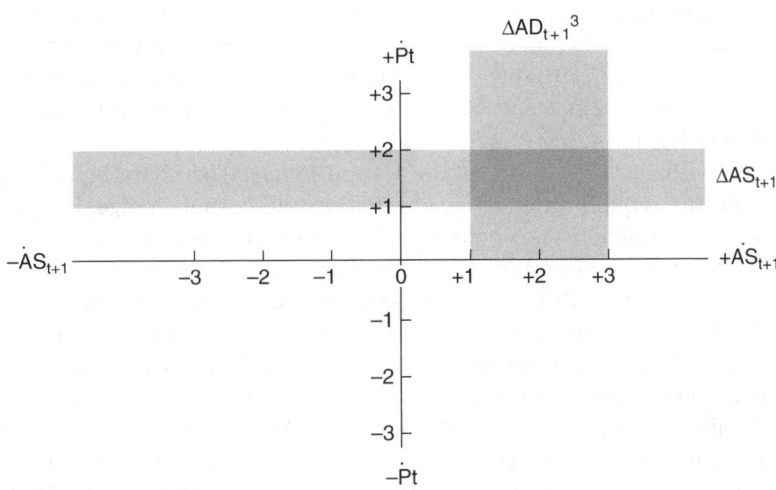

Figure 14.3 The AD–AS diagram

In Figure 14.2 the downward-sloping fractal AD's relationship illustrates the expected change in aggregate demand in the next period (ΔAD_{t+1}) is inversely related to the level of Bank Rate in the current period (BR_t). In complex systems all relationships are time-dependent, and exhibit only "demi-regularities." The current level of Bank Rate (BR_t) is associated with a fractal band of changes in AD over the subsequent period (ΔAD_{t+1}). The (ΔAD_{t+1}) curve is a fractal band that takes up space not a single-valued determinants relationship. The width of the AD band denotes the variability of the demi-regularity characterizing different complex relationships. The AD band shifts rightward during periods of expansion and leftwards during periods of contraction, induced by changes in (nonmeasurable) animal spirits. The level of BR_t is varied procyclically by the central bank (CB) in the attempt to hit its future policy target.

In Figure 14.3 the aggregate supply relation summarizing the price-setting and quantity-taking behavior of business firms in the subsequent period is a horizontal fractal band (ΔAS_{t+1}). The "core" inflation rate in the current quarter is predetermined by the excess of the average rate of increase in money wages above the average rate of growth of labor productivity in the previous quarter.[12] Increases in money wages in excess of the rate of growth of average labor productivity raise unit costs and prices, unless accompanied by a squeezing of business markups. Ordinarily firms maintain their markups and pass on increases in unit costs in higher prices. The rate of change in unit costs determines the "core" inflation rate. Changes in "animal spirits" in the current quarter directly change aggregate demand (ΔAD_t), not the current "core" inflation rate (P_t) since there are a large number of complex influences on prices and the inflation rate, is a fractal band ΔAS_{t+1}.

The position of the ΔAS band depicts the expected "core" inflation rate (shown between 1 and 2 percent) in period ($t+1$) predetermined by the change in unit costs in period (t). The inflation rate is largely independent of changes in aggregate demand (ΔAD) in the current period. The position and interest-elasticity of the ΔAD band, and the BR set by the CB in Figure 14.2, determine the change in aggregate demand in the subsequent period (ΔAD_{t+1}) in Figure 14.3. When the CB sets the level of BR at 3 percent, the expected change in AD in the sets segment period (ΔAD_{t+1}) (shown as 2 percent with a fan range of 1–3 percent in Figure 14.3) is derived from Figure 14.2.

The deeply shaded intersection of the AD and AS fractal bands in Figure 14.3 does not denote any "equilibrium" range of inflation and output change. It represents the change in inflation (1–2 percent) and output (1–3 percent) is expected in period (t) to occur in period (t+1).[13] Changes in output are demand-determined (ΔAD_{t+1}) by "animal spirits" and the level of BR. Changes in prices are cost-determined (ΔAS_{t+1}). The "core" inflation rate is equal to the excess of the average rate of wage inflation over the average rate of labor productivity growth.

"Animal spirits" (agents' expectations of other agents' future expectations) vary pro-cyclically over the cycle, and shift the vertical ΔAD relation rightward and leftward. The CB varies BR pro-cyclically over the cycle in pursuit of its stabilization goals. When the CB expects the ΔAS relation to shift rightward, it raises BR. When the CB expects the ΔAD to shift leftward, it lowers BR. Both the timing and the ordinal and cardinal change in BR are at the discretion of the CB.

The CB's "Policy Reaction Function" summarizes how the CB has changed BR in the past in response to deviations of the economy from its stabilization targets.[14] The CB's "Policy Reaction Function" is now termed the "Taylor Rule" (TR) after an important paper by John Taylor which successfully empirically described the past rate-setting behavior of the Federal Reserve System.[15] In Figure 14.2 the Taylor Rule TR is drawn as a horizontal line at the BR set by the CB (BR_t). As shown when the CB sets BR at 5 percent (TR_5), the expected change in AD (ΔAD) over the subsequent quarter is zero, with a fan range from -1 to $+1$ percent. When the CB sets BR at 3 percent (TR_3), the expected change in AD (ΔAD) over the subsequent quarter is +2 percent, with a fan range from +1 to +3 percent. In complex adaptive systems all relationships are time-dependent and exhibit only "demi-regularities."

14.4 Process analysis: the ΔBR–ΔAD diagram

Bank Rate is the CB's chief policy instrument, which is changed discretionarily and instantaneously in the pursuit of the CB's policy targets. The theoretical reasons why changes in AD (ΔAD) are inversely related to changes in BR are outlined in section 14.5. Most simply stated, the problem in analysing complex systems is that the *ceteris* never remain *paribus*.

Whenever interest rates are changed, it is necessary to decompose the change in AD into the change associated with the *level* of Bank Rate, and the change associated with the *change* in Bank Rate. Unfortunately there is usually insufficient information to distinguish the effects of the *change* in Bank Rate on AD, from the effects of the *level* of Bank Rate on AD. When Bank Rate is changed more frequently than once a quarter, the effects of the change in Bank Rate on AD cannot be empirically estimated, since GDP is only measured quarterly.

In Figure 14.4 the Taylor Rule curve is drawn for a 1 percent increase in the BR when the economy is expanding ($+\Delta TR_E$) and 1 percent decrease in BR ($-\Delta TR_R$) when the economy is contracting. Increases in BR are associated with reductions in AD, and reductions in BR are associated with increases in AD. The implicit assumption, which on the surface appears perfectly reasonable, is that *ceteris paribus*, AD remains unchanged in the absence of a change in BR. But this ignores that changes in "animal spirits" are directly related both to the change in AD and in BR. As was shown in Figure 14.2 in a business cycle the expected change in AD is zero only under an extremely restrictive set of assumptions: BR must be set exactly at 5 percent, if AD is to remain constant. But "animal spirits" change pro-cyclically over the cycle, irrespective of the level of BR. In the real world the change in AD is not primarily a function of the change in BR. AD rises when the economy is in an expansion phase, when the CB raises BR. AD falls when the economy is in a contraction phase when the CB reduces BR. As a result AD empirically varies *positively* rather than *inversely* with changes in BR.

The problem is that even when BR is held constant AD shifts pro-cyclically due to shifts in "animal spirits." Figure 14.4 does not illustrate the general case. It is valid only for the particular assumption that the current level of BR is set at the particular rate (5 percent in Figure 14.2) that keeps AD unchanged. Such an unrealistic

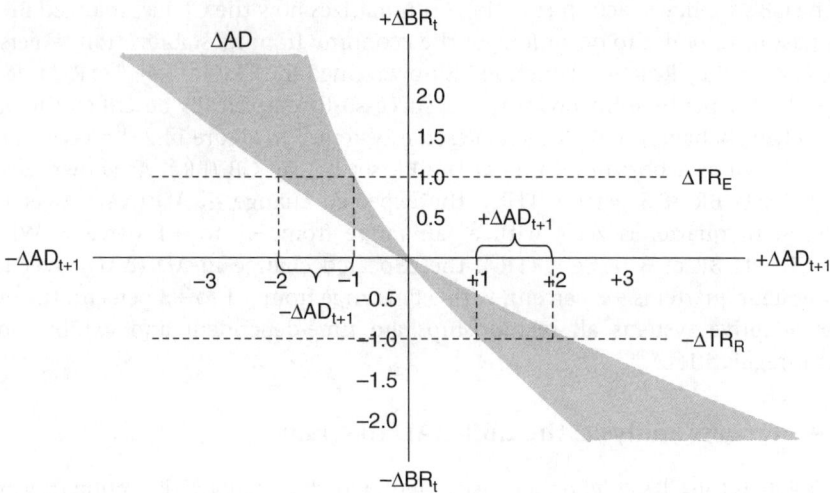

Figure 14.4 The ΔAD–ΔBR diagram

assumption must be imposed if AD is to remain unchanged over the cycle, and ΔAD is to be negatively related to the change in BR. However unobserved shifts in "animal spirits" cause the ΔAD relation to shift pro-cyclically over the cycle. Both the position and the shape of the change in aggregate demand band (ΔAD) and the change in BR, are highly time-dependent over the cycle.

Figures 14.5 and 14.6 illustrate how the ΔAD relation shifts rightward during expansions (E) and leftward during recessions (R). Even when the interest elasticity of AD is very substantial, as shown by the high elasticity of the fractal AD band in expansions in Figure 14.5, this will not generally result in an inverse relation between changes in AD and changes in BR. Due to CB countercyclical monetary policy, changes in BR (ΔBR_t) may be regarded as a proxy for the CB's expectations of changes in animal spirits and of future changes in inflation, output and AD (ΔAD_{t+1}).

The effects of a change in interest rate on AD will be substantial whenever the interest-elasticity of AD is high. But because changes in BR are a proxy for changes in "animal spirits," *changes in AD are positively correlated empirically with changes in Bank Rate*. BR and AD fall together in recessions and rise together in expansions. The empirical relationship between changes in AD and changes in BR is positive whenever BR is varied pro-cyclically over the business cycle. CBs shift BR pro-cyclically, so changes in BR are a proxy for the CB's expectations of changes in "animal spirits." As a result the estimated empirical relationship between changes in interest rates and changes in investment spending and AD is typically *positive* in both expansions and recessions.

The BR–ΔAD and ΔBR–ΔAD diagrams are shown in Figures 14.5 and 14.6 in periods of expansion (AD_E) and recession (AD_R). During expansions the change in AD_E is positive, and CBs raise BR. Expected returns on investment projects are high due

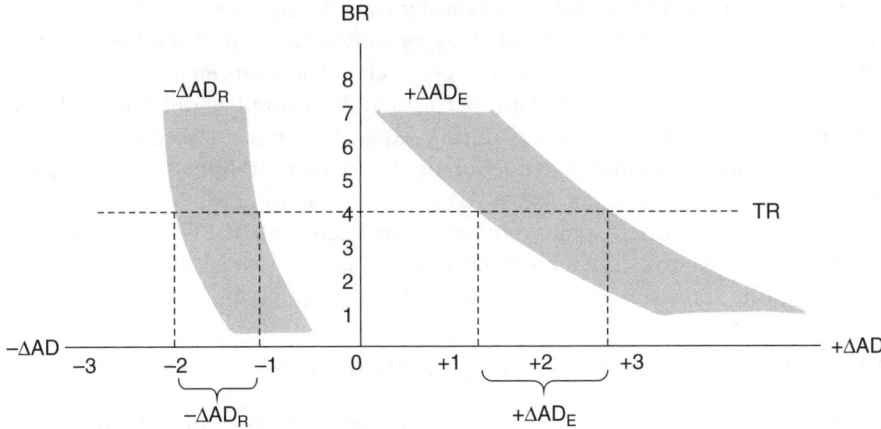

Figure 14.5 The BR–ΔAD diagram

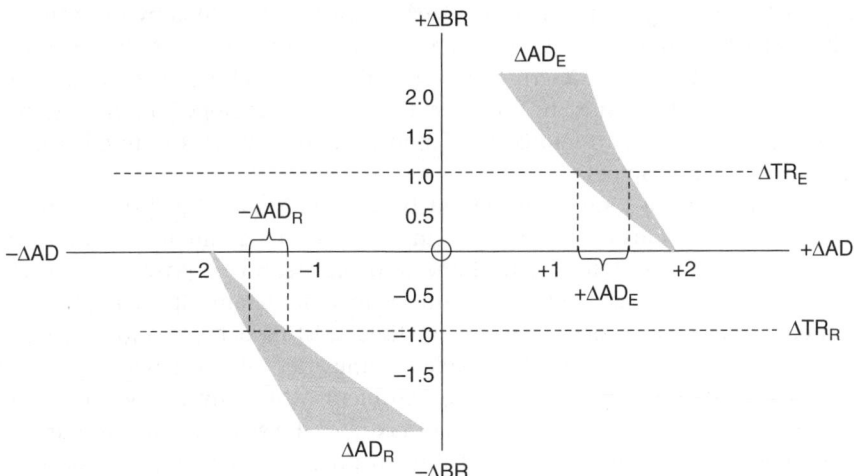

Figure 14.6 The ΔBR–ΔAD diagram

to expected increases in future ΔAD and accompanying higher capacity utilization. The demand for investment increases and becomes more responsive to changes in interest rates, as shown by the more interest-elastic BR–ΔAD$_E$ band. During recessions expected returns on investment projects fall, AD and capacity utilization rates decline, and CB's lower BR. The demand for investment falls and becomes less responsive to reductions in interest rates, shown by the less interest-elastic BR–ΔAD$_R$ band.

Figure 14.6 shows how the ΔBR–ΔAD diagram shifts pro-cyclically over the cycle. During expansions the ΔAD relationship expands (shifts right), and CBs raise BR. During contractions the ΔAD relationship declines (shifts left), and CBs reduce BR in all economies. CB's vary BR pro-cyclically over the business cycle. The inverse effect of interest rate changes on AD may be substantial as indicated by the high interest-elasticity of the ΔAD_E and the ΔAD_R relationships in Figure 14.6. But the observed empirical association of an increases in BR is simply a diminution in the rate of expansion of AD ($+\Delta AD_E$) during expansions not an absolute decrease. Similarly during recessions a reduction in BR is empirically associated with a diminution in the rate of decline of AD ($-\Delta AD_R$) not an absolute increase. Even when the interest elasticity of investment is extremely high, the effects of a change in interest rates on investment are typically outweighed by the pro-cyclical shifts in "animal spirits," investment, and AD as shown in diagrams 14.5 and 14.6.[16]

14.5 The interest elasticity of aggregate demand

The recognition that the level of short-term interest rates is a direct instrument of CB monetary policy and that CBs can affect the level of long-term rates by changing investor expectations of future short-term rates opens up whole new expectations for monetary policy. It had been thought that the level of real interest rates was largely beyond goverment control, exogenously determined by real forces of thrift and productivity. But as seen Keynes was very critical of the view that real interest rates were determined by real forces behind the supply and demand for loanable funds. In the *General Theory* he developed an entirely new theory of interest, and attempted to demonstrate interest rates were determined solely by monetary factors.

Interest rates have long been viewed by economists as the "price of time." Providing expectations are given, reducing the level of nominal rates raises the current market value of all financial and tangible assets that provide ownership rights to future pecuniary and non-pecuniary income streams. Reducing the level of interest rates enables debtors to reissue their existing debts at a lower interest cost, and to increase their net disposable income after interest payments. This is particularly important for the central government, which invariably is the economy's largest debtor. With a given level of tax rates the government can purchase more public goods when the interest burden on debt obligations is reduced. A reduction in interests rates raises the ratio of deficit spending as a share of GDP that governments can service at existing tax rates. Reducing the level of interest rates reduces the interest (carrying) cost of all long-lived investment and consumer goods that have been previously financed by the issue of debt. By reducing the level of interest rates, CBs reduce the rate that all future income streams are discounted, raise wealth values, and increase the total utility of all wealth-owners. There are a number of powerful theoretical reasons why changes in aggregate demand (ΔAD) are inversely related to the level of interest rates. At the limit AD would expand indefinitely if BR were reduced to zero, and the cost of borrowing and debt issue were eliminated.

One obvious problem is that if CBs were responsive to political pressure, they might be tempted to pursue short-term populist policies, reduce interest rates towards zero, and increase the current utility of all existing wealth holders, in order to gain poliical support. This would eventually result in an inflationary expansion of AD, and in the long run would raise inflation, result in higher interest rates, and reduce wealth owner utility. This is the main reason why in all countries Governors of CBs are appointed, not democratically elected. Many richer wealth owners have an underlying fear that populist politicians would be tempted to attract votes by setting interest rates at too low a level and generate AD inflation, to the long-run detriment of wealthowners.

Keynes' central vision was that market economies were demand-constrained. Once it is recognized that the level of short-term interest rates is set by the CB, the underlying reason why market economies are demand-constrained becomes obvious. AD is insufficient to generate a full employment level of output, and economies will typically remain below their production-possibility frontier, when CBs set interest rates at "too high" a level. The reasons why CBs set interest rates "too high" to achieve full employment AD are explored in depth in the next chapter. But it is very important to fully understand the multiple reasons why lower interest rates are expansionary. The following discussion enumerates 16 distinct reasons why a lower level of BR results in a higher level of AD and permits economies to operate closer to their production possibility frontier.[17]

1. Business firms rank all prospective capital projects by their expected rate of return, in their attempt to achieve a target rate of return on investment. To maximize share prices, they accept all projects whose expected risk-adjusted rate of return exceeds their estimated cost of capital. The latter is conventionally viewed as the weighted average of their cost of debt and equity capital. The inverse relationship between interest rates and investment spending is summarized by the "marginal efficiency of investment" (MEI). This plays the central role in explaining the volume of investment spending in macroeconomic textbooks.

2. The CB directly sets BR, the overnight wholesale rate at which bank reserves are provided. By a process of bank arbitrage, all short-term market rates are held equal to BR, correcting for all perceived differences in maturity, marketability, risk and returns in kind. Long-term interest rates are determined in a similar arbitrage process, and held equal to the average level of expected future short-term rates at each particular maturity. The long-term rate falls when capital markets anticipate BR will be reduced in the future. A lower cost of capital directly induces firms and governments to expand investment and undertake more investment projects, until the cost of capital exceeds expected risk-adjusted rate of return.

3. Asset values are equal the discounted present value of all (pecuniary and non-pecuniary) future income streams that accrue to the asset-owner. As a result their value is inversely related to the rate that the expected future income streams are discounted. Lower discount rates (R) result in an increase in asset values (V) in proportion to the maturity of the income stream and so raise wealth-owners total utility. The market value of financial assets with a constant expected income stream that extend *indefinitely* into the future varies inversely with the change in the discount rate [$V = X/R$]. The market value of financial assets with expected returns that extend a finite distance into the future vary less than inversely with the

change in the discount rate, depending on their maturity. The value of financial assets with expected future income streams expected to grow at the rate (g) (>0) vary more than proportionately with the change in the discount rate [$V = X/(R - g)$]. If the discount rate falls below the long-run expected growth rate of the economy, the market value of land, equities and any long-term rights to perpetual income streams will increase indefinitely.

4. Reductions in interest rates create capital gain income for all wealth-owners by raising the market prices of all assets. Even if assets undergo no real physical change, but simply experience price revaluation, the resulting "unearned" capital gain income represents an increase in command over real resources that is identical to "hard earned" labor income and "unearned" interest, rent and dividend property income. Increases in wealth values are necessarily utility-producing. Reductions in BR result in increases in wealth values and so in the total utility of wealth-owners, in proportion to the quantity and maturity of their assets. All wealth-owners are made better off by a reduction in the level of interest rates, since they then have command over a greater amount of real resources, in proportion to their existing wealth ownership and its maturity.

5. A reduction in the level of interest rates reduces the cost of borrowing of all debtor units, and leads to an improvement in their total utility. Past borrowers are able to refinance their outstanding debt at lower interest costs. The reduction in debt service costs results in a direct increase in disposable income. This is particularly important for the central government, which generally is the largest debtor in the economy.

6 Creditors are made worse off by a reduction in interest rates since their total current interest income is reduced. But the result of a reduction in interest rates is not a zero sum redistribution of given income streams and wealth values between creditors and debtors. Creditors are made worse off by lower rates of return on their investments. But they are simultaneously also made better off by increased capital gain income and increases in wealth values, due to the rise in the price of their financial and real assets.[18]

7. The increase in the capital value of long-lived reproducible capital assets gives an immediate signal to producers of such assets to initiate additional production. Additional units will be produced so long as the discounted present market value of the asset exceeds the replacement cost. This results in an increased demand for labor and other factors of production, and an increase in household's total net worth.

8. A reduction in interest rates reduces the carrying costs of debt to all owners of previously produced houses, apartments, and all other capital structures that yield pecuniary or non-pecuniary income. Investors considering the purchase of such capital projects are now willing to undertake additional investment, since the interest cost of new borrowing has been reduced. A reduction in rates is analogous to a reduction in the price of all lumpy assets purchased on credit. Agents are able to purchase a greater quantity of real and financial assets with a given income, and are able to obtain finance for them more cheaply. The expected income plus the

capital appreciation then exceeds the interest cost by a larger amount. As a result the rate of capital appreciation required for the projects to be undertaken is reduced.

9. Lower interest rates have the effect of raising the discounted present value of all structures and other real tangible assets in proportion to their expected maturity. Prospective purchasers are faced with the prospect of greater expected future discounted present values, and greater capital appreciation of existing assets. As a result a lower rate of capital appreciation is required to justify the interest expense of additional investment projects. Investment in housing in all economies is the sector most responsive to reductions in long-term interest rates.

10. In all open developing economies, a reduction in BR reduces the interest rate differential between the domestic rate and the lower rate prevailing in the center economies. This reduces short-term capital inflows, and in all flexible exchange rate regimes causes the exchange rate to fall, reducing the deficit or increasing the surplus in the current account. Lower domestic interest rates cause the exchange rate to depreciate, raising the domestic price of imports and reducing the foreign prices of exports. An increase in domestic rates has the opposite effect. For small open economies monetary policy has substantial effects on the inflation rate and on the rate of growth of real output through its to impact on capital flows and the exchange rate.

11. As BR approaches zero, so long as financial markets anticipate the rate will be maintained at the new lower level into the future, asset values and the ΔAD relation will increase. As BR is reduced towards zero, asset values theoretically approach infinity. Bank prime lending rates will have a positive floor level even when BR approaches zero. Bank lending rates are administered to cover the costs of financial intermediation by maintaining a spread of the lending rate charged over the cost of funds.

12. As long-term rates approach zero, the present value of all indefinitely lived assets (land, equities, and consuls) rise indefinitely. For all financial and tangible assets representing a claim to a growing income stream their market value may be expressed as: $V = X/(r-g)$ where: V = asset value, X= nominal income stream, r = real discount rate, and g = real growth rate of the income stream. When the CB reduces the level of real interest rates (r) below the long-term expected real growth rate of the economy (g), the present value of X increases indefinitely. This creates the underlying conditions for a speculative "rational bubble." The discounted present values of land and stock prices can rise indefinitely, and may reach "bubble" levels.

13. The $V = X/(R-g)$ relationship places a positive floor to the real interest rate, that CBs ignore at their peril. For all perpetually-lived assets like land and equities, as the real discount rate (R) is reduced towards the expected real growth rate of the asset's expected future income stream (g), asset prices increase indefinitely.

14. The level of interest rates affects the amount of volitional consumption and saving as well as the amount of volitional investment. As previously

demonstrated, most total saving in an economy is not volitional, since saving is the accounting record of investment. An increase in volitional saving (abstinence) implies a reduction in current spending on consumption, and so a reduction in AD.

15. Volitional savers may be grouped into two groups: target savers and residual savers. Target savers save with the "target" of acquiring sufficient resources to purchase a specific asset, for example, a house. For target savers a reduction in interest rates increases the amount that must be volitionally saved, since the funds saved accumulate at a lower rate. But most savers are non-volitional residual savers, for whom saving occurs because they do not spent all of their current income. Lower interest rates reduce the price of present goods in terms of future goods. This may induce residual savers to increase current consumption in response to a fall in interest rates. But if the increase in consumption spending is less than the increase in their income, their residual saving will increase.

16. Classical economists regarded saving as a volitional decision and viewed interest rates as the price of time. A rise in interest rates reduces the cost of future goods in terms of present goods, and a reduction in interest rates raises the cost of future goods in terms of present goods. Lower interest rates induce investors to purchase more capital goods, because their cost of future goods has fallen. But lower rates also induce residual savers to allocate a greater proportion of their income to the purchase of consumption goods, since their current income and wealth is higher. A reduction in interest rates increases the demand for both investment and consumption goods. As interest rates approach zero borrowing to acquire investment goods and consumer durables will increase indefinitely, so long as agents have a positive time preference (prefer present to future goods), and believe the sky will not fall in the future.

14.6 The Japanese conondrum

The Japanese economy presents a disturbing dilemma for monetary theorists. The case has been made that the reduction in BR is an extremely powerful instrument that permits CBs to stimulate aggregate demand. Yet after the crash of the stock market in 1990 the Bank of Japan gradually reduced the discount rate to zero, but was completely unsuccessful in stimulating AD. If low interest rates are of such importance for AD, why were cheap money and zero interest rates so ineffective in Japan over the post-1990 decade?[19]

Until the stock market crashed in 1990 the Japanese economy was widely hailed as the world's most striking economic success story. In the 45 years from 1945 to 1990 the economy grew at an average rate of 6 percent, resulting in an unprecedented 50-fold increase in GDP. This rapid growth over such a long period permitted Japan to attain a level of per capita GDP second only to the United States. During the 1980s, in response to a growing current account surplus with the United States the Bank of Japan gradually reduced the discount rate from 9.0 to 2.5 percent, in an attempt to reduce the rate of appreciation of the Yen. The

Japanese economy maintained its rapid growth pace over the 1980s. But by the end of the decade the low interest rate policy combined with rapid GDP growth and stable prices led to the development of a classic asset bubble in equity and land values.[20] The level of real long-term interest rates had been reduced below the expected real long-term growth rate of the economy. This laid the foundations for an enormous asset bubble, whose lingering effects are still painfully evident today.

The market value of long-lived income streams, particularly land and stock prices rose indefinitely. This increase in asset values created huge capital gain income which propelled individual net worth and overdraft facilities to unprecedented heights. In response to the easy money policy of the 1980s, many business firms were faced with a negative cost of capital. Banks have an incentive to lend as much as possible when asset prices are rising since the market value of their collateral rises. The increase in equity and land values served to justify huge increases in bank lines of credit to businesses and households. Japanese banks loaned billions of Yen on projects, which with hindsight wisdom were based on wildly over-optimistic expectations. The asset boom became self-fulfilling. Land prices, stock prices and balance sheets rose continually, and asset values, overdraft commitments, bank loans, net worth, and land values rose to astronomical heights.[21]

The Bank of Japan raised the discount rate from 2.5 to 6.0 percent from 1989 to 1991. Unfortunately the result was not a soft landing. The sharp rise in interest rates precipitated a stock market collapse which led to massive structural adjustments for the economy. In 1990 stock prices spiraled downward in apparent "free fall."[22]

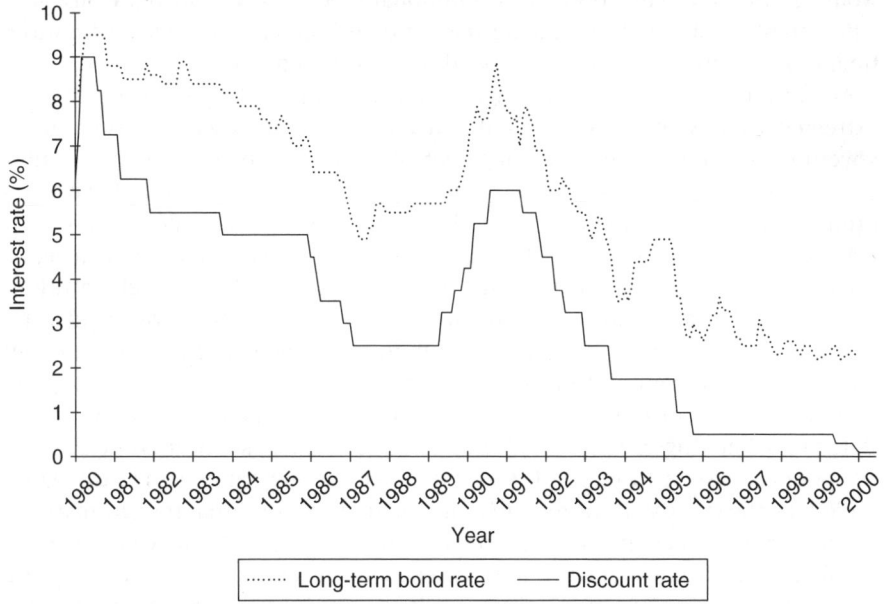

Figure 14.7 Interest rates, 1980–2000
Source: International Financial Statistics Yearbook (2000).

The year 1990 was an extremely painful experience for Japanese investors. Stocks fell by more than 50 percent, and rapidly approached their pre-bubble 1985 values. This crash in share values led to huge drops in individual and firm net worth, producing a crash in "animal spirits," and exceedingly negative expectations about the future of the economy.[23] As the value of their assets declined, economic agents learned to their dismay that a large proportion of their disposable income, net worth, and credit lines had vanished with desperately alarming prospects for how they were to survive retirement.

After the bubble burst the Bank of Japan rapidly reversed its stance. Over a two-year period from 1991 to 1993, the discount rate was reduced in a series of short steps from 6 to 2 percent. In 1996 the discount rate was dramatically reduced to 0.5 percent, and in 2000 was finally lowered to zero. Long-term rates fell from 9 percent in 1991 to 3 percent in 1995. By 2000 the long rate had fallen to 2 percent and monetary stimulation appeared exhausted. Several well-known economists concluded that Japan was mired in the infamous "liquidity trap." "Monetary policy [has] become ineffective, because [the Bank of Japan] cannot push interest rates below zero."[24]

In spite of the Bank's reduction of short-term interest rates to zero AD did not respond. Over the 1990s investment fell both absolutely and as a percentage of GDP in every year, except 1996. Business and households became increasingly anxious about further falls in asset prices. Consumption spending shut down as agents frantically attempted to build up liquid reserves. Negative demographic change reinforced expectations that National Net Worth and National Income would continue to fall, stimulating additional precautionary saving. Households when questioned stated that the purpose of their high current saving ratio was to finance their future consumption spending after retirement.

Apart from a brief interval of budget surpluses in early 1990–91 fiscal policy was extremely expansionary over the entire decade. Since the stock market crash, the government repeatedly injected huge deficit-financed capital expenditures none of which succeeded in lifting private spending. To date fiscal stimuli have served primarily to raise the national debt. The failure of monetary policy cannot be blamed on tight fiscal policy. Due to the very high past investment levels in response to near-zero financing costs, in the 1990s Japan found itself with huge excess capacity and low expected rates of return on new investments. The economy faced a variety of negative economic problems: excessive government regulations, very high cost of rice price supports, unresponsiveness of the economy to government monetary and fiscal stimulation, and an exceedingly fragile state of the banking system. People became increasingly skeptical of the ability of the political system to respond. Many doubted the government had the will to undertake the harsh actions required for structural institutional transformation.[25]

The familiar experience of the United States in the late 1930s when very low nominal interest rates failed to raise investment expenditures was widely attributed to expectations of future deflation, which raised the *ex ante* real interest costs of borrowing and made expansionary monetary policy impossible.[26] But unlike the US experience, when prices and wages fell by about one-third in the period

1929–33, and the average rate of deflation was 10 percent, the price level in Japan remained stable throughout most of the 1990s. CPI inflation fluctuated about zero for most of the period, and by the end of the 1990s a mild deflation of about 1 percent was experienced so unlike the US experience of the 1930s real *ex ante* interest rates in Japan were not kept apt by anticipated double-digit deflation. Due to its long average life time the housing sector in all economies is most sensitive to changes in interest rates. A large part of the key to the Japanese paradox is why in spite of the well-known cramped size of Japanese living accommodations did fail to provoke a housing boom.

Stocks are sold on well-organized markets with low transactions costs and prices rapidly adjust rapidly to reflect new information. Since new information appears randomly it was argued that stock prices follow a random walk.[27] This has now been refuted. But what is indubitably the case is that future changes in stock prices are unknown in advance. The volatility of stock prices has been much higher over the 1990s as shown in Figure 14.9, but the Nikkei index remained within a broad trading range of 14,000–20,000 (Figure 14.8). Apart from the sharp consecutive negative spikes in 1990, and the increase in volatility throughout the 1990s decade as shown in Figure 14.9 the monthly changes in stock prices was broadly similar in appearance over the entire period.

In sharp contrast to stocks, traded on well-organized national exchanges, land is the most heterogeneous of assets. Each unit of land is unique in its location. Most structures are highly specialized and exhibit novel individual features. Due to the extreme heterogeneity of real estate it is difficult to determine the true "market value" of land or houses, independent of sales transactions. Like old masters an individual unit of land or a house is within a broad band "worth what someone is willing to pay for it." Due to their heterogeneity houses are not traded in organized markets. Both land and real estate are extremely illiquid. Sellers must search and wait to find the "perfect" buyer. Real estate is characterized by high transactions costs.

It has often been argued that bubbles are more likely to develop in housing markets than in stock markets due to the much less perfect information. No two houses are exactly alike. With the absence of short sellers, optimists can keep driving prices up in selected areas. Buyers' expectations tend to be heavily based on recent trends, so a rise in prices frequently tends to boost demand further.

Japanese land prices behaved totally differently from stock prices. Since the 1991 crash land prices fell sluggishly and predictably in every year. Over the boom period from 1983 to 1991 land prices rose consistently at rates from 3 to 25 percent per year. As shown in Figure 14.10 in 1991 one year after the stock market crashed, land values commenced to fall. But in sharp contrast to stocks, the housing market never crashed. Due to their heterogeneity, illiquidity, and high transactions costs real estate transactions are relatively infrequent. Unlike stocks the price of a house or a plot of land typically changes slowly and does not continually adjust to reflect new information coming on the market. Due to land's heterogeneity, investors typically are not convinced the asking price of land reflects its "true" value. As a result extended negotiation and "price discovery" are commonly involved in housing and land transactions.[26]

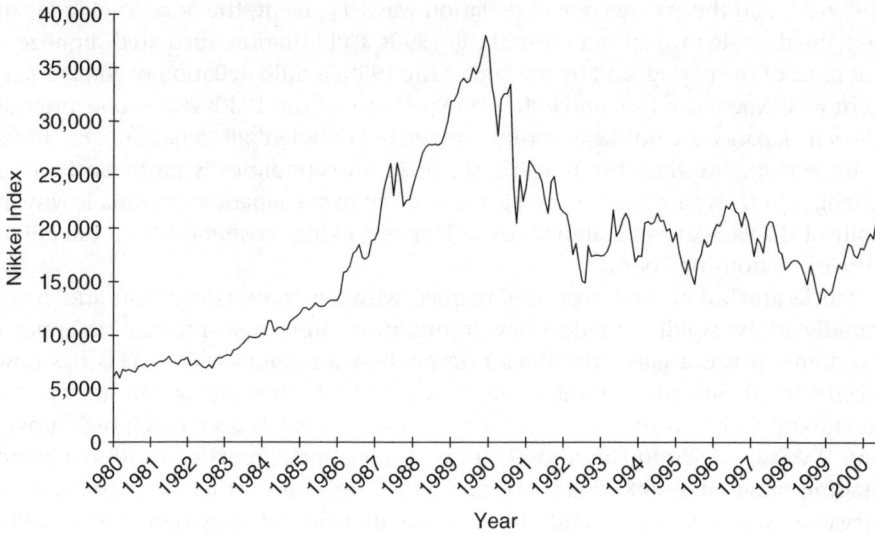

Figure 14.8 The Nikkei index, 1980–2000
Source: Bloomberg.

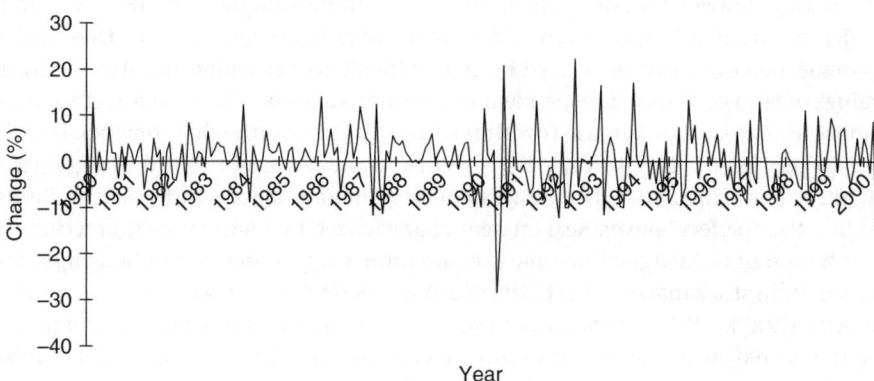

Figure 14.9 Monthly changes in the Nikkei index, 1980–2000
Source: Bloomberg.

As shown in Figure 14.11, over the decade of the 1990s housing prices fell regularly within a narrow band, at an average rate of about 10 percent for commercial property and 5 percent for residential property. Based on past experience in all years except the turning point investors could reasonably expect that the change in land values in the previous year offers a good estimate of the change in land values in the current year.

In the case of land there is an important asymmetry in investor response to expected price movements. To speculate on expected future land price increases, it

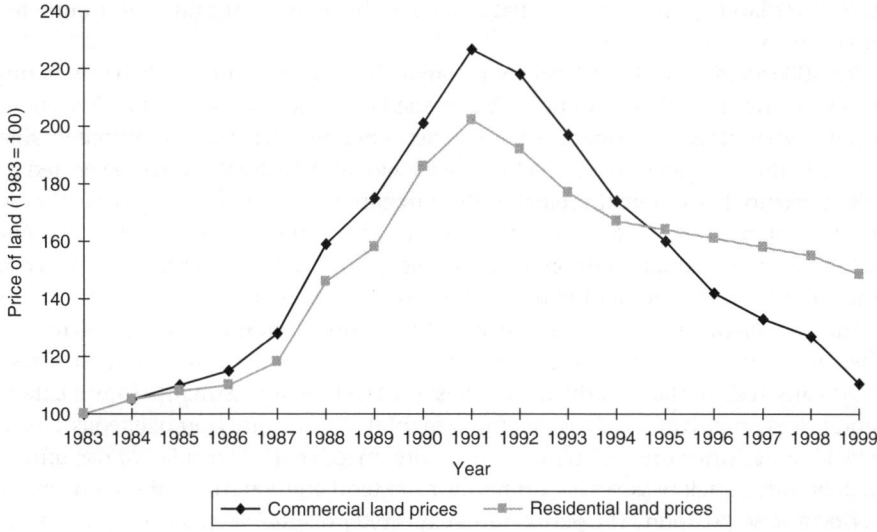

Figure 14.10 Commercial and residential land prices (1983 = 100)
Source: National Land Agency.

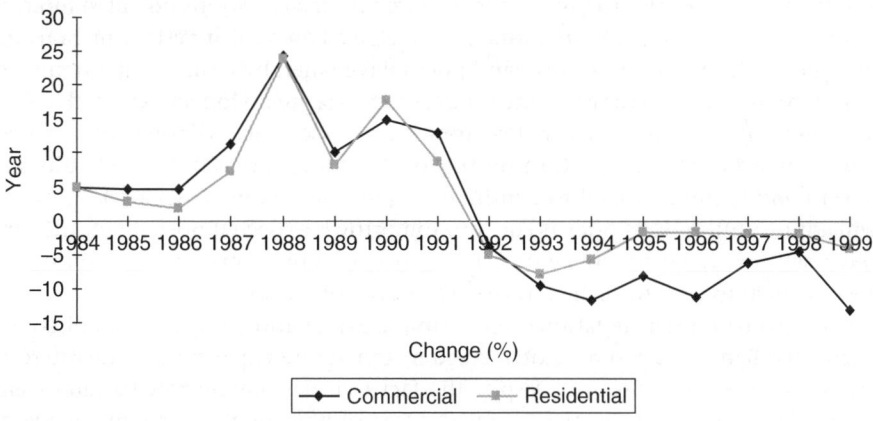

Figure 14.11 Annual changes in land prices, 1984–2000

is common practice to buy a plot of land on credit, and hold it "long" for anticipated capital gains, thus increasing the demand for land and adding to its price rise. But due to the heterogeneity of land and housing, it is not possible to borrow a similar unit and sell it "short." As a result it is very difficult to speculate against an expected fall in land prices. Since it is impossible to construct a close substitute for a heterogeneous asset, investors are unable to "short" land to speculate on a future fall in land values. When land prices are expected to fall all owners can do is hold their land off the market, that is reduce the amount supplied and hope for prices to level out.

By 2000 commercial land values in Japan had fallen close to their pre-boom levels, but residential land values still exceeded their 1983 values by 40–50 percent. From 1990 until 2003 residential land values remained well above their pre-bubble levels. Until land prices have reached a level where they are no longer expected to fall, households will remain reluctant to purchase new houses, irrespective of how low the interest cost of mortgage finance.[27] By 2005 both commercial and residential land prices had fallen to pre-boom levels, price deflation had come to an end, and commercial investment may now be expected to recommence.

Sluggish price changes operate to smooth the fluctuation of land prices, reduce their variance and so reduce the risk attached to land ownership. But they also drastically reduce the liquidity of land as a marketable investment. To the extent land prices are driven by the same fundamental forces as are homogeneous assets, whose values since they are traded in well-organized markets can fall or rise immediately, price stickiness serves primarily to extend the length of the adjustment period and so postpone the period until expected price stability is reached, and the prospect of price increases is restored.

When investors believe they will be able to purchase land at a cheaper price in the future, they have no incentive to buy land in the present, no matter how low the borrowing cost. Until land prices are widely believed to have bottomed out investors will chose not to invest in real estate. In such situations no fall in interest rates can make real estate investment attractive. Potential investors in housing have no choice but to wait until land prices have fallen by a sufficient amount so that they are expected to rise in the future, or at least are no longer expected to fall. So long as transactions costs are low, tomorrow's asset price will on average equal today's plus the expected return on the asset. As a result a fall in asset values is never confidently expected to continue. When transactions costs are low, prices will adjust until today's price is equal to tomorrow's expected price discounted by the asset's expected rate of return. The expected return on holding the asset is always equal to the "normal" return on the asset in question.[28]

Expected land price deflation offers a simple explanation why the zero discount rate of the Bank of Japan did not succeed in generating expansion in the interest-rate-sensitive housing sector. Despite the fact that *nominal* borrowing rates were reduced to very low levels, the *ex ante real* cost of housing finance remained very high, due to expected asset price deflation. Selective asset deflation has the same effect as general deflation in reducing expected real returns and in discouraging real investment in the particular sectors concerned.

Differences in mortgage finance result in large differences in the ease of borrowing and the availability of housing equity withdrawal among countries, and play a large role in translating gains in housing prices into consumer spending.[29] The quantitative importance of housing and equities in household portfolios is subject to wide variations among countries.[30] In many countries the value of mortgages as a proportion of housing values is limited by law. In most developed economies, though not in the US, the total market value of residential properties substantially exceeds the total market value of equities in household portfolios. Total household mortgage debt is 90 percent of GDP in the United States and less than 50 percent in the Euro area. This is due to the fact that in the United States the typical new mortgage debt contract is 90 percent of a home's value for an average period of 30 years. In the Euro area's less-developed mortgage systems, the typical mortgage contract is 50–70 percent of a home's value and the repayment period is only 15 years. In some countries lack of competition plus government transfer taxes result in high transactions costs for buying and selling homes (15–25 percent). This discourages owners from regarding property as a liquid asset and blunts the effect of changes in house price on spending.[31]

14.7 Conclusions: changes in Bank Rate are an excellent proxy for changes in "animal spirits"

CBs raise rates when they expect investment spending and AD to increase and lower rates when they expect investment spending and AD to decline. Changes in BR may be regarded as a proxy for the CB's expectations of changes in "animal spirits." Changes in BR may have extremely powerful inverse effects on capital spending, as illustrated by the high interest elasticity of ΔAD curves in Figure 14.5. But due to pro-cyclical movements in BR the observed empirical relationships between changes in AD and changes in BR are positive rather than negative in both expansions and recessions, was shown in Figure 14.6.

These empirical results have led many economists to conclude incorrectly that changes in interest rates have small and perverse effects on investment behavior.[32] But the true explanation for the failure to find significant negative coefficients on interest rates in investment and AD regressions and for the positive coefficients frequently found, is because changes in interest rates are a proxy for unobservable shifts in "animal spirits" which cause investment spending, ΔAD and ΔBR to shift pro-cyclical over the cycle. This explains why single equation estimates of the effect of changes in interest rates on changes in AD are hugely biased due to the "missing variable" problem. Empirically, AD is positively not inversely related to BR.

There is a separate set of reasons why economists have been unable to find strong negative empirical relationships between changes in BR and changes in AD. CBs directly administer the level of *nominal* BR. But real investment projects are influenced by *ex ante real long-term* rates rather than by current nominal short-term rates. To a changing degree inflation varies pro-cyclically, causing *ex ante* real rates to move counter-cyclically, and fall during expansions and rise during contractions. Unless the CB targets a pro-cyclical movement in *real* BR, the counter-cyclical variation in real rates reinforces the positive empirical coefficients found between changes in nominal interest rates and AD.

Monetary policy operates by changing BR and attempting to alter agents' expectations of future inflation and future ΔAD. Investment spending and *ex ante* long-term rates are dependent on capital markets' current expectations of changes in future inflation and future short-term rates. When CBs wish to lower current long-term rates to expand current AD, but can operate directly only on short-term rates, to be successful in reducing *ex ante* long-term rates they must persuade agents in financial markets that BR will be maintained at its current low level over a substantial future period. It is very difficult for CBs to succeed in such persuasion sufficiently to reduce the long end of the yield curve. The more successful CBs are in stimulating AD by lowering current interest rates, the greater will be market confidence that the economy will soon recover, and the more the market will expect that the CB will be forced to raise BR again in the future. The ability of the CB to alter market expectations of future inflation is the *sine qua non* for successful inflation targeting.

The ability of monetary policy to achieve its objectives depends on the effects of the nominal BR set by the CB on the position and interest-elasticity of the AD curve. Powerful theoretical grounds have been summarized why investment spending and AD are inversely related to interest rates. But economists have surprisingly found little empirical support for the expected strong inverse association between BR and changes in investment spending. Using single equation investment equations, regression analysis does not find a strong negative relationship between investment spending and the level of or the change in BR. The coefficient on the interest rate in investment equations is usually positive, and frequently statistically significant. Even using instrumental variables the data typically fail to reveal the theoretically expected powerful inverse relationship between interest rates, inflation and AD.[33]

"Animal spirits," the heterogeneous expectations of agents about the future heterogeneous expectations of other agents about future events, are generated by fundamental uncertainty. They constitute the central causal variable governing investment behavior and AD growth in complex economies. Regression analysis fails to find the theoretically expected strong negative relationship between interest rates and economic behavior because changes in BR act as a proxy for changes in "animal spirits." Changes in expectations, the key variable determining changes in investment spending and AD, are unquantifiable and nonmeasurable. In consequence "animal spirits," the single most important causal variable explaining investment spending cannot be quantified, and so cannot be directly entered as a causal variable in investment equations. Once changes in BR are recognized as a proxy for CBs' expectations of changes in "animal spirits," it is no longer surprising that changes in BR are positively rather than negatively empirically associated with changes in investment spending.

CBs vary BR pro-cyclically over the cycle, in an attempt to achieve their stabilization goals of price stability, full employment and rapid growth. Changes in BR may be regarded as the CBs' proxy for the change in "animal spirits." Investment spending and BR vary pro-cyclically with changes in animal spirits. Changes in investment spending and BR are positively correlated. The volatile quality of "animal spirits," and the looseness of the linkage between exogenous short-term rates and endogenous long-term rates, provide additional reasons why the empirical relationship between changes in AD and BR is time-dependent, portrayed graphically by the width of the fractal band representing the effect of interest rates on changes in aggregate demand (ΔAD) in Figures 14.4–14.16.

Changes in BR are a proxy for the CB's expectations of future changes in investment and AD over the subsequent quarter or year. As a result the change in BR is an excellent operational proxy for the CB's expectation of the future change in nonmeasurable "animal spirits." Agents' heterogeneous expectations of the future heterogeneous expectations of other agents in response to exogenous future changes are intrinsically un-measurable. Changes in BR reflect changes in the CB's expectations of agents' current and expected future changes in prices, expenditures and GDP. Once changes in BR are viewed as a proxy for the CB's expectations of the change in "animal spirits," it ceases to be surprising that changes in investment expenditure vary positively with changes in BR.

In the *General Theory* Keynes' argued that the most important goal of the monetary authorities was to set BR at a sufficiently low level to generate a level of AD consistent with the economy's full employment capacity:

> The justification for a moderately high rate of interest has been found hitherto in the necessity of providing a sufficient inducement to save. But we have shown that the extent of effective saving is necessarily determined by the scale of investment, and that the scale of investment is promoted by a **low** rate of interest provided that we do not attempt to stimulate it in this way beyond the point that leads to full employment. Thus it is to our best advantage to reduce the rate of interest to that point relatively to the schedule of the marginal efficiency of capital at which there is full employment.
>
> There can be no doubt that this criterion will lead to a much lower rate of interest than has ruled hitherto; and, so far as one can guess at the schedules of the marginal efficiency of capital corresponding to increasing amounts of capital, the rate of interest is likely to fall steadily, if it should be practicable to maintain conditions of more or less full employment—unless, indeed, there is an excessive change in the aggregate propensity to consume.
>
> I feel sure that the demand for capital is strictly limited in the sense that it would not be difficult to increase the stock of capital up to a point where its marginal efficiency had fallen to a very low figure.[34]

This chapter has argued the logical support for the proposition that investment spending and aggregate demand are inversely related to interest rates is particularly compelling. Business spending on capital goods, and household purchases of houses and lumpy consumer durable, vary inversely with the level of interest rates. The inability to find strong confirming empirical evidence for a highly interest-elastic demand for assets was explained by the strong pro-cyclical movement of changes in BR with pro-cyclical changes in unquantifiable "animal spirits." Changes in BR are an excellent proxy for the CB's expectations of the change in "animal spirits."

This recognition renders empirical estimates of low interest elasticity of investment spending extremely suspect. The special case of Japan where a zero BR completely failed to revive AD may be explained as due to the huge crash in "animal spirits," which led during the 1990s to the expectation of persistent deflation in land and housing markets. Unlike equity prices, land prices were prevented from falling by the banks' desperate price-supporting efforts to stabilize land values and ward off bankruptcy, aided by a widespread concern about the negative net worth of the banking system, and the impossibility of shorting land. This resulted in a persistent fall in land and housing prices over a decade-long period, generated strong expectations of future asset price deflation, reducing expected real returns on land and real estate. Expected selective asset price deflation operates like general deflation to raise the *ex ante* real cost of borrowing when deflationary expectations persist.

In the absence of an effective incomes policy, most CBs have more concern for the inflation rate and the goal of price stability than for the unemployment rate and full employment. CBs are the only government institution explicitly responsible for price stability. In developed economies CB inflation targeting over the past decade has proven highly successful in reducing inflation. But this attrition process is typically quite lengthy. The costs of additional unemployment in terms of foregone output have been extremely high. In several developing countries the social costs of additional unemployment have been judged unacceptable, and CBs have been forced to acquiesce to wage increases well above productivity increases. The resulting rate of inflation is regarded as the lesser of two evils.

In developed economies tight money has been successful in achieving dramatic moderation of wage increases, largely via conventional Phillips Curve (PC) effects. This success has chiefly involved reducing the bargaining power of labor unions by raising unemployment rates, and weakening unions' ability to push up wages. The PC is in fact alive and well. Wage moderation remains the fundamental prerequisite for price stability.

15
Monetary Policy: Non-Volitional and Volitional Saving

> An act of individual saving means—so to speak—a decision not to have dinner today. But it does not necessitate a decision to have dinner or to buy a pair of boots a week or a year hence, or to consume any specific thing at any specific date. Thus it depresses the business of preparing today's dinner without stimulating the business of making ready for some future act of consumption. It is not a substitution of future consumption demand for present consumption demand—it is a net diminution of such demand ... Moreover, the expenditure of future consumption is so largely based on present experience that ... [an act of saving] may reduce present investment demand as well as present consumption demand.
>
> John Maynard Keynes, 1936: 210

> The justification for a moderately high rate of interest has been found hitherto in the necessity of providing a sufficient inducement to save. But we have shown that the extent of effective saving is necessarily determined by the scale of investment, and that the scale of investment is promoted by a *low* rate of interest, provided that we do not attempt to stimulate it in this way beyond the point which corresponds to full employment. Thus it is to our best advantage to reduce the rate of interest to that point relative to the schedule of the marginal efficiency of capital at which there is full employment.
>
> John Maynard Keynes, 1936: 375

> Thus the remedy for the boom is not a higher rate of interest but a lower rate of interest! For that may enable the boom to last. The right remedy for the trade cycle is not to be found in abolishing booms and thus keeping us permanently in a semi-slump; but in abolishing slumps and thus keeping us permanently in a quasi-boom.
>
> John Maynard Keynes, 1936

15.1 The central role of monetary policy in AD growth

When nonbank agents borrow money from (i.e. sell their own IOUs to) other nonbank units, in exchange for previously accumulated money balances, the money supply does not change. The increase in current spending by borrowing units is roughly offset by the decrease in spending on current output by lending units. When the money supply is constant, there is no accompanying long-run growth in AD, unless the income velocity of money has a positive secular drift. When banks undertake no new net lending, the supply of credit money remains constant. Changes in AD and income reflect primarily changes in the income velocity of money.

So long as the income velocity of money remains stable, the proportional change in AD is well-explained by the proportional change in the money supply. The income velocity of money approximates a random walk with drift, so over the short run velocity is path-dependent, and its level drifts pro-cyclically. Secular increases or decreases in income velocity cause AD to grow at a rate above or below the rate of change in the money supply.[1]

When net new bank borrowing is positive, the percentage change in AD is equal to the percentage increase in bank borrowing (net deposit creation) plus (or minus) the percentage change in income velocity. When velocity follows a random walk with zero drift, its expected value in the next period is simply its current value. When velocity follows a random walk the short-run future change in AD cannot be foreseen, even when the money supply is constant.

From the point of view of individual depositors an increase in "convenience lending" to the banking system does not imply net diminution in aggregate spending. New bank lending finances most increases in AD for investment or durable consumption goods. The increase in bank deposits associated with additional bank lending is not regarded as a "loan" to the bank by bank depositors. Depositors experience no abstinence of consumption, and suffer no sacrifice of liquidity by holding bank deposits instead of currency. For some individual depositors the period of the loan may be extremely short, even measured in nanoseconds. But for depositors in the aggregate, the non-volitional lending of currency to the banking system *ex post* is long term, the entire period over which the newly-created bank deposits remain in existence.[2]

Deposits are non-volitionally held by depositors, and result in an increase in "convenience lending" to the banking system for the entire period until the bank loans are repaid, the securities are sold from bank portfolios, or the deposits are exchanged for cash. When bank loans finance increases in deficit-spending for investment goods, "convenience lending" by depositors represents an increase in "convenience saving." When bank loans finance an increase in deficit-spending for consumption goods, "convenience lending" by bank depositors represents an increase in "convenience dissaving." When bank loans finance expenditures on previously-existing tangible or newly-created financial assets there is no increase in demand for currently produced output, and neither saving nor dis-saving occurs. Deficit-spending to acquire non-GDP assets—like equities or mortgages—reduces the income velocity of money. The affect on AD and on the level of output in the subsequent period depend on what the sellers of the previously-existing assets purchase with the newly created money balances they received in exchange, and how this impacts on the income velocity of money.

For AD to grow over time, economic agents must demand currently-produced goods and services in the current period in excess of their money income in the previous period. Such spending must be financed. Newly-created bank loans and deposits provide most of the finance that permits credit-worthy agents to net deficit spend and AD to expand. In developed economies most "saving" takes the form of increases in non-volitional "convenience lending" to the banking system and the non-volitional accumulation of corporate equities whose market values have risen. These increases in equity values are due to earnings retention by firms, and/or increases in the valuation ratios and price–earnings ratios of corporations. New bank loans finance secular increases in spending on currently-produced goods and services, newly-created and previously-existing tangible and financial assets, and previously-existing financial and tangible assets, and cause the income-velocity of money to fall.

The increase in AD in excess of the inflation rate determines the rate real output growth. When wage increases exceed average labour productivity growth, unit labor costs and prices increase with the increase in the money supply. In consequence inflation is typically attributed to the "excess" rate of money growth. But the "true" cause of inflation is not the increase in the money supply but the excess of the average rate of increase in money wages over the average rate of labor productivity growth, so unit costs increase. Wage and cost inflation can persist for long periods, without any tendency to accelerate. Keynes described this phenomena as follows:

> If there are strong social and political forces causing spontaneous rises in the money production costs of reproducible goods, the control of the price level may pass beyond the power of the banking system.[3]

Secular increases in AD are financed by net money issue created by new bank borrowing. The percentage change in AD may be decomposed into the percentage change in the money supply, plus the percentage change in velocity. In the US business demand for fixed assets is about half financed internally out of retained earnings, and half financed externally by debt issue. Business demand for working capital is externally financed by bank loans as firms draw down pre-assigned credit facilities with their bankers.

If prices are stable, the proper stabilization goal of enlightened central banks (CBs) in closed economies is to set the level of Bank Rate (BR) at a sufficiently low level to generate a level of AD equal to the full employment capacity of the economy. Since AD is negatively related to interest rates, and BR is exogenously set by the CB, the obvious policy to achieve full employment is for CBs to lower interest rates. So long as money wage growth does not exceed the growth rate of average labor productivity, even rapid increases in bank borrowing, money supply growth, employment expansion, and growth of AD will generate neither cost-nor demand-inflation. Nevertheless the persistent achievement of full employment with stable prices has proven beyond most government's capability.

There are a number of ideological obstacles to pursuing a policy of cheap money. One of the most overlooked is false economic theory. In the *General Theory* Keynes had recognized that saving was the accounting record of investment, although he failed to state this proposition with sufficient clarity. An increase in planned saving by households denotes a decision to reduce the proportion of income consumed. So long as there is no concurrent increase in investment expenditures, and the CB fails to acknowledge its responsibility to ensure full employment by lowering BR, the effect of an increase in planned saving is to reduce the level of AD and AS. Keynes' logic would be correct. The appropriate policy response by the CB to restore AD would be to reduce interest rates.

> A boom is a situation in which over-optimism triumphs over a rate of interest which, in a cooler light, would be seen to be excessive.[4]
>
> The justification for a moderately high rate of interest has been found hitherto in the necessity of providing a sufficient inducement to save. But we have shown that the extent of effective saving is necessarily determined by the scale of investment, and that the scale of investment is promoted by a low rate of interest. ... Thus it is to our best advantage to reduce the rate of interest to that point relatively to the schedule of the marginal efficiency of capital at which there is full employment.[5]

In a world in which there are only consumption and investment goods, it is obvious that saving defined as income not consumed is simply the accounting record of investment. In the *General Theory* Keynes was nearly there. He had recognized that increases in investment were always accompanied by equal increases in saving. Lower interest rates call forth greater investment and greater non-volitional savings required to finance it. But he did not completely recognize that saving is identical to investment simply because it is the accounting record of investment. There is no volitional aggregate savings function in interest rate-output space, and no tendency for lower interest rates to reduce the supply of saving. To the extent lower interest rates stimulate investment spending, lower interest rates paradoxically *increase* the supply of saving.

Due to the extreme length and depth of the Great Depression by 1936 Keynes along with most of his contemporaries had grown disheartened and exceedingly pessimistic about the efficacy of cheap money policy. He still had occasional flashes of optimism:

> It may turn out that the propensity to consume will be so easily strengthened by the effects of a falling rate of interest that full employment can be reached with a rate of accumulation little greater than at present.[6]

Nevertheless he had persuaded himself that a low level of interest rates was not, "*sufficient by itself to determine an optimum rate of investment.*" He concluded reluctantly,

> it seems unlikely that the influence of banking policy on the rate of interest will be sufficient by itself to determine an optimum rate of investment. I conceive,

therefore, that a somewhat comprehensive socialisation of investment will prove the only means of securing an approximation to full employment.[7]

Keynes recognized that any proposal for increased state participation in the economy would involve,

> a terrific encroachment on individualism. ... The authoritarian state systems of today seem to solve the problem of unemployment at the expense of efficiency and freedom.[8]

Nevertheless he persisted with his advocacy of greater government spending, because his pessimism about the difficulty of increasing private investment demand had convinced him that to escape the depression,

> a large extension of the traditional functions of government, ... (was) ... the only practicable means of avoiding the destruction of existing economic forms in their entirety, and as the condition of the successful functioning of individual initiative.[9]

Economists and CBs are both very aware that expected deflation raises *ex ante* real borrowing rates. When combined with a collapse of animal spirits deflation is likely to prevent cheap monetary policy from successfully stimulating AD. Nevertheless political economy considerations explain much of the resistance of economic and political elites to cheap money, as interest rates are reduced to zero.

> the aggregate return from durable goods would ... just cover their labour costs of production, plus an allowance for risk and the costs of skill and supervision ... it would mean the euthanasia of the rentier, and consequently, the euthanasia of the cumulative oppressive power of the capitalist to exploit the scarcity-value of capital.[10]

There are a variety of reasons why capitalist economies characteristically operate at less than full capacity output. In the presence of fundamental uncertainty about future demand, profitable firms possessing market power build-in excess capacity to ensure their future capability to meet unexpectedly large increases in future demand, to discourage entry of competitors, and to protect their domestic market share. Some workers prefer to remain voluntarily unemployed, rather than accept employment offers below their reservation wage rate.

Nevertheless the above factors cannot explain the very high levels of output gaps and very high rates of involuntary unemployment that characterize many developing economies. Keynes insisted that most economies are demand-constrained and operate for long periods under slack conditions. Under the present institutional arrangements of flexible exchange rates, most CBs do not have the ability to lower short-term interest rates towards zero since they are forced to defend the current value of their exchange rate. CBs have a natural bias in favor of creditors, and are terrified that the apparition of runaway inflation or exchange rate depreciation might occur under their watch.[11]

So long as the inflation rate is positive by reducing the level of nominal rates below the inflation rate, CB's can reduce *ex ante* real short-term rates to negative levels. If they were to succeed in persuading markets that this policy would be continued into the indefinite future, the market value of long-term claims to growing income streams would rise sharply. Increases in Kaldor's "valuation ratio" (Tobin's "Q") provide strong incentives for managers acting in the interests of their shareholders to accumulate capital goods and so increase wealth values, current investment spending, and AD. This is reinforced by increased consumption spending out of Hicksian income by all households receiving capital gains on their assets.

In the process "animal spirits" eventually recover over time. When that time comes, CBs are likely again to decide that interest rates must be raised to moderate the growth of AD and dampen increasing threats of future inflation. These expectations make it impossible for CB to substantially reduce the level of long-term interest rates. Economic growth proceeds cyclically over time. The great danger of slumps is the possibility of deflation that accompanies them. By increasing *ex ante* real rates, deflation renders even very expansionary monetary policy and very low nominal interest rates ineffective in stimulating AD.

The rate of inflation in the current production-sales period is largely predetermined by the wage increases granted and productivity increases experienced in the previous period. Since prices are administered by firms on historic average variable costs, a shift in AD induced by a change in BR has the primary effect of increasing or decreasing real output, and does not directly affect inflation. Unless the CB can induce substantial wage moderation, the resulting "sacrifice ratio" (the output foregone by reducing the inflation rate through depressing AD) of restrictive monetary policy may be considered excessive. Wage–cost inflation may have to be tolerated as the lesser of two evils.

In addition to directly reducing current AD increases in interest rates moderate future wage increases by increasing unemployment via conventional Phillips Curve effects. Lowered expectations of future profits, higher current unemployment rates, and reductions in the bargaining power of labor are the result. When labor unions are supported by pro-labor governments, and labor remains militant in its demands and continues to demand wage increases in excess of average labor productivity growth in the face of high and rising unemployment, as is the case in South Africa, the costs of restrictive monetary policy in terms of foregone output and the psychic and social costs to the unemployed is likely to be judged unacceptably high. The CB must acquiesce to inflationary wage settlements, and the government is strongly tempted to pursue time-inconsistent behavior.[12]

Investment spending is highly dependent on expectations of high future AD and profitability, what Keynes termed "animal spirits." Expectations of the unknown future are weakly held, and potentially very fragile. When "animal spirits" collapse, positive expected returns on future investment projects quickly vanish, and profitable investment projects and new investment spending can rapidly dry up. Marketable asset prices fall and Hicksian disposable income, including capital losses on equities, land and real estate, shrinks below the value of current output. Banks become more restrictive in their requirements for credit-worthiness, and the quantity of credit supplied to borrowers who are now judged too risky rapidly declines. Investment and AD can plummet and the rate of unemployment rise rapidly. All that CBs can do in response is further reduce BR.

Suppose collective bargaining over wages were centralized and social contracts between labor, business and government negotiated to ensure unit labor costs and prices remain stable. Such an institutional arrangement has been created in Singapore, with brilliant results.[13] In such circumstances the CB is able to lower interest rates sufficiently to ensure full employment and rapid growth with no fear the reduction in unemployment will lead to increases in wages and greater inflation.

"Inflation targeting" works by having the CB impose high interest and indirectly high exchange rates. The threat of open unemployment and foreign competition rather than a social contract must be relied on to moderate money wage increases. Interest rates must be maintained at a sufficiently high level to keep the economy with sufficient slack, and the unemployment rate sufficiently high, to ensure wage moderation. In the absence of a social contract, the level of interest rates set by the CB ceases to be a problem of optimal control and becomes an exercise in game theory between government, business, and the unions. If price stability is to be achieved, the average rate of growth of money wages must not exceed the average rate of growth of labor productivity in the previous period. The greater is labor's ability to raise money wages the higher must be Bank Rate. To reduce wage demands towards the average growth rate of average labor productivity, unemployment rates must be held at higher levels.[14]

In place of a social contract "inflation targeting" has been adopted by many central banks in developed economies as a guide for monetary policy to achieve and maintain credibility for low inflation.[15] The mainstream literature conventionally indentifies five channels of monetary policy trasmission.[16]

1. The Interest rate channel: A reduction in Bank Rate leads to a reduction in longer term rates providing the public is persuaded the CB will lower rates in the future. This in turn expands business investment, investment in residential housing and consumer expenditure on durable goods. This interest rate channel lies at thse core of the "Science of monetary policy from a new Keynesian perspective," which hinges on a framework based on optimizing dynamic behaviour, rational expectations, and the existence of temporary price rigidities (e.g. Clarida and Gertler, 1999).
2. The assest price channel: There is no need to focus on only one assest price. Monetary policy has important effects on the prices of equities, foreign exchange, real estate and all durable assets. Lower Bank Rate leads to higher equity prices, making investment more attractive through raising Tobin's q, and increasing investment and AD. Higher equity prices also entail increased wealth values and capital gains, which further raise consumption and AD.

3. The exchange rate channel: Lower Bank Rate brings about a depreciation of the domestic currency through the interest rate parity condition. This in turn leads to higher net exports and stronger AD. Real depreciation raises the prices of imported goods, raising the inflation rate directly. The higher price of imported inputs increases aggregate supply prices, average variable costs and the inflation rate.
4. The credit channel: Price and output effects also occur due to information asymmetries between financial lenders and their borrowers. Increased net worth reduces perceives loan risk, and improves firms' cash flows through lower interest rates on outstanding debt contracts. Banks become more willing to supply additional credit and finance additional increases in AD (Bernanke and Gertler, 1995).
5. The "expectations" channel: All variables that have intertemporal implications are determined in a forward-looking way and shaped by beliefs of how the CB will react in the future. CB announcements of future lower inflation will have desired effects only when the CB is perceived as committed to its policies. The credibility of future monetary policy then becomes central.

Not all economies react in the same way to changes in monetary policy. The effectiveness of country transmission mechanisms will depend on specific features on the economy in question. Changes in Bank Rate differentially influence various assest markets and prices, affecting spending decisions by households and firms. Each step is affected by an economy's specific features, its stage of financial development, its openness to international trade and finance, and the state of solvency of its firms and households. The size and openness of the economy determine the importance of the exchange rate channel, and the ability of monetrary policy to determine domestic interest rates. In small open economies the pass-through from exchange rate changes to domestic inflation and output and the exchange rate regime in force take center stage. The pass-through of exchange rate depreciation to domestic inflation rate varies widely in different economies.

The estimate of the inflation coefficient in Taylor reaction functions varies widely among different countries, from 0.2 for S.A. to 1.5 for the U.S.[17] In many countries the CB appears to adjust to rather than oppose inflation increases. A high degree of policy inertia characterizes most CB's reaction functions. CB's typically attempt to maximize their credibility by keeping their policies stable and systematic. The more CBs are unsure about the impact of their policies, the more do they resist changes in their current policy stance. The more uncertain the CB is about the economy's future reaction to changes in Bank Rates the greater the inertia to changing the current policy stance. Countries with explicit inflation targets have been able to significantly reduce both the level and the volatility of inflation compared with a control group of countries. But output volatility is higher in countries with explicit inflation targets. When the CB has a greater preference for inflation control, but the government cares more about unemployment reduction, both interest rates (the CB's instrument) and the public sector deficit (the government's instrument) are biased upwards. There are huge potential benefits to generating institutional incentives, such as social contracts that permit coordination between the monetary and fiscal authorities.

The underlying reason why growth rates have been lower since the demise Bretton Woods in 1970 is because central bankers, in the absence of a social contract to maintain wage increases below average productivity increases, have been compelled to pursue more restrictive monetary policies to enforce money wage moderation. In the process interest rates have been maintained at much higher levels than is consistent with full employment AD.

In the absence of a social contract, money wage increases characteristically exceed the average rate of labor productivity growth before the economy has attained full employment levels of AD. CBs must pursue restrictive policies, even in the presence of high unemployment, in the attempt to preempt further wage increases, and hit their inflation targets, CBs face infeasible policy goals. To achieve internal balance, many CBs currently pursue inflation targeting. But they are able to lower the inflation process only by depressing AD and raising unemployment rates. The necessary wage moderation can be reached only through the costly Phillips Curve procedure of imposing higher interest rates and higher unemployment rates.

International considerations are important for all countries running current account deficits. With the exception of the center economies, most economies in a floating exchange rate regime when faced with external imbalance and a shortage of foreign exchange reserves, have no option but to maintain interest rates at a sufficiently high level to keep AD below the economy's full employment capacity. This is to ensure that the demand for imports does not persistently exceed export proceeds, and the deficit in the current account does not threaten the long-run stability of the exchange rate.[18]

When the income velocity of money follows a random walk and there is no secular drift in velocity, changes in AD and income are well-explained by the change in the money supply in the previous period. Increases in AD are financed by, and largely the consequences of, net deficit spending which in turn is financed largely by borrowing from the banking system. CBs can never refuse to accommodate credit expansion. They have an overriding obligation to provide the economy with sufficient liquidity and must provide the banking system with the cash reserves demanded. All they can do is raise the Bank Rate they charge banks for required reserves. In response to increases in the demand for credit, commercial banks do not raise their lending rates independently of BR. Competitive forces operate to maintain the spread of lending rates above deposit rates, and the markup of lending rates above BR reasonably stable. The level of the spread depends on the extent banking markets are concentrated.

Saving is the accounting record of investment, so the cause of inadequate investment can never be an inadequate supply of saving. There is no tendency for income to adjust automatically to equilibrate planned saving with planned investment at full employment. Saving is identical to investment by definition. Since the CB acts as the residual supplier of system liquidity, even if interest rates are much "too high" to achieve a full employment level of AD there can never be inadequate liquidity in financial systems. CB open market purchases of securities provide the banking system with additional reserves. Since the CB is continuously targeting BR, the effects of any exogenous open market purchase must immediately be reversed, before the slack in reserve deficiency pushes market rates below their targeted levels.

Once the level of BR has been chosen by the CB the supply of bank reserves becomes completely endogenous. Interest rates rise when investment increases because CBs characteristically vary interest rates pro-cyclically as they follow their Taylor Rule. Since the level the CB selects is discretionary interest rates do not generally follow a stable procyclical relationship. Rates may fall throughout an economic expansion if they were initially set at a very high level, as occured in the United States during the 1980s. The behavior of BR and other short-term rates over time depends on the CB's policy goals and its Taylor Rule.

15.2 Internal balance constraints on reducing Bank Rate to R_F

As shown in Figure 15.1 in complex economies the ΔAD_t curve is a downward-sloping fractal band in interest rate-output space. If the goal of monetary policy were exclusively full employment and if excess demand were the sole cause of inflation, in closed economies the CB's task is both straightforward and assured of success. So long as inflation does not increase in the presence of involuntary unemployment until full employment output has been reached, the aggregate supply (AS) relationship is horizontal until full employment at which point it becomes vertical.

The Taylor Rule dictates the CB lower BR from BR_t to BR_F until all involuntary unemployment of labor is eliminated. The CB will be uncertain *ex ante* how low the future level of Bank Rate (BR_F) must fall to assure future full employment. But it need only approach its full employment target incrementally. If the change in

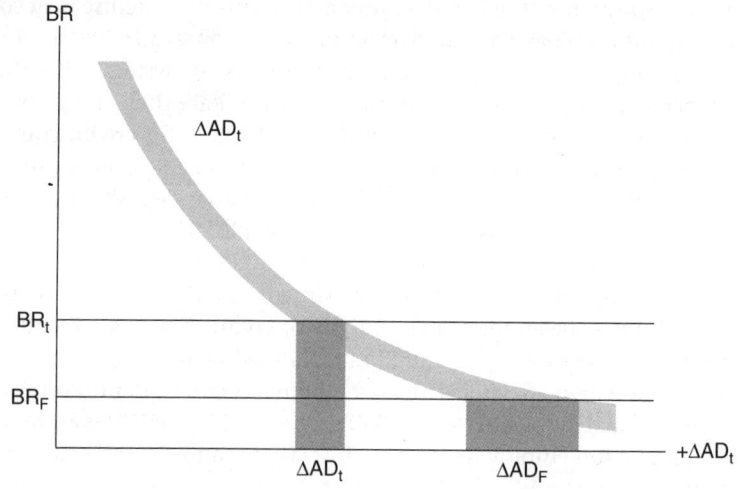

Figure 15.1 The BR–ΔAD relationship

AD is insufficient to induce full employment output, the current Bank Rate (BR_t) must be lowered to BR_F, until full employment AD is eventually attained. The expectation that future interest rates will decline is extremely encouraging for investment spending and "animal spirits".[19]

As shown in Figure 15.2, in complex economies the ΔAD_t curve is a vertical fractal band in inflation-output space, whose position depends on the state of "animal spirits," and Bank Rate (BR_t) as shown in Figure 15.1. The increase of costs and prices in each period is predetermined by the rate of wage increase and productivity growth in the previous period. When firms are price-setters and quantity-takers the AS relationship is a *horizontal* fractal band in inflation-output space. The change in AD relationship is a vertical fractal band at the intersection of BR and the ΔAD relationship. So long as income is demand-constrained, the change in output is determined by the change in aggregate demand (ΔAD). The deeply shaded intersection of the vertical AD band and the horizontal AS band in Figure 15.2 denotes the range of inflation and output growth expected in the subsequent period.

Unfortunately in the absence of a social contract, as unemployment rates decline in response to lower interest rates, the balance of bargaining power in wage negotiations shifts towards labor. Due to the development of supply bottlenecks and pockets of labor scarcity, as the unemployment rate falls firms are pushed to offer money wage increases that exceed the average rate of labor productivity growth. In response to a rise in average money wages ($\dot{w}$) above the average rate of labor productivity growth ($\dot{a}$), unit labor costs rise ($\dot{w} - \dot{a}$). Since firms set their prices as a stable mark-up over historical unit costs, the "core" inflation rate ($\dot{p} = \dot{w} - \dot{a}$) increases. In the next period inflation will equal the excess of the average rate of money wage increase over the average rate of growth of labor productivity in the current period.

Increased wage inflation generates increased price inflation, so the AS curve shifts upward. The economy soon finds itself in a wage–price spiral with prices and

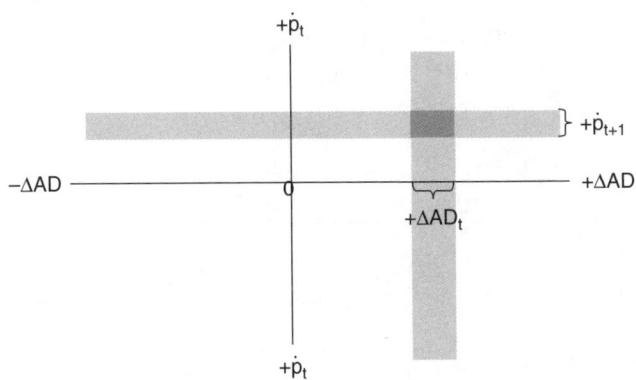

Figure 15.2 AS and AD determination of $\dot{P}$ and ΔY

wages chasing each other upwards. As the expected future rate of inflation rises the Phillips Curve (PC) shifts upwards. There is a whole family of PCs, each with a higher expected inflation rate. All the CB can do to restrain inflation is continue to raise BR, reduce AD, and permit unemployment to increase until wage growth moderates, and the price level finally stabilizes.

The combination of rising inflation and unemployment (stagflation), and the accompanying rise in the "misery index" (the sum of the inflation rate and the unemployment rate), eventually creates sufficient political dissatisfaction with inflation to force CBs to change their policy stance, and tighten monetary policy. When expectations of future inflation are well-entrenched, and both capital and labor have substantial market power, the result may be an extended period of stagflation. This occurred in the United States over the 1970s, in Europe over the 1980s, in Japan over the 1990s, and in SA since 1994. CBs have no choice but to raise BR, until the rate of growth of AD is sufficiently reduced and the level of unemployment sufficiently increased so inflationary expectations have been "wrung out" of the system deterring further wage increases. The misery index can approach stratospheric heights. But with the passage of time inflationary expectations recede and the PC curves shift leftward.

Higher rates of unemployment reduce union bargaining power, and result in lower rates of money wage increase and cost inflation. The PCs for more developed countries (PC_D), and less developed countries (PC_{LD}) are presented in Figure 15.3. In less developed countries a larger proportion of the labor force is unskilled, uneducated, and located in rural areas where there are fewer employment opportunities. In consequence in LDC's a larger share of total unemployment is "structural" and less responsive to increases in AD.

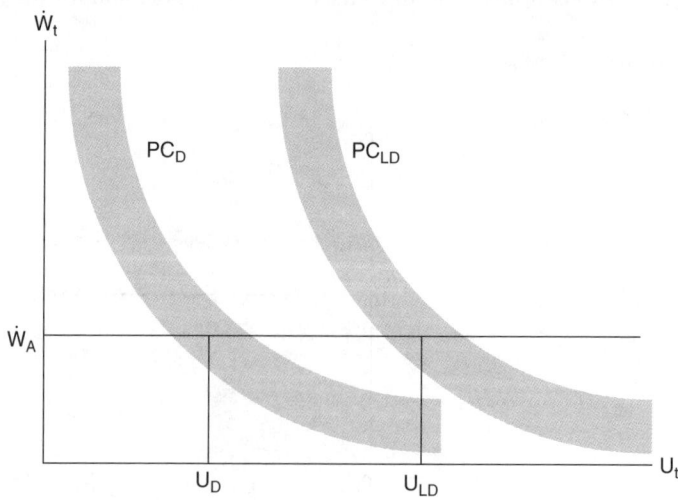

Figure 15.3 Phillips curves in developed and less developed economies

Monetary Policy: Non-Volitional and Volitional Saving 343

For less developed countries the Phillips Curve (PC_{LD}) is located further to the right, and the "NAIRU" is correspondingly higher. For price stability the CB must accept an unemployment rate of (U_D) in developed economies and (U_{LD}) in less developed countries, to assure that money wages do not increase at a rate in excess of ($\dot{w}_A$), the rate of average labor productivity growth. Less developed economies have both higher interest rates and higher unemployment rates, and are characteristically more demand-constrained than are developed economies.

In developed economies CBs are able to maintain BR at lower levels (BR_D) because the PC relationship is closer to the origin (Figure 15.3). In most developing economies, the CB must maintain BR at a sufficiently higher level (BR_{LD}) to keep the unemployment rate sufficiently high, to restrain money wage increases to the level of average labor productivity growth and so achieve price stability.

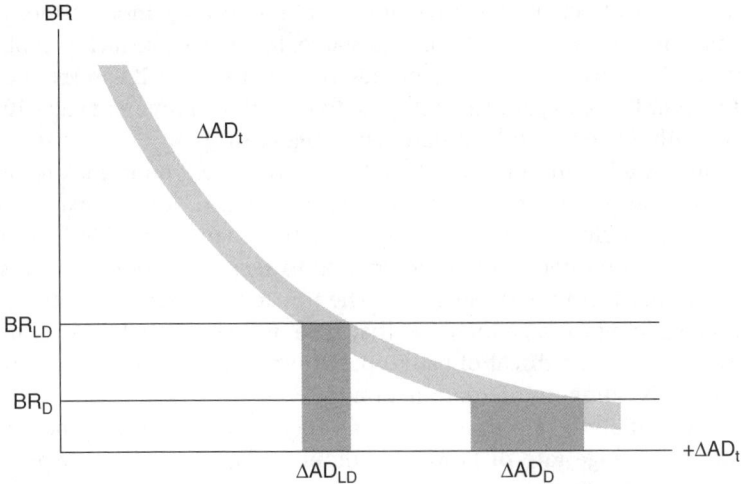

Figure 15.4 The BR–ΔAD relationship in developed and less developed economies

In many developed economies CB policy of "inflation targeting" has been quite successful over the past decade in reducing the rate of expected inflation by "squeezing inflation out of the system."[20] But the cost of such "inflation targeting" has been the redistribution of bargaining power towards business, and away from labor, and an accompanying shift in the distribution of real income and self-confidence towards management at the expense of workers.

So long as the income velocity of money remains stable changes in the rate of AD growth are paralleled by changes in the rate of growth of the money supply. Increases in AD are financed by net deficit spending which in turn is financed by new bank lending and net money creation. For the economy as a whole, the net deficits of the business, government, and "rest of the world" sectors are as an accounting relationship identical with the net surpluses of the household sector.

When bank loans externally finance investment expenditures and the economy has not reached full employment, the increase in disposable income is sufficient to purchase the increase in real output. Investment spending financed by new bank loans creates the "convenience saving" necessary to finance itself. Deficit spending for consumption goods and services increases AD in a similar fashion, but without creating an accompanying increase in AS. Bank financed consumption spending results in an increase in the economy's dissaving rate, reducing capital formation and net savings.

Additional bank borrowing, money supply growth, investment and consumption expenditure, and the associated employment expansion need not generate cost inflation as the unemployment rate falls and output expands. So long as money wage growth does not exceed the rate of average labor productivity growth, the inflation rate remains low. One way to achieve this is to have a social contract in place between business, labor, and government, as in Singapore to ensure money wage growth does not exceed the growth of average labor productivity. A social contract enables governments to attain wage moderation with the goal of full employment so prices remain stable. If a social contract is in place and wage demand equals average labor productivity gains, the CB can set short-term interest rates at BR_D and generate AD equal to the full employment capacity of the economy, without setting off a inflationary wage–cost spiral.

But in almost all economies social contracts have a very poor track record. One conservative way to ensure that money wage growth does not exceed average labor productivity growth is for a country to fix its exchange rate, eliminate all trade barriers, and rely on international competition to keep unit labor costs constant in all industries producing tradable goods. The threat of foreign competition deters firms from agreeing to wage increases that raise unit costs. Higher wage increases leave firms open to the threat of bankruptcy from imports when they raise prices above the levels ruling in international trade.

The "core" inflation rate in an economy in the current pricing period is the excess of the average rate of growth of money wages over the average rate of growth of labor productivity in the previous period. Increases in the wage bill are the largest single component of business demand for working capital. Under overdraft systems, firms are granted prearranged credit commitments by their bankers, so increases in the demand for working capital are automatically financed by increases in bank loans. The proportionate increase in the money supply equals the proportionate increase in bank loans, which in turn equals the proportionate increase in the wage bill in the current production-sales period. The rate of average wage inflation minus the rate of average labor productivity growth determines the rate of "core" inflation $\dot{p}_t = \dot{w}_{t-1} - \dot{a}_{t-1}$. Whenever wage growth is equal to average labor productivity growth, the "core" inflation rate is zero.

The increase in the credit money supply finances the increase in the wage bill. Net deficit spending, AD, and AS all vary together. The rate of growth of the wage bill, of the demand for working capital by firms, and the money supply rise *pari pasu*, raising the level of AD and AS. Conversely the repayment of bank loans causes the money supply to decline. By reducing income devoted to the purchase of currently produced goods and services, net loan repayment lowers the level of

AD. Once the supply of credit money is recognized as endogenous, the Pigou Effect (Real Balance or Wealth Effect) disappears. The nominal money supply grows at the same rate as inflation, and the real money supply is independent of the price level.

In overdraft economies increases in investment spending require no simultaneous increase in volitional saving. Increases in business investment for working capital are externally financed by increases in business borrowing from the banking system. The acceptance of newly-created bank deposits represents a non-volitional increase in "convenience lending" of fiat money to the banking system by bank depositors. The accumulation of bank deposits financing business deficit spending require no volitional abstention or deferral from current consumption, and no sacrifice of portfolio liquidity on the part of savers. The newly-created deposits will always be "accepted" by their recipients, so long as deposits retain their "moneyness" (general acceptability as a means of payment and a store of purchasing power). Prices are determined by unit variable costs. They will not rise with increases in AD unless average money wages rise more rapidly than the rate of average labor productivity growth.

The expenditure of deposits for goods has no effect on the money supply. Spending previously-existing deposits simply redistributes the ownership of existing deposits among economic agents. In the "circular flow" of money between households and firms, economic agents literally must "do nothing" when they increase their "convenience lending" to the banking system. They must simply ensure that all checks received are deposited into their accounts. Banks create money when they grant new loans, and provide newly-created deposits in exchange, which are always generally-accepted in exchange.

15.3 External balance constraints on reducing Bank Rate to R_F

Due to increasing globalization and the reduction in telecommunication costs, the value of international financial flows overwhelmingly dominates trade flows. Exchange rates are now influenced primarily by movements in financial flows, rather than by the change in the trade balance. Interest rate parity has replaced purchasing power parity as the driving force behind exchange rate movements.

The effectiveness of domestic monetary policy in open economies depends centrally on the exchange rate regime in place. Under flexible exchange rate regimes, with free capital mobility, a change in the level of domestic BR relative to rates existing in foreign financial centers can result in massive changes in exchange rates. Flexible exchange rate regimes greatly increase the importance of CBs, and the effectiveness of monetary policy. Changes in interest rates can now dramatically affect exchange rates, the domestic price of imports, the foreign price of exports, the trade balance, the inflation rate and the rate of growth of AD.[21]

Imports (M) respond to changes in domestic aggregate demand (ΔAD), while exports (X) are a function of the change in AD in the rest of the world. Increases in domestic ΔAD *ceteris paribus* raise the value of imports, and worsen the current account BOP (X − M). Unless countries use the same currency deficit countries, with the exception of the center, are faced with greater external imbalance and forced to take steps to depress the growth of AD to protect their exchange rate. Countries with BOP deficits generally raise interest rates and pursue more restrictive monetary policies to depress domestic AD, and so the rate of growth of imports. Countries with open economies are not free to set interest rates to manage domestic AD to target full employment and price stability (internal balance). When if they have a current account deficit, they have no choice but to raise short-term interest rates to protect their foreign exchanges, even when they are concurrently faced with substantial internal imbalance and high domestic unemployment.

As will be developed in Part V the requirement that most deficit countries must impose restrictive policies to protect their exchange rates imposes a huge deflationary bias on the global economy. CBs in deficit countries are compelled to raise BR and pursue restrictive policies to protect their exchange rates. But CBs in surplus countries are under no similar pressure to reduce BR and pursue expansionary policies. They are able to continue their current policy stance, enjoy their current BOP surplus and simply allow their foreign exchange reserves to accumulate, even if their trading partners are convinced their exchange rate is undervalued.

In open economies CBs in deficit countries are severely constrained to raise BR and pursue deflationary policies to depress the domestic economy. In most countries with BOP deficits, the authorities are unable to take expansionary steps to raise AD to a level consistent with domestic full employment. This would create even greater imbalances in their current account, and threaten the stability of their exchange rate. Depending on the extent labor and other factor resources are mobile, in all fixed exchange rate regimes domestic price and wage inflation will eventually fall into line with the average rates generated in the country's trading partners.

Under flexible exchange rate regimes the power of monetary policy is enormously increased. An increase in BR induces capital inflows which cause the exchange rate to appreciate until interest rate parity is restored. When BR is set above the level set in the center economies, the exchange rate will appreciate, and overshoot its expected current value until the expected rate of depreciation in the subsequent year equals the annual interest rate differential. These open economy effects are addressed more fully in Part V.

Figure 15.5 shows a situation when the country initially has an approximate balance on current account (T_0), but an increase in aggregate demand (ΔAD_o) greatly below the economy's full employment capacity output (ΔAD_F), so both the output gap and the unemployment rate are high. Suppose the CB is under considerable public pressure to reduce BR to expand (ΔAD_o) and move the economy closer towards its potential full employment output (ΔAD_F). Suppose that at the current exchange rate, the CB decides to reduce BR. In response AD expands and the economy moves towards its full employment ceiling. But the expansion in domestic demand increases the current demand for imports and worsens its current account balance (T_1). If the country continues to pursue this policy and persists unilaterally

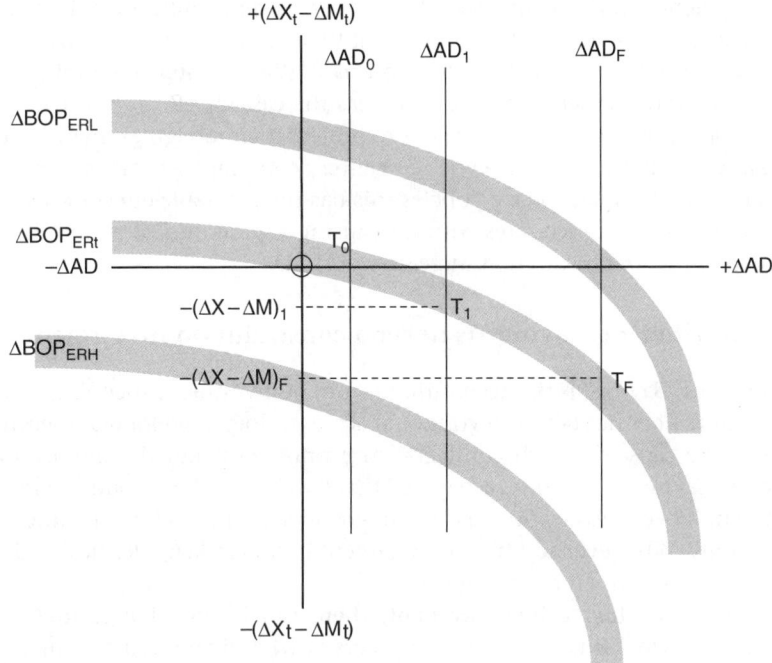

Figure 15.5 The ΔAD–ΔBOP relation in an open economy

with an expansionary policy to reduce unemployment the current account deficit (external imbalance) will increase alarmingly (T_F), threatening the stability of the exchange rate. The more AD increases, the larger will be the current account deficit as the rate of growth of imports outstrips the growth of exports. The CB will sooner or later be inhibited from further lowering BR and pursuing an expansionary domestic policy to achieve internal balance. It will eventually be forced to pursue restrictive policies to improve its BOP on current account and protect its exchange rate, and thus accept its current high unemployment rate.

When an expansionary monetary policy is pursued as BR is reduced capital outflows cause the exchange rate to depreciate (E_{RL}). If the exchange rate is permitted to depreciate, this operates to encourage exports and increase AD, and the current account balance will improve. But depending on the openness of the economy, the rise in the price of imports increases the domestic inflation rate. This sooner or later will force the CB to reverse gear and raise BR in an attempt to encourage capital inflows. It is forced to attain external balance at the expense of internal balance.

When a restrictive monetary policy is pursued as BR is increased this causes the exchange rate to appreciate (E_{RH}). By lowering the prices of imports, exchange rate appreciation reduces the inflation rate, and provides a relatively easy way for the CB to achieve its inflation target. Higher exchange rates reduce the domestic cost of imports and raise the foreign price of exports, so the current account deficit increases. Higher exchange rates (E_{RH}) reduce exports, increase imports, raise unemployment rates, and increase the current account imbalance. It is not the absolute level of domestic interest rates, but their relative differential over foreign rates that cause the exchange rate to appreciate. When center economies raise BR and pursue more restrictive policies, this has the cascade effect of forcing CBs in the developing world to raise their rates to protect their foreign exchanges, further depressing world AD. Conversely when center economics set low real bank rates and pursue more expansionary policies this has the favorable effect of permitting developing CBs to reduce rates without causing capital outflows, and to pursue more expansionary policies that increase world AD.

15.4 Insufficient "saving" is never a constraint on investment

In economics "Saving" is the accounting record of investment spending. "Saving" in economics does not denote a volitional act, as it does in colloquial speech. This has been the cause of much confusion in economics about the implications of volitional "saving." Once it is recognized that "saving" is the accounting record of investment it becomes clear there is no independent volitional saving function for the economy. Whenever additional investment is undertaken, identical additional "saving" is necessarily forthcoming.[22]

If there is no change in investment, there can be no change in "saving," irrespective of what financial behavior occurs or what financial assets are created. It is important to note that investment determines "saving," not the other way round. "Saving" does not "determine" investment. If there is no change in investment, there can be no change in "saving." If there is an increase in investment there must necessarily be an increase in "saving." If there is an increase in "volitional" saving, but no change in investment, there is no increase in "saving" for the economy unless unintended inventory accumulation occurs. The (literal) meaning of "an increase in volitional saving" is "a volitional increase in abstention from consumption." The direct result of in increase in volitional saving is a decrease in consumption, AD, AS, and nominal and real GDP.

Wealth-owner purchases of previously existing assets financed out of current income, for example stocks and bonds, although regarded as and termed "saving" in everyday speech, do not represent "saving" in economics if they do not result in an increase in investment. The purchase of previously-existing assets represents a change in the ownership of wealth, a redistribution of existing wealth claims among different agents. The purchase of previously-existing financial assets such as stocks or bonds out of current income does not represent "saving." It may, but need not, "cause" asset values to rise. Only the purchase of newly-created tangible assets (investment), or the purchase of newly-created financial assets issued to finance concurrent investment, constitutes "saving" for the economy.

Since "saving" is the accounting record of investment, investment creates its own saving. This saving may be entirely volitional, and take the form of the purchase of newly-created nonmonetary financial assets issued to externally finance deficit-spending. Or the saving may be entirely non-volitional, and take the form of the accumulation of newly-created money balances in exchange transactions, or the passive accumulation of previously-existing financial or tangible assets whose market values have risen over the period. The key point is that in economics "saving" and its accompanying asset accumulation does not denote volitional behaviour, as is implied by the verb *"to save"* in everyday speech.

In monetary economies investment must either be financed with money, or with promises to pay money in the future. Finance for investment spending may be internal or external. When the deficit-spending to acquire newly created capital goods (investment) is externally financed with bank loans and newly-created money balances, the accumulation of these balances represents an increase in "convenience lending" to the banking system. From the point of view of the economy, the increase in "convenience lending" represents an increase in "convenience saving" when the deficit-spending is directed at the purchase of investment goods, an increase in "convenience dis-saving" when the deficit spending is directed at the purchase on consumption goods, or merely the redistribution of existing wealth ownership when the deficit-spending is directed at the purchase of previously-existing assets.

Saving is identical to investment, and total surpluses are identical to total deficits, as accounting identities. AD expands whenever some agents volitionally deficit-spend (spend more than their current income) to acquire currently-produced goods and services. Total deficits are equal to total surpluses, so deficit-spending by some units must necessarily create surplus-spending by other units. If the surplus-spending results in an equal reduction in demand for currently-produced goods and services, this will offset the increase and AD by deficit-spending agents and AD will remain constant. If the surplus-spending takes the form of the non-volitional accumulation of wealth by surplus-spending agents, and does not involve any reduction in expenditure for currently-produced goods and services, there is no offsetting reduction in AD.

Changes in asset values are determined by changes in the expected future income stream accruing to the owners of the asset, or by changes in the rate at which the earning stream is discounted. Equity values change continuously over time with changes in the present value of expected future income streams. Saving is identical to investment by definition, but there is no causal relationship between an increase in volitional saving, and an increase in investment. When there is no increase in investment there is no increase in saving. An increase in volitional saving does not then result in an increase in saving, but in an equal reduction in consumption spending and AD.

When increased purchases of previously-existing assets out of current income are associated with a reduction in spending for currently-produced consumption goods, there is negative casualty between an increase in volitional saving, and an increase in investment spending. The abstention from consumption associated with the increase in purchases of previously-existing assets results in a reduction in AD. Since total deficits are equal to total surpluses, an increase in volitional saving results in a reduction of AD and unintended inventory accumulation. The short-run casualty between an increase in volitional saving, and an increase in planned investment, will be negative if firms reduce planned investment in response to perceived decreases in current consumption spending and so in future AD.

It is a popular misunderstanding that increases in investment spending *"put pressure on interest rates to rise."* But BR is set exogenously by CBs as an autonomous monetary policy instrument. There is no direct causal relation from changes in investment, to changes in interest rates. Changes in BR are solely due to CB monetary policy. Any empirical relationship between changes in investment, saving, income, inflation, or government deficits, and changes in BR is time-dependent. The relationships vary with the CB's reaction function, its expectations of where the economy is positioned in the business cycle, its macroeconomic goals, its Taylor Rule, and how rapidly it attempts to move the economy towards its stabilization goals.[23]

Depositors make no volitional sacrifice when they loan fiat money to the banking system in exchange for credit money. Most depositors do not even regard increases in their bank deposits as increases in "lending" to the banking system, but simply as increases in their money balances. So long as deposits are generally accepted in exchange, depositors are always willing to accept additional deposits. Deposits are created by new bank loans, and extinguished by the repayment of bank loans. Although the money supply is equal to the sum of individual agents deposit balances, the money supply is not determined by depositors' demand for deposits. It is determined by the quantity of bank loans extended by the banking system, the demand for net credit by bank borrowers.[24]

Volitional demand changes on the asset side of bank portfolios (loans and securities) and not volitional changes on the liability side (deposits) determine changes in the volume of bank intermediation. Agent exchange of deposit balances for currently-produced goods and services, and for previously-existing real and financial assets, has no direct effect on the money supply. Writing a check merely redistributes the ownership of the existing deposit balance among households and firms, leaving total deposits unchanged. Narrow monetary aggregates (M1) can be volitionally changed by depositor exchange of demand deposits into bank and nonbank less liquid near-money substitutes. Broad monetary aggregates (M3) can be volitionally reduced only by using existing deposits to replay bank loans, and to purchase securities held in bank portfolios.

Secular increases in AD are financed by net money issue created by new bank borrowing. The percentage change in AD over any period can be decomposed into the percentage change in the money supply, plus the percentage change in velocity. In many countries business demand for fixed assets is roughly one-half financed internally out of retained earnings, and one-half financed externally out of debt and stock issue. Business demand for short-term working capital is financed by bank loans, as borrowers draw down pre-assigned overdraft facilities with their bankers.

Bank credit represents the demand of bank borrowers to increase their money balances by going into debt, and issuing a promise to repay the money in the future (IOUs). Bankers are primarily concerned about borrower solvency. They stipulate the maximum amount they are prepared to lend to any individual borrower (credit ceiling), based on their (conservative) appraisal of borrower's ability to repay the loan.

Quantity-rationing is inherent in all lending processes. Borrowers who have exhausted their credit allocations or who have been judged noncreditworthy by their bankers, are credit-constrained, and have an excess demand for credit. Most poor households and most new and small micro-enterprises are deemed noncreditworthy by their bankers, and have no access to credit in the formal sector. All such potential borrowers are credit-constrained.

In developed economies the credit-utilization ratio, the ratio of total loans granted to total credit commitments extended, varies around 50 percent.[25] This implies that credit-worthy borrowers could, if they so wished roughly double the current volume of their loans under previously-created credit commitments, and so double the money supply. The response of the CB is confined to raising BR, holding it unchanged, or lowering it. This is why most CBs overshot or undershot their money supply targets when operating in money supply targeting regimes. This has nothing to do with CB efficiency or inefficiency, but simply reflects the interest inelasticity of the demand for bank credit.

In overdraft systems, bank loans are like credit cards. Bank borrowers and not banks decide the amount of credit they draw down. So long as borrowers remain within their credit allocations, banks are price-setters and quantity-takers in lending markets. The supply of credit money is determined by the quantity of bank credit demanded. Increases in the wage bill result in concurrent increases in bank loans and deposits. Firms administer their prices as a stable mark-up on historical average variable costs. Increases in unit labor costs and other factor costs are marked-up in prices in the subsequent production-sales period. Increases in money wages are the largest single component of factor costs. As a result changes in the wage bill are primarily responsible for changes in the money supply.

The price level and the money supply generally vary together. Increases in the money supply precede increases in the price level by the production-pricing period. The empirical finding that money "Granger-causes" inflation reflects the fact that bank loans are taken out during the construction period *before* the capital projects have been completed. The rate of inflation is "caused" by the excess of the rate of increase in money wages over the rate of average labor productivity growth, not by the excessive rate of growth of the money supply. The supply of credit money is always endogenously credit-driven.

The recognition that "Inflation Targeting" operates through old fashioned Phillips Curve effects makes the tendency for "tough" central bankers to treat relatively low inflation rates as a serious welfare reducing problem. "Inflation Targeting" operates by raising interest rates, reducing liquidity, and so reducing AD. But the measurement bias in CPI inflation in modern economies may be as high as 2 percent. In consequence AD restriction by a "tough" central banker is highly likely to be inappropriate.

Since it reduced the discount rate to 1 percent immediately after the stock market crash of 2001, the US Federal Reserve has raised the discount rate in measured steps of 25 basis points to its current level of 4.25 percent. It appears to fear that the current historically low rates in the center may result in an inflationary buildup of AD and possible overinvestment, since the current low levels of

BR are likely to prove temporary. But as long as the "core" inflation rate shows no sign of rising above 2 percent, historically unprecedented low levels of interest rates may be necessary to ensure that AD is sufficient to eliminate the output gap. There are many other countries in the world in addition to Japan, for example Switzerland, Singapore, and even the United States, with a combination of low expected returns on investment and high saving propensities, particularly if income is measured in a Hicksian sense.

For many countries historically unprecedented low levels of interest rates are likely to be necessary to maintain the high financial asset values and high investment–income ratios required for full employment AD. The Federal Reserve continues to raise BR because it believes the current levels are likely to generate future inflationary consequences. But US inflation is rising primarily because the Dollar is falling and oil and other import prices are increasing. Inflation changes tend to lag output movements by a lag of one–two years. Unit labor costs and the "core" inflation rate, the measures of inflation more responsive to AD constraint, are both now well under control. Raising BR towards more historically higher levels will operate to slow down the fall in the Dollar, and reduce import inflation. But it may result in a fall in equity and house prices from their current high levels, which could induce a withdrawal of funds from equities and houses. It will also slow the reduction in the current account deficit which reflects the huge deficit in the public sector. The expansionary effects of a loose fiscal policy may be overtaken by the restrictive effects of tight monetary policy. In this case the net effects of high government deficits may inadvertently have a net restrictive effect on AD.

15.5 The short run "exogeneity" and long run "endogeneity" of Bank Rate

A central achievement of endogenous money has been the recognition that BR is the main instrument of monetary policy, set exogenously by the CB to achieve its stabilization goals of price stability, full employment, rapid growth and current account balance. The present value of future income streams are inversely related to the rate at which they are discounted, and the market value of all private assets are inversely related to the level of interest rates. Economists have long regarded interest rates as the price of time. The control of BR permits CBs to directly affect asset values, capital gain income, investment, consumption and the level of AD.

Economists traditionally assumed the supply of saving in an economy was the aggregation of individual agent's volitional saving decisions. The amount saved was believed to be positively related to the level of interest rates.[26] Neoclassical economists attempted to "pierce the veil of money" and uncover the "real" forces determining interest rates. They concluded that the level of interest rates was endogenously determined by the intersection of an upward-sloping supply of savings function, reflecting "real" forces of time preference and thrift, with a downward-sloping demand for funds function, reflecting "real" forces of productivity and technology. As in the case of goods, the demand and supply of savings were regarded as separate and independent functions. Wealth-owners decided on the amount they wish to save, and investors decided on the amount they wish to invest.

The real interest rate was defined as the nominal rate minus the inflation rate, and was equal to the nominal rate only when the price level is stable. In the presence of inflation, the nominal rate was believed equal to the "real" rate, plus an inflation "premium" reflecting the capital markets' estimate of future inflation. The intersection of the saving and investment functions at a zero rate of inflation determined the real rate of interest. If the economy was at full employment, and the price level was stable, the resulting level of interest rate around which the system revolved was termed the "natural" rate. Lower rates of time preference, higher levels of thriftiness, and greater volitional saving were believed to result in lower real interest rates. The real interest rate was a "bribe" that society had to pay wealth-owners to persuade them to abstain from consuming their wealth.

> Everyone is aware that the accumulation of wealth is held in check, and the rate of interest so far sustained, by the preference which the great mass of humanity have for present over deferred gratifications, or in other words by their unwillingness to "wait."[27]

But by 1936 Keynes found that he fundamentally disagreed with the entire neoclassical paradigm of interest rates. He had persuaded himself that saving and investment determined the "equilibrium" level of income in an economy, not the "equilibrium" level of interest rates. Keynes gradually recognized that interest rates were determined by monetary, not by real forces. In the *General Theory* he attempted to develop an entirely new "Liquidity Preference" theory of interest. This held that interest rates were determined by wealthowners' demand to hold the existing supply of monetary and nonmonetary assets. A "Liquidity premium" was realized by holding perfectly liquid monetary.

> The rate of interest ... is a measure of the unwillingness of those who possess money to part with their liquid control over it.[28]

As stated above, in modern credit money economies CBs set BR *exogenously* as their chief instrument of monetary policy. In closed economies they have great discretion as to the interest rate they set, and when they change the rate. The recognition that the level of short-term interest rates is set exogenously by the CB as its chief instrument of monetary policy negates both the neoclassical and the Keynesian theory of interest. Even more importantly, it breaks the classical link between saving and investment behavior and the level of interest rates.

Keynes's insistence in the *General Theory* that market economies are demand-constrained may be taken as *prima facie* evidence that CBs typically err too much on the side of conservatism. They set interest rates at "too high" a level to generate AD equal to the economy's full employment potential output.[29] Today, with widespread CB independence, most CB Governors claim they have a mandate from the government to achieve long-run price stability. Their belief in the necessity of maintaining internal and external balance is derived from their desire to fulfill this mandate. It is widely believed by central bankers that price stability is a necessary precondition for successful long run economic performance. There are two separate reasons why CBs believe they must restrain AD below the economy's full employment "production possibility" frontier.[30]

First, from the point of view of maintaining "internal balance," CBs argue that price stability is the necessary precondition for both a healthy economy and a rapid rate of economic growth. To reach this goal the CB must keep AD below the economy's NAIRU (Non Accelerating Inflation Rate of Unemployment). The NAIRU is defined as the maximum level of output consistent with stable prices. As seen above, in most economies the NAIRU lies well inside the economy's maximum production possibility frontier. As full employment is approached, lower levels of unemployment raises the bargaining power of labor in wage negotiations. Firms attempt to bid skilled workers away from other firms to fill scarce bottle-neck positions. This generates money wage growth above the average rate of growth of labor productivity, and results in a rise in unit costs, and "cost" or "wage push" inflation.

Second, from the point of view of maintaining "external balance," CBs argue that AD must be maintained at a sufficiently low level to prevent persistent negative deficits in the current account. Persistent current account imbalance leads to an increasing probability of future exchange rate depreciation or devaluation, and so leads to a rise in import prices and a higher rate of inflation. Most CBs to be certain they achieve external balance, desire to maintain AD at a level consistent with a small positive balance in the current account.

As was shown in Chapter 7, saving is not an independent behavioral relationship but is equal to investment as an accounting identity. The identity between S and I does not come about by variations in the level of interest rates, as the classical economists maintained, nor by variations in the level of income, as Keynes envisaged. The vast majority of saving in modern economies is non-volitional, and takes two forms: the accumulation of newly-created bank deposits and other near-money liquid assets, and the accumulation (non-realization) of capital gains on equities and other assets whose market values have appreciated. In complex systems, planned saving is never equal to planned investment.

A rise in volitional saving denotes a decision to reduce consumption spending, and purchase additional financial or tangible assets. Volitional saving takes the form of increased purchases of tangible or financial assets. When the asset is currently-produced or currently-issued, the increase in saving and the reduction in consumption spending is identical with the increase in deficit spending on investment, so the level of AD remains unchanged. But if the asset is nonreproducible (such as land), or previously-existing (such as a used car, a house, or previous-existing financial assets), the effect of an increase in volitional saving is a reduction in current AD. Such individual saving behavior does not constitute "saving" from a National Income Account (NIA) viewpoint. The only increases in "volitional saving" that constitute "saving" in the NIA are purchases of currently-produced tangible consumer or producer durables, and purchases of currently-issued financial assets issued to finance deficit spending on real goods and services.

The attempt of agents to volitionally increase saving by reducing current consumption has a negative affect on the current level of AD. Consumption plus saving by definition exhaust total disposable income. When agents have a higher volitional propensity to abstain, this implies they have a lower volitional propensity to consume. The behavioral counterpart of volitional increase in saving is a volitional reduction in consumption. Unless the saving takes the form of internally-financed increases in the demand for currently-produced consumer and investor capital goods, AD for currently produced goods and services falls with increases in volitional saving. The vision that total saving is the sum of individual volitional saving decisions stems from a barter economy. In developed credit money economies, the vast majority of saving is non-volitional. Volitional saving constitutes only a small proportion of total saving in all modern economies.

The level of Bank Rate is an exogenous policy instrument of the CB. In economies where agents have high saving propensities and corresponding low consumption propensities, CBs must set BR at a lower level to achieve their stabilization goals. Asset prices represent the discounted present value of expected future income streams. Lower interest rates result in higher asset prices, and higher wealth values relative to income. When income is defined in the Hicksian sense to include capital gains on all marketable assets, lower interest rates result in higher wealth levels, higher capital gain income, and greater social utility. It follows that *ceteris paribus* a lower CB interest rate policy is preferable to a higher CB interest rate policy. With lower levels of interest rates, real income, real wealth and total utility are all higher at every level of current real output.

So long as the average rate of wage inflation does not exceed the average rate of labor productivity growth, unit labor costs and prices in the fix-price sector will remain constant. If the goal of price stability has been achieved, monetary policy can focus solely on the goal of full employment. In this fundamental sense, the neoclassical vision was correct. So long as CBs can be assumed to pursue **enlightened** monetary policy, and are persuaded of the benefits and desirability of lower rates, higher saving propensities become a *social virtue* and not a *social vice*. Even though in all developed economies interest rates are the exogenous policy instrument of the CB, higher saving propensities persuade the monetary authorities to reduce interest rates to lower levels, and to generate higher wealth values, higher wealth–income ratios, higher real disposable income, and higher total social utility, without creating accompanying inflationary demand pressure.

Economists finally have the knowledge to render Keynes' *General Theory* dream of full-employment price-stability prosperity realistic. The above relationship appears neoclassical—a higher propensity to save results in a lower level of interest rates. But the explanation of how this comes about is thoroughly Post Keynesian. Higher saving propensities do not *ceteris paribus* raise the supply of savings and "loanable funds," and so reduce the equilibrium level of interest rates as the neoclassical economists had believed Keynes' conclusions were correct, but over a shorter time scale, **assuming CB policy was unenlightened**. Higher volitional saving propensities, when not accompanied by a CB policy of discretionarily reducing the level of interest rates do have the negative Keynesian effect of depressing AD. If CBs do nothing, the result of higher volitional saving is a rise in unemployment and excess capacity, and a reduction in the level of real output and in total social utility. Under such behavior Keynes' view was correct.

But providing the monetary authorities are committed to stable prices and full employment and, so long as prices remain stable, are willing to set interest rates sufficiently low levels to achieve full employment levels of AD, cyclically depressed levels of AD can be interpreted as the result of higher volitional saving propensities. In such periods the monetary authorities should reduce the level of interest rates, and increase income, wealth, and wealth–income ratios, without provoking any accompanying demand inflation. **Enlightened** CBs have the responsibility and obligation to set interest rates at the lowest level possible consistent with price stability and zero excess demand. Higher saving propensities enable *enlightened* CBs to set BR at lower levels, and to realize higher levels of social utility and welfare.

So long as CB monetary policy is *"enlightened,"* lower rates of time preference and higher saving ratios become social virtues. In response to a fall in AD, *enlightened* CBs will lower BR. In consequence economies with higher levels of volitional saving will enjoy lower levels of interest rates, higher wealth–income ratios, higher levels of disposable income at full employment, and higher levels of and more rapid growth rates in real income and output. This contrasts sharply with the lower levels of AD anticipated by Keynesians from the reduction in AD associated with increases in volitional saving preferences, which follow when the CB maintains rates unchanged. Keynes was perfectly correct to emphasize the negative implications of higher saving preferences on AD. But he ignored the fact that higher saving propensities enable enlightened CBs to lower the levels of interest rates, and so create a higher full employment level of AD, and higher levels of wealth, disposable income, and social utility.

So long as CBs set the level of short-term interest rates at a sufficiently low level to achieve full employment AD, the classical vision comes into its own. Volitional saving becomes a *public virtue* and not a *public vice*. Very high levels of volitional saving preferences permit CBs the luxury to set BR at extremely low levels, without generating inflationary levels of AD. Just look at Japan! The result is higher wealth–income ratios, higher levels of disposable income, and more rapid growth rates of real GDP, all of which are utility-producing.

Keynes was correct. The goal of enlightened central bankers should be *"the euthanasia of the cumulative oppressive power of capital."*[31] In his discussion of monetary policy the *General Theory* in Keynes overlooked the inverse relationship between interest rates and the level of asset values. Whenever debt is the primary means of financing capital formation, and the level of AD is insufficient for full employment, the CB should lower BR, to encourage volitional investment, and discourage volitional saving. This has the effect of raising the level of Hicksian income, reducing the share of property income, and raising the real GDP. As the interest rate is reduced, debtors experience higher market values of their assets and their liabilities, and receive utility-increasing higher real capital gain income as the market value of their assets appreciates. The market value of their liabilities also increases but the face value of their liabilities remain unchanged, permitting outstanding debt obligations to be refinanced at lower rates. Keynes's "euthanasia" of the rentier is the precisely appropriate expression for the effects of lower interest rates on the economy.

In the case of equity securities, the situation is somewhat different. Equities represent ownership claims to a stream of future dividends that will be declared by the firm into the indefinite future. As Bank Rate is reduced the rate that future dividend income streams are discounted falls and the market value of equities rises. If CBs set the level of long-term interest rates below the expected future growth rate of the economy, this induces continuing increases in the prices of equity claims and other asset values. If the theoretical value of such streams becomes infinitely large, it can lead to the formation of "rational bubbles."

The real growth rate of the economy, and not zero, is the lower limit to the long-term level of interest rates that CBs can administer, without generating asset price inflation. If CBs set BR below the economy's real growth rate, and succeed in persuading wealthowners that these low levels of rates will persist into the future, land and stock prices can rise indefinitely with a stimulating affect on AD. But the downside is that asset bubbles will be generated, and sooner or later the CB will be forced to raise BR to deflate these bubbles. This may lead to a painfully long periods and of depressed "animal spirits" and recession.

The underlying "root" condition for "rational" asset bubbles is the fact that the CB has set BR "too low." During the bubble's expansion phase, the accompanying capital gains are exhilarating for animal spirits, for the growth of the economy, and for total social welfare. But when the asset price bubble eventually bursts, as it sooner or later must, this causes a collapse in asset values, capital losses, bankrupt debtors, nonperforming loans, negative net worth for all financial institutions who have lent against the collateral of land and equities, and an accompanying collapse of "animal spirits." Extreme damage to the solvency and health of the financial system and difficult decisions of how to divide the resulting capital losses among shareholders, creditors and taxpayers can create periods of slump, depression and stagnation, that can persist for decades. The US Wall Street bubble of 1928–29 was followed by the Great Depression of the 1930s, which lasted until war was declared in 1941. The Japanese stock market and real estate bubble of 1985–90 was followed by the long slump of the 1990s, from which the Japanese economy has still (2005) not completely recovered.

The recognition that CBs must set different levels of BR to achieve full employment in economies with different saving propensities presents a huge potential problem for all economies that wish to join a currency area, or to adopt a leading world currency such as the Dollar or the Euro.[32] Trading areas with a common currency and a common CB must have a single interest rate for all members. But as seen, countries with different saving propensities and investment prospects have different levels of BR consistent with a full employment level of AD. This suggests that countries seeking to join a trading group to finesse their external balance constraint are advised to associate with countries with similar saving propensities. Countries with higher saving propensities should join trading areas containing other countries with higher saving propensities. In this case lower levels of BR need not prove inflationary in economies with lower saving propensities. This provides an additional reason for a plurality of currencies and trading areas.

16
The Monetary Transmission Process

If the Keynes story is to be told properly (in its historical context) it should begin before Keynes. It begins with Hawtrey: *Currency and Credit* (1919). ... Neither of them held that the economic system is automatically self-righting. ... In Hawtrey as in Keynes, the system has to be stabilized, by policy and by some instrument of policy. It was over the instrument of this policy that they differed. As the difference began, it looked rather small. Both agreed that the instrument was a rate of interest, but Hawtrey looked to the short rate, Keynes to the long. At this point I would accept that Keynes was more up to date. ... But then Keynes discovered that his long rate was not only less directly susceptible to banking control than Hawtrey's short, but that it was very likely to be found that just when it was wanted, it could not move enough. So he moved away from monetary methods to the "fiscal" methods which have later been so associated with his name. ... Thus it was that what began as monetary theory became "fiscalism."

Sir John Hicks, 1976

Our desire to hold money as a store of wealth is a barometer of our distrust of our own calculations and conventions concerning the future. ... The possession of money lulls our disquietude.

John Maynard Keynes, 1937

The very notion of a "transmission mechanism" would be uncongenial to Keynes, for it suggests a dichotomy between the monetary and real aspects of the economy, where he saw the economy as inherently monetary.

Victoria Chick, 1983: 327

16.1 Process analysis of how aggregate demand grows over time

First, some definitions. Investment goods may be defined as all final goods with an expected life-time of more than one year. Consumption goods may be defined as all final goods with an expected life-time of less than one year. Consumption goods and investment goods thus exhaust total output. When saving is defined as income not consumed, it is immediately obvious why saving is identical to investment. Saving is not as it sounds a behavioral relationship, it is an accounting identity. Whenever there is an increase in investment the quantity of saving rises by the same amount. The question is, how does the increase in saving that satisfies the $S \equiv I$ identity come about?

As previously developed, in credit money economies the money supply is endogenously determined by the demand for bank credit, and the level of Bank Rate (BR) is set exogenously by the central bank (CB). Money income (GDP) grows with the money supply, and the ratio of money income to the money supply M/V is termed the income velocity of money. Since the supply of credit money is endogenous, money cannot be the ultimate "cause" of inflation, of the growth of money income, or of anything else. To understand the monetary transmission process in credit money economies, one must understand how money income grows.

For income and output to grow over time aggregate demand (AD) in the current period must exceed aggregate supply (AS) in the previous period. This implies that economic agents must spend more on currently produced goods and services in the current period than the total income they receive in the previous period. Agents in aggregate must be net deficit-spenders.[1]

Businesses on balance are a deficit-spending sector, and households on balance are a surplus-spending sector. The stage of the business cycle, and the monetary, fiscal and exchange rate policies in place, determine whether the government and the rest of the world sector will be in deficit or surplus. Investment spending is volitional, apart from unintended changes in inventory accumulation which are offset as soon as perceived by altering output levels. Since it is the accounting record of investment total saving cannot be volitional. Whenever some units increase their investment, spending, the saving of other units must (non-volitionally) increase. For AD to grow some units must deficit-spend, to permit AD in the current period to exceed AS in the previous period.

When some agents in the economy deficit-spend, other agents must necessarily run surpluses.[2] As an accounting identity, net surpluses of creditor sectors must be identical to net deficits of deficit sectors. But since total deficits of deficit units are always identical to total surpluses of surplus units, how does AD increase? If deficits are necessarily always equal to surpluses, how does AD grow? All agents cannot collectively deficit-spend, and all agents cannot simultaneously run deficits?

In monetary economies only money buys goods. Deficit-spending must be financed either with money, or with promises to pay money in the future (IOUs). As stated with the exception of unintended changes in inventories which are restored as soon as discovered, all investment spending behavior is volitional. As accounting identity deficits are identical to surpluses, so surplus-spending behavior, like saving behavior, must also be non-volitional.

The relationship between *volitional* deficit-spending units and *non-volitional* surplus-spending units is summarized below in the following 5 truisms:

1. In monetary economies only money buys goods. All purchases must be paid for with money or with promises to pay money.

2. The money balances that finance deficit-spending may be internally or externally acquired.
3. With the exception of unintended inventory accumulation, all consumption and investment spending behavior is volitional.
4. Deficit-spending units volitionally decide on the amount they wish to deficit-spend providing they can obtain the required finance.
5. Total deficits are identical to total surpluses as an accounting identity.

It follows that total saving, like total surplus-spending, must be non-volitional. Unfortunately the relationship between volitional deficit-spending, and non-volitional surplus-spending is non-transparent and confusing. In part this reflects the human difficulty of comprehending the unfolding of historical time. When one agent volitionally deficit-spends this necessarily results in another agent simultaneously becoming a surplus-spending unit, and either volitionally or non-volitionally acquiring an IOU.

One approach to modelling the complexity introduced by historical time is to follow the lead of Sir Denis Robertson and arbitrarily impose different time periods or "days."[3] This yields the following truisms:

Investment spending is exogenous. ($I_{(t)} \equiv I_{(o)}$)
1. Consumption in "day" (t) [$C_{(t)}$] is a function of income in the previous day (t − 1): $C_{(t)} = cY_{(t-1)}$. Spending in the current "day" is thus a function of yesterday's income.
2. The amount of saving [$S_{(t)}$] is then non-volitional. Saving each "day," the difference between total income and total consumption, is equal to investment, and becomes a function of the change in income: $S_{(t)} = Y_{(t)} - C_{(t)} = I_{(t)} = Y_{(t)} - CY_{(t-1)}$.
3. AD increases when aggregate spending in the current "day" exceeds aggregate income of the previous "day." If total deficit-spending by debtor units in the current "day" is a volitional function of income in the previous day, surplus spending in the current day becomes non-volitional. Changes in current income can never be known in advance but reflect volitional changes in today's spending.
4. Total saving in the current period is identical to total investment in the current period. $S(_t) \equiv I(_t)$. But if they are independent and identical both cannot be volitional. Saving, the net change in surplus-spending, is the result of exogenous changes in current investment. Today's consumption spending (C_t) is a volitional function of yesterday's income $c(Y_{t-1})$. Saving units cannot change their spending today in response to unknown concurrent changes in investment.
5. Non-volitional savings by creditor units is the accounting record of volitional deficit-spending by deficit units.

AD increases when spending units raise total consumption and investment expenditure, and falls when spending units reduce total consumption and investment expenditure. AD is constant when total spending is constant and today's total spending is equal to yesterday's income. AD rises when economic units net deficit-spend, (i.e.) spend more on currently produced goods in the current period than their current income from production in the previous period. The money to finance deficit-spending may be obtained either internally, from past or current saving, or externally, by borrowing from other units in monetary production economies; borrowing from banks results in an endogenous expansion in the credit money supply.

The quantity of bank credit demanded to finance current investment spending is a function of the expected return on investment projects, and the lending rate charged, the volume of credit banks are willing and able to make available. The last factor is directly under government influence. Banks administer their lending and deposit rates at a relatively stable mark-up or mark-down on Bank Rate (BR). So long as consumption is a stable function of yesterday's income, exogenous investment spending becomes the prime driver of changes in AD.[4]

In credit money economies Bank Rate (BR) is the exogenous policy instrument of the Central Bank (CB). In Chapter 15 the reason why output is demand- constrained (AD is below the economy's total potential output) was shown to be because CB's set BR at "too high" a level. Full employment demand management requires that CB's must set BR at sufficiently low level to generate AD, equal to the economy's potential full employment output. Providing interest rates are set at a sufficiently low level to achieve a full employment level of AD, the stabilization goal of the government is satisfied. For full capacity AD with a zero output gap it is irrelevant whether private units or public units deficit-spend.

Demand management requires that when AD is insufficient to generate full employment, CBs must lower BR to stimulate additional investment spending. The share of investment-spending undertaken by private and public units depends on the relative returns expected on private and public capital projects. The AD relationship slopes downward in interest rate-output space, and rises indefinitely as BR approaches zero. If, due to a long series of negative contingencies, and/or poor government policies, AD remains insufficient over long time periods, excess capacity becomes widespread and animal spirits become fatally depressed. In this case even zero levels of interest rates are insufficient to induce sufficient private investment spending to generate full capacity output. History has demonstrated that after the collapse of major investment bubbles it can take several decades before anticipated future returns revive sufficiently to generate full employment AD, even when BR is reduced to zero.

Since the great depression of the 1930s economists have recognized that the appropriate long-term fiscal response to an insufficiency of AD is the preparation of a shelf of investment public work projects, ranked by estimated rates of return. These projects should be prepared in advance in both the private and public sectors, and regularly updated. When additional deficit-spending is required, CBs should sequentially lower BR. Projects with the highest expected after-tax return should be chosen first, irrespective of whether they are in the public or the private sector. The initial responsibility to increase deficit-spending to restore full employment AD lies with monetary policy, not fiscal policy. Only after BR has been reduced to zero by the monetary authorities, and the private sector has failed to respond with sufficient increases in deficit-spending to generate full employment, should the fiscus be called on to deficit-spend.

When animal spirits have deteriorated to such an extent that there is widespread excess capacity, and no investment projects in the private or public sector have positive expected returns even at zero BR, the CB retains a number of options: It can subsidize the construction of selected capital projects, either directly through the award of lump sum subsidies or indirectly by announcing its willingness to purchase selective negative interest rate securities. The result is the subsidization of private investment to carry out selected capital formation.

The magnitude of the subsidy can be adjusted to the estimated external benefit of the projects, including the benefits of reduced unemployment. When governments have no existing tradition in the production of public services and very little capability to carry out capital formation, administration and utilization efficiently (as currently is the case in many developing economies) the provision of public goods (for example the construction and administration of public work projects such as schools and highways) can be privatized, and leased to local or foreign private sector firms for a management fee.

At the end of the day, if private deficit-spending has not responded to zero nominal BR "public works" constitute governments' final reserve to attain full employment. A useful "anti-boondoggle" requirement would be that to justify public deficit-spending, benefit–cost analysis must first be conducted. The estimated benefits of public investment projects at a zero discount rate should exceed the estimated costs of financing them. Once it is recognized that the level of short-term interest rates is the exogenous policy instrument of the CB and can if necessary be reduced to zero, the requirement of a positive expected return on investment projects is no longer a constraint.

16.2 "Convenience lending": the non-volitional finance of deficit-spending

Consider first a barter economy where no financial assets and liabilities exist so all agents must run a balanced budget. For such an economy Say's Law holds: AD for current output is identical to AS of all goods currently produced and available for barter. General deficiency of AD is impossible since changes in AS are identical to the changes in AD.[5]

Once time is introduced, it is necessary even in a barter economy to distinguish between currently-produced, and previously-existing goods (whether previously-produced or nonreproducible). AD for currently-produced goods can exceed or fall short of current AS in barter economies when income from currently-produced goods and services is exchanged for previously-produced, or nonproducible goods. This break in Say's law constituted the classical case against the purchasing and holding ("hoarding") of nonreproducible assets: land, gold, or commodity money. The purchase of previously-existing assets provides a temporary resting place for purchasing power, and results in a reduction in AD for currently-produced goods below current output, and so the breaking of Say's Law.

In commodity money economies where gold is used as the money commodity currently-produced goods are exchanged for previously-existing gold. Newly-created gold finances increases in net deficit spending and so in AD. Since deficit-spending may be financed with previously-existing gold, Say's Law no longer holds. AD for currently-produced goods and services is no longer identical to AS in every period. In commodity money economies when the supply of the money commodity (gold) is given, AD can rise or fall independently of AS, when either the income velocity of money, and/or the relative price of gold varies over time.

From the definition of income velocity ($V \equiv Y/M$), by fully differentiating the quantity identity ($Y \equiv MV$) the rate of increase of AD in any time period may be shown to equal the rate of increase in the money supply, plus the rate of change in velocity ($\dot{Y} = \dot{M} + \dot{V}$). If velocity remains constant an increase in M is necessary for AD to increase. Whether the increase in the money commodity is due to the domestic mining of gold, or the running of a current account surplus with other economies, money has only a first round distributional effect, and determines how the additional money is initially distributed among agents in the economy. In open economies government policy designed to reduce the current account surplus increases AD when it increases the money supply, so long as the income velocity of money remains unchanged.[6]

If demand for goods is to be effective in a money economy, it must be financed either with money, or with promises to pay money. The money balances to finance deficit spending may be obtained by agents either internally or externally:

1. The internal finance of deficit expenditures:
   a. Dishoarding: the expenditure (sale) of previously accumulated money balances.
   b. The sale of nonmonetary assets, either previously-accumulated financial or real assets for money to nonbanks, in exchange for previously-existing money balances. Nonmonetary assets must possess high liquidity if they are not to be sold at a loss.[7] In all cases of internal finance, the total quantity of monetary and nonmonetary financial assets remains unchanged. Any associated change in AD is due to changes in velocity associated with the redistribution of ownership of existing assets. Internal finance involves the sale of previously-accumulated nonmonetary financial, or real assets in spending units' portfolios for money, to acquire previously-existing or currently- produced real assets from other unit's portfolios.

2. The external finance of deficit expenditures:
   a. Borrowing from the Banking System: the sale (issue) of newly-created own financial assets (IOUs) to the banking system, in exchange for newly-created money balances created by the act of bank lending.
   b. Borrowing from NonBank Agents: the sale (issue) of newly-created own financial assets (IOU's) to nonbank units, in exchange for previously-existing money balances accumulated in earlier periods.

In all cases of external finance, the total quantity of monetary and nonmonetary financial assets and liabilities increases. External finance involves the issue of newly-created debt (IOUs) in exchange for newly-created money balances when the borrowing is from a bank, and in exchange for previously-existing money balances when the borrowing is from a non-bank. The resulting change in AD is due to the change in the existing quantity of financial assets and liabilities and/or to the redistribution of the ownership of existing money balances.

When the agent financing deficit expenditure is a non bank, the result is an increase in newly-created IOUs and a redistribution of previously-existing money balances among agents. If the money supply is unchanged, AD will increase only if the velocity of money rises. In case 1(a) (dishoarding), the velocity of money increases by definition. In cases 1(b) and 2(b) (the sale of IOUs or tangible assets to non-banks in exchange for money balances), a volitional act of abstention by creditor units is required, involving both reduction in the liquidity of the unit's wealth portfolio and volitional abstention from consumption by the creditor.

In the case of borrowing from the banking system [case 2(a)] the borrowing agent (debtor) and the lending agent (creditor) are the same unit. The acquisition of newly-created money balances by borrowing units results in an increase in the liquidity of their wealth portfolios. No abstention from current consumption is involved. Borrowing units take on the additional risk of incuring an IOU (obligation to pay money in the future), which is financed out of the expected future income from the investment.

Deficit spending financed by bank borrowing results in an increase in AD over the period equal to the proportionate increase in the money supply plus the proportionate change in income velocity. When the lending agent is a bank (2(a)), the change in AD is the result of the exchange of newly-created IOUs between the borrower and the bank. The result is an increase in total assets, total liabilities and the supply of credit money.

A bank loan represents an exchange of IOUs. The borrower gives its IOU (promise to pay money in the future) to the bank, and the bank gives its IOU (bank deposits) to the borrower. When agents sell their IOU to a bank, deposits are created in the process ("Loans create deposits"). Banks exchange their own highly liquid IOUs (transaction deposits) for the illiquid IOUs of borrowers that pay higher returns. Newly-created deposits are credit money which is non-volitionally accepted by all agents in the act of sale of goods and services. No change in asset prices, interest rates or income is required. The increase in "convenience demand" for deposits is due to the general acceptability of bank deposits in exchange (the "moneyness" of deposits).[8]

When financed by bank lending, deficit-spending creates additional non-volitional lending to the banking system. Such non-volitional lending is undertaken by all agents who permit their deposits to accumulate over the period. From the point of view of individual depositors, "convenience lending" is neither volitional nor long term and may even be measured in nanoseconds.[9] Even though demand deposits are perfectly liquid, from the point of view of the economy, convenience lending to the banking system is long term, until the nonmarketable IOUs (loans) or marketable IOUs (securities) acquired by the banking system expire, repaid or are sold. From the viewpoint of the economy, the collective maturity of "convenience lending" is the period the deposits remain in existence.

Increases in "convenience lending" by bank depositors are entirely non-volitional. They involve no reduction in current expenditures on consumption goods, and no sacrifice of liquidity. The liquidity of the lender actually increases. An increase in deficit-spending by bank borrowers financed by an increase in bank lending is not offset by any volitional reduction in spending or volitional increase in surplus-spending by bank depositors. An increase in "convenience lending" by depositors finances a net increase in demand for goods and financial assets.

16.3 "Convenience lending" and "convenience saving"

Depositors experience no sacrifice of liquidity from holding bank deposits rather than fiat money. Agents prefer to use credit money (bank deposits) over fiat money (currency) for many transactions. Unlike volitional lending, which involves an abstinence from current consumption and a reduction in portfolio liquidity on the part of the lender, the "convenience lending" of fiat money to the banking system involves no sacrifice of consumption or liquidity. Since it is associated with an increase rather than a reduction in lender liquidity, it requires no pecuniary reward. Like other financial intermediaries banks borrow short from their creditors (depositors) and lend long to their debtors (borrowers). This sounds counter- intuitive because depositors regard their bank deposits as "their" money, rather than as the accounting record of their loan of fiat money to the bank. Deposits are the bank's IOUs, the record of their debt of fiat money to their creditors.

When additional bank loans are demanded by credit-worthy borrowers, the credit granted takes the form of newly-created deposits. When new bank loans are extended, the quantity of bank deposits increases. When agents do not borrow bank credit, the money supply remains unchanged. In developed banking systems total bank credit commitments extended but unutilized are roughly as large as total loans granted.[10] Deposits are the banks' IOU of a debt of fiat money, the accounting record of bank credit granted. On the liability side of bank portfolios, changes in depositor demand for bank deposits have no effect on the quantity of deposits in existence. Deposits are the accounting record of bank assets. When depositors write a check, this represents the transfer of the ownership of a previously-existing deposit to another depositor.

During the initial stage of investment projects, increases in working capital are required to pay for the factors of production and finance all other costs of construction before the asset is completed, transferred to the buyer, and final payment is received. Most business' demand for working-capital finance is provided by bank loans. In overdraft economies unlike commodity money economies, increases in investment spending require no increase in volitional saving, with its implied decision to defer current consumption (abstinence). Similarly, additional bank lending does not reduce the liquidity of debtor portfolios for which an interest reward must be paid.

From the viewpoint of the economy, deficit-spending financed by new bank loans provides borrowers with newly-created deposits, which they spend and transfer to other agents. No bank creditor must volitionally abstain from current consumption when the total amount of "convenience lending" to the banking system increases.

Borrowing from the banking system increases the total supply of credit money, and the total value of liquidity and purchasing power in the economy. Increases in bank lending are financed by non-volitional increases in lending by all bank depositors whose deposit balances increase over the period. When increased deficit-spending by bank borrowers finances additional investment spending, the increase in "convenience lending" by economic units whose deposit balances have increased over the period becomes an increase in "convenience saving." Investment financed by new bank loans creates an increase in "convenience lending" sufficient to finance itself and an increase in purchasing power sufficient to purchase the increase in real output.

In contrast when deficit-spending by bank borrowers finances additional consumption spending from the viewpoint of the economy it generates an increase in "convenience dis-saving." When the increase in bank lending finances increased spending on previously-produced or on nonreproducible goods, e.g., previously existing land or securities there is no increase in AD. The effect is simply to redistribute the ownership of money balances, and reduce the income velocity Y/M. Since velocity broadly follows a random walk, this implies that other depositors are concurrently purchasing currently-produced goods and services over the period. AD increases at a rate equal to the rate of increase in the money supply plus the rate of change of velocity.

The decision by bank borrowers to repay bank loans constitutes a reduction of "convenience lending" to the banking system. From the viewpoint of the economy, if debt repayment results in a reduction in AD, current income is devoted to the repayment of previously-existing debt. The result of debt repayment is a reduction in "convenience lending" to the banking system, and an accompanying reduction in bank deposits and the money supply.[11]

Neither income nor interest rates adjusts to "equilibrate" saving and investment. Saving as an accounting identity is identical to investment, and is not a behavioral relationship. In overdraft economies, additional investment spending financed by new bank loans induces an identical increase in "convenience saving" by bank depositors, which requires neither abstinence from consumption nor sacrifice of liquidity. The demand for newly-produced investment and consumption goods creates a demand for additional working capital, which in overdraft systems is financed by an increase in bank borrowing. Borrowers receive newly-created deposits and exchange them for factors of production, finished and unfinished goods, and previously-existing real or financial assets. When new investment is externally financed by bank loans the newly-created deposits provide an identical increase in "convenience saving." No increase in volitional saving must be made by any agent.

Banks are prepared to make credit commitments to all borrowers whom they judge to be sufficiently credit-worthy to repay the loan. In developed economies bank loans and an increase in convenience lending is made at the initiative of credit-worthy borrowers not the banks.[12]

So long as public confidence in the banks "instant repurchase clause" is maintained, bank deposits function as the chief means of payment, and bank deposits are generally accepted in settlement of all debt obligations. Banks create additional deposits when they make additional loans and supply borrowers with newly-created deposits. As the accounting record of investment spending saving automatically increases with the construction of investment goods. The particular wealth form that saving takes after the initial act of investment evolves over time, from highly liquid and low-yielding deposits to less-liquid but higher-yielding financial and tangible assets.

Suppose the initial investment project were a building, that takes one year to construct, the contractor initially borrows short-term funds from her bank, to finance the working capital required for construction expense during the year. In one year's time when the project is completed, the new owner takes possession and pays the builder for the project. With the proceeds the builder repays her loan from the bank.

Investment and non-volitional saving occur concurrently as the building is under construction. Deposits are created by the new loans, and extinguished by loan repayment when the construction period ends. Investment and saving rise *pari pasu* over the period. At the end of the period the net change in bank loans and in the money supply is zero if the loan is fully repaid. Over the year in which the investment was made the accompanying nonvolitional saving took the form of increases in "convenience lending" of fiat money to the banking system by bank depositors.

All subsequent transactions that occur after the construction of the capital project are portfolio transactions (National Flow of Funds transactions) and do not enter the National Income Accounts (NIA). Portfolio transactions determine how ownership claims to assets are distributed among agents, and the different forms ownership claims take. In the above example the net change in the money supply over the period was zero. Focusing on final "equilibrium positions" hides bank financial loans and repayments and renders the lending process much less transparent and more impervious to understanding.

Assume the new owner is a firm that pays one-half of the cost of the building out of its current profits (retained earnings) and issues a long-term bond to finance the remaining half (corresponding broadly to current US behavior). Retained earnings raise the book value of share-holders' equity. The total market value of equities will increase by an amount that depends on the level of and the change in the firm's price–earnings ratio. When income is measured in the Hicksian sense, income in the form of capital gains increases. The marginal propensity to consume out of capital gain income is very low compared to earned income, and has been estimated at 0.02–0.05.[13] Most capital gain income is not consumed and becomes "convenience saving" by shareholders.[14]

Such "saving" does not correspond to the current National Income Accounts which excludes all capital gain income. Saving, the accounting record of investment, occurs *pari pasu* when investment is undertaken. If newly-issued bonds are initially purchased by nonbank financial institutions, they are financed by money received from the sale of secondary securities. Purchases of previously-existing and newly-created financial assets, although treated as "saving" by individual households, do not constitute "saving" for the economy. They are portfolio transactions which determine the ownership composition of claims to national wealth. In an uncertain world many agents demand liquid assets and lines of credit, access to immediately available funds to discharge future commitments that may arise under worst-case scenarios.

Keynes mistakenly argued saving was a two-step process: savers must first decide how to allocate their current income between consumption and saving, and must then decide how to allocate their saving among alternative asset stores of value, with differing liquidity and expected returns.[15] Keynes' account was mistaken since he (implicitly) assumed all "savings" are volitional. The acquisition of bank demand deposits does not constitute volitional act of lending and saving by bank depositors. It represents a non-volitional increase in "convenience lending," which may constitute "convenience saving," convenience dis-saving" or neither, depending on whether the goods purchased with the bank loan are currently-produced capital goods, consumption goods, or previously-existing tangible or financial assets.

"Saving" defined as income not consumed may include the acquisition of "previously-existing" as well as "newly-created" assets, and may or may not enter into the circular flow of income. The accumulation of credit money received in exchange for goods sold implies no volitional decision to "invest" or "save". In credit money economies a decision to "save" may denote a volitional decision to accumulate newly-created capital assets, in which case it is also an act of investment. But an increase in saving does not imply a volitional decision to refrain from consuming current income. Most saving undertaken in the United States is non-volitional, and is not accompanied by a volitional decision to refrain from consumption and accumulate capital assets.

Exchange denotes the act of supplying goods, accompanied by the act of demanding money. After being spent by business and household borrowers, newly-created deposits are always accepted by their recipients in exchange, so long as public confidence in the bank's "instant repurchase" deposit clause is maintained. From the viewpoint of the economy, the accumulation of newly-created deposits by bank depositors represents a non-volitional increase in "convenience-lending" of fiat money in exchange for credit money.

Saving is the record of investment. Once an act of investment is made an equal amount of saving is automatically forthcoming over the investment period, irrespective of the accompanying financial transactions that may occur. When new investment is financed by bank loans, the newly-created deposits represent an increase in non-volitional "convenience savings" identical to the investment undertaken. No increase in volitional saving occurs. Unless currently created financial assets are used to finance increases in investment expenditures, household purchases of previously-existing financial assets such as stocks and bonds do not constitute "saving" for the economy. The purchase of previously-existing financial assets, even if regarded as "saving" by the agents themselves, and commonly termed "saving," does not constitute "saving" for the economy. It constitutes instead the transformation of wealth into different forms and the redistribution of existing wealth ownership. Portfolio transactions are entered in the National Flow of Funds Accounts, not the National Income Accounts.

An increased demand for previously-existing or newly-created debt and equities may result in an increase in asset prices. The price of financial assets is the present value of expected future streams of asset income, discounted at the own rate of interest on the asset which varies with BR set by the CB. Financial valuations depend on the expected future stream of interest and dividends and the rate at which they are discounted. The National Accounting system in place determines whether capital gain income associated with changes in asset prices is ignored, or recorded as current income. There is no direct relation between changes in volitional saving, and changes in interest rates or asset prices.[16] The short-run relationship between changes in volitional saving and changes in investment is typically negative. The market does not invest in response to current saving decisions. As Keynes recognized, an increase in volitional saving initially implies a decline in current consumption:

> An act of individual saving means—so to speak—a decision not to have dinner today. But it does not necessitate a decision to have dinner or to buy a pair of boots a week hence or a year hence, or to consume any specific thing at any specified date.[17]

16.4 The demise of the Keynesian "multiplier"

In all overdraft economies, change in bank loans reflect changes in the demand for bank credit by bank borrowers who have been deemed credit-worthy by their banks. When new investment is financed by bank credit an increase in "convenience lending" to the banking system is transformed into an increase in "convenience saving" for the economy. Saving varies with investment. Keynes was mistaken. There is no Keynesian multiplier relation. No multiple change in income must occur for the $S \equiv I$ identity to hold. When financed by increase an in bank loans, additional investment creates the increase in non-volitional saving necessary to finance itself. The *ex post* propensity to save increases with no increase in volitional saving behavior and no volitional abstention from consumption. Increases in investment spending create identical increases in saving, with no multiple increase in output, employment or income.

The Keynesian "Multiplier" makes no reference to "convenience lending" or "convenience saving" in its explanation of the multiple expansion of income resulting from an increase in investment spending. More importantly the Keynesian multiplier ignores the question how the increases in investment spending are financed.[18]

The preceeding monetary transmission process negates the Keynesian "income multiplier" analysis. In each "round" of the conventional multiplier process, the "leakage" of income into the purchase of financial assets is held to constitute additional "savings." But "saving" is the accounting record of investment, and cannot occur independently of investment. If no additional investment is undertaken, there can be no concurrent increase in saving, irrespective of the abstinence from current consumption that may occur. Investment "determines" saving, rather than the reverse. Once an act of investment is made, over the same period an equal amount of saving is automatically generated, irrespective of the accompanying financial transactions.

Changes in investment spending are determined by investor expectations of the future profitability of the investment, relative to the present and future cost of finance. To emphasize the evanescent, unquantifiable, and unknowable nature of expectations about the changing future expectations of other agents, Keynes coined the term "animal spirits." Investment spending is forward-looking, driven by expected future returns. Unlike consumption spending, investment is not a function of current disposable income. In Keynes' vision, changes in expectations is the driver behind cyclical changes in AD and AS.

Keynes was correct that a change in investment (ΔI_{t0}) causes an identical change in AD in the current period, on a one-for-one basis: $\Delta I_{t0} = \Delta AD_{t0} = \Delta Y_{t0}$. But in the (General Theory), he argued that an increase in investment spending induces a "multiple" increase in future income, depending on the value of the marginal propensity to consume. Keynes' "multiplier" analysis is a comparative static equilibrium analysis. It traces out *ceteris paribus* the effects of a once-and-for-all change in autonomous investment on the level of GDP, until in the new equilibrium, the level of AS is equal to the higher level of AD. But to analyze the process of change in complex systems, all variables must be dated. Once this is done Keynes' "multiplier" analysis of the effect of current investment on future income may easily be shown to be erroneous.

Expectations about the future returns on autonomous investment projects change continually over time. For complex systems, it is illegitimate to consider the effects of a change in autonomous investment on income in some initial time period, and then assume *(ceteris paribus)* that autonomous spending remains constant throughout the adjustment period until all the effects of the initial change in investment on income and consumption have worked their way through the system. Yet this is exactly what the Keynesian multiplier process requires.

Once the multiplier process is recognized to occur over chronological time, in each "period" of the process, future expectations and autonomous investment will change. Unless expectations are "frozen," and held constant under the *ceteris paribus* clause, the system cannot reach any new determinate position of "equilibrium," where income has increased by some "multiple" of the initial change in autonomous investment.

Changes in consumption in any period are not determined solely by the change in disposable income. A multitude of other forces impact on consumption spending: current, lagged and expected future income, wealth, capital gains, tastes, fashion, and so on. The level of consumption in the next period is superficially well-explained by the level of consumption in the current period. But since consumption and income have unit roots, current shocks have permanent effects. Income is defined as consumption plus saving so consumption and income are co-integrated. First differences in consumption are not well-explained by first differences in income. Although co-integrated, since consumption is a component of income, both series broadly follow a random walk. In complex systems "equilibrium," whether defined as a position of balance, where all adjustments have ceased, or as a position of general market clearing, where all expectations are realized, can never occur.

The above is all very old hat. It simply states that the MPC does not remain constant over time. But what has not been recognized is that if a system is unpredictable, and has no tendency to move towards some determinate future "equilibrium" position, there can be no determinant income "multiplier."

The Keynesian multiplier (m) is customarily mechanically derived from the National Income identity plus a behavioural consumption relationship as follows:

$$Y \equiv C + I \tag{16.1}$$
$$C = C_0 + CY \tag{16.2}$$

Substituting equation 16.2 into equation 16.1 and solving for Y,

$$Y \equiv [c_0 + I][1/(1-c)] \equiv m[c_0 + I], \tag{16.3}$$

where $m \equiv [1/(1-c)]$ and $c \equiv (\Delta C/\Delta Y)$.

The nature of the multiplier identity is illustrated in Figure 16.1, the C + I + G diagram with the government sector omitted. The Keynesian multiplier is the ratio of the change in income to the change in autonomous investment spending: ($m \equiv \Delta Y/\Delta I$).

In the simplest case the multiplier may be rewritten $m \equiv 1/(1+c)$, where c is the marginal propensity to consume.

In Figure 16.1 the value of the multiplier expression is easily derived geometrically using comparative static equilibrium analysis:

$$\Delta Y \equiv \Delta C + \Delta I \tag{16.4}$$

Rearranging 16.4 and substituting $\Delta I \equiv \Delta Y - \Delta C$ into the definition of the multiplier in equation 16.3:

$$m \equiv \Delta Y/\Delta I \equiv \Delta Y/(\Delta Y - \Delta C) \tag{16.5}$$

Dividing the numerator and denominator of equation 16.5 by ΔY yields:

$$m \equiv 1/(1 - [\Delta C/\Delta Y]) \text{ or} \tag{16.6}$$
$$m \equiv 1/(1-c) \text{ [where } c \equiv \Delta C/\Delta Y] \tag{16.7}$$

As professors of macroeconomics love to show on the blackboard, the essence of the multiplier process is that given an initial equilibrium position $Y_{E(to)}$, an increase in

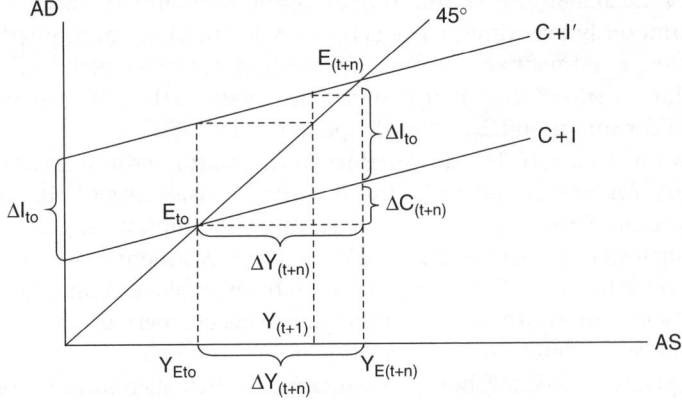

Figure 16.1 The Keynesian multiplier

autonomous spending of ΔI_{to} will, after n periods, yield a new equilibrium position $\Delta Y_{E(t+n)}$, where the change in income $\Delta Y_{(t+n)}$ is a "multiple" of the change in investment spending $\Delta I_{(to)}$. But the (implied) comparative static assumption that the Keynesian "multiplier" is "instantaneous," is both analytically bankrupt and highly misleading. It is simply a non-transparent way of getting rid of time, and with time all the complex events of the transition process in order to pursue comparative static equilibrium analysis. The Keynesian income-adjustment process evolves over chronological time. If multiplier theory is to shed light on real world behavior, all variables must be dated, and change must occur over chronological time.

In complex systems it is illegitimate to assume that "animal spirits" undergo a once-and-for-all change in the initial period, and are then "frozen" and held unchanged over the transition time period, when the multiplier works itself out. Yet this is exactly what must be assumed for a quantitative value of the multiplier to be derived. As shown in Figure 16.1, the change in investment (ΔI_{to}) is assumed to remain constant over the adjustment period (t+n). Only consumption (C_{t+n}) and income (Y_{t+n}) are allowed to change. But in a complex system all variables, production, income, investment, consumption, and output change continuously over time.

Keynes' comparative static equilibrium procedure assumes an initial exogenous change in "animal spirits" and so in investment spending. It then in effect waves a magic wand and traces out the consequences of this exogenous change in investment for the accompanying changes in income and consumption in logical time, holding investment constant at the new level over the adjustment period.

At the beginning of the second "period," income will increase by the change in exogenous spending to $Y_{(t+1)}$. But however this initial period is defined, once it is admitted to take place in chronological time, expectations of the future and animal spirits must be allowed to change, as well as income, consumption, and investment ($Y_{(t+1)}, C_{(t+1)}, I_{(t+1)}$). At every intermediate time period in the adjustment process e.g. (t + 1) the situation is analogous to the situation at the beginning of the process $Y_{(t0)}$. Change is continuous, and "autonomous" investment spending shifts continuously over time. There is thus no determinate "multiplier" relationship between investment and income. In any short run single period ($Y_{(t+1)}$) there is no "multiplier effect." The change in income is equal to the change in investment ($I_{(t+1)}$) and consumption ($C_{(t+1)}$) in the period.

As shown in Figure 16.1, if all variables in the multiplier process are dated, as is necessary for process analysis, the logical inconsistency of the analysis is revealed. In the final "equilibrium" position, consumption and income have both been allowed to change (ΔC_{t+n}, ΔY_{t+n},). But investment has been held at its initial period value (ΔI_{t0}). But in the real world of chronological time, expectations of future events are continually changing during each "period" of the transition process, and so is "autonomous" investment.

It is imperative to show how bank-financed deficit-spending is financed by increases in the money supply, which enables AD to grow over time. The hidden truth in the multiplier process is that although spending on current output has identical one-for-one effects on AD, irrespective of whether it is for investment or consumption goods, investment and consumption spending differ in the manner by which they are financed. Capital goods by definition have an expected future lifetime that extends beyond one year. Capital budgeting considerations dictate that only their current consumption ("depreciation") must be expensed and paid for in the current period. In consequence, a much larger proportion of investment expenditures are externally financed by newly-created money, compared with consumption expenditures.

Investment spending is generally financed to a greater degree than consumption spending by bank-financed deficit-spending. But as shown above deficit-spending financed by bank credit is the key to AD growth in market economies. Expected events are continuously changing and "autonomous" spending is changing with them. Unless future expectations are "frozen," it is not possible to determine the effects of current exogenous changes in investment on future income. Spending changes continuously over time and the system never approaches a new determinate "equilibrium" position.

The following counterfactual experiment would be logically required to demonstrate a determinate Keynesian "multiplier." Assume the existence of two hypothetical "identical" economies at the same point in calendar time. Let an exogenous change in investment occur in one economy, and observe how both economies change over future chronological time. The multiplier could then be directly calculated *ex post* as the difference in income and output between the two previously identical economies at future dates. There is no reason to expect such a "multiplier" would remain stable over different time periods.

The kernel of truth in the Keynesian multiplier is that, even though spending on current output has identical one-for-one effects on AD, irrespective of whether it is for investment or consumption goods, investment and consumption spending differ in the way they are financed. Capital goods have by definition an expected future lifetime that extends beyond one year. Capital budgeting considerations, dictate that only their current consumption ("depreciation") must be expensed and paid for in the current period. As a result a much larger proportion of investment expenditures compared with consumption expenditures will be externally financed with newly-created money. The consequence is that investment is financed to a much greater degree than consumption by deficit-spending financed by bank borrowing. As previously demonstrated deficit-spending financed by bank credit is the key to how AD grows over time in monetary economies.

An additional criticism of the Keynesian multiplier is that it fails to address how increases in exogenous investment are *financed*. It implicitly assumes that excess money balances ("hoards") are always available to internally finance any desire to deficit-spend, and the result is merely a rise in income velocity. But since such "hoards" do not in general exist, the finance for the deficit spending must be raised by new borrowing. When the borrowing is from the banking system, the money supply increases. In the real world complex systems a significant proportion of investment spending is financed externally, by borrowing from the banking system for the required working capital. In contrast a significant proportion of consumption spending is financed internally out of current income. This provides an alternative explanation for the differential effect of investment and consumption spending on AD.

16.5 The Quantity Theory of Money

The Quantity Theory of Money like the Multiplier theory is an identity:

$Y_t \equiv M_t V_t$
where Y_t = Income, M_t = Money Supply, V_t = Velocity $[Y_t/M_t]$ (16.8)

Unfortunately the variables in 16.8 are incommensurate. Income (Y_t) is a flow variable, while the money supply (M_t) is a stock variable. This dimensional incommensurateness is resolved by defining velocity (V_t) as the ratio of the flow of income to the stock of money, the average number of times money circulates as money income in one period (Y_t/M_t). Velocity is defined as the ratio of the flow of income over a one-year period to the stock of money at the beginning of the period: As such, its value depends on the length of the period over which income is defined.

$V_t \equiv Y_t/M_t$,   or $Y_t \equiv M_t V_t$ (16.9)

The level of income over any period may be expressed as the product of the money supply at the beginning of the period, times the average income velocity of money over the period. As an identity, the Quantity Theory is true at every instant of time and over every period of time. The quantity equation can also be totally differentiated with respect to time. The change in income is equal to the change in the money supply in the next period times the current income velocity of money, plus the change in the income velocity of money in the next period times the current supply of money.

$\Delta Y_t \equiv \Delta M_{t+1} V_t + \Delta V_{t+1} M_t$ (16.10)

Like other macro variables, velocity has a unit root and closely approximates a random walk. The velocity of money is continually changing. But since it has a unit root, the best estimate of next period's velocity is the current period's velocity and the expected change in velocity is zero ($\Delta V^e_{t+1} = 0$).[19] This radically simplifies the analysis since the second term in 16.10 disappears. But at the same time its explanatory power is radically reduced. Since the expected change in velocity is zero, the expected change in income over the next period becomes the expected change in the money supply in the next period, times the current value of income velocity.

$$\Delta Y^e_{t+1} = \Delta M^e_{t+1} V_t \tag{16.11}$$

Suppose the following two very strong but reasonable assumptions are made:

1. All changes in investment spending are financed by bank lending: ($\Delta I_{t+1} \equiv \Delta L_{t+1}$).
2. Bank lending only finances investment expenditures: ($\Delta L_{t+1} \equiv \Delta M_{t+1}$).

The change in investment is then equal to the change in the money supply: $\Delta I_{t+1} \equiv \Delta M_{t+1}$ Substituting the change in investment for the change in the money supply in equation 16.11, the expected change in income in the following period is equal to the change in investment in the following period, times the current income velocity of money.

$$\Delta Y^e_{t+1} = \Delta I_{t+1} V_t. \tag{16.12}$$

This states that over each individual time period the Keynesian multiplier, the ratio of the increase in income to the increase in autonomous spending ($m = \Delta Y/\Delta I$), is equal to the income velocity of money ($V = \Delta Y/\Delta M$).[20] The Keynesian multiplier is simply the income velocity of money! Both the Keynesian multiplier and velocity are identities, true over every period and at every instant of time.

There is one major problem. The length of the multiplier period over which income adjusts to a change in investment, and the length of the velocity period over which income adjusts to a change in the money supply are not identical. Velocity is arbitrarily defined for an income period of one year, while the time period of the multiplier is undefined. The time period (t+1) representing the change in income associated with a change in the money supply (equation 16.11) is not identical to the time period (t+1), representing the change in income associated with a change in investment spending (equation 16.12).[21]

The ratio of money to income (M/Y) is not governed, as the Monetarists asserted, by the demand for money, i.e. by the asset by preferences of bank depositors. The ratio of money to income is determined by the demand for credit, i.e., by the debt preferences of bank borrowers. Changes in the demand for credit on the asset side of bank balance sheets determine the change in the money supply. The money supply is endogenously determined by the demand for bank credit and not the demand for bank deposits.[22]

The quantity theory identity reveals that the rate of growth of money income may be expressed in terms of the behavior of the money supply, and of the income velocity of money:

Y = MV or $\dot{Y} = \dot{M} + \dot{V}$, where a dot over the variable denotes percentage change. In credit money economies the rate of change of money income depends on the rate of change of the money supply, and the rate of change of the income velocity of money.

Like most time series in economics, both money and velocity have a unit root, and loosely follow a random walk over time. Velocity varies pro-cyclically over the business cycle as the CB varies BR pro-cyclically to smooth fluctuations in AD. If these variables have a unit root the best forecast of the growth rate of income in the next period, is the growth rate of money and velocity in the current period. Changing technology in financial markets results in a positive drift in velocity.

Examination of the quantity theory identity reveals that, over longer periods, by far the largest share of the increase in AD is associated with the increase in the money supply. To the extent velocity is stable the rate of growth in AD is primarily attributed due to the rate of growth of the money supply. The money supply increases whenever deficit-spending is financed by bank borrowing, since deficit spending is financed by the issue of newly-created money. Newly-created money balances are always accepted in exchange, and represent a non-volitional increase in "convenience lending" and "convenience saving" to the banking system by bank depositors. No volitional increase in saving is required since saving is simply the accounting record of investment. The increase in bank-financed deficit spending for capital goods provides the "convenience saving" necessary to finance the capital accumulation and to increase AD, at the growth rate equal to the full capacity growth rate of the economy.

16.6 The simultaneous achievement of internal and external balance

The rate at which AD expands is determined by animal spirits and the level of BR set by the CB. Lower levels of BR result in a greater rate of deficit spending and capital formation and a more rapid growth of the money supply and AD. Keynes' insight, that capitalist economies are typically demand-constrained implies that CBs set "too high" a level of BR, that is a rate above the rate consistent with a full employment level of AD.

Why do CBs keep the level of interest rates so high, now that they have at last fully achieved their responsibility for setting the level of BR as a policy instrument? The reason is that under current institutional arrangements CBs are severely constrained in their ability to reduce BR by their other obligations. Their main constraint is their persistent obligation to achieve internal and external balance. As interest rates are reduced, bank borrowing increases and the rate of growth of the money supply and AD expands. Unfortunately in most economies wages and prices have a clear tendency to rise before full employment levels of output are reached.

In addition in most open economies higher AD growth results in greater current account deficits as import tend to expand more rapidly than exports. CBs are subsequently forced to raise BR to deter anticipated future increases in inflation, and in current account deficits. In consequence they are unable to achieve internal and external balance at a full employment level of output.[23]

It is widely believed that, at least in developed economies, restrictive monetary policy due to CB "Inflation Targeting" has been successful in reducing inflation rates by reducing agent expectations of future inflation. But this has been achieved primarily by Phillips Curve effects of raising unemployment rates and reducing the bargaining power of labor. For price stability, wages must not increase more rapidly than the growth rate of average labor productivity. Wage moderation is an absolute pre-requisite for low inflation. In the absence of an Incomes Policy, which experience has shown to be a nonstarter for all major economies, there remains the possibility of redesigning the international financial architecture, to permit the simultaneous elimination of external balance and internal balance constraints. This possibility will be addressed in the final section: Open Economy Considerations.

Appendix: A critique of the Quantity Theory of Money

In all transactions where money is exchanged for goods, the agents acquiring money are conventionally described as having a "demand" for money. Although the identical word is used, there are substantive differences in meaning between the "demand" for money, and the "demand" for goods. It will be argued that in the interests of analytical clarity, the expression "the demand for" money should be abandoned and be replaced by "the acceptance of" money. As in the case of the use of the verb "to save" rather than "to abstain" in the analysis of saving behavior, changes in terminology can result in new perceptions of existing theory, in this case the "Quantity Theory of Money."

Much unnecessary confusion has been created by the terminological use of "the demand for" money. Money is "generally accepted" in exchange, and is not "demanded" in exchange for money in the sense that goods are "demanded." The "portfolio demand" to hold money by asset-holders initially appears superficially analogous to the "demand" for goods. But on reflection this parallel is also false and misleading.

Although money is "accepted" in wealth portfolios, money does not have a "price" in terms of money, as is the case with goods. The "price" of holding money in wealth portfolios may be viewed as the "opportunity cost" of holding money, in terms of the income foregone. But such a "price" does not denote the meaning of "price" in the sense that is used for goods, the number of units of money for which the good can be exchanged. Goods have both a "price" in terms of money and a price in terms of "opportunity cost." But money does not have a money price. The "price" of one unit of money in terms of money is by definition unity.

Money does not have a money price at which it is exchanged to equilibrate supply and demand as in the case of goods, for the following reasons:

1. Money is not a "goods" but is rather a "token," the thing that by convention is generally accepted in exchange. Money is a generalized "store" of purchasing power, "generally accepted" in exchange for goods due purely to social convention, like a language.
2. The quantity of money demanded is not subject to "diminishing marginal utility" as in the case of goods, where satiation occurs as the quantity consumed increases.
3. The "acceptance" of money in exchange does not have the deliberative price-versus-quantity-demanded diminishing-marginal-utility characteristic of the "demand" for goods.
4. The quantity of goods demanded is a function of the money price charged. Money is always "accepted" in exchange for goods and its money price is always unity.

5. The "acceptance" of money is not functionally related to the "price" at which money is sold as is the case with the "demand" for goods.
6. The "price" of goods is the number of units of money for which it is exchanged. But the "price" of money in terms of money is always unity.
7. Goods have a money price, and a price in terms of opportunity cost. But money does not have a money price. The "price" of money can only be defined as the "opportunity cost" of holding money, the interest rate differential between the return on holding money and on holding interest-bearing money-substitutes. Moreover the "price" of money in the sense of opportunity, cost does not influence the quantity of money "accepted" in exchange for goods as is the case for the price of goods.
8. The "price" of money, in the sense of opportunity cost, varies with the expected rate of return on other assets.
9. The "opportunity cost" of holding money is very different from the "opportunity cost" of goods. It does not denote the money price to acquire money.
10. The "price" of money in the sense of opportunity cost is widely believed to determine the proportion of their wealth portfolios that wealth owners desire to hold in the form of money. But this is incorrect. Money is always accepted in exchange, irrespective of the price of money in terms of its "opportunity cost" or of the supply of money currently in existence.
11. Money is always accepted in exchange irrespective of the quantity of money held in wealth portfolios. The "acceptance" of newly-created deposits denotes a non-volitional increase in "convenience lending" of fiat money by depositors to the banking system.
12. Whenever spending on capital goods or durable consumer goods is financed by bank loans, the increase in investment spending is accompanied by an identical increase in non-volitional "convenience saving."
13. Bank deposits are both the banks' liabilities and the accounting record of bank assets. Changes in the supply of bank deposits are caused by changes in the demand for credit, not by changes in the demand for deposits.
14. Once created as a by-product of bank lending bank deposits are always "accepted" in exchange and are always held in wealth portfolios, irrespective of the "return on" or the "opportunity cost of" deposits.

The nature of "demand for money" has been critically considered above as a precondition for the analysis of the "Quantity Theory of Money." Despite minor differences in formulation, the Quantity Theory commands such assent among economists as to appear self-evident. But Quantity Theory analysis is seriously misleading as a description of monetary exchange, because the Quantity Theory incorrectly regards the "demand" for money as analogous to the "demand" for goods.

The Quantity Theory can be summarized in the following five propositions:

1. The quantity theory is simply an identity:

    $Y \equiv MV$

    where Y is nominal annual income, M is the money supply, and V is the income velocity of money (Y/M). Since money is a stock variable and income is a flow variable, V resolves the dimensional incommensurateness of the expression.
2. Money is neutral by assumption. All nominal variables can be deflated by the price level and transformed into "real" variables: $Y \equiv py$ where y is the level of real income (Y/p) and p is the price level.
3. The "demand" for money balances is assumed to be a broadly stable function of the level of income, and output, wealth and the rate of return on other assets $M/p = f(y, w, r_i)$.[24]
4. The income velocity of money (V = Y/M) is assumed to have some behavioural stability.

5. The supply of money is assumed to be under the control of the monetary authorities. It appears that when the money supply is changed, comparative static analysis implies that the price level will vary in proportion to the change in the money supply.

The quantity theory makes a number of very strong implicit assumptions:

(a) Additional money can autonomously be "injected" or "withdrawn" from the system, *ceteris paribus*.
(b) The public can be induced to hold more or less money than it desires to hold, and economic units can find themselves with an excess supply of or excess demand for money.
(c) Agents will spend more or less money on goods and services, due to an "excess" supply of or demand for money.
(d) Full employment, technology and the level of real output are all assumed to be given.
(e) If the quantity theory holds, prices must change until both the nominal and the real money stock are willingly held.

Working from the Quantity Theory paradigm Monetarists and their critics have devoted substantial analytical and empirical effort to explicating the "monetary transmission process." Each component of the Quantity Theory argument has been directly or indirectly challenged and defended:

(1) Can money be exogenously "injected" into the system, or is the money supply endogenous?[25]
(2) Is the supply of money independent of the demand for money?
(3) Is the demand for money empirically stable?
(4) Is monetary change neutral? Do interest rates change in the adjustment process?
(5) Is the level of real output independent of aggregate demand?
(6) Is "broad" or "narrow" money a better determinant of the price level?
(7) What is the time period required for the adjustment process to work itself out?

But none of these questions goes to the fundamental error in the Quantity Theory. The conclusion that the proportional change in the money stock determines the proportional change in the price level holds only for *comparative static general equilibrium analysis*. But real world economies as complex adaptive systems can never be in "general equilibrium." Expectations of the unknowable future change continuously, accompanied by continuous changes in demand and supply, expected returns and AD. Like all economic variables the money supply changes continually, in response to continual changes in the demand for bank credit and in the repayment of bank loans. Changes in the money supply are always "accepted" by depositors, irrespective of concurrent inflation rates and expected returns.

General Equilibrium (GE) is defined as a position where all markets are in a position of balance, and no prices or quantities change. GE is intended to be truly "General" and include all markets and all economic behavior. In GE analysis there are no *ceteris* that must remain *paribus*, since all variables are included.

The central goal of GE analysis is to discover if there exists a core set of prices and expectations consistent with general equilibrium, so all values are internally "congruent" and all markets are "clear." At this point there is no tendency for any variable to change. But complex systems have no tendency to approach any "equilibrium" position defined as a hypothetical position of "balance," where all change ceases.

If the price level is assumed to be given, the marginal utility of money is positive. From the viewpoint of individual agents the marginal utility of money can never be reduced to zero, no matter how much money the agent possesses. If "excess supply" is defined for money as it is for goods, as a position where the goods' own price must be lowered to induce additional demand, money can never be in "excess supply," since agents can never be in a position where they have "too much" money. Agents can never have an "excess supply of" or an "excess demand for" money.

Perpetual change is the essence of complex systems, so the assumption of GE is logically unattainable. GE cannot be incorporated into the analysis of complex systems, since GE denies the essence of complexity: perpetual change. In the complex real world the *ceteris* never remain *paribus,* and equilibrium analysis yields incorrect conclusions. "GE" is not a useful analysis for complex systems since the assumption of GE conflicts with the inherent dynamic nature of complexity. The conclusions of GE analysis cannot hold for complex systems since for complex systems a position of GE cannot be imagined.

For partial equilibrium analysis, the *ceteris paribus* clause must be invoked to close the system. For all empirical statements such a procedure is necessary. (E.g. all predictions in the social sciences implicitly assume the temperature of the interior of the sun remains broadly constant.) But a key contribution of complexity theory is the recognition that for complex systems, the *ceteris* can never remain *paribus*. All things are continuously changing over time, at different rates. Once economies are recognized as complex systems, all determinate relationships and deductive reasoning are seen to be mis-specified. Comparative static equilibrium analysis cannot capture the dynamic complexity of real world economic behavior.

Only partial equilibrium analysis can be used to analyze complex systems. But because money is defined as the asset that is **generally accepted** in exchange, it is not possible to conduct partial equilibrium analysis for money. Partial equilibrium analysis of money demand is illegitimate, since money is not an economic good but a social convention. Money is a general store of claims to purchasing power. Since money is generally exchanged for all other goods, a position of "partial equilibrium" for money logically implies a position of "general equilibrium."

Credit money is a debt, so any change in the money supply must necessarily be accompanied by an identical change in a financial liability. It is therefore not logically possible to assume, *ceteris paribus*, a change in the supply of credit money.

Since agents can never have an "excess supply" of money the Quantity Theory falls. So long as money retains its general acceptability or "moneyness," an "excess supply" of money cannot be imagined. The monetarist comparative-static "thought-experiment," that an exogenous change in the nominal money supply will lead to a proportionate change in all prices and incomes, is a logical *non sequitur*. It requires the commodification of the tokens that constitute money.

Monetarists, by defining the demand for money in real terms, finesse the objection that the demand for nominal money balances is unlimited. It may be legitimate for an economist as outside observer to convert nominal money balances into real balances by deflating nominal quantities by a price index so as to compare "real" positions at different points in time. But in real world economies, agents can only exchange goods for nominal money. So long as money retains its moneyness, nominal money balances are always accepted in exchange for goods, irrespective of the level of prices, incomes, inflation, or real value of money balances. The conversion of nominal money balances into real money balances represents an illegitimate injection of General Equilibrium into monetary analysis.

The deflation of nominal into real balances makes no difference to agent willingness to demand and supply nominal money in exchange. Economists are always able to convert nominal into real values, by deflating by the price level. But agent monetary behavior can apply only to nominal quantities of money since agents can only supply and accept nominal money in exchange.[26] To comprehend monetary behavior, economists must conduct their analysis in terms of nominal money.

"Excess supply" implies that agents find themselves with greater quantities of the good in question at the current price than they wish to hold. But additional money is always "accepted," at every moment in time, without any change in any price. So long as money retains its general acceptability in exchange, an "excess supply" of money balances involves a logical contradiction, and cannot be envisaged. Agents are always willing to accept (demand) additional units of money in exchange with no change in any price.

The conclusion that marginal utility declines as the quantity held increases due to the law of diminishing returns holds only for goods, and is not applicable to money. A situation of excess supply is conceptually possible only for goods, where the money price must be lowered to induce additional demand. In the case of a barter economy, where money does not exist, a position of general equilibrium where all markets clear is logically conceivable, since in a barter economy all markets can conceptually be envisaged to be in equilibrium.

The Quantity Theory thought experiment contains an intrinsic logical contradiction. In order to assume the supply of credit money can be exogenously given, time must be stopped and all expectations must be frozen. If one makes the assumption of a perfectly certain world, a position of GE would be logically conceivable for a barter economy. But in such a world, where all prices are known, there would be no need for money. **"The conditions necessary for a GE to exist in a monetary economy are the conditions necessary for a perfect barter economy where money has no function,"** QED.

For complex systems the quantity theory "thought-experiment," that agents may be imagined to be in a position of "monetary equilibrium," involves an inherent logical contradiction. It is literally nonsense. Additional units of nominal money are always accepted with no change in any price, irrespective of the price level or the real value of money in agents' possession. As there can be no "general equilibrium" in a monetary economy there can be no "partial equilibrium" demand for money.

As soon as the notion of "general equilibrium" is discarded, the Quantity Theory falls, since there can be no "GE" quantity of money demanded. Since money is defined as "the thing that is generally accepted in exchange," money is a social convention, not a commodity. As such, money does not have a "price", does not have a "demand", and can never be in "excess supply." (If there were an "excess supply" of money, money would not be generally accepted," and so would not be money).

The Quantity Theory thought experiment, that an increase in the supply of money will lead to an excess supply of money, is fallacious. Money is accepted, not demanded, can never be in "equilibrium" and can never be in "excess supply". The Quantity Theory vision, that in GE an exogenous change in the money supply will result in a proportional change in the price level, cannot logically be sustained. Money is not a commodity, the Quantity Theory is a misleading fiction, literally non-sense.

Part V
Open Economy Considerations

17
Using National Currencies in International Trade: The Case for Fixed Exchange Rates

> The weight of my criticism is directed against the inadequacy of the theoretical foundations of the laissez-faire doctrine upon which I was brought up and which for many years I taught—against the notion that the rate of interest and the volume of investment are self-adjusting at the optimum level, so that preoccupation with the balance of trade is a waste of time. ...
> John Maynard Keynes, 1936; CW VI: 339

> Years ago, money was an international thing: if you had the money of one country you could change it into the money of another at a fixed rate, and you never had to think which currency you held. Exchange control changes all that: before anyone accepted payment in a controlled currency, he had to discover where he could spent it and what he could buy with it. One by one the currencies of the world like their national economies were becoming independent of one another.
> John Maynard Keynes, 1940, CW XXV: 3

> The problem of maintaining equilibrium in the balance of payments between countries has never been solved since methods of barter gave way to the use of money and bills of exchange. During most of the period in which the modern world has been evolved ... the failure to solve this problem has been a major cause of impoverishment and social discontent and even of wars and revolutions.
> John Maynard Keynes, 1941, CW XXXV: 21

17.1 Open Economy Macroeconomics

Although international trade is conducted under different types of trading regimes, most countries continue to use their own national currencies in international transactions. Profound changes were introduced into the postwar world when the Bretton Woods fixed-but-adjustable exchange rate regime broke down in the early 1970s and the trading system evolved into a flexible exchange rate regime. The current flexible exchange system was not adopted volitionally. It was forced on countries by the inability to maintain fixed exchange rates under Bretton Woods.

Due to the memories of the 1930s the European Economic Community (EEC) has a long history of resistance to freely floating exchange rate regimes and "beggar-my-neighbor" exchange rate policies.[1] In response to the threatened disruption of Bretton Woods in 1969 the EEC announced that monetary union was the long-term goal of the Community, and a three-stage approach was proposed towards monetary union: (1) policy coordination, (2) realignment of exchange rates, and (3) a European central bank. The evolution of the European Exchange Rate Mechanism is a manifestation of the general skepticism about the operation of unregulated financial markets and the consensus on the desirability of limiting exchange rate flexibility.[2] Since the collapse of Bretton Woods in 1971, the elimination of restrictions on capital transactions has led to an astonishing increase in the volume of financial transactions and an explosion in new financial derivative instruments. The move to flexible exchange rates has greatly increased the complexity of the international trading system and the uncertainty about how the system worked. In the current flexible exchange rate regime economists are not only unable to predict future exchange rates movements, they are unable to explain why past exchange rate movements have occurred.

The increased openness of domestic economies to foreign disturbances has been accompanied by much controversy concerning the causes and consequences of the huge trade imbalances that have evolved among the major industrial economies. In less than ten years the United States went from being the world's largest creditor nation to the world's largest debtor.[3] This was accompanied by corresponding large sequential trade surpluses in Germany, Japan, the Asian Tigers and now China.

Public officials in all countries have been greatly alarmed by the huge fluctuations in exchange rates that have accompanied trade imbalances under the new flexible exchange rate regime. American negotiators have tended to attribute the US trade deficit to unfair trading practices on the part of creditor nations, and have sought to correct the imbalance by restricting US imports and bilaterally pressing other countries to purchase additional American exports. But most economists do not believe that "unfair" trade practices were the primary determinant of the huge trade imbalances. They have emphasized the causal role played by the different patterns of domestic investment and saving behavior.

Economies have a net deficit or surplus on external account when their domestic expenditures exceed, or fall short of, their domestic output. In the National Income Accounts (NIA) the current account balance is equal to the difference between domestic saving and domestic investment. Economists as a result have rather naturally interpreted trade surpluses and deficits as implying different national units have volitionally saved more or less than they have invested. Most US economists currently believe that the rise in the US trade deficit is a reflection of inadequate underlying national saving propensities. There is broad agreement that the root of the huge US balance of payments deficits lies in the sharp decline in the nation's saving rate. This has been accompanied by repeated calls for government policies to increase "domestic resource mobilization" and raise the national saving rate.[4] Economists have viewed total saving as determined by the sum of volitional saving decisions by ultimate wealth owners.

But as previously developed from the point of view of the economy saving is simply the accounting record of investment. $S \equiv I$ is an accounting identity so the two magnitudes are identical by definition. As shown in Chapter 8 in developed financial systems the majority of total saving is non-volitional, and takes the form of the passive accumulation of newly created bank deposits ("convenience lending" and "convenience saving") and the accumulation of equities and other financial and real assets of higher market value (the nonconsumption of capital gain income). Total saving is identical to total investment as an accounting identity. Although it is the sum of agents' saving behavior, saving is determined by investment behavior not by saving behavior.[5]

In the United States since the 1980s the deficits in the current account and in the government budget have been referred to as the "twin deficits." The emergence of large and rising current account deficits has been attributed to increases in the government's budget deficit and to the decline in the personal savings rate. During the 1990s large government deficits were transformed almost overnight into large government surpluses, but the current account deficit continued to grow. Its current level (2005) has reached the historically unprecedented amount of US$600 billion, or nearly $2.0 billion per day. Economists' have changed their lament about the unprecedented sharp decline in the private saving ratio in the late 1990s to the huge increase in the government's deficit since 2000.

As was shown in Chapter 7 whether income is defined to exclude or include capital gains critically affects the empirical measurement of saving and investment. When capital gains are included in income and investment, large private sector deficits can become large private sector surpluses. In National Income Accounting systems saving is the accounting record of capital formation. But capital may be measured at historical cost or at current market value. When saving is defined as equal to the net increase in wealth measured at current market value the definition of income must include capital gains and losses.

The exchange rate determines the relative price of domestic and foreign goods and services. The extent that changes in exchange rates influence changes in trade flows has long been the subject of substantial controversy. The story is not simple since many multinational firms vary their markups to gain market share. Before the 1980s most country current account surpluses and deficits were small and transitory. National saving and investment rates were closely linked, and moved up and down together.[6] In the 1980s the US national saving rate as conventionally calculated fell sharply in the public sector and in the 1990s also in the private sector. The gap between domestic saving and investment was filled by increases in local indebtedness and an inflow of finance from overseas.

This new international debtor–creditor configuration altered the traditional position of wealthy countries as net creditors who supply capital to the poorer debtor nations with greater unexploited investment opportunities. United States, the world's richest country, has as a result of the new de facto US Dollar trading regime accidentally become the world's largest debtor. American consumers have benefited enormously from the US economy's ability to run persistent current account deficits. But so has the rest of the world since other countries have been provided with a huge export market, and have been able to increase their annual current account surplus by $600 billion and accumulate equivalent foreign exchange reserves.

It is unfair that only Americans enjoy these delights of a "free lunch." Why should not other countries be allowed to join the party? There is also the potential problem that US consumers are now heavily dependent on the net inflow of foreign resources (purchases of US government securities) to support their high living standards. If foreigners were to decide to no longer accumulate US Dollars the US exchange rate could collapse and the world would be thrown into financial turmoil. Who would be able to pick up the pieces?

Advances in communications and calculations technology combined with the liberalization of controls on financial transactions have resulted in rapid development of international financial markets and enormous expansions of financial capital flows. Domestic saving no longer finances only domestic investment since domestic investment can now draw on a worldwide pool of finance. Domestic saving now flows abroad in response to increases in interest rate differentials.

The increase in capital mobility and the growth of international capital flows has been accompanied by a greater equalization of interest rates across international capital markets. This suggests CB autonomy to set interest rates exogenously is being gradually constrained. International interest rate differentials are increasingly important in determining funds flows and changes in exchange rates. The fact that a loan is financed from abroad has no effect on the spending decisions of borrowers. Buyers do not appear to view domestic and foreign goods as close substitutes, since large changes in exchange rates in response to interest rate differentials are associated with smaller changes in aggregate trade flows. This is in part due to firms applying their pricing markups more flexibly to retain market share.

The Federal Reserve's very high interest rate policy in 1979–80 led to a huge appreciation of the US exchange rate of about 50 percent. By the mid-1980s the US trade deficit had reached a peak of $150 billion, or 4 percent of GDP. After the Plaza Accord in 1985 the Dollar rapidly fell back toward its 1980 level. But the response of trade flows was disappointingly small, and the trade deficit remained about $100 billion. The US deficit has now (2005) risen the unprecedented levels of $600 billion or about 6 percent of GDP, and the dollar has been falling against most other currencies. A depreciating US Dollar will no longer be regarded as a "safe haven" by international investors. This has led to concern about a future "tipping point" which could lead to massive portfolio reallocation, and a sharp fall in the US exchange rate. One difficulty is that current NIA's exclude all capital gains, so increases in the market value of overseas direct investments are not measured in the calculation of US international net worth.

As stated exchange rates have been subject to excessive variations that are not well explained by existing theories. Uncovered interest rate parity states that in the presence of perfect capital mobility, with no capital controls, the expected real return on homogeneous assets should be equal, irrespective of their location. If one CB raises Bank Rate (BR) above the rate ruling in the center economies, short-term capital inflows will cause the domestic exchange rate to appreciate sufficiently until it has overshot its expected value, and is expected to depreciate over the next year by an amount equal to the interest rate differential. In this case borrowers and lenders are indifferent between borrowing and lending in domestic or overseas markets. This is termed 'Interest Rate Parity'.

The inability of economists to predict *ex ante* or even to explain or understand *ex post* exchange rate movements in flexible exchange rate regimes imposes a severe lack of transparency and a myriad of obstacles to modeling the behavior of open economies. What is clear is that the combination of flexible exchange rate regimes and more integrated capital markets has in all economies severely reduced the impact of fiscal policy on the level of domestic AD and real output as a stabilization tool. Through the links between changes in interest rates, exchange rates and capital flows, monetary policy is now widely regarded as more important than fiscal policy in affecting changes in aggregate demand and exchange rates.

17.2 Consistent capital budget accounting for open economies

One cause of the confusion in open economy macroeconomics is the widespread belief that changes in interest rates are a reflection of endogenous shifts in volitional saving and investment behavior. It is believed that declines in saving or increases in investment spending lead to a rise in interest rates. The recent recognition that the level of short-term interest rates is the exogenous policy instrument of the monetary authorities *reverses* the causal direction between interest rates and income flows and requires that many hypotheses about international relationships be revised.

The earlier chapters were concerned with closed economies so all transactions between economic units outside the domestic economy were ignored. When all contractual settlements are in terms of the domestic monetary unit, all transactions are recorded in the balance sheet of the domestic banking system. Double-entry bookkeeping ensures that total expenditures on final goods and services are identical to total income receipts, apart from any accounting errors.

The present section will summarize how National Income Accounting rules should be adjusted for the correct capital accounting of open economies. Different exchange rate regimes have widely different implications for international transactions when a Hicksian definition of income is adopted. The recognition that saving is the accounting record of investment implies that deficits to imports of capital finance goods represent an increase in the capital stock, not a reduction in domestic saving. By responding differently to trade imbalances different exchange rate regimes reduce or magnify the effects of the trade imbalance on AD, inflation, employment and output, and alter the relative effectiveness of monetary and fiscal policy.

In the real world most countries are deeply interlinked with other countries through their trade in goods, services, financial assets and immigration. Nevertheless most countries continue to use their own money in international exchange. Open economies include transactions between domestic units and units resident in foreign countries. The degree of openness of an economy is frequently measured by the ratio of the average of the sum of exports and imports to GDP.

Once international transactions are introduced, the identity between aggregate domestic expenditure and aggregate domestic income ceases to hold. The market value of the production of final goods by domestic agents is no longer identical to total expenditures by domestic agents on domestic final goods and services, or to total income earned by domestic residents. National Income Accounting in open economies is derived from double-entry bookkeeping. Every item that puts the domestic economy in debt to foreigners is recorded in the debit column, and every item that provides the domestic economy with a claim on foreigners is recorded in the credit column.[7]

The value of merchandise credits minus merchandise debits defines the Balance of Trade. Adding the net value of exports and imports of services, and net income received from or paid to foreigners, yields the Balance on Goods, Services and Income Account. Adding net unilateral transfer payments yields the Balance on Current Account. When the current account balance is positive, agents in the economy spend less on imports than they earn on net exports and other current receipts. When it is negative, they spend more on current imports than their net export earnings plus transfers.[8]

The current account balance is determined by the causes of changes in exports and imports: the behavior of foreign income (Y_f), domestic income (Y_d), and the relative prices of domestic and foreign produced goods and services. Trade in goods and services is the largest component of the current account balance, but there are many other kinds of income and wealth transactions among residents of different countries. When domestic residents make more payments to foreigners than foreigners make to domestic residents the current account is in deficit, and governments must decide how these payment deficits are to be financed.[9] Conversely when foreigners make more payments to domestic residents than residents make to foreigners the current account is in surplus, and governments must decide on the form in which these surpluses are to be held.

The capital account balance indicates how current account deficits or surpluses are financed or invested: by changes in short-term credits, the sale or purchase of long-term assets, and the sale or purchase of foreign reserves. As the product of double-entry bookkeeping, the Balance of Payments must always balance. When the current account is in deficit, the capital account must be in surplus. Conversely when the current account is in surplus, the capital account must be in deficit.

Under a flexible exchange rate regime future changes in the exchange rate are a perpetual concern to both exporters and importers since exchange rate changes can easily wipe out profits from international trade and turn them into losses. When two countries use the same currency, they have a common monetary system.[10] The great advantage of a common system is that all uncertainty about future relative exchange rates and future relative values of the two currencies is in one stroke eliminated.

When two countries use the same currency they no longer have an exchange rate between them. This leads to the biggest advantage of common currencies: they no longer need be concerned with the trade balance between them. Permanent or structural deficits can then continue indefinitely, as occurs among groups within a single economy.

When each country uses its own national currency in foreign transactions forward markets permit agents to hedge future short-term exchange rate changes, permitting exchange rate risk to be shifted from entrepreneurs to speculators. But hedging foreign exchange rate movements is not the same as using a single currency. Entering into hedging contracts to eliminate the risk of future changes in exchange rates imposes substantial transactions costs. Forward exchange markets are of short duration normally 90–180 days. Exchange rate uncertainty associated with longer time periods, as is applicable to most real investment decisions cannot be shifted. When two countries each use its own currency in international transactions, the exchange rate risk must be borne by at least one and usually two parties.

Following the basic terminology of the NIA, for open economies the National Income Accounting identities is conventionally written:

$$GDP = C + I + G + (X - M) \quad (17.1)$$
$$GDP = C + S + T \quad (17.2)$$

Equating 17.1 and 17.2,

$$(I - S) = (T - G) + (M - X) \quad (17.3)$$

Saving and investment appear to differ by sum of the government (T−G) and the foreign trade (M−X) deficit or surplus. Chapter 7 demonstrated that by using consistent capital budgeting and distinguishing public consumption and public investment activities saving remains identical to investment (S = I) after the inclusion of the government sector.

When the government sector is eliminated, equation 17.3 simplifies to:

$$(I - S) = (M - X) \quad (17.4)$$

It appears that in open economies, saving and investment differ by the deficit or surplus in the current account. But as in the case of public goods consistent capital budgeting requires that consumption goods and capital goods be carefully distinguished. Consumption (C) is the market value of domestically produced (C_d) and imported (C_m) consumption goods: $C = C_d + C_m$ Investment (I) is the market value of domestically produced (I_d) and imported (I_m) investment goods: $I = I_d + I_m$. Government spending is the market value of domestic and foreign public goods $G = G_d + G_m$.

Imports (M) are the total value of foreign consumption, investment, public, and intermediate goods (raw materials and goods-in-process) imported into the economy ($M = C_m + I_m + G_m$). Since all exports leave the economy there is no need to distinguish exports of consumption and investment goods, so X denotes the total value of all goods exported to other economies.

Equation 17.4, the accounting identity stating that the difference between saving and investment equals the current account imbalance, is thus incorrect. From the point of view of consistent capital budgeting it fails to distinguish imports of consumption goods from imports of investment goods. On a global basis, providing there is no measurement errors, the world current account balance must sum to zero. The world is a closed economy and world saving is the accounting record of world investment.[11] Once consistent capital budgeting is introduced, the identity between domestic saving and investment is restored in open economies.

The National Income Accounting identity (equation 17.1) must be rewritten to distinguish imports of consumption goods which represent domestic consumption, from imports of investment goods which represent domestic saving. GDP may be viewed as the sum of domestically produced consumption goods, investment goods, and government goods plus total exports:

$$GDP = (C - C_m) + (I - I_m) + (G - G_m) + X \qquad (17.5)$$

In closed economies aggregate domestic output is necessarily identical to aggregate domestic expenditures. In open economies the difference between aggregate domestic output and aggregate domestic expenditure (AD) is the value of total exports minus the value of total imports. This difference represents the economy's Current Account Balance (CAB) of Trade in Goods and Services:

$$GDP - AD = (X - M) = CAB \qquad (17.6)$$

The CAB summarizes all current transactions with foreigners; trade in goods and services (X−M); net factor income receipts (NFI); and net transfer payments (NTR):

$$CAB = (X - M) + NFI + NTR \qquad (17.7)$$

The real exchange rate (q) between two countries provides a measure of their relative price levels: it is equal to the nominal exchange rate (e) multiplied by the ratio of foreign to domestic price levels ($q = e \cdot (P_f / P_d)$). Following standard convention the nominal exchange rate e may be defined as the domestic currency price of a unit of foreign currency. A rise in e or q indicates a nominal or real devaluation or depreciation of the domestic currency.

$$(X - M) = f(Y_d, Y_f, q) \qquad (17.8)$$

Chapter 7 demonstrated why in all closed economies saving is the accounting record of investment. In open economies saving appears to differ from investment by the size of the current account surplus or deficit (X−M). Ignoring the government sector total saving (S) is equal to total domestic investment (I) plus the current account surplus or deficit (X−M).

$$S - I = (X - M) \text{ or } S = I + (X + M) \tag{17.9}$$

The current account surplus (X−M) is confusingly termed "Net Foreign Investment" in the literature. But (X−M) does not represent "net foreign investment" in the domestic sense of net capital formation. Although (X−M) is termed "net foreign investment," it is simply the net change in foreign exchange holdings. It denotes saving in the colloquial sense; the net accumulation of financial assets. But it does not denote saving in the economic sense, income not consumed, or net capital formation. Such a definition of "net foreign investment," the net change in foreign exchange receipts due to the trade imbalance, is no longer of interest even for explaining the behavior of foreign exchange rates, since financial transactions have increased enormously relative to trade in goods. Nor does it explain the rate of net capital formation, since it fails to perform capital budgeting on the trade account, and does not classify imports of investment goods as a form of domestic saving.

The CAB (X−M) equals the foreign exchange inflow from current exports minus the foreign exchange outflow for current imports. Innovations in communication technology have greatly reduced the cost and enormously increased the value of international financial transactions. In the US economy the **daily** volume of financial transactions now greatly exceeds the **annual** volume of trade in goods and services. The annual volume of financial flows are about 500 times the annual volume of commodity flows.

Consider the "rest of the world" sector in isolation. To measure net real capital formation consistently in an open economy, the "current account balance" must be presented in a capital budgeting framework. Under the conventional definition (X−M), although termed "net foreign investment," represents the extent total foreign exchange credits received from the sale of exports are in excess of total foreign exchange debits to pay for imports of consumer, investment and public goods.

But imports of investment goods (I_m) are not "consumed" in the current period like consumption goods. They are real capital assets with an expected lifetime greater than one year that have been produced in other countries. As such they properly belong in the capital account not in the current account. Saving is the accounting record of investment. Net domestic capital formation results in an identical increase in net domestic saving irrespective of where the capital goods are produced or of how they are financed.[12]

Consistent capital budget accounting distinguishes imports of consumption goods (C_m) which belong in the current account, from imports of investment goods (I_m) which belong in the capital account. Imports of capital goods constitute domestic capital formation. As such they are properly recorded in the NIA as an increase in saving. Saving is the accounting record of increases in domestic investment, including investment goods produced in the rest of the world.

$$M = C_m + I_m \tag{17.10}$$

A country's current account is not "balanced" from a capital budgeting point of view when the proceeds from total exports are equal to the costs of total imports. It is balanced when the proceeds from total exports are equal to the costs of imports of consumption goods plus the estimated depreciation costs of imported capital goods: $(X-(C_m + Dep_{im}) = 0)$. Imported consumption goods are consumed in the present and on proper capital budgeting grounds must be financed by current export proceeds. But imported capital goods bear a future stream of investment services that extend beyond one year into the future. Only the estimated depreciation of capital goods constitutes current consumption which must be financed in the current period by exports.

With consistent capital budgeting, imports of investment goods belong in the capital account not in the current account. Imports of capital goods need not be financed by current export proceeds in the year of purchase as is the case for imports of consumption goods. They should rather be expensed over the expected lifetime of the capital good, as the capital assets depreciate. As with other investment goods imports of capital goods are appropriately capitalized and financed by debt. Under proper capital budgeting only their current depreciation must be charged against current export proceeds. Depreciation represents the estimated amount of capital goods currently used up and "consumed."

When Gross National Product is taken as the measure of aggregate income, Gross National Investment (I_N) is the record of all investment goods undertaken by Nationals in the economy. In this case imported investment goods are excluded.

$$I_N = (I - I_m) = S_N \tag{17.11}$$

But when Gross Domestic Product (GDP) is taken as the measure of aggregate income, Gross Domestic Investment (I_D) is the record of all National Investment (I_N) plus all Imported Investment (I_m). Total domestic Saving (S) then remains the accounting record of total domestic Investment (I_D). Whether capital formation is undertaken by nationals or foreigners is irrelevant from the point of view of total capital formation in the economy. GNP, defined as the value of total income and output produced by nationals, is a misleading measure of capital formation and output for open economies. GDP, the value of total income and output produced within the geographic area of the country, is the more appropriate measure of an economy's income and output.

To calculate Gross Domestic Investment, imports of investment goods must be distinguished from imports of consumption goods and imports of investment goods must be included in Gross Investment. Using GDP as the measure of domestic income the appropriate definition of the current account balance is: $(X - C_m - Dep_{im})$. Only the annual depreciation of imported capital goods (I_m) is properly recorded as a current cost, which must be financed by current exports. The total value of imports of capital goods in excess of their current depreciation expenses represents domestic capital formation which on capital budgeting grounds is appropriately financed by the issue of debt. When the maturity of the debt is equal to the estimated lifetime of the capital goods the annual interest expense is the appropriate measure of the annual cost of the services on imported capital goods.

Using GDP as the measure of aggregate output, the balance on current account must be redefined. Under proper capital budgeting the CAB defines the position where the foreign exchange proceeds from exports are sufficient to finance imported consumption goods plus the depreciation charges on imported investment goods [X − (C_m − Dep_{im}) = 0]. Total domestic savings is then the accounting record of total domestic investment: (S = I).

$$CAB = (X - C_m - Dep_{im}) \qquad (17.12)$$

Domestic investment (I_D) is equal to total domestic capital formation irrespective of whether the capital goods are produced domestically, or in other countries. Gross Domestic investment (I_D) equals domestic investment goods produced by nationals (I_N) plus imported investment goods produced by foreigners (I_M). This holds irrespective of how investment goods are financed. Domestic saving is then the accounting record of domestic investment. The importation of investment goods constitutes an act of domestic investment from the point of view of the domestic economy, irrespective of whether the capital goods are made by, financed by, or owned by foreigners, and should be reflected in domestic saving.

When developing countries (DCs) experience cyclical growth of AD imports of capital goods typically rise sharply. Due to scale economies most capital goods are imported in DC's. Under conventional National Income Accounting, imports of capital goods are recorded as increases in the current account deficit, and are treated as a reduction in National Saving. Countries whose imports exceed their exports are frequently castigated as "living beyond their means" and are expected to expand their exports or restrict their spending on imports, to reduce the current account deficit. But once it is recognized that imported capital goods represent domestic investment, and not domestic dis-saving like imports of consumer goods, it is obvious that imported capital goods constitute domestic capital formation and saving like domestic capital goods.

Using consistent capital budgeting, countries that borrow to import capital goods are not "living beyond their means." Balance of payment deficits incurred to finance capital imports are similarly not an indication of "fiscal imprudence." They represent the state of "animal spirits," i.e. expectations on the part of domestic and foreign investors that the expected future returns on capital projects will be greater than the interest cost of borrowing. The imposition of restrictive policies to reduce a current account deficit that is due to capital imports (X−M) is totally inappropriate.

Correct policy decisions require consistent national accounting. Current and capital transactions must be distinguished in the external accounts as they are in the domestic accounts. Countries which borrow to import capital goods are simultaneously investing and saving. Under consistent capital accounting when a country borrows to finance the acquisition of capital goods, this is not recorded as a current account deficit. When the CAB is properly defined the value of a country's export proceeds must equal only the value of its imports of consumption goods, plus the estimated value of the annual depreciation on all imported capital goods.[13] Net imports of capital goods belong in the capital accounts, and are properly financed by the issue of debt.

17.3 The classical view of balance of payments adjustment

Whenever countries use separate national currencies for international transactions trade imbalances create a liquidity problem for both the debtor and the creditor nation. Deficit nations must decide how their excess of international payment obligations over international payments receipts are to be financed over the future. With consistent National Income Accounting current account deficits are only created when a country's exports receipts fail to cover its imports of consumption goods, plus the depreciation charges on its imports of capital goods. Exporters in exporting nations normally provide short-term trade-credit to finance capital imports. This gives the deficit nation's capital goods importers time to arrange the appropriate longer-term funding of imported capital goods.

Surplus nations have the much less pressing but potentially equally destabilizing problem of selecting the asset in which to store their claims to additional international resources. Countries typically seek a "safe haven" currency in which to hold their liquid reserves. Under current international trading practices, this has long been the US Dollar. Now that the Dollar is depreciating and is expected to continue to fall, there has been consideration on the part of CBs toward diversifying their "safe haven" portfolios to include other assets, such as Euros and gold in addition to Dollars.

Classical trade theory has traditionally considered international payments imbalances as temporary adjustment phenomena. Strong automatic market mechanisms were believed to operate to eliminate any permanent payments imbalance. Liquidity problems were regarded as a complication of the "real" problems faced in barter transactions. It appeared perfectly natural that the onus for making balance of payment adjustments should fall solely on deficit nations. After all debtors must pay for the goods they purchase even when they are faced with shortages of liquidity.[14] When unanticipated international payments deficits occur nations are expected to maintain sufficient liquid foreign reserves to be able to meet all short-term obligations. Since increasing foreign reserves is expensive, this may require debtor countries to engineer an "output gap," and maintain AD below the economy's full employment output potential (internal balance). But this is a "Loss-Loss' situation. Export growth is constrained by the inadequate growth of world AD, and import growth is constrained by the inadequacy of world foreign exchange reserves.

Classical trade doctrine relied on David Hume's specie-flow mechanism to illustrate the temporary nature of international payment imbalance problems. Under the gold standard, an excess of imports over exports was believed to lead directly to an outflow of gold from deficit countries to surplus countries. The resulting reduction in gold reserves would eventually force the money supply of the deficit country to contract, and the supply of money in the surplus country to increase.

Using quantity theory reasoning monetary change was regarded as "causal" in the short run, but "neutral" in the long run. AD shocks were assumed to have only short-term effects. Changes in relative money supplies were expected over time to produce relative changes in national cost and price levels between surplus and deficit countries, and so automatically reduce the surpluses of surplus countries and the deficits of deficit countries. The change in relative prices was assumed to continue until balance of payments deficits and surpluses were eliminated. Monetary change was regarded as "neutral" and changes in relative price levels were assumed to leave global real income unchanged.

The world is obviously no longer on the gold standard. But a similar argument is incorporated into the "monetary approach to the balance of payments" reasoning. Even though nations no longer operate on the gold standard, it is assumed:

> Balance of payments deficits or surpluses are by their nature transient and self correcting, requiring no deliberate policy to correct them. ... The reason is simply that deficits reduce money stocks whose excessive size underlies the deficit, and surpluses build up the money stocks whose deficiency underlies the surplus.[15]

Trade imbalances are viewed by mainstream economists as temporary phenomena. So long as wages and prices are flexible, it was believed current account payments (BOP) imbalance would be resolved automatically by accompanying relative price movements in both countries. Imports were considered to be close substitutes for domestically produced goods and services. The classical "gross substitution axiom" demonstrated that as residents in surplus countries increase their import purchases, residents in deficit countries will reduce their demand for imports. The current account export–import balance in each country would be endogenously restored.[16]

Exchange rate appreciation and depreciation are the major classical mechanisms for invoking relative price movements to eliminate payments imbalance between imports and exports. If deficit nations run out of reserve assets before relative prices have changed sufficiently to bring exports and imports into balance, governments may be forced to devalue their exchange rate. If the country is in a floating exchange rate regime, the exchange rate will depreciate. Either way the fall in exchange rates will raise the domestic cost of imports and reduce the cost of exports to foreigners. This must eventually result in a reduction in import quantities and an expansion in export quantities until eventually current account balance of payments (CABOPs) equilibria are restored.

Devaluation or depreciation of the exchange rate causes the physical volume of imports demanded to fall since with devaluation the domestic price of imports rises, and causes the physical volume of exports supplied to rise since the foreign price of exports falls. But as has long been recognized changes in the quantities of commodities traded do not automatically carry over into changes in the values of traded commodities. Depreciation or devaluation initially lowers the price received for exports, and raises the price paid for imports. Its initial impact, before quantities have changed is to worsen the trade balance. So long as the sum of the price elasticity of the demand for imports plus the price elasticity of the demand for exports is in excess of unity the monetary value of exports minus imports must increase, and eventually become positive.[17]

Agents do not immediately adjust the quantities they purchase in response to changes in prices. In the short run the sum of the price elasticities are typically less than unity, so the immediate effect of a fall in the exchange rate is to worsen the country's payments imbalance. Since demand elasticity's are low over the short run, the Marshall–Lerner conditions are not satisfied. The dynamic response of the trade balance to an exchange rate devaluation or depreciation is the famous "J-curve." Exchange rate devaluation and depreciation initially worsens the trade deficit for some unspecified time period, which can extend for several years, before it eventually turns up and an improvement in the trade balance occurs. If the short-run worsening of the trade balance provokes dynamic exchange rate depreciation the improved positive trade balance may never materialize.

17.4 The Keynesian view of balance of payments adjustment

Keynes disagreed with the laissez faire view that so long as wages and prices were flexible, market economies possess homeostatic properties and eventually would reach a full employment equilibrium position. Expectations of future profits determine current investment behavior. The future is unknowable and expectations of future events are frequently characterized by herd phenomena, and exhibit wide fluctuations of optimism and pessimism (animal spirits). These lead to cyclical fluctuations in investment spending and in the level of economic activity. Keynes argued that governments must accept the responsibility to manage the level of aggregate demand, to ensure that economies remain over time on, and not within their production possibility frontiers.

In the *General Theory* Keynes developed a theory of output determination that was independent of the presence or absence of market power in individual markets. His theory of "effective demand" was intended as a general theory, and held irrespective of whether prices were flexible and markets were perfectly competitive, or prices were administered and markets were highly concentrated. He recognized that due to the special incentive nature of employment contracts, and the special long-term nature of labor contracts, money wages were inflexible downward. Firms administer prices as a stable markup on unit costs, and money wages and prices are jointly codetermined in labor and product markets. Keynes argued that output and employment respond to cyclical changes in aggregate demand for currently produced private and public goods.[18]

Due to the unprecedented length of the Great Depression, Keynes like most economists finally became persuaded that market forces on their own could not be relied upon to generate full employment output. He argued that governments must explicitly assume the responsibility to manage the level of aggregate demand to ensure that economies performed at their full employment potential frontier. Writing in the 1930s Keynes argued that due to insufficient expansionary monetary and fiscal policy, outdated laissez faire notions of fiscal prudence, monetary conservatism and the way international payments institutions were organized, market economies do not reach full employment "equilibrium" on their own. They instead remained for long periods in "sub-normal activity" with less than full employment levels of AD and output:

> It is an outstanding characteristic of the economic system in which we live that whilst it is subject to severe fluctuations in respect of output and employment, it is not violently unstable. Indeed it seems capable of remaining in a chronic condition of sub-normal activity for a considerable period, without any marked tendency either towards recovery or toward complete collapse. Moreover the evidence indicates that full, or even approximately full, employment is of rare and short-lived occurrence.[19]

The centrality of Keynes' principle of insufficient effective demand is the major theoretical distinction between post-Keynesian and mainstream New Keynesian, neoclassical, Monetarist, and New Classical macroeconomics. Post Keynesians insist that investment spending concerning the unknowable future is nondeterminate. Expectations are the key element driving changes in AD and driven by changes in "animal spirits." The autonomy of investment spending from current income and output is the source of the openness and indeterminism of the Keynesian system.

Although there exist causal relationships between changes in investment and changes in income they are not reducible to a mechanical "multiplier" or "law of motion," from which the future evolution of income can be predicted. Consistent with the discovery that all economic time series have unit roots, the long run may be viewed as the inter-temporal sequence of short runs. Unanticipated and autonomous demand-side changes are paramount in determining the path of output. The level of economic activity evolves in response to changes in AD and technology. Bi-directional feedback processes are common. The level of AD indirectly influences investment spending through a loose accelerator process, which in turn impacts directly on the rate of technological progress, capital utilization and output growth. The medium-run growth trajectory of an economy is the result of a near-random sequence of short-run events.[20]

Volitional decisions to increase saving do not finance additional investment spending, as the mainstream view maintains. The behavioral implication of an increase in volitional saving is a reduction in consumption spending, and so a reduction in aggregate demand. Increases in volitional saving depress the current and expected future level of demand and lead to a fall not a rise in investment spending. Economies are not restrained by a "deficiency" of saving.

Investment spending creates its own non-volitional "convenience" lending and saving.

Mainstream economists have succeeded in persuading themselves that income and price elasticities are generally high, so sufficient substitution occurs to ensure that economies in the long run are supply-constrained. The Keynesian problem of aggregate demand deficiency is regarded as a special problem of the 1930s, relevant only to cases of extreme depression. Free trade and international capital mobility are unambiguously assumed to raise global income by reducing AS constraints, through the principle of comparative advantage. Competition in unregulated national markets is expected to lead eventually although not directly to global prosperity and full employment.

In striking contrast in the *General Theory* Keynes argued that unemployment was due to a systematic deficiency of "effective demand," and not to the failure of labor markets to clear because of the downward inflexibility of money wages. "In the long run you are always in the short run." Keynes developed his argument of effective demand in the context of a closed economy. But in the final chapters of the *General Theory* he extended the argument to demonstrate how open economy considerations reinforced his central vision of global demand deficiency in market economies. In his post-*General Theory* writing, he hugely advanced his analysis of the global economy.

Keynes first argued that as an empirical fact money wages were sticky and inflexible downward. If a general reduction of money wages were to be brought about by government policy, this would result in a redistribution of real income from workers toward entrepreneurs and rentiers, and would have the indirect effect of reducing the aggregate propensity to consume. But he added,

> If we are dealing with an unclosed system, and the reduction of money wages is a *reduction relative to money wages abroad*, ... it is evident that the change will be favourable to investment, since it will tend to increase the balance of trade.[21]

Keynes thus explicitly acknowledged that in the case of an open economy a cut in money wages could stimulate domestic employment, as classical economists had long maintained. But he continued:

> A reduction of money-wages, though it increases the favourable balance of trade is likely to worsen the terms of trade. Thus there will be a reduction in real incomes, except in the case of the newly employed, which may tend to increase the propensity to consume.[22]

In the *General Theory* Keynes introduced open economy considerations in his discussion of Mercantilism. He argued that the Mercantilists had been correct in their belief that a favorable balance of trade was desirable for a country, since increases in foreign investment increase domestic AD exactly like increases in domestic investment:

> When a country is growing in wealth somewhat rapidly, the further progress of this happy state of affairs is liable to be interrupted, in conditions of *laissez-faire*, by the insufficiency of the inducements to new investment. ... the well-being of a progressive state essentially depends ... on the sufficiency of such inducements. They may be found either in home investment or foreign investment ... which between them make up aggregate investment. ... The opportunities for home investment will be governed in the long run by the domestic rate of interest; whilst the volume of foreign investment is necessarily determined by the size of the favourable balance of trade.[23] ...
>
> Mercantilist thought never supposed that there was a self-adjusting tendency by which the rate of interest would be established at the appropriate level.[24]...
>
> In a society where there is no question of direct investment under the aegis of public authority, ... it is reasonable for the government to be preoccupied ... [with] the domestic interest rate and the balance of foreign trade. ... when nations permit free movement of funds across national boundaries the authorities have no direct control over the domestic rate of interest or the other inducements to home investment, measures to increase the favourable balance of trade [are] the only direct means at their disposal for increasing foreign investment; and, at the same time, the effect of a favourable balance of trade on the influx of precious metals was their only indirect means of reducing the domestic rate of interest, and so increasing the inducement to home investment.[25]

Keynes emphasized that any domestic employment advantage gained by export-led growth was a zero-sum game and *"was liable to involve an equal disadvantage to some other country."* He argued that export-led growth aggravates the unemployment problem for the surplus nation's trading partners, who are forced to engage in "an immoderate policy that (may) lead to a senseless international competition for a favourable balance, which injures all alike."[26]

The traditional approach to improve the trade balance has been to attempt to make the domestic export and import-competing industries more competitive, either by forcing down nominal wages to reduce domestic production costs, or by devaluing the exchange rate. Keynes argued that gaining competitive gains by reducing nominal price variables would tend indirectly to foster a state of global recession. One's trading partners would be forced to attempt to regain their competitive edge by instituting their own restrictive policies. When nations fail jointly to undertake expansionary policies to raise domestic investment and generate domestic full employment, free international monetary flows create a global environment where each nation has national advantages in a policy of export-led growth. The pursuit of these policies will lead to a race to the bottom, that *"injures all alike."*

> the weight of my criticism is directed against the inadequacy of the *theoretical* foundations of the *laissez-faire* foundations upon which I was brought up and which for many years I taught—against the notion that the rate of interest

and the volume of investment are self-adjusting at the optimum level, so that preoccupation with the balance of trade is a waste of time[27]

These apposite warnings of Keynes have gone virtually unnoticed as mainstream economists have waxed enthusiastic about the benefits of liberalized financial markets and the export-led economic miracles of the Asian "Tigers," and now the miracle of China.[28] Modern economies have become more open than when Keynes was writing, so it is imperative that Keynes' open economy analysis becomes better known.

In the concluding chapters of the *General Theory* Keynes developed his argument at length why capitalist economies were demand-constrained. He first developed the general case for lower interest rates and emphasized that cheap money policies were frequently frustrated by balance of payments considerations:

> Under the influence of this faulty theory, the City of London gradually devised the most dangerous technique for the maintenance of equilibrium which can possibly be imagined, namely, the technique of bank rate coupled with a rigid parity of the exchanges. For this meant that the objective of maintaining a domestic rate of interest consistent with full employment was wholly ruled out. Since, in practice, it is impossible to neglect the balance of payments, a means of controlling it was evolved which instead of protecting the domestic rate of interest, sacrificed it to the operation of blind forces.
>
> Never in history was there a method devised of such efficacy for setting each country's advantage at variance with its neighbours as the international gold ... standard. It made domestic prosperity directly dependent on a competitive pursuit of markets, and a competitive appetite for the precious metals.[29]

Keynes insisted that the law of comparative advantage holds only after nations have achieved full employment through expansionary domestic AD management, and are on their production possibility curves. When economies operate under laissez faire policy mentality, they are restrained by AD deficiency to remain well within their production possibility curves. Substantial global unemployment is then inevitable, and the law of comparative advantage no longer applies. Free trade under these conditions is not per se globally job creating:

> Under the system of domestic laissez-faire, and an international gold standard ... there was no means open to a government whereby to mitigate economic distress at home, except through the competitive struggle for markets ... if nations can learn to provide themselves with full employment by their domestic policy, ... there need be no important economic forces calculated to set the interest of one country against that of its neighbours. There would still be room for the international division of labour and for international lending in appropriate conditions. But there would no longer be a pressing motive why one country need force its wares on another, or repulse the offerings of its neighbour, not because this was necessary to enable it to pay for what it wished to purchase, but

with the express object of upsetting equilibrium in the balance of payment so as to develop a balance of trade in its own favour [export-led growth]. International trade would cease to be what it is, namely, a desperate expedient to maintain employment at home by forcing sales on foreign markets and restricting purchases, which, if successful, will merely shift the problem of unemployment to the neighbour which is worsted in the struggle, but a willing and unimpeded exchange of goods and services in conditions of mutual advantage.[30]

17.5 Keynes' proposal for an international clearing union (ICU)

In November 1940 Keynes received a request from a friend in the Ministry of Information to counter German proposals, by a Dr Funk, for a "New Order" in the new postwar world.[31] By 1941 Keynes had written his first memorandum on postwar currency policy.[32] It included the following introductory comments on the international currency problem:

> so far from currency laisser-faire having promoted the international division of labour, which is the avowed goal of laissez-faire, it has been a fruitful source of all those clumsy hindrances to trade which suffering communities have devised in their perplexity as being better than nothing in protecting them from the intolerable burdens flowing from currency disorder. Until quite recently nearly all departures from international laisser-faire have tackled the symptoms instead of the cause.[33]

Keynes suggested that the interval between the wars offered: "almost, as it was ... an intensive laboratory experiment [of] all the alternative false approaches to the solution."[34]

Keynes' "false approaches" merit quoting at length, since they provide a near-complete set of familiar international economic policies that Keynes regarded as "proven fallacies":

(i) the idea that a freely fluctuating exchange would discover for itself a position of equilibrium;
(ii) the provision of liberal credit and loan arrangements between the creditor and debtor countries;
(iii) the theory that unlimited free flow of gold automatically bring about adjustments of price levels and activity in the recipient country, which would reverse the pressure;
(iv) the use of deflation, and still worse, competitive devaluations, to force an adjustment of wage and price levels;
(v) the use of deliberate exchange depreciation, and still worse of competitive exchange deprecations, to attain the same objective;
(vi) the erection of tariffs, preferences, subsidies *ac hoc genus omne* to restore the balance of international commerce by restriction and discrimination.[35]

Keynes decided the best solution was to adopt the idea that Dr Schlacht had stumbled upon in the last month before the great crash of 1929:

> to cut the knot by discarding the issue of a currency having international validity, and substitute for it what amounted to barter (of national reserve balances), not indeed between individuals, but between different national economic units, ... which has allowed impoverished Germany to build up reserves without which she could scarcely have embarked on war.[36]

Keynes gradually, laboriously, and nearly single-handedly developed his insights into a full-fledged formal English proposal for an "International Currency Union" and an "International Clearing Bank" (ICB). These were then eventually put forward as the British government's official proposals for Bretton Woods:

1. The ICB was to have its own currency, for which Keynes suggested the name "Bancor."
2. Bancor was not to be a new world currency. It was to be held only by CBs.
3. Its value was to be fixed in terms of gold, and Bancor was to be accepted as the equivalent of gold by all member CBs.
4. Each national bank was to keep an international account with the ICU, and their exchange balances would be settled with one another in terms of bancor.
5. Countries having a favorable balance with the ICU would have a credit balance, and those having an unfavorable balance would have a debit balance.
6. Each member state was to be allowed overdraft facilities based on its foreign trade volume.
7. Each CB was required to guarantee one-way convertibility from Bancor into its own currency, but national CBs were not permitted to purchase Bancor with their own currency.
8. Bancor credits were simply transfers from the bank account of one member to the bank account of another.
9. Since total credits and debits are necessarily equal, the ICB itself *"could never be in difficulty"* and could safely make whatever advances it wished to any of its members.[37]
10. Countries individually would be in debit or credit balance with the ICU but there was to be no direct indebtedness between member states.

The central innovation of Keynes' plan was that unlike the present system both debtor and creditor countries were required to share the responsibility for BOP adjustment. A nominal charge, e. g. 1–2 percent per annum was to be payable to the ICB, based on the average amount the balance of a particular member state exceeded or fell below its quota, irrespective of whether it was a debtor or as a creditor. Surplus and debtor countries were required to discuss with the bank the measures most appropriate for the country to restore equilibrium of their Bancor balances: changes in expenditures, loans, and borrowings. If at the end of the year the credit balance of any member bank exceeded the total amount of its quota, the excess was to be transferred to the Reserve Fund of the ICB and distributed proportionally to all deficit members.

Keynes' ingenious plan was based on the recognition that from the point of view of the world economy, country bookkeeping deficit and surpluses entries most necessarily sum to zero. If countries maintained their own convertible national currencies and if surplus countries were forcibly kept within their reserve quotas, deficit country deficits would similarly be constrained. So long as surplus countries could be deterred from building up surplus reserves above a specified proportion of their annual international trade, deficit countries as a group could not have deficit balances beyond an equivalent proportion of their annual trade.

Keynes was persuaded that without such a clearing union an international payments system using different national currencies would severely depress global economic expansion. When trading countries experience persistent current account imbalances, they are forced to pursue restrictive AD policies in the attempt to reduce the deficit in the current account. These deflationary restrictions on AD are not offset by correspondingly expansionary policies on the part of surplus nations. Hence the net "deflationary bias."

Keynes' proposals for an International Clearing Union (ICU) were derived directly from his macroeconomic vision of an open economy. The ICU was designed to create incentives for each nation to pursue expansionary domestic AD policies designed to ensure full employment. Debtor and creditor nations were to be penalized equally for being below or above their quotas. The plan remained within the given political constraints: "no new world currency" and "no new world central bank." Only after full employment was experienced in all countries would the law of comparative advantage come into its own. Keynes recognized that due to the presence of unemployment and excess capacity, the law of comparative advantage would not hold. Each nation has a self-interest incentive to pursue "beggar my neighbor" policies and export their unemployment to others.

In the end politics prevailed.[38] Despite Keynes' verbal pyrotechnics at Bretton Woods, the United States held all the cards. By the end of the war the United States was by far the world's largest GDP and also by far the world's largest creditor country. Keynes was unable to persuade the Americans that a financial penalty was an appropriate reward for being a wealthy creditor country. The ICB became the International Monetary Fund (IMF), and the World Bank was added to provide postwar reconstruction finance for developed countries and later development finance for developing economies.[39]

17.6 Conclusions: the Bretton Woods system—success and failure[40]

Bretton Woods and the IMF was America's compromise for Keynes' Clearing Union. It was designed in the same climate of opinion that produced the US Employment Act of 1946, and was comparable to progressive national economic policy legislation in many other countries at the time. Its institutional framework derived directly from the vivid experience of the Second World War and the world slump of the 1930s accompanied by the common determination that such tragedies must never again be permitted. The Bretton Woods Agreement comprised four central features:

1. Exchange rates between countries were to be fixed. This was clearly influenced by the turbulent background of flexible exchange rates in the 1920s and 1930s that contrasted sharply with the nineteenth century's successful experience with the gold standard.
2. All currencies were fully convertible in exchange for goods and services. This was influenced by the extensive wartime history of exchange controls by Nazi Germany, and the tight wartime restrictions on trade and payments levied by all allied countries. It was recognized that countries were unlikely to be able to pursue their domestic economic policies independently, and still maintain fixed exchange rates and convertibility, except by good luck or coincidence.

In order to obviate potential conflict, two important additional features were added.

(a) Temporary balance of payment deficits were to be covered by generous new short-term international lending. The IMF was created to channel this new low cost short-term lending to debtor countries.
(b) When faced with "a fundamental disequilibrium," exchange rates could be altered exogenously by a discrete amount, with the explicit permission of the IMF authorities.

The central flaw in the Bretton Woods arrangement was that no formal provision was provided for the secular growth of international reserves. It was (implicitly) assumed that, as in the past new gold production would be sufficient to provide for adequate growth in monetary reserves. At the end of the war US gold reserves amounted to more than 70 percent of the total world gold pool. Over the next 25 years $10 billion was gradually transferred to the rest of the world from the United States, and about $5 billion was added in new gold production. After an initial period of redistribution of the world's gold stock, surplus countries were no longer expected to convert their dollars into gold but were to accumulate interest-bearing reserves of US dollars. The US Dollar with its fixed price in terms of gold evolved into the world's international currency, and became the currency of intervention to assure that exchange rates remained fixed.

The Bretton Woods system essentially involved a bargain between the United States and the rest of the world. The United States was to maintain its domestic economic prosperity and to keep its domestic price level relatively stable. Other countries were to fix their currencies to the Dollar and to accumulate reserves in the form of gold-convertible Dollars. As an unintended result the United States no longer had to be concerned as did other countries on how to finance current account payments deficits. The United States was in effect able to act as the world's CB.

With hindsight wisdom, the Bretton Woods system may now be seen to have two major intrinsic flaws. It would eventually have broken down even without the burst of US inflation associated with the Vietnam War in the late 1960s which precipitated its demise:

1. The gold convertibility of the dollar was bound to become increasingly doubtful. The US position was precisely analogous to that of a CB whose cash reserve ratio is falling secularly over time. US Dollar liabilities continued to rise relative to US gold reserves. Although all currencies were formally symmetrical, the US Dollar was the only currency that guaranteed convertible into gold on demand at a fixed rate. Most countries continued to accumulate Dollars, but total reserve growth was insufficient.[41] A new international reserve asset—IMF Special Drawing Rights—aptly described as paper gold—was finally created in the late 1960s as a substitute for Dollar balances. But the change came too little and too late.
2. Equally important was the system's exclusive reliance on exogenous changes in exchange rates to correct payment imbalances. Once a country had persisted long enough for a current account imbalance to become "fundamental," the future direction of the change in the exchange rate was clear to everyone. This produced huge one-way invitations for currency speculators. Speculators could move into or out of a currency cheaply before they thought the "jump" was likely to occur, and then take their gains and run after the devaluation occurred. The result was a sloshing tidal wave of international currency flows which completely swamped the resources of individual country CBs, and left them virtually defenseless against global currency attacks by private speculators.

The Bretton Woods architects had anticipated this problem, and had stipulated that currencies were to be fully convertible only for current account transactions, not for the capital account. Capital controls were both operative and allowed in the Bretton Woods system. In a sense they were required by its internal logic. The free movement of capital is incompatible with a system of fixed exchange rates among national currencies, which is occasionally changed by huge and consequential amounts in predictable directions.

The Bretton Woods architects could not anticipate the enormous increase in financial capital movements that occurred over the postwar period. Due to technological innovations capital could be moved around the world instantaneously, at increasingly lower cost. Intra-corporate transactions grew ever more complex and international in nature. Payments for trade and for finance became inextricably mixed, and financial flows came to dominate and eventually overwhelm trade flows. The ratio of capital to trade transactions shot up whenever changes in exchange rates were anticipated. The subsequent movement of such funds greatly complicated the management of domestic policy. It became increasingly difficult to separate capital from current transactions, and to control capital transactions.[42]

The rise of US inflation rates in the late 1960s, directly connected with the US government's deficit due to the unpopular Vietnam War, resulted in ever-increasing gold outflows which eventually strained the system to its breaking point. In the face of hemorrhaging gold sales, President Nixon finally suspended the gold convertibility of the Dollar on July 13, 1971. After a short transition period Bretton Woods was abandoned and in 1973 the world embarked on its new experiment: floating exchange rates.

With hindsight wisdom the Bretton Woods period has since been termed the "Golden Age" of world economic performance. World trade expanded at a historically unprecedented rate. Inflation and unemployment rates were on average very low, growth rates were very high, and inflation rates were very moderate.

Adelman concluded that during Bretton Woods "productivity growth in OECD countries was more than triple that of the industrial revolution era."[43] From 1946 to 1970 the average annual growth of real GDP attained unprecedented heights in both developed and in developing countries. Over the entire period real growth averaged 6 percent in industrialized nations and 5.5 percent in developing nations. In per capita terms the growth rates of Developed Countries and Less Developed Countries attained an unprecedented long-term average of 5 and 3 per cent respectively. The difference was entirely due to the greater population growth rate of the developing world.

Bretton Woods was a great success until its demise. The framework of fixed but adjustable exchange rates combined with the ample international reserves made available by the Marshall Plan's recycling of US current account surpluses, permitted most countries to pursue expansionary monetary and fiscal policies simultaneously. International liquidity was for most periods in ample supply and the sharply reduced exchange rate uncertainty made rapid growth in international trade and output possible. For the first time in the twentieth century countries were able to pursue expansionary domestic policies simultaneously.

Interest rates were maintained at low levels throughout the period, and cheap monetary policy was pursued generally. Governments were given the freedom to pursue autonomous national economic policy, and to realize their domestic stabilization goals of full employment, price stability, and rapid growth. As a result of Bretton Woods for the first time countries were able to achieve external balance and internal balance simultaneously. Exchange rates remained stable and balance of payments crises was largely avoided. With hindsight wisdom, until its very end Bretton Woods was truly a "Golden Age."

18
Using National Currencies in International Transactions: The Case for Flexible Exchange Rates

To suppose that there exists some smoothly functioning automatic mechanism of adjustment which preserves equilibrium if only we trust to methods of *laisser-faire* is a doctrinaire delusion which disregards the lessons of historical experience without having behind it the support of sound theory.

Keynes, 1941, CW XXV: 21–2

There is no doubt that contractionary monetary and fiscal policies implemented in defence of the fixed parity put a serious drag on real economic performance

Buiter *et al.*, 1998: 37

It is characteristic of a freely convertible international standard that it throws the main burden of adjustment on the country which is in the debtor position on the international balance of payments. ... that is, on the country which is (in this context) by hypothesis the weaker and above all the smaller in comparison with the other side of the scales which (for this purpose) is the rest of the world. ... The contribution in terms of the resulting social strains which the debtor country has to make to the restoration of equilibrium by changing its prices and wages is altogether out of proportion to the contribution asked of its creditors ... the process of adjustment is compulsory for the debtor and voluntary for the creditor. If the creditor does not choose to make, or allow, his share of the adjustment, he suffers no inconvenience. For whilst a country's reserve cannot fall below zero, there is no ceiling which sets an upper limit. The same is true if international loans are to be the means of adjustment. The debtor must borrow; the creditor is under no such compulsion.

Keynes, 1941, CW XXV: 27–8

18.1 The current international payments system: flexible exchange rates

After the demise of Bretton Woods the world trading system has been characterized by lower growth, higher inflation, gyrating exchange rates, recurring international liquidity crises and secularly rising rates of unemployment. In the process a variety of flexible exchange rate regimes have evolved. These have created perverse incentives to compete for limited reserves, set trading partner against trading partner and perpetuated the stagnant world economy that Keynes had so presciently anticipated. The resulting degree of exchange rate volatility has been greater than ever previously experienced. Economic performance, whether measured in terms of growth rates or unemployment rates was dramatically below the exceptionally strong experience of the Bretton Woods period under fixed exchange rates.

Nevertheless after 1971 the attempt to maintain fixed-but-adjustable exchange rates would have required countries to impose draconian controls on capital transactions. If individual country experiences provide any guide, any attempt by the IMF to impose fixed exchange rates would have broken down. Capital controls can be used effectively to dampen short-run speculative pressures. But they are gradually eroded over time as agents learn to get around them. Capital controls alone cannot provide the long-run independence desired by national monetary authorities.

> Capital controls, always leaky over the long run, work during a crisis because they put a cap on the amount of assets that can be transferred per unit of time. They provide a breathing space to organize a realignment without ever abandoning the fixed exchange rate regime[1]

Most economists have now come to believe that floating exchange rates are a necessary evil in the modern world of inexpensive and rapid capital transfer. They are widely regarded as the least unsatisfactory solution for the new global economy, with which all countries must somehow come to terms.

Even though all currencies were formally symmetrical under the Bretton Woods system the US dollar, as "first among equals", was the only currency freely convertible into gold. Most other countries continued to accumulate dollars after the fixed gold convertibility of the dollar was suspended in 1971. One completely unanticipated and regressive consequence of the breakdown of Bretton Woods has been that the world's richest country, the United States, was able to enjoy a perpetual "free lunch." It alone was able to run huge current account deficits, amounting to up to 6 percent of its annual gross domestic product (GDP), with little fear of external imbalance.

The United States has been the sole country that has not been forced to compromise its internal balance objectives for the sake of maintaining external balance. It alone has been able to lower its domestic short-term rate towards zero in response to increases in unemployment rates with no concern for the ensuing current account deficit. It has even felt sufficiently confident of the position of the dollar as a "safe haven" to actively encourage a fall in the external value of the dollar to reduce its current account deficit. In contrast most other countries must stabilize their dollar exchange rate by holding their domestic Bank Rate (BR) significantly above the level of the US federal funds rate.

The high level of non-transparency about the workings of the current flexible international trading system, combined with the near-complete inability of economists to predict future exchange rate movements, or even to account for past movements, has resulted in a dangerously low general level of understanding of the international financial system. Few observers, whether politicians or economists, have a clear idea of the future direction in which exchange rates will move, or how the international payments system will evolve over the longer run. The resulting redistribution of capital flows from poor to rich countries is widely decried as unfair and regressive. But in the absence of a complete collapse of the payments system and a flight from dollars into alternative currencies or other stores of wealth, until a superior alternative to the current system is proposed the current *status quo* appears extremely likely to persist.

18.2 The case for flexible exchange rates

The astonishing success of the Keynesian Revolution and Bretton Woods in the immediate post-Second World War period in establishing global full employment led to an unforeseen process of wage–cost inflation whose appearance Keynes had prophesied just before his death. Cost inflation became increasingly endemic in most developed countries in the late 1960s and 1970s. Without the persistent threat of large-scale unemployment, which Marx termed the "Reserve Army of the Unemployed," bargaining power over wages shifted dramatically from being in favor of business to being in favor of labor. Workers and their unions became increasingly truculent and aggressive in their wage demands. In consequence money wages rose at a greater rate than average labor productivity growth. This in turn led to increases in unit costs which were passed on by firms to consumers in the form of higher prices.

Wage increases greater than average labour productivity growth led to the infamous wage–price spiral and eventually stagflation. Rising wages led to rising costs, which led to rising prices, which led back to ever higher wage demands. It became impossible empirically to disentangle the causal forces creating high inflation rates. Firms viewed themselves, quite correctly, as merely attempting to pass on past wage increases, which since the increases were in excess of average labor productivity growth had caused unit labor costs to increase. Workers viewed themselves equally correctly as merely attempting to keep up with past rises in prices, which if not offset by rises in money wages would reduce future real wages. By the late 1960s most developed nations found themselves pursuing "stop–go" policies. Such policies generated government-generated planned recessions, which increased the unemployment rate, to reduce the bargaining power of labor. These recessions were then followed by expansionary domestic spending policies by the subsequent government, moving the economy back toward full employment, until the next round of inflationary wage demands were tabled by workers and their unions. Hence the nomenclature "stop–go" policies.

Since the Bretton Woods systems broke down in 1971 the world has practiced a variety of flexible exchange rate arrangements, characterized by gyrating exchange rates, higher interest rates, periodic bouts of inflation and deflation, recurring international liquidity crises, slower growth and secularly rising rates of unemployment. The flexible exchange rate system that evolved since 1973 created disastrously perverse incentives, and set trading partner against trading partner to perpetuate the stagnant world economy that Keynes had foreseen.[2]

Since 1971 the degree of exchange rate flexibility has been much greater than ever previously experienced. *Ex post* economic performance, whether measured in terms of growth rates or unemployment rates, has been dramatically inferior to the Bretton Woods fixed exchange rate period. But as stated any attempt to maintain fixed but adjustable rates would have required draconian restrictions over capital movements, and would have led all down a slippery slope. Most economists now believe that floating exchange rates are the necessary evil with which we must all learn to live.

A typical assessment of the modern floating rate era begins by noting just how wrong Milton Friedman was when he envisaged flexible exchange rates adjusting smoothly and slowly to small differentials in relative national price levels.[3] Nothing could be further from the truth. As is now well known exchange rates fluctuated wildly in comparison with goods prices. Early in the flexible rate experience economic theorists offered what appeared to be an attractive explanation for the more substantial exchange rate movements. Currencies are assets, and their prices reflect market expectations of their future flow of services, not their spot value at a point in time. According to this "asset" view of exchange rates it is not so surprising that exchange rates fluctuate as wildly as stock prices.

This asset view is useful, but incomplete. Financial flows now thoroughly dominate quantitatively flows of goods and services. Exchange rates are now explained on "interest rate parity" rather than "purchasing power parity" grounds. Interest rate parity states that if capital mobility is high and there are no capital controls imposed by governments, the expected real rate of return on all homogeneous securities should be equalized. This requires that when a CB raises domestic bank rate above that ruling in the center economies, the domestic exchange rate will rise and overshoot its expected level, so that it is expected to depreciate over the next year by an amount equal to the annual interest rate differential.

In this way exchange rates correct for expected differences in national interest and inflation rates. But they characteristically overshoot, so nominal exchange rates will vary by even greater amounts. The exchange rates of the three major currencies, the Dollar, the Euro, and the Yen have with the exception of the Yen been allowed to float more or less freely by their corresponding CB. But most other countries have been forced to pursue "dirty floating" and attempt to smooth and manage the relative value of their currencies against each another.

It is important to remember that the collapse of the Bretton Woods system was not due the conscious adoption of floating rate regimes as a superior option over fixed rate regimes. Floating was accompanied by serious attempts by international organizations to frame rules to guard against competitive devaluation.[4] How has the flexible exchange rate system fared over the past 30 years? A number of points can be made. (See Goodhart, 2002):

(1) Due to their "asset" character, exchange rates have varied in a much more volatile manner than most observers had expected. In response to interest rate differentials exchange rates will adjust until the expected real returns on financial assets are equalized across countries.
(2) Interest rate differentials and financial capital movements are the principle driver of short-term changes in exchange rates. Deep and liquid capital markets have shown the capacity to discount into today's prices a huge variety of factors affecting expectations of future payment flows. As a result exchange rates fluctuate endogenously in response to interest rate differentials, increasing the influence of monetary policy.[5]
(3) Contrary to what many had feared when the Bretton Woods system collapsed, there has been only infrequent evidence of aggressively competitive exchange rate practices.
(4) Floating exchange rates require a domestic monetary anchor in the center country to contain inflation.
(5) The past 20 years have seen a much greater incidence of currency crises than was experienced in the earlier postwar years. The result has been a strengthening of the external balance constraint for most CBs.
(6) Countries with high unemployment have been increasingly reluctant to pursue expansionary domestic policies due to fear of precipitating current account deficits and currency crises.
(7) The post-1973 period has produced a wide variety of exchange rate regimes: wider bands, crawling bands, asymmetric bands, target zones, basket pegs and other forms of exchange rate management, none of which has ultimately proven successful.
(8) A substantial amount of active intervention continues to characterize the behavior of most "floating" currencies.
(9) With free capital mobility exchange rates have a tendency to "jump" from one level to the next. The timing of these abrupt changes in exchange rates has proven impossible to predict or even to explain *ex post*.
(10) Floating exchange rates behave like other financial asset prices traded in highly organized markets with low transaction costs. The current price tends to reflect all public information bearing on their immediate future value which makes accurate prediction of future movements virtually impossible. The resulting huge uncertainty about the volatile future level of the exchange rate has severely increased the risk of developed country investment in developing countries.

18.3 The case against flexible exchange rates

There are two fundamental *intrinsic* defects of flexible exchange rate regimes. The first problem is the presence of "crowd" or "bandwagon" effects in the trading community. Given the unknown level of future exchange rates, expectations feed on the expectations of other agents. Due to the complexity and non-transparency of the system no one knows for sure how to interpret the "news." "Fundamentals" are easily overwhelmed in the short run by market- driven speculative dynamics, based solely on technical issues about expected future price movements.[6]

In consequence exchange rate volatility and overshooting are typical. When sufficiently severe, for example the Asian crisis of 1997, such fluctuations produce liquidity crises that derail economic growth for entire regions for substantial periods. Movements in real exchange rates cannot easily be controlled by the usual instruments of national economic policy. Unpredictable movements in exchange rates and unpredictable responses of exchange rates to government actions greatly aggravate the problem of successful macroeconomic management. In short freely flexible exchange rates are unsatisfactory as a long-run solution, since major movements in exchange rates have substantial and unwelcome effects on prosperity and growth rate of national economies.

The second problem is that since exchange rates define the conversion ratio between different currencies, governments have a self-interest incentive to manipulate the exchange rate for purely domestic ends. This is usually done in the fight against inflation, since monetary tightening produces an immediate reward in terms of a reduced inflation rate due to an appreciated currency. So long as foreigners do not respond in kind, this gain will be largely at the expense of increased depression in other countries.

Exchange rate manipulation is highly useful to combat unemployment. Expansionary monetary policy depreciates the currency and increases exports at the expense of other countries. Such manipulation represents self-interested national policy since it passes the underlying problem of inflation or unemployment on to other economies. The plus side of such actions is that reduction of interest rates in the center economies exerts an expansionary effect over much larger geographic areas. CBs in smaller economies are able to reduce their BR in response to their now greater positive differential, with less fear of exchange rate depreciation.

Members of the International Monetary Fund (IMF) are explicitly mandated to avoid the manipulation of their exchange rate to improve external balance. The IMF has general responsibility for surveillance over unfair exchange rate practices. Unfortunately such surveillance has never really gotten off the ground, and it is very difficult to see how it can. What can an IMF do when a United States achieves a dramatic unexpected reduction in its inflation rate through an extremely tight monetary policy which causes a sharp appreciation of the dollar against other countries and a resulting higher general level of world interest rates precipitates a third world debt crisis? Or when a Sweden or a U.S. pursues a very low interest rate policy to depreciate its exchange rate and promote its exports?

After the stock market crash of 2000 the Federal Reserve rapidly and dramatically reduced the federal funds rate to 1 percent in an attempt to resuscitate the US economy. One intended effect was a general slow depreciation of the exchange rate designed to reduce the US current account deficit. This greatly benefited countries such as China and Hong Kong whose exchange rate was pegged to the US dollar. The Fed has now (2005) changed course, and is gradually increasing the federal funds rate by 25 basis points at every monetary policy meeting. This has produced in a "Chinese Water torture" effect on the US stock market as speculators attempt to forecast when this process is likely to cease.

Such interest rate manipulation represents self-interested national policy, which passes the problems of inflation and unemployment on to other countries. The effects of a rate change are asymmetrical. The indirect effects of a reduction in rates in the center are "good" for the rest of the world, since lower rates in the center enable CBs in the periphery to lower rates, and generally lower rates operate to stimulate aggregate demand (AD) in a world economy that suffers from a aggregate demand deficiency bias. Conversely the effects of an increase in rates in the center are "bad" for the rest of the world, since higher rates in the center lead to generally higher rates in the periphery, and higher rates operates to restrict AD in a world economy that already suffers from a recessionary bias.

One result of the increased non-transparency of future interest rate and low exchange rate movements has been that both agents and macroeconomists are much less confident of the longer future in open economies as compared with closed economies. No one knows when or by how much future exchange rates are going to change, and the consequences are undecipherable. To model an open economy it is necessary to distinguish the financial regime in place: freely floating, managed floating, or firmly fixed exchange rates. One must distinguish the degree of and manner in which capital movements are controlled and regulated. No real-world exchange rate has ever been fixed forever. So the time period over which the exchange rate has been pegged and the period over which it is expected to be pegged in the future must be considered. As the complexity increases, the modeling task eventually becomes insuperable.[7]

The degree that exchange rates are fixed determines the degree of autonomy domestic CBs possess to set the key domestic short-term rate (bank rate) relative to the rates ruling in the center. In a closed economy the CB is the monopoly supplier of system liquidity and its interest rate-setting procedure is unambiguous. But in open economies so long as capital controls do not prohibit all capital movements, a degree of control that in practice is impossible to sustain, funds can usually be obtained from foreign lenders and so indirectly from foreign CBs. How are an economy's interest rate and exchange rate then determined?

If the exchange rate is permanently fixed and financial capital is perfectly mobile, the domestic CB will lose all ability to exogenously control the short-term rate. In the absence of capital controls domestic banks are able to lend to and borrow from foreign banks and nonbank institutions outside the domestic economy, and will do so whenever the rate set by the domestic CB is below or above the rate set by the central dominant CB of the global financial system. The country must simply accept the interest rate that is set by the CB in the dominant economy.

A perfectly freely floating exchange rate regime requires that the domestic CB never intervenes in foreign exchange markets to influence the value of the exchange rate. But the central responsibility of any CB is to assure that liquidity is always maintained in all financial markets, including the market for foreign exchange. In practice CBs oversee and smooth out all sharp short-term fluctuations in security prices and foreign exchange in all economies, in the process of ensuring market and system liquidity. It is not possible for CB intervention to be perfectly neutral in this process. Smoothing out large short-term fluctuations affects longer-term "trend" movements, which are simply the cumulative sum of short-term movements. As a result perfectly "clean" floats are never observed. All CBs engage in "dirty" floating to the extent they intervene to smooth out short-run fluctuations and permit their reserves to vary over time.

Whenever the exchange rate is permitted to "float" in response to changes in the supply and demand for foreign exchange, the CB has some freedom to set BR at a differential above or below the rate ruling in foreign financial centers. So long as capital movements are not totally controlled and some capital mobility is possible, exchange rates will adjust until interest rate "parity" is achieved. Interest rate parity assures that expected effective real borrowing and lending rates are the same all over the system. This condition is brought about as international financial institutions engage in arbitrage to eliminate perceived differences in real lending and borrowing costs. The satisfaction of interest rate parity conditions leads to overshooting of spot exchange rate levels and so increases the variability of exchange rates. This increased variability of exchange rates, combined with the near total inability of agents to predict future exchange rate movements, enormously increases the degree of uncertainty about future exchange rates in international trade, and acts like a tax in discouraging entry to international trade.

Many mainstream economists are optimistic that CB "Inflation Targeting" is sufficient to provide the stability required for an anchor to the price level. Many countries lack the internal discipline, labor market traditions, and market institutions necessary to reach a successful domestic commitment to price stability. But the larger issue is: "What is the process by which inflation targeting operates?"

In the short run the core inflation rate is predetermined by the behavior of unit costs, in particular the rate of money wage inflation in excess of the rate of average labor productivity growth. The AS relationship is then a fractal horizontal band in inflation-real output space. In open economies movements in the exchange rate play a critically important role, and shift the AS band upward or downward as the currency depreciates or appreciates. With an endogenous money supply the AD relationship is vertical in inflation-real output space, since with endogenous money there is no "Pigou," "Keynes," or "real balance" effect. Output is demand-determined in all market economies.

Keynes' central point was there are no endogenous market forces that push an economy toward any full employment "equilibrium" position. The recognition that economies are complex systems permits understanding why economies have no tendency whatsoever to approach any "equilibrium" configuration. Change is the only constant. Many countries lack the internal discipline, labor market tradition and market institutions necessary for successful long-run commitment to price stability. Mainstream economists have been largely supportive of central bank "Inflation Targeting" to provide the price stability required for an anchor in flexible exchange rate systems. But the issue remains: What is the process by which "inflation targeting" operates?

Changes in interest rates clearly produce inverse changes in AD. Most markets are highly concentrated, and most prices of current output are administered at relatively stable markups on average variable costs. Since labor is by far the largest variable cost component for the economy, the "core" price level and inflation rate are driven by the behavior of unit labor costs. In most economies inflation is cost-determined and not demand-determined. The "core" inflation rate, derived by deducting changes in flex prices in agriculture and raw materials, taxes, interest rates and import prices from the "headline" rate, is equal to the excess of the current rate of average money wage increases over the rate of growth of average labor productivity in the previous period. In the short run the core inflation rate is predetermined by unit cost and the exchange rate in the previous period.

In most small open economies movements in the exchange rate play a crucially important role in determining the inflation rate. With endogenous credit money there is no "Pigou" or "Keynes" effect. Output is demand-constrained in all market economies. As a stylized fact the AS relationship is horizontal and the AD relationship is vertical in inflation-output space. The CB attempts to manage the level of AD by varying interest rates to ensure full employment is achieved.

Given expectations of future profits, the position of the vertical AD curve moves inversely with changes in the level of interest rates. A change in interest rates produces an inverse change in AD and induces a rightward or leftward shift in the AD relationship. Since the AS relationship is horizontal changes in AD directly determine changes in the quantity of goods sold and the level of real output. The price level and the inflation rate are determined by cost factors while changes in output are determined by demand factors.

Restrictive monetary policy by raising interest rates reduces AD and causes the AD curve to shift leftward. The direct effect of restrictive monetary policy is to reduce the level and change the composition of GDP. Reduced demand for labor and decrease in AD raise the unemployment rate. The impact of unemployment on wage and price inflation depends on the position and slope of the Phillips curve relationship.

Given the expectations of future profits, AD is inversely related to the level of interest rates. A change in interest rates produces an inverse change in AD, represented diagrammatically as rightward (expansionary) or leftward (restrictive) shift in the vertical AD band. Changes in AD directly determine changes in the quantity of goods sold, and so the level of real output. The primary effect of a rise in interest rates is to reduce the level of nominal and real GDP. This reduces the demand for labor and raises the unemployment rate. Its indirect effect on the level of wage inflation depends on employment effects on future expected inflation, the position and slope of the Phillips Curve.

Once inflation expectations have taken hold, prices and wages frequently chase each other in the infamous "wage–price spiral." Inflation becomes the side effect of a conflict between labor and business over distributive shares. This battle was fought in most developed economies during the stagflation of the 1970s, and is still being fought today in many developing economies where unemployment rates remain stubbornly in double digits.

During an inflationary wage–price spiral the Phillips Curve typically flattens so that given expected future inflation rates, higher unemployment rates lose their ability to reduce the future rate of wage inflation. Under such conditions the main effect of restrictive monetary policy is to restrict the rise in AD, and keep real income growth below the full employment output gap of the economy. The exercise of "Inflation Targeting" by CBs becomes the means to provide a new political consensus under which nominal interest rates can be significantly raised and real rates held at higher levels. The resulting slower growth and higher employment rates and slack are tolerated as a "necessary evil."

Free floating among the "core" G3 exchange rates appears very likely to remain unless the system somehow implodes. When economic performance and expectations about a major region strengthen, the exchange rate appreciation of the region serves the valuable function of stimulating demand in the rest of the world and restraining inflation in the more rapidly growing region. Unless exchange rate variability becomes excessive, international response is likely to be the intensification of existing *ad hoc* cooperation.[8]

Fluctuations in real exchange rates are not easily controllable by the usual instruments of economic policy. Flexible exchange rates can exist simultaneously with severe and persistent misalignment of relative international prices and exchange rates. Exchange rates are characterized by excess volatility and other manifestations of speculative bubbles in foreign exchange markets with obvious trade and investment-deterring consequences. Unpredictable movements in exchange rates, and the unpredictable responses of exchange rates to government actions, greatly aggravate the problem of successful macroeconomic management. Because unanticipated large movements in exchange rates have major negative effects on national economies, most economists continue to regard freely flexible exchange rates as unsatisfactory as the long-run solution to world trading problems. But since fixed exchange rates are unattainable, exchange rate flexibility is believed to be a necessary evil.

A flexible exchange rate system is much less transparent than a fixed exchange rate system, since it is not possible to predict future exchange rate values or state how they are determined. Due to their inability to understand the forces driving flexible exchange rates, macroeconomists are much less confident of their understanding and analysis of open-economy issues compared with closed economies. Under current institutional arrangements to model an open economy it is necessary to carefully distinguish the financial regime in place: freely floating, managed floating, or firmly fixed exchange rates. The model must distinguish the degree and manner in which capital movements are controlled and regulated. Since no real-world exchange rate has ever been fixed forever, the time period over which the exchange rate has been pegged, and the period over which it is expected to remain pegged in the future must also be established. A near impenetrable cloud of uncertainty about the world economy is cast by economists' inability to forecast or even understand the dynamics and movements of exchange rates.

The "impossible trinity" maintains that countries cannot simultaneously have free capital mobility, an independent monetary policy and fixed exchange rates.[9] The degree to which the exchange rate is fixed determines the autonomy the CB possesses to set BR autonomously. In closed-economies the CB is the monopoly supplier of system liquidity and its interest-rate-setting procedure is clear and unambiguous. So long as the exchange rate is expected to stay fixed, there is much less uncertainty about the future. Even the strictest capital controls cannot prohibit all capital movements in open economies. Capital controls are impossible to sustain in practice over the longer run. Funds can always be obtained from or lent to foreign lenders and investors and so indirectly foreign CBs. How are interest rates then to be modeled? Only in the United States as the center economy can the Fed set the federal funds rate to satisfy internal balance, with little need to be concerned with the implications of the level of interest rates for the level of the exchange rate or for future current account deficits.

In the case when the exchange rate is permanently fixed, and financial capital is perfectly mobile with no exchange controls, the domestic CB loses all ability to exogenously set the level of BR. Domestic banks are able to borrow and lend funds to foreign banks and non-banks outside the domestic economy, and do so whenever the interest rate set by the domestic CB is sufficiently below or above the rate set by the dominant CB in the global financial system to make arbitrage profits. The country's monetary authorities must accept the interest rate set by the authorities in the dominant financial system when their exchange rate is fixed, even when this interest rate happens to be quite inappropriate to their internal balance goals.

A perfectly freely-floating exchange rate regime requires that the domestic CB *never* intervene in foreign exchange markets to influence the value of the exchange rate. But the central responsibility of any CB is to assure the liquidity of the financial system. All CBs must smooth out sharp short-term fluctuations in security prices and foreign exchange in all economies in the process of providing market and system liquidity. It is not possible for CB intervention to be completely "neutral." Whatever it does has some effect. Smoothing out large short-term fluctuations must affect the course of longer term "trend" movements since the "trend" is simply the cumulative sum of short-term movements. Perfectly "clean" floating is impossible. All CBs engage in "dirty" floating when they intervene to smooth out short-run exchange rate fluctuations. A perfectly freely floating exchange rate is an oxymoron.

When the exchange rate is permitted to float in response to changes in supply and demand for foreign exchange, CBs will set the domestic short-term rate at some differential above or below the rate ruling in foreign financial centers. Depending on the rate set, so long as some capital mobility exists exchange rates will adjust until interest rate "parity" is approximated.

Interest rate "parity" describes the situation when expected real borrowing and lending rates are the same over the entire system. This condition is brought about as financial institutions engage in arbitrage to eliminate perceived differences in real lending or borrowing costs. The fulfillment of the interest rate parity condition leads to overshooting of spot exchange rate movements which increase the variability of exchange rates over time. The resulting increased variability of exchange rates, combined with the near total inability to predict future exchange rate movements greatly increase uncertainty about future rates and the future profitability of international trade. This acts like a tax in discouraging new entrants into the international trading system.

18.4 Endogenous speculation in flexible exchange rate regimes

The recognition that economies are complex systems whose future is unknowable implies that agents are unable to construct "rational" conditional probabilities based on past observations. Advocates of the efficient market hypothesis (EMH) maintain that the "intrinsic value" of stocks and exchange rates are defined by "fundamentals." Observed fluctuations in prices are due the continuous random arrival of new information affecting future prospects. Efficient market theory holds that agents analyze past and present market data to form "rational" expectations for utility-maximizing decisions. Observed price volatility is attributed to "shocks" that push the system away from its long-term equilibrium path. Economic "fundamentals" lead to statistically reliable conditional probabilities concerning the future path of the economy. Stiglitz has argued that financial markets:

> affect how the pie is divided, but not the size of the pie. ... The most important social function of financial markets is to correctly allocate real capital among industries in accordance with reliable information about future rates of return determined by fundamentals.[10]

But if markets were truly "efficient," market forces must eliminate all "noise traders" who persistently make errors in financial markets. To resolve this dilemma and explain the consistency of efficiency with the persistence of financial volatility over time, Stiglitz appeals to P.T. Barnum's dictum, *"There's a sucker born every minute."* He argues some irrationality is pervasive in economics.[11]

Short-term traders consist of two groups, *"noise traders, and those who live off them."*[12] Volatile financial market prices are movements *away* from "fundamental" values. Volatility is attributed to the existence of "noise traders" who mistakenly believe they know how the market works. Rational short-term market traders feed off these foolish noise traders and ultimately return the market to its fundamental values.

Alternatively financial markets can be viewed as dynamic nonlinear systems, that generate chaotic prices which appear random, but behind which lies chaotic order. Complex processes generate numbers that cannot be distinguished from random numbers. When stock markets are complex systems price fluctuations are determined endogenously by the market's internal nonlinear dynamics, not by exogenous "random shocks." In complex systems, today's prices are related by complex changing nonlinear functions to yesterday's prices. Stock prices can change endogenously even when no new information comes onto the market. In complex systems it is not possible to describe expectations as "rational" since there is no single "correct" *ex ante* forecast.[13]

Speculators on the floor of the exchange do not base their trades on "fundamentals," but on how they believe market participants expect other participants to react to news. The major market news is usually the most recent past movement in an asset's price. Markets are driven by endogenous complex processes, and have long memories. When each agent has independent and inelastic short-run expectations, there must exist credible market-makers to assure orderliness is maintained. Previous price movements form the data that non-linearly determine future price movements. Some market participants (technicians and noise traders) extrapolate from past changes, while others (analysts and economists) focus on "fundamentals." This leads to ever-changing positive short-run serial price correlation. But after some point the market overadjusts in the other direction, as the initial overreaction becomes obvious, leading to ever-changing negative longer-run serial correlation. In short stock markets feed on and react to their own volatility, and exhibit the endogenous price-driven instability characteristic of complex systems.

In liquid financial markets it is desirable to have a substantial number of market participants who independently hold differing expectations about the future, to ensure that small changes in market prices bring significant market reaction in the other direction. The result of broader markets will be more stable spot prices over time and higher liquidity. Market stability requires both a dense spectrum of bull and bear opinion, and participants with different expectation horizons. Keynes explicitly recognized the importance of heterogeneous expectations.

> The liquidity of financial markets often facilitates, though it sometimes impedes, the course of new investment. ... it is interesting that stability ... and its sensitiveness ... should be so dependent on the existence of a variety of opinion about what is uncertain. Best of all that we should know the future. But if not, then, if we are to control the activity of the economic system, it is important that our opinions differ.[14]

It has recently been found that stop-loss orders reinforce price movements. Changes in exchange rate and stock prices are systematically larger when prices reach levels where stop-loss orders cluster. Clusters of stop-loss orders propagate trends which are triggered in waves or "price cascades." This explains the well-known "fat tails" in the historical distribution of stock and exchange rate returns, and the high frequency and volatility of financial asset prices.[15]

Exchange rate crises can be caused by self-fulfilling speculative behavior, for example sudden shifts from low to high expectations of devaluation while economic fundamentals appear to remain unchanged. In a world with incomplete markets, the existence of multiple currencies with flexible conversion rates creates many additional markets through which endogenous speculative volatility can be injected into the system. Exchange rate flexibility breeds excess volatility and temporary misalignment. Such changes may become permanent, and add to rather than filter out the exogenous irreducible fundamental uncertainty. Capital controls temporarily permit a greater degree of exchange rate autonomy, by dampening speculative pressures. Different exchange rate regimes transmit fundamental shocks differently, and generate different kinds of endogenous speculative movements. Most mainstream economists have now convinced themselves that freely fluctuating exchange rates are a necessary evil.

Some neoclassical economists have even argued that freely flexible exchange rates are efficient, for the following reasons:

1. With freely flexible exchange rates, nations are able to pursue independent monetary and fiscal policies to maintain full employment.
2. With freely flexible exchange rates, it is impossible for all countries except the center to persistently run balance of payments deficits.
3. Real returns are higher in poor nations where capital is relatively scarce. Capital will flow from richer creditor nations to poorer debtor nations, until the return on capital at the margin is equalized. This operates to raise the growth rate of developing countries (DCs).

Unfortunately all of the above statements have very little empirical support. All minimize the negative effects of the increase in uncertainty associated with exchange rate volatility. The record of the postwar period is flatly inconsistent with the neoclassical position. Growth rates have been very substantially lower and interest rates have been substantially higher in post 1971 flexible exchange rate regimes, compared with the fixed-but-flexible low interest rate regime under Bretton Woods.

Many countries have experienced persistent deficits in their balance of payments over the postwar period. In few countries do governments have the freedom to pursue independent monetary and fiscal policy to achieve internal balance. Most CBs are continually forced to pursue restrictive domestic AD policy and maintain high domestic interest rates to defend their balance of payments, in the attempt to sustain external balance. The flight of highly mobile international capital to "safe havens" drains resources from the poorer nations of the world towards the United States, and continually poses the threat of a severe collapse of the exchange rate, resulting in an ever more unequal distribution of global reserves and incomes.

With a fixed exchange rate regime CBs must continually intervene to keep the exchange rate within a narrow target band. There is some discretion in the position and width of the band. But for exchange rate stability to persist, agents must be convinced that the CB has adequate reserve assets on hand to "fix" the market price, or, if reserves are not available, that the CB can obtain reserves as desired *via* "swap" lines from other CBs.

Once reserve holdings are perceived to be inadequate, markets frequently decide that selling a currency which must be defended offers a one-way bet. The only defense for the besieged CB is to attempt to borrow more additional reserves from the IMF. Such loans are never available in unlimited supply and come with increasingly severe restrictive strings attached. They are typically accompanied by critical comments of "Treasury imprudence" and also need for "greater fiscal discipline."

When exchange rate movements are expected to be temporary, the elasticity of expectations approaches zero, and, exchange rate perturbations set off strong self-stabilizing market forces. By adjusting the leads and lags of trade payments, importers and exporters will hold more of those currencies whose values are expected to rise relative to their current value, and less of those currencies whose values are expected to decline. Endogenous market forces can then operate to restore the "normal" exchange rate level, with no need for CB intervention.

When the exchange rate value is widely regarded as "flexible," in the case of an unanticipated exchange rate change no agent can be sure whether the rate will continue to move further away from the original value or move in the reverse direction. When the preponderant market view becomes that current short-term weaknesses are a signal of larger declines to follow, the elasticity of expectations rises. Leads and lags can then become powerfully destabilizing, and operate to reinforce exchange rate variability.

Where the elasticity of expectations is equal to unity marks the dividing line between stability and instability. The more flexible the exchange rate, the more current weaknesses will induce expectations of greater uncertainty concerning the ability of the authority to maintain a stable future value of the currency and the greater will be the tendency of asset holders to adopt a "fast exit" strategy, producing destabilizing "crowd" and "bandwagon" effects. Expectations about the long-run economic future are anchored by social conventions. Even when based on beliefs about "fundamentals" social conventions can be fragile and precarious.

Fixed exchange rates, although highly desirable from the viewpoint of reducing uncertainty and encouraging trade, have proven impossible formally to maintain since the demise of Bretton Woods, even with the application of strict capital controls. History strongly suggests that in finite time, all managed exchange rate regimes will break down with a probability of one. It is not possible for monetary authorities to hold exchange rates perpetually fixed at the same level in any regime where capital mobility is high, and market-clearing values of the exchange rate are continually changing. A strong case will be made that the only credible fixed exchange rate regime is a single currency regime. Individual countries then become like geographical regions of a single country and have no exchange rate.[16]

Free floating among the "core" G3 exchange rates appears extremely likely to persist over the foreseeable future. When the economic performance of one major region strengthens, its exchange rate appreciation serves the useful function of stimulating demand and output in the rest of the world and restraining inflation within the more rapidly growing region. Unless exchange rate variability becomes excessive, the future global response is likely to be merely the intensification of the existing of *ad hoc* policy cooperation among CBs at different stages of the cycle.[17]

18.5 The deflationary bias in the current flexible exchange rates regime

Keynes developed his vision on how the existing international payments system led to a global deficiency of aggregate demand at great length in his post-*General Theory* writings, which are unfortunately much less widely known. He emphasized that when governments do not have the political will to stimulate domestic AD, due then to a self-imposed belief in the desirability of a "balanced budget," and now to the fear of missing self-imposed inflation "targets," each country's international advantage can easily become at variance with that of its neighbors.[18] He argued that neoclassical theory ignored many implications of a money-using economy, in particular the central necessity for CBs to continuously maintain system liquidity. These implications impede understanding of the central problems of international finance: the need for liquidity, for growing debt obligations, and for "stable" versus "flexible" exchange rates. Nowhere is the difference between Keynes' position and that of the supporters of *laissez-faire* more evident than in the issue of the desirability of free international capital movements and of flexible exchange rates.

Keynes argued forcibly that government regulation of international capital movements to promote exchange rate stability was both necessary and in the public interest. He observed many international financial flows were the result of anti-social activities. In a *laissez-faire* system of international finance there is no way to distinguish the short-term movement of funds used for new real investments, from speculative funds taking refuge in one nation after the other in the continuous search for speculative gains, or to avoid the tax collector.[19] Exogenous capital movements easily can have detrimental effects on individual countries' balance of payments, unemployment, and exchange rates. The international flow of "hot" money in the form of precautionary and speculative funds is frequently disruptive, and can result in seriously impoverishing nations whose current accounts would otherwise be balanced:

> Loose funds ... sweep round the world, disorganizing all steady business. Nothing is more certain than that the movement of capital funds must be regulated. ... There is no country which can in the future safely allow the flight of funds for political reasons or to evade domestic taxation, or in anticipation of the owner turning refugee. Equally, there is no country that can safely receive fugitive funds which cannot safely be used for fixed investments, and might turn it into a deficiency country, against its will, and contrary to the real facts.[20]

So long as countries trade with the rest of the world, they must avoid all expansionary domestic policy that threatens external imbalance. Countries that engage in international trade must attempt to maintain expected future conversion rates of their currency at their current values. If the exchange rate is expected to fall, CBs must pay a risk premium to attract funds to compensate foreign portfolio holders for expected capital losses. Since currencies represent a store of wealth in asset portfolios, countries are doubly concerned about the current size of their foreign exchange reserves and the future value of their exchange rate. When a country's current foreign exchange outflows consistently exceed its foreign exchange receipts, it has limited choices. It must either pay out foreign currencies from its reserves, borrow foreign currencies to cover its negative balance, let the exchange rate depreciate, or devalue its currency.

This situation of conflict between internal and external balance is illustrated in Figure 18.1. In process analysis all variables are expressed in terms of percentage rate of change from the present value (t_0) to the expected value one period in the future (t_1), where the period depends on the commodity and the market on which it is traded. The vertical axis measures the change in the current account deficit or surplus ($\Delta X_t - \Delta M_t$), and the horizontal axis represents the change in aggregate

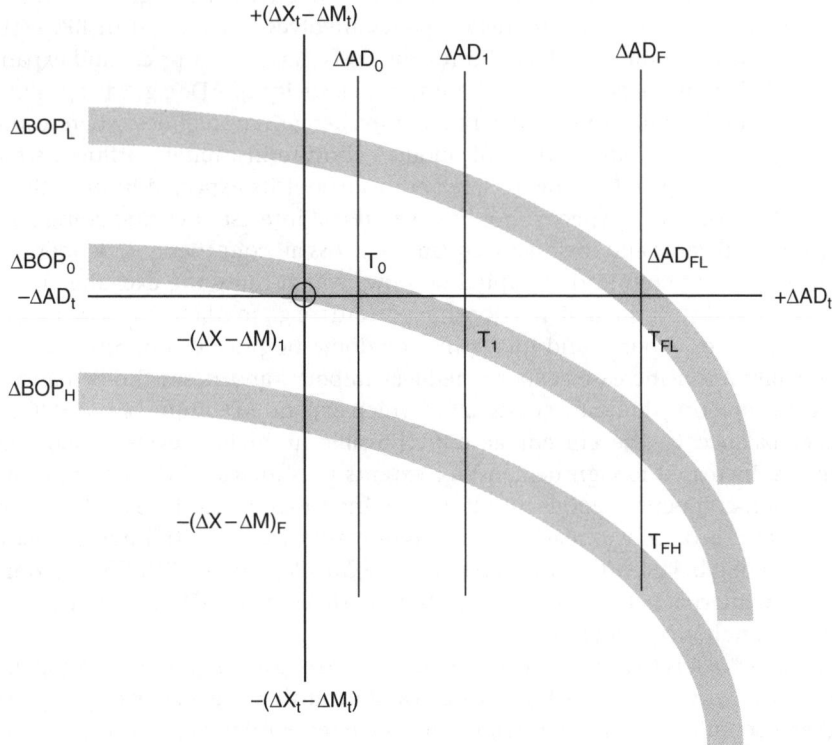

Figure 18.1 The ΔAD–ΔBOP relation in an open economy

demand (ΔAD_t). The vertical line ΔAD_F represents the change in AD required for full capacity output. Imports are positively related to domestic AD while exports are dependent on foreign AD. Given the current exchange rate (E_{T_0}) and Bank Rate (BR_{T_0}), increases in the level of domestic AD increase imports and cause the balance of payments (BOP) to worsen. The fractal band ΔBOP_0 illustrates how the current account balance deteriorates as AD increases. The ΔBOP_0 relationship slopes downward since increases in ΔAD result in greater imports, and worsen the BOP.

In Figure 18.1 the current account is in balance at the level of income where the ΔBOP_0 relationship intersects the horizontal axis (T_0). The economy is assumed to be initially at a level of AD_0 sufficiently below full capacity so the value of imports is equal to the value of exports and the current account is balanced. The current change in aggregate demand (ΔAD_0) is insufficient to reach the economy's potential capacity (ΔAD_F). The CB anticipates that even though sharply lowering BR would increase employment and raise ΔAD_0 towards ΔAD_F, the current account deficit would greatly increase (T_2), and the resulting outflow of foreign exchange would reduce the current level reserves and jeopardize the exchange rate. As a result the CB decides to forego more expansionary monetary policy, and acquiesces to the levels of unemployment and excess capacity at the modest current account deficit (T_1).

Figure 18.1 illustrates the extent the power of monetary policy is increased in floating exchange rate regimes when changes in BR have a much greater effect on ΔAD. A more expansionary monetary policy involves a reduction in BR, which e.g., in closed economies reduces borrowing costs, raises asset prices and expands aggregate demand depending on the interest elasticity of ΛD, e.g. to (T_1). But in open economies operating under floating exchange rate regimes where capital mobility is high, a reduction in BR induces short-term capital outflows, which cause the exchange rate to depreciate and overshoot its expected future value in the next period, until expected holding period real interest rates (including anticipated capital gains and losses) are equalized across all countries and periods.

Lower interest rates lead to capital outflows which cause the exchange rate to depreciate and shift the BOP relationship upwards, e.g., to ΔBOP_L. By lowering the foreign price of exports, and increasing the domestic price of imports exchange rate depreciation increases exports, reduces imports, and raises the demand for import-competing domestic goods, all of which expand AD, improve the BOP, and render balance in the current account possible at higher levels of aggregate demand. Increased foreign demand for exports plus increased domestic demand for import-competing goods result in an increased interest-elasticity of AD, enabling the economy to realize higher employment (ΔAD_F) with internal balance (T_{FL}). External balance (the intersection of the ΔBOP_L relation with the horizontal axis), and internal balance (the intersection of ΔBOP_L with AD_F) can now both be realized simultaneously (T_{FL}).

The drawback is that in open economies a more expansionary monetary policy, with lower interest rates (BR), greater capital outflows, lower exchange rates, higher asset prices and higher AD, results in a temporary increase in the inflation rate as well as an increase in AD. This inflation comes about not due to excess demand, but to the higher prices of imported goods that accompany exchange rate depreciation. The result is a one-shot rise in the inflation rate associated with the fall in the exchange rate, assuming all induced secondary cost and price increases are avoided. In open economies a reduction in BR induces capital outflows which cause the exchange rate to depreciate and the prices of imported goods to rise when the exchange rate falls. Depending on the openness of the economy exchange rate depreciation leads to a one-shot increase in the inflation rate until the exchange rate stabilizes at a lower level. This makes it more difficult for the CB to meet its inflation targets interest rates when it lowers.

In contrast more restrictive monetary policy with higher interest rates causes the exchange rate to appreciate, and shifts the ΔBOP_H relationship downward. In closed economies higher BR raises the cost of borrowing and lowers asset prices, directly reducing AD and shifting ΔAD_0 leftward depending on the interest elasticity of AD. But in open economies higher BR also induces short-term capital inflows, causing the exchange rate to appreciate and overshoot its expected value in the subsequent period, until expected real rates (including capital gains and losses) have been equalized across countries and holding periods. The appreciation of the exchange rate raises the foreign price of exports and reduces the domestic price of imports, reducing exports, increasing imports and causing the inflation rate to decline. The reduced demand for exports and the increased demand for imports raises the interest-elasticity of AD and increases the reduction in AD that accompanies any given increase in BR. The current account deficit at full employment is then substantially increased (T_{FH}), so the CB is unable to achieve external balance at full employment (AD_F).

For an inflation-targeting CB, a higher BR has the desirable effect of directly reducing the inflation rate by reducing the price of imports, depending on the openness of the economy. Higher interest rates lead to capital inflows and higher exchange rates, which by reducing import prices lower the inflation rate and enable the CB to more easily attain its inflation target. With a higher level of BR and a higher exchange rate, as the economy expands toward AD_F, the current account balance (ΔBOP_H) becomes increasingly negative as the excess of imports over exports increases (T_{FH}).

A highly unfavorable trade balance superficially appears to imply that the economy is in danger of overheating and must be restrained by still higher interest rates, and even more restrictive monetary policy.[21] But paradoxically lower interest rates by induction of short-term capital outflows, lower exchange rate and improved current account balance (ΔBOP_L), make the simultaneous attainment of external (current account) balance and internal (full employment) balance much more feasible (T_{FL}).

The root problem of inflation remains. The core inflation rate is only permanently reduced if the government can moderate the rate of increase of money wages. Unit labor costs will be stabilized only when the average rate of growth of money wages has been brought down to the average rate of labor productivity growth.

Countries running large current account deficits frequently believe they have no choice, but are forced to restrict domestic demand to protect their exchange rate and reduce their imports. Countries persistently running current account *deficits* are widely viewed as "attempting to live beyond their means." In contrast *surplus* countries are under no pressure to increase expenditures on imports or to raise foreign investment. They can accumulate reserves indefinitely. The net effect of trade imbalances on global AD is thus highly restrictive. Debtor countries are forced to pursue more restrictive policies, but surplus countries are under no similar pressure to pursue expansionary policies.

Developing countries (DCs) are heavily dependent on imported capital goods during the growth process. In response to the higher expected returns on investment projects, they attempt to undertake additional capital formation financed by debt issue. For many developing countries (DCs) the marginal propensity to import borrowed capital goods rises above unity when the economy enters the boom phase of the business cycle.[22] Lenders must bear the exchange rate risk that in the future the country may find itself unable to service its total foreign borrowing, in which case they will be repaid at some fraction of the face value. As a result DCs typically face high borrowing costs and find it difficult to finance capital imports in excess of their export proceeds. Cyclical expansions must frequently be deflated by draconian monetary policy to depress AD growth, reducing their debt ratios and the growth rate of GDP.[23] But capital budgeting must be applied to the external sector and imports of consumer and capital goods be sharply distinguished. Increased imports of capital goods represent an increase in both investment and saving.

18.6 Empirical estimates of the deflationary bias

For the twenty year period 1980–2000 annual averages were calculated for the real growth rate of per capita GDP, the inflation rate, Bank Rate (BR), and real BR for 50 countries (25 DCs and 25 LDCs)[24]. Two proxies for the degree of external imbalance were calculated.

(a) the ratio of the stock of foreign exchange reserves to current imports,
(b) the ratio of the current account balance of payments surplus or deficit to current imports.[25]

(Note that a lower value of each proxy indicates a higher degree of external imbalance, so the sign of the estimated coefficients on the proxies must be reversed.)[26]

Figures 18.2 and 18.3 reveal that countries with greater external imbalance (lower values of the proxy) are associated with higher levels of BR. Figures 18.4 and 18.5 reveal a clear negative association between the degree of external imbalance (lower values of the proxy), and the rate of growth of real per capita GDP. Finally Figures 18.6 and 18.7 indicate that higher levels of nominal and real bank rate are associated with lower levels of per capita GDP growth.

Regressions summarizing the empirical relationship between Bank Rate (BR) and the two proxies for the degree of external imbalance, and the relationship between growth rate of real per capita GDP, and the proxies for the degree of external imbalance and Bank Rate over the period 1980–2000 are presented in Table 18.1.[27]

Equations (1) and (2) find a positive relationship between BR and both proxies for the degree of external imbalance, although only the BOP/Import proxy is

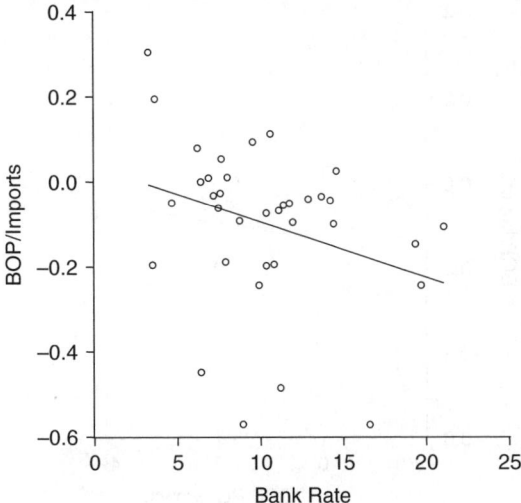

Figure 18.2 BOP/imports vs Bank Rate

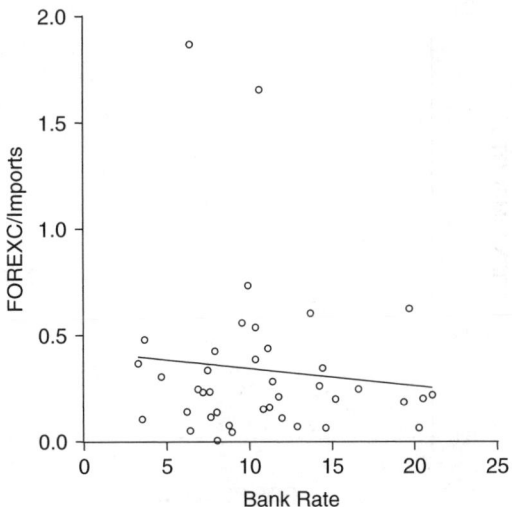

Figure 18.3 FOREXC/imports vs Bank Rate

statistically significant. This provides empirical confirmation that higher degrees of external imbalances are associated with more restrictive monetary policy and higher interest rates. Equations (3) and (4) reveal that both proxies for the degree of external imbalance are negatively related to real per capita GDP growth, although only the Foreign Exchange/ Imports ratio is significant. This confirms greater external imbalance is associated with a lower rate of GDP growth.

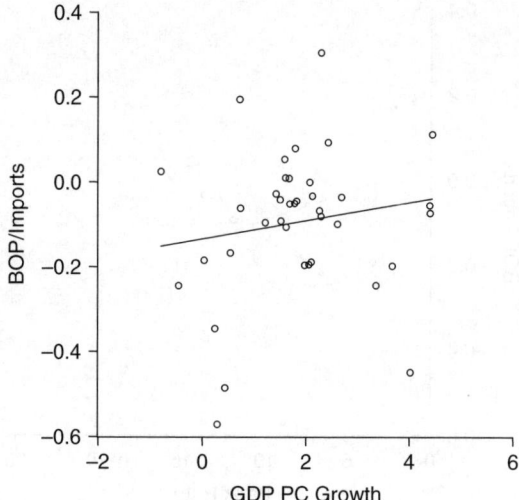

Figure 18.4 BOP/imports vs GDP PC growth

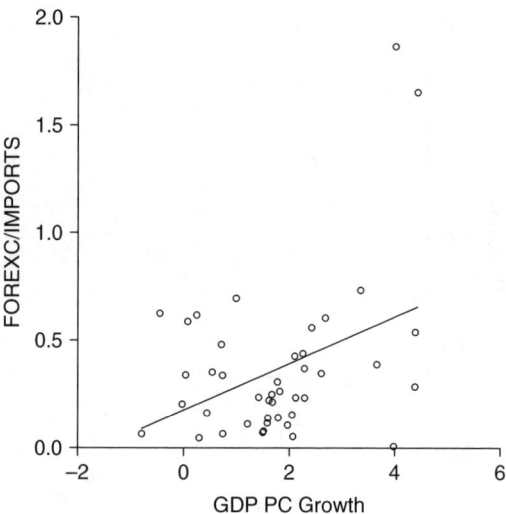

Figure 18.5 FOREXC/imports vs GDP PC growth

Equations (5) and (6) reveal that both nominal and real BR are negatively associated with the growth rate of real per capita GDP, though only the nominal rate is statistically significant. Finally Equation (7) presents the multiple correlation between real per capita GDP growth, and bank rate and the Foreign Exchange/Imports proxy for external imbalance. The growth rate is significantly negatively related to both variables, implying that higher bank rates and a greater

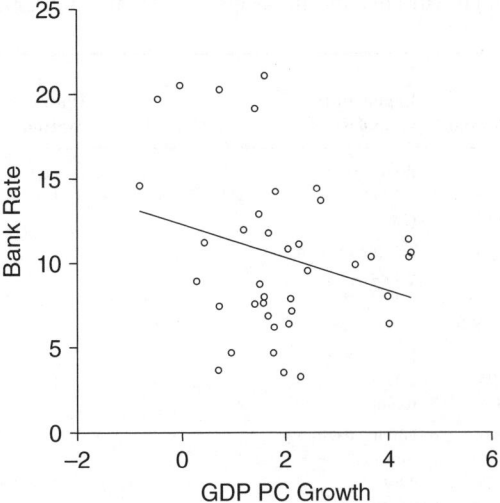

Figure 18.6 Bank Rate vs GDP PC growth

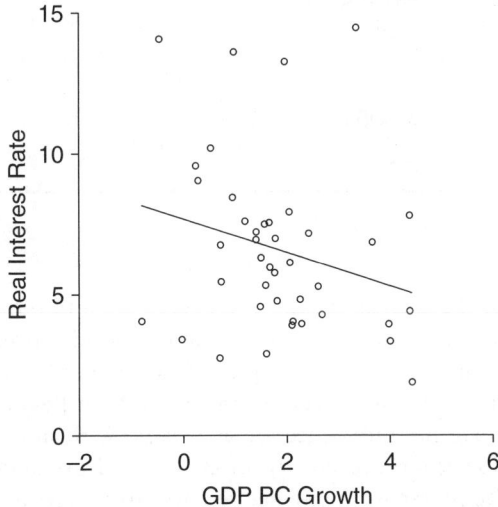

Figure 18.7 Real Bank Rate vs GDP PC growth

degree of external imbalance, proxied by a lower Foreign Exchange/ Imports ratio, were associated over the period with a lower real rate of growth of real income.

Countries with both flexible and fixed exchange rate regimes must keep AD depressed, and strive to sustain surpluses in their current account in response to negative external imbalance, in order to satisfy potential creditors that the current exchange rate will maintain its existing value in the future. This is consistent with

Table 18.1 Bank Rate, growth rate, and the degree of external imbalance 1980–2000 (t-stats in parenthesis)

Equation	Dependent variable	Constant	Explanatory variables		R^2	Durbin–Watson	Mean of dependent variable	No. observations
1	Bank Rate	9.58 (11.91)	BoP/imports −7.032 (1.85)		0.065	1.91	10.3	36
2	Bank Rate	11.29 (10.92)	Foreign exchange/ imports −1.33 (0.64)		−0.01	2.17	10.8	40
3	GDP PC growth	1.95 (8.20)	BoP/imports 1.17 (0.96)		−0.01	1.78	1.8	38
4	GDP PC growth	1.25 (4.71)	Foreign exchange/ imports 1.39 (2.69)		0.13	2.28	1.7	4.3
5	GDP PC growth	2.93 (5.45)	Bank Rate −0.12 (2.59)		0.12	1.81	1.6	42
6	GDP PC growth	2.51 (5.36)	Real Bank Rate −0.10 (1.60)		0.03	2.53	1.8	41
7	GDP PC growth	1.78 (4.46)	Bank Rate −0.06 (2.76)	Foreign Exchange/ Imports 1.50 (2.63)	0.21	2.07	1.5	46

Source: IMF International Financial Statistics.

the significant positive association found between BR and the degree of external imbalance, and the significant negative association found between the growth rate of per capita GDP, bank rate, and the degree of external imbalance.

These regression results provide empirical support for Keynes' hypothesis that higher degrees of external imbalance are associated with more restrictive monetary policies and lower rates of growth of GDP. In all exchange rate regimes all countries except the center are compelled to strive to achieve a surplus position in their current account, to satisfy their potential creditors that their exchange rate will preserve its relative value in the future.

19
Using a Common Currency in International Transactions: The Post Keynesian Case for No Exchange Rates

> Years ago, money was an international thing; if you had the money of one country you could change it into the money of another at a fixed rate, and you never had to think which currency you held. Exchange control changed all that: before anyone accepted payment in a controlled currency, he had to discover where he could spend it and what he could buy with it. One by one the currencies of the world, like their national economies were becoming independent of one another.
>
> J.M. Keynes, 1940, CW XXV: 3

> It is characteristic of a freely convertible international standard that it throws the main burden of adjustment on the country which is in the debtor position on the international balance of payments. ... The contribution in terms of the resulting social strains which the debtor country has to make to the restoration of equilibrium by changing its prices and wages is altogether out of proportion to the contribution asked of its creditors. Nor is this all. ... The social strain of an adjustment downwards is much greater than that of an adjustment upwards. ... The process of adjustment is compulsory for the debtor and voluntary for the creditor. If the creditor does not choose to make, or allow, his share of the adjustment, he suffers no inconvenience. For whilst a country's reserve cannot fall below zero, there is no ceiling which sets an upper limit. The same is true if international loans are to be the means of adjustment. The debtor must borrow; the creditor is under no such compulsion.
>
> J.M. Keynes, 1941, CW XXV: 27–8

> The problem of maintaining equilibrium in the balance of payments between countries has never been solved since methods of barter gave way to the use of money and bills of exchange. During most of the period in which the modern world has been evolved ... the failure to solve this

problem has been a major cause of impoverishment and social discontent and even of wars and revolutions.

J.M. Keynes, 1941, CW XXV: 21

19.1 The choice of a national payments medium: a critically important policy decision

Confidence is fundamental for the general acceptability of money. In all international systems using convertible national currencies, foreigners can never be completely confident that the foreign currency they accept will always remain exchangeable into their own country's currency at the current exchange rate. This is particularly the case when the foreign country runs a deficit on current account or holds very small foreign exchange reserves.

The necessity for countries to maintain "external balance" to keep their exchange rates stable, stems at root from the fact that countries are using their national currency over a foreign geography where they have no jurisdictional ability to proclaim their debt as "legal tender" at a fixed value. Whenever countries use their own currency in international trade, they must persuade potential creditors that the conversion rate of their currency into other currencies will remain constant over the foreseeable future. This belief is necessary to persuade wealth owners to accumulate foreign currency in their portfolios. To persuade foreigners to accept its currency a country must demonstrate its ability to maintain the external value of its currency stable over time, either by accumulating foreign exchange reserves and/or by running a positive balance on current account. If the currency is expected to depreciate in the future, the country must pay a higher rate of interest to foreigners from whom it wishes to borrow and include a risk premium sufficient to offset any expected future depreciation.

When countries share a common currency, they become like states and regions within a single country. Since they no longer maintain a separate exchange rate, it becomes irrelevant whether their current and capital account balance is in deficit or surplus. Since they no longer have an exchange rate, the size of their current account balance ceases to be of interest.[1] Countries then no longer have an "external balance" constraint, and no longer must pay risk premiums to foreign lenders. So long as individual borrowers can make a persuasive case to individual lenders, wherever they may be located, that their project is credit-worthy they will be granted credit, irrespective of the area in which they are located and whether it has a preponderance of debtor or creditor units.

Suppose all countries used the same currency in international trade. Countries would then no longer have an exchange rate and their governments would no longer have to ensure "external balance," to persuade foreign lenders that future convertibility will be maintained at the existing exchange rate. Government policy no longer need attempt to persuade foreigners that the domestic economy will not be allowed to approach its full employment ceiling to an extent that might jeopardize the value of future exchange rates.

Economists must learn "to think outside the box" on exchnge rates. To illustrate the manner in which a single currency removes the external balance constraints for national political entities, assume the world monetary system consisted of a single currency, with a single branch bank and a single central bank (CB). Individual countries would then become comparable with individual states or regions in existing political units, and their current account balance would become irrelevant. Regions running current account deficits are no longer pressured to raise the domestic interest rate, restrict total spending on imports, or raise the value of their exports. Regions would no longer be viewed as "living beyond their means" when they run a deficit on current account.

By using a single currency the relationship among economies becomes much more transparent, permitting greatly improved economic analysis and understanding of open economy phenomena. International macroeconomics then becomes part of macroeconomics and "International Trade" and "International Finance" would disappear as separate sub-disciplines. All the learned technical papers concerning the various forces that influence exchange rates, all the irresolvable problems of understanding, predicting, and explaining future changes in exchange rates, and nominal and real international asset returns would disappear.

In branch banking systems, the head office is indifferent whether individual branches or individual geographic areas run a deficit or a surplus. Branches in less developed, less capital intensive, and more rapidly growing regions where more borrowing firms are located will on balance be deficit branches, and total loans will exceed total deposits. Branches in more developed and established regions, where more large depositors are located will on balance be surplus branches, and total deposits will exceed total loans.[2] Such deficits or surpluses may be structural and permanent in nature. But this is of absolutely no concern to head office.

In a one bank system, changes in total bank deposits are necessarily equal to changes in total bank earning assets.[3] Branches that consistently run current deficits need not be located in cyclically depressed regions and their individual loan applications need not be judged less credit-worthy. In fact if loan officers have uniform lending parameters, deficit branches would more likely be located in regions where future income is expected to grow more rapidly, and investment prospects are more favorable.

Within their own domestic territory, governments can simply declare by fiat the asset to be "generally accepted" in settlement of debt and in payment of taxes, with no formal consideration of alternative media. Historically governments have proclaimed their own debt as "legal tender," in order to appropriate the seigniorage income.[4] At a deeper level money is based on a social convention about the asset to be generally accepted in exchange. Social conventions are grounded on mutual trust and obligation: all economic agents unconditionally agree to accept a particular asset as their means of payment, unit of account, and store of value, even though the asset itself may be intrinsically worthless. Within their territorial jurisdiction, governments are able to set the money asset's nominal exchange value.

The central point is that the particular asset accepted as "money" is based solely on social convention. Like a language, money is acceptable and useful to me only if it is acceptable and useful to you. Governments have the inherent power to declare the asset that will be "legal tender" in payment of taxes and through their administration of the courts the asset that will be "legal tender" in settlement of private debts. Governments also have the ability to validate or change this convention within the geographic areas under their jurisdiction. With current technological changes occurring in communication and processing, chronological and physical distances between geographic areas are perceptively rapidly shrinking. The global economy is approaching the global village. What language will this global village speak, and what money will it use?

Social conventions like languages and money are themselves complex systems whose past can never be uncovered, and whose future can never be forecast. Languages, money, and economies are all characterized by powerful scale economies. In the case of language the more people who speak a language, the more important becomes its literature, the more is it used in books and on TV, and the greater is the incentive of others to learn it.[5] As the global village is approached the number of living languages is falling rapidly.[6] Many parents are now for the first time able to decide the language they would like their children to learn. It is beneficial for children to learn the language most likely to improve their life chances.[7]

It is easier for governments to change the asset that is generally accepted as money than to alter the language that is generally spoken in the community. Fiat money denotes the asset that is generally accepted by government fiat in settlement of debt and in payment of taxes. Historically most countries have chosen to endow their own noninterest-bearing liabilities with the status of legal tender.

But it is nowhere written that they must do this forever. If one thinks what particular asset a government should rationally denote as "legal tender" in exchange, like a language it is desirable to select the asset that is generally accepted by the largest and most influential country with whom one trades. If a country chooses as its domestic money the asset that is generally accepted as money by the most important countries with which it trades, it instantaneously reaps large benefits. At one stroke it is able to exchange goods and services more efficiently and more cheaply with the largest number of other agents. By choosing to make the noninterest-bearing debt of another country the money asset, rather than its own noninterest-bearing debt, the country foregoes its seignorage income. But it gains direct access to a much larger transaction economy, and is able to eliminate the resource costs of exchanging one money into another. It is much easier for governments to change their money than to change their language.

It is not generally appreciated that the policy tradeoff governments face between internal and external balance, which as was shown depresses the expansion of global aggregate demand (AD), stems entirely from governments' decision to use their own national money in international trade. When, as in the European Monetary Union (EMU), a group of countries combine to adopt a common currency as legal tender, all the unsolvable problems that bedevil international trade and cloud our understanding of open economy economics—fluctuating and unpredictable exchange rates, conflict between internal and external balance, shortages of foreign exchange reserves, deflationary bias, higher average levels of interest rates—at one stroke disappear. Each country becomes analogous to a domestic state from the point of view of the payments system.

When all countries use a common currency, they cease to have an exchange rate between them. The world economy can then be analyzed as if it were a single country. All uncertainty concerning the future value of exchange rates, the relative prices of exports and imports, the real resources utilized in the markets for foreign exchange, the transactions and financial costs of exchanging and converting one currency into another, the problems created by a country's foreign imbalance, the size of the current account deficit or surplus, the necessity of earning foreign exchange by the sale of exports to finance import demand, are all eliminated.

When using its national currency a country may find itself in deficit on current account because, at the current exchange rate, its wage levels are "too high" relative to their average labor productivity relative to other countries. Its relative prices may be "too high" because its exchange rate is "overvalued," and sooner or later the rate may have to fall. But a country may also have a current account deficit because it is at an earlier stage of economic development, has more attractive investment prospects than its neighbors, and a larger proportion of deficit spenders relative to surplus spenders. As in a branch banking system such deficits and surpluses may be entirely structural, and need not indicate that the exchange rate is overvalued. It may instead be the case that borrowers in the particular region have more attractive investment projects, with higher expected returns, and desire to invest and deficit-spend larger amounts. When this occurs in branch banking systems, there is no cause for concern. Greater deficits in one area are always exactly offset by greater surpluses in other areas.

In an individual branch, bank loan officers are given lending criteria that apply over the entire system, irrespective of whether the particular branch or geographic area is predominately in surplus or deficit.[8] In multi-currency systems borrowers in areas with higher investment prospects are in effect "redlined" and discriminated against. Their projects are regarded as more risky and less credit-worthy, simply because they are located in a country with deficits in the current account. When a country is spending on imports an amount in excess of its receipts from the sale of its exports, lenders tend to regard the country's exchange rate as overvalued. All borrowers become suspect, are "redlined" and are forced to pay higher interest rates on their loans to cover the greater "country risk."

Similarly with convertible currencies all lenders are exposed to the flight of short-term capital, and the possible collapse of the exchange rate due to speculative considerations. So long as separate national currencies remain in existence, markets may suspect that in the future new operating guidelines will be adapted, existing legislation repealed, or constitutions amended. No country is able to maintain fixed rates in the face of persistent speculative pressures. These constitute extremely strong arguments for dropping the use of the domestic currency in international transactions. When a country avails itself of a medium of exchange of unquestioned stability, it has no need to defend the foreign exchange value of its currency with high domestic interest rates.

It is not widely appreciated that exiting from a fixed exchange rate need not be viewed as the defeatist adoption of being forced to abandon a fixed peg. Countries can instead be viewed as moving in the opposite direction of making the peg more viable. What considerations apply to this kind of shift? Decisions to Dollarize have in the past typically been made against a background of crisis and chronic inflation. These are not ideal circumstances for calm consideration of exit criteria.[9] If the hypothesis of the "disappearing middle" has empirical validity, the increasing integration of goods and capital markets will make it more difficult for noncore countries to maintain pegged but adjustable regimes. Countries must now choose between adopting a floating exchange rate regime, or making a fixed peg more credible by adopting a common currency.

If a common currency is the obvious preferred solution to the deflationary bias imposed by a convertible-currency system, why has it not been proposed by the economic(s) profession? Most economists would probably agree that a world CB and a world currency are the logical solution to the problems of the global trading system, and at some distant date will probably occur.[10] But the insuperable political problems preliminary to agreement on a world CB have rendered the goal of a world bank so impossible in the short run that its espousal appears hopelessly utopian.

After the demise of Bretton Woods, Cooper made a powerful persuasive case that the emergent monetary arrangements do not constitute a durable system, and must in the long run evolve into something else.[11] Cooper concluded the world would eventually evolve to a system of fixed exchange rates. We now understand exchange rates can be credibly fixed for long periods only if they are eliminated altogether, and all transactions take place using a common currency.

If a common payments system could be devised that encouraged all nations to operate closer to their full employment potential, countries would be provided with a "free lunch" in the form of lower interest rates, more rapid rates of economic growth, and global full employment. This end can only be accomplished by moving to a common currency. All transactions and exchange rate costs, all price uncertainty due to exchange rate volatility, and all deflationary bias due to forced debtor restrictions of AD in the quest for "external balance" would be thereby totally eliminated.

But unfortunately in the foreseeable future it is inconceivable the world could unite into a single global trading federation, with a single CB and a single currency. Consider the insuperable difficulties such a polyglot global CB would face in the political sphere, even when set up as only a loose federation: hundredfold differences in per capita incomes, deep historical prejudices among different religious, ethnic, racial and geographic groups, multiple languages, histories, and cultures, political representation with hundreds of languages, an uncountable number of political parties, an unresponsive and unrepresentative world legislature, and a colossal, inefficient, and impossible to monitor administrative bureaucrat monstrosity.

In his 1984 paper, "A Monetary System For The Future," Cooper concluded,

> For such a bold step to work at all presupposes a certain convergence of political values as reflected in the nature of political decision-making and the basic trust and confidence to which these give rise. ... Countries with different values, circumstances, and systems of government are bound to introduce into the negotiations leading toward a common Bank of Issue elements which are of greater concern to them, thus broadening the area of negotiation, and rendering impossible an already difficult negotiation.[12]

Unfortunately it is inconceivable that such an entity could be created in the foreseeable future. If by some fortuitous miracle it were somehow to be imposed, it would soon dissolve in widespread alienation, dissatisfaction, and failure. There is a serious question whether a world government and world CB will ever become feasible. It is hard to imagine the US public would ever accept that countries with oppressive and autocratic political regimes should have a vote on monetary policy affecting interest rates and monetary conditions in the United States. Similar reservations hold for other wealthy countries.

There is also the question whether a single global CB is appropriate. Rogoff has argued it would be undesirable to pursue currency consolidation all the way to a single global currency, since it would be extremely difficult to establish adequate checks and balances on a monopoly global CB.[13] Even though currencies are a natural monopoly, there are persuasive reasons why it might be desirable to entertain competition among separate CBs. A monopoly world CB might constrain future financial innovation, out of a desire to maintain its monopoly or simply due to misjudgment, inefficiency or the clash of personalities. Like the European Central Bank (ECB) it might be founded on unenlightened monetarist principles, be reluctant to permit governments to deficit-spend by more than an arbitrary percentage of gross domestic product (GDP), and be reluctant to lower interest rates sufficiently to reach full employment AD, out of fear of future excess demand inflation.

In contrast currency consolidation through Dollarization or Euroization is clearly feasible. It might be preferable to retain two or three competing currencies, rather than establish a single global currency. There is also the questions of the stability of a single inflation anchor, the rapidity of required inflation conversion, and the feasibility of a common nominal interest rate for countries with widely different inflation histories.

19.2 Efficiency gains from a common currency

The transactions costs benefits of using of a common currency are conventionally regarded as the main factors favoring currency unions. Countries are likely to abandon their national currency if they are small, have a history of high inflation and interest rates, and have a large volume of trade with the anchor country, as reflected in a history of stable real exchange rates. With globalization, the rapid expansion of telecommunications technology has rendered trade-enhancing considerations increasingly important. These are the reasons why the world has been inching away from the "one country-one currency" doctrine toward common currencies. The costs of a separate national currency in terms of forgone trade have been ruled unacceptably high by most new countries created since 1946. It is not generally known that more than 60 countries currently use another country's money, or are members of currency unions.[14] Trade barriers differ among countries, depending on geographic proximity, common languages, and regional trade agreements. By lowering these barriers currency unions lead to higher trade and welfare.

Rose examined the trade patterns of countries in currency unions. By comparison with analogous countries not in currency unions, he attempted to estimate the effects of a common currency on trade volume.[15] Holding constant an array of variables that affect trade flows Rose estimated using a common currency was associated with a 200–400 percent expansion in trade volume! He concluded that separate national monies impose very substantial barriers to the expansion of trade.

Trade barriers take various forms. In cases where trade barriers are low, and previous trade among members of a currency union were high, the impact of a currency union will be lower. These considerations imply that the EMU had a smaller effect on bilateral trade flows than most currency unions. Rose and van Wincoop estimated the trade-creating effects of different currency unions.[16] They found huge effects of currency unions on increasing trade volume, from 50 percent for the EMU to more than 100 percent for the hypothetical dollarization of Argentina and Equador. Estimates of the welfare gains from a common currency generally exceed 10 percent. The Euro will eventually result in enormously increased intra-European trade and accompanying rapid economic growth. Rose and van Wincoop concluded that the case for a common currency was very much stronger than is commonly regarded.

Rose's estimates of the trade barriers from national money may seem implausibly high. But their magnitude accords with recent empirical studies for Canada and the United States where extremely strong home bias in trade has again been identified.[17] Borders appear to matter a great deal, both for trade and financial integration. Crossing a border implies changing moneys, which itself leads to a large home bias in trade patterns. Multinational convertible currencies impose huge barriers on international trade. Reducing these barriers by using a common currency results in a greatly increased volume of international trade, with accompanying high welfare gains. In the future the use of a common currency will almost certainly be endorsed by many additional countries.

It is widely believed that the main cost to a country of giving up its currency is the elimination of independent domestic monetary policy. But since domestic monetary authorities at the periphery are unable to reduce interest rates to the levels ruling in the center, the expansionary gains of policy independence are largely nonexistent. It is little advantage to have an independent monetary policy if the authorities are unable to pursue an expansionary policy. Another consideration favoring the growth of currency unions is that as cyclical fluctuations become more coordinated the gains from independent policy are reduced. As price level stability is valued above active stabilization policy, the benefits attributed to more active monetary policy have diminished. Many economists now view the benefits of "fine-tuning" monetary policy as chimerical.[18]

19.3 Stabilization gains from a common currency

The transactions costs of multiple currencies are in fact merely a small proportion of the total burden imposed by the use of multiple currencies. More importantly, the use of a common currency removes policymakers' conflict between "external balance" and "internal balance," by effectively eliminating the "external balance" constraint. The authorities are then free to concentrate on "internal balance" and reduce interest rates to expand domestic AD, thereby reducing the output gap.[19]

When individual countries use their own currency, "internal balance" goals are overridden by the necessity to maintain "external balance" and assure the stability of the exchange rate. This constraint is binding in both fixed and flexible exchange rate regimes. But it is more restrictive in flexible exchange rate regimes, where the uncertainty of future exchange rate value is greater. The need to assure the future value of the exchange rate, and the accompanying desire to accumulate increased reserves of foreign exchange, prevents governments from pursuing expansionary domestic policy, preventing internal balance from being attained. Keynes argued the restraint on expansionary monetary and fiscal policies imposed by separate currencies was the major defect of using multinational currency standards.[20]

Unlike the case of domestic currency, the accumulation of foreign exchange reserves has important opportunity costs. Foreign exchange reserves can be increased only by running surpluses on current account, or by borrowing on capital account. Countries not using the major currency as the domestic payments media are constrained from pursuing policies that increase the probability of a severe fall in their foreign exchange reserves in a fixed exchange rate regime, or would result in a severe fall in their exchange rate in a flexible exchange rate regime.

As seen the use of multiple national currencies forces all countries, apart from the center, to pursue restrictive AD policies to ensure "external balance." Protection of the foreign exchanges necessitates restrictive domestic policies, higher levels of interest rates, higher taxes, duties and quotas, and reduced government expenditures, all of which depress the level of domestic AD. The macroeconomic domestic policy objectives of full employment, more rapid capital formation, and more equal distribution of income must all be abandoned.

So long as countries wish to trade with the rest of the world, they must avoid all policies that threaten their external balance since they must preserve the expected future conversion rate of their currency at the current rate. If the exchange rate is expected to fall, the CB must set higher domestic interest rates and pay a risk premium to compensate foreign holders for expected capital losses. Since all currencies must be able to act as a store of wealth in asset portfolios, in successful multinational trading relationships all CBs must remain focused on the quantity of their current foreign exchange reserves, and the future value of their exchange rate. Whenever foreign exchange payments exceed foreign exchange receipts, CBs must either pay out foreign currencies from their reserves, borrow foreign currencies to cover their negative current balance of payments, let their exchange rate depreciate or devalue their currency. None of these options is attractive. This explains why external balance considerations dominate internal balance considerations in CB policy priority.

By far the most common response to a negative foreign balance is for CBs to raise the level of domestic short-term interest rates, to attract additional net short-term funds and appreciate the exchange rate. This has the undesirable side effect of depressing the level of domestic AD, to reduce the demand for imports and increase the supply of exports, and conflicts directly with the goal of maintaining internal balance. Deficit countries, if they cannot impose trade barriers, have no choice but to restrict domestic demand to restrain their demand for imports to reduce the deficit. Countries that are prone to run current account deficits are widely viewed as "attempting to live beyond their means."

Developing countries (DCs) are heavily dependent on imported capital goods. In response to higher expected returns on investment projects, they finance capital formation by debt issue. For many DCs the marginal propensity to import capital goods substantially exceeds unity in boom phases of the cycle. Lenders must bear the exchange rate risk that the country in the future may find itself unable to service its total foreign borrowing, in which case they will be repaid only at some fraction of face value. In consequence DCs typically face higher borrowing costs, and still find it difficult to persuade lenders to finance capital imports greatly in excess of their export proceeds. Their cyclical expansions are characteristically deflated by restrictive monetary policy and their long-term GDP growth rates are correspondingly reduced.

Under present institutional arrangements, the pressure to adjust falls solely on deficit countries. Deficit countries are compelled to reduce the imbalance in their current accounts by depressing AD, thus increasing the value of exports and reducing the value of imports. Surplus countries are under no similar pressure to raise expenditures on imports or to make foreign investments. They can simply accumulate foreign exchange reserves indefinitely. In consequence the net effect of trade imbalances on global AD is highly restrictive.

19.4 Post Keynesian open economy macroeconomics

Mainstream economists have succeeded in convincing themselves that most modern economies are supply-constrained. The Keynesian problem of aggregate demand deficiency is regarded as a problem of the 1930s, no longer relevant outside of cases of severe depression. Free trade and greater international capital mobility are held to raise global income, by reducing aggregate supply constraints through the principle of comparative advantage. Unregulated national markets are believed to lead directly to greater global output and employment.

In the *General Theory* Keynes argued that unemployment was primarily due to deficiency of "effective demand," and not to the failure of labor markets to clear because money wages were downwardly sticky. In the *General Theory* Keynes developed his argument in the context of a closed economy. But he indicated how open economy considerations reinforced his vision of a global deficiency of effective demand (AD).

Keynes first argued that as an empirical fact, wages were sticky and inflexible downwards, due as we now know to the widespread existence of implicit contracts in long-term relationships. If a general reduction of money wages were somehow to be brought about, it would affect a redistribution of real income away from workers toward entrepreneurs and wealth-owners, and reduce the aggregate propensity to consume. But he immediately added,

> If we are dealing with an unclosed system, and the reduction of money wages is a reduction relative to money wages abroad ... the change will be favourable to investment, since it will tend to increase the balance of trade.[21]

Keynes explicitly acknowledged that in the case of an open economy, cuts in money wages would increase domestic employment as the classical economists had argued. They were also likely to raise exports and generate additional employment. He added:

> A reduction of money-wages is also likely to worsen the terms of trade. Thus there will be a reduction in real incomes, except in the case of the newly employed, which may tend to increase the propensity to consume.[22]

In the *General Theory* Keynes first introduced open economy effects in his discussion of Mercantilism. He maintained that Mercantilists had been correct that a favorable balance of trade was desirable for a country, since increases in exports and foreign investment increase domestic AD, exactly as increases in domestic investment:

> When a country is growing in wealth somewhat rapidly, the further progress of this happy state of affairs is liable to be interrupted, in conditions of laissez-faire, by the insufficiency of the inducements to new investment. ... The well-being of a progressive state essentially depends ... on the sufficiency of such inducements. They may be found either in home investment or foreign investment ... which between them make up aggregate investment. ... The opportunities for home investment will be governed, in the long run, by the domestic rate of interest; whilst the volume of foreign investment is necessarily determined by the size of the favorable balance of trade.[23] ...

> Mercantilist thought never supposed that there was a self-adjusting tendency by which the rate of interest would be established at the appropriate level.[24]

> In a society where there is no question of direct investment under the aegis of public authority ... it is reasonable for the government to be preoccupied ... [with] the domestic interest rate and the balance of foreign trade. ... When nations permit free movement of funds across national boundaries, the authorities have no direct control over the domestic rate of interest or the other

inducements to home investment, ... measures to increase the favorable balance of trade [are] the only direct means at their disposal for increasing foreign investment; and, at the same time, the effect of a favourable balance of trade on the influx of precious metals was their only indirect means of reducing the domestic rate of interest and so increasing the inducement to home investment.[25]

Keynes argued, the domestic employment advantage gained by export-led growth was a zero sum game since it *was liable to involve an equal disadvantage to some other country*. Export-led growth aggravates the unemployment problem for the surplus nation's trading partners, who are then forced to engage in, "a senseless international competition for a favorable balance, which injures all alike."[26]

The traditional approach to improve the trade balance was to make domestic industries more competitive by forcing down nominal wages to reduce domestic production costs, or by devaluing the exchange rate. Keynes argued that gaining competitive gains by reducing nominal variables tended to foster global recession, since one's trading partners were induced to regain their competitive edge by similar deflationary policies. If nations failed to mutually undertake expansionary policies to increase domestic investment and generate domestic full employment, free international monetary flows create a global environment where each nation has national advantages in a policy of export-led growth, but the pursuit of these policies leads to a race to the bottom, which *injures all alike*.

These alarmist warnings of Keynes have gone virtually unnoticed as mainstream economists have waved enthusiastically about the benefits of liberalized financial markets and the export-led economic miracles of the Asian "Tigers."[27] Modern economies are now more open than when Keynes was writing. This makes it imperative that Keynes' open economy macro-analysis becomes better known. In the concluding chapters of the *General Theory*, Keynes outlined his argument why capitalist economies were typically demand-constrained, and developed his case for a low interest rate policy:

> The weight of my criticism is directed against the inadequacy of the theoretical foundations of the laissez-faire doctrine upon which I was brought up and which for many years I taught;—against the notion that the rate of interest and the volume of investment are self-adjusting at the optimum level so that preoccupation with the balance of trade is a waste of time. ... Under the influence of this faulty theory, the City of London gradually devised the most dangerous technique for the maintenance of equilibrium which can possibly be imagined, namely the technique of bank rate coupled with a rigid parity of the exchanges. For this meant that the objective of maintaining a domestic rate of interest consistent with full employment was wholly ruled out. Since in practice it is impossible to neglect the balance of payments, a means of controlling it was evolved which instead of protecting the domestic rate of interest, sacrificed it to the operation of blind forces.[28]

Never in history was there a method devised of such efficacy for setting each country's advantage at variance of such efficacy with its neighbours as the international gold ... standard. For it made domestic prosperity directly dependent on a competitive pursuit of markets and a competitive appetite for the precious metals.[29]

Keynes insisted that the law of comparative advantage holds only *after* individual nations have achieved full employment through domestic aggregate demand management, and are on their production possibilities curves. When economies operate under a *laissez faire* mentality, substantial global unemployment is virtually inevitable. The law of comparative advantage no longer applies and free trade under such conditions is not *per se* globally job creating:

> Under the system of domestic laissez-faire and an international gold standard ... there was no means open to a government whereby to mitigate economic distress at home, except through the competitive struggle for markets ... if nations can learn to provide themselves with full employment by their domestic policy, ... there need be no important economic forces calculated to set the interest of one country against that of its neighbours. There would still be room for the international division of labour and for international lending in appropriate conditions. But there would no longer be a pressing motive why one country need force its wares on another, or repulse the offerings of its neighbor, not because this was necessary to enable it to pay for what it wished to purchase, but with the express object of upsetting equilibrium in the balance of payment so as to develop a balance of trade in its own favour [export-led growth]. International trade would cease to be what it is, namely, a desperate expedient to maintain employment at home by forcing sales on foreign markets and restricting purchases, which if successful, will merely shift the problem of unemployment to the neighbor which is worsted in the struggle, but a willing and unimpeded exchange of goods and services in conditions of mutual advantage.[30]

Keynes developed his vision of how the existing international payments system led directly to a global deficiency of aggregate demand at greater depth in his post-*General Theory* writings, which are much less well known. He emphasized that when governments did not have the political will to stimulate domestic AD (in Keynes' day due to self-imposed beliefs in the desirability of a balanced budget, today due to the fear of missing similarly self-imposed inflation targets), each country's international advantage becomes at variance with its neighbors. The result is a "race to the bottom."[31]

Keynes believed neoclassical logic assumed away most questions fundamental to a money-using economy, in particular the necessity to continually maintain system liquidity and balance of payments surpluses in an uncertain world. These problems are particularly relevant for understanding international financial phenomena: portfolio liquidity, growing debt obligations, and fluctuating exchange rates. Nowhere is the difference between Keynes' position and that of supporters of the "Washington Consensus" more evident than the question of the freedom of international capital movements and the advantages of stable exchange rates. Keynes was convinced that government regulation of international capital movements to promote stability of exchange rates was in the public interest. He noted that

> Many international financial flows were the result of anti-social activities. In a *laissez faire* system of international financial markets there is no way to distinguish the movement of funds used to promote new investments, from speculative funds that are seeking a safe haven and attempt to take refuge in one nation after the other, either in a continuous search for speculative gains, or to hide from the tax collector.[32]

Anti-social activities to one side, exogenous capital movements if not offset can have severely detrimental effects on individual countries balance of payments, exchange rates, GDP growth, and unemployment rates. The international flow of "hot" money in the form of precautionary and speculative funds can be seriously disruptive, and result in the impoverishment of nations whose current accounts could otherwise be balanced:

> Loose funds ... sweep round the world disorganizing all steady business. Nothing is more certain than that the movement of capital funds must be regulated. ... There is no country which can in the future safely allow the flight of funds for political reasons, or to evade domestic taxation or in anticipation of the owner turning refugee. Equally, there is no country that can safely receive fugitive funds which cannot safely be used for fixed investments and might turn it into a deficiency country against its will and contrary to the real facts.[33]

19.5 Currency unions

The number of countries in the world has more than doubled since the Second World War. In 1946 there were 76 independent countries, while in 2000 there were nearly 200.[34] Since it was largely taken for granted that proper countries must have their own currency, the expansion of countries led to an accompanying proliferation of new moneys. Over the past decade the identification of currencies with countries has weakened, and much discussion has shifted to the type and area of possible currency unions.

The EMU with a new currency the EURO was recently formed with 15 European countries. Fifteen additional eastern European countries have now been admitted into the EURO, and more have been proposed.[35] Three countries in the Americas have adopted Dollarization, and others are contemplating it. There have been proposals for a North American Monetary Union (NAMU) with its own new currency the AMERO.[36] South America and Africa are currently considering free trade areas and currency unions.

Why the shift? Conventional wisdom maintains that the costs of joining a currency union are high, because member countries loose the ability to pursue an independent monetary policy. So long as countries operate in a flexible exchange rate regime, each monetary authority is able to set its Bank Rate and tailor monetary policy to its particular domestic economic situation. In fixed exchange rate regimes, domestic monetary policy must be rigidly subordinated to maintenance of the exchange rate. When capital is highly mobile, the domestic monetary authorities lose all ability to set Bank Rate autonomously.

Most economists appear to believe the positive benefits of a common currency are modest. But conventional wisdom is again seriously mistaken. Independent national currencies impose substantial transaction barriers on international trade. Even more important, as developed in Chapter 18 the authorities' attempts to stabilize the value of convertible national currencies have the unintended side effect of depressing global AD. Under the present international regime all countries apart from the "center" must try to maintain "external balance" (balance in their current account), and when possible generate a positive balance. This creates a severe conflict with "internal balance" objectives, and for most countries precludes expansionary domestic policy. All countries with BOP deficits are forced to pursue restrictive policies to various degrees. This deflationary bias operates both in fixed and flexible exchange rate regimes, but is greater under flexible exchange rates.

The adoption of one country's money by another country makes the costs of turning back extremely expensive. Joining a common currency is a much stronger commitment device than a government's promise to peg the exchange rate.[37] One unanticipated benefit of currency unions is that, when countries are linked by a common currency, the benefits of belonging to a larger political union are diminished. When the benefits of free trade and a common currency are no longer linked with political union, it is less costly for regions to secede. In consequence, in Europe the demand for greater regional political autonomy is currently showing renewed vigor.[38]

The theory of optimal currency areas suggests that a currency union is most beneficial when there is a large degree of trade integration, when the regions are not subject to asymmetrical shocks, and when income transfer mechanisms exist to cushion regional disparities in economic activity. Within a currency union it is possible to provide every country with a "free lunch," in the form of lower interest rates, more expansionary monetary policy, full employment, and greatly increased growth rates. Since the establishment of the EMU, the literature on currency unions has gathered increased momentum.[39]

The long transition period necessary before agreement on a European Currency Union could be reached, even for a relatively homogeneous group of European countries, has given currency union proponents occasion for pause. The European Central Bank was formed only after a deliberative process lasting nearly half a century. The original European countries, who constituted the OECD formed the European Free Trade Area (EFTA) immediately after the Second World War. The EFTA first undertook to confine exchange rate movements for the group within a specified band, subject to periodic renegotiation when they became questionable. The choice of a currency for the union was politically highly charged with strong emotional ties and objections to each participating national currency. Eventually the Euro was born as a completely new currency, with much greater adjustment costs than would have had been imposed had the currency with most widespread use, the British Pound, been adopted. In the end the UK decided not to join the Euro zone.

The OECD maintained economic convergence should precede monetary union, and a strong fiscal position was required of all individual members. In a currency union, domestic inflation is no longer an option to deal with high nominal debt service obligations. Market confidence in a government's ability to meet its debt service obligations must first be established, otherwise the risk premiums on outstanding debt can rise without limit threatening unsustainable debt dynamics. Similar inflation rates are necessary, since in order for sustainable trade to continue, countries must keep their domestic inflation rates in line with the average of the trading block.

The Maastricht Treaty early proposed five "convergence criteria":

(i) Government budget deficits under 3 percent of GDP
(ii) Government debt levels under 60 percent of GDP
(iii) Inflation rates not more than 1.5 percent above the average of the three countries with the lowest inflation rates
(iv) Long-term interest rates not more than 2 percent above the average of the three countries with the lowest interest rates
(v) Exchange rates within the normal ERM bands for two years prior to entry to union.

Fines were liable if countries exceeded these limits. Both Germany and France have since breached these numbers, and negotiations are underway for more a flexible dispensation. Within the Euro area balance-of-payments adjustment has now disappeared, as in the case of different states and regions in a single country. Regional underemployment and overemployment is still substantial, but can be cushioned by fiscal transfers and encouraging greater labor mobility. The major unresolved problem for the ECB is how low should interest rates be set, when different countries are at different stages of the business cycle and have very different output gaps and unemployment rates? The theoretical answer is the lowest interest rate consistent with overall price level stability. But the ECB has not yet reached this position, and violent disagreement continues over the level of Bank Rate to be set. Perhaps the major significance of the establishment of the Euro is the clear demonstration that currency areas need no longer be confined to a single country.

A currency union is very difficult to negotiate since it means giving up an important degree of domestic economic sovereignty, and finding satisfactory means to pool decision-making authority in the monetary and fiscal sphere. Its creation involves a long and intricate process of common institutional creation over a variety of dimensions. In the case of Europe, the development of the Euro went hand-in-hand with broader economic and political integration. Even so the realization proceeded slowly over several early rocky stages, took half a century, and has still to reach fruition.

The main economic purpose of a single currency is to deepen integration among its members, by reducing the costs of cross-border commerce. The European

Economic Commission maintains that cyclical convergence in the Euro is gradually occurring. The standard deviation of quarterly GDP growth rates for the nine countries that publish quarterly growth rates fell from 1.8 to 0.9 from 1997 to 2001 but has recently increased to 1.2.[40] This divergence in growth rates conceals a much larger divergence in the components of GDP, C, I, G, and X. Consumption, the largest component has been buoyant in Spain and France, but low in Germany and Italy. Investment fell cumulatively by 6 percent in Germany from 1998 to 2004, but rose in Spain by 26 percent. Inflation rates as measured by GDP deflators have also diverged leading to differences in real exchange rates, even though nominal exchange rates are fixed. Europe's single interest rate has served to widen the gap. Monetary policy has been too tight for sluggish Germany, but too loose for fast-growing Spain and Ireland. While different parts of America also grow at different rates, America has the labor market flexibility and the fiscal mechanisms to reduce divergences, and smooth the system. On both these fronts Europe lags.

19.6 Dollarization and Euroization

The experience of the prewar gold standard, and the prosperity of the period of Bretton Woods, demonstrated that fixed exchange rates can result in a major reduction in uncertainty in international transactions, lower Bank Rates, and much higher rates of economic growth. But they also provide ample evidence that exchange rates between countries can be permanently fixed only if they are eliminated altogether and all transactions are conducted in a common currency.

It had long been presumed that the formation of a global monetary authority required independent national states to turn over the determination of monetary policy to a supranational authority, responsible collectively to all governments of the national states.[41] This seemed to imply the institutional organization of a global currency and a global CB empowered to set interest rates for the world. While such an outcome may some day occur, it will only be in the far distant future, after the world has converged toward a more homogeneous global culture. On purely pragmatic grounds, a world CB appears to be politically inconceivable in the foreseeable future.

But the creation of a global CB, or a global currency union with its manifold political and organizational problems, is no longer a precondition for the existence of a common currency. Dollarization and Euroization are much less utopian and clearly more feasible alternatives. While they may not be first-best, they very clearly dominate the current international financial architecture. All the political difficulties that accompany the formation of a global world organization can be finessed, and no collective agreements must be negotiated. Country A must simply decide unilaterally to adopt the currency of Country B. This implies granting the CB of country B the authority to vary Bank Rate for both countries.

A large collection of independent countries that do not easily fit into any obvious currency union now have the option to abandon their national currencies and Dollarize or Euroize. Instead of having to imagine all countries of the world inconceivably uniting under a global CB, or a global currency union, each country must merely choose to adopt the currency of its largest trading partner as its currency. In so doing, countries can sequentially and incrementally free themselves from external balance constraints and gradually become able to focus primarily on expansionary domestic policy to achieve internal balance.

The case for such action is extremely strong in all countries with a history of high inflation and weak CB/government credibility, and in all countries where the economy is stagnant and the government is constrained by external balance considerations from pursuing a sufficiently expansionary domestic monetary policy to reduce a high unemployment rate. With Dollarization or Euroization, so long as the currency link is secure, the level of interest rates and inflation rates in the periphery must gradually fall to the levels existing in the center.[42]

Most countries have neither the tradition nor the implicit social contracts in place to maintain unit labor costs constant when employment rises, the output gap declines, and unemployment rates fall toward frictional levels. Most economies are forced to remain demand-constrained so as to preserve external balance. If the internal balance (wage–cost inflation) and the external balance (current account) deficit constraint were both absent, the appropriate goal of CBs would be exceedingly straightforward. The aggregate supply (AS) curve becomes a horizontal band up to where full employment was reached, when the band becomes vertical. CBs must then continue to reduce the level of interest rates sequentially, until AD has been raised to the level of potential full employment GDP and the output gap is completely eliminated.

Wages are not a good control variable. Governments cannot implement a law requiring that average money wage increases do not exceed the level of average labor productivity growth in the previous period. As a result, CBs have no discretion to reduce interest rates to the level that results in domestic full employment. They are compelled to keep nominal rates sufficiently high, and keep the economy sufficiently depressed, to achieve their inflation and external balance targets. All governments faced with negative current account balances must maintain Bank Rate at a sufficiently high level to attract short-term funds to be able to defend their exchange rate. As Keynes argued, this injects a huge deflationary bias into the world economy.

Before a country can successfully Dollarize or Euroize, it must decide on the rate at which it will convert its currency into the currency of the center (Begg and Wyplosz, 1993). If a country is experiencing inflation at a greater rate than the center, it must choose an initial exchange rate that sets its current domestic prices below existing prices in the anchor, so that it initially has a positive current account balance. So long as its inflation rate exceeds the inflation rate of the center it will find its positive current account balance will decline. To successfully Dollarize or Euroize, countries must bring their domestic inflation rate down to the inflation rate of the anchor. For price level stability, average wage increases must not exceed the average rate of labor productivity growth. When the domestic inflation rate exceeds that of the center locally produced goods will sooner or later be unable to compete with cheaper foreign goods. The result will be an inflow of imports, a collapse of local production, and political pressure for trade protection.

Either way the local economy will undergo a massive slump, with accompanying huge increases in unemployment rates. This situation will continue, until union power to demand wage increases above the rate of average labor productivity growth has been eliminated. Such a deflationary process will shift the distribution of income toward nonlabor income. Countries desiring to Dollarize or Euroize are strongly advised to first achieve a low rate of inflation and approximate price level stability, before they attempt entry. They can do this either by means of social contracts that keep unit labor costs constant, or by the successful pursuit of restrictive monetary policy and inflation targeting.

As neighboring countries Dollarize or Euroize, only the external balance constraint will incrementally dissolve. The freedom from being required to depress domestic activity to protect the exchange rate permits CBs to lower interest rates and pursue generally more expansionary domestic, monetary, and fiscal policies. Foreign competition forces workers and firms to keep wage growth below average labor productivity growth, to keep prices competitive and stable. Successful Dollarization and Euroization will lead to lower inflation rates and more rapid growth rates. This will have a strong demonstration effect, and encourage additional countries to Dollarize or Euroize, resulting in a general movement toward fewer currencies.

Alesina and Barro (A&B) attempted to estimate the empirical contours of future currency areas. They conclude that Mexico and Canada were excellent candidates for Dollarization since their trade focus is primarily with the United States, and NAFTA is encouraging further economic integration. Their gains from dollarization and deeper financial integration with the United States are likely to be quite substantial.[43] The case is similarly strong for most Central America countries. For some countries the Dollar is the best anchor, while for others that trade more heavily with Europe the Euro dominates. In Asia, Philippines, Korea, Hong Kong, and Singapore all belong in the dollar area. All of Eastern Europe, most of Africa, and most of Asia belong in the Euro area. The Japanese economy is relatively closed, and few prospective clients have a high share of their exports to Japan. With the possible exception of Indonesia, there is not a natural yen area beyond Japan. As a result Yenization is not an appealing option. The recent rapid growth of China may induce China to Dollarize even though it is no longer fixing its currency to the dollar. Its size and growth rate in the future may alternatively induce China to merge with Japan, and form a new Asian currency block.

The loss of seigniorage with Dollarization or Euroization is an important consideration. A major cost of Dollarization or Euroization is the loss of seigniorage in the client country. While large in absolute amount, in most countries seigniorage is less than 1 percent of GDP. Most governments' budgets will be more than compensated by the lower interest costs of public debt.[44]

Seigniorage is not a social waste or inefficiency but represents a redistribution of property income among countries. In principle, the anchor should return all seigniorage to the client. A & B suggest the allocation of seigniorage be part of a compensation scheme between anchors and clients, to provide anchor countries the incentive to consider the interest of clients in formulating their monetary policy. As the process of Dollarization and Euroization proceeds, client countries will eventually be allocated a share of seigniorage income, and probably some sort of representation on Interest Rate Committees.[45]

There have as yet been few empirical studies of the gains from Dollarization. One exception is the recent paper by Edwards and Magendzo (E & M).[46] Supporters of Dollarization claim two major positive effects on economic performance:

1. The inflation rate will be lower since the economy is then hooked into the financial system of the anchor. This will prevent firms from passing on higher labor costs in higher prices. As a result there is likely to be a sharp reduction in union market power, and with it a reduction in union ability to achieve higher wages for their members.[47] The gains will come in lower output gaps and higher total employment and real income.
2. The growth rate will be higher through several channels: lower interest rates, higher investment spending, higher AD, reduced costs of foreign exchange dealings, better structural adjustment, lower exchange risk, greater imports and exports, and a generally higher level of globalization, trade and financial mobility.[48]

E & M found that for the period 1978–98 Dollarized countries had substantially lower rates of inflation. The mean and median difference from the matching control group was a highly significant 2 and 5 percent reduction in inflation. Surprisingly, no similar positive growth benefits were identified. In fact Dollarized economies had an (insignificant) 1 percent lower annual growth rate. No differences were found in measures of macroeconomic stability between Dollarized and nonDollarized economies.

E & M conjectured that the inability to find a higher growth rate in Dollarized countries might be due to countries being more likely to Dollarize when their economies are in trouble, and they are having difficulties accommodating external disturbances, or simply be due to small sample size effects. Taken the evidence at face value, it appears that the few economies that have Dollarized have not yet succeeded in finding their way free to eliminate the external balance constraint, and pursue vigorous expansionary domestic policies. The benefits of Dollarization in removing the external balance constraint become increasingly important only after additional trading partners Dollarize. For example, South American or African countries would strongly benefit if they Dollarized or Euroized as a group, rather than serially, since the external balance constraint would then be relaxed more rapidly.

Convergence on the money of the core is generally in a country's self-interest. As Dornbusch put it, "For many countries monetary convergence is simply a no-brainer."[49] But if Dollarization or Euroization were to succeed it must be market driven. Countries must individually demonstrate the macroeconomic advantages of adopting the center currency: lower interest rates, lower inflation rates, higher employment, greater investment, and more rapid growth of real GDP.

The center must also recognize the existence of reciprocal gains. Fewer crises on the periphery, and more stability and growth across the border, make the center also better off. This recognition will increase the activity of centers in promoting

Dollarization or Euroization. It is then but a short step to discussion of how the accompanying seigniorage should be shared.

At root the argument for Dollarization and Euroization is the ability of currency blocks to pursue more expansionary monetary policy than individual countries acting on their own. They are able to reduce Bank Rate to the level required to achieve full employment and simultaneously to have stable prices, due to the competitive power of international competition. Since currency blocks have a much higher total level of GDP than individual countries, and a much lower ratio of exports and imports to GDP, they have much weaker external balance constraints. Since there will probably be only two or three currency blocks, there will be competition among CBs as to which currency area performs most successfully. This competition gives each center an incentive to keep Bank Rate at the lowest level consistent with price stability. Blocks will then be able to operate closer to their full capacity potential output, and will no longer be demand-constrained by the external balance constraint to protect the current value of exchange rate.

20
Financial Barriers to Demand-led Growth

> The outstanding faults of the economic society in which we live are its failure to provide full employment, and its arbitrary and inequitable distribution of wealth and incomes.
>
> John Maynard Keynes, 1936: 372

> It is the policy of an autonomous rate of interest unimpeded by international pre-occupations, and of a national investment programme directed to an optimum level of domestic employment which is twice blessed, in the sense that it helps ourselves and our neighbours at the same time. And it is the simultaneous pursuit of these policies by all countries together which is capable of restoring economic health and strength internationally, whether we measure it by the level of domestic employment or by the volume of international trade.
>
> John Maynard Keynes, 1936: 349

> We should not conclude from this that everything depends on waves of irrational psychology. ... The state of long term expectations is often steady. ... We are merely reminding ourselves human decisions affecting the future, whether personal, or political, or economic, cannot depend on strict mathematical expectations, since the basis for making such calculations does not exist. ... it is our innate urge to activity which makes the wheels go round.
>
> John Maynard Keynes, 1936: 162–3

> At the time of his death [April 21, 1946] he was beginning a post-budget memorandum for the Chancellor, arguing that a gradual and controlled rise in prices and wages desirable. ... He also prophesied that in the future inflation was more likely to be caused by changes in costs than by excess demand. He offered no solution.
>
> Moggidge, 1992: 835

20.1 Why market economies are demand-constrained?

Keynes disagreed strongly with the *laissez faire* view that market economies possess strong homeostatic properties and if only prices were flexible would tend in the long run towards full employment equilibrium. Keynes emphasized that the future is unknowable and economic behavior nondeterministic. Continuously changing expectations of future aggregate demand (AD) and future profitability drive current investment spending, and govern current AD. He characterized agents' expectations about future AD as "animal spirits," self-fulfilling waves of optimism and pessimism about the unknown future state of the economy. This expectations process generates unpredictable fluctuations in future economic activity.

Keynes urged that with our current increased understanding of how economies function, for the first time governments now have the ability and the responsibility to manage aggregate demand (AD), to ensure no workers are involuntarily unemployed, and the economy performs at its production-possibility frontier with stable prices. Firms administer their prices over the current pricing period as a relatively stable mark-up over historic unit variable costs in the previous pricing period. Prices in the current pricing period are thus pre-determined by average costs and mark-ups in the previous period. In labor markets money wages, which constitute by far the most important component of business costs, in most sectors are inflexible downwards, due primarily to "implicit contracts" that evolve in all long-term relationships (marriage being the classic example). The behavior of wages from one pricing period to the next is central to an understanding of how the inflation rate changes, and how interest rates and unemployment respond. As developed in Chapter 12 money wages are determined in labor markets by market power in a collective bargaining process between labor and business. Prices are co-determined in product markets as a stable markup on unit costs.

In the *General Theory* Keynes developed a general explanation of how output was determined, which was independent of the degree of market power in labor and product markets. He believed his theory of "effective demand" held generally, irrespective of whether prices were flexible and markets were perfectly competitive, or prices were administered and markets were highly concentrated. Keynes emphasized that as an empirical fact, money wages were highly inflexible downwards, due to the special nature of labor markets and employment contracts, what are now termed "implicit contracts." He maintained that stable wages and prices were welfare-enhancing, compared to the alternative of wage and price flexibility since they reduced the degree of uncertainty about expected future price levels and profits. He insisted insufficient AD and not sticky wages was the core explanation for unemployment, excess capacity, and output gaps. When firms are price-setters and quantity-takers, the short-run aggregate supply (AS) relation becomes a horizontal fractal band in price-output space. Output and employment respond directly to changes in "effective demand," Keynes' term for AD for currently produced consumption, investment, and public goods and exports.

Keynes insisted that market economies did not self-equilibrate. Due to the fundamental uncertainty of future events firms are never sure what their future sales quantities will be. It is impossible for market forces to provide firms with accurate information concerning future AD. Markets on their own cannot be relied upon to produce full employment levels of output: "full, or even approximately *full employment is of rare and short-lived occurrence.*"[1]

Keynes argued it was the responsibility of governments to manage the level of AD to ensure that economies performed at their full employment potential. Writing in the 1930s, he argued that as a result of insufficiently expansionary monetary and fiscal policy, associated with *laissez faire* notions of fiscal prudence, monetary conservatism, and the way in which the international financial architecture (then the gold standard) was organized, market economies generally did not reach their full employment potential. They remained stuck for long periods below their full capacity level of output:

> It is an outstanding characteristic of the economic system in which we live that whilst it is subject to severe fluctuations in respect of output and employment, it is not violently unstable. Indeed it seems capable of remaining in a chronic condition of sub-normal activity for a considerable period, without any marked tendency either towards recovery or toward complete collapse. Moreover the evidence indicates that full or even approximately full employment is of rare and short-lived occurrence.[2]

In the *General Theory* Keynes recognized that interest rates were not endogenously determined by real forces of productivity and thrift as the classical economists had argued, but by capital market expectations of the future supply of money and bonds. In his post *General Theory* writings, Keynes explicitly stated that Bank Rate was set by the CB on its exogenous policy instrument, and it could set it at whatever level it liked. The level of AD was determined by business expectations of future profitability (animal spirits) and by the level of Bank Rate. The AD curve is then a downward-sloping fractal band in interest-rate-output space. Bank Rate set by the CB then determines the level of AD, so in inflation-output space, the AD curve can be visualized as a *vertical* fractal band.

The underlying reason why market economics are typically demand-constrained may now be seen to be because CBs do not set BR at a sufficiently low level to achieve a full employment level of AD. This is because CBs are preoccupied with ensuring that inflation remains low, and the balance of payments remains balanced. Under existing labour market procedures, in most economies wages rise well before the full employment capacity of the economy is approached.

Most monetary authorities, who are in all economies appointed by governments and not publicly elected, rank price stability above full employment as a policy objective. This is rationalized since rapid inflation is widely believed to be extremely destabilizing for the economy, and must be controlled by proactive increases in interest rates before it accelerates even though this has negative effects on the growth of AD. In most economies CBs are the sole government agency mandated to achieve price stability.

20.2 Neoclassical supply-side models of economic growth

Mainstream economics has accepted the central importance of short-run countercyclical monetary and fiscal AD management. But it continues to embrace neoclassical long-run theories of economic growth. These offer solely supply-side explanations of output determination and are deeply inconsistent with Keynes' central belief that market economies are inherently demand-constrained.[3]

For example Solow's well-known growth model derives the steady-state "natural" rate of growth as dependent on two fundamental supply-side forces: the rate of population growth and the rate of labor-augmenting technical progress.

> The new wrinkle I want to describe is an elementary way of segregating variations in output per head due to technical change from those due to changes in the availability of capital per head.[4]

In the Solow model, exogenous increases in the savings rate raise the rate of capital accumulation, the level of capital stock per worker, and the level of potential output, but do not affect the "natural" growth rate of the economy. Changes in the long-run rate of growth of real per capita income are explained by changes in the rate of population growth and in the rate of technical progress, both of which are exogenous to the model.

In most neoclassical growth models, full employment is simply assumed due to the (implicit) operation of Say's Law. All such models offer purely supply-side explanations of economic growth, completely independent of monetary and fiscal policy and all other demand-side factors, which are considered to have only short-run transitory real effects. Real interest rates are assumed to be determined by real factors reflecting the marginal productivity of capital and the rate of time preference of economic agents. Such models embody the "classical dichotomy," and are characterized by a "natural" rate of growth determined solely by real supply-side forces. Monetary change is assumed to be "neutral" in the long run, and to affect only nominal values, like the price level and the inflation rate.

New Classical real business cycle economists have recently developed models that generate endogenous trends and cyclical fluctuations in aggregate income.[5] These models assume all markets clear and the economy is continually in a general equilibrium (GE) configuration. Fluctuations in output are attributed to exogenous productivity shocks and to demand-side monetary "surprises," which impact on the aggregate production function. All such models offer purely supply-side explanations of business fluctuations. They are aggressively "equilibrium" models: all unemployment is voluntary and the "natural" growth rate is derived as the "center of long-run gravitation" for the model. Actual output is assumed to converge eventually on the potential output path:

> The resulting real business cycle approach simply denies that there is in fact any significant effect of monetary policy on output: observed money-output correlations are said to be the consequence of "reverse causation," i.e. responses of the money stock to output fluctuations. These fluctuations are brought about, to finish the story, by random real shocks to technology.[6]

The goal of monetary and fiscal policy is to stabilize the path of actual output around potential output by minimizing fluctuations in AD. Whenever actual output is subject to large negative or positive "shocks," monetary and fiscal policy can be used to speed up the adjustment process. Income fluctuations are explained in terms of informational and strategic considerations (e.g. "menu" costs) which dictate whether firms will change prices.[7] In New Keynesian models recessions are generated by reductions in the level of AD due to negative demand "shocks," which reduce the rate of investment spending and temporarily lower the rate of growth of the economy. Since the steady-state capital–labor ratio and the level of potential output remain unchanged, the effects of any such demand-side recessions are only temporary. Recessions are costly, in the sense that they cause a loss in the flow of output that can never be recovered. But they leave behind no permanently lower capital–labor ratio or rate of population growth, and so no permanently lower "natural" rate of output growth.

Supply-side models are in fundamental conflict with Keynes' central vision: due to fundamental uncertainty about the environment and the behavior of other agents, and the innate conservatism of monetary and fiscal authorities, interest rates are held at too high a level. As a result there is a persistent shortage of aggregate demand. Real world economies get stuck in less than full employment positions and remain there for long periods of time. Keynes emphasized the centrality of "effective demand," and the volatility of investment spending, due to swings in expectations of future events associated with changes in investor "animal spirits."

New endogenous growth models (NEG) now recognize a range of behavior by economic agents that renders the rate of technological progress endogenous. Changes in the stock of human capital and in the level of investment spending both affect, and are affected by the rate of technological change. In such models investment serves to expand the real capital stock to feed technological innovations into the production process, and to uncover further possibilities for real innovation.[8]

In NEG models by making the rate of labor-augmenting technical progress endogenous, the rate of potential output growth also becomes endogenous. The rate of technical progress can be affected by AD policies, and can influence capital stock per worker and the flow of investment per worker. Positive externalities are recognized in firms' production functions, which lead to various processes of cumulative causation. The accumulation of capital can accelerate the rate of technical change and the growth rate, and affect cross-country convergence or divergence of growth rates.[9]

In NEG models, monetary and fiscal policies impact on AD and affect the flow of investment spending, the level of output, and the growth of technological change. Expansionary AD policies are recognized as consistent with increases in both the level and growth rate of AS. Restrictive AD policies create excess supply, and reduce the level and rate of growth of real output. Expectations of the future are now incorporated in NEG models on the demand-side as well as the supply side of the model:

> In this essay the focus is on aggregate demand, as in fact was standard in the old Keynesian tradition. Both the new and the old Keynesians are trying to answer a question of the 1950's and 1960's: why are prices sticky? But the question that

needs to be asked is: why are prices sticky in certain historical episodes, and rapidly adjusting in others?[10]

In NEG models, physical and human capital need not as in the Solow model exhaust their contribution to production at the margin. The growth rate can be sustained through a steady process of accumulation. Given the conventional neoclassical vision that "saving determines investment," anything that affects the saving rate affects the long-run rate of growth. But long-run effective demand failure is not recognized in the model. Autonomous short-falls in AD only impact on the utilization of resources in the short run due to various expectational errors, and nominal wage rigidities.

Whereas old growth theory was totally inconsistent with Post Keynesian theory, NEG theory at least offers the prospect of a reconciliation of subsets of Post Keynesian and mainstream theory.[11] But so long as NEG models derive an "equilibrium" or "natural" rate of growth for the economy, even if they include demand-side variables, they diverge fundamentally from Keynes' vision of the economy as a complex adaptive system (CAS) whose long-run growth rate is inherently chaotic and hysteretic in character.

Keynes' *General Theory* focused on explaining short-run changes in GDP, and purported to determine the equilibrium *level* of output not the growth rate. This is generally regarded as a flaw by mainstream economists. But all long-run equilibrium growth models are incompatible with Keynes' vision of the macroeconomy. Given the presence of fundamental uncertainty, the economy's future long-run output path can never be formulated in advance. Economies are complex adaptive systems driven by agents' ever-changing expectations of future events. Complex adaptive systems can never exhibit steady-state "equilibrium" configurations or "natural" rates of long-run growth, for any variable. For Keynesi, the economic system is inherently complex, and its future inherently unknowable. Change is the only constant. All long-run "equilibrium" analysis is fundamentally incompatible with the view of the economy as a complex adaptive system.

A recent salient World Bank study dramatically showed how the volatility of country growth rates may be due simply to "luck."[12] The economic "miracles" of the postwar period, Germany, Japan, the Asian "Tigers," and now China have been intensively studied by analysts, eager to apply and generalize their explanations for such rapid growth rates to other economies. The unquestioned assumption has been that differences in long-run economic growth rates among countries are solely due to supply-side factors. But in most countries economic success and failure is very shortlived. Most countries' performance is characteristically outstanding one decade, and disappointing in the next. Very few countries, only the so-called Asian "tigers," have experienced successful growth processes that have persisted from one decade to the next. In most countries growth episodes have been shortlived. The correlation of growth rates for roughly 100 countries for the two 14-year periods, 1960–73, and 1974–88, was below 0.2. This indicates less than 20 percent of the differences in growth experienced between countries in the first 14-year (1960–73) period persisted into the subsequent (1974–88) 14-year period.

The primary lesson to be drawn from past economic growth performance is that "failures" can become "successes" and vice versa with surprising speed.[13]

Political and policy indicators display much higher cross-decade correlations (0.7–0.9) than do country per capita growth rates (0.1–0.2). Consequently they offer little help in explaining a transitory growth process. "Shocks" appear to have a major effect on growth rates over most periods less than one decade in length. Only over substantially longer periods can supply-side variables be shown empirically to significantly affect growth rates.

Supply-side factors are strongly related with longer-run economic performance. The data show that over 30-year periods, countries with the most rapid long-term growth rate have on average: double the investment rate, half the inflation rate, twice the export share, one-fifteenth the black market premium for the exchange rate, four times the secondary enrolment, and twice the primary enrolment of the slowest growth economies.[14] Nevertheless the Asian Tigers have been the only economies to consistently perform in the top tier while only the African economies have consistently been at the bottom. For the rest cyclical fluctuations in AD best explain why short- and medium-run performance diverge sharply from the supply-side full employment potential production-possibility frontier.

20.3 Post Keynesian demand-led models of economic growth

Mainstream economics has followed the neoclassical lead, and paid near-exclusive attention to the supply-side analysis of economic growth. There was a hiatus in mainstream growth theory during the 1970s and early 1980s, until the appearance of the NEG models of Romer and Lucas in the late 1980s. In contrast Post Keynesian economists continued to make key contributions to the theory of demand-led growth throughout the entire postwar period.[15]

In 1972 Cornwall identified the reconciliation of the rate of growth of demand with the rate of growth of supply as the central issue in growth theory.[16] Rejecting the neoclassical claim that demand adjusts passively to accommodate real supply, he argued for the central relevance of the Keynesian principle of "effective demand." Cornwall termed the economic process by which the expansion of supply and potential output responds to the expansion of demand and actual output, "Say's law in reverse." The central question becomes "what factors shape the elasticity of the supply response to an expansion of demand," and "what factors encourage or inhibit AD growth?"[16]

In the early 1970s Kaldor championed Myrdal's notion of "cumulative causation" as a basis for a nonequilibrium Keynesian growth theory. In Kaldor's theory the rate of growth of exports was the proximate determinate of income growth.[17] Kaldor recognized that export growth provided a basis for faster expansion of domestic demand without producing a situation of external imbalance, and creating balance of payment difficulties that inhibited the successful use of expansionary AD policies and the successful realization of internal balance.

It is not possible for all countries simultaneously to expand their export growth rate, unless there is more rapid growth of global AD. Subsequent development of Kaldor's theory has led to Thirlwall's "Balance-of-Payments-Constraint Growth" (BPCG), theory, and "Thirlwall's Law." "Thirlwall's Law" demonstrates that when countries each use their own currencies in international trade, the rate of growth of each country's income is bounded by the rate of growth of the demand for its exports and the income elasticity of its demand for imports. By endogenizing income elasticities for imports and exports, the output path in the BPCG model can be rendered more chaotic.[18]

Demand-led growth models focus both on the *composition*, and the *level* of demand in explaining the growth rate. Cornwall envisioned a country's growth rate as a movement through a commodity hierarchy, in which demand for the output of various sectors of the economy—agriculture, manufacturing, and services—is characterized by a series of Engel curves.[19] Nell's Transformational Growth theory attempted to develop these insights into a grand historical account of the links between the development of AD and the structural change in AS through the entire course of capitalist history.[20] These insightful Post Keynesian contributions to demand-led growth theory have been near-completely neglected by the mainstream.[21] NEG models focus on a relentlessly supply-oriented account of the growth process. Demand is assumed passively to accommodate all expansion of potential output.

So long as firms are price-setters and quantity-takers the aggregate supply function is horizontal, and AD directly determines the level of utilization of productive resources. With a horizontal AS relationship, there is no supply-determined "equilibrium" level of full employment output that acts as a center of gravity towards which the level of economic activity is inexorably drawn. At every point in time, the extent that existing productive resources are put in place and utilized is entirely demand-determined. This renders the output path of capitalist economies inherently demand-driven.

> The sequence of short-run outcomes associated with the demand-determined utilization of productive resources traces out the economy's long-run growth trajectory in a manner that is relatively autonomous of the conditions of supply defining the potential output path of the economy, which does not act as a strong attractor as in neoclassical growth theory.[22]

Keynes' principle of *effective demand* is the *major* conceptual distinction between Post Keynesian economics on the one hand, and mainstream, neoclassical, and classical economics on the other. Capitalist economies are complex adaptive systems and investment spending is both forward-looking, and nondeterminate. In Keynes vision investment spending is the key element driving AD. The relative volatility and autonomy of "animal spirits" in a world of fundamental uncertainty is the source of the openness of the Post Keynesian vision.

There exist causal relationships between changes in investment and changes in output. But they are not reducible to any mechanical "multiplier" or "law of motion," from which the evolution of future income can be deduced or predicted. The discovery of unit roots in economic time series is consistent with the Post Keynesian insistence that the long run is the intertemporal sequence of more volatile short-run sequences. For stock prices and other chaotic series, short-run booms and busts account for the major proportion of long-run "trend" movements. Over longer run periods, unanticipated and nondeterministic demand-side changes are paramount. Economic activity evolves in response to demand side changes, and bidirectional feedback processes are characteristic of all complex adaptive systems.

Total saving is simply the accounting record of investment. In consequence decisions to increase saving cannot directly finance additional investment spending as the mainstream view maintains. In the short-run, causality is reversed. Increases in volitional saving are likely to result in a reduction in consumption spending, in current aggregate demand, and in expectations of future AD. An increase in volitional saving is more likely to cause a fall rather than a rise in investment spending and in the growth rate of the economy. When financed by bank borrowing, investment creates its own saving in market economies. Most saving is non-volitional.

The growth of AD determines changes in investment spending through an accelerator process that impacts on the rate of technological progress and output growth. The long-run growth trajectory of an economy is the path-dependent record of a historical sequence of short-run outcomes. Economies have no pre-determined "equilibrium" or "natural" growth corridor along which they "tend." There are no "conditional" or "provisional" equilibria positions that provide stability properties of conventional neoclassical equilibria, and which are reproduced as a "state of rest" that the economy can "get into" at some point in time.

The expansion of productive resources is at root dependent on the continually changing expectations of present and future profitability. Since no firm knows for certain what its future level of income will be, firms build-in excess capacity when they construct new plants. By maintaining excess capacity, their profits increase automatically whenever additional demand occurs. Supply conditions do not define any prospective "natural" output path of an economy independent of the demand-determined time-dependent hysterical path of actual output. The supply of labor and capital is dependent on the level of actual and expected future AD, and on the realized quantity of economic activity. The existing level of AD and output determines the quantity of labor force skills, participation rates, migration patterns, capital formation, and the general allocation of labor and capital.

Capital accumulation is influenced by both currently realized and expected future output. Investment responds to expected future AD via accelerator effects. Technological progress is also demand-determined: different vintages of capital embody different states of technology. Investment contributes to both AD and AS, the available stock of capital, and average productivity. The growth process is endogenously demand-led and the investment process is inherently forward-looking. Physical ceilings to the level of economic activity are ordinarily not approached. The supply of new capital created is sensitive to the expected rate of growth of future AD, and the confidence with which these expectations are held.

Potential "full capacity" as well as actual levels of output are always demand-led. This leads to the general importance of "path dependence" in the Post Keynesian literature, and the general hostility to OLS regression studies of past growth rates. Macroeconomics constitutes the attempt to understand, explain and when possible predict the forces determining short-run ordinal changes in AD and AS. Long-run behavior can only be understood as the historical sequence of short-run changes. Both the actual and potential rate of long-run growth are path-dependent.

> The long-run trend is ... a slowly changing component of a chain of short-period situations.[23]

Econometric investigation of the relationships between income, investment, government spending, exports, and the broad money supply, when all variables are tested for unit roots, is highly supportive of the theory of demand-led growth. In the US economy GDP, investment, government spending, exports, and M2 are all integrated of order one. In sharp contrast to neoclassical claims that the level of output is uniquely determined by supply-side forces, significant unidirectional causality is found from interest rates, government spending, and exports to nominal and real GDP, and significant bi-directional causality is found between output, investment, and the money supply. This reveals the existence of strong bi-directional relationships between demand-side and supply-side forces, as highlighted by Keynesian theory and ignored by assumption in neoclassical theory. The data are also supportive of significant feedback effects from output, to investment to money supply growth, as hypothesized by the Post Keynesian theory of endogenous money.[24]

20.4 A demand-side explanation for the low-growth rates of African economies

One central implication of the Solow model is the "convergence" hypothesis. Countries with similar capital–labor ratios and technology should have similar growth rates. From a supply-side perspective, knowledge, technology, and education are all public goods. Since poorer countries can use the latest technologies discovered by richer countries, this should provide them with huge "catch-up" advantages. The flow of technology from richer to poorer countries should cause growth rates to converge. But in fact growth rates have been diverging between the richest and the poorest economies over at least the past 50 years.

Why growth rates should very positively with the level of per capita income is difficult to explain from a conventional supply-side perspective. Mainstream growth models predict longer-run per capita GDP convergence. Poorer countries should grow at more rapid rates than richer countries. This "convergence" result conflicts with much empirical evidence, and it has been formally challenged by NEG theorists by replacing the assumption of decreasing returns, to scale by the assumption of increasing returns.

Solow himself has acknowledged:

> There was one bad by-product of this focus on the description of technology. I think I paid too little attention to the problems of effective demand.[25]

Divergence and convergence is in fact occurring at both ends of the income scale in the global village. There have been many striking examples of convergence over the postwar period: Japan, the Asian "Tigers," and now China and India have experienced dramatic growth rates. But the poorest and least developed countries, mostly located in Africa, have been falling drastically behind for the past half-century. In most African countries real output growth has been below the rate of population growth and per capita income has declined. On average per capita income in Africa is lower now than it was half a century ago, when the countries were European colonies. Multiple theories have been advanced to explain the failure of African economies to catch up with the pack in spite of their ability to take advantage of the latest inventions and techniques discovered in the developed economies. The single most important explanation for the low growth rates of *per capita* income is rather clearly their very high rate of population growth.[26]

Mainstream economists have focused exclusively on supply-side factors in their search for explanations of country growth rates. But Keynes's emphasis on the central role of demand in the growth process suggests the role of demand-side factors should be reconsidered in any examination of the inability of the African economies to close the gap with the developed world. Keynes's vision of how AD forces constrain economic growth was developed in a developed country context, but it applies equally to developing economies.

As described in the previous chapter, in developed market economies output is characteristically demand-constrained. Due to the fear of provoking cost inflation on the part of organized labor, and to the need to maintain positive current account surpluses to protect their exchange rates, CBs in all countries using their own money in international transactions must keep their economies with a substantial output gap, as a consequence of their pursuit of restrictive monetary and fiscal policy to achieve internal and eternal balance.

CBs in low income economies fail to pursue expansionary policies with sufficiently low interest rates to induce a volume of investment spending consistent with full employment AD. In fact the opposite is the case. Although most low income economies are characterized by much higher levels of unemployment than high income economies, CBs are forced to set interest rates at significantly higher levels in low income than in high income economies. This is conventionally attributed to the higher level of lender risk in less-developed economies.

In developed economies the fix-price sector dominates and most prices are administered by firms possessing market power. In developing economies the flex-price agricultural sector is more important than in developed economies. But in most of the poorest countries the agricultural sector is dominated by subsistence farming. Government policies tend to keep food prices low to feed urban populations. But in both developed and developing economies as is driven by the growth of AD and in both developed and developing economies the AS relationship may be envisaged as a stylized fact as a horizontal fractal band in inflation-output space.

Developing countries have a larger agricultural sector, and so a larger flex price sector than developed economies. Since they are more exposed to crop failures, both prices and real income have a higher variance than in developed economies. In both the "core" rate of inflation in the fix-price sector can be expressed as the excess of the percentage change in the average rate of wage inflation over the average growth in labor productivity. Depending on the share of the flex-price sector, and the openness of the economy, the inflation rate is also affected by the rate of exchange rate depreciation and import inflation.

The expansion of domestic AD depends on the relative amount of bank financed deficit spending. The credit money supply is fully endogenous in all economies. There is no "real balance" effect, and the money supply varies pro-cyclically over the cycle with changes in money income. In both developed and developing economies as a stylized fact the AD relation may be visualized as a vertical fractal band in inflation-output space, which shifts rightward and leftward due to changes in interest rates, in the terms of trade, and in the prices of primary commodities.

In pre-capitalist economies the growth of AD was much lower than in capitalist economies. Economic activity was primarily subsistence agriculture with little or no manufacturing or service activity, and no commercial banking. Although today all developing countries do have commercial banking systems in place, in poor economies where most families are subsistence farmers there are very few creditworthy borrowers with the collateral to borrow from the banking system. Most micro firms and poor households are regarded as noncreditworthy, and receive little or no credit from the formal banking system. In consequence there is very little rightward shift of AD due to deficit-spending financed by bank lending. The growth of private AD is dependent on the growth of AS, since with no collateral there is no bank lending available to finance private investment spending. In most African economies most bank lending is to governments, in the form of the purchase of Treasury Bills, since governments are only the borrowers who are considered credit-worthy by the banking system. And as well known governments are not well-suited to conduct efficient investment programs.

In market economies GDP has a unit root. This implies that in each period AD is equal to the level of AD in the previous period, plus or minus current net deficit-spending. In all economies, increases in AD are financed primarily by new bank borrowing and net money creation. The level of Bank Rate is set by the monetary authorities in all countries. The markup over Bank Rate determines bank lending and deposit rates, and so the cost of bank finance for loans for working and fixed capital. The demand for bank credit and the volume of bank borrowing is inversely related to the lending rate charged. In all credit-money economies AD is increased by net borrowing from the banking system, and decreased by the net repayment of bank loans.

The World Bank classifies countries into four income groups:

Group 1 = High Income countries,
Group 2 = Upper-middle Income countries,

Group 3 = Lower-middle Income countries,
Group 4 = Low Income countries.

In an empirical study of the extent of monetary endogeneity in developing economies, the growth rate of per capita income for a random sample of 25 developed and 25 developing countries was collected for the 20-year period 1980–99.[27] The sample of 50 countries contained 25 High Income developed countries, 10 Low Income developing countries, 7 countries classified as Upper-middle and 8 as Lower-middle Income. As may be seen from visual inspection of Figure 20.1, the 20-year growth rates for the sample of 50 countries varied from −2 to above 4 percent. Note that all countries with average growth rates below 0.5 percent were developing economies.

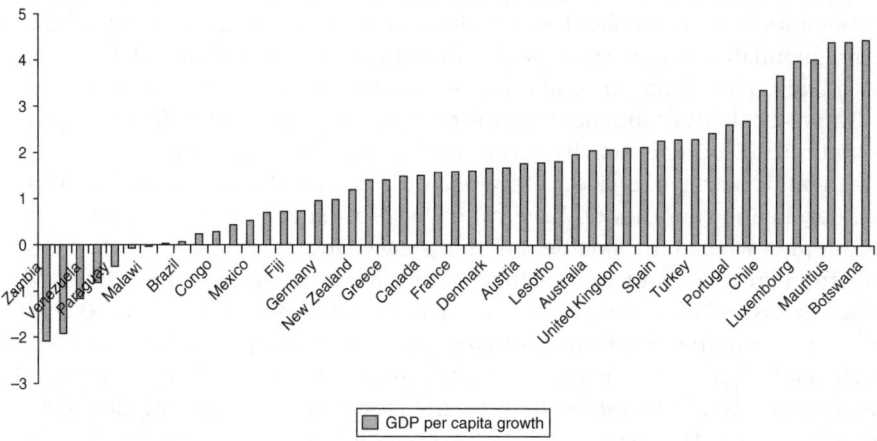

Figure 20.1   GDP per capita growth rates 1980–2000

Figure 20.2 presents the average real GDP per capita growth rates for the 25 High Income and the 10 Low Income countries in the sample, (all of whom were African), for the period 1980–2000. Over this 20-year period, country growth rates diverged rather than converged. In High Income countries per capita GDP grew on average by 2.1 percent and in Low Income countries per capita GDP grew on average by 0.2 percent. At these growth rates, per capita real income doubles every 34 years in High Income countries but every 350 years in Low Income countries. To what extent are these huge differences in growth rates between High Income and Low Income countries explainable by demand-side factors?[28]

As previously developed, the growth of AD in market economies is well-explained by the growth of the credit money supply. Bank credit finances deficit spending by issuing newly created deposit balances. Banks only lend to borrowers whom they believe are credit-worthy and able to repay the debt. The growth of the money supply depends on the demand for bank credit by credit-worthy borrowers,

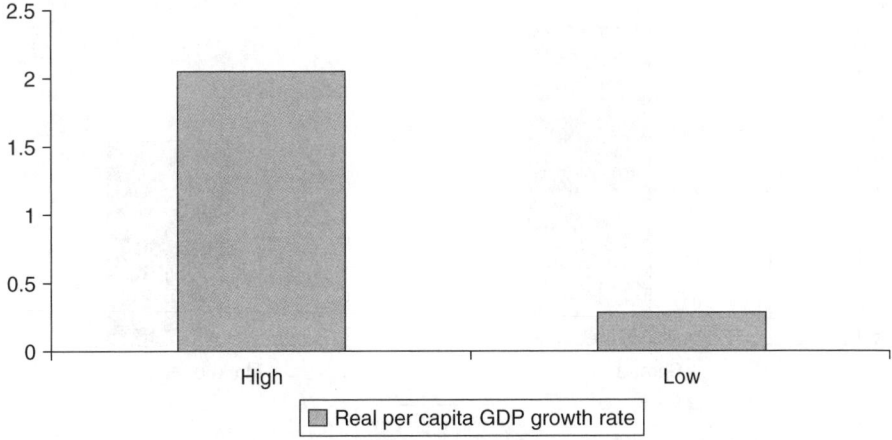

Figure 20.2 High and Low Income countries: real per capita growth rates, 1980–2000

and the lending rate set by the banking system. There are a number of demand-side factors that constrain the growth of the supply of credit money.

1. Banks set their lending rates as a markup on Bank Rate set by the CB. The first reason for the lower growth rates of the supply of credit money in developing countries than in developed countries is the higher level of Bank Rate set. As shown in Figure 20.3, the average level of Bank Rate set in developing countries was 16.2 percent, nearly double the average rate of 8.9 percent set in developed

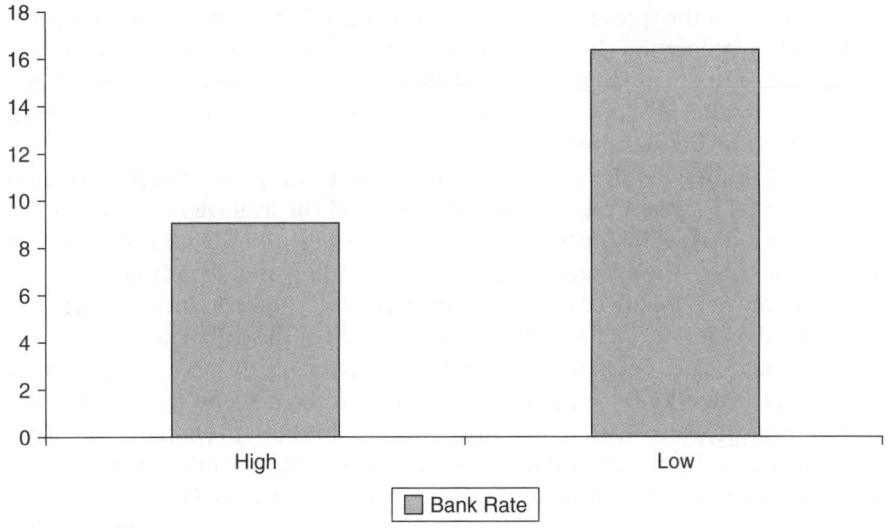

Figure 20.3 Bank Rate, developed and developing economies

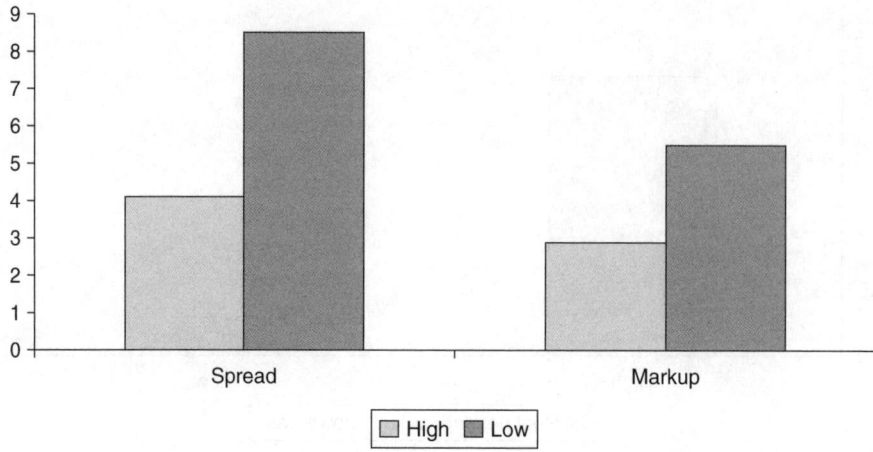

Figure 20.4 Average markups and spreads: High Income and Low Income countries

countries over the same 20-year period. In general the Bank Rate set in by the center CBs is traditionally much lower than Bank Rate set in the periphery. This difference is conventionally explained by higher levels of lender risk.

2. In all countries commercial banks set their lending rate at a relatively stable markup over Bank Rate, and at a relatively stable spread over the deposit rate. In developed economies banking systems are generally less efficient than in developing economies, and also exhibit much lower levels of technology. In addition the banking sector is much more highly concentrated in developing countries, reflected in the significantly higher markup of bank lending rates over Bank Rate, and in the size of the spread over deposit rates in developing economies compared to developed economies. In consequence Low Income developing country borrowers face substantially higher lending rates than High Income developed country borrowers, and developing country lenders receive substantially lower deposit rates on their saving accounts.

Figure 20.4 presents the average spread of the lending rate charged on loans over the average interest rate paid on deposits, and the average markup between the lending rate as set by the banks and Bank Rate set by the CB for High and Low Income countries. The average spread between lending and deposit rates was 8.5 percent in the developing economies, more than twice the 4.1 percent charged in developed economies. Similarly the average markup of the bank lending rate over Bank Rate was 5.5 percent in the developing economies, nearly twice the 2.9 percent markup in the developed economies. To the extent the demand for bank loans is interest inelastic, banks with monopoly power are able both to charge higher lending rates to bank borrowers and to pay lower saving rates to bank depositors, thus reducing money/income ratios and the ratio of bank loans to GDP.

In consequence bank borrowers in the Low Income developing countries pay substantially higher lending rates for bank credit, since substantially higher spreads and markups are charged by banking systems. Borrowers in Low Income developing countries pay both a substantially higher price for credit and receive a lower rate of return on deposits. Average bank lending rates charged (the sum of Bank Rate plus the markup), were 22 percent in the Low Income developing countries, nearly double the 12 percent charged in the High Income developed economies. On these grounds alone, the demand for bank credit would be expected to be a much smaller proportion of GDP in the poorest countries compared to the richer countries, even if all other factors were equal.

Figure 20.5 presents the average 4-firm concentration ratio in banking in the High and Low Income countries. Due to the presence of significant scale economies in banking, bank concentration is high in all countries. The 4-firm concentration ratio was 62 percent in the High Income countries, and 85 percent in the Low Income countries. With such high concentration ratios banks are able to raise their spreads and service charges with impunity. Both implicit and explicit pricing agreements are much easier to maintain.

3. In all economies commercial banks are willing to lend money only to borrowers whom they believe are able to repay the loan when it comes due. In Low Income developing economies, a much higher proportion of business firms are micro-enterprises, and a much higher proportion of households are located in the informal sector. Based on ample experience, such informal sector borrowers are widely viewed by first-world multinational banks as noncredit-worthy. Banks are ordinarily quite willing to accept deposits from microenterprises and households in the informal sector. But they are typically quite unwilling to provide them with credit to finance their deficit spending projects.

An additional reason for higher bank lending rates in the poorest economies is the existence of substantial economies of scale in banking. Making small loans is much more expensive than larger loans. Making small loans to micro borrowers

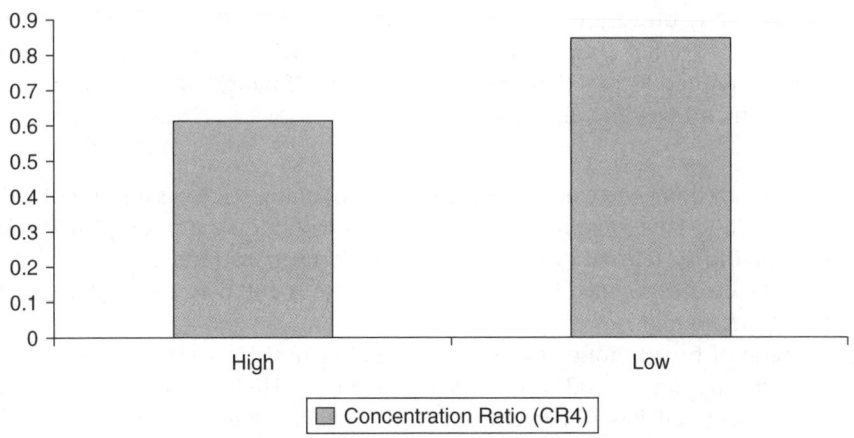

Figure 20.5 Four firm banking concentration ratios: High Income and Low Income countries

is completely unprofitable for banks in the formal sector. They typically pay formal sector salaries to their lending officers, find it more difficult to access borrower risk, and the overhead cost of making and servicing loans as a proportion of the amount lent is very much higher for small loans than for larger loans. Small borrowers have little credit history, and do not keep the bookkeeping records expected and required by first world bankers. In consequence small loans are much more expensive to service, are viewed as bearing higher risk, and are charged much higher lending rates.

In Low Income African economies a much higher proportion of economic agents are regarded as noncreditworthy by the formal banking sector. As a result they receive no bank credit, and are unable to bank finance planned deficit expenditures, no matter how attractive their investment projects. There is also typically no history of successful business practices, no tradition of mutual trust and honesty and no custom of "my word is my bond" in informal business relationships except in exclusive minority groups. Corruption is high in all transactions concerning the government sector, which still tends to be antagonistically regarded as was the case under colonialism, as "the enemy."

In consequence there are few compunctions about stealing from the government sector in the developing world. Ethnicity, color, and class differences are all much more important. As a result personal and business relationships are more antagonistic, more short-sighted, and more exploitative. For all of the above reasons, it is much more difficult to establish mutually binding profitable contractual relationships in Low Income African developing economies than in High Income developed economies.

Unfortunately data on the existence and quantity of outstanding overdraft lines for Low Income bank borrowers in developing economies are still unavailable. CBs of Low Income economies do not collect, or at least do not publish data on lines of credit, or overdraft commitments for the domestic banking system. Researchers are forced to rely on various proxy measurements in the attempt to quantify the extent credit is available, and credit rationing is experienced, by borrowers in Low Income economies. Figure 20.6 presents four proxy "financial deepening" indicators for High and Low Income economies:

1. The ratio of domestic credit provided by the banking sector as a share of GDP (DC/GDP): In Low Income economies the share of domestic credit provided by the banking system is 35 percent of GDP. In High Income economies total domestic credit provided by the banking system is 100 percent of GDP, nearly three times as high.
2. The ratio of broad money (M3) as a share of GDP (M3/GDP): In Low Income countries the ratio of M3 to GDP is 30 percent. In High Income countries the ratio of M3 to GDP is 75 percent, again nearly three times as high.
3. The ratio of claims on the private sector by deposit money banks to GDP (Bank loans/GDP): In Low Income economies the ratio of bank loans GDP is

15 percent. In High Income economies the ratio of bank loans GDP is 60 percent, four times as high as in Low Income economies.
4. The ratio of the change in bank credit to the change in GDP ($\Delta C/\Delta GDP$): In Low Income countries the ratio of the change in bank credit to the change in GDP is 40 percent. In High Income economies the ratio of the change in bank credit to the change in GDP is nearly 200 percent, five times as high as in Low Income economies.

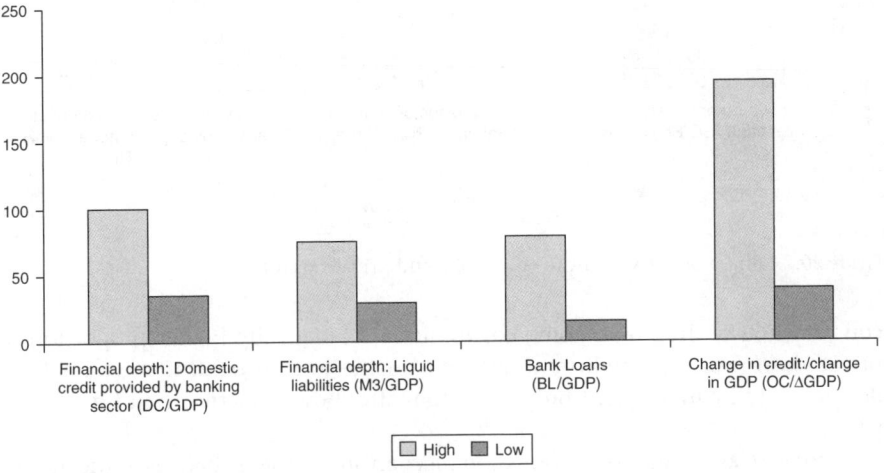

Figure 20.6 Indicators of "financial deepening"

The share of bank credit that goes to the private and public sector is more than reversed in Low and High Income economies as shown in Figure 20.7. In Low Income economies, two thirds of total bank credit is allotted to the government sector, more than four times the 15 percent share of total bank credit received by the government sector in High Income economies. In High Income economies three quarters of total bank credit goes to the private sector, three times the 25 percent of total bank credit received by the private sector in Low Income economies. In High Income economies bank credit received by the private sector is 60 percent of GDP, more than four times the 13 percent share of bank credit received by the private sector in Low Income economies. Due to the lack of credit-worthy borrowers in the private sector formal sector financial institutions direct most of their lending to the government, the sole borrower who is regarded as credit-worthy.

The combination of these three factors: a higher Bank Rate set by the CB, higher markups and spreads set by the banking system, and so higher lending rates and lower deposit rates, and a smaller proportion of borrowers who are judged credit-worthy by the banking system, due to poverty and the lower tradition of honesty in business practices, when taken together have the consequence that the share of total bank credit to the private sector in Low Income economies (16%) about one quarter of the share of bank credit to the private sector in the High Income

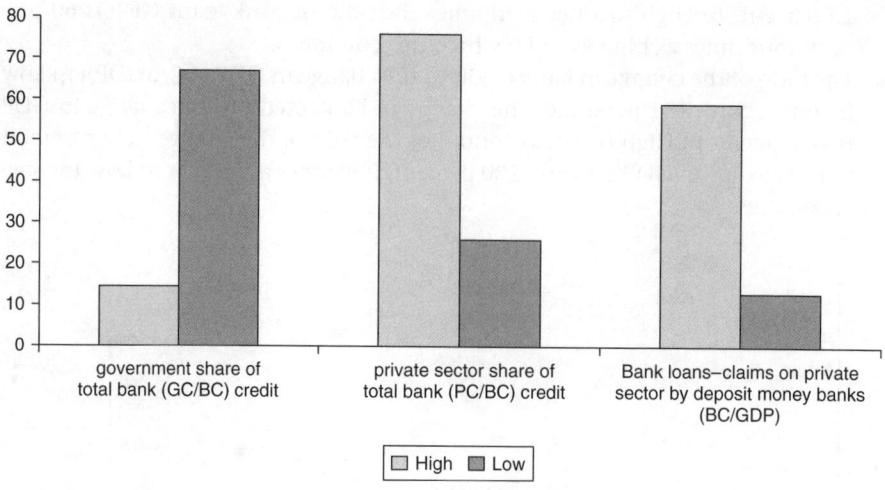

Figure 20.7 Share of bank credit to the public and private sector

countries (60%). In Low Income economies a dramatically higher proportion of private borrowers are credit-rationed and unable to find bank finance for their deficit-spending investment proposals, no matter how attractive their investment projects.

Chapter 16 analyzed the transmission mechanism between changes in the money supply and changes in money income. New money creation was shown to finance most of the increase in deficit spending that permits AD to increase and the level of output to grow. Low Income economies have many more frustrated borrowers with attractive investment projects who are unable to access bank finance than in High Income economies. Even if due to the scarcity of capital relative to labor, investment projects with highly attractive returns were in fact a higher proportion of GDP in the Low Income than in High Income economies, as the mainstream maintains, it is not possible for AD and GDP to grow at as high a rate in Low Income developing economies as in High Income economies. Due to the inability and unwillingness of private banks to finance micro deficit-spending units with bank credit, the growth of AD is lower in Low Income economies than in High Income economies, irrespective of differences in expected rates of return.[29]

20.5 Conclusions

The above analysis has provided an alternative demand-side explanation for slow growth. Instead of converging, the rate of growth of per capita GDP in Low Income African developing economies has steadily fallen behind the rate of growth of per capita GDP in developed High Income economies, increasing the variance in international income distribution. The rapid growth of market economies is comparatively speaking a relatively recent phenomenon. Before the industrial revolution and the development of commercial banking, the growth rate of all pre-capitalist economies was by modern standards extremely low. Most households were subsistence farmers who were unable to borrow. In the absence of commercial banking, and the existence of credit money, the growth of GDP was primarily due to growth in supply-side factors, primarily the growth of population and the contingency of favorable weather harvests for accumulating agricultural surplus.

Although commercial banking is highly developed in modern economies, in today's poorest economies, largely located in Africa, most businesses are unable to access bank credit since they are regarded as credit-worthy. "The rich get credit and the poor get children" holds particularly for the global village. As a result they are unable to finance their investment projects.

Notes

Preface: Complex Adaptive Systems (CAS)

1. Thuan (2001) provides a dazzling introduction to the development of ideas that led to the vision of a world where indeterminacy and emergence predominate. Auyang (1998) provides a nontechnical and wide-ranging introduction to the key concepts and general methods used in studying complexity in the physical, biological, and social sciences.
2. See Arthur, 1994; David, 1985.
3. As Alfred Marshall long insisted, "time" was the most difficult concept economists had to comprehend and somehow incorporate meaningfully into their theories. Marshall though First Wrangler [in mathematics] at Cambridge was quite hostile to the use of mathematics in economics. So, very inconveniently to his mainstream followers, was Keynes. Mathematical models can give one's ideas tremendous insight, order, power, and clarity. But when misapplied they can equally provide tremendous distractive diversion, and an unfortunate tendency to formalism for its own sake. Much of the mathematicization of neoclassical economics has involved the "dressing up" of pedantic observations in rigorous "rational expectations," "choice-theoretic," "utility maximizing," "general equilibrium" models which offer little new explanatory or revelatory power. See the discussion on the relationship between mathematics and economics in JPKE, Summer, 2003 by Davidson, Dow, Katzner, Rosser and Weintraub.
4. S. Keen, *Debunking Economics*, 2001: xiii. Keen argues the reason why economists persist with such theories lies in the way economics is taught. It has given them, "*the behavioral traits of zealots rather than dispassionate intellectuals.*"
5. See Day, 1996; Keen, 2001.
6. As Kirman has argued, economic theory has seen off many attacks, not because it has been strong enough to withstand them but because it has been strong enough to ignore them. "*Many economists are not even concerned over the sea-worthiness of the vessel in which they are sailing*" (Kirman, 1989: 126–39).
7. Lawson, T., 1997, 2003.
8. This gap has recently been addressed by the new field of behavioral economics. See Thaler, 2003; Shefrin, 2002.
9. This was central to Keynes' criticism of econometrics (Keynes, 1939).
10. Keen, 2001: 5.
11. Personal conversations, Cambridge, 1970–71.
12. Keen, 2001: 179.
13. This has the great virtue that all articles on "equilibrium" modeling embracing "rational expectations" need only be cursorily pursued.
14. For a more comprehensive discussion see Moore, 1988.
15. But possibly not. See Arestis and Howells, 2002 for an endogenous money explanation of the sixteenth-century European inflation is conventionally attributed to the exogenous inflow of specie from the New World.
16. See Moore, 1988a.
17. A successful career could be made by young scholars who chose to devote their efforts to writing clear and simple presentations of the central Post Keynesian insights designed to persuade and convince mainstream economists of their correctness. The goal would be publication in those mainstream journals devoted to keeping teachers abreast of new developments. The PK message must be hammered home by extensive confrontation with ever-more comprehensive data series using ever-more sophisticated techniques.

18 One characteristic of economic editors whose effect is to protect the mainstream core is reluctance to publish material that is non-orthogonal to the ruling paradigm. As a result heterodox economists have great difficulty in getting their work published in leading mainstream journals. This phenomenon is not confined to economics.
19 For example, the current European "stability conditions" mandating a maximum 3 percent deficit for member governments are senseless, misleading, and dangerous unless current and capital expenditures are carefully distinguished for the government sector as well as the private sector. As another important example the calculation of current account deficits and surpluses is misleading and senseless for any country, unless imports of consumption goods and capital goods are sharply distinguished. Borrowing to purchase assets is not in itself reprehensible. See chapters 7 and 17.
20 One obvious *caveat* on the introduction of proper capital budgeting is that when capital spending is believed desirable, politicians and bureaucrats have a huge incentive to reclassify expenditure as capital, and to never meet a capital expenditure they don't like. This may not be inappropriate for expenditures on education or health services whose durability is difficult or even impossible to quantify. But what about military and other spending close to politicians hearts? Most white elephants are capital goods.
21 I would like here to express my current astonishment at my earlier degree of naiveté. In 1988 having persuaded myself of the validity of endogenous money, and having discovered Keynes' then not well-known adoption of endogenous money in the *Treatise*, I took for granted that endogenous money would soon be embraced and adopted by the profession. Now, in 2005, 17 years after the publication of HORIZONTALISTS & VERTICALISTS, only one mainstream and graduate Money and Banking text (Walsh, 2003) has incorporated endogenous money into its formal discussion.
22 King, 2002: 1.
23 King, 2002: 265–6.
24 Smithin, 2001: 259.
25 Davidson, 2003–04: 245–50, 271.
26 Keynes, 1936: 383.
27 Keynes, 1936: 38.
28 McCloskey, 2002.
29 In Kuper *et al.*, 2001.

1 Marshall's Tides

This chapter has been inspired by John Sutton, *Marshall's Tendencies, What Can Economists Know?* 2002.

1 Since economies are complex systems, the *ceteris* never remain *paribus*.
2 Sutton, 2002: 5.
3 The meteorological universe would have been a more appropriate metaphor for the social universe.
4 See Sutton, 2002: 6–7.
5 For a review of this exchange see Sutton, 1993, 2002: 7–9.
6 Sutton, 2002: 9.
7 Morgan, 1990.
8 Robbins, 1932.
9 Robbins, 1932: ch. 4.
10 Sutton, 2000: 11.
11 Sutton, 2002.
12 Sutton, 2000: 13–14.
13 Haavelmo, 1944.
14 Haavelmo, 1944, quoted in Sutton, 2002: 15.
15 Hayek, 1935.

16 *Collected Writings of J. M. Keynes*, XIV: 285–6.
17 *Collected writings of J.M. Keynes*, XIV: 285–300, 315–6. Because of changes in animal spirits over the business cycle which cannot be quantified or directly measured, yet which in his mind were supremely important, Keynes believed that econometrics was unsuitable and misleading for analysis of business cycle behavior.
18 Pesaran and Smith (1985) re-estimate Tinbergen's work to show how sensitive the results were to the issues raised by Keynes.
19 Sutton, 2002: 26–31. For a general discussion of these issues see Backhouse, 1995.
20 See Sutton, 2002: 35–58.
21 Sutton, 2002: 32–3.
22 Sutton, 2002: 26–30.
23 Lorenz, 1993.
24 Galbraith, 1993: 107–110.
25 Solow, 1986, has been extremely critical of this approach.

2 Complexity and Contingency

This chapter has been greatly influenced by discussions on complexity and post modernism with Paul Cilliers. The chapter closes with a bibliography on Complexity and Chaos Theory.

1 As someone presumably a Frenchman said, "A snowflake is complicated, but a mayonnaise is complex" (Cilliers, 1998).
2 This insight puts "paid" to the entire project of long-run equilibrium growth models.
3 In statistical mechanics this is called "coarse graining." Conventional linear statistical measures such as correlation functions are inadequate to describe chaos. A chaotic process can appear to be completely uncorrelated, and yet in fact be completely deterministic. Linear properties like autocorrelation or covariance cannot provide us with the proper information to characterize chaotic behavior accurately. Statistical descriptions based on nonlinear statistical averages, such as entropy, and Lyapunov exponents, must be used (Gleick, 1988).
4 Our empirical measurements reduce continuous time observations to a stream of discrete symbols. Changing the level of coarse graining may be regarded as analogous to changing the resolution of our instruments (Pagels, 1988).
5 Prigogine quoted in Horgan, 1996: 220.
6 Horgan, 1996.
7 Cilliers, 1998. The *sine qua non* of a CAS is its capacity to produce novelty or "surprises." Markose, 2005. Cooperative behavior may be an emergent phenomenon rather than arising from rational calculation.
8 Dupré, 1993.
9 Wilson, 1998.
10 Van Regenmortel and Hull, 2002.
11 R. Williams, in Van Regenmortel and Hull, 2002.
12 "Modeling aggregation requires us to transcend the level of individual cells. In dealing with systems with large numbers of components, we must make recourse to 'holistic concepts,' and refer to the macro behavior of the system as a whole. These system properties need not ultimately be definable in terms of the states of the individual components. Yet this fact does not make them fictions. They are causally efficacious (hence real), and have definite causal relationships with other system variables, and even to the states of the individuals" (Van Regenmortel, 2004a).
13 Cilliers, 1998.
14 Vanderwert, 1997.
15 Bak, 1996: 132.
16 Bak, 1996. The identical statement could be made with equal truth about stock prices.
17 In some cases this inverse proportionality appears in such an astonishing manner that when expressed in logs their ranking is linearly inversely related to their frequency!

Compare the probability frequency that a word is used in the English language with its relative use ranking. "The" is the most commonly used word in English, and the probability of its use is on average 10 percent (0.1). The tenth most commonly used word is "I," and the frequency with which it is used is on average 1 percent (0.01). The one-hundredth most frequently used word is "say" and its frequency of use is on average one-tenth of 1 percent (0.001). The one-thousandth most frequently used word is "quality" and it is used on average once every 10,000 words (0.0001)! This astonishing relationship is known as Zipf's law (Zipf, 1954).
18   Mandelbrot, 1971, 1994.
19   "Cockroaches are extremely likely to outlast humans" (Per Bak, 1996).
20   These characteristics have been derived from Nicolis and Prigogine (1989), Jen (1990), and Cilliers, 1998 and embody the Red Queen Principle (Robson, 2005).
21   The behavior of the system is not determined by the number of interactions associated with any specific element. If there are enough elements in the system, some of which are redundant, a set of more sparsely connected elements can perform the same function as a more richly connected element.
22   Economies are determined by their history. In the very short run their behavior is largely predetermined, as today's output, wages, costs, prices, capital stocks, and technology are determined by yesterday's history. For most prices and quantities, expectations of future values ordinarily change slowly. But expectations of prices of homogeneous assets, traded in well-organized markets with low transactions costs like stocks or foreign exchange or tulips, can vary sharply and discontinuously, as associated with rapid changes in the collective consensus about the economy's future prospects. Low transaction costs generate high asset liquidity.
23   In this light it is certainly strange that, when it comes to the formal description of private enterprise economies, there is such strong emphasis among today's mainstream economists on the desirability of building macro-models on rigorously well-defined micro-foundations, to yield closed-form equilibrium models. One of the reasons for this predisposition is that economics like other behavioral sciences has inherited its methodology from a classical analytical tradition, which is at its core deeply deterministic.
24   This section has been strongly influenced by John Horgan's *The End of Science*, New York, Addison-Wesley, 1996.
25   Steven Gould has attributed the essential complexity of paleontology to the simple fact of contingency. Historical events depend on "freak" accidents of history. Just think how different life on earth would have been if dinosaurs had not been extinguished by a meteor hitting the earth instead of continuing in orbit. See Gould, 1987, 1989, 1991; Thuan, 2001.
26   Complex computer simulations represent a kind of meta-reality, within which we can play with and to a limited degree test scientific theories. But they should not be confused with reality itself. By giving scientists more power to manipulate different symbols, in different ways to simulate a natural phenomenon, simulations may even eventually undermine scientists' faith that their theories are exclusively and absolutely true (Cilliers, 1998). Vanderwert, 1997.
27   Horgan, 1996.
28   Prigogine and Stengers, 1984: 129.
29   Shannon, 1948.
30   Chaitlin, 1975: 48.
31   Chaitlin, 1975: 49.
32   Talking only about series of numbers may seem a little superficial. But via Gödel's numbering system, all formalism can be expressed as a series of numbers (Godel, 1931; Cilliers, 1998).
33   For example, the contingent impact of an asteroid.
34   Diamond, 1999: 424.
35   Diamond has recently posed the nature–nurture question of European colonial world domination—why did human development proceed at such different rates on different

continents? By comparing the stage of development of relatively recent Polynesian populations living on islands differing naturally in resource abundance he makes an extremely persuasive case for environmental and against biological explanations of racial differences in intelligence (Diamond, 1999).

36 As Kierkeguard put it, *"Life is understood backwards, but must be lived forwards"* (Horgan,1996).
37 "Any more than a rat can solve a differential equation." McGinn, 1993.
38 See I. Prigogine, 1980; B. Mandelbrot, 1989; J. Feder, 1988; M. Schroeder, 1991.
39 Dawkins, 1984; Kauffman, 1995, 2000.
40 Market activity lends itself to precise measurement of prices and quantities. Markets are the sole reason much economic behavior can be quantified and expressed in the form of algebraic equations, and why economics exists as discipline with a tight theoretical core, the "queen" of the social sciences.
41 The battle over the appropriateness of reductionism is being fought over all disciplines. In a chapter in his biography entitled "The Molecular Wars" the evolutionary biologist Edward Wilson describes the grim determination with which molecular biologists have fought to extirpate ecological research in biology (Wilson, 1994). Diamond has termed this professional hostility "the latest in a long history of frequent and deep-seated disagreement among scientists, pitting so-called reductionists, who seek explanations at the cellular, molecular or atomic level – against scientists interested in higher levels of organization. The battle alternatively pits 'hard scientists,' working in fields where controlled repeated laboratory experiments are feasible, against so-called 'soft scientists,' who are dependent on other methodologies" (Diamond, 1995:18). Diamond continues "It ought to be obvious that both reductionist understanding and higher level understanding are essential, and that it is pointless to berate scientists for failing to do controlled experiments on subjects for which controlled experiments would be immoral, illegal, orimpossible. ... Unfortunately in their belief that only reductionist experimental approaches qualify as true science, many molecular biologists continue to try to strangle evolutionary biology, ecology, and related fields. The strangulation takes the form of vigorously opposing academic appointments and research funds for evolutionary biologists" (Diamond, 1995:18). The situation is similar between mainstream and heterodox economists.
42 Jen, 1990, introduction.
43 Pagels, 1988; Gould, 1989.
44 See Arthur, 1994; Waldrop, 1992.
45 Kauffman, 2000.
46 Wilson, 1998: 88.
47 Wilson, 1998: 86–7.
48 Real time does not attempt to define a future "equilibrium" state toward which the system is tending. Equilibrium, based on the analytic fiction of a tendency toward some hypothetical future "steady state," is a timeless concept and useless for studying complex systems.
49 For a more extended discussion see Horgan, 1996.
50 Horgan, 1996, introduction.
51 Richard Feynman has offered the following dark prophecy about the future of physics:

> We are very lucky to live in an age in which we are still making discoveries. It is like the discovery of America—you only discover it once. The age in which we live is the age in which we are discovering the fundamental laws of nature, and that day will never come again. It is very exciting, it is marvelous, but the excitement will have to go. Of course in the future there will be other interests. There will be the interest of the connection of one level of phenomena to another—phenomena in biology and so on, or if you are talking about exploration, exploring other planets, but there will not be the same things we are doing now ... The philosophers who are always on the

side making stupid remarks will be able to close in, because we cannot push them away by saying, "If you were right we would be able to guess all the laws." Because, when the laws are all there, they will have an explanation for them ... There will be a degeneration of ideas, just like the degeneration great explorers feel is occurring when tourists begin moving in on a new territory. (Horgan, 1996)

52 Nicholas Rescher, 1984, quoted in Horgan, 1996: 29.
53 The quest for knowledge is the noblest and most meaningful of all human endeavors. "We are here to figure out why we are here" (Horgan, 1996).
54 A phrase like "the edge of chaos" though didactically enlightening does not provide any formulation of measurable quantities or qualities.
55 See "Getting the Goat," *The Economist*, Feb. 20, 1999, 90. Genes and culture interact in a nonlinear way so the question, what proportion of intelligence is due to genes and what proportion due to culture is simply unanswerable.
56 Dawkins, 1986.
57 *Mind and Brain Scientific American, Special Report*, 1994.
58 "It's simply hubris to think we've somehow now got all the correct cognitive instrument in our heads" (McGinn, quoted in Horgan, 1996: 58).
59 The majority of people watching a fair coin being tossed believe that an alternate sequence: e.g. – H – T – H – T – H is more likely than one with repeated groupings: for example, – H – H – H – T – T. But both are equally probable.
60 Wilson, 1998.
61 Most of us are unable to keep more than seven unrelated single numbers in our head at one time.
62 See Wilson, 1998; Pinker, 1997; Mackean, 1990.
63 *Mind and Brain, Scientific American, Special Report*, 1994; Machean, 1990; Hall, 1992.
64 Here again complex behavior emerges from the interaction between many simple processes, which respond in nonlinear fashion to local information.
65 Rose, 2004.
66 Kahnemann, 2003.
67 Cilliers, 1998.
68 Wilson, 1998: 123.
69 Cilliers, 1998.
70 *Mind and Brain*, Scientific American, Special Report, 1994.
71 As Marvin Minsky put it, "We humans are really just dressed up chimpanzees." Quoted in Horgan, 1996: 187.
72 Wilson, 1998.
73 Corry, 1999, 2000.
74 Pinker, 1997.
75 Corry, 2000; MacLean, 1990.
76 Van Regenmortel, and Hull, 2002, 2004a, 2004b.
77 Bak has contended that economic phenomena are more like sand than water.
    The obsession with the simple picture of equilibrium stems from the fact that economists long believed that their field had to be as "scientific" as physics, meaning everything had to be predictable. What irony! In physics detailed predictability has long ago been devalued and abandoned as a largely irrelevant concept. Economists have been imitating a science whose nature they did not understand (Bak, 1996: 185).
78 In the case of traffic flows, it has been shown that traffic jams characterize all "efficient" states, defined as those with the highest throughput of cars. It is neither possible nor desirable to eliminate such fluctuations. "Friction" is absolutely central to the story. We can never attain a perfectly "efficient" state, only the best that is dynamically achievable (Bak, 1996).
79 In a complex world a position of general equilibrium cannot exist. General equilibrium implies at least the hypothetical existence of some long-run position toward which the

system is tending. Economic phenomena are continuously evolving. There is no underlying deterministic trend path that acts as a center of gravity.
80 The most economists can really say with confidence about most economic questions is, "One the one hand it could be this, or on the other it could be that". As soon they try to simplify their models to be able perform "rigorous" analysis, for example, by assuming that all investors have "perfect information," or "rational expectations," the results are deterministic models that immediately become unrealistic, and usually uninformative.
81 Anderson *et al.*, 1988.
82 Waldrop, 1992; McCloskey, 1994.
83 Arthur *et al.*, 1997.
84 Van Regenmortel, 2004a.
85 Van Regenmortel, 2004b.
86 This Appendix is based on "The Copenhagen Interpretation" Henry Pierce Stapp. *American Journal of Physics*, 1972, 40 (8), 1098–1116. Reprinted in Vandervert, 1997: 25–52.
87 Horgan, 1996.
88 Stapp, 1972.
89 Quoted in Stapp, 1972.
90 Bohr, 1934; quoted in Stapp, 1972.
91 Bohr, 1934; quoted in Stapp, 1972.
92 Bohr, 1934; quoted in Stapp, 1972.
93 Bohr, 1934; quoted in Stapp, 1972.
94 Bohr, 1934; quoted in Stapp, 1972.
95 The bulk of Einstein's scientific life was spent in a frustrated unsuccessful effort to make field theory ideas work at the microscopic level.
96 James used the term *"Hypersensitive realities."*
97 There are many situations where one is unable to find out the truth from inside: for example, unless it should come to us we will never know if life exists in other solar systems. Are mathematical truths invented, or discovered? We may engage in informal speculations which may lead to high probabilities. But we can never be certain about questions concerning, for example, the origin of the universe, because it lies so distant from us in space and time. We can easily be deceived into thinking we understand the world when actually we do not. If the world has a fractal structure there may be no limit to the number of things we can investigate. We may live in a universe of fractal expansions, but they are structured in a way we will never be able to fully comprehend.

3 Chaos Theory: Unpredictable Order in Chaos

1 Keen, 2001: 246. There are now computer programs that enable the "n-body problem" to be simulated.
2 For references on chaos theory see the Bibliography on Complexity and Chaos. Rosser, 1999.
3 Many people believe that twentieth-century science will be remembered for three central discoveries: relativity, quantum mechanics, and chaos theory.

> Relativity eliminated the Newtonian illusion of absolute space and time; quantum theory eliminated the Newtonian dream of a controllable measurement process; and chaos eliminates the Laplacian fantasy of deterministic predictability. (Gleick, 1987: 6)

4 For an excellent introduction to the epistemological and methodological implications of chaos theory see Kellert, 1993.
5 "Complexity theory" or "Complex systems theory" provides a better description of the subject matter but the term Chaos theory has now become widely accepted.
6 Linear dynamic systems are differentiable, and the relevant variables change in a smooth and continuous way. The evolution equations (the rules governing the changing

state of the system) can be written down in the form of differential equations specifying the rate of change of all the variables.
7 See Gleick, 1987: 306.
8 In the last decade researchers have begun to investigate visual preferences for fractal patterns. In visual perception tests, participants consistently express a preference for D values in a range of 1.3–1.5, regardless of the pattern's shape or origin. Mid-range D values have been found to put people at ease, for example, clouds have a D value of 1.3. It has recently been discovered that Jackson Pollock's famous drip paintings are fractals. As Pollock continued to refine his technique over the last decade of his life, their complexity as measured by their D value increased from 1.1 to 1.7 (R.P. Taylor, 2002).
9 Gleick, 1987: 104.
10 Gleick, 1987: 96–7.
11 Barnesley, 1988, quoted in Peters, 1994: 10.
12 A simple analogy is the way two paper cups placed together at the top of a waterfall reappear yards apart at the bottom. We are never able to predict which cup will emerge first.
13 Any task that grows exponentially in difficulty can be made so hard that the universe cannot provide enough mass or energy to write down all the numbers involved. Any task which is technologically impossible is thus theoretically impossible. See Kellert, 1993
14 Kellert, 1993.
15 For an introduction to modeling dynamic systems, see Day, 1994; Rosser, 2004.
16 Population is expressed as a fraction between zero and one, zero representing extinction and one the greatest conceivable population.
17 Yorke, 1975.
18
>   For want of a nail, the shoe was lost;
>   For want of a shoe, the horse was lost;
>   For want of a horse, the rider was lost;
>   For want of a rider, the battle was lost;
>   For want of a battle, a kingdom was lost!

And all for the want of a nail. Small causes can have large effects. It is not widely known that Hitler very narrowly escaped death in 1931 when an automobile in which he was riding collided with a large truck. The twentieth century would then have evolved very differently.
19 Gleick, 1987: 16–17.
20 Lorenz, 1963.
21 The actual equations were: 1. $dy/dt = a(y-z)$, 2. $dx/dt = x(b-z)$, and 3. $dz/dt = xy - cz$. Keen, 2001: 180–3.
22 Keen, 2001: 183.
23 A strange attractor is the limit per set of a chaotic trajectory. It can also be termed a fractal attractor. Such objects are called strange because they reconcile two seemingly contradictory effects. They are attractors, which means that nearby trajectories converge onto them. They also exhibit sensitive dependence on initial conditions, which means that trajectories initially close together on the attractor diverge rapidly. This apparent contradiction is reconciled by the geometrical feature of strange attractors, a combination of stretching, which takes nearby points apart in a certain direction, and folding, which causes a convergence of trajectories in a different direction. Keen, 2001: 181–3.
24 Keen, 2001: 181–3.
25 See Kellert, 1993.
26 Quoted in Gleick, 1987: 137.
27 Fama, 1970.
28 There are traditionally three degrees of market "efficiency," depending on whether the stock price fully reflects all past stock price information (weak form efficiency), all public

information impacting on the value of the company (semi-strong form efficiency), and all information both public and private about the company (strong form efficiency).
29 Haugen, 1999.
30 Mandelbrot, 1989, 1994.
31 Bachelard, 1994: 102.
32 Prigogine, 1980: 214. Striving for total predictability never had omniscience as its goal, and total predictability was never considered more than a theoretical possibility. Nevertheless determinism has been properly termed the "founding myth" of classical science. Chaos theory is causing quantum physicists to accept what Einstein rejected: God does play dice with the universe.
33 Einstein exclaimed that the problem of the "Now" worried him seriously. "Now" means something special for man, essentially different from the "past" and the "future." This important difference does not and cannot occur within physics (R. Carnap, quoted in Prigogine and Stengers, 1984: 214).
34 Gleick, 1987.
35 Crutchfield *et al.*, 1986: 56. As you read this book chaos algorithms are being continually applied to predict stock prices and exchange rates.
36 Kaldor, 1985.
37 Chirikov, 1979: 265. Quoted in Crutchfield, 1986.
38 Einstein famously maintained that "The past, present and future are only illusions, even if stubborn ones" (Davies, 2002: 41). For a discussion see, *"A Matter of Time"* Special Issue, *Scientific American*, 2002. See also Davies, 1987, 2002; Gleick, 1987.
39 Our conception of time depends on the way we measure it. It is not widely known that before the expansion of railroads in the nineteenth-century local towns used the sun to determine local time. Because noon occurs in Boston three minutes before it does in Worcester Mass., Boston's clocks were set three minutes ahead of those in Worcester. The 24 universal time zones were finally established only in 1984 at the International Meridian Conference in Washington, DC (Andrews, 2002: 83).
40 A. Marshall, 1920: vii.
41 In academic year 1970–71 as a young scholar I was fortunate to be given a sabbatical year at Trinity College Cambridge, where to my astonishment and delight I was assigned an office in the Faculty beside Joan Robinson. That year Joan's favorite syllogism was, *"Time is a device to prevent everything happening at once. And Space is a device to prevent everything happening in Cambridge."* I was properly enlightened.
42 F. Knight, 1921: 313.
43 Many people are familiar with the everyday fact that for a single position of a water tap, the water may flow differently out of the faucet depending on whether the pressure has been turned on from the "off" position, or turned off from the "on" position.
44 Toulmin, 1961: 30.
45 Toulmin, 1961.
46 Predictability is not the same as understanding. But the enabling of qualitatively new predictions, and the accounting of the limits of predictability are signs of greater understanding.
47 Hirsch, 1984: 11.
48 Prigogine and Stengers, 1984: 144–5.
49 Kellert, 1993: 114.
50 In this sense chaos theory has much in common with non-western intellectual traditions.
51 Kellert, 1993: 115.
52 Cartwright, 1999.
53 Cilliers, 1998.
54 Vetter, *et al.*, "Phase Transitions in Learning," in Vandervert, 1997: 233–48.
55 This remains the case when the data is transformed to logs to make nonlinear relationships more amenable to linear description.

56 This section is derived from a special issue of *The Journal of Mind and Behavior, Understanding Tomorrow's Mind; Advances in Chaos Theory, Quantum Theory and Consciousness in Psychology*, Vol.18, No. 2 and 3, Spring and Summer, 1997.
57 See B. West, "Chaos and Related Things: A Tutorial," in Vandervert, 1997: 1–24.
58 The view that "scientific" theories can only be quantitative is of little assistance to economists attempting to reach a decision concerning the quality of life of economic agents.
59 See Mandelbrot, 1977, 1982.
60 Consider Ohm's law: E = IR, where E is voltage, measured across resistance R, through which flows a current I.
61 Mandelbrot, 1977, 1984, 1994.
62 See Crutchfield *et al.*, 1986.
63 Rossler, 1976.
64 Lyotard, 1984: 15.
65 In this respect it is diametrically opposed to the rule-based tradition of neoclassical economics. The choice of the word "paralogy" is significant. Paralogism designates false reasoning, an illogical argument, a fallacy of which the reasoner is unaware. Paralogy literally means "beside," "beyond," or "past" logic. Lyotard employs it to show logical descriptions, which may be inadequate when dealing with the richness and contradictions of complex systems (Lyotard, 1984); Lemert, 1997.
66 Lyotard, 1984: 15.
67 Lyotard's description fits perfectly academic e-mail networks, for example, Post Keynesian Theory: pkt@csf.colorado.edu
68 Counter-factuals raise interesting questions. What if Charles I had avoided the Civil War? What if Wolfe had been defeated at Quebec? What if Britain had stood aside in 1914? What if Hitler's chauffeur had not avoided the truck in 1931?
69 Lyotard, 1984: 61.
70 Cilliers, 1998.
71 See McCloskey, 1990, 1994, 2000.
72 Hausman, 1992.
73 "As a growing snowflake falls to earth, typically floating in the wind for an hour or more, the choices made by the branching tips at any instant depend sensitively on such things as the temperature, the humidity, and the presence of impurities in the atmosphere. The six tips of a single snowflake, spreading within a millimeter space, feel the same temperatures, and because the laws of growth are purely deterministic, they maintain a near-perfect symmetry. But the nature of turbulent air is such that any pair of snowflakes will experience very different paths. The final flake record records the history of all the changing weather conditions it has experienced, and the combinations may well be infinite" (Gleick, 1987: 311).
74 Franks, 1989: 65–6.
75 Kellert, 1993: 120.
76 Franks, 1989: 65.
77 Rouse, 1996: 229.
78 Glieck, 1987: 24.
79 Quoted in Kellert, 1930. Markose, 2005; Axtell, 2005; Robson, 2005; Durlauf, 2005.
80 Merchant,1980: 234.
81 Rouse, 1996: 236.
82 Schachtel, 1959: 171, quoted in Keller, 1985: 120.
83 Quoted in Merchant, 1980, 130; James Gleick, 1987.

4   Econometrics, Data Mining, the Absence of a Stable Structure and the Pervasiveness of Contingency

1 See Morgan, 1990, ch. 1.
2 Yule, 1926, reprinted in 1971. Quoted in Morgan, 1990.

3 Yule, 1926, reprinted in 1971: 328. Quoted in Morgan, 1990.
4 Yule, 1926, reprinted in 1971: 326–30. Quoted in Morgan, 1990.
5 Yule, 1926, reprinted in 1971: 350. Quoted in Morgan, 1990.
6 Slutsky, 1927, 106–114. (quoting from the 1937 English translation). Morgan, 1990.
7 See for example, Fama, 1971.
8 Brealey, 1972.
9 See Chapter 12 of this volume for a discussion of markup pricing.
10 Frisch, 1933: 198. Quoted in Morgan, 1990.
11 Robbins, 1935: 101. Quoted in Morgan, 1990.
12 Persons, 1924: 11. Quoted in Morgan, 1990.
13 Frisch, 1948: 370. Quoted in Morgan, 1990.
14 Keynes, 1939: 567. Quoted in Hendry and Morgan, 1995.
15 Keynes, 1936.
16 Hendry and Morgan, 1995: 44.
17 Haavelmo, 1944: preface, iii.
18 Haavelmo, 1944: preface, iii.
19 Haavelmo, 1944: 43.
20 See Hendry, 2000.
21 Leamer, 1978.
22 Haavelmo, 1944: 18.
23 See Morgan, 1990: 243; Hendry, 2000.
24 Haavelmo, 1944, 3.
25 Tinbergen, 1970: 19–20.
26 Tinbergen, 1970: 195.
27 This was why Keynes in his critique of Tinbergen's book argued that econometrics could not be applied successfully to business cycle fluctuations. Changes in investor expectations about the unknown future are critically important, but as nonmeasurable phenomena are necessarily omitted from the model.
28 For an extended discussion see Charemza and Deadman, 1997.
29 Christ, 1966: 4.
30 Christ, 1966: 4–6. These properties all implicitly presuppose that the economy is in essence predictable. The last criterion, forecasting ability, explicitly assumes that the economy is predictable. Once the economy is recognized as a complex system, successful forecasting can no longer be a criterion for model desirability.
31 Durbin, 1990. The latter sense is particularly important when something has gone wrong and a new beginning or new direction is needed to solve a problem. A less serious but equally useful view of methodology is due to Leamer: "Methodology like sex is better demonstrated than discussed, though often better anticipated than experienced" (1983: 40).
32 Leamer, 1978, 1983.
33 For a survey see Granger and Newbold, 1986: 287–92.
34 See Charemza and Deadman (1997: 8–9) for additional negative comments about current practices.
35 Desai, 1994: vii.
36 Leamer, 1978: 39. The potential misuse of the student-t ratio is shown in the following simple example: suppose we choose 100 "explanatory" variables whose distributions are identical and independent, none of whom are correlated with the dependent variable. If we proceed to fit 100 OLS regressions, at a significance level of 0.05 about 5 of these regressions will be "significant." If we select these five models, and ignore the rest, we will be left with five "good" models in spite of the fact that by construction all explanatory variables are uncorrelated with the dependent variable. For the case of orthogonal "explanatory" variables, Lovell (1987) was able to calculate the probabilities that regressors not correlated with the dependent variable appear significant.

37 Charemza and Deadman give the following example: After running 100 trials on a consumption function with one explanatory variable and four seasonal dummies, the highest student-t value on the explanatory variable was 2.48, indicating a highly significant positive relation. But the explanatory variable chosen was a series of random numbers with zero mean and unit variance. "Statistical evidence" thus demonstrates that consumption in the United Kingdom is determined by random numbers! (Charezma and Deadman, 1997: 16).
38 See the Symposium, 'Econometric Tools', Journal of Economic Perspectives, 2001. Note that all participants shared the implicit belief that stable underlying relationships existed to be discovered.
39 Lovell, 1987.
40 Charemza and Deadman, 1997.
41 Summers, 1991.
42 Charemza and Deadman, 1997.
43 Pagan, 1987.
44 Hendry, 2000.
45 Leamer, 1978: 36.
46 Leamer, 1978: 33.
47 Leamer, 1978.
48 Sims, 1980.
49 Darnell and Evans, 1990: 129.
50 Pagan, 1987: 21.
51 McCloskey, 1990: 14.
52 Klein (1943, 1985: 35) in McCloskey, 1994.
53 McCloskey, 1994: 36–59.
54 McCloskey, 2000: 230. See also McCloskey and Ziliak, 2002.
55 Dow, 1996a: 727.
56 Dow, 1996a: 727–9.
57 Lawson, 1997. See also Lawson, 2003.
58 Lovell, 1987.
59 Summers, 1991.
60 Charezma and Deadman, 1997.
61 A stationary process is invariant with respect to displacement in time. If a series is stationary, its mean, variance, and covariance for any lag k are also stationary, and its probability distribution is unchanged over time. Its shape can be inferred by looking at a historogram of the time series observations that make up the series. An estimate of the mean can be obtained from the sample mean of the series, and an estimate of the variance from the sample variance. A random walk with drift is an example of a nonstationary process for which it is possible to construct an algebraic model whose stochastic properties are invariant with respect to time.
62 For most economic time series first differencing is sufficient to assure stationarity. The price level is an important exception since the first difference of the price level is the inflation rate which both accelerates and decelerates, twice differencing is necessary for stationarity.
63 The types of misspecification arising from inappropriate detrending may be illustrated by considering the properties of residuals from a regression of a random walk on time. The autocorrelation of any such residuals is a spurious statistical artifact, since if the series is a random walk any autocorrelation must be accidental and time dependent. But in fact trend residuals in such regressions display strong positive autocorrelation at low lags, and psuedo-periodic behaviour at long lags (Nelson and Kang, 1981). See also Nelson and Plosser, 1982.
64 McCulloch, 1975.
65 Slutsky (1927) in Morgan, 1990; Hendry and Morgan, 1995.

486 Notes

66 For example Schiller (1979) found that when short rates are assumed stationary around a fixed mean, the variance of holding period returns on long-term bonds is much larger than is consistent with a rational expectations version of the term structure. But when short rates are assumed stationary only after differencing, the variance was no longer excessive. Similarly in a subsequent paper Cambell and Shiller (1987) found that the variance of linearly detrended stock returns was excessive if dividend yields are assumed to be stationary around a linear trend. But the variance is not excessive if dividend yields are assumed to be stationary only after differencing.
67 Nelson and Plosser, 1982.
68 Nelson and Plosser, 1982: 144–5.
69 The explanation of the significant positive autocorrelation at lag one lies in how the series are constructed. Annual series are created by averaging shorter interval observations, which are themselves generated by a DS process. Working (1960) showed that positive autocorrelation at lag one approaches + 0.25 for a random walk as the underlying observations being aggregated becomes large.
70 Real per capita GDP, the GDP deflator, unemployment rate, consumer prices, money stock, and the bond yield, exhibit some persistent autocorrelation of first differences. Such series must be twice differenced and are d(2).
71 Nelson and Plosser, 1982: 152.
72 Dickey and Fuller, 1979, 1981; Fuller, 1976; Charemza and Deadman, 1997. For a recent survey of the literature on unit roots see the symposium "Econometric Tools," *Journal of Economic Perspectives*, Fall 2001.
73 Unnecessarily including the time trend or any other irrelevant regressors, reduces the power of the test.
74 See Peron, 1989; Hanson, 2001.
75 Hanson, 2001: 125.
76 Charemza and Deadman, 1997. If economies are complex systems on theoretical grounds cointegration will be confined to variables linked together by accounting relationships, for example, income and consumption, or short-term and long-term interest rates. Paul Davidson (2002) claims that by repeated differencing it is possible to find cointegration between any two series, even series that by construction are random walks. This speaks to the weakness of the Dicky–Fuller procedure when data are generated by complex systems.
77 Suppose two random walks are both purely by chance drifting upwards. A computer may estimate a significant positive correlation between them. But if their changes are random there is no structural relationship between the two variables, no matter how strong the correlation.
78 Haavelmo, 1944: 14–15.

5 The Implications of Complexity for Economic Analysis

1 A list of "Devastating Internal Criticisms of Modern Economics That Have Not Been Answered," may be found in McCloskey, 2002: 244. See Eichner, 1983; Dow, 1992; 1996b; Heilbroner and Milberg, 1996; Colanda, 2001; Lawson, 2003.
2 What Heilbroner and Milberg have termed *"Rigor Mortis"* (1996).
3 See McCloskey, 1990, 1994, 2000.
4 They are unable to formulate the "optimum" move in of chess. Life is much more complex than a chess game.
5 These phenomena may have a genetic basis and an epigenetic history (Wilson, 1998).
6 See Thaler, 1993, 1994, 2003. There is a whole new area of "behavioral" finance, for example, Shefrin, 2002. Kahnemann *et al.*, 2000.
7 Marx, quoted in Heilbroner and Milberg, 1996.
8 Hayek, quoted in Horgan, 1996.

9   Popper, quoted in Horgan, 1996.
10 For example, Davidson, 1972; Donaldson, 1984, 1988; Hendry, 2000; Leamer, 1978; McCloskey, 2000: Ormerod, 1994; Lawson, 2003.
11 Leontief, 1971: 104.
12 McCloskey, 1985, 1990, 2000.
13 Lawson, 1997, 1999, 2001, 2003.
14 Fisher, 1932, Presidential Address to American Statistical Association, quoted in McCloskey, 1990.
15 See Lawson, 1997, 2003.
16 Lawson, 1997, 2003.
17 This section is heavily influenced by Lawson, 1997, 2003.
18 Its proponents refer to themselves simply as "theorists"(Hahn).
19 Hahn, 1984: 5. See also Hahn, 1965, 1970, 1973, 1977, 1981, 1984.
20 Hahn, 1984: 3.
21 Hahn, 1984: 50. See also Hahn, 1965, 1970, 1973, 1977.
22 Solow, 1999: 22.
23 Ingrao and Israel, 1990.
24 Hahn, 1984: 7.
25 Hahn, 1984: 11–13.
26 Even though all formulations that entail closure are bound to be unenlightening in an open world unsusceptible to closure, the demonstration that the formal system is internally coherent does provide a semblance of achievement. See Hahn, 1984.
27 This has been termed by Hausman the "rational greed" assumption (Hausman, 1992: 208).
28 Lawson, 1997: xxx.
29 Hahn, 1977, 1984.
30 Hahn, 1984: 246.
31 The term "stylized facts" is due to Kaldor, 1985.
32 Above economic classrooms stand the words: "ABANDON HISTORY ALL YE WHO ENTER HERE" (David, 1985).
33 The technical definition of ergodicity is as follows: Time series statistics are data calculated from single realizations over a period of calendar time. Cross-section statistics are data calculated over a space of realizations at a fixed point in time. If the underlying process is ergodic, as the number of observations increases, over infinite time realizations, space and time distributions will eventually converge. The property of Ergodicity was rediscovered and emphasized among Post Keynesians by Paul Davidson, 1994.
34 This discussion follows that of Davidson, 1994, 1996.
35 Friedman, 1977, 150. Note the strong (implicit) assumption that there exists a stable underlying path that real world outcomes tend to approach. Since the world is a complex system, in fact no such objective trend exists.
36 Grandmont and Malgrange, 1987: 9.
37 Mankiw, 1992: 561.
38 Knight himself believed that uncertainty was due to the fact that the particular probability distribution could not be known: "The reason (for uncertainty) being in general that it is impossible to form a group of instances, because the situation dealt with is in a high degree unique" (Knight, 1921: 233). Unique events occur because agents possess only "partial knowledge" of the universe. He agreed that "the universe may not be knowable." But he maintained, "the objective phenomenon … is certainly knowable to a degree far beyond our actual powers … .[therefore] any limitation of knowledge due to lack of real consistency in the cosmos may be ignored" (Knight, 1921: 210).
39 Knight, 1921: 233.
40 As James Dean used to say *Ratex* would be a much more appropriate term, since it sounds like Rat Poison.
41 Samuelson, 1969: 184–5.

42 Davidson has termed this the ergodic axiom of neoclassical economics (Davidson, 1994).
43 Model builders typically refrain from assigning probabilities to general economic variables but attach them instead to different and presumed mutually exclusive "states of the world" (Lawson, 1997: 47–8). Lawson, 1999, 2001, 2003.
44 Keynes, 1936: 210.
45 Keynes, 1936: 149–50.
46 Keynes, 1937: 214.
47 Keynes, 1938: 154–6.
48 Keynes, 1936: 154–6.
49 Shackle, 1955, 1968, 1971, 1983.
50 See Robson, 2005.
51 Astronomy is the sole exception and is the polar opposite of meteorology. In astronomy intrinsic states are stable over the time period with which people are usually concerned, the human life span. But over longer scales, such as billions of years, we know the behavior of the solar system is extremely complex, and is subject to massive disruption and change; Diamond, 1999.
52 Keynes insisted, "A decision to consume or not to consume truly lies within the power of the individual; so does a decision to invest or not to invest" (Keynes, 1936: 65).
53 Within minutes of being born, human infants instinctively mimic the external facial expression of the adult onlooker.
54 Machiavelli, 1532.
55 Hofer, 1991. When walking in the mountains, hikers unquestioningly follow the path taken by earlier travelers.
56 Behavioral convergence leading to cascade effects explains the observed sharp fluctuations in stock prices, exchange rates, investment spending, and bank runs.
57 Hahn, 1984.
58 Kaldor, 1972, 1985.
59 Frank Hahn is here quite explicit: "The [general equilibrium] assumption that intertemporal and contingent markets exist for all commodities has the effect of collapsing the future into the present" (Hahn, 1973, 1977, 1989).
60 Loasby, 1976: 220; Katzner, 1999.
61 Accurate forecasts are impossible in economics. This has the direct implication that long-run deterministic equilibrium growth models are of no value in understanding system behavior. The fact that long-run growth models are non-refutable lends them a temporary false credulity. We now know why the future of the meteorological universe cannot be predicted beyond a short-run period: sensitive dependence on initial conditions. Why should the economic universe, which is made up of sentient actors and so even more complex, be any different? Balanced growth models are about as useful for understanding economic growth as solving a chess problem.
62 Like meteorologists economists must give up attempting to make long-run predictions. They must publicly acknowledge that all long-run forecasting models are worthless and have no predictive ability. A successful model must be as complex as the system to be modeled. If such a model could ever be constructed it is unlikely it would be understandable. Stock markets and exchange rates clearly have important macroeconomic effects. Consider economists' complete inability to predict the ordinal movement of stock prices and exchange rates. In the short run levels of most variables are well-explained statistically by the lagged value of the dependent variable. The process of vector regressions provides great promise for process analysis. See Stock and Watson, 1988. The most that can be attempted from long-run analysis of complex systems is to propose alternative possible "scenarios." Thaler, 1994.
63 When a time series is sufficiently long the estimated coefficient on the lagged dependent variable can ordinarily be shown not to be statistically different from unity. Dickey and Fuller, 1979, 1981. Stock and Watson, 1988.

64 Farmer, 1993.
65 Lawson, 2003.
66 Hendry, 2000.
67 Hacking, 1990; Dupter, 1993; Durlauf, 2005; Markose, 2005.
68 Luhman, 1984; Crurchfield *et al.*, 1986; Mandelbrot, 1988; Kauffman, 1995, 2000; Day, 1997; Lovelock, 2000; Davies, 2002; Markose, 2002, 2003; Dupter, 2005; Freuken, 2005.
69 Process analysis models the process of complex systems over calendar time without imposing any future "equilibrium" outcome. It attempts to explain how economic variables change from their current value to their value in the subsequent period. Franks, 1989; Finch, 2005.
70 This explains why there is continuing controversy about the world's future temperature, the "Greenhouse effect."
71 See Arthur, 1994; Rosser, 2000; Darlauf, 2005; Markose, 2005.
72 Waldrop, 1992; Holland, 1995; PerBak, 1996; Day, 1997; Albin, 1998; Ball, 1999; Cartwright, 1999; Collandu, 2000, 2001; Dopfer, 2005; Finch, 2005; Markose, 2005.

6 Sorites' Paradox: The "Looseness" of Economic Concepts

1 This chapter is heavily indebted to Kamark, 1983.
2 See Hacking, 1990; Cartwright, 1999, and Haasman, 1992.
3 Imagine that all economic activity occurred in a pre-capitalist economy with no formal markets. All production would then be for own consumption. Under autarky agents would be much poorer since they would be unable to take advantage of the economies of scale from specialization. But the decisions concerning how much to produce, and how much to consume, and how to allocate resources among different ends would remain unchanged. But in such an economy rigorous analysis of economic behavior would not be possible since without markets no prices and quantities would be generated. Economists could attempt to construct units of value based on estimated number of labor hours in production. But in the absence of prices and quantities, the extreme heterogeneity of labor and capital and the inability to reconcile past and present factor inputs would render quantitative analysis impossible. Without prices, it would be impossible to compare the value of apples and oranges. Economists currently face this problem when they analyze household activity. But the problem would then be severely compounded, since no market prices would be available by which opportunity costs of household activity could be estimated. Without prices economic behavior cannot be quantified. Economists then find themselves in the same position as all other social scientists.
4 Oscar Wilde was precisely correct: "An economist is someone who knows the price of everything, and the value of nothing."
5 The arbitrariness and inexactness of empirical measurement of continuously distributed analytical classes was given the term "Loose concepts" by Max Black, 1970.
6 This colorful presentation of Sorites' dilemma is by Joseph Rouse, Wesleyan Professor of Philosophy of Science. Sorites' dilemma is less colorfully defined in the Shorter Oxford Dictionary: "*a series of propositions leading by gradual steps from truth to absurdity, based on the absence of precise numerical limits to items that are continuously distributed.*"
7 A simple metaphor can help communicate the meaning of the term "loose concept." Suppose we observe someone is "short," or "heavy." Both height and weight are meaningful empirical statements and correspond to objective numerical dimensions. These measurements may be operationally corroborated (confirmed or refuted) by empirical observation. Someone less than four feet high may unambiguously be described as "short." Someone more than six feet high may unambiguously be described as "tall." Nevertheless, in spite of our ability to measure height and weight with utmost precision, it is impossible to provide a nonarbitrary empirical definition of the concept "short" or

"tall." Wherever the empirical boundary is defined it is always possible to suggest another slightly higher or slightly lower boundary which cannot be refuted. If someone who measures four feet is "short," how is someone who is four feet one inch to be classified? Or four feet two inches? Within a limited range, one inch does not make a difference to "shortness." But we cannot conclude that inches do not matter. The statement "short" is in no sense devoid of meaning even though we are unable to give it a precise empirical magnitude. We can describe and measure the empirical distributions of many phenomena objectively. But a precise empirical classification of short or tall or any other theoretical concept can only be arbitrarily imposed. The same argument holds for the terms "rich" or "poor."

8 This is the well-known problem faced in attempting to describe and categorize different wines. Because tastes are subjective it is impossible to refute or confirm any evaluation no matter how effusively it may be expressed. It is at root "a matter of taste." See Desai, 1994.
9 Marshall was fully aware of this. As he commented in the preface to the first edition of his *Principles*; "There is a temptation to classify economic goods in clearly defined groups to gratify the desire for logical precision. But great mischief seems to have been done by yielding to this temptation. ... There is not in real life a clear line of division between things that are and are not Capital, or that are or are not Necessaries, or again between labour that is and is not Productive" (1964: viii). He could have continued with other examples *ad infinitum*.
10 See for example, Streeten, 2000, McCloskey and Zihak, 2002.
11 Pareto emphasized the absurdity of assuming that it would ever be possible to obtain the amount of data necessary to calculate from his system of equations the prices and quantities of all goods and services actually sold in an economy (Hayek, 1975: 35).
12 Kamarck, 1983: 20.
13 Kamarck, 1983: 3–4.
14 Zinman, 1978: 28.
15 Relationships in geology and astronomy appear to be precise and constant. But this is solely because geological and astronomical events dance to a different time scale, one in which we humans are merely "one day flies." Within the span of a human lifetime geological and astronomical relationships are for all practical purposes completely constant. But as we now know, over uncountable eons the position of the continents and mountains and the movement of the planets has varied enormously.
16 Positivism holds that the "truth value" of a scientific statement is contingent on its ability to successfully predict future events. Friedman has taken the positivist position to extreme and argued that the only thing that matters for the usefulness of a hypothesis is its ability to make successful predictions. He maintains that it is unimportant whether the assumptions of the hypothesis are realistic or unrealistic. He has even perversely maintained that "to be important ... a hypothesis must be descriptively *false* in its assumptions." This argument confuses abstraction—separating relevant factors from a cloud of irrelevant detail—with the difference between falsehood and truth. Abstractions attempt to reproduce the "signal" but not the "noise." All abstractions are by definition incomplete and so in this sense are "false" when compared with the complexity of the real world. But this is not a defect but an intention due to the finite capability of our minds and our inability to comprehend complex systems. Friedman's purely positivist position ignores the primary function of theory: to provide greater understanding of how and why events occur. If a theory based on unrealistic assumptions has provided a successful prediction in the past, one can have little confidence that it will continue to provide successful prediction in the future. The result is likely to be a coincidence and the conclusions suspect. "True" theories must be based on assumptions that are isomorphic to reality.
17 See Kamark, 1983; Fisher, 1999.
18 The current controversy over the issue of abortion in the United States is a disagreement about *exactly when* does a human entity (zygote, embryo, or fetus) become a human

being? There is a similar controversy about when a human entity should be considered dead? How do we classify someone who is on a life-support system? When does an individual motor car cease to exist? How many of its parts must we take away without destroying the existence of the individual car? Rear-view mirror? Certainly. Driver's seat or tires? Surely. Breaks or clutch? Probably yes. Motor? Probably not. Body or Frame? Certainly not.

19 Kaldor, 1972.
20 Eisner, 1989: 2.
21 US Department of Commerce, 1954: 30.
22 Kuznets in Moss, 1979: 579; Kuznets, 1948.
23 F. Schneider and Enste, 2000; Schneider, 2002.
24 A recent study of 18 transition economies from 1989 to 1994 estimated the share of the "Unofficial" economy as a share of official GDP was on average 28 percent, with a range between 10 and 70 percent (Rosser *et al.*, 2003). See also Feige, 1979; Gutmann, 1977.
25 D. Farrell, 2004.
26 D. Farrell, 2004.
27 The preparation of meals in restaurants, cleaning services, and the laundry washing of clothes is included. But the greater value of home-cooked meals, home cleaning, and the services of all user-owned washers, dryers, appliances and other consumer durables are not. The transportation services of taxis, buses and rented cars is included, but the greater value of transportation services of family cars are excluded. When a man marries his housekeeper, services provided consequently increase but National Income declines.
28 Like individual goods most inventory items last less than one year. But collectively inventories exist forever.
29 Increases in GDP associated with the movement of women into the labor force signify a much smaller proportional gain in total output. Nonmarket child-care makes way for nursery schools, nursing homes, hospitals, restaurants and others whose sales are recorded as current output and income. Exclusion of nonmarket output brings significant changes to various measures of the distribution of income by size, age, sex, urban–rural status, and so on. Measures of inequality are also exaggerated since the proportion of income relating to nonmarket output is much larger for women, the poor, the aged, and people living in rural areas. Lipsey and Tice, 1989.
30 In the United States computer software, which had previously been treated as a business expense, is now treated as investment and so a component of GDP. Inflation has been recalculated by the "geometric mean" method back to 1978. The result has been a revision of economic growth upward since 1959 by an average of about 0.5 a percent to 3.4 percent per year. The productivity slowdown of the 1970s now appears much less severe. Productivity growth began accelerating in the 1980s, when the computer boom took off.
31 Using official international statistics is like comparing apples and oranges because of differences in the way GDP is measured in different countries. American statisticians count spending on computer software as investment, so it contributes to GDP. In Europe it is generally counted as a current expense and so excluded from final output. The recent surge in software spending has inflated America's growth rate relative to Europe's.
32 Police services purchased by government are final product while services of guards or watchmen purchased by private business are intermediate. The repair of state-owned highways is a final product while the repair of private railroad tracks is intermediate. If the highways were to become private toll-ways and the railways were nationalized these classifications would be reversed.
33 Government defense and police services are considered final rather than intermediate goods, and so are included in GDP while private police services are excluded. The amusement and entertainment services of movies watched in theatres, on cable television, and on public television are included in GDP. Similar services provided by commercial television are not included since they are paid in the form of non-capitalized advertising expenses by one firm to another. Travel expenses paid directly by business firms are an

intermediate product and so are excluded in the value of "final' output. When firms pay their employees higher wages and let them pay their own travel costs, this counts as final consumption. Their value enters directly into GDP, in addition to the value of whatever output the firm is producing. In each of these issues judgment is involved as to where to draw the line. Individually they appear to be minor but in aggregate as will be shown they can become very substantial.

34 Kuznets, 1953: 197–8.
35 Kuznets, 1953: 199.
36 Kuznets, 1953: 200.
37 Kuznets, 1948: 8. Kuznets expressed his position on government expenditures as follows:

> It is particularly true of such activities as are directed at domestic peace and the international position of the country that they provide the precondition of economic activity; but that they themselves cannot be conceived as yielding a final economic product ... These activities of government ... are in the nature of costs rather than returns; and if wisely chosen and pursued, will increase the flow of economic welfare—the latter to be realized when it materializes in a greater flow of goods to individuals.

38 Police services are counted as final product if purchased by government and as intermediate product if purchased by business. But police services to protect the activity and profitability of production represent a cost of that output. Unless they provide a final product enjoyed for its own sake they are intermediate in nature. Treating police services as intermediate goods would avoid the anomaly of showing the effects of an increase in police efforts to hold back an increase in crime as an increase in nominal and real GDP.
39 A case can be made that the boundary needs to be shifted in the other direction to include selected "intermediate" business output in consumption, such as business lunches, entertainment, and a host of employee health and welfare benefits not purchased on their own account by the employees who enjoy them.
40 Another potential adjustment of the final–intermediate product classification concerns the vast amount of entertainment and information media services for advertising. Commercial television supported by business advertising is not counted in real GDP, while pay-per-view and public television is included. The present convention implies that when public television is privatized and financed by private advertisers, GDP will decline.
41 Eisner, 1994: 22. With many imputations there are frequently substantial differences between market cost and opportunity cost estimates of the value of nonmarket output. The question is again, where do we draw the line?
42 When a private company buys an automobile this constitutes "investment" expenditures. When the same car is purchased by government it shows up as "government purchases of goods and services." When purchased by households it is included in "personal consumption expenditures." From the point of view of economic theory all of the above expenditure on automobiles are Gross Investment, just like the expenditure on any durable producers' good.
43 In addition to vitiating international and inter-temporal comparisons the exclusion of capital formation from official measures of investment makes more difficult the explanation of economic growth. Some extremely difficult conceptual questions of taxonomy must also be faced. How should changes in relative prices be considered? Since Net investment constitutes an addition to the value of capital, should we not include changes in the real value of capital stemming from changes in the relative price of capital and output? Since saving corresponds to the accumulation of wealth, should we not include wealth accumulation from relative price changes and capital gains? Should we adjust real product when the terms of international trade change? A constant value of domestic output is then exported in exchange for more (or less) imports from other countries? Should productivity be affected by a shift in the composition of consumer expenditures? See Nordhaus, 2000.

44 Machlup, 1962. Extended accounts include the acquisition of durable assets and the additions to inventories in all sectors of the economy, not solely in the business sector. Investment could include expenditure on intangible productive services, research and development, education, training, health, advertising, information, and intangible human capital.
45 Investment in land could be evaluated on the basis of costs or on changes in value. Due to externalities changes in the aggregate value of capital may exceed the total costs of investment. But all economic activity that reduces value must be regarded as capital consumption.
46 See Machlup, 1980.
47 Should one treat human beings as human capital? If what proportion of the costs of child rearing should be viewed as investment? Should birth and immigration count in the formation and accumulation of human capital? What are the total costs of such investment? Should we calculate the present value of the earnings of the new-born, and the newly arrived immigrants? If humans are to be viewed as capital goods, should we measure their earnings net of depreciation or maintenance, that is, net of consumption? In view of these horrendous problems, should the extension of investment to the production of human capital simply be arbitrarily omitted from the Income Accounts?
48 If income is defined in the Hicksian sense: the total amount that can be consumed while keeping wealth values intact, saving becomes the difference between this measure of income and current consumption, and both income and saving will include capital gains. The failure to include capital gains causes a huge disparity between income statements and changes in the value of balance sheets reflecting changes in the market value of assets, and further distorts measures of the wealth distribution within nations and the distribution of income and wealth among nations. See Chapter 8.
49 See Machlup, 1962.
50 The omission of stock market revaluations in income and savings explains why the recorded saving rate of US households fell to negative figures in the stock market boom of the late 1990s. Saving was actually very high. See Chapter 8.
51 Consumption expenditures for consumer durables may be reclassified as investment. Estimates of the value of the services of durables may be put into consumption. Government expenditures on goods and services may be broken down into consumption, capital accumulation, and intermediate product, with imputations for the value of services of government capital on the basis of a classification of government activities by function. Activities of the nonprofit sector may be taken out of the household sector and classified separately, or combined with an expanded "enterprise" sector.
52 Imputations of the value of production by nonmarket labor have been attempted on the basis of the costs of comparable market labor and on opportunity costs. Rates of remuneration per hour have been applied to time use estimates to get the value of the nonmarket output. These estimates differ substantially depending on whether they are based on opportunity costs, or on the wages of market labor devoted to similar market output.
53 Should my time spent reading to my son be evaluated at my marginal opportunity as an economist, at the rate of pay of a professional reader, or at the rate for a baby-sitter?
54 Eisner, 1989.
55 Eisner, 1989: 33.
56 Eisner, 1989, appendix E, tables E.16, E.17, E.18, E.19, E.20.
57 As will be shown in the final section this is another powerful argument for the use of a common world currency.
58 In 1998 in South Africa the Central Statistical Service released a new official estimate that 23 percent of the workforce was officially out of a job. It had previously been reported that the unemployment rate was 38 percent. The previous method deemed respondents jobless if they had not worked during the last seven days before being interviewed, wanted to work, and were available to start work within a week. The new definition added a fourth requirement, that respondents should have taken active steps

to look for work or to start some form of self-employment in the four weeks prior to the interview. The 15 percent difference represents the "discouraged worker effect," the huge band of people who have become so disenchanted with the prospect of gaining meaningful employment that they have given up looking. Are they unemployed?
59 See Stigler, 1961; Boskin, 1996, 1998; Boskin and Baker, 1998; Baker, 1997.
60 R. Gordon, 2004: 31.
61 Boskin, 1996, 1998, 2004; Schultze, 2003. See also Lebow and Rudd, 2003.
62 Boskin, 1996: 77.
63 See Schultze (2003) Symposia, Nordhaus, 1988; Hausman, 1994, Consumer Price Index, in *The Journal of Economic Perspectives*, 17 (1) Winter.
64 Changes in the level of nominal income can be expressed as the sum of the change in real income and the change in the price level. Since real income is equal to nominal income deflated by a price index, the rate of change in real income may be written as the rate of growth of nominal income, minus the inflation rate. A substantial upward bias in the inflation rate results in a substantial downward bias in the real growth rate.
65 Such a bias has major political and redistributional implications and consequences for government tax and revenue programs indexed to inflation, the time path of the government budget deficit, and the national debt. It produces misleading estimates of inflation for monetary policymakers for whom the inflation rate is a critical target. The suggestion that the upward bias in the CIP caused excessive growth in Social Security and other benefits provoked a sharp political reaction by the AARP (American Association of Retired Persons), which with the miraculous disappearance of the deficit derailed the movement for indexation. It is quite possible that official estimates of the inflation rate have an upward bias of as much as 2 percent.
66 Fischer, 1999.
67 Deaton, 2004.
68 Sala-i-Martin, 2002.
69 Chen and Ravallion, 2000.
70 Deaton, 2004.
71 Deaton, 2004.
72 On any estimate poverty is most impervious in sub-Saharan Africa. These are not only the poorest countries in the world, but also the slowest growing. It is difficult to claim that these countries are the victims of globalization, since one characteristic of African economies is that they are comparatively isolated from the rest of the world economy. For most African countries per capita income in 2000 was less than when they were a colony in 1960. On average Africa has not been growing as fast as its population has been increasing, and per capita income has been declining secularly.

7 Saving is the Accounting Record of Investment

1 Competitiveness Policy Council, 1993, 303. Quoted in Baker, 1997, 36. See Bosworth, 1993.
2 Summers, 1990: 153. Quoted in Pollin, 1997: 2–3. See Friedman, 1988.
3 See the discussion in Pollin, 1997.
4 Tobin, 1997: 300.
5 Feldstein and Horioka, 1980. In a subsequent study they concluded that more recent data supported their earlier conclusions that domestic investment responds to changes in domestic saving. They concluded that government budget deficits therefore "crowd out" private investment (Feldstein and Bacchetta, 1991). For a critique see Dalziel and Harcourt, 1997; Coakley et al., 1996.
6 Sawyer, 1996.
7 Solow, 1997: 230.
8 To the extent mainstream economists embrace the Keynesian multiplier process, where AD drives income and saving in the short run, they exhibit in Solow's terms, "a lack

of real coupling between the short run picture and the long run picture" (Solow, 1997: 232).
9 See for example, Keynes, 1936; Davidson, 1990, 1994.
10 Equilibrium analysis cannot be reconciled with causality. Simultaneous determination cannot be distinguished from mutual interdependence. See Pasinetti, 1974: 43–4. Mathematical theorists sometimes argue that since everything is related to everything else, the concept of causality is otiose. Such a position is unenlightening for understanding economic activity and unhelpful for policy analysis.
11 As Abba Lerner delighted to proclaim, "*In the long run we are always in the short run.*" Class notes, The John Hopkins University, 1957.
12 The World Bank is currently pursuing a major international saving study on what factors drive private saving rates: www.worldbank.org/research/projects/savings/policies.htm
13 Keynes, 1936; Davidson, 1994.
14 The World Bank research project identifies eight independent factors that drive saving: income, growth, fiscal policy, pension reform, financial liberalization, external borrowing and foreign aid, demographics, and uncertainty.
15 A precisely analogous argument applies to the supply and demand for money. Individual agents by changing the amount spent or borrowed can volitionally increase their own money balances or reduce them to zero. But when one agent reduces her balances by writing checks, another agent necessarily acquires deposit balances. Individuals are unable collectively to reduce their aggregate holdings of money balances, unless they purchase marketable financial assets or repay the nonmarketable loans held in bank portfolios.

Individuals do not "demand" to hold money balances as a function of their income, wealth and relative interest rates as they "demand" individual commodities. The total quantity of money supplied is always identical to the total quantity of money demanded. Money as the payments medium is always accepted ("demanded"). The total quantity of money balances outstanding is not determined by summing individual depositors' volitional demands for money. Money is generally accepted in exchange for goods. But this implies no accompanying volitional demand to increase or reduce the share of money balances in wealth portfolios. The quantity of credit money in existence is determined by the quantity of bank loans demanded by credit-worthy borrowers, not by the quantity of deposits demanded by bank depositors. "Loans create deposits" (Moore, 1988). The recognition that saving is the accounting record of investment leads directly to the insight that in monetary economies most deposit accumulation and "saving" undertaken is non-volitional.

If the total quantity of money supplied were exogenously determined by the amount of reserves provided by the central bank as the mainstream view maintains, the total supply of money would then not be determined by the total quantity of money demanded by individual depositors. Post Keynesians emphasize that the supply of credit money is endogenously credit-driven and demand-determined. As will be demonstrated in Part III, the supply of bank money is determined neither by the high-powered base nor by the quantity of deposits demanded by bank depositors. It is determined by the amount of bank credit demanded by credit-worthy bank borrowers and by the total amount of securities purchased by the banking system. The belief that the total supply of deposits outstanding is governed by the total quantity of deposits demanded is another fallacy of composition.

Consider the "hat check theory of money." Suppose tokens given out in the check room of a leading opera house became generally accepted as money. Individuals would then demand to hold tokens as a function of their income, wealth, and relative interest rates. But the total quantity of tokens in existence in the economy is determined by the number of hats checked by opera patrons, not by the transactions demand for tokens. With credit money bank loans correspond to hats in the hat check theory. "Loans make deposits." See Chapters 9–10.
16 Since the savings–income ratio is the inverse of the consumption-income ratio, if there is a stable behavioral relationship between consumption and income there must also be

a stable behavioral relationship between saving and income, the "savings function." Keynes, 1936, chs. 8–10.
17 Even though the relation is frequently expressed as actual saving equals actual investment.
18 This logically implies that there is no stable behavioral "consumption function" for the economy.
19 This alone provides conclusive proof that "saving" cannot be a volitional relationship.
20 See Eisner, 1989. The US National Income Accounts have recently been revised to include computer services for example, computer software, as investment.
21 Such a revision was recently undertaken in the United States.
22 This offers conclusive proof that saving when defined as "income not consumed" is simply an accounting identity.
23 This issue is discussed at length in the following chapter, where the advantages and disadvantages of defining current income to include capital gains and losses are considered.
24 Equities represent a complication to the above argument. Equities constitute ownership claims to business net worth. Their book value is equal to the accounting value of business net worth, total assets minus total liabilities. Standard accounting principles measure business tangible assets at historical cost minus estimated depreciation. This constitutes the book value of equities. But the market value of equities as determined on stock exchanges represents the market's weighted consensus of the discounted present value of all expected future dividends and capital gains by all participants. Kaldor termed the ratio of the market value of equities to their replacement value the "Valuation" ratio. Tobin termed the ratio the "Q" ratio. When firms chose to retain earnings rather than distribute them as dividends, and when wealth-holders expect the future growth of corporate earnings to increase, stock prices concurrently rise and shareholders receive income in the form of capital gains. Capital gain income is not included in the NIPA measure of GDP since GDP is a measure of the value of real output and includes only the income derived from current output.

Measured consumption and saving 'ratios' are sensitive to how income and saving are defined and whether capital gains on existing assets are excluded or included in the definition of income. If capital gains are excluded, total saving becomes the accounting measure of total investment spending measured at historical cost. But the historical cost or book value of business capital provides a distorted measure of the role of wealth in consumption and investment behavior and the value of total household assets. Due to their very high marketability, equities are conventionally valued by their owners at their current market price.

Capital gains received by households were particularly relevant for US consumption spending in the 1990s, when equity price-earning ratios soared and accompanying capital gains amounted to nearly 70 percent of Total Personal Income. The total market value of equities in the United States in the 1990s was more than 200 percent of Personal Income. It follows that current NIPA income data substantially understate the value of wealth ownership and the flow of resources to the household sector. Capital gains on corporate equities financed the rapid growth of consumption expenditures which provided the foundation for the prosperity of the 1990s. In the decade of 2000 capital gains on housing has played a similar role in sustaining household consumption expenditures, and household saving is similarly misleadingly stated as a near zero or even negative figure (1996, 1998).
25 In the 1990s there was widespread concern about the rise in household debt and the fall in the personal saving rate. But if properly calculated household debt in fact fell as a ratio of household assets. When realized capital gains are included in income the US personal saving rate, rather than falling below zero, remained broadly constant at about 10 percent. When unrealized capital gains are included in income the personal saving rate rose very substantially to about 40 percent of income. To adequately explain recent consumption behavior income must be redefined along Hicksian lines to include capital

gains and losses. In this case NIPA conventions must be fundamentally revised (See, Peach and Steindal, 2000).

26 Changes in asset prices result in capital gains and losses to asset-owners. If saving is defined as net wealth accumulation and as income not consumed, income must be redefined to include holding gains and losses. The following chapter makes the case for following a Hicksian definition of income in the NIA's. The identity of changes in saving with changes in investment, and the non-volitional character of most household saving are then highlighted, so the saving relationship becomes more transparent.

27 The required capital budgeting changes in the ROW accounts are even more important for theory and policy. They are considered in Chapter 17 under Part V, Open Economy Considerations in this volume.

28 As argued in Chapter 6 where the line is drawn between limit consumption goods, investment goods, and intermediate goods and services must frequently be arbitrary. If it were recognized that many public goods are really intermediate rather than final goods, for example, police services, national defense, measured GDP would be smaller. See Eisner, 1989.

29 Keynes could not define saving as the net accumulation of wealth, because he had accepted Simon Kuznet's definition of National Income as the value of current output and current earned income excluding all capital gains. As will be shown in Chapter 8, under even moderate rates of inflation most nominal wealth accumulation is attributable to changing wealth values, not to net real capital formation. Substantial capital gain income is generated in all economies even when inflation is quite modest.

30 For a summary of this literature see Lerner, 1939.

31 Under rudimentary financial conditions—a barter economy where all investment is internally financed—the two meanings are identical. But in modern financial environments, where more than half of total investment spending is typically deficit-financed, the two concepts differ substantially.

32 Consider the supply of credit money. Economic units demand to hold deposits as a function of their income, wealth, and relative interest rates. Each individual unit decides on the amount of deposits it wishes to hold. Since a deposit cannot exist without an owner, the total quantity of deposits outstanding is identical to the sum of deposits held by all depositors. But the money supply is not *determined* by the total quantity of deposits demanded by individual economic units. The mainstream holds that total deposits are exogenously determined by the CB by controlling the high-powered base. Post Keynesians hold deposits are endogenously created by the act of bank lending. In overdraft systems bank loans are determined by the demand for credit by bank borrowers. Total deposits outstanding represent the accounting record of bank loans and securities, and in individuals decide on the amount of deposits they wish to hold. But the total amount of deposits outstanding is *determined* by the total amount of deposits created, and so by the amount of loans granted or securities purchased. Total liabilities in bank balance sheets are the accounting record of the total volume of loans and securities in bank asset portfolios (See Moore, 1988, 2000).

33 If instead of using the verb "to save", economists were to use the more correct verb "to abstain," the statement that saving (abstention) is the accounting record of investment would not appear so controversial. Income consists of two kinds of goods, consumption goods and investment goods. When saving is defined as to abstain from consuming all one's income, it becomes transparent that total abstention is identical to total investment.

34 The analysis of investment behavior when financial assets are absent is illuminating. National Income Accounting, with the exception of rent on owner-occupied housing, does not attempt to impute the value of consumption or production services-in-kind received on durable assets. But the non-pecuniary services from many tangible assets can be "saved," in the colloquial sense, by volitional abstention. Such "saving" results in an equal increase in internally financed net investment and is defined as the net accumulation of tangible assets. For wealth owners the decision to "save" (in the sense of "conserve" rather than to consume) is entirely volitional. As a result, such volitional

saving "causes" investment. This serves powerfully to reinforce our robust colloquial understanding of "saving" as volitional.
35 The extent corporate decisions to finance investment spending by retain earnings induce household decisions to abstain from consumption of wealth will be explored in Chapter 8. Such household savings does not involve volitional action. Agents must simply do nothing, and take no action. The consequence is to hold assets of greater market value.
36 Services-in-kind on tangible assets in monetary economies correspond to barter economies, where financial assets do not exist. Only in such circumstances do the colloquial and accounting meanings of "saving" coincide. "To accumulate" then denotes "to spend less on consumption goods." All decisions to spend on investment goods are volitional, and are accompanied by identical volitional decisions to save. This is an example how institutional circumstances can determine the validity of theoretical propositions.
37 Most nonmarket saving and investment goes unrecorded. All saving and investment that involves the conserving of the services-in-kind on tangible assets does not involve a market transaction and so is excluded from the National Income Accounts. Helm, 1984.
38 Classical economists emphasized the antisocial consequences of saving to accumulate money balances. They denoted the accumulation of money balances as "hoarding," which resulted in a reduction in AD since they regarded the supply of the money commodity as exogenous (Moore, 1988). As Keynes repeatedly emphasized saving directed to the accumulation of land has a similar negative effect on the level of AD. Depending on their liquidity, nonreproducible and previously produced assets may be used as temporary stores of purchasing power, and the accumulation of such assets reduces AD for current output. Kuznets, 1953; Gertler, 1988.
39 When investment is deficit-financed by bank credit it is technically correct to state that "investment creates the saving necessary to finance itself." But since saving is the accounting record of investment, the statement is also misleading, since it appears to imply that saving is something that can be independently "created."
40 If consumption is financed by bank credit, this implies a simultaneous decrease in volitional saving.
41 This explains why Crusoe metaphors so aptly and persuasively illustrate mainstream theorems.
42 See Nell (2001) on Hicks' evolving views on the institutional changes accompanying the evolution of the money asset.
43 Keynes, 1936, chs. 13–18.
44 Keynes, 1936, ch. 18. *"We can sometimes regard our ultimate independent variables as consisting of ... (3) the quantity of money as determined by the action of the central bank"* 247.
45 Economic recessions are associated with falls in AD which may be viewed as an increase in volitional saving. If the reduction in AD results in a sufficiently large reduction in income, the total quantity saved will decrease. Assuming that the CB attempts to reach its full employment stabilization objective, the CB will respond by lowering short-term interest rates. Keynes' paradox of thrift was a description of the process where a rise in planned saving rates reduces AD and investment and actual saving. If households and firms persistently maintain high volitional saving rates, the CB would be forced to lower interest rates to achieve its stabilization goals. Depending on the CB's reaction function, a raise or reduction in volitional saving may indirectly affect the volume of investment by inducing the CB to reduce or increase the rate of interest. This is discussed at greater length in Chapters 15 and 16.
46 Levuer, 1939; Peach and Steindel, 2000.
47 Keynes, CW XIV: 222.

8 Capital Gains: Toward a Hicksian Definition of Income

1 See e.g. Friedman, 1988, 2000.
2 For collections on the "shortfall" of US saving see Lipsey and Tice, 1989; Bernheim and Shoven, 1991; Friedman, 1988.

3 For a discussion see Bradford, 1990, 1991, 16; Bernheim and Shoven, 1991.
4 This loosely corresponds to the difference between financial historical cost accounting as a measure of the net worth of business firms, versus the equity market valuation of the firm. See Bradford, 1991, in Bernheim and Shoven, 17–18.
5 See Bradford, Bernheim and Shoven, 1991.
6 Hicks, 1946. A similar definition was long ago suggested by Haig (1921) and Simons (1938).
7 Hicks, 1946.
8 Hicks, 1946, ch. 14.
9 Hicks, 1939, ch. 14.
10 Hicks, 1939, Helm, 1984.
11 "We shall be well advised to eschew income and saving in economic dynamics. They are bad tools which break in our hands." Hicks, 1939: 53–6, Helm, 1984.
12 Hicks, 1939, ch. 14.
13 Hicks, 1939, ch. 14.
14 Hicks, 1939, ch. 14.
15 See for example Friedman, 1957; Ando and Modigliani, 1963; Bhatia, 1987, and Campbell, 2004.
16 As Argentineans and South Africans are only too aware, sharp depreciation of the exchange rate renders all nationals drastically poorer in their ability to command foreign goods.
17 Bradford, 1990, 1991.
18 See Moore, 1988.
19 Since deposits dominate fiat money for many purposes, depositors make no sacrifice of liquidity or abstention from consumption, as is the case with other lending behavior. In consequence they do not even regard the accumulation of deposits as an act of increased lending of fiat money to the banking system.
20 Graziani, 1990.
21 Graziani, 1989.
22 Longitudinal studies are required to determine how gross and net changes in asset values are associated with the expansion and decline of AD over time.
23 "Financial accounting is not designed to measure directly the value of a business enterprise. But the information it provides may be helpful to those who wish to estimate its value." Financial Accounting Standards Board, 1978, excerpted in Gibson and Frishkoff, 1986: 19.
24 Bradford, 1990, 1991, Bernheim and Shoven, 1991.
25 Note for the two common overlapping years, 1986–87, the reported ratio of equities to net worth is 20 percent higher in the 1984 source compared to the 2002 source (65 percent compared to 45 percent). This difference should be investigated.
26 If stocks were priced rationally, how can the fall of 25 percent in asset values in a single day in 1987, in the absence of any major change in real fundamental events, be accounted for?
27 In nonmonetary barter economies all economic units must run a balanced budget, so deficit spending is impossible. All investment spending is internally financed, and volitional saving becomes a precondition for investment to occur. The classical vision that saving 'governs' investment is appropriate only for a barter or "Crusoe" economy.

9 The Endogeneity of Credit Money

1 Hicks, 1967, 1977. Chick, 1984.
2 Keynes' formulation of the essential properties of money, an asset with an approximately zero elasticity of production and substitution, refers to commodity and fiat money.
3 This phenomenon is known as Gresham's Law, "Bad money drives out good."
4 Huge fines were imposed on anyone who tampered with the King's money.

5 In the 1811 British debate on the gold standard, David Ricardo conceded that precious metals, "are themselves subject to greater variations than it is desirable a standard should be subjected to. They are, however, the best with which we are acquainted." Ricardo argued that without a precious metal standard money "would be exposed to all the fluctuations to which the ignorance or the interests of the issuers might subject it" (Ricardo, 1951: 59, 62).
6 Hicks, 1989.
7 Hicks, 1967, 1977, 1980, 1982. See Nell, 2001 for an incisive exposition of the evolution of Hick's position on money.
8 Hicks, 1967.
9 Mainstream theory is appropriate to a commodity money world. Rochon, 1999.
10 See Moore, 1988.
11 This is the "reflux" principle in "circuit" theory. See Lavoie, 1992, ch. 4; Lavoie, 2005b.
12 Stiglitz, 1987.
13 Davidson and Weintraub, 1973.
14 Phillips, 1920; Cannan, 1921; Crick, 1927; Chick, 1986; Desai, 1987; Dow, 1996a.
15 For a thorough discussion with citations see Moore, 1988.
16 Higher interest rates induce banks to reduce their holdings of noninterest-bearing excess reserves, leading to a higher multiplier.
17 Moore, 1988, preface. The terms "Verticalist" and "Horizontalist" were suggested in correspondence by Axel. Leijonhufvud.
18 Friedman, 1970, 1977, 1982, 1999.
19 Whenever the ratio between any two variables (X / Y) remains constant, if one knows the value of one variable it is possible to "predict" the value of the other, and conversely. But this usage of "predict" does not imply "explanation." A good "prediction" requires only that the ratio remain stable over the period in question. Such "explanations" are really simply "tautologies," and imply nothing about causality. For X → Y causality to be empirically "proven" it must be demonstrated that X is exogenously determined. This point has been very effectively made by Charles Goodhart, 1985: Suppose total academic salaries (S) were a stable proportion α of national income (Y): $S/Y = \alpha$. It is always possible to write this identity as $S = \alpha Y$. Y can then be "explained" as a stable "academic multiplier" $(1/\alpha)$ of S and $Y = 1//\alpha\, S$. So long as α remains stable, the change in GDP can be successfully "predicted" by the change in academic salaries. But academic egos notwithstanding, and despite its any huge *ex post* predictive power the "academic multiplier" does not provide a true *explanation* of the forces determining GDP. In addition the value of the "academic multiplier" would be subject to "Goodhart's Law" if the government attempted to use academic salaries to control GDP. See Goodhart, 1984.
20 Moore, 1988, ch. 2.
21 For empirical support, see: Hendry and Ericsson, 1985, 1989; Cottrell, 1986, 1994; Desai, 1987; Goodheart, 1989; Wray, 1990, 1998; Pollin, 1991; Nell, 1996; Howells, 2001; Lavoie, 2001; Arestis and Sawyer, 2005.
22 Dow, 1996; Chick, 2000; Rockon, 2000; Lavoie, 2005a.
23 Taylor estimated that over the 1980s the Fed raised the Federal funds rate on average by 0.2 percent for every 1.0 percent the inflation rate exceeded its target level, and reduced the funds rate on average by 0.1 percent for every 1.0 percent the unemployment rate exceeded its target level (Taylor, 1993).
24 This is how it is recognized by mainstream economists. See for example, Walsh, 2003.
25 Stiglitz, 1987.
26 Arestis and Sawyer, 2002, 2005; Arestis *et al.*, 2005.
27 De Kock Report, 1985: 182–4. See Moore, 1988, ch. 5.
28 Holmes, 1969: 73–4. For additional central banker quotations see Moore, 1988: 88–92.
29 For a detailed description of German and Swiss "pragmatic" monetary targeting see Bernanke *et al.*, 1999.

30 Lavoie, 2005a, 2005b.
31 See Moore, 1988.
32 Moore, 1979, 1985, 1988a; Cottrell, 1986, 1994.
33 Several economists have criticised "convenience lending." as a term: Wray, 1990; Pollin, 1991; Arestis and Howells, 1996; Dav, 1996; Palley, 1998.
34 Particular implications of "convenience lending" by depositors are developed in the Appendix of Chapter 16 *"The Quantity Theory of Money."*

10 Commercial Bank Intermediation

1 Hicks, 1989.
2 "Stable" does not imply "constant." But some stability of the mark-up is necessary for mark-up pricing to have operational meaning. Otherwise mark-up pricing would be the near-tautology that banks set prices above unit variable costs. Chick, 1986, 2002.
3 See Moore, 1988.
4 Gurley and Shaw, 1960; Cannan, 1921; and Robertson, 1933.
5 The development of securitization, which permits a wide variety of heterogeneous assets to be bundled together and sold as a more or less homogeneous package, is an important institutional exception. To the extent securitization occurs primarily within the banking system, from debt on to surplus banks, the argument that total quantity of bank loans is determined by borrowers' demand for credit remains valid for the banking system as a whole. But bank sale of securitized bundles of securities to nonbanks permits the banks to control the quantity of their individual loan portfolios.
6 The term used for the overnight rate at which CBs lends reserves to the banking system varies over different financial systems, but it is often termed "Bank Rate." In the United States the key CB overnight lending rate to the banking system is termed the "federal funds rate." Goodhart, 1984.
7 See Moore 1988. The difference between Post Keynesian and mainstream theory centers on the particular time period considered over which pegging occurs. Most mainstream theorists would acknowledge that if central banks "pegged" the price of securities kept the rate unchanged at some specified target level for some specified time period, and ignored all quantity implications of such behavior for the high-powered base, the money supply would be endogenously credit-driven. Over such periods the supply function would be horizontal. But the time period of such a peg is (implicitly) viewed to be a substantial. Only if the rate were maintained at "too high" or "too low" a level indefinitely would such behavior be destabilizing. This scenario is regarded as so unusual as to safely be ignored. In practice CBs keep the rate pegged only for the short- run periods between monetary policy committee meetings, usually four- or six-week periods. In all short-run periods between when the interest rate target is set and changed, "pegging" or rate-setting behavior accurately describes CB behavior. If the period over which the rate is changed is instantaneous, the economy always finds itself in a situation when the interest rate is being pegged or "smoothed," but level at which it is pegged changes over time.
8 Crick, 1927; Tobin, 1963; Ingham, 2005.
9 Tobin, 1982. See also Tobin, 1963.
10 See any mainstream textbooks, for example, Goodhart, 1984; Walsh, 2003.
11 Collateralization eliminates the heterogeneity of bank loans by merging them into homogeneous maturity portfolios.
12 Moore, 1988: 215–21.
13 Moore, 1988, Howells and Mariscal, 2002; Wray, 1998, 2004; Rochon, 1999, 2000; Rochon and Matias, 2001; Rochon and Sergio, 2004.
14 See Moore, 1988, ch. 3.
15 See Moore, 1988, ch. 5, 2–3.

16 As the Great Depression song put it, "Banks won't lend you anything, unless you don't need it."
17 Moore, 1988.
18 Desai, 1987.
19 Had there been no banks to provide working capital finance there would have been no industrial revolution.
20 Whenever inventories rise in value at a greater rate than the firm's profit mark-up on sales, increases in inventory costs absorb *more* than the increase in profits (Godley and Cripps, 1983).
21 See Chapter 20.
22 An ongoing debate in the accounting profession concerns the accounting conventions that best assure profits are correctly measured during periods of rapid inflation. The cumulative cash generated by any rapidly growing business will fall short of its recorded profits, which are therefore not available for distribution. Given its profit mark-up and its production-sales period, the faster sales expand, the greater will be the discrepancy between profits and cash flow.
23 If banks make no other loans will the increase in total bank loans (ΔL) equal the increase in the total value of business inventories (ΔI)? If bank loans were the sole bank asset the change in total bank deposits will equal the change in total business loans ($\Delta L = \Delta M$). The change in finance supplied is equal to the change in the total value of inventories, and in the value of new investment ($\Delta M = \Delta L = \Delta I$).
24 Moore, 1988; Wray, 1991. It has recently been discovered that this relationship does not hold for many developing countries, where borrowers are small and uncredit-worthy. Banks do not then typically provide overdraft facilities to the private sector and governments receive a much larger share of total bank credit. See Chapter 20, this volume.
25 This figure adapted from Goodfriend, 1987. Although designed for the United States a similar presentation can be made for any banking system.
26 The Discount Window Official will ask frequent borrowers why they need more funds, and may demand to see their books.
27 This non-transparent procedure amounted to interest rate targeting. The Fed directly set the discount rate, the reserve shortage that banks were forced to make up at the Discount Window, and administered the price at which it was willing to lend funds at the Discount Window. It then claimed disingenuously that the federal funds rate was a market rate, so the Fed was not responsible for its unpopular high level. This was attributed to excessive government deficit-spending and the overissue of Treasury debt.
28 Moore, 1988, ch. 11.
29 Credit commitments vary pro-cyclically since when rates are higher, bad debt losses are offset more quickly by interest earnings. When interest rates are 15 percent the earnings from $7 of performing loans offset $1 of bad debt losses in one year. Alternatively expressed, when rates are 15 percent it takes 7 years of interest earnings to offset $1 of bad debt losses. When interest rates are 2 percent $50 of interest earnings are required to offset $1 of bad debts losses in one year. Alternatively expressed it then takes 50 years of interest earnings to offset $1 of bad debts.
30 This pro-cyclical variation in credit commitments operates to smooth cyclical variations in the credit utilization ratio.
31 Approximately, because banks hold small quantities of other assets in addition to loans and securities and have other net liabilities in addition to deposits and net worth.
32 Moore, 1988, ch. 10.
33 The situation was analogous to Japan throughout the 1990s and early 2000s.
34 See Moore, 1988.
35 Paul Volcker, 1978.
36 Volker, 2002.
37 Some texts have at last recognized that US monetary policy operates by using the Federal funds rate and not reserves as its policy instrument. (See Walsh, 2003).

38 It was recently reported that the Euro declined when the European Central Bank refused to reduce bank rate, and rose when the ECB reduced bank rate, the reverse of the normal response of exchange rates to changes in Bank Rate. If a reduction in Bank Rate stimulates the economy sufficiently it can attract foreign funds and raise the exchange rate.
39 See Moore, 1968.
40 Lavoie, 1992, 2001, 2005b.

11 The Exogeneity of Interest Rates

1 For an extended discussion of different theories of interest see Moore, *H&V*, 1988, chs. 10 and 11.
2 The real rate (r) is the equivalent nominal interest rate (R) if prices were constant: $r = (1 + R)/(1 + p)$. For moderate inflation rates, this may be approximated by the nominal rate minus the inflation rate: $r = (R - p)$. Rewriting the nominal rate can be viewed as the real rate plus the inflation premium. $R = r + p^e$.
3 Wicksell, 1895, 1898.
4 See Rogers, 1989.
5 See Rogers, 1989.
6 Ricardo, 1951, V. 4: 290.
7 Keynes, 1936: 82.
8 Keynes argued that the general level of short-term interest rates was determined by the monetary authorities by controlling the supply of liquidity. It is now gradually becoming recognized that the CB controls the price of credit, and the quantity of credit demanded and granted is endogenously demand determined (Walsh, 2003). See Keynes, 1923, 1930 for a development of his views on interest rare-setting procedures.
9 Fontana, 2004. Goodfriend, 1983; Howells and Mariscal, 2002, Laurie and Seccareccia, 2004; Rochon and Rossi, 2004.
10 Goodhart, 2003.
11 "Pegging" interest rates was the characteristic policy of most CBs before the Second World War. I still remember my astonishment when doing research for my dissertation at The Johns Hopkins University, The Effects of Counter-Cyclical Monetary Policy on the Earnings of Canadian Chartered Banks (1958) on discovering that the Bank of Canada kept BR unchanged over decade-long periods between the two World Wars. I was convinced this must be a typographical error. See Moore, 1988.
12 See Moore, 1988, chs. 10, 11, Evans and Marshall, 1998; Campbell, 1995; McCulloch, 1975; Montic, 1998.
13 Taylor, 1993; Walsh, 2003.
14 For a detailed summary of Federal Reserve operating procedures and the instrument-choice problems, see Walsh, 2003.
15 Goodfriend, 1980, 1989.
16 Moore, 1988, chs. 3–7.
17 Moore, 1988, ch. 2.
18 Volker, 2002. This explains the ineffectiveness of cheap money policy in inducing additional borrowing in the United States in the second half of the 1930s. Nominal rates had been reduced to near zero, but *ex ante* real rates had risen due to expectations of future deflation.
19 See *Financial Innovation and Monetary Transmission, Economic Review*, Federal Reserve Bank of New York, 8(1), 2001; Walsh, 2003; Lavoie and Seccareccia, 2004; Rochon and Rossi, 2004; Arestis *et al.*, 2005.
20 Bernanke *et al* (BLMP), 1999: 6. Due to the short observational time period BLMP largely forego econometric analysis, and develop a case-study approach of countries that adopted inflation targeting.

21 Chapter 13 provides a critique of the mainstream argument.
22 Friedman, 1953, 1959, 1968, 1970, 1977, 1982, 1999. Phelps, 1968.
23 BLSP, 1999: 15–16.
24 Bruno and Easterly, 1998; see Andersen and Gruen, 1995 for a survey.
25 Bank of England, Monetary Policy Committee, 1999.
26 Bank of England, 1999. This represents belated admission of the endogenous money theory long endorsed by Post Keynesians, which at last is finding its way into mainstream textbooks. See Arestis and Sawyer, 2002.
27 See the summary of empirical effect of money and interest rates on output in Walsh, 2003; Woodford, 2003.
28 Walsh, 2003.
29 Walsh, 2003.
30 Woodford, 2003.
31 See Moore, 1988, ch. 11.
32 Walsh, 2003.
33 Alan Greenspan, the Chairman of the US FED, has stated that if people could understand what he was saying, he would not be doing his job properly .
34 In a one commodity world the commodity ("corn") must *first* be saved *before* it can be invested.
35 See Goodhart, 2002; Arestis *et al.*, 2005; Lavoie, 2001, 2005a.
36 The level of borrowed reserves was a function of the interest rate differential between the Fed Funds rate and the official discount rate. The Fed chose a desired Fed Funds rate and then derived the implied borrowed reserves target (Thorton, 1983; Goodfriend, 1986, 2000).
37 Goodhart, 2002: 17.
38 Holmes, 1969; Moore, 1988.
39 This has led to some confusion between a "policy-determined," and an "exogenous" variable. An "exogenous" variable is interpreted as one that is not set in response to current, past, or future developments in the economy, but is fixed at some arbitrary level, or varied randomly. But it would be extraordinarily rare and stupid for economic policy to be set in such an "exogenous" way. All economic policy instruments are set in response to current, past or expected future developments in the economy. It can easily be shown that if interest rates were to be set "exogenously," the price level would be indeterminate, whereas if the monetary base were to be set "exogenously," the price level will be determinate. But this distinction has no implications for policy whatsoever, since no CB would consider setting the interest rate "exogenously" in this manner. Nevertheless among economists who thought that monetary base control should be the adopted policy mechanism, this was somehow thought to prove that a policy of setting H was preferable to a policy of setting. See Goodhart, 2002.
40 Keynes, 1936, chs 13–18.
41 Moore, 1988, ch. 8.
42 Saving by definition is simply the accounting measure of investment (Chapter 7).
43 Keynes, XXVII: 392.
44 Keynes, 1937a: 247.
45 In the heat of the debate Keynes appears to have completely forgotten his endogenous credit money model of the *Treatise*, that additional demand for bank finance automatically results in additional newly created money balances.
46 Keynes, 1937b: 668–9.
47 Keynes, 1936: 382–3.
48 Keynes, 7, p. 184.
49 Dimand, 1986: 4.
50 Keynes, 1936: 246–7.
51 Keynes, Vol. VI: 211.
52 Keynes, V; 275.
53 Keynes, 1937b: 669.

54 Keynes, 1937b: 669.
55 Keynes, Vol. XXV; 149 (Letter to Harrod, 1942).
56 Keynes, Vol. XXVII; 390–92 ('Minutes for the National Debt Inquiry'), 1945.

12 Markup Pricing and the Aggregate Supply Relationship

1 Thaler has argued that in the future *homo economicus* will become a slower learner and more emotional, that is, more like *homo sapiens*, thus reversing a 50 year trend where "The IQ of *homo economicus* became bounded only by the IQ of the smartest economic theorist." Thaler, 2000. See Kahnemaun, 2000, 2003.
2 Keynes, 1936; ch. 12, 156–57. The author is old enough to remember in the 1930s staring long and hard at the two middle pages of the TORONTO STAR, with its pictures of 50 beautiful women, trying to discern who would be the readers' choice to enable me to win the $100 prize. This clearly required first estimating of the type of reader who was most likely to enter the competition. I was never able to reach a decision on this initial step, other than recognizing that they were probably as poor a judge as I was.
3 Suppose you did not believe sunspots caused the economy to expand, but most other agents believed this was true. If you observed an increase in sunspots, it is then "rational" for you to believe that the economy will expand. As Keynes said when the world has gone mad, nothing is worse that rationality.
4 See Downward, 2000, 2001, Godley and Nordhaus, 1972, Marris, 1998.
5 Downward, P.,1999: 45; Lee, F. 1998; Eicknen, 1973, 1978, 1987; Bils, 1997; Coast, 1999.
6 Hall and Hitch, 1939.
7 Hall and Hitch, 1939: 28.
8 Hall and Hitch, 1939: 28.
9 Hall and Hitch, 1939: 28–33.
10 Andrews, 1949: 58–9.
11 Andrews, 1949: 59, 78.
12 Andrews, 1949: 81.
13 Andrews, 1949: 153.
14 Kalecki, 1971a: 165.
15 Hall and Hitch's influence on Kalecki was direct and strong. Kreisler, 1987: 53–54.
16 Kalecki, 1954: reprinted in Kalecki, 1971: 44.
17 Kaldor, 1934.
18 Means, 1972: 292–3.
19 Means states that the ubiquitous objective of businessmen is to maximize profits. But this unfortunate use of neoclassical language is not indicative of the essence of his analysis. By insisting that prices are set in advance of trade, by adding some markup to average direct costs, and that the markup is indeterminate, Means avoids the deductive determinism of neoclassical work.
20 Eichner, 1973: 2–4. See Hart, 1982; Fedderke, 1992.
21 Eichner, 1973: 43.
22 Solow, 1998; Downward, 1999.
23 Sylos-Labini, 1979: 6, 1983.
24 Steindl, 1990: 123.
25 Lavoie, 1992: 61.
26 The determinism of some Post Keynesian theorizing, drawn from Sraffa and the classical economists and sharing the neoclassical agenda of equilibrium, and widely referred to as neoRicardian analysis (Okun, 1980; Lavoie, 1992; Lee, 1998) is inconsistent with the open system methodological position required for complex systems analysis.
27 Little, 1962; Kiug, 1993; Bils and Klendo, 2004.
28 McCallum, 1970: 147.
29 McFetridge, 1973.

30 Eckstein and Fromm, 1968.
31 Godley and Nordhaus, 1972; Coutts et al., 1978.
32 Smith, 1982.
33 Sylos-Labini, 1979.
34 Sawyer, 1983.
35 Geroski, 1991, and Fedderke, 1992.
36 Dorwald, 1987.
37 Reynolds, 1987: 82.
38 Gilbert, 1986.
39 The problem of identification arises in qualitative as well as in quantitative empirical work.
40 Downward, 1999.
41 Early, 1956.
42 Kaplan, 1958; Lanzillotti, 1964.
43 Gordon, 1981.
44 Samiee, 1987.
45 Blinder, 1998.
46 Blinder, 1998: 84–85.
47 Blinder, 1998: 84–92.
48 Blinder, 1998: 93–101.
49 Blinder, 1998: 99–105.
50 Blinder, 1998: 99–105.
51 Blinder, 1998: 99–105.
52 Blinder, 1998: 99–105.
53 Blinder, 1998: 300.
54 Blinder, 1998: 301.
55 Blinder, 1998: 302.
56 Blinder, 1998: 302.
57 Blinder, 1998: 308. Sibly has suggested that firms may be viewed as possessing a stock of goodwill associated with past price behavior, which is accumulated when price increases are delayed and drawn down when price are hiked. So long as clients display "*loss aversion,*" price increases cost more goodwill than price reductions produce gain. This operates strongly to reinforce price rigidity. Sibly, 1995.
58 Miller, 2000, 2001.
59 Miller, 2000.
60 Miller assembled a substantial bibliography of empirical studies that support fixed proportions in production. 2000, 2001.
61 Robinson, 1956: 247–8.
62 Kalecki, 1971: 105–6.
63 Marris 1964: 9.
64 Shapiro and Sawyer, 2003: 364.
65 The PK price equation is a useful informative relationship. See Atesoglu, 1997. It is frequently decomposed to show the relationships between the markup and the real wage given average labor productivity and the value of the mark-up as follows: $P = (1 + \mu)(ulc) = (1 + \mu)(WL/y) = (1 + \mu)(W/(y/L)\text{-}1 + \mu)(W/a)$ where $a = (y/L)$ = average labor productivity. Solving for the real wage: $W/P = 1(1 + \mu)(a)$ The real wage varies directly with average labor productivity and inversely with the markup. Solving for the markup: $(1 + \mu) = 1/(WL/pY)$ The markup is thus equal to the inverses of labor's share in GDP. Taking logs of both sides and differentiating with respect to time gives the relationship between percentage changes in the variables. Using the convention that a dot over a variable denotes the percentage changes: $\dot{P} = (1 + \dot{\mu}) + \dot{W} - \dot{a}$ So long as the markup remains stable the rate of inflation equals the excess of the rate of wage inflation [$\dot{W}$] over the average rate of labor productivity growth [$\dot{a}$]. The "core" rate of inflation represents the

underlying rate of inflation in the economy, excluding short-term flex-price causes of inflation due to variation in for example, food or oil prices, taxes or interest rates.
66 This is the sense of the Post Keynesian expression: "Output is demand-determined." When prices do not adjust to changes in demand and all adjustment is in terms of quantities, the economy may be regarded as in "equilibrium," in the sense that there are no excess demand or excess supply forces causing prices to change. This is one interpretation of Fisher Black's vision that "markets are always in equilibrium." Black, 1995.
67 Bloch and Sapsford, 1991–92; Sapsford and Morgan, 1994.

13 The "Raffishness" of Mainstream Macroeconomics: a Post Keynesian Critique

1 Solow, 1997: 230.
2 Solow, 1997: 230.
3 Solow, 1997: 231.
4 Blanchard, 1997: 245.
5 Taylor, 1997: 233.
6 Blanchard, 1997: 245.
7 Solow, 1997: 231.
8 Blinder, 1997: 240.
9 Eichenbaum, 1997: 238.
10 Taylor, 1997: 235.
11 Moore, 1988.
12 Taylor, 1997: 234.
13 Eichenbaum, 1997: 238; Blinder, 1997: 242.
14 Solow, 1997: 231.
15 Solow, 1997: 231.
16 Blinder, 1997: 242.
17 Solow, 1997: 232.
18 New endogenous growth (NEG) models are specified over long-run periods when parameters as well as variables change. As a result they can never yield refutable hypotheses. Many long-run growth models can be constructed to simulate the same empirical data set. As a result they can never be refuted by new empirical data, but can only be recalibrated. The NEG models are certain to follow the same fate as the once-heralded neoclassical growth models of the 1960s.
19 This has been encouraged by the common practice of fitting trend lines to log transformations of economic time series.
20 See e.g. Kennedy, 2003; Hendry and Ericsson, 2003.
21 Blinder, 1998: 242.
22 Blanchard, 1997: 246.
23 Eichenbaum, 1997: 236.
24 Taylor, 1997: 233; Blanchard, 1997: 244.
25 Davidson, 1991: 92. See Rowthorn, 1977; Sarantis, 1991; Sarantis and Stewart, 2000; Atesoglu, 1997.
26 Keynes, 1936; 269–70. Moore, 1997.
27 Hicks, 1979.
28 This lies behind the businessman's classical question to the economist: "Have you ever met a payroll?"
29 As Patinkin mildly puts it, "The absence of the asset side of bank balance sheets is a lacuna of great significance" (1956).
30 The author has personally demonstrated this equilibrium "proof" to his students for the past 50 years!

31 The proportional change in income over any period is an identity equal to the proportional change in the money supply plus the proportional change in the income velocity of money over the period. $\dot{Y} \equiv \dot{M} + \dot{V}$, price level.
32 Since price-setting is not coordinated in the economy the AS curve will rise over one-quarter or one year at the rate at which average money wage growth exceeds the average rate of growth of labor productivity: $\dot{p} \equiv \dot{w} + \dot{a}$.
33 To the extent they induce greater investment lower interest rates will result in greater non-volitional saving.
34 For a critique IS–LM see Hicks, 1980; Rotheim, 1981, 1998; Modigliani, 1983; Davidson, 1984, 1994; Solow, 1984, 1990; Darity, 1985; Diamond, 1971, 1988; Fields and Hart, 1990; Blaug, 1997; Chick, 1997b, 2002; Galbraith, 1997.
35 The explanation for the mainstream Monetarist direction of causality from monetary change to income change, historically derives from the Quantity Theory identity: MV=PY. The assumption of monetary exogeneity was more accurate for commodity and fiat money when the quantity of money could be assumed an exogenous government policy instrument. The supply of credit money is assumed to depend on CB open-market operations, which are added-to or subtracted-from the high-powered base. Through the "money multiplier" relationship, a change in the base was held to effect a "multiple" change in the money supply. Historically the supply of credit money was long assumed to be the exogenous instrument of the CB. The level of interest rates was assumed to rise and fall endogenously with changes in the level of income, investment and saving, and with changes in the demand and supply of money.
36 See Kalecki, 1939, 1943, 1971: Diamond, 1971; Phelps 1968; Minsky, 1975; Eckstein, 1969; Bernanke and Blinder, 1988; Bernanke, 1993; Hahn and Solow, 1995; Delaplace and Nell, 1996; Blaug, 1997; Harcourt and Riach, 1997; Fitzgibbons, 1988; Tobin, 1982.
37 Davidson and Weintraub, 1973; Fields and Hart, 1990.
38 Many authors have noted the many difficulties and complications due to possible feedbacks between AD and AS: Hall and Treadgold, 1982; Fields and Hart, 1990, 1998; Barro, 1996; Bhaduri *et al.*, 2003. Collander, 1996, 2000; Krugman, 1996.
39 This was one of Keynes' central insights in Ch. 19 of the *General Theory*. In the short run the level of prices and wages may be taken as predetermined, since wages are sticky downwards. But even if most wages and prices were downwardly flexible, it is incorrect to conclude that wage and price flexibility will be automatically stabilizing. Wage flexibility would lead to a deflationary wage–price spiral, which would significantly raise real interest rates *ex ante*. As a result monetary policy would invariably become restrictive, in spite of the best intentions of the monetary authorities. On these grounds Keynes concluded that stable wages were the best policy. See Solow, 1980, 1998; Moore, 1997.
40 Blinder reported the median pricing period in his questionnaire for the US economy was one year. This makes Fisher Black's vision that economies should be modeled as if all markets are continually in equilibrium more acceptable. If equilibrium is defined as a situation where there is neither excess demand nor excess supply, all markets where sellers are price-setters may be viewed as in "equilibrium," since there is no tendency for prices to change over the period. Since such economies are characterized by excess productive capacity and involuntary unemployment, it is accurate to say that they are demand-constrained (Black, 1987). See Akerlof and Yellen, 1985.
41 Kalecki, 1971; Blinder *et al.*, 1998; Hall, 2003.
42 Keynes, 1936: 156, 161, 163. See also Skidelsky, 2000.
43 Blaug, 1997; Tobin, 2002.

14 Interest Rates and Aggregate Demand

1 Keynes, 1936, Ch. 19.
2 Keynes, 1936, Ch. 2.

3   Keynes, Vol XIV:411; Hall, 2003.
4   *"The outstanding fact is the extreme precariousness of the basis of knowledge on which our estimates of prospective yield have to be made. Our knowledge of the factors which govern the yield of an investment some years hence is usually very slight, and often negligible"* (Keynes, 1936: 149).
5   *The Trade Cycle is best regarded, ..., as being occasioned by a cyclical change in the marginal efficiency of capital. ... which depends not only on the existing abundance or scarcity of capital—goods, and the current cost of production of capital-good, but also on current expectations as to the future yield of capital goods. In the case of durable assets it is therefore natural and reasonable that expectations of the future should play a dominant part in determining the scale on which new investment is deemed advisable. But as we have seen the basis for such expectations is very precarious. Being based on shifting and unreliable evidence they are subject to sudden and violent changes.* (Keynes, 1936: 313–15)
6   By convention a dot over a variable (·) denotes the percentage rate of change. Real output is calculated by deflating nominal GDP by a price index and is sensitive to the accuracy of the price index used. Upward bias in the estimated price level and inflation rate leads to downward bias in the estimate of the level and growth of real output and real wages.
7   Domestic AD deficiency is aggravated by open economy considerations when countries use their own currencies in international trade. As will be shown under the current institutional framework, each country has an incentive to run a current account surplus. But for the system as an accounting identity total surpluses must equal total deficits. In the *General Theory* Keynes argued for lower interest rates which if pushed far enough would result in the *"euthanasia of the rentier"* (Keynes, 1936: 376).
8   This occurred most clearly in the United States during the recent invasion of Iraq when the highly concentrated newspaper and TV networks failed to vigilantly analyze and instead passively acquiesced in the government's flawed case for a "war against terrorism."
9   The textbooks are now at last slowly being revised. A new mainstream textbook by Walsh (2003) and a new monograph by Woodford (2003) recently concluded that CBs now control the overnight interest rate, not the money supply. Neither author referred to the large Post Keynesian literature on monetary endogeneity and interest rate exogeneity.
10 The author has spent the last decade in South Africa where the new Governor of the Reserve Bank has been mandated by the Treasury to target the annual inflation rate at 3–6 percent. Thoroughly indoctrinated by the professional elite of the IMF and the World Bank, he has learned to regard high interest rates as an indicator of a Central Banker's fortitude and machismo. Over the past few years inflation has fallen, due largely to the Reserve Bank's double-digit interest rates, and the Rand has enjoyed the world's highest rate of appreciation. In consequence South Africa currently has the world's highest unemployment rates (30–50%) combined with one of the world's highest real BRs, and a large relative current account deficit.
11 By focusing solely on the final state-change in variables, equilibrium analysis ignores events that occur during the transition process, but disappear when changes cease. See Stock and Watson, 2003; Rogoff, 2003.
12 Blinder, *et al.* 1998; Davidson, 1992.
13 In complex economies there is no "equilibrium" level of income, no "natural" rate of unemployment, no "normal" rate of interest, and no "warranted" rate of growth of output uniquely determined by supply-side forces.
14 Moore, 1988; Thorton, 1983.
15 Taylor, 1993.
16 See Romer and Romer, 2000; Minsky, 1983, 1986; Goodfriend, 1986; Heise, 1991; Cochrane, 1995; Ball, 1999; Campbell, 1999; Crockett, 2000; Fontano, 2000; Campbell and Cocco, 2004; Diamond, 2004.

17 There is a huge literature, on the effects of interest rates on AD. See Keynes, 1938, 1939; Minsky, 1977; Fazzari, 1993; Markin, 1998; Ball, 1999; Poterba, 2002; Mizen, 2003; Stock and Watson, 2003.
18 Keynes prophetically termed this effect the "*euthanasia*" of the rentier.
19 In the United States in the late 1930s the Treasury Bill rate fell to 5–10 basis points, but the bank Prime Lending Rate never fell below 1.5 percent.
20 There is a huge literature on the Japanese experience with cheap money. See, eg., Romer and Fischer, 1986; Blanchard and Sammers, 1987; Ito, 1992; Krugman, 1995; Friedman, 2000; Goodfriend, 2000; Nogami, 2000; Poterba, 2002.
21 In 1989 the value of the land under the Emperor's palace in Tokyo was worth more than the value of all the land in the State of California! (*The Economist*, 1991).
22 The bubble was at root attributable to the Bank of Japan's maintenance of long-term interest rates below the long run growth rate of the economy. The formula for the discounted value of a perpetual income stream (X), growing at the rate g, and discounted at the rate r, is $P = X/(r-g)$. As the real growth rate (g) approaches the real discount rate (r), the value of $(r-g)$ approaches zero, and the theoretical value of P increases indefinitely. As price/earningts ratios rose to unprecedented levels, this provoked increasing fear of ever-larger future capital losses should the growth rate decline in the future or the interest rate be increased. The increased risk of capital losses raises the required rate of return sufficiently to keep asset prices from rising indefinitely.
23 In one month "Black August," stock prices fell by more than 20 percent.
24 Krugman (1995).
25 See Butler,1998; Economic Planning Agency, 2000; Nogami, 2000.
26 Japanese bank accounting is characterized by a serious lack of transparency. Some banks have never recorded price decreases on their portfolios, keeping their assets valued at historical cost, and their net worth artificially high. Lags in calculation and purposeful miscalculation have hidden the huge negative net worth of many banks since the 1990 crash: "*Bad debt held by Japanese banks is far worse than admitted, and has been estimated at nearly $1 trillion, as compared with the official estimate of $620 billion. Each time a financial institution has collapsed in recent years investigators have discovered piles of bad loans stashed in the books of affiliated firms, raising the actual levels of bad debt far above previous disclosures*" (Butler, 1998).
27 See Butler, 1998; Ito, 1992; Hondai, 1998; Nogami, 2000; Bremner, 1998.
28 Keynes himself became pessimistic in the late 1930s of the efficacy of cheap money to stimulate AD. Although a natural economic conservative, he was driven to recommend increased government deficit spending on public goods, the "socialization of investment," as the only effective instrument in major slumps (Keynes, 1936).
29 See Lo and MacKinley, 1988; Thaler, 1993; Tversky, 1992.
30 The difficulty of establishing the "true" price of land without a sales transaction, and the resultant ease of price manipulation played an important role in the fragile and non-transparent nature of Japanese bank balance sheets. During the period of the bubble numerous loans were made against land values whose recipients after the bubble burst turned out to be non-credit-worthy, so the banks were forced to take over the collateralized land. As land prices fell, banks typically neglected to record the drop in the market value of asset prices in their balance sheets, and continued to record their value at historical cost to prevent further erosion of their net worth. Asset values on bank balance sheets are not marked to market, and artificially high prices are frequently sustained on landholdings at the expense of illiquidity. Banks frequently sold smaller properties to one another to establish an artificially high price. Large properties were totally illiquid, and remained without a market.
31 See *The Economist*, December 11, 2004.
32 See Fazzari, 1993. For a summary of the empirical literature see Walsh, 2003.

33 See Cochrane, 1989; Taylor, 1993; Christiano *et al.*, 1996; Bernanke and Woodford, 1997; Evans and Marshall, 1998; Bernanke *et al.*, 1999; Ronner and Ronner, 2000; Clarida *et al.*, 2000, Christiano *et al.*, 1999; and Walsh, 2003; Woodford, 2003.
34 Keynes, 1936: 375.

15 Monetary Policy: Non-Volitional and Volitional Saving

1 Eichenbaum, 1997; Realfonzo, 1998; Berhauke *et al.*, 1999; Sims, 2001; Issing, 2004; Chick, 1984; Colander, 1984.
2 Keynes recognized that saving and investment are *"so defined that they are necessarily equal in amount, being for the community as a whole merely different aspects of the same thing"* (Keynes, 1936: 74). He also recognized that different definitions of investment lead to different definitions of income. But he had not totally freed himself from the false belief that saving and investment could differ under some definitions (74–85). Rather than defining saving as the accounting measure of investment, he argued that saving was a *"two-sided affair."* The attempt to save more or less than current investment would necessarily change incomes *"to a level at which the sums which individuals choose to save add up to a figure exactly equal to the amount of investment"* (1936: 84).
3 Keynes, 1930, II, 351 Translation: If due to union demands average money wages rise more rapidly than the growth rate of average labor productivity, the control of the price level will pass beyond the power of the banking system.
4 Keynes, 1936: 322.
5 Keynes, 1936: 375.
6 Keynes, 1936: 377.
7 Keynes, 1936: 378.
8 Keynes, 1936: 380, 81.
9 Keynes, 1936: 380–1.
10 Keynes, 1936: 375–6.
11 In 2001 the US Federal Reserve, in response to the puncture of the bubble in stock prices and a sharp fall in AD dramatically lowered the federal funds rate to 1.0 percent, the lowest level in 50 years. This was partly due to the fear of possible future deflation if no dramatic actions were taken. Such a fall in AD in effect constitutes a temporary sharp rise in volitional savings ratios. To achieve full employment, CBs must reduce the level of interest rates sufficiently to induce the volume of additional investment spending required for a full employment level of AD. It is appropriate for CBs to lower interest rates rapidly toward zero and attempt to stimulate animal spirits before the slump has persevered too long. Once animal spirits have been severely demoralized, experience suggests it can take decades before full employment can be restored.
12 This is behind the case for central bank independence and the appointment of conservative central bankers with high intolerance for inflation. See Taylor, 1999.
13 Due to its early populist history and extremely strong Premier, the government of Singapore has been successfully able to cultivate the image of a "wise uncle" who can be relied on to act in the best interest of all his people. There is no need for labor unions, since "uncle" looks after workers' employment conditions and needs. In Singapore labor unions are prohibited and striking is illegal. Incomes policy takes the form of centralized collective bargaining. The average rate of annual money wage increases is based on the average rate of labor productivity growth in the previous year. The result is to maintain domestic unit labor costs and prices constant. Imported inflation is suppressed by allowing the exchange rate to appreciate to stabilize import prices, while it is set at a level that encourages sufficient exports to achieve full employment. Banks lend at low nominal rates but are prohibited from lending to foreigners. The Monetary Authority of Singapore is free to set domestic interest rates at a sufficiently low level to realize full employment

AD growth, low inflation, and low unemployment rates. Since its founding in 1965 Singapore's long-run real growth rate has averaged 7 percent, while inflation and unemployment rates have averaged below 1 percent. Such rates would be unthinkable in the absence of a successful income policy.

14   At the other end of the spectrum consider the new South Africa. After years of apartheid suppression, black labor unions have become highly organized, aggressive, resentful, and suspicious of white management as racist. Demands for money wage increases to reduce the black–white wage gap have proven politically impossible for the new Black government to resist. In consequence the Reserve Bank has been forced to maintain high double-digit nominal interest rates, in a losing attempt to restrain wage increases and lower the inflation rate. The unemployment rate has averaged between 30 and 50 percent while money wage increases and inflation rates have averaged 5–10 percent. The depreciation and then appreciation of the Rand have been unprecedentedly volatile, and the growth rate of real per capita income has remained low. It was recently estimated that the "natural" rate of unemployment or (NAIRU) was 40 percent for South Africa.
15   See Goodfriend (2003) for a sympathetic description of how the Fed by its interest rate policy succeeded in reducing US inflation over the period from 1987 to 2000; Gordon, 1988.
16   Mishkin (1995) and Taylor (1995) provide an exposition of the main channels of transmission, and the role of each in the context of the US experience. See Bank of England (2001) for the UK economy.
17   See Arestis and Sawyer, 2004.
18   Under the current international financial architecture, most CB's in developing countries are forced to maintain domestic interest rates at higher levels than rule in foreign financial centers. This is due to the existence of country risk and their desire to accumulate additional reserves when operating in a fixed exchange rate regime, or to prevent their exchange rate from depreciating when operating in a floating exchange rate regime.
19   Anderson, 1995; Barro, 1996; Bernanke *et al.*, 1997; Eichenbaum, 1997; Sims, 2001; Dow, 2004; Meyer, 2001.
20   See Bernanke *et al.*, 1999.
21   See Calvo, 2000; Davidson, 2002; Crockett, 2004.
22   Such "saving" need not be volitional. Most saving is in fact non-volitional.
23   During the 1980s the Federal Reserve reduced interest rates over an extended period while income and investment spending were increasing, although admittedly from a very high initial level.
24   French "Circuit" theorists have traced the flow of money through the economy to reveal the intrinsic endogeneity of money supply changes and the exogeneity of changes in interest rates. See Graziani, 1990; Lavoie, 1992; Rochon, 1999; Parguez, 2001.
25   Moore, 1988.
26   It was recognized that for "target" savers who desire to acquire a particular asset in the future, like a car or house, saving is negatively related to the level of interest rates. But saving was regarded as the demand for future consumption, and the demand for future consumption was believed to be "residual," income not currently consumed. The behavior of target savers simply served to make the supply of saving less interest-elastic. But though total saving is equal to the sum of individual agents, saving it is not determined by saving behavior since saving is the accounting record of investment.
27   Marshall, *Principles*, 1964, Quoted in Keynes, 1936: 242.
28   Keynes, 1936: 167.
29   Central bankers are conventionally perceived as having the duty to remove the punch, bowl when the party threatens to get too lively. But life can be a party. See Gordon, 1981; Solow 1998.
30   The small and super-efficient city-state of Singapore is perhaps the sole exception to this generalization. With its highly disciplined labor force (most unions are forbidden, and striking is not permitted), elite civil service, and "nanny" style of micro-management, the government has been able to design a supremely successful incomes policy. By a

process of centralized collective bargaining between business, labor and government, the average rate of money wage growth in the current year is set equal to the average rate of productivity growth in the previous year. In consequence domestic unit labor costs are held approximately constant. The Singapore economy is extremely open, and its ratio of exports and imports to GDP is well in excess of 100 percent. The Monetary Authority of Singapore (MAS) does not permit completely free capital mobility (firms are not permitted to borrow at low domestic interest rates to invest oversees), and manages the exchange rate at a sufficiently low level to maintain export demand sufficient to produce approximate full employment in the export industries. At the same time the MAS administers the exchange rate to appreciate by an annual amount equal to the rate of imported inflation, to keep import prices constant. In this manner the Singapore authorities have succeeded in freeing themselves from the need to pursue restrictive AD policies to maintain internal and external balance and stabilize unit labor costs. Since its founding in 1959, Singapore has been able to keep domestic interest rates at a sufficiently low level to maintain a sufficiently high level of AD to generate full employment, full capacity utilization, and rapid growth. Since 1960 Singapore has enjoyed average rates of unemployment and inflation below 2 percent, and average rates of growth of real wages and real GDP above 6 percent. Singapore is now termed the "Garden City."
31 Keynes, 1936: 373–6.
32 Davidson, 2002.

16 The Monetary Transmission Process

1 Bank of England, 2000.
2 The argument is identical to that earlier used to establish that saving as the accounting record of investment must be a non-volitional accounting relationship, and not a behavioral relationship.
3 D. Robertson, 1933b; Keynes, 1936: 78.
4 Robust and ebullient investor "animal spirits" and well-defined property rights are essential for the successful performance of market economies (Schultz, 2001).
5 In many respects such a barter model is implicit in the macroeconomic vision of mainstream economics where output is viewed as supply constrained by the production-possibility frontier, and the decision to invest is viewed as accompanied by another unit's volitional decision to save.
6 Keynes recognized that this insight provided theoretical support for the oft-maligned but widespread policy of Mercantilism in early commodity money economies (Keynes, 1936, Ch. 23).
7 When an economic unit spends previously accumulated money balances, the increase in deficit-spending on current output by the borrowing unit is offset to a greater or lesser degree by a decrease in spending by the lending unit. So long as the money supply remains unchanged, the change in AD is due solely to the change in income velocity. If income velocity has a unit root, it is impossible to predict the future change in AD associated with changes in velocity. A long-run positive secular change in AD depends on the presence of a positive secular "drift" in velocity.
8 Moore, 1988, ch. 2.
9 Moore, 1998, ch. 12.
10 Moore, 1988, ch. 12: 290–300.
11 Bernanke and Gertler, 1995; Taylor, 1995, 1999; Docherty, 2005; Dullien, 2004; King, 1994; Loayza and Schmidt-Hebbel, 2002; Woodford, 2003.
12 Moore, 1988, ch. 12: 290–300.
13 Poterba, 2000.
14 Poterba, 2000.

15 See for example, Davidson, 2002: 81.
16 The relation between an increase in volitional saving and a change in investment is more likely to be inverse, since firms respond to a decrease in current AD by reducing investment spending.
17 Keynes, 1936: 210.
18 See Moore, 1994; Chick, 1997a; Cottrell, 1994b; Docherty, 2005.
19 Nelson and Plosser, 1982.
20 This paradox was first put forward in *Horizontalists and Verticalists* (Moore, 1988).
21 Formally, the (t+1)'s represent different time periods and the equality is only apparent.
22 Estimates of money "demand" equations are really estimates of money "supply" relationships. All single-equation empirical estimates of the "demand for money" are thus misspecified. They are in fact estimates of the demand for bank credit (Moore, 1988, 1994).
23 Calvo, 1999; Calvo and Reinhart, 2001; Davidson, 2002.
24 This is the sense in which the "demand" for money is incorrectly analogous to the "demand" for goods. The Quantity Theory treats the "demand for" money as analogous to the demand for goods, although the "demand" for money denotes the "acceptance" of money. The particular term used influences the ease with which propositions are accepted in economics.
25 The idea that money is simply "injected" into the economic system ("money rain" or "helicopter money") is particularly heroic. It implies that the money stock can be changed exogenously without anything else happening, or that if other changes occur, they can be left unspecified because they are on balance unimportant.
26 Moore, 1988, Part I.

17 Using National Currencies in International Trade: The Case for Fixed Exchange Rates

1 Buiter *et al.*, 1998: 22; Tobin, 1996.
2 This process has been termed the *"quest for exchange rate stability in Europe"* (Giavazzi and Giovannini, 1989).
3 This reversal in the US creditor status was as completely unanticipated as the fall in the Berlin wall, or the collapse of communism.
4 See for example, B. Friedman, 1988, 2000.
5 So long as capital budgeting is performed correctly, total saving is identical to investment by definition. The belief that saving is determined by the sum of individual behavioral saving decisions is erroneous. Individual agents are free to decide how much money they wish to hold, and the money supply is equal to the sum of all agents' deposit balances. But the supply of money is *determined* by the demand for bank credit and by the amount of credit granted by the banking system.
6 Feldstein and Horioka, 1980.
7 Davidson has provocatively argued that double-entry bookkeeping which developed along with banking in the late Middle Ages in the Italian merchant states, was the most important economic invention ever developed, since it enabled the organization of production and exchange. Without double-entry bookkeeping, the industrial revolution could never have occurred (Davidson, 2002).
8 A negative current account is conventionally characterized as evidence that a nation is "living beyond its means." When a negative balance persists, conventional wisdom holds that a nation must "tighten its belt" and reduce its expenditures on imports. It is important to note this characterization follows solely from the fact that nations use their national money in international transactions. When countries use a common currency their current account balance become a matter of no importance, as is the case with individual states or provinces in national federal systems, or individual countries in the EMS. Borrowing to finance increased investment goods need not imply profligacy but optimistic expectations of future returns from investment projects.

9   With the advent of multinational corporations a proportion of a nations exports and imports represents the transfer of goods from a subsidiary of a multinational corporation in one country, to a subsidiary in another country. The question then arises at what price should these international shipments be valued? The transfer price need not be a market price, and is frequently arbitrarily set to avoid tax liabilities in the country with the higher tax rates. The transfer price selected will affect the balance of payments of the two countries, and if significant can bias the measures of trade and account balances.
10 See Davidson, 2002.
11 If all countries were to use the same money, the world could be analyzed as a single economy. The $S = I$ identities hold for the world economy as a closed accounting system.
12 Since exports are sold to foreign agents and so exit the economy the composition of exports is of no significance for the level of domestic capital formation. Conventional National Income Accounting is appropriate for exports since capital budgeting need not be applied to export goods.
13 Since most countries are demand-constrained, from the viewpoint of the world economy the appropriate policy response would be for center economies to lower their interest rates, and encourage additional debt-financed capital formation.
14 Keynes argued that the one-sided pressure on deficit nations to reduce AD and "tighten their belts," with no corresponding equivalent pressure on surplus nations to expand AD, produces a global deflationary bias that depresses AD and reduces the well-being of all nations, including trading partners with current surpluses.
15 Johnson, 1976: 16.
16 The "monetary approach to the balance of payments" is based on the validity of the classical axioms of "ergodicity," "gross substitutability," and "neutrality of money." See for example, Calvo, 2002, Calvo and Reinhart, 2001; Davidson, 2002, and Crockett, 2004.
17 This is the "Marshall–Lerner" condition.
18 There is no predetermined path along which the economy "tends," no positions of conditional "equilibrium" which possess the stability properties of conventional neoclassical equilibrium, and no "states of rest" that the economy can "get into." Change is continuous.
19 Keynes, 1934: 262.
20 Kalecki, 1971.
21 Keynes, 1936: 262.
22 Keynes, 1936: 263.
23 Keynes, 1936: 335.
24 Keynes, 1936: 341.
25 Keynes, 1936: 335–6. Many modern governments fear that deliberately stimulating domestic AD may unleash inflationary forces. For this reason export-led growth is regarded as a much more desirable alternative path for expanding domestic employment.
26 Keynes, 1936: 338–9.
27 Keynes, 1936: 339.
28 Davidson, 2002.
29 Keynes, 1936: 339, 349. Keynes was here incorrect. Flexible exchange rates are even more efficacious in setting each country's advantage at variance with its neighbors.
30 Keynes, 1936: 382–3.
31 Keynes' immediate reply to the Minister of Information, commenced with the pungent comment,

> Your department think that they are making a good joke at Funk's expense by saying "gold will have no place in this brave new world" and quoting German propaganda to the effect that "gold will no longer control the destinies of a nation," etc. Well obviously I am not the man to preach the beauties and merits of the pre-war gold standard. In my opinion about three-quarters of the passages quoted from the German broadcasts would be quite

excellent if the name of Great Britain were substituted for Germany or the Axis, as the case may be. If Funk's plan is taken at its face value, it is excellent and just what we ourselves should be thinking of doing. Keynes, Vol. XXV Activites 1940–4 Shaping the Postwar World – The Clearing Union, 21–22.

32 The various permutations of Keynes' ideas on international monetary reform, finalized in his proposal for an International Clearing Union, are documented at length in Keynes CW XXV, 1980; See Tobin, 1995, 2003.
33 Keynes, Vol. XXV.
34 Keynes, Vol. XXV, 22–23.
35 Keynes, Vol. XXV, 23.
36 Keynes, Vol. XXV, 23.
37 Keynes, Vol. XXV, 23.
38 For a brilliant and incisive summary of this struggle, see Skidelsky, 2000.
39 This entire project at playing the role of the world's "Philosopher King" must have given Keynes enormous personal satisfaction. Yet with hindsight wisdom the economics profession and the world would have been better served had he diverted his talent and creative energies to rewriting the *General Theory* for an open economy.
40 This section is indebted to the summary of Bretton Woods by Cooper, 1984.
41 The French under De Gaulle were the irritating exception since they refused to play by the rules. Whenever France received net US Dollars, De Gaulle hastened to convert them into gold.
42 Edwards, 1999, 2001.
43 Gordon, 1988; Adelman, 1991, 1999.

18 Using National Currencies in International Transactions: The Case for Flexible Exchange Rates

1 Begg and Wyplosz, 1993: 31.
2 Calvo, 2000; Calvo and Reinhart, 2001; Broda, 2001.
3 Friedman, 1953.
4 IMF, 1974.
5 See for example, Dornbusch, 1976; Galbraith, 1990; Eichengreen, 1994; Krugman, 1996; Obstfeld and Rogoff, 1995; Tobin, 1998; Davidson, 1999a, 2002; Crockett, 2004.
6 Dornbusch, 1976; Obstfeld and Rogoff, 1995; Buiter *et al.*, 1998, Davidson, 1999a; Frankel and Rose, 1999; Arestis and Sawyer, 2002
7 The gold standard that worked so well in the nineteenth century did not prevent chaos and depression in the 1930s. Eichengreen has plausibly argued that the credibility and cooperation that were strong in the period of the classical gold standard, had largely disappeared by the 1930s. For exchange rate stability market participants must believe current exchange rates are sustainable and are supported by official policy (Eichengreen, 1994).
8 Crockett, 2004: 26–8.
9 Crockett, 2004.
10 Stiglitz, 1989: 102–3; Obstfeld and Rogoff, 1995.
11 *"Even among by brightest economic students, three quarters believe they are in the top half of the class"* (Stiglitz, 1989).
12 Stiglitz, 1989: 106; Potenba and Summers, 2002.
13 Robbins, 1932: 101.
14 Keynes, 1936: 160, 172.
15 Schiller, 1981, 1990; Campbell, 1989, 2005; Welch, 2000; Osler, 2005; Sheffrin, 2002; Thalor, 1993, 1999, 2003; Toporowski, 2005.
16 This case will be developed in Chapter 19.
17 Crockett, 2004: 26–8.

18 Keynes' analysis makes clear that the huge current account deficits of the United States throughout the 1990s have provided a critically important direct stimulus to AD in the rest of the world. The huge US deficits have prevented the world from falling into even deeper recession and unemployment than has occurred.
19 Keynes, CW XXV, 1980, Proposals for an International Currency Union, 1941: 42.
20 Keynes, CW XXV, 1980, Proposals for an International Currency Union, 1941: 87. There has recently developed a new 'Behavioral' analysis of capital markets, and a recognition that exchange rates and stock prices fluctuate endogenously. See, Haugen, 1999; Schiefer, 1999, 2000: 10; Shiller, 2000; Sornette, 2003; Kahnemann, 2000, 2003a, 2003b; Welch, 2000; Sheffrin, 2002; Toporowski, 2005.
21 This situation describes the case of South Africa today (Tversky 1992, 1995, 2000, 2003, 2005), where the measured unemployment rate is 30 percent, on the strict definition that the unemployed must be looking for work, and 40 percent dropping the work-seeking criterion. Despite such high unemployment rates the SA Reserve Bank feels compelled to keep nominal and real interest rates high relative to rates in the center, on the grounds that its directive from the government is to hit its inflation target, 3–6 percent. The current inflation rate has fallen to 4–5 percent, due in part to the doubling of the value of the Rand over the past two years. The differential between domestic short term rates, 8–10 percent, and short term rates in the center, 2–3 percent implies that for interest rate parity, the Rand must appreciate to a sufficiently high level, so that it is expected to depreciate by 6–7 percent over the next year. In such situations, when inflation is primarily cost inflation and high unemployment rates have little deterring effect on wage settlements, the practice of "inflation targeting" serves primarily to maintain a high level of nominal interest rates, and keep the economy permanently below its full capacity frontier.
22 In South Africa the Marginal Propensity to Import (MPM) exceeds 100 percent during booms. Ben Smit, Director, Bureau of Economic Research (BER), Stellenbosch University.
23 As argued in Chapter 17 the importation of capital goods, because it represents an increase in domestic capital formation, constitutes an increase rather than a decrease in national saving.
24 Data limitations required excluding a small number of LDC countries in each regression, as indicated in Table 18.1.
25 Somewhat surprisingly although these ratios are closely interrelated (since foreign exchange reserves are the accumulation of past balance of payments surpluses and deficits), for this particular 20-year sample period the two proxies evidence considerable statistical independence. Usually only one was statistically significant in explaining the relationships of interest.
26 A lower Balance of Payments/Imports ratio, and a lower Foreign Exchange/Imports ratio indicate a greater degree of external imbalance.
27 From inspection of the scatter diagrams, outliers with 20-year average nominal bank rate in excess of 25 percent were excluded from the regression. These were South American countries that had experienced massive hyperinflation over the period, and in consequence had extremely high nominal interest rates, and extremely low real interest rates.

19 Using a Common Currency in International Transactions: The Post Keynesian Case for No Exchange Rates

1 Current account imbalances among units using a common currency become such a nonissue that as in the United States individual state balance of payments are unknown and not generally reported in government statistics.
2 If there were more than one branch bank, some banks would run surpluses and others deficits of identical amounts. Deficit banks finance their deficits by borrowing from

(selling their short-term CD's to) surplus banks. Total bank assets and liabilities are larger in multiple bank systems than in the case of a single banks, due to interbank lending and borrowing.
3 Individual branches in a branch banking system, or individual geographic areas do not have total loans equal to total deposits. From the head office point of view surpluses and deficits of individual branches balance out. The use of separate national moneys is as if individual branches in a branch banking system decided each to use their own currency. If they did, they could no longer behave as net debtors, no matter to what extent their deficits were structural, and were due solely to an excess of economic units in that geographic area who desire to deficit-spend, over those who decide to surplus-spend because they anticipated higher returns on their investment projects.
4 The view that governments are responsible for creating money is termed Chartalism. See Keynes, 1930, Vol. 1. Commercial banks, by gaining and maintaining their depositors' absolute confidence that their "demand" deposits will be exchanged into legal tender fiat money "on demand," and by offering a host of transactions services attractive to wealth owners, have been able to confer "moneyness" (general acceptability in exchange) on their deposit liabilities, and so are able to reap seignorage income from the issue of credit money.
5 Over the past few decades more and more children from all over the world are being taught English. English is increasingly accused of taking on a hegemonic character as it tends to "beat up on" smaller languages. In consequence governments frequently decide that the "home" language needs official protection to help it survive, *vide* the extreme measures taken to support French in Canada, and Afrikaans in South Africa. In the year 1000 who would have predicted that English, the language spoken by the inhabitants of a wet miserable little island off the coast of Europe, would one day be the indispensable language of global business and the world language of choice?
6 It has been estimated that the world now has more than 6800 distinct languages. Well over 500 are currently close to extinction with only a few elderly speakers left. All experts agree that in 100 years the number will be much smaller, but disagree widely by how much. Some experts expect that in 100 years about 90 percent will be gone, and that in a few centuries the world will be left with less than 200 tongues (*The Economist*, January 1, 2005: 58–60).
7 The same logic applies to moneys. Language is a much more important social convention than money, as evidenced by the fact that the 15 members of the European Union agreed to have 1 money, but to retain 11 different official languages. Regulation No. 1 of the European Commission states that it will accommodate any member's official language. But again there is a paradox. Even though nationalistic and emotional concerns are more intense for languages than for money, many countries continue to use the language of their former colonial rule but reject its currency, on the nationalistic grounds that an important country must have its own money. In many cases the language an individual country speaks appears to be valued primarily out of national pride.
8 There is one important problem faced by domestic economies that characterizes international lending, which even when ruled illegal has proven extremely difficult to eliminate. This is the problem of "redlining" where lending officers use different credit standards for different borrowers based on their ethnic, racial or locational characteristics, and not on the innate quality of the borrowers' loan requests. This same problem characterizes international lending to individual borrowers in debtor countries.
9 Consider the very different experience of currency boards in Hong Kong and Argentina. Hong Kong, with a strong position in each of the above criteria, has been able to maintain its currency board with relatively little pressure, and much less cost in terms of domestic economic growth, than has Argentina.
10 See for example, Cooper, 1984.
11 Cooper, 1984.

12 Cooper, 1984: 184.
13 Rogoff, 2001.
14 Alesina and Barro, 2000, 2001.
15 Rose, 2000a.
16 Rose and van Wincoop, 2001.
17 McCallum, 1995; Helliwell, 1998.
18 See Clarida, Gali and Gertler, 2000; Calvo and Reinhart, 2001, 2002; McCallum, 2001; Meyer, 2001; Arestis and Sawyer, 2002.
19 This problem is known in macroeconomics as "goal inconsistency," the inability to attain simultaneously internal and external balance. But "goal inconsistency" is incorrectly viewed as the natural outcome of market forces. The external balance constraint is solely attributable to the use of national currencies for international transactions.
20 His post-*General Theory* views on open economies have not yet been sufficiently absorbed by mainstream scholars (Keynes, CW, XXV, 1980).
21 Keynes, 1936: 262.
22 Keynes, 1936: 263.
23 Keynes, 1936: 335.
24 Keynes, 1936: 341.
25 Keynes, 1936: 335–6. Many modern governments fear that deliberately stimulating domestic AD will unleash inflationary forces, so export-led growth is widely regarded as a desirable alternative path for expanding domestic employment.
26 Keynes, 1936: 338–9.
27 Davidson, 2001; Bhaduri, 2003.
28 Keynes, 1936: 339.
29 Keynes, 1936: 349. Keynes was incorrect since there was then very little experience with exchange rates. Flexible exchange rates are equally efficacious at setting each country's advantage at variance with its neighbors.
30 Keynes, 1936: 382–3.
31 The huge current account deficits of the United States throughout the 1990s have operated as a direct stimulus to AD in the rest of the world, and have prevented the world from falling into even deeper recession.
32 Keynes, CW XXV, 1980, Proposals for an International Currency Union, 1941: 42.
33 Keynes, CW XXV, 1980, Proposals for an International Currency Union, 1941: 87.
34 Alesina and Barro, 2000.
35 See Ponsot, 2002.
36 See for example, Grubel, 1999, 2000.
37 Grubel, 2000; Hanke and Schuler, 1994; Schuler, 1999.
38 Goodhart, 1995; Dowd and Greenway, 1993; Buiter, 1997; Alesina, et al. 2000; Guosch et al., 2000; Rose, 2000a; Rose, 2000b; Cerba, 2001; Dornbusch, 2001; Rose and Winccop, 2001; Magendzo, 2002.
39 Europe no longer has a serious external balance constraint, since its external trade has fallen substantially as a proportion of its GDP. It could eliminate virtually all exchange rate risk if the European Central Bank (ECB) were to enter into an agreement with the Federal Reserve System to keep the Euro/$ rate constant. Europe's current difficulty is that the ECD is mandated by statute to maintain price stability as its sole objective, without the area first having adopted any sort of incomes policy. Since prices are cost- determined, and wages are the most important cost, the ECB must keep interest rates sufficiently high to maintain AD in the economy sufficiently below the level of full employment output to ensure that money wage increases do not exceed the rate of average labor productivity growth. Providing the ECB can focus on internal balance and full employment its potential will be assured. One possible future problem is that the German inflation rate has been below that of the Euro area, so Germany's export prices are lower and its rate of export growth is more rapid than its Euro partners.
40 "Economics Focus: Growing Apart" *The Economist*, October 2, 2004: 78.

41 This occurred in the origins of the US Federal Reserve System, which blended separate regions of the country, and banks subject to diverse state banking jurisdictions into a single system. But it occurred within the confines of a single country.
42 See Helliwell, 1996, 1998; McCallum, 1995; Calvo, 1999; Grubel, 1999; Schuler, 1999; Bogetic, 2000; Cohen, 2000; Weintraub, 2000; Calvo and Reinhart, 2001; Dellas and Tavlas, 2001; Salvatore, 2001; Studart, 2001; Douglas and Vives, 2002; Edwards and Magendzo, 2002; Klein, 2002; Ize and Yeyati, 2003; Jameson, 2003.
43 In the case of Canada, the emotional desire to remain independent of the United States is the major political obstacle. See Grubel, 2000.
44 Alesina and Barro, 2001.
45 This has already been raised for South America by some US Congressmen. See Schuler, 1999; Grubel, 2000.
46 Edwards and Magendzo, 2002, 2003.
47 Grubel, 2000.
48 E & M did not explicitly acknowledge the Keynesian benefits from using a common currency. With no exchange rates, countries are no longer forced to accept internal imbalance and to depress domestic AD to achieve external balance.
49 Dornbusch, 2001. See also Hanke and Schuler, 1994; Calvo, 2000; Gosh et al., 2000.

20 Financial Barriers to Demand-led Growth

1 Keynes, 1936: 250.
2 Keynes, 1936: 249–50.
3 See, for example, Setterfield, 1995, 1997a, 1997b, 1997c, 1998, 2002.
4 Solow, 1956: 312; Robinson, 1956; Durlauf and Quak, 1999; Mankiw 1992.
5 See Long and Plosser, 1985.
6 McCallum, 1988: 464.
7 Mankiw, 1985, 1996; Barro, 1994, 1996.
8 Romer, 1986, 1990, 1994; Lucas, 1975, 1988; Scott, 1989.
9 This process was anticipated by Kaldor, 1957. See Tobin, 1972; Kaldor, 1972, 1996; Lucas, 1975, 1988; Long and Plosser, 1983.
10 King, 1993: 70.
11 Palley, 2002: 30; Romer, 1994; Schultz, 2001.
12 Easterly and Pritchett, 1993.
13 Easterly and Pritchett, 1993: 40.
14 Easterly and Pritchett, 1993: 40. See Barro and Lee, 1994.
15 See Cornwall, 1972, 1980, 1991, 1994; Cornwall and Cornwall, 2001; Setterfield, 2002.
16 The recognition that most firms are price-setters and quantity-takers so the AS relationship is horizontal in price- and inflation-output space, make it clear why the supply elasticity to changes in demand is unity.
17 Kaldor, 1972, 1981; Hahn, 1989.
18 Thirwall, 1979, 1997; McCombie and Thirwall, 1994, 1997; Blecker, 1998.
19 Cornwall, 1970, 1980. See also Pasinetti, 1981; Petit, 1986.
20 Nell, 1992, 2002; Davidson, 1990.
21 Setterfield, 2002.
22 Setterfield, 2002: 4.
23 Kalecki, 1971: 165.
24 See for example, Atesoglu, 1997, 2002: 55–63.
25 Solow, 1988: xiv.
26 Here is Paul Theroux's vivid description in his book *Dark Safari*: of his recent return to Africa, where he had worked for five years in the 1960s as a teacher in Malawi and Uganda

> All news out of Africa is bad. It made me want to go there, though not for the horror, the hot spots, the massacre-and-earthquake stories you read in the newspaper. I wanted the pleasure

of being in Africa again. ... Africa is now materially more decrepit than it was when I first knew it—hungrier, poorer, less educated, more pessimistic, more corrupt. ... Africans, less esteemed than ever, seemed to me the most lied to people on earth—manipulated by their governments, burned by foreign experts, befooled by charities and cheated at every turn. ... To be an African leader was to be a thief. ... But evangelists stole people's innocence, and self-serving aid agencies gave them false hope, which seemed worse. In reply Africans dragged their feet, or tried to emigrate, they begged, they pleaded, they demanded money and gifts with a rude, weird sense of entitlement. ... Not that Africa is one place. It is an assortment of motley republics and seedy chiefdoms. (Theroux, 2003: 1)

27 N Theron, PhD. Stellenbosch University, 2003.
28 Schumpeter, 1934; Thirwall, 1979, 2001; Lucas, 1988, 1990; Easterly and Pritchett, 1993; Durlauf, 1999; Denton, 2002, 2004; Sali-i-Martin, 2003.
29 Assume that the money supply were to grow at the same rate in both Low Income and High Income economies. Assume also that velocity follows a random walk, the expected change in velocity is zero in both economies, and that deficit spending financed by new bank credit is the sole reason why AD increases in both economies that even if the increase in the money supply due to bank credit-financed deficit-spending resulted in an equal increase in AD in both economies, because of greater financial deepening, the percentage growth in AD would be greater in High Income economies than in Low Income economies so their growth rate will be higher. Since financial deepening is greater in High Income economies than in Low Income economies, the ratio of M/Y and $\Delta M/\Delta Y$ will be greater in High Income economies. If the ratio of financial deepening were 1.0 in High Income economies, and 0.2 in Low Income economies. If bank loans financed all deficit spending on investment goods in both economies and if the money supply and bank credit grew by 10 percent in both economies, the rate of growth of AD in High Income economies would be 10 percent, while in Low Income economies the growth rate would be 2 percent.

Bibliography

Adelman, Irma (1991) "Should there be a Marshall Plan for Eastern Europe?" in Paul Davidson and Jan Kregel (eds) *Economic Problems of the 1990s: Europe, the Developing Countries and the United States*, Aldershot, UK, Edward Elgar.

Adelman, I., (1999) "The Role of Government in Economic Development," *University of California Department of Agricultural and Resource Economics and Policy (CUDARE)* Working Paper, 890, May, 28.

Akerlof, George, and Yellen, Janet (1985) "A Near-Rational Model of the Business Cycle, with Wage and Price Inertia," in Gregory Mankiw and Romer David (eds) (1991) *New Keynesian Economics*. Vol 1. *Imperfect Competition and Sticky Prices*, Cambridge MA. MIT Press.

Alesina, Alberto, and Barro, Robert, (2000) Currency Unions, *National Bureau of Economic Research* (Cambridge, MA) Working Paper, No. 7927, September.

Alesina, Alberto, and Barro, Robert, (2001) "Dollarization," *American Economic Review*, May, 91 (2), 381–5.

Alesina, Alberto, Spolaore, Enrico, and Wacziarg, Romain, (2000) "Economic Integration and Political Disintegration," *American Economic Review*, December, 90 (5), 1276–96.

Andersen, Palle, and Gruen, David (1995) "Macroeconomic Policies and Growth," in Palle Andersen, Dwyer Jacqueline, and Gruen David (eds) *Productivity and Growth*, Sydney, Reserve Bank of Australia, 279–319.

Andrews, Paul W. (1949) *Manufacturing Business*, London, MacMillan.

Arestis, P., and Howells, P.G.A. (1996) "Theoretical Reflections on Endogenous Money: The Problem with "Convenience Lending," *Cambridge Journal of Economics*, 20, 539–51.

Arestis, Philip, and Howells, Peter (2002) "The 1520–1640 'Great Inflation' An Early Case of Controversy on the Nature of Money," *Journal of Post Keynesian Economics*, 24 (2), 181–203.

Arestis, Philip, and Sawyer, Malcolm (2002) "An Evaluation of the Tobin Transactions Tax," in Sheila Dow and John Hillard (eds) *Beyond Keynes*, Vol. 2, *Keynes, Uncertainty and the Global Economy*, Chelyenham, UK, Edward Elgar.

Arestis, Philip, and Sawyer, Malcolm (2004) "On the Effectiveness of Monetary Policy and of Fiscal Policy," *Review of Social Economy*, December, 62 (4), 441–63.

Arestis, Philip, and Sawyer, Malcolm (2005) "The Nature and Role of Monetary Policy when Money is Endogenous," *Cambridge Journal of Economics*, forthcoming.

Arestis, Philip, Baddeley, Michelle, and McCombie, John (2005) *The New Monetary Policy: Implications and Relevance*, Cheltenham, UK, Edward Elgar.

Asimalopulos, Athanasios (1983) "Kalecki and Keynes on Finance, Investment and Saving," in Malcolm Sawyer (ed.) (1999) *The Legacy of Michal Kalecki*. Vol. 2, Cheltenham, UK. Elgar.

Atesoglu, Sonmez (1997) "A Post Keynesian Explanation of U.S. Inflation," *Journal of Post Keynesian Economics*, Summer, 19 (4), 639–49.

Atesoglu, Sonmez (2002) "Growth and Fluctuations in the USA: A Demand-Oriented Explanation," in Mark Setterfield (ed.) *The Economics of Demand-led Growth: Challenging the Supply-Side Vision of the Long Run*. Cheltenham, UK, Edward Elgar.

Bachelard, Gaston (1994) *Water and Dreams: An Essay on the Imagination of Matter*, Dallas, TX, Dallas Institute Publications.

Backhaus, Juergen (ed.) (2005) *Entrepreneurship, Money and Coordination*, Cheltenham, UK, Edward Elgar.

Backhouse, Roger (2000) *Macroeconomics and the Real World*, Vol. 2, Oxford, Oxford University Press.

Baker, Dean (1997) (ed.) "Does the CPI Overstate Inflation?," in D. Baker, *An Analysis of the Boskin Commission Report. Getting Prices Right: The Debate over the Consumer Price Index*. Armonk, NY and London, Sharpe, 1998, 79–155.

Ball, Laurence (1999) "Aggregate Demand and Long-term Unemployment," *Brookings Papers on Economic Activity*, 2, 189–236.

Barro, Robert (1996) *Getting It Right: Markets and Choices in a Free Society*, Cambridge, MIT Press.

Barro, Robert, and Lee, Jong-Wha (1994) "Losers and Winners in Economic Growth," in Bruno, Michael and Pleskovic, Boris (ed.) *Proceedings of the World Bank Annual Conference on Development Economics*, Washington, DC, World Bank, 267–97.

Bhadhuri, Amit, and Dutt, Amitava (2003) "Selling the Family Silver or Privatization for Capital Inflows: The Dual Dynamics of the Balance of Payments and the Exchange Rate," in Ros, Jaime (ed.) *Development Economics and Structuralist Macroeconomics*, Cheltenham, UK, Edward Elgar, 169–78.

Begg, David, and Wyplosz, Charles (1993) *Making Sense of Subsidiarity: How Much Centralization for Europe?* Monitoring European Integration Series, Vol. 4, London, Centre for Economic Policy Research.

Berg, Andrew, and Borensztein, Eduardo (2000) "The Dollarization Debate," *Finance and Development*, 37 (1), 38–41.

Bernanke, Ben (1993) "Credit in the Macroeconomy," *Federal Reserve Bank of New York Quarterly Review*, Spring, 18, 50–70.

Bernanke, Ben, and Blinder, Alan (1988) "Credit Money and Aggregate Demand," *American Economic Review*, Papers and Proceedings, May, 7 (2), 435–9.

Bernanke, Ben, and Gertler, Mark, (1995) "Inside the Black Box: The Credit Channel of Monetary Transmission," *Journal of Economic Perspectives*, 9, Fall, 27–48.

Bernanke, Ben, and Woodford, Michael (1997) "Inflation Forecasts and Monetary Policy," *Journal of Money, Credit and Banking*, November, 29 (4), part 2, 653–84.

Bernanke, Ben, Laubach, Thomas, Mishkin, Frederick, and Posen, Adam (1999) *Inflation Targeting: Lessons from the International Experience*, Princeton, NJ, Princeton University Press.

Bernheim, D., and Shoven, John (eds) (1991) *National Saving and Economic Performance*, Chicago, IL, University of Chicago Press.

Bhadhuri, Amit, and Dutt, Amitava (2003) "Selling the Family Silver or Privatization for Capital Inflows: The Dual Dynamics of the Balance of Payments and the Exchange Rate," in J. Ros, Jaime (ed.) *Development Economics and Stucturalist Macroeconomics*, Cheltenham, UK, Edward Elgar, 169–78.

Bibow, Jorg (2000) "The loanable funds fallacy in retrospect," *History of Political Economy*, 32 (4), 790–831.

Bibow, Jorg (2004) "Reflections on the Current Fashion for Central Bank Independence," *Cambridge Journal of Economics*, 28 (4), 549–76.

Bils, Mark (1987) "The Cyclical Behavior of Marginal Cost and Price," *American Economic Review*, December 77, 838–55.

Black, Fisher (1986) "Noise," *Journal of Finance*, 41, 529–43.

Black, Fisher (1987) *Business Cycles and Equilibrium*, New York, Blackwell.

Black, Fisher (1995) *Exploring General Equilibrium*, Cambridge, MA, MIT Press.

Blanchard, Oliver (1990) "Why does Money Affect Output? A Survey," in Ben Friedman, and Frank Hahn (eds) *Handbook of Monetary Economics*, Amsterdam, North-Holland, 779–835.

Blanchard, Oliver (1997) "Is There a Core of Usable Macroeconomics?," *American Economic Review*, May, 87 (2), 244–6.

Blanchard, Oliver, and Summers, Laurence (1987) "Hysteresis in Umnemployment," *European Economic Review*, 31(2), 288–95.

Blaug, Mark (1997) "Ugly Currents in Modern Economics," *Opinions Politiques*, September, 3–8.

Blecher, Robert A. (1998) "International Competitiveness, Relative Wages and the Balance of Payments Constraint," *Journal of Post Keynesian Economics*, 20, 495–526.

Blinder, Alan (1997) "Is There a Core of Practical Macroeconomics That We should All Believe?," *American Economic Review*, May, 87 (2), 240–3.
Blinder, Alan, Canetti, E., Lebow, D., and Rudd, J. (1998) *Price Stickiness in the United States*, New York, Russel Sage.
Boehm-Bawerk, (1923) (Innsbruck, 1912) *The Positive Theory of Capital* (translated by William Smart), New York, Stechert.
Bogetic, Zelijko (2000) "Full Dollarization: Fad or Future?," *Challenge*, March/April, 43(2), 17–48.
Bordo, Michael and Eichengreen, Barry (1993) *A Retrospective on the Bretton Woods System: Lessons for International Monetary Reform*, NBER Project Report, Chicago, University of Chicago Press.
Boskin, Michael, and Baker, Dean (ed.) (1998) "Toward a More Accurate Measure of the Cost of Living," in *Getting Prices Right: The Debate Over the Consumer Price Index*, Armonk, NY Sharpe, 5–77.
Boskin, M., Dulberger, E.R., Gordon, R.J., Griliches, Z., and Jorgenson, D.W. (1998a) "Consumer Prices, the Consumer Price Index and the Cost of Living," *Journal of Economic Perspectives*, 12 (1), 3–26.
Bradford, David (1990) "What is National Saving? Alternative Measures in Historical and International Context," NBER Working Papers 3341.
Bradford, David (1991) "Market Value versus Financial Accounting Measures of National Savings," in *Taxation, Wealth and Saving*, Cambridge, MA, MIT Press.
Bradford, David (2000) *Market Value versus Financial Accounting Measures of National Savings*. Cambridge, MA, MIT Press.
Brealy, Richard, (1972) *An Introduction to the Risk and Return From Common Stocks*, Oxford, Blackwell.
Brealey, Richard (1991) *Principles of Corporate Finance*, New York, McGraw-Hill.
Brealey, Richard, and Myers, Stuart (1983) *An Introduction to Risk and Return from Common Stocks*.
Broda, Christian (2001) "Coping with Terms-of-Trade Shocks: Pegs Versus Floats," *American Economic Review*, May, 91 (2), 376–80.
Brock, William (1993) "Pathways to Randomness in the Economy: Emergent Nonlinearity and Chaos in Economics and Finance," *Estudios Económicos*, 8, 3–55.
Bruno, Michael, and Easterly, William (1998) "Inflation Crises and Long Run Growth," *Journal of Monetary Economics*, 41 (1), 3–26.
Buiter, Willem (1997) "The Economic Case for Monetary Union in the European Union," *Review of International Economics*, 5 (4), 10–35.
Buiter, W., Corsetti, G., and Pesenti, P., (1998) *Financial Markets and European Monetary Cooperation*, Cambridge, Cambridge University Press, 179.
Calvo, Guillermo (1999) "Inflation Stabilization and BOP Crises in Developing Countries," in John Taylor and Michael Woodford (eds) *Handbook of Macroeconomics*, Amsterdam, New York, Elsevier Science, North-Holland, 1531–614.
Calvo, Guillermo (2002) "On Dollarization," *Economics of Transition*, 10 (2), 393–403.
Calvo, Guillermo, and Mendoza, Enrique (2000) "Contagion, Globalization and the Volatility of Capital Flows," in Sebastion Edwards (ed.) *Capital Flows and the Emerging Economies: Theory, Evidence and Controversies*, Chicago, University of Chicago Press.
Calvo, Guillermo, and Rheinhart, C. (2001) "Reflections on Dollarization," in A. Alesina and R. Barro (eds) *Currency Unions*, Stanford, Hoover Institute Press.
Calvo, Guillermo, and Reinhart, Carmen (2002) "Fear of Floating," *Quarterly Journal of Economics*, 117 (2), 378–408.
Campbell, John (1995) "Some Lessons from the Yield Curve," *Journal of Economic Perspectives*, Summer, 9(3), 129–52.
Campbell, John (1996) "Consumption and the Stock Market: Interpreting International Experience," NBER Working Papers 5610.
Campbell, John (1999) "Asset Prices, Consumption and the Business Cycle," in John Taylor and Michael Woodford (eds) *Handbook of Macroeconomics*, 1C, Amsterdam, Elsevier, 1231–303.

Campbell, John, and Cocco, Joao (2005) "How Do House Prices Affect Consumption? Evidence from Micro Data," NBER Working Papers 11535.
Campbell, John, and Mankiw, Gregory (1987) "Permanent and Transitory Components in Macroeconomic Fluctuations," *AEA Papers and Proceedings*, 77, May, 111–17.
Campbell, John, and Mankiw, Gregory (1989) "Consumption, Income and Interest Rates: Reinterpreting the Time Series Evidence," NBER Macroeconomics Annual, Cambridge, MA, MIT Press.
Campbell, John, and Shiller, Robert (1989) "The Dividend-Price Ratio and Expectations of Future Dividends and Discount Factors," in A. Lo (ed.) (1997) *Market Efficiency: Stock Market Behavior in Theory and Practice*, Cheltenham, UK, Edward Elgar.
Campos, Julia, Ericsson, Neil, and Hendry, David (eds) (2005) *General-to-Specific Modelling*, 2 Vols, Cheltenham, UK, Edward Elgar.
Cannan, E. (1921) "The Meaning of Bank Deposits," *Economica*, 1 (1), 28–36.
Cartwright, Nancy (1999) *The Dappled World: A Study of the Boundaries of Science*, Cambridge, Cambridge University Press.
Caserta, M., and Chick, Victoria (1997) "Provisional Equilibrium and Macroeconomic Theory," in P. Arestis, G. Palma, and M.C. Sawyer (eds), *Markets, Employment and Economic Policy: Essays in Honour of G.C. Harcourt*, Vol. 2, London, Routledge, 223–37.
Cecchetti, S.G. (2000) "Making Monetary Policy," *Oxford Review of Economic Policy*, 16 (4), 43–59.
Cencini, A., (1995) *Monetary Theory: National and International*, London, Routledge.
Charemza, W.W., and Deadman, D.F. (1997) *New Directions in Econometric Practice: General to Specific Modelling, Cointegration and Vector Autoregression*, 2nd edn, Cheltenham, UK, Edward Elgar.
Chick, Victoria (1984) "Monetary Increases and their Consequences: Streams, Backwaters and Floods," in Phillip Arestis and Sheila Dow (eds) (1992) *On Money, Method and Keynes*, New York, St Martins Press.
Chick, Victoria (1986) "The Evolution of the Banking System and the Theory of Saving, Investment and Interest," *Economies et Societes*, 'Monnaie et Production', 3, 95–110.
Chick, Victoria (1997a) "The Multiplier and Finance," in G.C. Harcourt and P.A. Raich (eds) *A Second Edition of the General Theory*, London, Routledge, 154–72.
Chick, Victoria (1997b) "Order out of Chaos in Economics", in S.C. Dow and J. Hillard (eds) *Keynes, Knowledge and Uncertainty*, Cheltenham, UK, Edward Elgar, 25–42.
Chick, Victoria (1998a) "A Struggle to Escape: Equilibrium in the General Theory," in S. Sharma (ed.) *John Maynard Keynes: Keynesianism into the Twenty-first Century*, Cheltenham, UK, Edward Elgar, 40–50.
Chick, Victoria (1998b) "On Knowing One's Place: Formalism in Economic Theory," *Economic Journal*, 108, 1859–69.
Chick, Victoria (2000) "Money and Effective Demand," in Smithin, John (eds) *What is Money?*, Ch. 6, London, Routledge, 124–38.
Chick, Victoria (2002) "Monetary Policy with Endogenous Money and Liquidity Preference: A Nondualistic Treatment," *Journal of Post Keynesian Economics*, 24 (4), 587–607.
Chick, Victoria and Caserta, M. (1997) "Provisional Equilibrium in Macroeconomic Theory," in P. Arestis, G. Palma, and M. Sawyer (eds) *Markets, Unemployment and Economic Policy, Essays in Honour of Geoff Harcourt*, Vol. II, London, Routledge, 223–47.
Christ, Carl (1966) *Econometric Methods and Models*, New York, Wiley.
Christiano, Lawrence, Eichenbaum, Martin, and Evans, Charles (1999) "Monetary Policy Shocks: What Have We Learned and To What End?" in J. Taylor, and M. Woodford (eds) *Handbook of Macroeconomics*, Vol. 1A, Amsterdam, Elsevier North-Holland, 65–148.
Christiano, Lawrence, Eichenbaum, Martin, and Evans, Charles (2000) "The Effects of Monetary Policy Shocks: Evidence from the Flow of Funds," *Review of Economics and Statistics*, February, 78 (1), 16–34.
Clarida, Richard, and Gertler, Mark (1999) "The Science of Monetary Policy," *Journal of Economic Literature*, December, 37, 1661–707.

Clarida, Richard, Gali, Jordi and Gertler, Mark (2000) "Monetary Policy Rules and Macroeconomic Stability: Evidence and Some Theory," *Quarterly Journal of Economics*, February, 115 (1), 147–80.
Coakley, Jerry, Kulasi, Farida, and Smith, Ron (1996) "Current Account Solvency and the Feldstein-Horioka Puzzle," *Economic Journal*, May, 106 (4), 620–7.
Coase, Ronald (1999) "Interview with Ronald Coase," *Newsletter of the International Society for New Institutional Economics*, Spring, 2 (1).
Cochrane, John (1989) "The Return of the Liquidity Effect: A Study of the Short Run Relation between Money Growth and Interest Rates," *Journal of Business and Economic Statistics*, January, 7 (1), 75–83.
Cochrane, John (1998) "What DO the VAR's Mean? Measuring the Oputput Effects of Monetary Policy," *Journal of Monetary Economics*, April, 41 (2), 277–300.
Cohen, Benjamin, J. (2000) "Political Dimensions of Dollarization," *Federal Reserve Bank of Dallas*, March 6–7, 1–12.
Colander, David (1994) "The Art of Monetary Policy," in (2001) *The Lost Art of Economics: Essays on Economics and the Economics Profession*, Cheltenham, UK, Edward Elgar.
Colander, David (1996) *Beyond Microfoundations: Post Walrasian Macroeconomics*, Cambridge, Cambridge University Press.
Colander, David (ed.) (2000) *The Complexity Vision and the Teaching of Economics*, Cheltenham, UK, Edward Elgar.
Colander, David (2001) *The Lost Art of Economics: Essays on Economics and the Economics Profession*, Cheltenham, UK, Edward Elgar.
Coley, T. and LeRoy, Steven (1981) "Identification and Estimation of Money Demand," *American Economic Review*, December, 71, 825–44.
Comer, A, McCloskey, Donald, and Solow, Robert (1988) *The Consequences of Economic Rhetoric*, Cambridge, Cambridge University Press.
Cooper, Richard (1984) "A Monetary System for the Future," *Foreign Affairs*, Fall, 63 (1), 66–84.
Corbo, Vincent (2001) "Is it Time for a Common Currency for the Americas?" *Journal of Policy Modeling*, 23 (3), 241–8.
Cornell, Bradford (1999) *The Equity Risk Premium*, New York, John Wiley & Sons.
Cornwall, John (1970) "The Role of Demand and Investment in Long Term Growth," *Quarterly Journal of Economics*, February, 84 (1), 48–69.
Cornwall, John (1972) *Growth and Stability in a Mature Economy*, London, Martin Robertson.
Cornwall, John (1977) *Modern Capitalism: Its Growth and Transformation*, London, Martin Robertson.
Cornwall, John (1991) (ed.) *The Capitalist Economies: Prospects for the 1990's*, Aldershot, UK, Edward Elgar.
Cornwall, John (1994) *Economic Breakdown and Recovery: Theory and Policy*, Armonk, NY, Sharpe.
Cornwall, John, and Cornwall, Wendy (2001) *Capitalist Development in the Twentieth Century: An Evolutionary-Keynesian Analysis*, Cambridge, Cambridge University Press.
Cottrell, Allin (1986) "The Endogeneity of Money and Money-Income Causality," *Scottish Journal of Political Economy*, February, 33 (1), 2–27.
Cottrell, Allin (1994a) "Post Keynesian Monetary Theory," *Cambridge Journal of Economics*, December, 18 (6), 587–605.
Cottrell, Allin (1994b) "Endogenous Money and the Multiplier," *Journal of Post Keynesian Economics*, Fall, 17 (1), 111–20.
Coutts, Ken, Godley, Wynne, and Nordhaus, William (1978) *Industrial Pricing in the United Kingdom*, Cambridge, Cambridge University Press.
Crick, W.F (1927) "The Genesis of Bank Deposits," *Economica*, 7, 191–202.
Crockett, Andrew (2004) "Exchange Rate Regimes in Theory and Practice," *Essays in Honour of Charles Goodhart*, London, Macmillan.
Daltzeil, Paul, and Harcourt Geoff (1997) "A Note on Mr. Meade's Relation and International Capital Movements," in Harcourt Geoff (2001) *Fifty Years a Keynesian and Other Essays*, New York, Palgrave.

Darity, W. Jr., and Young, W. (1995) "IS-LM An Inquest," *History of Political Economy*, Spring, 27 (1), 1–41.
Darity, Sandy (1987–88) "Labor Supply Response in Keynes' Theory of Involuntary Unemployment," *Journal of Post Keynesian Economics*, Winter, 10 (2) 183–210.
David, Paul, (1985) "Clio and the Economics of QWERTY," in Harald Hagemann, Michael Landesmann, and Roberto Scazzieri (eds) *The Economics of Structural Change*, Cheltenham, UK, Edward Elgar, 556–61.
Davidson, Paul (1982) *International Money and the Real World*, London, Macmillan.
Davidson, Paul (1983) "Rational Expectations: A Fallacious Foundation for Crucial Decisionmaking Processes," *Journal of Post Keynesian Economics*, Winter, 5(2), 289–318.
Davidson, Paul (1984) "Reviving Keynes' Revolution," *Journal of Post Keynesian Economics*, 6 (4), 561–75.
Davidson, Paul (1990) "A Post Keynesian Positive Contribution to Theory," in Davidson, Louise (ed.) (1999) *The Collected Writings of Paul Davidson, Vol. 3. Uncertainty, International Money, Employment and Theory*, New York, St. Martin's Press.
Davidson, Paul (1991) "Is Probability Theory Relevant for Uncertainty? A Post Keynesian Perspective," *Journal of Economic Perspectives*, 5 (1), 129–44.
Davidson, Paul (1994) *Post Keynesian Macroeconomic Theory: A Foundation for Successful Economic Policies in the Twenty-First Century*, Aldershot, UK, Edward Elgar.
Davidson, Paul (1996) "Reality and Economic Theory," *Journal of Post Keynesian Economic Theory*, 18 (4), 479–508.
Davidson, Paul (1999a) "Is a Plumber or a New Financial Architecture Needed to End Global International Liquidity Problems?," in *Uncertainty, International Money Employment and Theory*, Collected Writings of Paul Davidson, Vol. 3.
Davidson, Paul (1999b) "Thoughts on Speculation and Open Markets," in Paul Davidson, and Jan Kregel (eds) *Full Employment and Price Stability in a Global Economy*, Cheltenham, UK, Edward Elgar, 91–108.
Davidson, Paul (2002) *Financial Markets, Money and the Real World*, Cheltenham, UK, Edward Elgar.
Davidson, Paul, and Weintraub, Sidney (1973) "Money as Cause and Effect," *Economic Journal*, Dec, 83, 332, 1117–32.
Deaton, Angus (2003) "Measuring Poverty in a Growing World (or Measuring Growth in a Poor World), Working Papers, Princeton University, No, 9822, July.
De Long, Bradford (1999) "Should We Fear Inflation?," *Brookings Papers on Economic Activity*, (2), 225–41.
Deleplace, G., and Nell, E.J. (eds) (1996) *Money in Motion: The Post Keynesian and Circulation Approaches*, New York, Macmillan.
Dellas, Harris, and Tavlas, George (2001) "Lessons of the Euro for Dollarization: Analytic and Political Economy Perspectives," *Journal of Policy Making*, 23.
Desai, Meghnad (1987) "Endogenous and Exogenous Money," in J. Eatwell, M. Milgate, and P. Newman (eds), *The New Palgrave: A Dictionary of Economics*, London, Macmillan, 146–50.
Desai, Meghnad (1989) "The Scourge of the Monetarists: Kaldor on Monetarism and on Money," *Cambridge Journal of Economics*, 13(1), March, 171–82. Reprinted in Tony, Lawson, G. Palma, and John Sender (eds) *Kaldor's Political Economy*, London, Academic Press.
Diamond, Peter (1971) "A Model of Price Adjustment, " in Gabszewicz, Jean and Thisse, Francois (eds.) *Microeconomic Theories of Imperfect Competion: Old Problems and New Perspectives*, Cheltenham, UK, Edward Elgar.
Diamond, Peter (1982) "Aggregate Demand Management in Search Equilibrium," in G.K Shaw, (1988) *The Keynesian Heritage*, Vol. I, Aldershot, UK. Elgar.
Dickey, D.A., and Fuller, W.A. (1979) "Distribution of the Estimators for Autoregressive Time Series with Unit Roots," *Journal of the American Statistical Association*, 74, 427–31.
Dickey, D.A., and Fuller, W.A. (1981) "Likelihood Ratio Statistics for Autoregressive Time Series with Unit Roots," *Econometrica*, 49, 1057–72.
Dimand, Robert (1986) "The Road to the General Theory: Keynes Lectures on the Monetary Theory of Production, 1932–33." (mimeo) Carleton University.

Dimand, Robert (1988) *The Origins of the Keynesian Revolution: The Development of Keynes' Theory of Employment and Output*, Stanford, CA, Stanford University Press.

Dimand, Robert (2004) "James Tobin and the Transformation of the IS-LM Model," *History of Political Economy*, Supplement, 36, 165–89.

Docherty, Peter (1995) "Endogeneity in Wicksell's Monetary Theory," *History of Economics Review*, Winter, 0 (23) 20–36.

Dopfer, Kurt (ed.) (2005) *Economics, Evolution and the State: The Governance of Complexity*, Cheltenham, UK, Edward Elgar.

Dornbush, Rudi (2001) "Fewer Monies, Better Monies," *American Economic Review*, May, 91 (2), 238–42.

Dornbusch, Rudiger (1976) "Expectations and Exchange Rate Dynamics" in R. MacDonald, and M. Taylor (1992) (eds.) *Exchange Rate Economics*, Aldershot, UK. Elgar.

Douglas, Gale, and Vives, Xavier (2002) "Dollarization, Bailouts, and the Stability of the Banking System," *Quarterly Journal of Economics*, May, 467–502.

Dow, Sheila (1992) "Postmodernism and Economics," in J. Doherty, E. Grahem, and M. Malek (eds) *Postmodernism and the Social Sciences*, London, Macmillan, 148–61.

Dow, Sheila (1996a) "Horizontalism: A Critique," *Cambridge Journal of Economics*, 20, 497–508.

Dow, Sheila (1996b), *The Methodology of Macroeconomic Thought: A Conceptual Analysis of Schools of Thought in Economics*, Aldershot, UK, Edward Elgar.

Dow, Sheila (2004) "Uncertainty and Monetary Policy," *Oxford Economic Papers*, 56 (3), 539–61.

Dowd, K., and Greenway, David (1993) "Currency Competition, Network Externalities and Switching Costs: Towards an Alternative View of Optimum Currency Areas," *Economic Journal*, September, 103 (420), 1180–9.

Downward, Paul (1999) *Pricing Theory in Post Keynesian Economics: A Realist Approach*, Aldershot, Edward Elgar.

Downward, Paul (2000) "A Realist Appraisal of Post Keynesian Pricing Theory," *Cambridge Journal of Economics*, June, 24 (2), 211–24.

Driver, C., and Moreton, D. (1992) *Investment, Expectations and Uncertainty*, Oxford, Blackwell.

Dullien, Sebastian (2004) *The Interaction of Monetary Policy and Wage Bargaining in the European Monetary Union: Lessons from the Endogenous Money Approach*, New York, Palgrave-Macmillan.

Durbin, John (1975) "The Techniques for Testing the Constancy of Regression Relationships over Time," in A. Harvey (ed.) *Critical Writings in Econometrics* (1994), Aldershot, UK. Edward Elgar.

Durlauf, Stephen and Quah, Danny (1999) "The New Empirics of Economic Growth," in J. Taylor, and M. Woodford (eds.) *Handbook of Macroeconomics*, Vil. 1A, Amsterdam, Elsevier Science, North-Holland, 235–308.

Easterly, W., and Pritchett, R. (1993) "The Determinants of Economic Success: Luck and Policy," *Finance and Development*, 30, December, 38–41.

Eckstein, Otto (1969) "Wage Price Dynamics, Inflation, and Unemployment: Discussion," *American Economic Review*, May 59 (2), 162–64.

Eckstein, Otto (1984) "Foundations of Aggregate Supply Price," *American Economic Review*, May, 74 (2) 216–20.

Edwards, Sebastian (1999) "How Effective Are Capital Controls?" *Journal of Economic Perspectives*, 13 (4), 65–84.

Edwards, Sebastian (2001) "Dollarization: Myths and Realities," *Journal of Policy Modeling*, 23, 249–65.

Edwards, Sebastian, and Magendzo, Igal (2002) "Dollarization and Economic Performance: What Do We Really Know?," Working Paper 65, Oesterreische National Bank, February.

Edwards, Sebastian, and Magendzo, Igal (2002) "Independent Currency Unions, Growth and Inflation," *Monetary and Economic Studies*, December, 20 (0), 215–32.

Edwards, Sebastian, and Magendzo, Igal (2003) "Dollarization and Economic Performance; What Do We Really Know?" *International Journal of Finance and Economics*, October, 8 (4) 351–63.

Eichenbaum, Murray (1997) "Some Thoughts on Practical Stabilization Policy," *American Economic Review*, May, 87 (2), 236–9.

Eichengreen, Barry (1992) "Is Europe an Optimum Currency Area?" in Sylvio Borner, and Herbert Grubel, (eds) *The European Community after 1992*, London, Macmillan, 138–61.

Eichengreen, Barry (1994) *International Monetary Arrangements for the 21st Century*, Washington, DC, Brookings Foundation Press.

Eichner, Alfred (1973) "A Theory of the Determination of the Markup under Oligopoly," *Economic Journal*, 83/332, December, 1184–200.

Eichner, Alfred (ed.) (1978) *A Guide to Post Keynesian Economics*, White Planes, NY, Sharpe.

Eichner, Alfred (1983) "Why Economics is Not Yet a Science," in Eichner (ed.) *Why Economics is Not Yet a Science*, London, Macmillan, 205–41.

Eichner, Alfred (1987) *The Macrodynamics of Advanced Market Economies*, Armonk, NY, M.E. Sharp.

Eisner, Robert (1989) *The Total Incomes System of Accounts*, Chicago, IL, University of Chicago Press.

Eisner, Robert (1994) *The Misunderstood Economy: What Counts and How to Count It*, Boston, MA, Harvard Business School.

Evans, Charles, and Marshall, David (1998) "Monetary Policy and the Term Structure of Nominal Interest Rates: Evidence and Theory," *Carnegie-Rochester Conference on Public Policy*, Fall, 49, 53–111.

Farmer, Roger (1993) *The Macroeconomics of Self-fulfilling Prophecies*, Cambridge MA, MIT Press.

Farmer, Roger (1999) *The Macroeconomics of Self-Fulfilling Prophecies*, Cambridge, MA, MIT Press.

Farrall, Diana (2004) "The Hidden Dangers of the Informal Economy," *McKinsey Quarterly*, No. 3.

Fazzari, Stephen (1993) "Monetary Policy, Financial Structure and Investment," in G. Dymsky, G. Epstein, and R. Pollin (eds.) *Transforming the US Financial System: Equity and Efficiency for the 21st Century*, EPI Series, Armonk, NY, Sharpe.

Feige, Edward (1997) "Revised Estimates of the Underground Economy: Implications of US Currency Owned Abroad," in Owen Lippert, and Michael Walker (eds), *The Underground Economy: Global Evidence of Its Size and Impact*, Vancouver, BC, Fraser Institute, 151–208.

Feldstein, M., and Horioka, C. (1980) "Domestic Saving and Intellectual Capital Flows," *Economic Journal*, 90, 314–29.

Feldstein, Martin (1983) "Domestic Saving and International Capital Movements in the Long Run and the Short Run," in G. de-Menil, and R. Gordon (eds.) (1991) *International Volatility and Economic Growth*, North-Holland, New York, Elsevier.

Feldstein, Martin, and Bacchetta, Philippe (1991) "National Saving and International Investment," in D. Bernheim, and J. Shoven (eds.) *National Saving and Economic Performance*, NBER, Chicago, University of Chicago Press.

Feyerabend, Paul (1975) *Against Method: Outline of an Anarchistic Theory of Knowledge*, London, Verso.

Fields, Windsor, and Hart, William (1990) "Some Pitfalls in the Conventional Treatment of Aggregate Demand," *Southern Economic Journal*, January, 56 (3), 676–85.

Fields, Windsor, and Hart, William, (1998) "Theoretical Inconsistencies in the AD–AS Model: Can the Model be Rehabilitated?" in Bhaskara Rao (ed.) *Aggregate Demand and Supply: A Critique of Orthodox Macroeconomic Modeling*, London, Macmillan Press.

Fischer, Stanley (1999) "On the Need for an International Lender of Last Resort," *Journal of Economic Perspectives*, Fall, 13 (4), 85–104.

Fisher, Irving (1930) *The Theory of Interest*, New York, Macmillan.

Fitzgibbons, Athol (1988) *Keynes Vision: A New Political Economy*, Oxford, Oxford University Press.

Fontana, Guiseppi (2000) "Post Keynesians and Circuitists on Money and Uncertainty," *Journal of Post Keynesian Economics*, 23 (1), 27–48.

Fontana, Guiseppi (2004) "Rethinking Endogenous Money: A Constructive Interpretation of the Debate between Horizontalists and Structuralists," *Metroeconomica*, November, 55(4), 367–85.

Frankel, Jeffrey, and Rose, Andrew (1999) "An Estimate of the Effect of Common Currencies on Trade and Income," *Quarterly Journal of Economics*, May, 117 (2), 437–66.

Friedman, Benjamin (1988) *Day of Reckoning: The Consequences of American Economic Policy Under Reagan*, New York, Random House.

Friedman, Benjamin (2000) "The Japanese Banking Crisis and the US S&L Collapse–Parallels and Lessons," in Mikitani Ryoichi, and Adam Posen (eds) *Japan's Financial Crisis and its Parallels to US Experience*, Washington, DC, Baker and Taylor, Ch. 9.

Friedman, Milton (1953) "The Methodology of Positive Economics," in Friedman, M. (ed.) *Essays in Positive Economics*, Chicago, IL, University of Chicago Press, 3–43.

Friedman, Milton (1968) "The Role of Monetary Policy," *American Economic Review*, 58, 1–17.

Friedman, Milton (1970) "Comment" (on Nicholas Kaldor), *Lloyds Bank Review*, October, 98, 52–3.

Friedman, Milton (1977) "Nobel Lecture: Inflation and Unemployment," *Journal of Political Economy*, 85 (3), 451–72.

Friedman, Milton (1982) "Monetary Policy," *Journal of Money Credit and Banking*, February 14, 98–118.

Friedman, Milton (1999) "Conversations with Milton Friedman," in Brian Snowden, and Howard Vane (eds) *Conversations With Leading Economists: Interpreting Modern Macroeconomics*, Cheltenham, UK, Edward Elgar.

Fuller, A.J. (1976) *Introduction to Statistical Time Series*, New York, Pergamon Press.

Furstenberg, George von (2000) "A Case Against U.S. Dollarization," *Challenge*, July/August, 43 (4), 108–120.

Galbraith, James (1997) "Time to Ditch the NAIRU," *Journal of Economic Perspectives*, 11 (1), 93–108.

Galbraith, John Kenneth (1961) *The Great Crash*, Harmondsworth, Penguin Books.

Gertler, Mark (1988) "Financial Structure and Aggregate Activity: An Overview," *Journal of Money, Credit and Banking*, August, 20 (3), Part 2, 559–88.

Gertler, Mark, Goodfriend, Marvin, Issing, O., and Spaventa, L. (1998) *Asset Prices and Monetary Policy: Four Views*, Centre for Economic Policy Research and Bank for International Settlements, London and Basle.

Gilbert, R. Alton (1980) "Lagged Reserve Requirements Implications for Monetary Control and Bank Reserve Management," *Review, Federal Reserve Bank of St Louis*, May, 62 (5), 7–20.

Gilbert, Christopher (1986) "Professor Hendry's Econometric Methodology," in C. Granger (ed.) (1990) *Modeling Economic Series: Readings in Econometric Methodology*, Oxford, Oxford University Press.

Giovannini, Alberto, and Giavazzi, Francesco (1989) "The European Currency Experience," in A. Giovannini (1995) *The Debate on Money in Europe*, Cambridge, MA, MIT Press, 129–34.

Godel, Kurt (1931) "On Formally Undecidable Propositions of Principia Mathmatica and Related Systems," (Translation in English) in (Shankar, S.G. ed.) *Godels Theorem in Focus*, London, Croom Helm, 1988.

Godley, Wynne, and Cripps, Francis (1983) *Macroeconomics*, Oxford, Fontana Paperbacks, Oxford University Press.

Godley, Wynne, and Nordhaus, William (1972), "Pricing in the Trade Cycle," *Economic Journal* 82, 853–82.

Goodfriend, Marvin (1983) "Discount Window Borrowing, Monetary Policy, and the Post-October 1979 Federal Reserve Operating Procedure," *Journal of Monetary Economics*, September, 12 (3), 343–56.

Goodfriend, Marvin (1986) "Monetary Mystique: Secrecy and Central Banking," *Journal of Monetary Economics*, 17, 63–82.
Goodfriend, Marvin (2000) "Overcoming the Zero Bound on Interest Rate Policy," Federal Reserve Bank of Richmond, Working Paper 3, 2000.
Goodfriend, Marvin (2003) "The Phases of U.S. Monetary Policy: 1987–2001" in P. Mizen (ed.) *Central Banking, Monetary Theory and Practice: Essays in Honour of Charles Goodhart*, Vol. 1, Cheltenham, UK. Elgar.
Goodhart, Charles (1975) *Money, Information and Uncertainty*, New York, Macmillan.
Goodhart, Charles (1984) *Monetary Theory and Practice: The UK Experience*, New York, Macmillan.
Goodhart, Charles (1989) "Has Moore Become Too Horizontal?," *Journal of Post Keynesian Economics*, Fall, 12 (1), 29–34.
Goodhart, Charles (1995) "The Political Economy of Monetary Union," in P. Kennen (ed.) *Understanding Interdependence: The Macroeconomics of the Open Economy*, Princeton, NJ, Princeton University Press, 450–505.
Goodhart, Charles (2002) "The Foreign Exchange Market: A Random Work with a Dragging Anchor," in Terence Mills (ed.) *Forecasting Financial Markets*, Vol. 1, Cheltenham, UK, Edward Elgar.
Gordon, Robert (1981) "Monetarist Interpretations of the Great Depression: An Evaluation and Critique," *NBER Working Papers*, 0300.
Gordon, Robert (1988) "The Rules versus Discretion Debate in the Light of Recent Experience," in H. Giersch (ed.) *Macro and Micro Policy for More Growth and Employment*, Symposium 1987, Tubingen, 64–71.
Gordon, Robert (2004) *Productivity Growth, Inflation, and Unemployment: The Collected Essays of Robert J. Gordon* (Foreword by Robert M. Solow), Cambridge, Cambridge University Press.
Gosh, Attish, Guide, Anne-Marie, and Wolf, Holger (2000) "Currency Boards: More Than a Quick Fix," *Economic Policy*, 31, October, 269–335.
Graham, B., and Dodd, D.L., (1951) *Security Analysis: Principles and Technique*, New York, McGraw-Hill.
Grandmont, Jean-Michel and Malgrange, Piere (1987) *Nonlinear Economic Dynamics: Economic Theory, Econometrics and Mathematical Economics*, Boston, MA, Academic Press.
Graziani, Augusto (1989) "The Theory of the Monetary Circuit," *Thames Papers in Political Economy*, Spring.
Graziani, Augusto (1990) "The Theory of the Monetary Circuit," *Economies et Societes, Series Monnaie et Production*, 7, 7–36.
Groenewegen, Peter (1995) *Soaring Eagle: Alfred Marshall 1842–1924*, Aldershot, UK, Edward Elgar.
Grubel, Herbert (1999) *The Case for the Amero: The Economics and Politics of a North American Monetary Union*, Vancouver, BC, Fraser Institute.
Grubel, Herbert (2000) "The Merit of a Canada – US Monetary Union," *North American Journal of Economics and Finance*, 11, 19–40.
Gurley, John, and Shaw, Edward, (1960) *Money in a Theory of Finance*, Washington, DC, Brookings Institution.
Guttmann, Peter (1977) "The Subterranean Economy," *Financial Analysts' Journal*, 34 (6), 24–34.
Haavelmo, Trygve (1944) "The Probability Approach in Econometrics," Supplement to *Econometrica*, July, 12, 1–118.
Hahn, Frank (1965) "On Some Problems of Proving the Existence of Equilibrium in a Money Economy," in Frank Hahn, and Frank Brechling (eds) *The Theory of Interest Rates*, London, Macmillan.
Hahn, Frank (1969) "On Money and Growth," in *Equilibrium and Macroeconomics* (1984) Cambridge, MA. MIT Press, 95–213.
Hahn, Frank (1973) "On the Foundations of Monetary Theory," in *Equilibrium and Macroeconomics* (1984) Cambridge, MA, MIT Press, 58–74.
Hahn, Frank (1973) *On the Notion of Equilibrium in Economics*, Cambridge, Cambridge University Press.

Hahn, Frank (1977)"Keynesian Economics and General Equilibrium Theory," in Geoff Harcourt (ed.) *Microfoundations of Macroeconomics*, London, Macmillan, 25–40.
Hahn, Frank (1981) *Money and Inflation*, Oxford, Blackwell.
Hahn, Frank (1989) "Kaldor on Growth," *Cambridge Journal of Economics*, March, 13 (1), 79–101.
Hahn, Frank and Solow, Robert (1995) *A Critical Essay on Modern Macroeconomic Theory*, Cambridge, MA, MIT Press.
Haig, Robert (1921) "The Concept of Income, Economic and Legal Aspects," in Robert Haig (ed.) *The Federal Income Tax*, New York, Columbia University Press.
Hall, R.L., and Hitch, C.J. (1939), "Price Theory and Business Behavior," *Oxford Economic Papers*, 2, 12–45, Reprinted in Wilson, T. and Andrews, P., *Studies in the Price Mechanism*, Oxford, Clarendon Press.
Hall, Robert (2003) "The Modern Theory of Unemployment Fluctuations," *American Economic Review*, May, 93 (2), 145–50.
Hanke, Steve, and Schuler, Kurt (1994) *Currency Boards for Developing Countries: A Handbook*, San Francisco, CA, ICS Press.
Hanson, Bruce (2001) "The New Econometrics of Structural Change: Dating Changes in U.S. Labor Productivity," *Journal of Economic Perspectives*, 15 (4), 117–28.
Harcourt, Geoff, and Riach, Peter (eds) (1997) *A Second Edition of the General Theory*, 2 vols, London, Routledge.
Harris, Richard, I.D. (1995) *Using Cointegration Analysis in Econometric Modelling*, London, Prentice Hall.
Haugen, R. (1999) *The Inefficient Stock Market*, New Jersey, Prentice Hall.
Hausman, Daniel (1992) *Essays on Philosophy and Economic Methodology*, Cambridge, Cambridge University Press.
Hausman, Jerry (1994) "Sources of Bias and Solutions to Bias in the CPI," *Journal of Economic Perspectives*, 17 (1), 23–44.
Hausman, Ricardo (1999) "Should There Be Five Currencies or One Hundred and Five?," *Foreign Policy*, 116, 65–79.
Hayek, Friedrich von (1932) *Monetary Theory and the Trade Cycle*, New York, Harcourt Brace.
Hayek, Friedrich (1935) *Prices and Production*, London, Routledge.
Heilbroner, Robert, and Milberg, William (1996) *The Crisis of Vision in Modern Economic Thought*, Cambridge, Cambridge University Press.
Heise, Arne (1991) "Monetary Theory of Production: The Still Unsolved Task," *Osaka City University Economic Review*, 26 (2).
Helleiner, Eric (2003) "Dollarization Diplomacy: US Policy Towards Latin America Coming Full Circle?," *Review of International Political Economy*, August, 10 (3), 406–29.
Helliwell, John (1996) "Do National Borders Matter for Quebec's Trade?" *Canadian Journal of Economics*, August 29 (3) 507–22.
Helliwell, John (1998) *How Much Do National Borders Matter?* Washington, DC, Brookings Institution.
Helm, Dieter (1984) *The Economics of John Hicks*, Oxford, Basil Blackwell.
Hendry, David (2000) *Econometrics: Alchemy or Science? Essays in Econometric Methodology*, 2nd edn, Oxford, Oxford University Press.
Hendry, David, and Ericsson, Neil (1985) "Assertion Without Empirical Basis: An Econometric Appraisal of *Monetary Trends in the United Kingdom*, by Milton Friedman and Anna J. Schwartz," Board of Governors of the Federal Reserve System (U.S.), International Finance Discussion Paper: 270.
Hendry, David, and Ericsson, Neil (1989) "An Econometric Analysis of UK Money Demand in *Monetary Trends in the United States and the United Kingdom*, by Milton Friedman and Anna J. Schwartz," Board of Governors of the Federal Reserve System (U.S.), International Finance Discussion Papers: 355.
Hendry, David, and Morgan, Mary (1995) *The Foundations of Econometric Analysis*, Cambridge, Cambridge University Press.

Hicks, Sir John (1939) "Mr Hautrey on Bank Rate and the Long Term Rate of Interest," in (1982) *Collected Essays on Economic Theory*, Vol.1, Oxford, Basil Blackwell.
Hicks, Sir John (1946) *Value and Capital*, 2nd edn. Oxford, Clarendon Press.
Hicks, Sir John (1967) "The Two Triads: Lecture I," Hicks, *Critical Essays in Monetary Theory*, Oxford, Oxford University Press.
Hicks, Sir John (1976) "Some Questions of Time in Economics," in A. Tang, F. Westfield, J. Worley (eds), *Evolution, Welfare and Time in Economics*, London, Lexington Books.
Hicks, Sir John (1979) *Causality in Economics*, New York, Basic Books.
Hicks, Sir John (1980) "IS-LM: An Explanation," *Journal of Post Keynesian Economics*, Winter, 4 (2), 291–307.
Hicks, Sir John (1982) *Money, Interest and Wages*, Vol II of *Collected Essays on Economic Theory*, Oxford, Basil Blackwell.
Hicks, Sir John (1989) *A Market Theory of Money*, Oxford, Clarendon Press.
Hilferding, R. (1981) (eds) *Finance Capital*, T. Bottomore (German Original 1910), Routledge and Kegan Paul.
Holmes, Alan (1969) "Operational Constraints on the Stabilization of Money Supply Growth," in *Controlling Monetary Aggregates*, Federal Reserve Bank of Boston, 73–4.
Hondai, Susumu (1998) *Japan: Why it Works, Why it Doesn't*, Honolulu, University of Hawaii Press.
Howells, P.G.A (2001) "Real Balance Effects and Endogenous Money," Berlin Conference.
Howells, Peter, (2001) "The Endogeneity of Money," in P. Arestis, and M. Sawyer (eds) *Money, Finance and Capitalist Development*. Cheltenham, UK, Edward Elgar, 134–78.
Howells, Peter, and Iris Biefang-Frisancho Mariscal (2002) "Central Banks and Market Interest Rates," *Journal of Post Keynesian Economics*, Summer, 24 (4), 569–86.
Ingham, Geoffrey (ed.) (2005) *Concepts of Money: Interdisciplinary Perspectives from Economics, Sociology and Political Science*, Cheltenham, UK, Edward Algar.
Ingrao, B., and Israel, G. (1990) *The Invisible Hand: Economic Theory in the History of Science*, Cambridge, MA, MIT Press.
International Monetary Fund (1974) "Guidelines for the Management of Floating Exchange Rates," Decision no. 4232.IMF.
Issing, Otmar (2004) "Inflation Targeting: A View from the ECB," *Federal Reserve Bank of St Louis Review*, July–August, 86 (4), 169–79.
Ito, Takatoshi (1992) *The Japanese Economy*, Cambridge, MA, MIT Press.
Ize, Alain, and Yeyati, Eduardo (2003) "Financial Dollarization," *Journal of International Economics*, 59.
Jameson, Kenneth, P. (2003) "Dollarization in Latin America: Wave of the Future or Flight to the Past?" *Journal of Economic Issues*, 3 September, Vol. XXXVII, 643–63.
The Japanese Economy: Recent Trends and Outlook. Coordination Bureau, Economic Planning Agency, Japan (2000).
Johansen, S. (1991) "Estimation and Hypothesis Testing of Cointegrated Vectors in Gaussian Vector Autoregression Models," *Econometrica*, 59, 1551–80.
Johnston, Jack (1984), *Econometric Methods*, New York, McGraw Hill.
Kahnemann, Daniel, (2003) "Maps of Bounded Rationality: Psychology for Behavioral Economics," *American Economic Review*, December, 93 (5), 1449–75.
Kahneman, Daniel, and Tversky, Amos (1979) "Prospect Theory: An Analysis of Decisions under Risk," in J. Shogren (ed.) (2003) *Experiments in Environmental Economics*, Vol. 2, Aldershot, UK, Ashgate.
Kahneman, Daniel, and Tversky, Amos (1981) "The Framing of Decisions and the Psychology of Choice," in J. Shogren (ed.) (2003) *Experiments in Environmental Economics*, Vol. 2, Aldershot, UK, Ashgate.
Kayneman, Daniel (1994) "New Challenges to the Rationality Assumption," in D. Kahneman, and A. Tversky (eds.) (2000) *Choices, Values and Frames*, Cambridge, Cambridge University Press.
Kaldor, Nicholas (1957) "A Model of Economic Growth," *Economic Journal*, 67, 591–624.

Kaldor, Nicholas (1970) "The New Monetarism," *Lloyds Bank Review*, 97, July, 1–18.
Kaldor, Nicholas (1972) "The Irrelevance of Equilibrium Economics," *Economic Journal*, 82, 1237–55.
Kaldor, Nicholas (1981) "The Role Of Increasing Returns, Technical Progress and Cumulative Causation in the Theory of International Trade and Economic Growth," *Économie Appliquée*, 34 (4), 1981, 593–617.
Kaldor, Nicholas (1982) *The Scourge of Monetarism*, Oxford, Oxford University Press.
Kaldor, Nicholas (1985) *Economics Without Equilibrium*, Armonk, NY, Sharpe.
Kaldor, Nicholas (1996) *Causes of Growth and Stagnation in the World Economy*, Cambridge, Cambridge University Press.
Kalecki, Michael (1939) *Essays in the Theory of Economic Fluctuations*, London, Allen and Unwin.
Kalecki, Michael (1943) *Studies in Economic Dynamics*, London, Allen and Unwin.
Kalecki, Michael (1971) "Costs and Prices," in M. Kalecki (ed.) *Selected Essays on the Dynamics of the Capitalist Economy* 1933–70, Cambridge, Cambridge University Press, Ch. 5.
Kamark, Andrew (1983) *Economics and the Real World*, Philadelphia, PA, University of Pennsylvania Press.
Katzner, Donald (1998) *Time, Ignorance and Uncertainty in Economic Models*, Ann Arbor, MI, University of Michigan Press.
Katzner, Donald (1999) "Hysteresis and the Modeling of Economic Phenomena," *Review of Political Economy,* April, 11 (2), 171–81.
Keen, Stephen (2001) *Debunking Economics: The Naked Emperor of the Social Sciences*, London, Zed Books.
Kennedy, Peter (2003) *A Guide to Econometrics*, 5th edn, Cambridge, MA, MIT Press.
Keynes, John Maynard (1913a) *Indian Currency and Finance, Collected Writings of J.M. Keynes*, Vol. 1.
Keynes, John Maynard (1913b) "How Far Are Bankers Responsible for the Alternations of Crisis and Depression?," *Collected Writings of J.M. Keynes*, Vol. 12, 2–14.
Keynes, John Maynard (1923) *A Tract on Monetary Reform, Collected Writings of J.M. Keynes*, Vol. 6.
Keynes, John Maynard (1930) *A Treatise on Money*, 2 vols, *Collected Writings of J.M. Keynes*, Vol. 5, Vol. 6.
Keynes, John Maynard (1933a) "A Monetary Theory of Production," *Collected Writings of John Maynard Keynes*, Vol. 13, London, Macmillan, 408–11.
Keynes, John Maynard (1933b) "The Characteristics of an Entrepreneur Economy," *Collected Writings of John Maynard Keynes*, Vol. 29, London, Macmillan, 87–101.
Keynes, John Maynard (1936) *The General Theory of Employment, Interest and Money*, London, Macmillan.
Keynes, John Maynard (1936a) "The 'ex-ante' Theory of the Rate of Interest," *Economic Journal*, 47, *Collected Writings of J.M. Keynes*, Vol. 14, 109–23.
Keynes, John Maynard (1937) "Alternative Theories of the Rate of Interest," *Economic Journal*, 48, *Collected Writings of J.M. Keynes*, Vol. 14, 201–215.
Keynes, John Maynard (1938a) "The General Theory of Employment," *Quarterly Journal of Economics*, 51, 209–23.
Keynes, John Maynard (1938b) "D.H. Robertson on 'Mr. Keynes and Finance': A Comment," *Collected Writings of J.M. Keynes*, Vol. 14, 229–33.
Keynes, John Maynard (1939) "The Process of Capital Formation," *Collected Writings of J.M. Keynes*, Vol. 14, 279–85.
Keynes, John Maynard (1945) "Minutes for the National Debt Inquiry" (1980) *Collected Writings of J.M. Keynes*, Vol. XXVII, 390–92.
Keynes, John Maynard (1980) *Collected Works, XXV Activities 1940–1944: Shaping the Post-War World*.
Kirman, Allan (1989) "The Intrinsic Limits of Modeling Economic Theory: The Emperor Has No Clothes," *Economic Journal*, Supplement, 99, 395, 126–39.

King, John (2002) *A History of Post-Keynesian Economics since 1936*, Cheltenham, UK, Edward Elgar.
King, Mervyn (1994) "The Transmission Mechanism of Monetary Policy," *Bank of England Quarterly Bulletin*, August, 34 (3), 261-7.
King, Robert, Plosser, Charles, Stock, James, and Watson, Mark (1991) "Stochastic Trends and Economic Fluctuations," *American Economic Review*, September, 81, 819-40.
Klein, Michael (2002) "Dollarization and Trade," NBER Working Paper Series, No. 8879.
Knight, Frank (1921) *Risk, Uncertainty and Profits*, Boston, Houghton Mifflin.
Kreisler, Peter (1987) *Kalecki's Microanalysis: The Development of Kalecki's Analysis of Pricing and Distribution*, Cambridge, Cambridge University Press.
Krugman, Paul (1995) *Currencies and Crises*, Cambridge, MA, MIT Press.
Krugman, Paul (1996) "Are Currency Crises Self-Fulfilling?" in B. Bernanke and J. Rotenberg (eds) *NBER Macroeconomics Annual*, Cambridge, MA. MIT Press.
Kuhn, T.S. (1962) *The Structure of Scientific Revolutions*, Chicago, IL, University of Chicago Press.
Kuper, Gerard, Sterken, Elmer, and Wester, Els (2001) *Coordination and Growth: Essays in Honour of Simon K. Kuipers*, Boston, MA, Kluwer Academic.
Kuznets, Simon (1948) *Economic Change: Selected Essays in Business Cycles, National Income and Economic Growth*, London, Heinemann.
Kuznets, Simon (1953) *Shares of Upper Income Groups in Income and Savings* (assisted by Elizabeth Jenks), New York, National Bureau of Economic Research.
Lavoie, Marc (1992) *Foundations of Post Keynesian Economic Analysis*, Aldershot, UK, Edward Elgar.
Lavoie, Marc (2001) *Endogenous Money in a Coherent Stock-Flow Framework*, Berlin Conference website.
Lavoie, Marc (2005a) "Monetary Base Endogeneity and The new Procedures of the - Asset-Based Canadian and American Systems," *Journal of Post Keynesian Economics*, Summer, 27 (4) 687-707.
Lavoie, Marc (2005b) "Endogenous Money": "Accomodationists," in Philip Arestis and Malcolm Sawyer (eds) *Handbook of Alternative Monetary Economics*, Cheltenham, UK, Edward Elgar.
Lavoie, Marc, and Seccareccia, Mario (2004) *Central Banking in the Modern World*, Cheltenham, UK, Edward Elgar.
Lawson, Tony (1989) "Abstraction, Tendencies, and Stylized Facts: a Realist Approach to Economic Analysis," in T. Lawson, G. Palida, and J. Sender (eds.) *Kaldor's Political Economy*, London, Academic Press.
Lawson, Tony (1997) *Economics and Reality*, London, Routledge.
Lawson, Tony (1999) "Connections and Distinctions: Post Keynesianism and Critical Realism," *Journal of Post Keynesian Economics*, Fall, 22 (1), 3-13.
Lawson, Tony (2001) "The Varying Fortunes of the Project of Mathematising Economics: An Evolutionary Explanation," *European Journal of Economic and Social Systems*, 15(4), 241-68.
Lawson, Tony (2003) *Reorienting Economics*, London, Routledge.
Leamer, Edward (1978) *Specification Searches: Ad Hoc Inferences with Nonexperimental Data*, New York, Wiley.
Lee, Fred (1998) *Post Keynesian Price Theory*, Cambridge, Cambridge University Press.
Leontief, Wassily (1971) "Theoretical Assumptions and Nonobserved Facts," in *Essays in Economics: Theories, Theorizing, Facts and Policies* (1985) Oxford, Transactions Books.
Lerner, Abba (1939) "Saving and Investment: Definitions, Assumptions and Objectives," *Quarterly Journal of Economics*, LII. No. 4, 611-19.
Lipsey, Robert, and Tice, Helen (1989) *The Measurement of Saving, Investment and Wealth*, Chicago, University of Chicago Press.
Little, Ian (1962) "Higgledy Piggledy Growth," *Oxford Institute of Statistics*, 24, November, 387-412.
Loasby, Brian (1976) *Choice, Complexity and Ignorance*, Cambridge, Cambridge University Press.
Loasby, Brian (1999) *Knowledge, Institutions and Evolution in Economics*, London, Routledge.

Loayza, Norman and Schmidt-Hebbel, Klaus (eds.) (2002) *Monetary Policy: Rules and Transmission Mechanisms*, Santiago, Central Bank of Chile.

Lo, Andrew (1999) *A Non-Random Walk Down Wall Street*, Princeton, NJ, Princeton University Press.

Long, John and Plosser, Charles (1983) "Real Business Cycles," in F. Kydland (ed.) (1995) *Business Cycle Theory*, Ashgate, UK, Edward Elgar, 301–31.

Lovell, Michael (1987) "Tests of the Rational Expectations Hypothesis," *American Economic Review*, March, 76 (1), 110–24.

Lucas, Robert (1975) "An Equilibrium Model of the Business Cycle," in K. Hoover (ed.) (1999) *The Legacy of Robert Lucas*, Cheltenham, UK, Edward Elgar.

Lucas, Robert (1977) "Understanding Business Cycles," in K. Brunner and A. Meltzer (eds) *Stabilization of the Domestic and International Economy*, Amsterdam, North-Holland, 7–29.

Lucas, Robert (1981) *Studies in Business Cycle Theory*, Cambridge, MA, MIT Press.

Lucas, Robert (1988) "On the Mechanics of Economic Development," in (2002) *Lectures on Economic Growth*, Cambridge, MA, Harvard University Press.

Lucas, Robert (1990) "Why Doesn't Capital Flow from Poor to Rich Countries?," *AEA Papers and Proceedings*, May, 80, 92–6.

Lyotard, J.F. (1984) *The Postmodern Condition: A Report on Knowledge*, Manchester, Manchester University Press.

McAleer, Michael, Pagan, Adrian, and Volker, Paul (1985) "What Will Take the Con Out of Econometrics?," *American Economic Review*, June, 75 (3), 293–307.

McCallum, Bennett (1978) "The Political business Cycle: An Empirical Test," in D. Mueller (ed.) (2001) *The Economics of Politics*, Cheltenham, UK, Edward Elgar.

McCallum, John (1995a) "National Borders Matter: Canada–U.S. Regional Trading Patterns," in R. Pomfret (2003) *Economic Analysis of RegionalTrading Arrangements*, Cheltenham, UK, Edward Elgar.

McCallum, John (1995b) "National Borders Matter: Regional Trade Patterns in North America," *American Economic Review*, June, 85(3), 615–23.

McCombie, John S. (1997) "The Empirics of Balance of Payments Constrained Growth," *Journal of Post Keynesian Economics*, 15, 345–505.

McCombie, John S., and Thirwall, Antony P. (1994) *Economic Growth and the Balance of Payments Constraint*, London, Macmillan.

McCulloch, J. Husten (1975) "An Estimate of the Liquidity Premium," in S. Ross (ed.) *The Debt Market*, Vol. 1, Cheltenham, UK, Edward Elgar.

McCloskey, Donald (1985) *The Rhetoric of Economics*, Madison, WI, University of Wisconsin Press.

McCloskey, Donald (1990) *If You're So Smart: The Narrative of Economic Expertise*, Chicago, IL, University of Chicago Press.

McCloskey, Donald (1994) *Knowledge and Persuasion in Economics*, Cambridge, Cambridge University Press.

McCloskey, Dierdre (2000) *How To Be Human, Though An Economist*, Ann Arbor, MI, University of Michigan Press.

McCloskey, Dierdre, and Stephen Ziliak (ed.) (2002) *Measurement and Meaning in Economics*, Cheltenham, UK, Edward Elgar.

McCombie, John, and Thirlwall, Antony (1997) "Economic Growth and the Balance of Payments Constraint Revisited," in P. Arestis, G. Palma, and M. Sawyer (eds) *Markets, Unemployment and Economic Policy: Essays in Honour of Geoff Harcourt*, Vol. 2, London, Routledge, 498–511.

McFetridge, Donald (1973) "Market Structure and Profitability in Canadian Manufacturing Sector," *Canadian Journal of Economics*, 6, 3, 344–55.

McGinn, Colin (1993) *Problems in Philosophy*, Cambridge, MA, Blackwell.

MacLean, Peter (1990) *The Triune Brain in Evolution: Role in Paleocerebal Functions*, New York, Plenum Press.

Machiavelli, Niccolo (1954) *The Prince*, London, Penguin Books.

Machlup, Fritz (1955) "The Problem of Verification in Economics," in B. Caldwell, (ed.) (1984) *Appraisal and Criticism in Economics: A Book of Readings*, Boston, Allen and Unwin.
Machlup, Fritz (1958) "Equilibrium and Disequilibrium: Misplaced Concreteness and Disguised Politics," *Economic Journal*, 68, March, 1–24.
Machlup, Fritz (1958) "Equilibrium and Disequilibrium: Misplaced Concreteness and Disguised Politics," in M. Perlman (ed.) (1991) *Economic Semantics*, 2nd ed. London, Transaction.
Machlup, Fritz (1982) "Issues in the Theory of Human Capital: Education as Investment," *Pakistan Development Review*, Spring, 21 (1) 1–17.
Mack, Connie (1999) "Basics of Dollarization," *Joint Economic Committee Staff Report*, July, updated January 2000.
Makin, John, H. (1998) "The Fed's Miracle Cure," *AE Economic Outlook*, December.
Mandelbrot, Benoit (1971) "When Can Price Be Arbitraged Efficiently? A Limit to the Validity of the Random Walk and Martingale Models," *Review of Economics and Statistics*, 53, 225–36.
Mandelbrot, Benoit (1994) "A Multifractal Walk Down Wall Street," *Scientific American*, 280, February, 70–3.
Mankiw, Gregory (ed.) (1994) *Monetary Policy: Studies in Business Cycles*, Vol. 29, Chicago, IL, University of Chicago Press.
Mankiw, Gregory, Romer, David, and Weil, David (1992) "A Contribution to the Empirics of Economic Growth," in E. Wolff (ed.)(1997) *The Economics of Productivity*, Vol. 2, Cheltenham, UK. Elgar.
Marris, Robin (1964) *The Economic Theory of Managerial Capitalism*, Glencoe, Free Press.
Marris, Robin (1998) *Managerial Capitalism in Retrospect*, London, Palgrave Macmillan.
Marshall, Alfred (1920) *Principles of Economics*, 8th edn, London, Macmillan.
Mayer, Thomas (2000) *Doing Economic Research, Essays on Applied Methodology of Economics*, Aldershot, UK, Edward Elgar.
Means, Gardiner (1940) "The Economics of Administered Prices: Introductory Explorations for an Atomistic Economy," in F. Lee and W. Samuels (eds.) *The Heterodox Economics of Gardiner C. Means: A Collection*, Armonk, NY. Sharpe.
Means, Gardiner (1972) "The Administered Price Thesis Reconfirmed," *American Economic Review*, June 62 (3) 292–306.
Means, Gardiner (1994) "The Determinants of Aggregate Demand," in F. Lee and W. Samuels (eds.) *Studies in Institutional Economics*, Armonk, NY, Sharpe, 135–40.
Means, Gardiner (1994) "A Monetary Theory of Employment," in F. Lee and W. Samuels (eds.) *Studies in Institutional Economics*, Armonk, NY, Sharpe, 143–57.
Merchant, Carolyn (1980) *The Death of Nature: Women, Ecology and the Scientific Revolution*, New York, Harper & Row.
Meyer, Laurence (2001) "Does Money Matter?" *Federal Reserve Bank of St. Louis Review*, September, 2001 83 (5), 1–15.
Miller, Richard (2000) "Ten Cheaper Spades: Production Theory and Cost Curves in the Short Run," *Journal of Economic Education*, Spring, 31 (2), 119–30.
Miller, Richard (2001) Firms' Cost Functions: A Reconstruction, *Review of Industrial Organization*, March, 18 (2), 183–200.
Minsky, Hyman (1975) *John Maynard Keynes*, New York, Columbia University Press.
Minsky, Hyman (1977) "The Financial Instability Hypothesis: An Interpretation of Keynes and an Alternative to 'Standard' Theory," *Challenge*, March–April, 20 (1), 20–35.
Minsky, Hyman (1983) *Can 'It' Happen Again? Essays on Instability and Finance*, Armonk, NY, Sharpe.
Minsky, Hyman (1986) *Stabilizing an Unstable Economy*, New Haven, CT, Yale University Press.
Mirowski, P. (1989) *More Heat than Light*, London, Cambridge University Press.
Mirowski, Philip (2000) *Machine Dreams, How Economics Became a Cyborg Science*, New York, Cambridge University Press.
Mizen, Paul (2003) (ed.) *Essays in Honour of Charles Goodhart*, Cheltenham, UK, Edward Elgar.

Modigliani, Franco (1983) "Comments," in James Tobin (ed.) *Macroeconomics, Prices and Quantities*, Washington, DC, Brookings Institution, 235–8.

Moggridge, Donald (1992) *Maynard Keynes, An Economist's Biography*, London, Routledge (Letter to O.T. Falk, 19 February 1936).

Monti, M. (1972) "Deposit, Credit and Interest Rate Determination under Alternative Bank Objective Functions," in G.P. Szego and K.Shell (eds) *Mathematical Methods in Investment and Finance*, North-Holland.

Moore, Basil (1979) "The Endogenous Money Stock," *Journal of Post Keynesian Economics*, Fall, 2 (1), 49–70.

Moore, Basil (1983) "Unpacking the Post Keynesian Black Box," *Journal of Post Keynesian Economics*, Summer, 5 (4) 537–56.

Moore, Basil (1988) *Horizontalists and Verticalists: The Macroeconomics of Credit Money*, New York, Cambridge University Press.

Moore, Basil (1988a) "The Endogenous Money Supply," *Journal of Post Keynesian Economics*, 10 (3), 372–85.

Moore, Basil (1994) "The Demise of the Keynesian Multiplier: A Reply to Cotrell," *Journal of Post Keynesian Economics*, 17, 121–34.

Moore, Basil (1996) "The Money Supply Process: A Historical Reinterpretation," in G. Deleplace and E. J. Nell (eds) *Money in Motion: The Post Keynesian and Circulation Approaches*, New York, Macmillan, 89–101.

Moore, Basil (1997) "Why Wage and Price Flexibility is Destabilizing," in P. Arestis (ed.) *Method, Theory and Policy in Keynes*, London, Edward Elgar.

Moore, Basil (1998) "Money and Interest Rates in a Monetary Theory of Production," in Rotheim, Roy (ed.) *New Keynesian Economics/Post Keynesian Alternatives*, London, Routledge, 339–55.

Moore, Basil (2004) "A Global Currency for a Global Economy," *Journal of Post Keynesian Economics*, Summer, 26 (4), 631–53.

Moreno-Villalaz, J. (1999) "Lessons from the Monetary Experience of Panama: A Dollar Economy with Financial Integration," *Cato Journal*, Winter, 18 (3) 421–39.

Morgan, Mary (1990) *The History of Econometric Ideas*, Cambridge, Cambridge University Press.

Morris, Stephen, and Hynn Song Shin (1999) "Risk Management With Independent Choice," *Financial Stability Review*, Bank of England, November.

Mundell, Robert (1961) "A Theory of Optimum Currency Areas," *American Economic Review*, September, 51 (4), 657–65.

Mundell, Robert (2000) "A Reconsideration of the Twentieth Century" (Nobel Memorial Prize Lecture), *American Economic Review*, June.

Nell, Edward J. (1992) *Transformational Growth and Effective Demand*, London, Macmillan.

Nell, Edward (1996) "The Circuit of Money in a Production Economy," in G. Delaplace and E.J. Nell (eds) *Money in Motion: The Post Keynesian and Circulation Approaches*, New York, Macmillan, 245–304.

Nell, Edward (2001) "Notes on Hicks on Money and Monetary Theory," in Louis-Philippe Rochon, and Matius Vernengo, *Credit, Interest Rates and the Open Economy*, Cheltenham, UK, Edward Elgar.

Nell, Edward J. (2002) "Notes on the Transformational Growth of Demand," in M. Setterfield (ed.) *The Economics of Demand-led Growth*, Cheltenham, UK, Edward Elgar, 251–72.

Nelson, Charles, and Ploser, Charles (1982)"Trends and Random Walks in Macroeconomic Time Series," *Journal of Monetary Economics*, November, 10, 139–62.

Nelson, Charles, and Ploser, Charles (1988) "Trends and Random Walks in Macroeconomic Time Series: Some Evidence and Implications," *Quarterly Journal of Economics*, November, 102, 857–80.

Nelson, Richard, and Winter, Steven (2002) "Evolutionary Theorising in Economics," *Journal of Economic Perspectives*, 16 (2), 23–46.

Nogami, Shozaburo (2000) "Bank of Japan's 'Tankan' Survey Offers Hope, Warning," *Japan Inc. Magazine*, January.

Nordhaus, William (1998) "Quality Changes in Price Indexes," *Journal of Economic Perspectives*, 12(1), 59–68.
Obstfeld, Maurice and Rogoff, Kenneth (1995) "Exchange Rate Dynamics Redux," in L. Sarno and M. Taylor (eds.) (2002) *New Developments in Exchange Rate Economics*, Cheltenham, UK, Edward Elgar, 69–105.
O'Driscoll, Gerold Jr., and Rizzo, Mario (1996) *The Economics of Time and Ignorance*, Oxford, Blackwell.
Okun, Arthur (1980) *Prices and Quantities*, Washington, DC, Brookings Institute.
Olekains, Nilss, and Sibly, Hugh (1992) "Credit Rationing, Implicit Contracts, Risk Aversion, and the Variability of Interest Rates," *Journal of Macroeconomics*, Spring 14 (2), 337–47.
Ormerod, Paul (1994) *The Death of Economics*, London, Faber & Faber.
Ormerod, Paul (1998) *Butterfly Economics: A New General Theory of Social and Economic Behaviour*, London, Faber & Faber.
Osler, Carol (2005) "Stop–Loss Orders and Price Cascades in Currency Markets," *Journal of International Money and Finance*, 24, March, 2, 219–41.
Palley, Thomas (2002) "Keynesian Macroeconomics and the Theory of Economic Growth: Putting Aggregate Demand Back in the Picture," in M. Setterfield (ed.) *The Economics of Demand-led Growth, Challenging the Supply-Side Vision of the Long Run*, Cheltenham, UK, Edward Elgar.
Palley, Tom (1998) "Accomodation, Structualism and Superstructuralism," *Journal of Post Keynesian Economics*, 21, 171–3.
Parguez, Alain (2001) "Money without Scarcity: From the Horizontalist Revolution to the Theory of the Monetary Circuit," in Louis-Philippe Rochon, and Matais Vernengo (eds) *Credit Interest Rates and the Open Economy: Essays on Horizontalism*, Cheltenham, Edward Elgar.
Pasinetti, Luigi (1974) "The Rate of Profit in an Expanding Economy," in C. Panico and N. Salvadori (eds.) (1993) *Post Keynesian Theory of Growth and Distribution*, Aldershot, UK, Edward Elgar.
Pasinetti, Luigi (1981) *Structural Change and Economic Growth: A Theoretical Essay on the Wealth of Nations*, Cambridge, Cambridge University Press.
Pasinetti, Luigi (1993) *Structural Economic Dynamics: A Theory of the Economic Consequences of Human Learning*, Cambridge, Cambridge University Press.
Patinkin, Don (1965) *Money Interest and Prices*, 2nd edn, New York, Harper & Row.
Peach, R., and Steindel, C. (2000) "A Nation of Spendthrifts? An Analysis of Trends in Personal and Gross Saving," *Current Issues in Economics and Finance*, Federal Reserve System, 6 (10).
Penrose, Roger (1989) *The Emperor's New Mind: Concerning Computers, Minds and the Laws of Physics*, Oxford, Oxford University Press.
Peron, P. (1989) "Testing for a Unit Root in Time Series Regressions," *Biometrika*, 75, 335–46.
Pesaran, M. Hashem (1987) *The Limits to Rational Expectations*, Oxford, Basil Blackwell.
Phelps, Edmund (1968) "Money-Wage Dynamics and Labor-Market Equilibrium," *Journal of Political Economy*, 76 (4), 678–711.
Phillips, Chester (1920) *Bank Credit*, New York, Macmillan.
Pollin, Robert (1991) "Two Theories of Money Supply Endogeneity: Some Empirical Evidence," *Journal of Post Keynesian Economics*, Spring, 13 (3), 366–96.
Pollin, Robert (1997) *The Macroeconomics of Saving, Finance, and Investment*, Ann Arbor, MI, University of Michigan Press.
Ponsot, Jean-Francois (2002) "The European Experiences of Currency Boards," in L.P. Rochon and M. Vernengo, *Monetary Unions and Dollarization: Lessons from Europe*, Cheltenham, UK, Edward Elgar.
Poole, William (1970) "Optimal Choice of Monetary Policy Instruments in a Simple Stochastic Macro Model" *Quarterly Journal of Economics*, May, 84, 197–216.
Popper, Karl (1961) *The Logic of Scientific Discovery*, New York, Basic Books.
Popper, Karl (1985) *Popper Selections*, David Miller (ed.) Princeton, NJ, Princeton University Press.
Poterba, James (2000) "Stock Market Wealth and Consumption," *Journal of Economic Perspectives*, Spring, 14 (2), 99–118.

Poterba, James and Summers, Lawrence (2002) "Mean Reversion in Stock Prices: Evidence and Implications," in L. Gallager and M. Taylor (eds.) *Speculation in Financial Markets*, Vol.1, Cheltenham, UK, Edward Elgar.

Prigogine, Ilya (1997) *The End of Certainty: Time, Chaos and the New Laws of Nature*, New York, Free Press.

Putt, A.K. (1990) *Growth, Income and Uneven Development*, Cambridge, Cambridge University Press.

Quandt, Richard, and Rosen, Harvey (1988) *The Conflict between Equilibrium and Disequilibrium Theories: The case of the U.S. Labor Market*, Kalamazoo, MI, W.E. Upjohn Institute.

Realfonzo, R. (1998) *Money and Banking: Theory and Debate (1900–1940)*, Cheltenham, UK, Edward Elgar.

Rescher, Nicholas (1984) *The Limits of Science*, Berkeley, CA, University of California Press.

Reynolds, Peter (1987) *Political Economy: A Synthesis of Kaleckian and Post Keynesian Economics*, New York, St. Martin's Press.

Riach, Peter (1995) "Wage-Employment Determination in a Post Keynesian World," in Phillip Arestis, and Mike Marshall, *The Political Economy of Full Employment*, Aldershot, UK, Edward Elgar.

Riccardo, David (1951) *The Works and Correspondence of David Ricardo*, Vol. 4, Pamphlets, 1815–23, Piero Sraffa (ed.) Cambridge, Cambridge University Press.

Robbins, Lionel (1937) *An Essay on the Nature and Significance of Economic Science*, London, Macmillan.

Robertson, Dennis (1933) *A Note on the Theory of Money*, London, Macmillan.

Robertson, Sir Dennis (1940) "Mr. Keynes and the Rate of Interest," in D. Robertson (ed.) *Essays in Monetary Theory*, London, Staples.

Robinson, Joan (1952) *The Rate of Interest and Other Essays*, London, Macmillan.

Robinson, Joan (1956) *The Accumulation of Capital*, London, Macmillan.

Robinson, Joan (1970) "Quantity Theories Old and New: A Comment," *Journal of Money Credit and Banking*, 4, November, 504–12.

Robinson, Joan (1979) "Unwinding the Stagflation Puzzle," *Journal of Portfolio Management*, Summer, 5 (4), 5–10.

Robinson, Joan (1985) *The Accumulation of Capital*, 3rd edn, London, Palgrave Macmillan.

Rochon, Louis-Philippe (1999) *Credit, Money and Production*, Cheltenham, UK, Edward Elgar.

Rochon, Louis-Philippe (2000) "1939–58; Was Kaldor an Endogenist?" *Metroeconomica*, May, 51 (2), 191–220.

Rochon, Louis-Philippe, and Vernengo, Matias (eds) (2001) *Credit, Interest Rates and the Open Economy: Essays on Horizontalism*, Aldershot, UK, Edward Elgar.

Rochon, Louis-Philippe, and Rossi, Sergio (2004) *Modern Theories of Money*, Cheltenham, UK, Edward Elgar.

Rogers, Colin (1989) *Money, Interest and Capital, A Study in the Foundations of Monetary Theory*, Cambridge, Cambridge University Press.

Rogoff, Kenneth (2001) "Why Not a Global Currency?," *American Economic Review*, May, 91 (2), 243–7.

Rogoff, Kenneth (2003) "The Evolution and Performance of Exchange Regimes," IMF Working Papers, 243.

Romer, Paul (1986) "Increasing Returns and Long Run Growth," *Journal of Political Economy*, 94, 1002–37.

Romer, Paul (1990) "Endogenous Technical Change," *Journal of Political Economy*, 98, 71–102.

Romer, Paul (1994) "The Origins of Endogenous Growth," in P. Stephan and D. Audretsch (eds.) (2000) *The Economics of Science and Innovation*, Cheltenham, UK, Edward Elgar.

Rose, Andrew (2000a) "Currency Unions: Their Dramatic Effect on International Trade," *Economic Policy*, 28, April, 9–45.

Rose, Andrew (2000b) "One Money, One Market: Estimating Effects of Common Currencies on Trade," *Economic Policy: A European Forum*, April, 30, 7–33.

Rose, Andrew and Van Wincoop, Eric (2001) "Nominal Money as a Barrier to International Trade: The Real Case for a Currency Union," *American Economic Review*, May, 91 (2), 386–90.

Rose, Stephen (2004) *The 21st Century Brain*, London, Jonathan Cape.

Rosser, J. Barkeley (1998) "Complex Dynamics in New Keynesian and Post Keynesian Models," in Rotheim, Roy (ed.) *New Keynesian Economics/Post Keynesian Alternatives*, London, Routledge, 288–302.

Rosser, J. Barkeley, Rosser, M., and Ahmed, E. (2003) "Multiple Unofficial Economy Equilibria and Income Distribution Dynamics," *Journal of Post Keynesian Economics*, 25 (3), 425–47.

Rosser, J. Barkeley Jr. (ed.) (2004) *Complexity in Economics*, 3 vols, Cheltenham, UK, Edward Elgar.

Rotheim, Roy (1981) "Keynes' Monetary Theory of Value (1933)," *Journal of Post Keynesian Economics*, Summer, 3 (4), 568–85.

Rotheim, Roy (1998) (ed.) *New Keynesian Economics/Post Keynesian Alternatives*, London, Routledge.

Rouse, Joseph (1996) *Engaging Science, How to Understand Its Practices Philosophically*, New York, Cornell University Press.

Rowthorn, Robert E. (1982) "Demand, Real Wages and Economic Growth," *Studi Economici*, 18, 591–624.

Rudebusch, Glenn (1998) "Do Measures of Monetary Policy in a VAR Make Sense?" *International Economic Review*, 39 (4), 907–31.

Rusek, Antonin (2002) "Pros and Cons of Official Dollarization in Eastern Europe," *International Advances in Economic Research*, 8 (4), 305–13.

Rymes, Phobus (1989) *Keynes' Lectures, 1932–35, Notes of a Representative Student*, London, Macmillan.

Salvatore, D. (2001) "Dollarization for the Americas?," *Journal of Policy Modeling*, 23 (3), 237–39.

Sali-I-Martin, Xavier (2003) "Convergence and Divergence – Theoretical Underpinnings," in G. Tumpel-Gugerell and P. Mooslechner (eds.) *Economic Convergence and Divergence in Europe*, Cheltenham, UK, Edward Elgar. 117–27.

Sapsford, David, and Morgan, Wyn (1994) *The Economics of Primary Commodities: Models, Analysis and Policy*. Aldershot, UK, Edward Elgar.

Samuelson, Paul (1969) "What the Classical and Neoclassical Monetary Theory Really Was," *Canadian Journal of Economics*, February, 1 (1), 1–15.

Sawyer, Malcomb (1988) *Post Keynesian Economics*, Aldershot, UK, Edward Elgar.

Sawyer, Malcomb (1996) "Money, Finance and the Interest Rates: Some Post Keynesian Reflections," in P. Arestis (ed.) *Keynes, Money and the Open Economy: Essays in Honour of Paul Davidson*, Vol. 1, Cheltenham, UK, Edward Elgar.

Sawyer, Malcolm (2002) "Market Structure, Uncertainty and Unemployment," in Malcolm Sawyer, Nina Shapiro, Sheila Dow, and John Hillard (eds), *Beyond Keynes*, Vol. 2, *Keynes, Uncertainty and the Global Economy*, Cheltenham, UK, Edward Elgar.

Seccareccia, Mario (1996) "Post Keynesian Fundism and the Circulation Approach," in Deleplace and Nell (eds), 400–16.

Schelling, Thomas (1978) *Micromotives and Macrobehaviour*, New York, Norton.

Shiller, Robert (1981) "Do Stock Prices Move Too Much to be Justified by Subsequent Changes in Dividends?" in L. Gallager and M. Taylor (eds.) *Speculation and Financial Markets*, Vol.1, Cheltenham, UK, Edward Elgar.

Shiller, Robert (1990) "The Term Structure of Interest Rates," in S. Ross (2000) *The Debt Market*, Vol.1, Cheltenham, UK. Elgar.

Schliefer, H. (2000) *Inefficient Markets: An Introduction to Behavioral Finance*, London, Oxford University Press.

Schmitt, Bernard, and Greppi, S. (1996) "The National Economy Studied as a Whole: Aspects of Circular Flow Analysis in the German Language," in Deleplace and Nell (eds), 341–64.

Schneider, Friedrich (2002) "Size and Measurement of the Informal Economy in 110 Countries Around the World," World Bank, Working Paper, July.
Schneider, F., and Enste, D. (2000) "Shadow Economies: Size, Causes and Consequences," *Journal of Economic Literature*, 31 (1), 77–114.
Schuler, Kurt (1999) "Basics of Dollarization," Joint Economic Committee Staff Report, Office of the Chairman, Washington, DC, July.
Schultz, C.L. (2003) "The Consumer Price Index: Conceptual Issues and Practical Suggestions," *Journal of Economic Perspectives*, 17 (1), 3–22.
Schultz, Walter (2001) *The Moral Conditions of Economic Efficiency*, Cambridge, Cambridge University Press.
Schumpeter, Joseph (1934) *The Theory of Economic Development*. Translation by Redvers Opie of 2nd edn of German Original (1926) (1st edn, 1911) Boston, MA, Harvard University Press.
Schumpeter, Joseph (1954) *A History of Economic Analysis*, London, Oxford University Press.
Setterfield, Mark (1995) "Historical Time and Economic Theory," *Review of Political Economy*, 7, 1–27.
Setterfield, Mark (1997a) *Rapid Growth and Relative Decline: Modeling Macroeconomic Dynamics with Hysteresis*, London, Macmillan.
Setterfield, Mark (1997b) "Should Economists Dispense with the Notion of Equilibrium?" *Journal of Post Keynesian Economics*, 20, 47–76.
Setterfield, Mark (1997c) " 'History versus Equilibrium' in the Theory of Economic Growth," *Cambridge Journal of Economics*, 21, 365–78.
Setterfield, Mark (1998) "History versus equilibrium: Nicholas Kaldor on Historical Time and Economic Theory," *Cambridge Journal of Economics*, 22, 21–37.
Setterfield, Mark (2002) *The Economics of Demand-led Growth*, Cheltenham, Edward Elgar.
Shackle, George (1955) *Uncertainty in Economics and Other Reflections*, Cambridge, Cambridge University Press.
Shackle, George (1968) *Expectations, Investment and Income*, 2nd edn (1st edn 1938), Oxford, Clarendon Press.
Shackle, George (1971) Discussion of R.W. Clower's Paper in G. Clayton, J.C. Gilbert and R. Sedgwick (eds), *Monetary Theory and Monetary Policy in the 1970s*, Oxford University Press, 32–7.
Shackle, George (1983) "Levels of Simplicity in Keynes' Theory of Money and Employment," *South African Journal of Economics*, September, 51 (3), 357–67.
Shapiro, Nina, and Sawyer, Malcolm (2003) "Post Keynesian Price Theory," *Journal of Post Keynesian Economics*, 25 (3), 355–65.
Sharpe, William (1970) *Portfolio Theory and Capital Markets*, New York, McGraw-Hill.
Sheffrin, H. (2002) *Beyond Greed and Fear: Understanding Behavioral Finance and The Psychology of Investing*, New York, Oxford University Press.
Shiller, Robert (1979) "The Volatility of Long-Term Interest Rates and Expectations Models of the Term Structure" in Robert Shiller, and Hersh Shefrin (eds) (2001) *Behavioral Finance*. Cheltenham, UK, Edward Elgar, 383–412.
Shiller, Robert (2000) *Irrational Exuberance*, Princeton, NJ, Princeton University Press.
Shmitt, Bermard (1966) *Monnaie, Salaires et Profits*, Paris: Presses Universitaire de France.
Simons, Henry (1938) *Personal Income Taxation; the Definition of Income as a Problem of Fiscal Policy*, Chicago, University of Chicago Press.
Sims, Christopher (1972) "Money, Income and Causality," *American Economic Review*, September, 510–52.
Sims, Christopher (1980) "Comparison of Interwar and Postwar Business Cycles," *American Economic Review*, May, 70 (2), 250–7.
Sims, Christopher (1992) "Interpreting the Macroeconomic Time Series Facts: The Effects of Monetary Policy," *European Economic Review*, June, 36 (5), 975–1000.
Sims, Christopher (2002) "Evolving Post World War II: US Inflation Dynamics: Comment," in B. Bernanke and K. Rogoff (eds.) *NBER Macroeconomics Annual 2001*. Vol. 16, Cambridge, MA, MIT Press, 373–79.

Skidelsky, Robert (2000) *John Maynard Keynes, Vol. 3, Fighting for Freedom*, New York, Putnam.
Smithin, John (1996) *Macroeconomic Policy and the Future of Capitalism: the Revenge of the Rentiers and the Threat to Prosperity*, Cheltenham, UK, Edward Elgar.
Solow, Robert (1956) "A Contribution to the Theory of Economic Growth," *Quarterly Journal of Economics*, February, 70, 65–94.
Solow, Robert (1957) "Technical Change and the Aggregate Production Function," in J. Hartley *et al.* (1998) *Real Business Cycles: A Reader*, London, Routledge.
Solow, Robert (1971) "Discussion," *American Economic Review*, Papers and Proceedings, May, 61(2), 63–8.
Solow, Robert (1980) "On Theories of Unemployment," in G.K. Shaw (ed.) (1988) *The Keynesian Heritage*, Vol. 2, Aldershot, UK. Elgar.
Solow, Robert (1984) "Mr.Hicks and the Classics," *Oxford Economic Papers*, November, 36, 13–25.
Solow, Robert (1990) *The Labor Market as a Social Institution*, Cambridge, Basil Blackwell.
Solow, Robert (1997) "Is There a Core of Usable Macroeconomics We Should All Believe In?," *American Economic Review*, May, 230–2.
Solow, Robert (1998) "Some Macroeconomic Implications of Monopolistic Competiton," in *Monopolistic Competition and Macroeconomic Theory*, Cambridge, Cambridge University Press.
Solow, Robert (2001) "Another Look at Whether a Rising Tide Lifts All Boats" in James Hines, Hillary Hoynes, Allan, Krueger, and Robert Solow (eds) *The Roaring Nineties: Can Full Employment be Sustained?* Russell Sage Foundation, New York, Century Foundation Press, 493–537.
Solow, Robert, and Taylor, John (1998) "How Cautious Must the Fed Be?" in B. Friedman (ed.) *Inflation, Unemployment and Monetary Policy*, Cambridge, MA, MIT Press.
Sornette, Didier (2003) *Why Stock Markets Crash*, Princeton, Princeton University Press.
Stein, Daniel (1989) *Lectures in the Sciences of Complexity*, Proceedings of 1988 Complex Systems Summer School, Santa Fe, NM, Addison-Wesley.
Steindl, Joseph (1990) *Economic Papers 1941–88*, London, Macmillan.
Stiglitz, Joseph, and Weiss, Andrew (1987) "Macroeconomic Equilibrium and Credit Rationing," *NBER*, Working Paper, 2164.
Stiglitz, Joseph (1989) "Using Tax Policy to Curb Speculative Short-Term Trading," *Journal of Financial Services*, 3–17.
Stock, James, and Watson, Mark (1988) "Variable Trends in Economic Time Series," *Journal of Economic Perspectives*, Summer, 2, 147–78.
Stock, James, and Watson, Mark (2003) "Forecasting Output and Inflation: The Role of Asset Prices," *Journal of Economic Literature*, September, 41 (3), 788–829.
Streeten, Paul (2000) "What's Wrong with Contemporary Economics?" *Pakistan Development Review*, Autumn, 39 (3), 191–211.
Studart, Rogerio (2001) "Dollarization: An Intellectual Fad or a Deep Insight?," *Journal of Post Keynesian Economics*, Summer, 23(4), 639–51.
Summers, Larry (1983) "The Nonadjustment of Nominal Interest Rates: A Study of the Fisher Effect," in J. Tobin (ed.) *Macroeconomics, Prices and Quantities*, Washington, DC, Brookings Institution.
Summers, Larry (1991) "The Scientific Illusion in Empirical Macroeconomics," *Scandinavian Journal of Economics*, 93, 129–48.
Summers, Larry (2000) "International Financial Crises: Causes, Prevention and Cures," *American Economic Review*, May, 90 (2), 1–16.
Sutton, John (2002) *Marshall's Tendencies*, Cambridge, MA, MIT Press.
Sylos-Labini, Paolo (1979) "Industrial Pricing in the United Kingdom: Review Article" *Cambridge Journal of Economics*, June, 3 (2) 153–63.
Sylos-Labini, Paolo (1979a) "Prices and Income Distribution in Manufacturing Industry," *Journal of Post Keynesian Economics*, Fall, 3–25.
Taylor, John (1979) "Staggered Wage Setting in a Macro Model" in F. Kydland (1995) *Business Cycle Theory*, Cheltenham, UK, Edward Elgar.

Taylor, John (1991) *Income Distribution, Inflation and Growth*, Cambridge, MA, MIT Press.
Taylor, John (1993) "Discretion versus Policy Rules in Practice," *Carnegie-Rochester Conference Series on Public Policy*, December, 39, 195–214.
Taylor, John (1995) "The Monetary Transmission Mechanism: An Empirical Framework," *Journal of Economic Perspectives*, 9 (4), 11–26.
Taylor, John (1997) "A 'Core' of Practical Macroeconomics," *American Economic Review*, May, 87 (2), 233–5.
Taylor, John (1999) "A Historical Analysis of Monetary Policy Rules," *Monetary Policy Rules*. NBER Conference Report Series, Chicago, University of Chicago Press.
Taylor, John (1999) "Staggered Price and Wage Setting In Macroeconomics," in John Taylor, and Michael Woodford (eds) *Handbook of Macroeconomics*, Vol. IB, Amsterdam, Elsevier, 1009–50.
Thaler, Richard (1985) "Does the Stock Market Overreact?" in S. Maital and S. Maital (eds.) (1993a) *Economics and Psychology*, Aldershot, UK Elgar.
Thaler, Richard (1993) *Advances in Behavioral Finance*, New York, Russell Sage Foundation.
Taylor, R. (2002) "Order in Pollock's Chaos," *Scientific American*, 287 (6), 116–21.
Thaler, R. (1985) "Mental Accounting and Consumer's Choice", *Marketing Science*, 4, 199–214.
Thaler, R. (ed.) (1993) *Advances in Behavioral Finance*, New York, Russell Sage Foundation.
Thaler, Richard (1995) "Myopic Loss Aversion and the Equity Premium Puzzle," in D. Kahneman and A. Tversky (2000) *Choices, Values and Frames*, Cambridge, Cambridge University Press.
Thaler, Richard (1999) "Mental Accounting Matters," in D. Kahneman and A. Tversky (eds.) *Choices, Values, and Frames*, Cambridge, Cambridge University Press
Thaler, Richard, and Barberis Nicholas (2003) *A Survey of Behavioral Finance*, in G. Constantinides, M. Harris, and R. Stultz (eds.) *Handbook of the Economics of Finance* Vol. 1B, *Financial Markets and Asset Pricing*, Amsterdam, Elsevier, North Holland.
Theil, Hener (1971), *Principles of Econometrics*, New York, Wiley.
Theroux, Paul (2003) *Dark Star Safari*, London, Penguin Books.
Thirwall, Antony, P. (1979) "The Balance of Payments Constraint as an Explanation of International Growth Rate Differences," *Banca Nazionale del Lavoro Quarterly Review*, March, 128, 45–53.
Thirwall, Antony, P. (1983) "A Plain Man's Guide to Kaldor's Growth Laws," *Journal of Post Keynesian Economics*, Spring, 5 (3), 345–58.
Thirwall, Antony P. (1997) "Reflections on the Concept of Balance-of-payments-constrained Growth," *Journal of Post Keynesian Economics*, 19, 375–85.
Thirwall, Antony, P. (2001) "The Mobilization of Saving for Growth and Development in Developing Countries," *Investigacion Economica*, April–June, 232, 13–44.
Thomas, L. (1983) *The Youngest Science: Notes of a Medicine Watcher*, New York, Viking Press.
Thorton, Daniel (1983) "Why Does Velocity Matter?" (1987) in J. Wilcox (ed.) *Current Readings on Money, Banking and Financial Markets*, Boston, Little Brown.
Thorton, Daniel (1983a) "Lagged and Contemporaneous Reserve Accounting: An Alternative View," *Review*, Federal Reserve Bank of St. Louis, November, 26–33.
Thorton, Daniel (2001) "The Federal Reserve's Operating Procedure, Nonborrowed Reserves and the Liquidity Effect," *Journal of Banking and Finance*, September, 25 (9) 1717–39.
Tobin, James (1963) "Commercial Banks as Creators of Money," in Dean Carson (ed.) *Banking and Monetary Studies*, Homewood, IL, Irwin.
Tobin, James (1970) "Money and Income: Post Hoc *ergo* Propter Hoc?," *Quarterly Journal of Economics*, May, 84 (2), 301–17.
Tobin, James (1972) "Inflation and Unemployment," *American Economic Review*, 62, 1–26.
Tobin, James (1982) "The State of Exchange Rate Theory: Some Skeptical Observations," in (1996) *Essays in Economics* Vol. 4, Cambridge, MIT Press, 601–16.
Tobin, James (1982) "Money and Finance in the Macroeconomic Process," in *Essays in Economics* Vol. 4, Cambridge, MIT Press, 23–66.

Tobin, James (1991) "Comment," in Douglas Bern Cheim and John Shoven (eds) *National Saving and Economic Performance*, Chicago, IL, University of Chicago Press, 301–4.

Tobin, James (1998) "Financial Globalisation: Can National Currencies Survive?," Annual World Bank Conference on Development Economics.

Tobin, James (2002) "An Overview of The General Theory," in Geoff Harcourt, and Raich Peter (eds) *A 'Second Edition' of the General Theory*, Vol. 2, London, Routledge.

Tobin, James (2003) *World Finance and Economic Stability: Selected Essays of James Tobin*, Cheltenham, UK, Edward Elgar.

Tobin, James, Eichengreen, Barry, and Wyplosz, Charles (2003) "Two Cases for Sand in the Wheels of International Finance," in S. Eijffinger and J. Lemmen (eds.) *International Financial Integration*, Vol. 1, Cheltenham, UK. Elgar.

Toporowski, Jan (2002) "Keynes and Monetary Policy in Speculative Markets," *Investigacion-Economica*, October–December 62 (242), 13–32.

Toulmin, Steven (1961) *Foresight and Understanding: An Inquiry into the Aims of Science*, Bloomington, IN, Indiana University Press.

Tversky, Amos, and Fox, Craig (1995) "Weighing Risk and Uncertainty," in D. Kahneman, and A. Tversky (eds.) (2000) *Choices, Values, and Frames*, Cambridge, Cambridge University Press.

Tversky, Amos and Kahneman, Daniel (1992) "Advances in Prospect Theory: Cumulative Representation of Uncertainty," in J. Hey (ed.) *The Economics of Uncertainty*, Cheltenham, UK. Elgar.

Tversky, Amos and Kahneman, Daniel (1992) (eds.) *Choices, Values, and Frames*, Cambridge, Cambridge University Press.

Vetter, M., Stadler, and Hayes, J. (1997) "Phase Transitions in Learning," in L. Vanderwert, "Understanding Tomorrow's Mind: Advances in Chaos Theory, Quantum Theory, and Consciousness in Psychology," *The Journal of Mind and Behavior*, Spring/Summer, 13, 2 & 3.

Vickers, Douglas (1999) *The Tyranny of the Market: A Critique of Theoretical Foundations*, Ann Arbor, MI, University of Michigan Press.

Volcker, Paul (1978) "The Role of Monetary Targets in an Age of Inflation," *Journal of Monetary Economics*, April, 4, 329–40.

Volcker, Paul (2002) "Monetary Policy Transmission: Past and Future Challenges," *Economic Policy Review*, Federal Reserve Bank of New York, May, 8 (1), 7–11.

Waldrop, M. (1992) *Complexity: The Emerging Science at the Edge of Order and Complexity*, New York, Touchstone.

Walsh, Carl (2003) *Monetary Theory and Policy*, 2nd edn, Cambridge, MA, MIT Press.

Weintraub, E. Roy (2002) *How Economics Became a Mathematical Science*, Durham, NC, Duke University Press.

Weintraub, Sidney (1978) *Capitalism's Inflation and Unemployment Crisis: Beyond Monetarism and Keynesianism*, Reading, MA, Addison-Wesley.

Weintraub, Sidney (2000) "The Dollarization Debate," *Issues in International Political Economy*, 2, 1–3.

Weitzman, Martin (1985) "Increasing Returns and the Foundations of Unemployment Theory," *Journal of Post Keynesian Economics*, Spring, 7(3), 403–9.

Welch, I. (2000) "Herding among Security Analysts," *Journal of Financial Economics*, 58 (3), 369–96.

West, B. (1997) "Chaos and Related Things: A Tutorial," in L. Vanderwert (ed.) "Understanding Tomorrow's Mind: Advances in Chaos Theory, Quantum Theory, and Consciousness in Psychology," *The Journal of Mind and Behavior*, Spring/Summer, 13, 2 & 3, 1–24.

Wicksell, Knut (1895) "Influence of the Rate of Interest on Commodity Prices," in Erik Lindahl (ed.), *Selected Papers on Economic Theory*, London, Allen and Unwin (1958).

Wicksell, Knut (1898) *Interest and Prices* (Translation by Richard Kahn, 1936), London, Macmillan.

Wolff, Edward (2004) *What Happened to the Quality of Life in Advanced Industrialized Nations?*, Cheltenham, UK, Edward Elgar.

Woodford, Michael (2003) *Interest and Prices. Foundations of Theory of Monetary Policy*, Princeton, NJ, Princeton University Press.

Working, Holbrook (1960) "A Random Difference Series for Use in the Analysis of Time Series," in T. Mills (ed.) (2002) *Forecasting Financial Markets*, Cheltenham, UK, Edward Elgar.

Wray, Randall (1990) *Money and Credit in Capitalist Economies: The Endogenous Money Approach*, Aldershot, UK, Edward Elgar.

Wray, Randall (1998) *Understanding Modern Money: The Key to Full Employment and Price Stability*, Cheltenham, UK, Edward Elgar.

Wray, Randall (2004) *Credit and State Theories of Money*, Cheltenham, UK, Edward Elgar.

Yule, Udny (1932) *An Introduction to the Theory of Statistics*, London, Griffen.

Zellner, Arnold (1979) "Causality and Econometrics," in *Three Aspects of Policy and Policymaking: Knowledge, Data and Institutions*, Carnegie-Rochester Conference Series on Public Policy, 10, 9–54.

Index

AS curve 278, 288, 289, 291, 298–300, 341, 350, 508
   horizontal 279
abstain from consumption 165, 168, 293, 498 n.35
the academy xxiv
AD–AS diagram 289, 297
African economies 460, 464–465, 470, 494 n.72
   low growth rates of 463
Aggregate Demand (AD) 157, 216, 242, 282, 304, 360, 415, 436, 455
   growth over time 360
   interest elasticity of 312, 314, 316, 323, 328, 426
   insufficiency 362
   management 9, 74, 285, 306, 402, 456–457
aggregate saving 159, 160, 166, 167, 170, 334
aggregate supply (AS) 142, 159, 236, 261–279, 284, 304, 312, 338, 340, 360, 442, 450, 455, 461, 505
Alesina, A. 451
analytical classes 133, 489 n.5
   classification of the distribution 133
   "loose" concepts 132, 137, 489 n.5
Andrews, P.W. 263, 264, 267, 482 n.39, 505 n.10–13
"animal spirits" 116, 132, 205, 230, 293, 294, 301, 312–314, 327, 336, 341, 357, 373, 461, 513 n.4
   changes in 301, 312–313, 327
   importance of art of persuading 301–302
ARIMA *see* autoregressive invertible moving average processes
Aristotle's law 134
Arrow–Debreu Walrasian system 114, 115
Arthur, B. (1994) 474 n.2
Artificial Emotion (AE) 32
Artificial Intelligence (AI) 32
AS–AD analysis, post Keynesian 300–301
Asian crisis of 1997 414
Asian "Tigers" 386, 460
asset market values 181, 188
asset valuations 143
Augmented Dickey–Fuller (ADF) tests 101

autoregressive invertible moving average processes (ARIMA) 97
   forecasts xxi
average variable cost (AVC) 276

Bak, P. 479 n.77
balance of payments adjustment 396, 398, 448
   classical view of 396–398
   Keynesian view of 398–403
balance sheet relation 225–226
banks
   borrowing 208, 210, 222–224, 229, 251, 252, 291, 332, 333, 344, 350, 365, 367, 375, 377, 462, 465
   credit 200, 362
   customer relation 221
   deposits 175, 186, 209, 216, 219
   intermediation 215–237
   lending 220, 224, 226, 319
   liability management 221, 232
   liquidity 221
   loans 175, 216, 219, 224–225, 365
   portfolio management 218
   as retailers of credit 200, 201, 205, 211, 216
Bank of England 248
Bank of Japan 320–322, 326
Bank Rate 217, 249, 252, 327, 340, 345, 352, 467
   changes in 327–330
   exogenous policy instrument of the central bank 252–255
   external balance constraints on reducing 345–348
   internal balance constraints on reducing 340–345
   short run exogeneity and long run endogeneity 352–358
banking system 171, 225, 231, 367
   assets and liabilities of 227
   origins 199
Barnum, P.T. 420
Barro, R. 451
Base-multiplier process 307
Bayesian approach 89
Blanchard, O. 281

Blinder, A. 270, 272, 274, 277, 281, 283, 508 n.40
Blinder's survey 275
Bohr, N. 36, 38
Borrowed Reserves (BR) 226
borrowing 207
Boskin, M. 494 n.61
Boskin Commission 151
BR–AD diagram 307–309
BR–ΔAD diagram 309–313
ΔBR–ΔAD diagram 313–316
Bradford, D. 175
branch banking systems 435, 518 n.3
Brealey, R. 79
Bretton Woods 339, 385, 386, 404–408, 410, 411–413, 422, 423, 438, 449
 Agreement 406
 collapse of 412–413
 success and failure 405–408
 system 405, 412
Buiter, W. 409
Bureau of Economic Analysis (BEA) 139
Bureau of Labor Statistics (BLS) 151
"butterfly effect" 55, 126

capital account balance 390, 434
capital accumulation 462
capital budgeting 163, 374, 391, 393, 475 n.20
 accounting for open economies 389–396
 for the government sector 163–164, 475 n.19
capital controls 410, 419, 422
capital gains 174–194
 Addendum to National Income Accounting 1983–1987 184
 income 496 n.24
celestial mechanics 66
central bank 55, 170, 173, 183, 208, 216–218, 222, 241, 337
 administration of supply price of reserves 230–232
 and bank rate 226, 246, 341, 426, 428, 430, 468
 inflation targeting 247–248
 interest rate setting behavior 241–243
 liabilities 206
 purchases of securities 208–209
 "reaction" function 243
 regulation of the supply of money 201, 205
 Taylor Rule 243
 ultimate supplier of system liquidity 208–212

Chaos Game 47, 48
chaos theory 43–74, 125
 application of 49–56
 definition 44
Charemza, W.W. 485 n.37
cheap money policies 402
Chick, V. 303, 359
China 149, 152–153, 386, 402, 415, 451, 459, 464
"Chinese Box" phenomenon 19
"Chinese Water torture" effect 415
choice theory 107
Christ 484 n.30
Churchill, W. 155
(C + I + G) diagram 289–291
Cilliers, P. 476
classical economists 112–113, 157, 170, 238–239, 262, 275, 299, 320, 354–355, 400, 422, 443, 498 n.38
classical trade theory 396
commercial banking 219, 473
commercial banks
 intermediation 215–237
 as retailers of credit 216–222
commodity money 198
common currency 434, 438–439, 441, 447
 efficiency gains from 439–441
 stabilization gains from 441–442
common monetary system 391
comparative static equilibrium analysis 55, 123, 305, 310
Competitiveness Policy Council 157
Complex Adaptive Systems (CAS) xvi–xxvi, 14–21, 459
complex economies 55, 242, 296, 302, 341
complex systems xiv–xv, 14, 20, 23–27, 29, 34–36, 66, 71, 80, 84, 91, 102, 111, 122
 challenge to modeling 25–28
 characteristics of 17–20, 35
 conclusions 33–36, 102–103
 and contingency 13–42
 equilibrium 372
 inability to comprehend 36
 introduction 14–17
 process analysis xx–xxii, 122–127
 randomness 23
 reductionist approach 16, 35
 relational structure of 20–21
 and science 22–25
 structure of 26
 unique characteristics of 17–20
complexity theory 15, 27, 108, 137, 381, 480 n.5

Index 549

connectionist systems *see* neural networks
Consumer Price Index (CPI)   298
consumption and investment
  distinction between   142–143
contingency   75–103
  pervasiveness of   75–77
convenience lending   213, 251, 332, 345, 349, 363, 366, 377
  and "convenience saving"   366–370
  non-volitional finance of deficit-spending   363–366
convenience saving   344, 377
conventional economics *see* orthodox economics
"convergence" hypothesis   463
convertible currencies   437, 440
convertible national moneys   434
Cooper, R.   438–439
Copenhagen interpretation   36
Cornwall, J.   460–461
Cowles Commission   84, 86, 88, 93
credit money   186, 197–198, 212, 220, 230, 381, 467
  commodity money   198
  and "convenience lending"   212
  economies   168, 360, 369
  endogeneity of   197–214
  fiat money   198
  growth   467–469
  supply of   230–235
creditors   318
credit ceiling   216
credit rationing   212, 220, 222
credit-utilization
  rate   245
  ratio   351
credit-worthiness   216
crucial choice   118
Crusoe economies   167
"cumulative causation"   460
currency blocks   453
currency unions   446–449
current account balance of payments (CABOPs)   397
current account deficits   427

Darwinism   24
data mining   75, 87–88, 93, 269
David   474 n.2
Davidson, P.   xxv
Dawkins, R.   43
Day   474 n.5
Deadman, D.F.   485 n.37

debtor and creditor
  configuration   387
  nations   405
deficit
  banks   227
  countries   346
  expenditures   364
  spending   193–194, 360, 365, 367
deflationary
  bias, empirical estimates of   424–432
  process   451
"Delphic" pronouncements   211
demand   303–330
demand constraints   340–347
  led growth, financial barriers to   454–473
  management   362
depreciation   397–398
deterministic system   59
devaluation   397–398
developed countries   342, 343
developing countries (DCs)   428, 442
Diamond, R.   478 n.41
Difference Stationary (DS) process   96
"dirty" interest rate targeting   234
discount window   244
Disposable Personal Income (DPI)   191
Dollarization   439, 446, 449–453
domestic investment   388
Domestic National Investment   394
Dorwald   269 (Author please provide the full name)
double-entry bookkeeping   161, 389–391, 514 n.7
Dow, S.   93
Durbin, E.F.M.   86, 484 n.31
Durbin–Watson
  ratios   87
  statistics   86
dynamic analysis   54–55
dynamic systems theory   63
dynamical equations   66–67

Eckstein, O.   268
econometric analysis   136
  of business cycles   77–85
  limitations of   136–138
econometrics, data mining   75–103
econometric theory   103
economic analysis   104
  implications of complexity   104–127
Economic Aspects of Welfare (EAW)   147
economic concepts   131, 136
  looseness of   131–155
  measurement and quantification of   136–138

economic growth 456–460
  neoclassical supply-side models of 456–460
  post Keynesian demand-led models of 460–463
economic measurement 139, 154
economic theory xx, xxv 109
  axioms of 109
  central significance of non-ergodicity for xxv
economic time series 96–102
economic variables 56
  innate instability of 56–58
Edgeworth, F.Y. 4
Edwards, S. 452
efficient market hypothesis (EMH) 56, 420
Eichenbaum, M. 281, 283, 286
Eichner, A. 267
Einstein, A. 43, 59, 131
Eisner, R. 144, 147–150, 175
Eisner's total income system 144–150
electronic funds transfer (EFT) system 201
endogenous money xxii–xxiii, 217, 237, 245, 248, 283, 301, 307, 352, 416, 463
endogeneity of the base 205–207, 228–230, 307–315, 331–347
endogeneity of base 205–07
epistemological uncertainty models 113
equilibrium analysis xx–xxii, 70, 81
  case against 119–122
  methodological choice of 70
equities 126–127, 309, 318, 319, 326–332, 333, 337, 352, 496 n.24
  market value of 171, 175–176, 177, 181, 182, 187, 188, 191
  ownership 187
ergodicity 113–115, 487 n.33
Euro 327, 357, 412, 440, 446, 448–449, 451, 501 n.38
Euroisation 439, 449–453
European Central Bank (ECB) 439
European Currency Union 447
European Economic Commission 448
European Economic Community (EEC) 386
European Exchange Rate Mechanism 386
European Free Trade Area (EFTA) 447
European Monetary Union (EMU) 436
evolutionary biology 24
exchange rate
  crises 422
  fixed *see* fixed exchange rates
  flexible *see* flexible exchange rates
  G3 423
  manipulation 414
  no *see* no exchange rates
  regime 338

exogenous
  interest rates xii–xxiii, 217, 238–251, 252–55
  money supply *see* money supply
  shocks 6, 11, 55, 57, 83, 114
  variables 7, 10, 89, 203
expectations theory 226, 232, 246, 249
expected fall in land prices (Japan) 320–328
external balance 206, 243, 306, 354, 434
  achievement of 377–378
  constraints on reducing bank rate 345–348, 358
external imbalance 339, 346–347, 410, 425–432, 460

Fedderke, J.W. 269
Federal Reserve 244, 246
  rate setting policy 246
federal funds rate 231–35
Feldstein, M. 158
Feynman, R. 36, 478 n.51
fiat money 115, 171, 185, 198–201, 206, 213, 243, 345, 350, 366, 369, 379, 436
final output 139
  definition of 139
financial markets 421
fiscal deficit 250
Fisher, B. 224
fix-price sector 265, 287, 291, 294, 300, 305
fixed exchange rates 385–408
flex-price sector 299
flexible exchange rate regimes 420, 424
  endogenous speculation in 420–424
  deflationary bias in the current 424–427
flexible exchange rates 409–432
  case against 413–420
  case for 411–413
foreign exchange reserves 434
Foundations of Economic Analysis 6
fractal structures 45, 47, 53, 68, 480 n.97
  static 67
France 448–449
Friedman, M. 113, 232, 202, 247, 412
Frisch, R.A.K. 81–82, 84
  "rocking horse" model of 1933 80
Fromm, E. 268
fundamental uncertainty 125, 240, 262, 276, 286, 302, 328, 335, 422, 455, 458–459, 461
  non-probabilistic nature of 112–122

G3 exchange rates *see* exchange rate
Galbraith, J. 11
Galileo 64

Index 551

General Equilibrium   115, 121, 380, 479 n.79
  configuration   457
  defined as   380
  paradigm   282
General Linear Model   86
General Theory   255–58
Germany   386, 404, 406, 448–449, 459
Geroski, P.   269
Gleick, J.   43, 483 n.73
global
  currency union   450
  income inequality   152–154
Godel, K.   64
Godley, W.A.H.   268
Goodhart, C.   253, 502 n.19, 504 n.39
Goods as saving   389–395
Gordon, R.J.   270
Government sector   162–64
Granger–Sims causality tests   249
Great Depression of the 1930s   104, 357, 362
Greenspan, A.   234
Gresham's Law   501 n.3
Gross Domestic Investment   394
Growth rates   150

Haavelmo, T.   6–7, 82–84
  "The Probability Approach in Econometrics"
  probability revolution   6–7, 82
Hahn, F.   108–111
Hall, R.   263, 267
Haugen, R.   57
Hayek, F.   7–8, 106
Heisenberg, W.   36
Helm, D.   174
Hendry, D.F.   89
  LSE approach   89
herding   119
Hicks, Sir J.   104, 131, 175, 178, 180–181, 197, 215, 331
  definition of income   174–194, 390
Hicksian income   177–183, 188, 192, 356; see also income
  estimates of   188–192
  and saving behavior   192–194
High Income
  developed countries   466, 470
  developing economies   469
  economies   472
Hitch, C.J.   263, 267
Hong Kong   415, 451
Horgan, J.   43, 477 n.24
  The End of Science   477 n.24
Horioka, C.   158
horizontalism   218–19

horizontalists   218, 236
human
  behavior   16, 105, 135
  brain   16–17, 29–33, 44, 61
  capital   182, 190, 493 n.47
Hume, D.   396
hysteresis   61, 62, 112, 126

identities   xxiii
  and consistent capital budgeting   xxiii–xxiv
IMF Special Drawing Rights   407
imports of capital goods as saving   389–395
income
  distribution of   104
  expected   86
  Hicksian definition of   174–194
  inequality   139
  labor   179
  money   21
individual depositors   213
individuals spending   495 n.15
inflation
  crises   248
  rate   247
  targeting   247, 337, 343, 351, 378, 416–418
inflationary wage–price spiral   418
informal economy   139
interactive systems   34
interest rates   238–258, 303–330
  different theories   238–241
  exogeneity of   238–258, 307–315
  loanable funds theory of elasticity of AD   316–320
  "parity"   420
  reductions in   318
  "smoothing" of   242
incomes policy,
  "dirty" targeting of   241–47
interdependence with foreign exchange rate   112, 135, 300
internal and external balance   377
  achievement of   377–378
  external balance constraints on   345–348
  internal balance constraints on   340–345, 378
  "too high"   307–309
  zero   320–330
international capital movements   446
International Clearing Bank (ICB)   404
international clearing union (ICU)   403
  Keynes' proposal for   403–405
International Currency Union   404
international monetary flows   401

International Monetary Fund (IMF)
    405, 414
international monetary system   435
international payments system   410, 445
    current   410–411
international trade   385
    using national currencies in   385–408
international transactions   409, 433
    using a common currency in   433–453
    using national currencies in   409–432
investment   374
    financed   374–377
    –saving relationship   294
    spending   168
"ironic" science   16
IS–LM
    analysis   307–309
    diagram   294–297
    paradigm   8
Italy   449

James, H.   xix
James, W.   36–38
    philosophical pragmatism   38
Japan/Japanese   459
    bank accounting   510 n.26
    conondrum   320–327
    land and housing prices   324–325
Jevons, W.   77
Johnston   88
Jorgensen, W.L.   147–149

Kahn, R.   255
Kaldor, N.   60, 112, 125, 190, 266, 336, 460–461
    valuation ratio   336
Kalecki, M.   265–267, 269, 277, 280, 300
Kaplan, T.A.   270
Keen, S.   xix, 474 n.4, 481 n.23
Kendrick, B.   147–150
Kepler, J.   22
Keynes, J.M.   498 n.43, 44, 516 n.31
    changing views on interest rates   255–258
    effect   417
    "euthanasia"   357
    General Theory   116, 240, 170, 172, 304, 316, 329, 334, 353, 355, 398, 400, 402, 424, 442–444, 455–456, 459, 508 n.39
    "multiplier"   370–376
    new models *see* new Keynesian models
    paradox of thrift   169
    pricing theory   269
    revolution   411
    skepticism   7–10

Keynesian Cross   291–294
    diagram   294, 297
King, J.   xxiv–xxv
Kirman   474 n.62
Knight, F.   114, 487 n.38
Koch curve   45–46
Kuhn, T.S.   28
Kuznets, S.   139, 141, 150, 497 n.29

labor   291
    income   179
Lagrange, J.L.   66
land prices in Japan *see* Japan
Lanzillotti   270
Lawson, T.   93, 474 n.7
Leamer, E.   84, 90, 270, 484 n.36
    Bayesian approach   89
Lebergott, K.   150
less developed countries (LDCs)   395
less developing countries (LDCs)   427
liquid financial markets   421
liquidity   243
    crises   414
    –money relationship   295
    trap   230
"Loanable Funds" theory of interest   239
loans and deposits   200
Locke, J.   198
"loose" concepts   131–138
Lorenz, E.   52–53, 55
Low Income   472
    developing countries   468–469
    economies   471
    and High Income economies   521 n.29
Lucas, R.   115
"luck"   459–460
Lyotard, J.F.   68–69, 483 n.65

Machcup   493 n.44
Maastricht Treaty   448
McCallum, I.   268
McCloskey, D.   71, 91–92, 106
McFetridge, D.   268
Machiavelli, N.   74
Magendzo, I.I.   452
mainstream
    "core"   281–286
    economics   137
    economic theory   110, 288
    economists   115, 400, 416, 474 n.17
    macroeconomics   281–302
    methodology   124
    theory of income determination   289–294
Malthusian world   49

Index 553

Mandelbrot, B.   44–45, 58
Marginal Cost (MC)   199, 211, 262, 267, 273–274, 276, 299, 304
marginal efficiency of investment (MEI)   317
marginal physical product (MPP) curve   276
marginal propensity to invest (MPI)   292
market economies   306, 454, 465
   demand-constrained   454–456
markup pricing   261–280
   post Keynesian theory of the firm   262–267
Marshall, A.   3–7, 84, 89, 223, 474 n.3, 490 n.9
   middle ground position   5–6
Marshall–Lerner conditions   398
Marshall Plan   408
Marshall's tidal metaphor   3–12, 81
   conclusions   10–12
   introduction   3–6
Marx, K.   105
mathematics   xvii, 135, 138
   in economics   135, 138
maximization
   impossibility of   261–262
   profit see profit maximization
May, R.   50
Measure of Economic Welfare (MEW) index   145
measurement and quantification   136–138
Menger Sponge   47
Mercantilism   400, 443, 53 n.6
meteorological universe   125
methodology of positivism   102
mind–body problem of consciousness   30
"misplaced concreteness"   108–111
mismeasurement, of National Income   138–144
   external balance constraints on   345–348, 424–427
   internal balance constraints on   340–345
modern econometrics   85
   methodology of   85–94
monetarists   376, 381
Monetary Authority of Singapore (MAS)   512 n.30
monetary conservatism   456
monetary endogeneity   284
monetary policy   247, 250, 322, 327–328, 331–358
   in AD growth   331
   five channels of transmission   337–338
   new consensus on   247–252
   and volitional saving   331–358

monetary transmission process   359–384
money   122, 213, 216, 436
   Credit money   221
   Commodity money   221
   legal tender   436
   -multiplier identity   202–205
   -multiplier theory   xxiii
   supply see money supply
money market mutual funds (MMMF)   235–236
money supply   350
   endogeneity of   236–237, 198–199, 205–206
   horizontal   250
Monte Carlo experiments   98
Moore, B.J.   237
Moore, H.   77
Morgan, M.   49
multiple currencies   441
Myrdal's notion   460

NAIRU see Non Accelerating Inflation Rate of Unemployment
NAMU see North American Monetary Union
National Accounting systems   138, 387
national currency   437
National Flow of Funds Accounts   175–176
national income   102, 140, 147, 149, 153–154
   mismeasurement of   138–144
   identity   156
National Income Accounting (NIA)   138, 139, 140, 177, 184, 389, 390, 396, 497 n.29, 515 n.12
   double-counting   140
   identity   392
National Income Accounts (NIAs)   292, 309, 368, 386
National Income and Product Account (NIPA)   176
   conventions   161
   definitions   141
national payments medium   434
   choice of   434–439
national saving   157, 175, 183, 387–388; see also saving
Negotiable Certificates of Deposits (NCDs)   214
Nelson, C.   97–98, 100
neoclassical economics   104
   tensions in   104–108
neoclassical economists   239, 422
neoclassical supply-side models   456
   of economic growth   456–460
neoclassical synthesis (NCS)   287

neoclassical theory 108
neo-Walrasian general equilibrium models 240
Neumann, Von 73
neural networks 33
new endogenous growth (NEG) models 458, 507 n.18
new Keynesian models 458
Newton, I. xvi, 59, 112
Newtonian model 67
nihilism 60
Nikkei index, 1980–2000 323
NIPA *see* National Income and Product Account
Nixon, R. 408
no exchange rates 433, 520 n.48
  post Keynesian case for 433–453
"noise" xvi–xviii, 4–5
nominal rate 230–231, 239, 241–242, 246, 316, 336, 353
Non Accelerating Inflation Rate of Unemployment (NAIRU) 354
Non-Borrowed Reserves (NBR) 226
non-equilibrium paradigm, new 11
nonergodic 112–119
nonlinear
  dynamical systems approach 64
  models 11
  systems 16, 65, 72
non-stationary processes 96
  stochastic 98
non-traditional truths 65–68
non-volitional saving 171, 175–177, 186, 251, 293
Nordhaus, W. 145, 147–149, 268
North American Monetary Union (NAMU) 446

Occam's razor 30
Off balance sheet committments 216–222
Ohlin, B. 255–256
Okun, A. 274
Okun's theory 272
"one country-one currency" 440
open economies 385–453
  capital budgeting for 389–395
  small 417
  macroeconomics 386–389, 442
  post Keynesian 442–446
open market operations 204
  defensive 202–205
orthodox economists 107
overdraft systems 166, 220, 351

over-shooting of exchange rate 442–445
Oxford Economics Research Group 263

Pagan, A. 89
Partial Equilibrium 120–121, 381–382
pattern search 75
pedagogy xviii–xix
persuading the academy xxiv–xxvi
Phelps, E. 247
Phillips Curve (PC) 287, 330
  effects 351
  mechanism 378
  procedure 339
physics, definition 136
Pigou, A.C. 416–417
Pigou Effect 298, 345
planned saving 294, 310
Plato 32
Plosser, C. 97–98, 100
Pluralism 33–34
Poincaré, H. 18, 43, 72
Policy reaction function 315
Popper, K. 106
positivism 490 n.16
post Keynesian
  demand-led models of economic growth 460–463
  theory of pricing 275–278
postmodernism 68
  and economics 68–72
poverty line, definition of 153
pre-capitalist economies 465
predictable system *see* deterministic system 59
price level 150
  and the inflation rate 150–152
  stability 330, 450
"primary" non-monetary financial assets 293
private savings 157, 163–164, 176–177, 387
probabilistic models 5
probability theory 81
process analysis xx–xxii, 27, 122–127, 309, 313–16
production
  boundary 139
  valuation of 143
profit maximization 278
  banks 211
protoreptilian structure 33

quantification, importance of 131–132
quantity theory 199, 375
  paradigm xxii

Quantity Theory of Money
  critique of 378–382
quantum mechanics chaos 55
quantum theory 16–17, 26, 38

"Raffishness" of mainstream
  macroeconomics 281–302
randomness 76
random shocks 80
rational bubbles 357
"Rational Expectations" theorists 114
Ravallion, M. 153
reaction function 243
"real balance" effect 298, 416
Real Business Cycle models 286
real interest rate
real theory of interest
real values
reductionism 35
reductionist neuroscience 31
regression
  analysis 328, 432
restrictive monetary policy 418
reverse causation 308
Ricardo, D. 502 n.5
Robbins, L. 5
Robertson, Sir D. 261, 276, 361
Robinson, J. xix, 303
Rogers, W. 281
Rogoff, K. 439
Rorschach tests 29
Rose, A. 440
Ruggles, N. 147
Ruggles, R. 147

"safe haven" currency 396
Samuelson, P. 6, 115
saving
  as accounting record of investment
    156–173
  definition 161
  government 162–163
  identical to investment 159–162
  insufficient 348–352
  national *see* national saving
  non-volitional *see* non-volitional saving
  planned *see* planned saving
  private *see* private savings
  volitional *see* volitional saving
  volitional and non-volitional 156–159,
    167–170
  words and terms 164–167
Sawyer, M. 269
Say's Law 306, 363, 457

Schackle, G.L.S. 104, 118, 238
  different theories of 238
Schlacht Dr 404
securitization 500 n.5
seigniorage 451
self-organizing system 18
Serpinski Triangle 47
Shefrin 474 n.8
shareholders 171
Sims' a-theoretical approach 90
Singapore 344
single currency 435
Slutsky, E. 78, 79, 96
Smithin, J. xxiv
Social contract 337
Solow, R. 281, 285, 457
Solow model 459, 463
Sorites' dilemma 131, 134, 138, 149
Sorites' Paradox 131–155, 182
South Africa 139, 248, 336, 493 n.58,
  512 n.14
Spain 449
Sraffian models 114
Stapp, H.P. 480 n.86
stationarity, importance of 94–96
Sterken, E. 215
Stiglitz, J. 420
Stock, J. 488 n.62
stock market crash of 2000 414
stylized facts 60, 112, 125, 138, 267, 487 n.31
Summers, L. 157
supply-side models *see* neoclassical
  supply-side models 458
survey evidence 270–275
Sutton, J. 475
Sylos-Labini, P. 267, 269

targeting of interest rates 307–09
  of exchange rates 386–89
  of money supply 225
  of wage increases 337
Tarshis, L. 304
Taylor, J. 281
Taylor Rule 207, 243, 248, 251
  curve 313
tensions in neo classical economics 104
textbook theory 203
"The Probability Approach in
  Econometrics" 6
Theroux, P. 521 n.26
theoretical concepts 132
  classical economics 104
  empirical approximation 132
  formulation 118

theory of optimal currency areas   447
thermodynamics   23
Thirlwall's Law   461
Thomas, L.   156
Thuan, T.   13, 474 n.1
time series analysis   94–95
  "classical" method of   95
Tinbergen, J.   82, 84–86
Tinbergen's Statistical Testing of Bussiness–Cycle Theories   8
Tobin, J.   xxiii, 131, 145, 147–149, 156, 220
Total Incomes System of Accounts (TISA)   144
trade balance   444
traditional truths   65–68
transmission mechanism   359–63
Treasury–Federal Reserve Accord of 1951   231
Treatise on Money   257
Trend Stationary (TS) process   96

(fundamental) uncertainty   112
unemployment   150, 299
unquantifiable complex phenomena   134
US Dollar   410
  liabilities   407
US inflation   407–408

"valuation" ratio   496 n.24
Van Ees, H.   215
Van Regenmortel   476 n.12
vector auto-regressions   90
Verticalists   (218), 204, 236
Volcker, P.   233, 253
volitional savers   320
volitional saving   171, 348, 331–358, 399;
  see also saving
Volker, P.   246

wage
  –cost inflation   411
  increases   450
  inflation   355
  moderation   330, 337
  –price spiral   341
Walras, L.   200, 239
Walrasian General Equilibrium   114
Watson, M.   488 n.62
way of the world   xiv–xv
Weinberg, S.   36
Wicksell, K.   239–240
Wilson, E.   3, 33
Wittgenstein, L.   281
working capital
  bank finance of   222–224
  finance   224
World Bank   153–154, 405
  study   459
world trading system   410

Yorke, J.   50
Yule, G.   77–78

Ziliak, S.   92
Zolotas, X.   147–148